LIDC Contributions on Antitrust Law, Intellectual Property and Unfair Competition

For further volumes:
http://www.springer.com/series/11817

Pranvera Këllezi • Bruce Kilpatrick •
Pierre Kobel
Editors

Antitrust for Small and Middle Size Undertakings and Image Protection from Non-Competitors

Springer

Editors
Pranvera Këllezi
Meyerlustenberger Lachenal
Geneva
Switzerland

Bruce Kilpatrick
Addleshaw Goddard
London
United Kingdom

Pierre Kobel
Etude Hirsch Kobel
Geneva
Switzerland

ISBN 978-3-642-53999-2 ISBN 978-3-642-54000-4 (eBook)
DOI 10.1007/978-3-642-54000-4
Springer Heidelberg New York Dordrecht London

Library of Congress Control Number: 2014937793

Printed on acid-free paper

Springer is part of Springer Science+Business Media (www.springer.com)

Preface

The International League of Competition Law (LIDC) carries out a leading work every year in studying two topical questions selected among the fields of antitrust law, intellectual property or unfair competition. On each question, the key themes in the major jurisdictions are reflected in a series of national reports, whilst an international report identifies common features and trends from the national reports and draws conclusions on potential solutions or ideas to be explored in the future. The works of the LIDC have been a well of practical guidance for generations of lawyers, whether or not they are members of the LIDC, and for regulatory authorities.

Parts of the studies, international reports and recommendations were made available on the Web and disseminated to a selected audience. For the first time, LIDC decided to publish the entire reports for the benefit of the legal practitioners, academics and authorities active in the field of antitrust, intellectual property and unfair competition. LIDC is therefore making full use of this unique opportunity to contribute in the development of these fascinating fields of law.

This publication provides unparalleled comparative analysis of two "hot topics" in the field of antitrust and unfair competition laws.

Part I of this publication examines whether small- and middle-sized businesses could or should be subject to specific competition rules or other adjustments. SMEs account for 99 % of all enterprises in Europe and the United States. The papers consider both public and private enforcement in relation to SMEs across a range of jurisdictions. A detailed international report prepared by Professor Michele Carpagnano identifies general trends and highlights differences and the most interesting features of national regulations.

Part II of the book gathers contributions from various jurisdictions on an unfair competition question: whether businesses could or should be protected against the use of their trademarks, distinctive signs and other components of their image and identity by non-competing undertakings. The papers focus on the fundamental requirement of a competitive relationship as a possible condition of protection under unfair competition acts and review other types of protection, usually in the context of intellectual property. The comprehensive and insightful international report prepared by Maître Martine Karsenty-Ricard puts these issues in perspective.

The editors would like to thank all the authors for their contributions and their patient collaboration during the editing of this book. They would like to express their sincere gratitude to the Members of the Bureau, of the Council and of the Scientific Committee for their kind support and encouragement during the preparation of this book.

Geneva, Switzerland — Pranvera Këllezi
London, UK — Bruce Kilpatrick
Geneva, Switzerland — Pierre Kobel

Abbreviations

BGBl.	Bundesgesetzblatt (Germany)
cf.	Compare
CFREU	The Charter of Fundamental Rights of the European Union, OJ 2010 C 83, p. 389
CHF	Swiss franc
CJEU (or ECJ)	Court of Justice of the European Union (after 1 January 2009)
De minimis Notice	Commission Notice on agreements of minor importance which do not appreciably restrict competition under Article 81(1) of the Treaty establishing the European Community (de minimis), OJ 2001 C 368, p. 13
DKK	Danish krone
DM	Deutsche mark
e.g. or eg	For example
EC	European Community
ECHR	Council of Europe, European Convention for Human Rights of 4 November 1950
ECJ (or CJEU)	European Court of Justice
ECR	European Court Reports
EU	European Union
ff	And following
GBP	Pound sterling (UK)
GDP	Gross Domestic Product
Guidelines on the effect on trade concept	Commission Notice – Guidelines on the effect on trade concept contained in Articles 81 and 82 of the Treaty, OJ 2004 C 101, p. 81
HRK	Croatian Kuna (*hrvatska kuna*)
HUF	Hungarian Forint (*Magyar forint*)
i.e.	Id est (that is)
Id./Idem	The same as previously mentioned
IP	Intellectual property

m	Million
MFN	Most Favoured Nation
NAAT-rule	The non-appreciable affectation of trade rule
OECD	Organisation for Economic Co-operation and Development
OJ	Official Journal
p./pp.	Page(s)
para/paras	Paragraph(s)
Paris Convention	Paris Convention for the protection of industrial property of 20 March 1883
pt	Point
R&D	Research and development
Recommendation 2003/361	Commission Recommendation of 6 May 2003 concerning the definition of micro, small and medium-sized enterprises (2003/361/EC), OJ 2003 L 124, p. 36
Recommendation 96/280	Commission Recommendation of 3 April 1996 concerning the definition of small and medium-sized enterprises (96/280/EC), OJ 1996 L 107, p. 4
Regulation 1/2003	Council Regulation No 1/2003 of 16 December 2002 on the implementation of the rules on competition laid down in Articles 81 and 82 of the Treaty, OJ 2003 L 1, p. 1
Regulation 139/2004	Council Regulation (EC) No 139/2004 of 20 January 2004 on the control of concentrations between undertakings, OJ 2004 L 24, p. 1
SEK	Swedish Krona
SMEs	Small and medium size enterprises
TEC	Treaty Establishing the European Community
TFEU	Treaty on the Functioning of the European Union
UK	United Kingdom
US/USA	United States of America
v	Versus

Contents

List of Contributors

Boris Andrejaš Babić & Partners, Zagreb, Croatia

Linda Arcelin Université de la Rochelle, La Rochelle, France

Gusztáv Bacher Szecskay Law Office, Budapest, Hungary

David Bailey Brick Court Chambers, London, UK

Nicolas Birkhäuser Niederer Kraft & Frey Ltd, Zurich, Switzerland

Gabriel Bleser Kleyr Grasso Associés, Luxembourg, Luxembourg

Kinga Bölcskei Bán, S. Szabó & Partners, Budapest, Hungary

Mathilde Boudou Jean-Claude Coulon et Associés, Paris, France

Sébastien Calmont Institut de recherche en propriété intellectuelle (IRPI), Paris, France

Michele Carpagnano University of Trento and Osservatorio Antitrust, Trento, Italy

Gianni, Origoni, Grippo, Cappelli & Partners, Rome, Italy

Laurence Charvoz Cabinet Charvoz, Angers, France

Lenka Čížková Associated Law Offices Všetečka Zelený Švorčík Kalenský and Partners, Prague, Czech Republic

Marianne Decker Decker & Braun, Luxembourg, Luxembourg

Nicolas Decker Decker & Braun, Luxembourg, Luxembourg

Meinrad Dreher Johannes Gutenberg-University of Mainz, Mainz, Germany

Gábor Fejes Oppenheim, Budapest, Hungary

Gerhard Fussenegger bpv Hügel Rechtsanwälte OG, Brussels, Belgium

Leila Ghassemi Farreras University of Neuchâtel, Neuchâtel, Switzerland

Petr Hajn Metropolitan University Prague, Brno, Czech Republic

Christian Handig Chamber of Commerce, Vienna, Austria

Zoltán Hegymegi Barakonyi Baker & McKenzie, Budapest, Hungary

Frauke Henning-Bodewig Max Planck Institute for Intellectual Property and Competition Law, Munich, Germany

Márton Horányi Baker & McKenzie, Budapest, Hungary

Alexander Jute Advokatfirman MarLaw AB, Stockholm, Sweden

Martine Karsenty-Ricard J.P. Karsenty & Associés, Paris, France

Márton Kocsis Oppenheim, Budapest, Hungary

Ágnes Eszter Komári Ministry of Rural Development, Budapest, Hungary

Julia Körner Johannes Gutenberg-University of Mainz, Mainz, Germany

Jean-Patrice de La Laurencie Independent Lawyer, Paris, France

Francesca La Rocca Studio Legale Sena e Tarchini, Milan, Italy

Arnaud Latil Université Paris-Sorbonne, Paris, France

Zsófia Lendvai Baker & McKenzie, Budapest, Hungary

Ádám Liber Bogsch & Partners, Budapest, Hungary

Ben Longstaff Hogarth Chambers, London, UK

Péter Lukácsi SBGK Law Office, Budapest, Hungary

Aurélia Marie Beau de Loménie, Paris, France

Zoltán Marosi Oppenheim, Budapest, Hungary

Robert Moldén Gärde Wesslau, Göteborg, Sweden

Max W. Mosing Gassauer-Fleissner, Vienna, Austria

Norman Neyrinck University of Liège, Liège, Belgium

Dehin & Brüls, Brussels, Belgium

Álmos Papp Bán, S. Szabó & Partners, Budapest, Hungary

Sune Troels Poulsen Centre for European Studies of Economic Law, University of Copenhagen, Copenhagen, Denmark

Boglárka Priskin Hungarian Competition Authority, Budapest, Hungary

Tamás Riba Bozzay & Partners Law Office, Budapest, Hungary

Olivier Sautel Microeconomix, Paris, France

Véronique Sélinsky Independent Lawyer, Montpellier, France

Katalin Szamosi SBGK Law Office, Budapest, Hungary

Pál Szilágyi Pázmány Péter Catholic University, Faculty of Law, Oppenheim, Budapest, Hungary

Izabella Szoboszlai Hungarian Competition Authority, Budapest, Hungary

Emilio Varanini Antitrust Section, California Office of the Attorney General, San Francisco, CA, USA

Alexander Vida Danubia Patent and Trademark Ltd., Budapest, Hungary

Péter Virág Hungarian Competition Authority, Budapest, Hungary

Clare Zammit Independent Lawyer, Milan, Italy

Part I

Antitrust for Small and Middle Size Undertakings

International Report 1

Michele Carpagnano

1.1 Introduction: The Scope of the International Report

The scope of this International Report is to foster a debate on whether small and medium-sized enterprises should be treated differently or not from other legal entities (and in particular large enterprises) under competition law provisions.

To contribute to the above-mentioned debate, the present International Report carries out a comparative analysis of the relevant legislative provisions, case law, as well as policy options and practices in 15 national legal systems.[1] In the following pages, we report the most interesting policy trends, legislative developments, and practices related to SMEs under competition laws. The national legal systems analysed belong to very different legal cultures and traditions, including the civil law system, common law system, and Eastern European legal traditions. It is also important to bear in mind that 11 of the 15 legal systems analysed belong to the European Union, thus having in common—at least since 1996—a relevant set of rules, case law, or policy options.

Notwithstanding the aforementioned cultural and "structural" differences, the present contribution shows a surprisingly high degree of common features in the treatment of SMEs in the field of competition law. Such common features, as well as differences, are described in detail in the following chapters.

[1] Austria, Belgium, Brazil (not published in the present volume), Croatia, Czech Republic, Denmark, France, Germany, Hungary, Italy, Luxembourg, Sweden, Switzerland, United Kingdom, and United States of America.

M. Carpagnano (✉)
University of Trento and Osservatorio Antitrust, Trento, Italy

Gianni, Origoni, Grippo, Cappelli & Partners, Rome, Italy
e-mail: Michele.Carpagnano@unitn.it

P. Këllezi et al. (eds.), *Antitrust for Small and Middle Size Undertakings and Image Protection from Non-Competitors*, LIDC Contributions on Antitrust Law, Intellectual Property and Unfair Competition, DOI 10.1007/978-3-642-54000-4_1, © Springer-Verlag Berlin Heidelberg 2014

The International Report consists of four sections and is structured so as to take into full account the role of SMEs under competition law. The role of both the infringer and the victim of competition rules' infringements has been taken into account, as well as the different levels of competition law enforcement (public and private). The International Report is structured as follows.

The first section revolves around SMEs in their economic and legal context. This chapter describes the nature and the role of SMEs in the economy, their legal definitions (where existing), and their treatment under competition law.

The second section is focused on the position of SMEs in the context of the public enforcement of competition law and analyses SMEs from two different perspectives: SMEs as infringers and SMEs as victims. Public enforcement of competition law is understood as the enforcement of competition law provisions by a public body (most often an agency) capable of detecting infringements and putting an end to illegal practices and of ensuring deterrence through appropriate fines and other remedies. Advocacy is also included in the scope of our contribution.

The third section analyses the role of SMEs in the context of private enforcement of competition law, such as enforcement of competition rules by civil courts in a private judicial litigation. Specific attention is paid here to burdens and limits that may eventually jeopardise the full effective exercise of SMEs' rights in courts.

The fourth section illustrates the policy recommendations submitted for discussion in the LIDC Congress 2012 and the resolution adopted by the LIDC. The International Report is based on data and information contained in the 15 national reports published in the present LIDC Series.

1.1.1 SMEs in Context

In the vast majority of the countries analysed, SMEs play a pivotal role in the national economies and represent the most common form of economic entity active in their markets.[2] Taking this into account, several countries have already adopted specific legislative measures and policy programmes to support the establishment, the growth, and the financing of SMEs.[3]

The OECD also fosters the adoption of ad hoc policy programmes that are conscious about the relevance of SMEs in a globalised context.[4] Within the

---

[2] For more information about the role of SMEs, see OECD, *SME and Entrepreneurship Outlook*, 2005, p. 17, available at http://www.oecd.org/cfe/oecdsmeandentrepreneurshipoutlook-2005edition.htm.

[3] See *Bailey*, United Kingdom, Part I, Chap. 14, p. 235; *Zammit*, Italy, Part I, Chap. 10, p. 160. *Communication from the commission to the council, the European parliament, the European economic and social committee and the committee of the regions "Think Small First" a "Small Business Act" for Europe*, 25.6.2008, COM(2008) 394 final.

[4] For more information about the role of SMEs, see OECD, *SME and Entrepreneurship Outlook*, 2005, p. 17.

European Union, the European Commission is leading an SME-friendly policy under the motto "Think small first". The "Small Business Act" enacted in 2008 can be considered as a milestone for Europe and for the due definition of companies with less than 250 employees.[5] The United States of America and Japan also share this SME-friendly approach, since the relevance of SMEs is also crucial in their respective economies.[6]

1.1.2 The Economic Perspective

All national contributions confirm that SMEs play a key role in national economies. In Europe, SMEs account for 99 % of enterprises, whereas 92 % are considered micro enterprises.[7] They also play a main role in the growth of the economy, in particular in crisis periods. According to public data available, SMEs generate two-thirds of employment and they are the main source of new jobs.[8] In the US, SMEs represent nearly 99 % of all employer firms.[9]

This data constitute illustrative evidence for the outstanding importance of SMEs in the world economy.[10] Although their business may typically have a local or regional scope, especially micro enterprises, it is worth mentioning that SMEs are also active beyond their national borders.[11] This means, from a legal point of view, that SMEs' business is potentially relevant not only under national competition law but also under international competition law provisions, such as competition law of the European Union.

1.1.3 Legal Definitions

1.1.3.1 Legal Definitions of SMEs

What are SMEs from a legal perspective, and how are they defined by national laws?

It is not always easy to answer these questions despite the fact that several jurisdictions have legal definitions of SMEs, since legislators, in most cases, have

---

[5] Small Business Act, COM (2008) 394, final 25 June 2008.

[6] For more information about the role of SMEs, see OECD, *SME and Entrepreneurship Outlook*, 2005, p. 17.

[7] See Report from the Commission to the Council and the European Parliament, *Minimizing regulatory burden for SMEs. Adapting EU Regulation to the needs of micro-enterprises*. Brussels, 23.11.2011, COM (2011) 803 final, available at http://eur-lex.europa.eu/LexUriServ/LexUriServ.do?uri=COM:2011:0803:FIN:EN:PDF.

[8] OECD, *SME and Entrepreneurship outlook 2005*, p. 15.

[9] OECD, *SME and Entrepreneurship outlook 2005*, p. 362.

[10] See hereto OECD, *SME and Entrepreneurship outlook 2005*.

[11] OECD, *SME and Entrepreneurship outlook 2005*.

introduced these definitions in different areas of law such as tax laws, commercial laws, labour laws, rather than in a single law.[12]

National Constitutions do not usually set the legal definition of SMEs, and some Civil or Commercial Codes only refer to "entrepreneur" or "trader" but do not contain any reference to SMEs.[13] In this respect, different countries have spread their definitions and rules for SMEs in different rules: one interesting example can be found in the Swedish labour rules that foresee that certain employment protection rules are not applicable to SMEs with less than ten employees.[14] France also limits its labour representation rules for SMEs.[15] Accounting and tax laws can also provide for softer rules for SMEs than for bigger undertakings.[16]

Nonetheless, within the EU, a certain degree of harmonisation in the legal definition of SMEs has been reached through the European Commission Recommendation of 6 May 2003 concerning the definition of micro, small, and medium-sized enterprises.[17] According to such Recommendation, SMEs are all enterprises with less than 250 employees and having a maximum EUR 50 million turnover or EUR 43 million balance sheet totals (equivalent to USD 65 million and USD 56 million). Micro enterprises are the smallest category of SMEs, with less than ten employees and a turnover or balance sheet equal to or less than EUR 2 million (equivalent to USD 2.6 million).[18] This definition, mandatory within the EU since 2005, has been adopted in all EU Member national legislations.

In countries that do not belong to the EU, the definitions of SMEs are also often based on the number of employees and other factors such as turnover.[19] In general, the OECD countries apply a variety of definitions, where the number of employees is important, but it is not the sole defining criterion: financial assets also play a key role in defining SMEs. The most frequent upper limit is 250 employees, but some countries have set the limit to 200 employees or, as in the US case, to 500.[20] Small firms usually have less than 50 employees, while the limits for micro enterprises vary from five to ten employees.[21] In Japan, the definition of an SME also depends on the market or sector where the company carries out its activities. In the

---

[12] OECD, *SME and Entrepreneurship outlook 2005*, p. 7.

[13] See *Zammit*, Italy, Part I, Chap. 10, p. 160.

[14] See *Moldén*, Sweden, Part I, Chap. 12, p. 192 f.

[15] See *Boudou et al.*, France, Part I, Chap. 7, p. 104 ff.

[16] See, for instance, *Moldén*, Sweden, Part I, Chap. 12, p. 192.

[17] OJ 2003 L 124, p. 36.

[18] See the Report from the Commission to the Council and the European Parliament, *Minimizing regulatory burden for SMEs. Adapting EU Regulation to the needs of micro-enterprises*, Brussels, 23 November 2011, COM (2011) 803 final, available at http://eur-lex.europa.eu/LexUriServ/LexUriServ.do?uri=COM:2011:0803:FIN:EN:PDF.

[19] See OECD, *SME and Entrepreneurship outlook 2005*.

[20] OECD, *SME and Entrepreneurship outlook 2005*, p. 17.

[21] OECD, *SME and Entrepreneurship outlook 2005*, p. 17.

Table 1.1 Employees and turnover

Country	Employees	Turnover or	Balance sheet	Market share
EU: Medium	$\leq$ 250	$\leq$ EUR 50 m	$\leq$ EUR 43 m	Not relevant
EU: Small	$\leq$ 50	$\leq$ EUR 10 m	$\leq$ EUR 10 m	Not relevant
EU: Micro	$\leq$ 10	$\leq$ EUR 2 m	$\leq$ EUR 2 m	Not relevant
USA	$\leq$ 500	Not relevant	Not relevant	Relevant
Japan	$\leq$300 (depending on the sector)	$\leq$ 300 m–500 m Yen	$\leq$ 300 m–500 m Yen	Not relevant
Brazil (small/medium)		USD 180.000–1.800.000	Not relevant	Only individual shareholders
Brazil (micro)		$\leq$ USD 180.000		

Source: LIDC National Reports and OECD

manufacturing or construction sectors, companies with fewer than 300 employees or attaining a turnover of less than Yen 300 million (equivalent to EUR 2.9 million or USD 3.8 million) are considered SMEs, whereas in the services sector the thresholds are stricter: the capital has to be less than Yen 500 million (equivalent to EUR 4.8 million or USD 6.35 million)[22] or the number of employees should be below 100.[23] Brazil defines SMEs with reference to their turnover, which has to be below USD 1,800,000 (equivalent to EUR 1,382,310.00), and establishes a special category for micro enterprises with a turnover below USD 180,000. The Brazilian legislation expressly excludes companies that do not belong to individual shareholders and are branches of international companies.[24]

Table 1.1 summarises the different criteria followed in legal systems analysed to define SMEs. It is interesting to underline that what constitutes an SME in one country may not be considered as such in another country.

1.1.3.2 Definition of Competition Law

The International Report refers to "Competition Law", also referred to as antitrust law, in a narrow (and selective) sense, as a set of laws that prevents and sanctions (1) "agreements" between economic entities with the aim/effect of distorting competition in the market and (2) unilateral practices by operators with substantial market power (the "abuse of dominance" in Europe or monopolisation in the US). State Aid and Merger control rules fall outside the scope of this report. In all legal systems analysed, Competition Law, as defined above, applies to all economic entities that are active in a market. Thus, as a general rule, Competition Law does

[22] Official exchange rate on 5 October 2012.

[23] OECD, *SME and Entrepreneurship outlook 2005*, Country report Japan.

[24] National Report Brazil, not published in the present volume, p. 1. Official exchange rate on 20 December 2012.

apply to SMEs as far as their conducts harm even potentially effective competition in the market.[25]

The Court of Justice of the European Union established that "the concept of an undertaking encompasses every entity engaged in economic activity regardless of the legal status of the entity and the way in which it is financed".[26] The main point is therefore to determine if the entity is engaged in an economic activity. The legal status is not relevant to determine if an entity is subject to Competition Law or not.[27] Therefore, even individuals or SMEs are subject to competition rules within the European Union. This does not, obviously, mean that conduct of economic entities that have very small or insignificant market power fall under antitrust scrutiny. In the definitions of SMEs, the approach followed by the United States of America appears more coherent with competition law rationale since SMEs are defined in relation to the market share of the economic enterprise in the relevant market, irrespective of the amount of assets or number of employees.[28]

As discussed later in the Report, both the EU and US definitions of SMEs (though based on conceptually different approaches) have, at least in the field of Competition Law, a very similar scope.

1.1.3.3 Legal Definitions of SMEs in the Field of Competition Law

Even in those countries where SMEs are properly defined by legislation, specific definitions of SMEs are rare in the field of competition law. As we will see, the definition of SMEs based on annual turnover or number of employees may not be considered as reliable indicator of market power under competition law.

Indeed, if under some circumstances the annual turnover of an enterprise may roughly constitute an indication of the market power of such company, the number of employees does not mean anything from a competition law perspective.

Germany constitutes one of the few exceptions to the absence of specific provisions for SMEs under competition law. Indeed, the German Act against Restraints of Competition contains a rule that refers explicitly to cartels engaged in by SMEs and to larger companies dealing with SMEs.[29] The specific provision under German Competition Law, Section 20(1), protects dependent SMEs on large companies.[30] According to this protection rule, undertakings are prohibited from abusing their position with respect to dependent SMEs. If the company is relatively

[25] ECJ, case C-309/99, *Wouters v Algemene Raad van de Nederlandsche Orde van Advocaten*, ECR 2002 I-1577, pt 57. R. Whish, D. Bailey, Competition Law 2011, p. 84; A. Calvo Caravaca, 2010 Derecho Antitrust Europeo, Vol. I, p. 179. While this International Report focuses on Competition Laws as defined herein, some national reports has also covered state aid and unfair competition rules.

[26] Van Bael & Bellis, Competition Law of the European Community, 2010, p. 17; ECJ, case C-41/90 *Höfner and Elser v Macrotron*, ECR 1991 I-1979, pt 21.

[27] Van Bael & Bellis, Competition Law of the European Community, 2010, p. 18–19.

[28] See *Varanini*, United States of America, Part I, Chap. 15, p. 258.

[29] See *Dreher & Körner*, Germany, Part I, Chap. 8, p. 130.

[30] See *Dreher & Körner*, Germany, Part I, Chap. 8, p. 134.

small compared to the other market participants, then the specific protection rules apply. Taking into account that, in practice, establishing the position of the companies could be a very difficult exercise, so far, as referred by the German National Reporter, German practitioners may use the merger control thresholds as a first indication.[31] In France, there are also special provisions for SMEs, distinguishing the size of the company and exempting *certain agreements, in particular when their purpose is to improve the management of small or medium-sized enterprises*. Notwithstanding this, in practice, the agreements in place referred to in this text are extremely limited.[32] In Belgium, the competition law system contains references but not a clear definition of SMEs in competition law, although there have been some legislative attempts to introduce a clear definition under Belgian laws.[33] Outside the EU, the US antitrust laws define SMEs with respect to their market power, excluding them from liability in case of unilateral conduct, and when they do not have market power and there is no negative effect in the market.[34] Of course, this liability limitation does not apply to hard-core infringements, to restraints with negative effects, and if the restraint is market-wide.[35]

1.2 Special Treatment of SMEs Under Competition Law

1.2.1 The Nature and Scope of Special Treatment for SMEs in Competition Law

As said, even though SMEs are legally defined in most of the legal systems analysed, competition law systems do not differentiate between undertakings because of their size, either as competitors or as trading partners.[36] There is a minor exception to this general approach in Germany, where national competition law foresees an additional rule for SMEs for the abuse of the bargaining position of bigger companies against dependent SMEs.[37]

[31] See *Dreher & Körner*, Germany, Part I, Chap. 8, p. 131, referring to Section 35 of the German Act against Restraints on Competition.

[32] There is also a specific jurisdiction rule about local anticompetitive practices that indirectly refers to SMEs; see *Boudou et al.*, France, Part I, Chap. 7, pp. 190 ff.

[33] See *Neyrinck*, Belgium, Part I, Chap. 3, pp. 44 ff.

[34] See *Varanini*, United States of America, Part I, Chap. 15, pp 258 and 260.

[35] See *Varanini*, United States of America, Part I, Chap. 15, p. 258.

[36] See *Andrejaš*, Croatia, Part I, Chap. 4, p. 67; *Bailey*, United Kingdom, Part I, Chap. 14, p. 236 and 237; *Papp et al.*, Hungary, Part I, Chap. 9, p. 142.

[37] See *Dreher & Körner*, Germany, Part I, Chap. 8, p. 134.

It shall also be noted that when certain sectors are (partially) excluded from competition rules, for instance agriculture in the EU,[38] more favourable treatment in these sectors is afforded to the economic entity itself independently from its size.[39] Thus, even big enterprises may apply for favourable treatment under special regulation.

1.2.2 Specific Programmes Addressed to SMEs

A recent study published by the OECD shows that the lack of awareness of competition rules and enforcement practice is one of the prominent reasons leading to competition law infringements by SMEs in several jurisdictions across the globe.[40] The majority of National Reports seems to confirm this statement. It must be noted however that according to the National Reports, some countries, namely UK and Germany, have adopted policies and programmes on compliance and enhancement of competition enforcement specifically addressed to SMEs.[41] Notwithstanding this, in general, those programmes are addressed to all market players. In the UK, the Office of Fair Trading launched a campaign addressed to SMEs in 2005 (Championing Competition) to inform them and highlight the positive aspects of competition rules.[42] This campaign was based on a research commissioned by the same OFT, which showed that only 49 % of the employees of small companies with 10–19 employees were aware of the Competition Act, whereas 80 % of the employees of corporations with more than 200 employees had knowledge of competition law.[43] This campaign was followed by a campaign against cartels. Six years later, the OFT carried out a similar study categorising the companies according to their number of employees, and the following interesting results came up: the knowledge of competition law increased with the number of employees, whereas micro enterprises had in general no knowledge of competition law.[44]

---

[38] See Article 42 TFEU (ex-36 TEC); on block exemptions in general, see R. Whish & D. Bailey, Competition Law 2011, p. 168.

[39] See Article 125 *quater*, Council Regulation 1234/2007 of 22 October 2007 establishing a common organisation of agricultural markets and on specific provisions for certain agricultural products, OJ 2007 L 299, p. 1, according to which "an organization of producers shall not be recognized when it holds a dominant position in a market".

[40] OECD (2012), *Promoting Compliance with competition law*, p. 211, available at http://search.oecd.org/officialdocuments/publicdisplaydocumentpdf/?cote=DAF/COMP(2011)20&docLanguage=En.

[41] See *Bailey*, United Kingdom, Part I, Chap. 14, and *Dreher & Körner*, Germany, Part I, Chap. 8.

[42] See OFT, *SMEs missing out on benefits of competition*, press release of 24 May 2005, available at http://www.oft.gov.uk/news-and-updates/press/2005/92-05.

[43] *Bailey*, United Kingdom, Part I, Chap. 14, p. 241

[44] *Bailey*, United Kingdom, Part I, Chap. 14, p. 241.

Furthermore, in Germany, the Competition Authority (*Bundeskartellamt*) issued an informative brochure about cooperation between SMEs that explained the German *de minimis* rules and the type of cooperation allowed and forbidden by the law.[45] As stated above, other jurisdictions (such as USA, Italy, Belgium, Switzerland, Croatia) also have programmes regarding compliance and programmes about SMEs but no specific policies that seek the improvement of competition law awareness for SMEs.[46] To reach SMEs and awake their interest in competition law can be quite difficult since, as described in the above-mentioned OECD Study, managers of SMEs usually have other priorities than competition law compliance.[47] A manager of an SME is much more involved in the day-to-day business and problems; he is probably in direct contact with clients, providers, and employees and worries about each invoice more than about the last developments in compliance policies.[48]

Therefore, as stated by the same OECD, in order to enhance the compliance level for SMEs, it seems necessary to design tailor-made programmes and tools for them that can really reach, educate, and "convince" small economic operators showing the advantages of competition law compliance rather than promoting high fines once infringements have been committed. These compliance tools should be spread not only through National Competition Authorities (hereafter referred to as "NCAs") but also through local authorities (at regional and local levels), which have more direct contact with SMEs, and maybe through trade and business associations.

Last but not least, the complexity in competition law can also become a big hurdle for an SME.[49] Predictability and legal certainty are crucial aspects in the decision-making process of businesses. While a legal evaluation error can cause harm in a big company, the same error can have fatal consequences for an SME.

[45] See *Dreher & Körner*, Germany, Part I, Chap. 8, p. 133.

[46] See Part I: *Neyrinck*, Belgium, Chap. 3; *Andrejaš*, Croatia, Chap. 4; *Poulsen*, Denmark, Chap. 6; *Zammit*, Italy, Chap. 10; *Moldén*, Sweden, Chap. 12; *Birkhäuser*, Switzerland, Chap. 13; *Varanini*, United States of America, Chap. 15.

[47] OECD (2012), Promoting Compliance with competition law, p. 264.

[48] OECD (2012), Promoting Compliance with competition law, p. 264.

[49] B. Lasserre, Market Definition: a resilient feature of competition enforcement?, Contribution to the 39th Annual Conference on International Antitrust Law and Policy, Fordham Competition Law Institute, September 2012, available at http://www.autoritedelaconcurrence.fr/doc/article_fordham_sept12.pdf.

1.2.3 The Role of Trade and Business Associations

Trade and business associations have a crucial role in most of all countries analysed.[50] These associations embrace SMEs (as well as big enterprises and other types of companies, such as cooperatives, individual professionals) normally for a specific sector or market segment and usually represent companies before the authorities and defend their interests.[51] On the one side, trade associations provide expertise to their members and have a number of important functions that benefit the market. They can support SMEs, help to educate, and update businesses on applicable rules and regulations or enhance consumer protection by developing standard terms and conditions, product safety standards, technical norms, etc.[52] In the UK Report, it is specified that the OFT has expressly recognised trade and business associations as potential effective partners to enhance compliance, using them to disseminate their guidelines.[53] On the other side, it must be recalled that trade associations are also a common vehicle to carry out anticompetitive conduct, especially by small and medium enterprises.[54] By their nature, they often bring together a number of—in some cases even all—competitors in a particular sector.[55] It is thus commonly believed that specific *caveat* must be adopted in order to avoid that business and trade associations may result in a *forum* for horizontal coordination that may, under certain circumstances, result in possible infringements of competition law provisions (such as anticompetitive agreements), with possible detrimental effects to market dynamics and to consumers.[56]

In order to increase the awareness of SMEs on more complex competition law issues (and prevent the opening of administrative proceedings against them), NCAs (*ex officio* or after receiving a complaint) could be empowered to send an official warning to SMEs or trade associations representing them. The warning, similar to those warnings addressed to bigger players in case of abuse of dominance cases, may alert SMEs on possible misconduct in a specific market and may force them to a voluntary compliance.[57] In case of non-compliance, NCAs must open a formal proceeding. Such moral persuasion activity aimed at obtaining voluntary

---

[50] J. Leibowitz (2005) The Good, the Bad and the Ugly, available at http://www.ftc.gov/speeches/leibowitz/050510goodbadugly.pdf.

[51] OECD (2012), Promoting Compliance with competition law, p. 209.

[52] OECD (2012), Promoting Compliance with competition law, p. 209.

[53] See *Bailey*, United Kingdom, Part I, Chap. 14, p. 7.

[54] OECD (2012), Promoting Compliance with competition law, cited, p. 209.

[55] OECD(2012), Promoting Compliance with competition law, cited, p. 209.

[56] J. Leibowitz (2005), The Good, the Bad and the Ugly, available at http://www.ftc.gov/speeches/leibowitz/050510goodbadugly.pdf.

[57] B. Lasserre, Market Definition: a resilient feature of competition enforcement?, Contribution to the 39th Annual Conference on International Antitrust Law and Policy, Fordham Competition Law Institute, September 2012, available at http://www.autoritedelaconcurrence.fr/doc/article_fordham_sept12.pdf, p. 12; ECJ, case C-322/81, *NV Nederlandsche Banden Industrie Michelin v European Commission*, ECR 1983 3461.

compliance by market operators is successfully carried out in Italy by the National Competition Authority in relation to consumer protection law cases.

1.2.4 Policy Recommendations for Discussion

- Legal definition: there is no need to set a specific legal definition for SMEs in the field of competition law. Soft law tools, such as guidelines, may suffice in order to provide a common definition of SMEs based on market share and power.
- Information activities specifically addressed to SMEs (who): NCAs (and the European Commission at EU level) should design and implement specific information/compliance actions/programmes to improve the knowledge of competition law within smaller businesses. Those programmes may be conducted with the strategic partnership of trade and business associations and other public authorities both at national and local levels.
- Information activities specifically addressed to SMEs (how 1): *ad hoc* compliance guides/models based on common standards approved by NCAs could be used by SMEs in order to avoid expensive individual legal assessment/competition law compliance. These models should be promoted by the NCAs and their networks and disseminated by trade associations and local authorities. SMEs that adhere to such programmes may indicate it to clients.
- Information activities specifically addressed to SMEs (how 2): it could be certainly useful that NCAs establish an "information point" or tool kits, even virtually on their web page, specifically addressed to SMEs.
- Information activities specifically addressed to SMEs (how 3): business and trade associations should assist SMEs in competition law compliance programmes and audit. They could, for instance, disseminate information on issues related to cartels and collusive conduct, including information regarding relevant developments in international and regional forums; provide training, prevention, due diligence, and general advice on diligence in carrying out compliance programmes; and advise on how to resist opportunities for collusive conduct.[58]
- Specific recommendations or warnings for risk groups: NCAs could address specific warnings to associations or other risk groups that could be suspected of being a vehicle for anticompetitive conduct.

[58] See, on this point, OECD (2012), Promoting Compliance with competition law, p. 283.

1.3 Public Competition Law Enforcement and SMES

1.3.1 Substantive and Procedural Rules Applicable to SMEs

1.3.1.1 Introduction

The majority of the legal systems analysed in this International Report does not distinguish between SMEs and other undertakings when applying competition rules. As an example, it is worth to mention that in the UK competition rules are applied without "uncritical sentimentality" to SMEs.[59] This mirrors the European approach to competition rules that, as known, are applicable to all persons and undertakings irrespective of their legal nature and size.[60] Notwithstanding this, in at least two of the jurisdictions examined, there are specific substantive rules applicable to certain competition law infringements (i.e., in the field of abuse of dominant position) that protect SMEs in relation to larger companies. It is the case of Germany, where specific rules applicable to SMEs define how larger companies with relative or significant market power have to deal with smaller undertakings, prohibiting impediments and discrimination in vertical and horizontal relationships.[61] This rule intends to protect retailers from anticompetitive practices such as low price strategies imposed by bigger companies.[62] Austria also has similar rules for dominant companies and a specific rule to protect local suppliers.[63] No distinction of treatment seems to be made from a procedural point of view, since, in principle, the same rules seem to be applied to all economic entities in the vast majority of jurisdictions examined. It seems possible, however, to detect some distinctions in the practice and enforcement by the NCAs and courts when they assess a potential involvement of SMEs. The size of the undertaking, for instance, is a factor that is taken into account in Hungary when the Competition Authority establishes the amount of fine in sanctioning proceedings for horizontal conduct.[64] Public interest rules may also play a significant role since in the same country the competition authorities "may" start investigations and proceedings if there is potential harm to public interest.[65]

In many jurisdictions, the national authorities could consider that small markets or regional markets (where SMEs act) are not as interesting or important as the bigger trans-regional markets (where bigger companies play an important role). Therefore, the national competition authorities tend to concentrate their efforts on "bigger" issues, ignoring the areas where SMEs act regularly.

---

[59] See *Bailey*, United Kingdom, Part I, Chap. 14, p. 242.

[60] See above, p. 3.

[61] See Section 20 of the German Act against Restrictions of Competition.

[62] See *Dreher & Körner*, Germany, Part I, Chap. 8, 134 ff.

[63] See *Fussenegger*, Austria, Part I, Chap. 2, pp. 32 and 33.

[64] See for instance *Papp et al.*, Hungary, Part I, Chap. 9, p. 144.

[65] See for instance *Papp et al.*, Hungary, Part I, Chap. 9, pp. 146 and 147.

1.3.1.2 Safe Harbours for SMEs

Taking into account that self-assessment is becoming more relevant in competition law systems across the globe, and in order to maintain predictability, safe harbours have been created such as Block Exemption Regulations, R & D agreements, specialisation agreements, or technology licensing agreements.

All these instruments are based on market share thresholds. The object of these tools is to *enable firms, especially SMEs, which will be in most cases indisputably under the relevant thresholds, to proceed safely with their business activity, while only bearing in mind the clear red lines in the said Regulations, i.e. the so-called "hard-core" restrictions.*[66] Notwithstanding the above, we shall question whether these tools are really helpful for SMEs or if they can in practice easily detect the "clear red lines". Several guidelines and regulations are based on market assessment and on the market definition. To define a relevant market can be a very complex task that needs expertise and specialised knowledge that could not be affordable for a micro enterprise. However, the national reporters coincide that there are no specific safe harbour rules for SMEs. This notwithstanding, each of the jurisdictions analysed has *de minimis* rules, block exemptions, and sector-specific rules that indirectly consider the size of the companies, usually due to their turnover.[67] For instance, competition rules in the UK foresee certain immunity rules for parties to a "small agreement", where small agreements are those between undertakings whose combined turnover in the business year preceding the agreement does not exceed GBP 20 million (equivalent to EUR 25.2 million and USD 31.8 million).[68] The USA enforcers also apply market screens to protect SMEs if they consider the conduct pro-competitive.[69] Notwithstanding this, SMEs in the US, as in other jurisdictions, are also liable for direct anticompetitive effects, joint hard-core conduct, and market-wide restraints, as in other jurisdictions.[70] It is important to remember the key facts of the European *de minimis* rules, since it is logical that SMEs fall easily under these rules based on the turnover thresholds having usually smaller turnovers than the bigger companies. They also act locally or, at most, regionally, as stated by the European Commission in its *De Minimis* Notice.[71] Furthermore, there is a safe harbour for SMEs if there is "no appreciable

[66] B. Lasserre, Market Definition: a resilient feature of competition enforcement?, Contribution to the 39th Annual Conference on International Antitrust Law and Policy, Fordham Competition Law Institute, September 2012, available at http://www.autoritedelaconcurrence.fr/doc/article_fordham_sept12.pdf, p. 15.

[67] Notice on agreements of minor importance which do not appreciably restrict competition under Article 101 (1) TFEU, OJ 2001C 368, p. 13, para 3. See also R. Whish & D. Bailey, Competition Law, 2011, p. 140.

[68] See *Bailey*, United Kingdom, Part I, Chap. 14, p. 3. Official Exchange rate on 5 September 2012.

[69] See *Varanini*, United States of America, Part I, Chap. 15, p. 260.

[70] See *Varanini*, United States of America, Part I, Chap. 15, p. 261.

[71] Notice on agreements of minor importance which do not appreciably restrict competition under Article 101 (1) TFEU, OJ 2001C 368, p. 13, para 3.

effect on trade".[72] According to the Notice of the European Commission regarding the effect on trade, agreements will not appreciably affect trade between Member States if the aggregate market share of the parties on the relevant markets within the European Community does not exceed 5 % and in case of horizontal agreements or the turnover of the involved undertakings does not exceed EUR 40 million (GBP 31.6 million, USD 50.3 million[73]) or, in case of vertical agreements, the aggregate annual Community turnover of the supplier in the affected products does not exceed EUR 40 million.[74] This definition establishes that the individual market share of each party to the agreement at stake should not exceed 15 % in case of non-competitors and 10 % in case of competitors.[75] However, SMEs have to assess themselves if they fall under a *de minimis* rule. Again, this could be more difficult for a micro enterprise or SME in comparison to a big corporation with experience, skills, and resources in competition law. However, this problem will be more relevant for bigger SMEs or for micro enterprises with an important position in small markets.

Table 1.2 compares the applicable safe harbour rules.

1.3.1.3 Access to Justice

In principle, SMEs enjoy the same procedural rights as other companies or individuals in all jurisdictions. There may be some specific differences between legal persons and persons rather than a size-based differentiation. Important case law also shows that SMEs have access to justice if bigger corporations abuse of their dominant position.[76]

There is consensus between the national reporters that no difference should be made between SMEs and larger firms from the procedural perspective apart from the differences that will be analysed in the following points.

1.3.2 Fundamental Rights of SMEs (as Infringers and Victims)

The national reporters agree that fundamental rights should be equally applied to all undertakings. The current legal systems only treat differently legal entities and individuals, this being relevant for micro enterprises or one-person entities. Broader differences could be considered discriminatory.

---

[72] Notice on agreements of minor importance which do not appreciably restrict competition under Article 101 (1) TFEU, OJ 2001C 368, p. 13, para 50.

[73] Official Exchange rate on 5 September2012.

[74] Notice of the Commission: Guidelines on the effect on trade concept contained in Articles 81 and 82 of the Treaty, OJ 2004C 101, p. 7, para 52.

[75] *Zammit*, Italy, Part I, Chap. 10, pp. 174 and 175. Notice of the Commission: Guidelines on the effect on trade concept contained in Articles 81 and 82 of the Treaty, OJ 2004C 101, p. 7, para 52.

[76] See, for instance, the German experience, *Dreher & Körner*, Germany, Part I, Chap. 8, p. 134.

Table 1.2 Safe harbour rules

Country	Horizontal conducts	Vertical conducts	Hard-core conducts	Annual turnover
EU	10 %	15 %	–	–
Sweden	15 % (non hardcore)	–	–	SEK 30 m
Hungary	10 %	No limitation	–	–
US	20–30 % pro-competitive assessment	20–30 % pro-competitive assessment	–	–
Austria	5 % national market 25 % regional market	–	Yes	–

1.3.2.1 Complaints

Complaints are a useful tool for the enforcement of competition law provisions. Any person that has knowledge of anticompetitive conduct may contact (in some countries anonymously) the Competition Authorities, which (at their discretion), may start an investigation about the reported conduct.[77] This means that the Competition Authorities in their discretion have no obligation to open proceedings.[78] Practice has shown that SMEs can be reluctant to directly complain since they fear loss of business or clients if they report about partners, clients, or providers.[79] In any case, sensitive information, such as business secrets, is usually handled confidentially by NCAs, so that SMEs can easily communicate with the authorities. Nevertheless, this confidentiality has to be balanced with the right of access to the administrative files of third parties.[80] Some of the national jurisdictions examined do protect complainants, preserving their anonymity during the proceedings. In other jurisdictions, the NCAs interpreted the confidentiality rules widely in order to protect complainants from other undertakings.[81] The German system contains an interesting anonymous tip-off mechanism that could be an option to follow. The system has two main advantages: (1) the competition authority can initiate the proceedings without indicating the name of the complainant in the files in order to help companies that do not want to take the risk of losing their business partner by reporting the conduct[82]; (2) the system allows to file complaints on unlawful conduct anonymously. This complaint mechanism is included in the website of the *Bundeskartellamt* and guarantees full anonymity

[77] On the complaints system before the European Commission, see Van Bael & Bellis, 2010, p. 986.

[78] See *ex multis Birkhäuser*, Switzerland, Part I, Chap. 13, p. 223.

[79] See *Dreher & Körner*, Germany, Part I, Chap. 8, p. 138. See, for instance, Bundeskartellamt: https://www.bkms-system.net/bkwebanon/report/clientInfo?cin=2bkarta151.

[80] *Zammit*, Italy, Part I, Chap. 10, p. 177.

[81] *Zammit*, Italy, Part I, Chap. 10, p. 177.

[82] See *Dreher & Körner*, Germany, Part I, Chap. 8, p. 138.

during the entire complaint process. According to the *Bundeskartellamt*, the guarantee of anonymity by the tip-off system has been certified by a publicly appointed expert. The information provided cannot be traced back to the informant so long as he does not enter any data that allow for inferences about his identity.[83] The established system also enables communication with the *Bundeskartellamt* if necessary and allows the complainant to cooperate without revealing its identity. Furthermore, the German Authority also accepts tip-offs filed through traditional channels such as post and telephone.

However, there are also jurisdictions where the protection of complainants is not yet considered a relevant issue, probably due to their short experience with competition law rules.[84] Notwithstanding this, Austria has an interesting rule established in section 6 of the Austrian Cartel Act, which prohibits retaliatory measures of dominant undertakings in relation to complaints against an alleged abuse of dominance. This rule also prohibits the refusal to supply if it is a retaliatory measure in reaction to injunctive relief claims of the discriminated resellers. France, and Italy have similar protection rules in order to help smaller companies who fear losing their contracting partner if they report possible anticompetitive conduct or give necessary proof to the authorities.[85]

1.3.2.2 Access to File as a Complainant or Third Party

In public enforcement, access to file in competition law proceedings is possible for parties under investigation in order to comply with the constitutional principles of defence and of equality of arms between parties.[86] In some legal systems, under specific circumstances, access to file (at least to the non-confidential version) is allowed to third parties that are able to demonstrate a concrete and legitimate interest to access to such information.

In private enforcement matters, the access to file by a complainant or other party in order to obtain information and evidence for potential claims is also a crucial point, since the claimants bear the burden of proof.[87] However, in principle, the

[83] See http://www.bundeskartellamt.de/wEnglisch/FurtherInfo/whistleblowing_infoW3DnavidW2631.php.

[84] See, for instance, *Andrejaš*, Croatia, Chap. 4; *Poulsen*, Denmark, Chap. 6; *Papp et al.*, Hungary, Chap. 9.

[85] See *Fussenegger*, Austria, Part I, Chap. 2, p. 34; *Boudou et al.*, France, Part I, Chap. 7, pp. 123 ff; *Zammit*, Italy, Part I, Chap. 10, pp. 176 and 177.

[86] See about the access to the file before the European Commission: Van Bael & Bellis, 2010, p. 1042.

[87] L. Idot, Access to evidence and files of Competition Authorities in J. Basedow, S. Franq, L. Idot: International Private Antitrust Litigation, 2012, p. 20. See also J. Suderow, El acceso a las pruebas en expedientes de la Comisión Europea y los límites establecidos por su programa de Clemencia, in L. Velasco et al.: La aplicación privada del Derecho de la Competencia, 2011, p. 535.

initial position is the same for all types of undertakings.[88] SMEs may face more difficulties than other companies if they are not well assessed and informed or if they are not party to the administrative proceeding. Complainants are considered as third parties without or with limited access to file in some jurisdictions.[89] In the US, SMEs also have the same rights of access to evidence against them as individuals; they receive enhanced due process rights if the SME is ran by individuals and have a sole owner. This distinction is based on the corporate form rather than size.[90] After receiving a complaint and if the NCA decides to start a proceeding, it may be interesting to inform the complainant specifically about the next steps of the proceedings and his rights.

1.3.3 Leniency, Settlements, and Commitment Decisions for SMEs

Leniency programmes are used by undertakings to confess their participation in secret cartels to NCAs. If the cooperation is successful, the authority in most jurisdictions that have taken part in this study will grant immunity for the administrative fine.[91] Usually, there are two types of immunity from fines in favour of a company disclosing its participation in a cartel.[92] The first undertaking to submit information and evidence that enables the authorities to carry out an inspection in connection with the alleged cartel will benefit from complete immunity from the fine. The other undertakings that submit information and evidence can only obtain a partial reduction of the fine.[93] It is important to highlight that a company will have to file as much evidence as possible and will have to cooperate throughout a long investigation proceeding. Therefore, companies that want to benefit from leniency programmes will need resources, time, and specialised advice, yet SMEs can often not afford this. SMEs might, because of these circumstances, refuse to apply for leniency, so that they would be disadvantaged in relation to more powerful undertakings.[94] In the jurisdictions examined, leniency programmes do not contain specific procedures for SMEs. Nevertheless, some of the jurisdictions taking part in this study do not have any experience with leniency since their leniency programmes have only been recently introduced.[95]

[88] See *Birkhäuser*, Switzerland, Part I, Chap. 13, p. 225.

[89] See, for instance, *Andrejaš*, Croatia, Part I, Chap. 4, and *Bailey*, United Kingdom, Part I, Chap. 14, pp. 247 ff; OFT, *Involving third parties in Competition Act investigations*, OFT 451, April 2006, para. 3.22.

[90] See *Varanini*, United States of America, Part I, Chap. 15, p. 259.

[91] See, about the leniency process before the European Commission, Van Bael & Bellis, 2010, p. 1125. A. Calvo Caravaca, 2010 Derecho Antitrust Europeo, Vol. I, p. 347.

[92] V. Bael & Bellis, Competition Law of the European Community 2010, p. 1125.

[93] V. Bael & Bellis, Competition Law of the European Community 2010, p. 1127.

[94] See *Birkhäuser*, Switzerland, Part I, Chap. 13, p. 229.

[95] See, for instance, *Andrejaš*, Croatia, Part I, Chap. 4, p. 72.

It has been stated that SMEs could be disadvantaged in the leniency race since their resources are limited.[96] Furthermore, a leniency application filed by the market leader or a subsidiary of a worldwide operator can lead to the disappearance from the market of SMEs.[97] In addition, leniency applicants are better positioned in case of damage claims, since the authorities will protect them more than other undertakings that did not cooperate or whose attempts to file a leniency application arrived too late.[98] On the other side, it should also be highlighted that SMEs have a more direct access to the competition authorities, since they do not have the bureaucratic and hierarchical structures of bigger undertakings.[99] In this respect, it could be helpful to point out the obligations, such as cooperation duties, and rights, such as right to non-self-incrimination, of an SME during the leniency and sanctioning proceeding.

1.3.4 Sanctions: Different Penalties for Different Size?

SMEs are indeed often involved in sanctioning proceedings regarding cartels, vertical agreements, and even abuse of dominance. Cartels can be detected in different local or regional markets and sectors such as taxi transport, plumbing services, bus transport, driving schools, and even funeral services. SMEs have also in some occasions been sanctioned for vertical restraints or even abuse of dominance in sectors such as funeral services.[100]

As we know, sanctions for competition law infringements can be very high and even affect the economic balance of big and small companies. In most of the jurisdictions examined, the amount of the fine is calculated on the basis of the turnover of the sanctioned company.[101] In the European systems, sanctions are capped to a maximum amount of 10 % of the turnover of the company.[102] On the other side of the Atlantic, courts can take into account the special status of SMEs, but they are still jointly and severally liable for all damages caused by their illicit conduct.[103] Therefore, and despite the mentioned cap, sanctions can be very

---

[96] See *Bailey*, United Kingdom, Part I, Chap. 14, p. 251, and *Birkhäuser*, Switzerland, Part I, Chap. 13, p. 229.

[97] See *Boudou et al.*, France, Part I, Chap. 7, p. 122.

[98] See *Boudou et al.*, France, Part I, Chap. 7, p. 122. Van Bael & Bellis, 2010, p. 1125. A. Calvo Caravaca, 2010 Derecho Antitrust Europeo, Vol. I, p. 571.

[99] See *Bailey*, United Kingdom, Part I, Chap. 14, p. 251.

[100] See, for instance, *horizontal agreements*: taxi drivers (Sweden, Brazil, Hungary), plumbers (Sweden), bus transporters (Sweden, UK), driving schools (Brazil), bakeries (Brazil and Italy), pasta producers (Italy), funeral service providers (Sweden, Brazil); *vertical agreements*: funeral service providers (Hungary); *abuse of dominance*: transport providers (UK), pharmaceutical companies (UK), funeral service providers (UK).

[101] A. Calvo Caravaca, 2010 Derecho Antitrust Europeo, Vol. I, p. 571.

[102] A. Calvo Caravaca, 2010 Derecho Antitrust Europeo, Vol. I, p. 572.

[103] See *Varanini*, United States of America, Part I, Chap. 15, p. 259.

harmful for undertakings. Nevertheless, a strict sanctioning policy guarantees also the effectiveness of the system and promotes more competition.[104] For this reason, sanctions should in principle be equally applied to all companies.

The French report contains an interesting analysis of the differences in sanctions against major companies and SMEs. According to the conclusions of the French Reporters, SMEs in France are more often involved in cartel cases than in other types of competition law violations: "in relative terms, SMEs that originate practices are thus more often found guilty than major companies, with equivalent types of practices". This asymmetry can be caused by lack of knowledge or resources. Major companies could have the necessary funds for an effective defence. Finally, SMEs do not appeal as often as major companies do: only 20 % of French SMEs appeal against a decision of the competition authorities, whereas 63 % of larger companies do appeal.[105] Another conclusion of the French report that should be highlighted is that bigger companies are not fined so often as SMEs, but the sanctions imposed on big corporations are usually higher than the level of fines imposed on SMEs.[106] We cannot ignore that being an SME reduces appeal probabilities because of lesser resources.[107] Therefore, the risk of paying the wrong fine is higher for SMEs than for bigger corporations that can invest more time and human and legal resources in costly appeal proceedings through different instances.[108] Nevertheless, in the UK, the CAT considers that it would be "inappropriate for the OFT to hold directors of smaller companies to a lower standard of compliance".[109] The UK competition rules are contradictory to this statement, establishing immunity from fine for conduct of minor importance if the parties have an aggregated turnover that is less than GBP 50 million (equivalent to EUR 61,460,958.37).[110]

Notwithstanding the above, the competition authorities should somehow establish the necessary balance in their sanctioning policy as proposed below. Negligence can be considered in some cases as a mitigating circumstance. In the European practice, this mitigating circumstance is not applied very often. In order to infringe the European prohibitions, it is sufficient that the undertaking could not have ignored that the conduct had the object to restrict competition.[111] Notwithstanding this, there is no clear red line for business people with limited time and

[104] See V. Bael & Bellis, Competition Law of the European Community 2010, p. 1125.

[105] See *Boudou et al.*, France, Part I, Chap. 7, p. 108.

[106] See *Boudou et al.*, France, Part I, Chap. 7, pp. 108 and 119.

[107] See *Boudou et al.*, France, Part I, Chap. 7, pp. 108, 119 ff.

[108] See *Boudou et al.*, France, Part I, Chap. 7, p. 121.

[109] CAT Case Nos, etc, 1125/1/1/09 *Barret Estate Services, Ltd & Ors v OFT* (2011), CAT 8; see *Bailey*, United Kingdom, Part I, Chap. 14, p. 251.

[110] See *Bailey*, United Kingdom, Part I, Chap. 14, p. 244.

[111] A. Calvo Caravaca, Derecho Antitrust Europeo, Vol. I, 2010, p. 573.

access to competition law. The exchange of information within a trade association is a clear example. Even companies with compliance programmes do not really know when the exchange of information is anticompetitive or not. The manager of an SME that takes part in regular association meetings where the participants discuss the market conditions and developments, even assisted by the legal advisors of the association, is not always aware of the limits between infringements and authorised exchange of information.[112] Limited involvement is also considered a mitigating circumstance in some jurisdictions,[113] which could be used to rebalance sanctions against SMEs if the effect of their conduct was limited or insignificant in comparison to the conduct carried out by other undertakings.

1.3.5 Policy Recommendations for Discussion

SMEs typically face more obstacles than big companies in dealing with competition law proceedings due to lack of human and financial resources.

In order to redress this asymmetry, the following policy recommendations could be taken into account:

- Anonymity for SMEs that help to uncover a competition law infringement—NCAs should guarantee the anonymity of complainants during the proceedings if SMEs ask for this special protection. SMEs should be given more incentives to access to leniency programmes—preventing cartel leaders from benefiting from any type or immunity within the leniency programmes. Cartels involving big and small companies are usually initiated by the bigger company that assumes the leading role in the cartel. This measure would indirectly help SMEs in the race to blow the whistle.
- The US failing-company doctrine could help to hinder the removal of SMEs from the market. Essentially, the doctrine allows a company, having a serious probability of business failure, to complete an otherwise illegal merger, provided no alternate good faith purchaser exists.[114] In Europe, according to the Commission notice on fines, in exceptional circumstances, the European Commission can reduce the fine if the company provides sufficiently clear and objective evidence that the fine is likely to affect seriously the economic viability of the

[112] See recent developments of the jurisprudence regarding exchange(s) of information, for instance ECJ, case C-8/08, *T-Mobile Netherlands BV, KPN Mobile NV, Orange Nederland NV and Vodafone Libertel NV v Raad van bestuur van de Nederlandse Mededingingsautoriteit*, ECR 2009 I-4529.

[113] See International Report prepared for the LIDC Congress in Oxford in September 2011 Question A: Fines in Antitrust, p. 26, and A. Calvo Caravaca: Derecho Antitrust Europeo, Vol. I, 2010, p. 574.

[114] M. P. Blum, The failing company doctrine, p. 1, in Boston College Law Review 1975 (16).

undertaking.[115] The analysis looks in detail at various company-specific factors and aims to be as objective and quantifiable as possible to ensure equal treatment and maintain deterrence.[116] This rule is applicable to all kinds of companies, and some national jurisdictions have similar rules. Notwithstanding this, it is more likely that an SME suffers the consequences of the fine more than a big corporation would. Therefore, it could be interesting to include size and market position as factors to be taken into account when setting the fines. Other mitigating circumstances such as negligence or limited involvement could also be applied to SMEs on a case-by-case analysis.

1.4 Private Competition Law Enforcement and SMEs

It is a common belief that victims of anticompetitive behaviour may face harsh difficulties in obtaining effective compensation for the damages suffered.[117] This is particularly true in the European legal system, where a legislative intervention aimed to foster litigation in competition law issues is expected in the near future. The reform is aimed to remove some substantial and procedural obstacles, such as rules on access to evidence, that still impede the full effectiveness of right of compensation by victims of anticompetitive conduct within the EU.

Irrespective of the specificities of the legal system where they are brought, actions for damages based on competition law violations are inherently difficult and expensive to pursue in courts. This is due to the difficulties to demonstrate the existence of an antitrust infringement (especially in stand-alone actions), the causal link between the misconduct and the damage, and the difficulty to quantify the damages suffered, where complex economic analysis is often required. Another complex aspect one may consider, according to the specificity of the case, is that these kinds of claim may involve several parties in multiple jurisdictions (this means that problems of joint liability, jurisdictions, conflict of laws may also arise).[118] SMEs, as well as consumers, especially when the economic harm they suffered is not relevant, are particularly disadvantaged in this kind of litigation. Limited resources can oblige SMEs to renounce their compensation rights even if they learn about the anticompetitive practice on time.

---

[115] See Van Bael & Bellis, Competition Law of the European Community, 2010, p. 1113.

[116] Guidelines on the method of setting fines imposed pursuant to Article 23(2) (a) of Regulation No 1/2003, OJ 2006C 210, p. 2.

[117] See, on the international perspective of private enforcement, J. Basedow, S. Franq, L. Idot, International Antitrust Litigation, 2012.

[118] J. Basedow, S. Franq, L. Idot, International Antitrust Litigation, 2012, p. 3. E. Castellanos, Competencia Judicial internacional en las acciones de reparación de daños y perjuicios por infracción del Derecho Antitrust in L. Velasco et al.: La aplicación privada del Derecho de la Competencia, 2010, p. 619. Ashton, D. Vollrath, D., Choice of court and applicable law in tortious actions for breach of Community competition law, in ZweR 2006, pp. 1–26.

1.4.1 Substantive Rules, Procedural Aspects for SMEs in Civil Suits

1.4.1.1 Obstacles

In all the legal systems analysed, in judicial proceedings, it is the claimants who have to prove the facts necessary to substantiate claims.[119] This can be particularly expensive and time consuming in comparison to the success rates. Risks, such as the payment of the defendant's costs, the fear of losing a good business partner, or passing on defence may affect victims' intention to claim damages.[120] Obstacles can be of two different categories, depending on the anticompetitive conduct. In the first case—exclusionary practices—SMEs may be interested in claiming, but if the practice is irreversible they could just "leave the market" in order to avoid further costs and losses.[121] On the other hand, in vertical restraints the claiming tendency may be lower since SMEs fear exclusion or further discrimination by the stronger undertakings that are infringing the law.[122] Furthermore, SMEs may ignore the existence of the cartel itself or even the sanctioning decision of the competent authorities. SMEs do not always have easy access to the information in the hands of competition authorities.[123] Although the manager of an SME may be informed about a cartel that affected his business, he may not even know how and where to start in order to check if the firm suffered any damage at all.

Quantification of damages is also a very complex matter that affects all parties involved. Again, the limited human and financial resources can weaken the litigation possibilities of SMEs against larger companies, since quantification often requires expertise and complex price and costs analysis and market definition.[124] Access to the competition authority's file can be quite difficult, particularly if the defendant filed for leniency.[125] Last but not least, complex claims such as competition law claims are very costly; therefore, the funding of the litigation can also represent a harsh burden on SMEs.

1.4.1.2 Best Practices

There does not seem to exist any "best practice" in private litigation in the civil courts of the different jurisdictions. Furthermore, there are no concrete protection mechanisms for SMEs in civil proceedings.

---

[119] L. Idot, Access to evidence and files of Competition Authorities in J Basedow, S. Franq, L. Idot: International Private Antitrust Litigation, 2012, p. 20. See also J. Suderow: El acceso a las pruebas en expedientes de la Comisión Europea y los límites establecidos por su programa de Clemencia, in L. Velasco et al.: La aplicación privada del Derecho de la Competencia, 2011, p. 535.

[120] See *Bailey*, United Kingdom, Part I, Chap. 14, pp. 253 ff.

[121] See *Boudou et al.*, France, Part I, Chap. 7, p. 123.

[122] See *Boudou et al.*, France, Part I, Chap. 7, p. 124.

[123] See *Neyrinck*, Belgium, Part I, Chap. 3, p. 58.

[124] See *Neyrinck*, Belgium, Part I, Chap. 3, p. 58.

[125] See recent developments in Germany and ECJ, case C-360/09, *Pfleiderer AG v Bundeskartellamt*, ECR 2011 I-5161.

In the US, SMEs are jointly and severally liable for all damages caused by the cartel. In this respect, it is important to highlight that US law, like other jurisdictions, does not allow SMEs to argue that other cartel members should pay more because of their leading role or market share.[126] Moreover, treble damages also apply to SMEs. This circumstance, coupled with the joint and several liability and the absence of a right to contribution, could, in the worst scenario, eliminate SMEs from the market. In this respect, the US National Reporter has proposed to accept the failing firm defence for trebled damages if the damages drive SMEs to bankruptcy.[127] This proposal should indeed be discussed not only for treble damages but also for public sanctions in European jurisdictions. The bankruptcy of any market player, particularly SMEs, provoked by competition law penalties would have negative effects on competition.[128]

1.4.2 Collective Redress

The International Report follows the definition of the European Commission for "Collective Redress". Under this definition, collective redress is any mechanism that "may accomplish the termination or prevention of unlawful business practices which affect a multitude of claimants (consumers and/or SMEs) or the compensation for the harm caused by such illegal practices".[129]

As already mentioned, it is a matter of fact that SMEs are reluctant (especially in the EU) to bring forward an action for damages if such damages are small in comparison to the costs of litigation.[130] The current European systems are not effective in promoting access of SMEs to collective redress instruments.[131] The asymmetry *vis-à-vis* the infringers against SMEs is similar to that of consumers.[132] The debate around SMEs and collective redress starts with the discussion of whether SMEs should have access to the same mechanisms as consumers. The European Commission, in June 2013, issued a recommendation on common principles for injunctive and compensatory collective redress mechanisms in the Member States concerning violations of rights granted under EU law that clearly includes SMEs among subjects entitled to bring collective actions.[133] Some authors

---

[126] See *Varanini*, United States of America, Part I, Chap. 15, pp. 259 ff.

[127] See *Varanini*, United States of America, Part I, Chap. 15, pp. 259 ff.

[128] See *Varanini*, United States of America, Part I, Chap. 15, pp. 276 ff.

[129] See P. Buccirossi, M. Carpagnano, L. Ciari, M. Tognoni, C. Vitale: Collective Redress in Antitrust, Study requested by the European Parliament's Committee on Economic and Monetary Affairs, p. 15, available at http://www.europarl.europa.eu/committees/fr/studiesdownload.html?languageDocument=EN&file=74351.

[130] European Parliament Study on Collective Redress in Antitrust, cit., p. 15.

[131] European Parliament Study on Collective Redress in Antitrust, cit., p. 38.

[132] European Parliament Study on Collective Redress in Antitrust, cit., p. 64.

[133] See Commission Recommendation C(2013) 3539/3. The same approach has been followed by the European Parliament in its Resolution of 2 February 2012 on the coherent European approach to collective redress.

consider that collective redress mechanisms have to protect consumers' interests, and no other interests. But on the other hand, the asymmetry is similar to consumers, particularly in micro businesses against big companies.[134] Nevertheless, the European definition of SMEs may be too broad, since it embraces companies with an annual turnover of up to EUR 50 million.[135] The asymmetry in this kind of company is probably not as obvious as in micro enterprises.[136]

Furthermore, collective redress mechanisms only work if the claims have common elements. Although SMEs may also be subject to standard contracts, their contractual conditions may be different across various countries. This could hinder the courts in determining the common ground for the action.[137] With respect to Europe, some of the national reports describe the existing collective redress mechanisms, such as representative actions or group litigation orders, but practical experience and case law with SMEs seem to be limited.[138] In the US, the situation is completely different. US class actions are open for SMEs and other types of companies, whereas large corporations usually file their own individual claims.[139] As stated by the US report, class action is a useful tool both for the defendant and for the victims that are SMEs and consumers. Indeed, the former can obtain a global release of claims, while the latter can obtain compensation for the damages suffered. However, even in the US there is limited experience with respect to SMEs and class actions for competition law infringements.[140] Table 1.3 summarises the existing collective redress mechanisms.

1.4.3 Should Trade Associations Have Standing in Collective Redress Claims?

As of today, trade associations cannot bring claims on behalf of their members in most of the jurisdictions, with some exceptions such as the German and Italian associations.[141] Also in this case, in the United States SMEs can file class actions through associations, as long as one member of the association can show that it suffered an economic injury causally connected to the illegal conduct of the defendant.[142] In Europe, specific consumer bodies are authorised to bring forward claims on behalf of their members.[143] Furthermore, according to several civil

[134] European Parliament Study on Collective Redress in Antitrust, cit., p. 69.

[135] Equivalent to USD 65,108,405.50 Official exchange rate on 21 October 2012.

[136] European Parliament Study on Collective Redress in Antitrust, cit. p. 69.

[137] European Parliament Study on Collective Redress in Antitrust, cit. p. 69.

[138] See *Bailey*, United Kingdom, Part I, Chap. 14, pp. 253–255.

[139] See *Varanini*, United States of America, Part I, Chap. 15, pp. 270 ff.

[140] See *Varanini*, United States of America, Part I, Chap. 15, pp. 270 ff.

[141] See *Varanini*, United States of America, Part I, Chap. 15, p. 270, and *Zammit*, Italy, Part I, Chap. 10, p. 182.

[142] See *Varanini*, United States of America, Part I, Chap. 15, p. 269.

[143] See *Bailey*, United Kingdom, Part I, Chap. 14, p. 255.

Table 1.3 Collective redress mechanisms

Country	Collective redress available for SMEs?	What the NRs think about it
EU	No	Why not? Maybe in the future
UK	Yes	Seems to be in favour
Sweden	Yes	Not very useful No standing for trade associations
USA	Yes	No extensive case law

procedural rules, claimants need to have a personal, direct, and immediate interest in the claim, whereas associations would in principle not need to fulfil these requirements.[144]

1.4.4 Policy Recommendations for Discussion

- As mentioned above, the British government has recently launched a public consultation about private actions in competition law.[145] One of the main aims is "to make it easier for businesses, especially SMEs, to challenge anticompetitive behaviour that is harming them". It should be highlighted that the British government is even considering creating a "fast track" procedure for SMEs before the CAT, which should be cheap, quicker, and simpler[146]. This fast track seems to be an interesting option for the parties involved, reducing costs and asymmetric situations for SMEs, as well as for defendants, because it would enable the courts to deliver fast decisions, reducing their own costs.
- Moreover, the Hungarian presumption could also be a potential solution. According to this presumption, unless otherwise proved, horizontal price fixing and/or market-sharing arrangements are assumed to determine an increase equivalent to 10 % of the contractual prices. This option certainly has some disadvantages, since the price increase could easily be over the 10 % threshold for long duration cartels or below, in the case of cartels having a shorter duration. Nonetheless, both parties would save litigation costs, and the courts would be able to take fast decisions.
- Legal aid tools cutting litigation costs made available to SMEs by the government or by bar associations would be an easy option that reduces the unbalanced situation in proceedings between SMEs and big companies.
- Arbitration proceedings should also be promoted. Bar associations and arbitration courts could create specialised panels for competition law litigation. This way, the parties involved would know where and how to claim. Also, the

[144] See, for instance, *Neyrinck*, Belgium, Part I, Chap. 3, p. 61.

[145] See *Bailey*, United Kingdom, Part I, Chap. 14, p. 256, and OFT, Private actions in Competition Law: a consultation on options to reform, April 2012.

[146] See *Bailey*, United Kingdom, Part I, Chap. 14, p. 256, and Private actions in Competition Law: a consultation on options to reform, April 2012.

defendants would probably prefer the arbitration approach due to the significantly reduced duration of the proceedings.
- As stated by certain national reporters, allowing standing for trade associations is also another positive approach that could help re-establish the balance between the involved parties.[147]

1.5 Resolution Adopted by the LIDC

The League recognises the importance of small and medium-sized enterprises, especially micro enterprises, in the world economy and society. From a competition law perspective, the LIDC underlines the importance of an approach mainly irrespective of the size.

In the light of the above, the League recommends that

- there is no need for a sector-specific legal definition of SMEs in the field of competition law. Soft law tools, such as guidelines, may suffice in order to provide a common and simplified definition of SMEs based on market realities.
- there should be more competition law culture and compliance programmes specifically addressed to SMEs: Antitrust Authorities should pay particular attention to, and further, the awareness and knowledge of competition law by SMEs (e.g., help desk, website, standard compliance models, etc.).
- anonymity should be organised for SMEs that denounce competition law infringements in a way that is consistent with the rights of defence: Antitrust Authorities should guarantee the anonymity of complainants during investigations if SMEs ask for this special protection.
- SMEs should be given more incentives to access leniency programmes.
- fining methodology should take into account the following in assessing mitigating circumstances and ability to pay: size, finances, and market position.
- if collective redress mechanisms were adopted, countries should further consider appropriate means to lower financial and organisational hurdles faced by SMEs in bringing a damage action.
- a rebuttable presumption on suffered damages should be considered as an option, especially to SMEs (e.g., in hard-core violations).
- legal aid tools in reducing litigation costs should be made available to SMEs.

Acknowledgment The Author is very grateful to Julia Suderow, Rechtsanwältin and Abogada, from the Antitrust Observatory, Trento for her valuable research and academic assistance. The International Reporter wishes to thank Pierre Kobel, Muriel Chagny, and the members of the Scientific Committee of the LIDC for their useful insights and feedback on this report and preliminary research. A warm thanks to all national reporters for their excellent contributions and valuable insights on national legal systems.

[147] See *Papp et al.*, Hungary, Part I, Chap. 9, p. 155.

Austria 2

Gerhard Fussenegger

2.1 SMEs in Context

2.1.1 SMEs' Economic Context and Legal Definition

2.1.1.1 Legal Definitions of SMEs

SMEs are not legally defined in Austria in the Austrian legislation on the protection of competition. Therefore, also in accordance with practice in Austria, the answers in Table 2.1 refer to the definition of SME as defined by the European Commission.[1]

2.1.1.2 The Economic Perspective

Concerning the number of employees, 403,601 in a total of 404,690 undertakings in Austria are SMEs in the meaning of the above-mentioned definition. In other words, more than 99.7 % of all undertakings in Austria are SMEs. Within these SMEs, more than 92 % of the undertakings are so-called micro undertakings with less than ten employees.[2]

[1] Recommendation 2003/361/EC.

[2] See Wirtschaftskammer Österreich (Austrian Economic Chambers), "KMU-Daten für Österreich" available at http://wko.at/Statistik/KMU/WKO-BeschStatK.pdf.

G. Fussenegger (✉)
bpv Hügel Rechtsanwälte OG, Brussels, Belgium
e-mail: Gerhard.Fussenegger@bpv-huegel.com

P. Këllezi et al. (eds.), *Antitrust for Small and Middle Size Undertakings and Image Protection from Non-Competitors*, LIDC Contributions on Antitrust Law, Intellectual Property and Unfair Competition, DOI 10.1007/978-3-642-54000-4_2, © Springer-Verlag Berlin Heidelberg 2014

Table 2.1 Definition of SME

Company category	Employees	Turnover or Balance sheet total
Medium sized	< 250	$\leq$ EUR 50 m or $\leq$ EUR 43 m
Small	< 50	$\leq$ EUR 10 m or $\leq$ EUR 10 m
Micro	< 10	$\leq$ EUR 2 m or $\leq$ EUR 2 m

2.1.1.3 Relevant Cases

Driving Schools

To date, the Cartel Court has issued two decisions regarding SMEs. Both decisions related to regional driving schools, the first concerning the area of Graz[3] in 2005/2006 and the second with regard to Innsbruck[4] in 2008.

In the first decision of 2005/2006, six local driving schools in Graz fixed prices for driving licenses. One of the driving schools was granted full leniency status; the aggregate fine for the other schools amounted to EUR 80,000. Similarly, in Innsbruck, seven driving schools fixed prices for driving licenses. Two driving schools applied for and obtained a leniency status. One of them was exempted from fines, and the remaining six schools were fined by the Cartel Court, with a total amount of EUR 70,000.

The size of the SMEs was taken into account in imposing relatively low fines; for instance, two driving schools concerned got a fine of EUR 12,500 each. However, it is unknown whether this amount was solely based on the (low) turnover of the SMEs or whether the Cartel Court additionally took as a mitigating factor the fact that the undertakings were small and regional driving schools.

Plumbers

The Austrian Federal Competition Authority (hereafter referred to as "Bundeswettbewerbsbehörde" or "BWB"[5]) has currently opened proceedings at the Cartel Court with regard to an alleged bid-rigging cartel of plumbers in Vienna. According to BWB, more than 40 plumber undertakings in Vienna participated in a price and market allocation cartel in the context of bids to the City of Vienna in relation to its community-subsidised tenement buildings. The allegations are fiercely contested by the plumbers concerned.

Shopping Centres

There is also some case law in Austria with regard to clauses in leasing agreements of shopping centres prohibiting the tenants to open further shops in other shopping

[3] Judgment of the Cartel Court of 28 October 2005, case number 25 Kt 30/05-18, '*Grazer Fahrschulen*'. The judgment is not published. Graz is the second biggest city in Austria with approximately 260,000 inhabitants.

[4] Judgment of the Cartel Court of 29 August 2008, '*Innsbrucker Fahrschulen*'. The judgment and its case number is not published. Innsbruck is the fifth biggest city in Austria with approximately 120,000 inhabitants.

[5] See http://www.bwb.gv.at/Seiten/default.aspx.

centres within a special radius.[6] Based on a wide relevant market, including all shopping possibilities within the respective radius, and not only shopping centres, the Supreme Cartel Court decided that the clause does not have any effect and therefore does not infringe competition law. However, these cases are not considered to be covered by the scope of the report, as the parties involved are not SMEs but major players like Spar or internationally active Outlet Centres. Furthermore, the Court decided exclusively on the basis of EU and not national competition law.

2.1.2 Specific Treatment of SMEs Under Competition Law

2.1.2.1 The Nature and Scope of Specific Treatment for SMEs

In general, there are neither specific public or private enforcement rules nor specific programmes (such as compliance, information policies, enhancement of competition enforcement) in Austrian competition law directly addressing SMEs. Therefore, the general approach in Austria is quite clear: each undertaking, regardless of its size, falls under the same substantive and procedural rules.

However, as outlined below in detail, there are some substantive rules that indirectly address SME issues in particular.

2.1.2.2 Size and Economic Power in Decisions of the National Competition Authorities and Courts

The size and economic power of the undertakings concerned are reflected, if even, within the sanctions imposed, mainly as a mitigating factor. Therefore, reference is made to Sect. 2.1.4 of this chapter.

2.1.3 The Role of Trade Associations

With regard to trade associations, there are neither specific rules nor specific programmes (compliance, information policies, enhancement of competition enforcement) in Austrian competition law directly addressing SMEs.

2.1.4 Policy Recommendations

In the author's view, every natural and legal person, regardless of economic size, should have the same rights concerning access to justice or remedies. Thus, SMEs should not have any special rights in Austrian competition law.

---

[6] Cf. judgment of the Cartel Supreme Court of 12 December 2011, case number 16 Ok 8/10, '*Radiusklausel II*'.

2.2 Public Antitrust Enforcement and SMES

2.2.1 Substantive and Procedural Rules Applicable to SMEs

2.2.1.1 Introduction

There are no specific rules that aim to protect SMEs. However, the Austrian competition law provides far-reaching substantive rules with regard to undertakings that are confronted with dominant undertakings (see section 'Far-Reaching Definition of "Abuse of Dominance"') or strong suppliers (see section "Regulation on Local Supplies"). Therefore, again, also SMEs can profit from these far-reaching rules.

2.2.1.2 Substantive Rules Applicable to SMEs

Far-Reaching Definition of "Abuse of Dominance"

In Austria, the legal wording of dominance in Section 4 of the Cartel Act[7] not only includes undertakings that are "not or only marginal exposed to competition"[8] but also encompasses an "outstanding" position compared to other competitors or its suppliers or buyers.

Therefore, the term "dominance" in Austrian competition law is far reaching. Undertakings claiming that other undertakings are dominant do not have to prove that there is no competition on the market but can demonstrate that they are economically dependent on the business relationship on the alleged dominant undertaking.

Furthermore, Section 6 of the Cartel Act prohibits any retaliatory measures of dominant undertakings in relation to complaints against an alleged abuse of dominance.

Regulation on Local Supplies

Besides the general abuse of dominance rules (see Section 4 of the Cartel Act), the Austrian legal regime includes the Act on Local Supplies ("Nahversorgungsgesetz", "NahVersG"), a far-reaching legislation protecting SMEs.

Section 2 of the Act on Local Supplies provides that suppliers that offer different conditions to its resellers that operate under the same conditions and without objective justifications can be addressees of an injunctive relief. Dominance of the supplier is not a precondition for submission of such a claim.

By including all undertakings which resell their **(also processed)** goods under the term "reseller", the scope of Section 4 of the Act on Local Supplies is widely defined. Based on this legal clause, there had been an (in)famous decision of the

[7] Bundesgesetz gegen Kartelle und andere Wettbewerbsbeschränkungen, BGBl. I Nr. 61/2005, available at http://www.bwb.gv.at/Fachinformationen/rechtlicheGrundlagen/Seiten/Kartellgesetz.aspx.

[8] Referring to EU law, which defines dominance as "the power to behave independently of its competitors, customers and consumer"; see, e.g., ECJ case C-27/76, *United Brands Company and United Brands Continentaal BV v Commission*, ECR 1978, p. 207, pt 65.

Cartel Supreme Court in 2008,[9] following which the Bavarian state forests had to terminate long-term supply agreements with Bavarian sawmills on the basis of a price level that was more than 5 % under the price that other buyers, amongst them Austrian sawmills, had to pay. The jurisdiction of the Austrian courts was, inter alia, reasoned by the fact that the given supply agreements impeded competition, also for Austrian undertakings.

Similar to Section 6 of the Cartel Act, Section 3 of the Act on Local Supplies prohibits any refusal to supply if it constitutes a retaliatory measure in response to an injunctive relief claim of the discriminated reseller.

2.2.1.3 Safe Harbours for SMEs

De Minimis Rule

So far, the Austrian *de minimis* rule, as stated in Section 2 (2) (1) of the Cartel Act, provides a specific safe harbour for SMEs in so far as cartels are completely excluded from the scope of competition law, if the combined market share of the participant does not exceed 5 % on a national basis or 25 % on a regional market.

Therefore, if trade between Member States is not affected and if thresholds are not met, SMEs are free to agree on prices and to allocate markets.

However, with the current reform of the Austrian Cartel Law, which comes into force on 1 March 2013, the clause will be deleted and replaced by a new provision that reflects the EU's *de minimis* rule.

First, the market share thresholds will be adapted to the EU's *de minimis* approach, i.e. the *de minimis* exception will only apply if the respective market shares of the undertakings concerned are not more than 10 % (if competitors are involved) or 15 % (concerning non-competitors).

Second, and this will be of essential importance to SMEs' hard-core cartel infringements, price fixing, limit or control production, and market allocation will not be exempted anymore from the scope of the Cartel Act, whether the market shares are met or not. Hence, the safe harbour for SMEs, as currently reflected in the *de minimis* rule of the Austrian Cartel Act, will be abolished once the adapted Austrian Cartel Act will come into force.

National Regulation to Austrian Cartel Act 1988

Until 2005, there had been a national regulation in force, which excluded certain forms of cooperation from the scope of competition law.[10] Based on this far-reaching regulation, e.g. purchasing groups under certain circumstances, common R&D projects and consortiums were exempted from the scope of the Austrian Cartel Law. With regard to SMEs (based on a market share threshold of below 5 %), the regulation allowed common advertising, even with regard to coordinated prices.

[9] Judgment of the Cartel Supreme Court of 16 July 2008, case number 16 Ok 3/08, '*Bayrische Staatsforste*'.

[10] Reg. BGBL 1989/185.

However, with the reform of the Austrian Cartel Act in 2005, the regulation was abolished.

2.2.2 Fundamental Rights of SMEs as Infringers and Victims

2.2.2.1 Complaints

SMEs do have the same rights as any other undertaking, independently of their size and turnover.

In the author's view, a mechanism to protect SMEs in the form of leniency applications would, on the one side, surely help in enabling SMEs to inform the national competition authority about alleged infringements.

However, on the other side, also an undertaking that is allegedly abusing its dominance in the market should be able to defend itself by getting access to file or cross-examining the complainant. It should be also noted that in Austria only courts are legally allowed to impose fines, while the competition authorities can exclusively submit an application before the court for a fine. Hence, especially in proceedings in front of courts, the "defendant" should be protected by wide-ranged rights of defence.

Therefore, in balancing the rights of SMEs and defending undertakings, it seems difficult to consider a system in practice where the SME is protected without infringing the rights of defence of the undertaking indicted.

In general, the Austrian Cartel Supreme Court[11] always avoided clarifying whether the abstract threatening of a fine according to Section 29 of the Cartel Act results in a direct application of Art 6 ECMR, which applies to criminal fines.

However, the Cartel Supreme Court follows the ECJ's approach that certain legal clauses of the ECMR do apply in cartel proceedings, for instance:

- Art 6 (2) ECMR, with regard to its principle of presumption of innocence[12];
- Art 6 (3) lit d ECMR, with regard to right to be heard.[13]

The Cartel Supreme Court furthermore confirmed that the decision and the calculation of the fine must be revisable on appeal.[14]

2.2.2.2 Access to File

According to Section 39 (2) of the Austrian Cartel Act, access to file in cartel proceedings can only be provided to third parties if all parties to the proceedings agree. This rule is a special rule in the Austrian Cartel Law, as opposed to civil and

---

[11] Judgment of the Cartel Supreme Court of 4 October 2010, case number 16 Ok 5/10, '*Printing Chemicals*'.

[12] Judgement of the Supreme Court of 6 November 2011, case number 5 Ob 154/07v.

[13] Judgements of the Cartel Supreme Court of 12 September 2007, case number 16 Ok 4/07 and of 15 July 2009, case number 16 Ok 6/09, '*Pressegrosso I*'.

[14] Judgment of the Cartel Supreme Court of 4 October 2010, case number 16 Ok 5/10, '*Printing Chemicals*'.

criminal procedural laws, which empower courts to grant access to file following a balancing of opposing interests.

On 12 October 2011, the Vienna Higher Regional Court sitting as Cartel Court referred a case[15] on the right of access to a cartel file to the Court of Justice of the European Union. The Cartel Court was seeking guidance as to whether the above-mentioned Section 39 (2) of the Cartel Act banning access to cartel files unless all parties to the cartel procedure have consented to such access is in line with EU law, particularly in light of the ECJ's recent judgment in the Pfleiderer case.[16]

The reference for preliminary ruling is based on a national proceeding, in which an association representing companies in the printing sector filed a damage claim. The claims follow an infringement decision adopted by the Cartel Court against companies active in the wholesale trade for printing chemicals.

2.2.3 Leniency, Settlements, and Commitment Decisions for SMEs

Compared to other undertakings, no different rules apply for SMEs in connection with settlements and commitment decisions in Austria.

In principle, the same can be noted with regard to leniency applications; no different levels of severity do apply for SMEs. The BWB, especially for the first leniency applicant, does accept a form with only essential information and therefore a low evidential threshold with regard to the alleged cartel. SMEs can take advantage of the leniency system. Reference in this regard can be made to the BWB's "Leniency Handbook", where the leniency procedure is explained in detail.

According to Section 11 (3) Austrian Competition Act,[17] the BWB can grant full immunity or a reduced fine to a leniency applicant only if the undertaking concerned did not, inter alia, "take steps to coerce other undertakings to participate in the infringement". However, if SMEs are market leaders in their niche and therefore able to coerce other undertakings to participate in a cartel, they might be excluded from applying as leniency applicants.

It appears that mostly leniency applicants tend to be undertakings belonging to major market players and not SMEs. However, there are also some exceptions.

In the Freight Forwarding Cartel,[18] the leniency applicant was Schenker. Other undertakings involved were more than 40, also small Austrian freight forwarding companies. In the Elevator Cartel,[19] the leniency applicants were Thyssen Krupp und Otis; other undertakings involved were, on the one side, global active

[15] Referral for a preliminary ruling of Cartel Court of 12 October 2012, case number 29 Kt 5/09.

[16] ECJ, case C-360/09, *Pfleiderer AG v Bundeskartellamt*, ECR 2011 I-5161.

[17] Which is the second antitrust law in Austria besides the Cartel Act.

[18] Referral for a preliminary ruling of the Cartel Supreme Court of 5 December 2011, case number 16 Ok 4/11, *Freight Forwarding Cartel.*

[19] Judgment of the Cartel Supreme Court of 8 October 2008, case number 16 Ok 5/08, *Elevator Cartel.*

undertakings Kone and Schindler and also Austrian-based Haushahn Aufzüge GmbH and Doppelmayr Aufzüge AG.

In the Chemical Industry Wholesale Cartel,[20] the Donau Chemie Group, which did not apply for leniency, unsuccessfully referred to its minor role compared to the successful leniency applicant Brenntag by arguing that the cartel was based on an initiative of the leniency applicant and that there had been substantial pressure to participate. Furthermore, Donau Chemie Group brought forward that they were substantially smaller than the leniency applicant and argued that this fact should be reflected in the gravity of default. This argument was also rejected.

Contrary to the cases listed above, the leniency applicants in the above-mentioned plumber and in the driving licence cartel proceedings were SMEs involved in the cartels.

2.2.4 Sanctions: Different Penalties for Different Sizes?

SMEs do fall in Austrian competition law under the same sanction regime as bigger market players. Therefore, in general, a fine is based on the turnover in the relevant market. Aggravating and mitigating factors are considered on a case-to-case assessment.

However, based on the following criteria, the size of SMEs will at least indirectly be taken into account:

- As it is the undertaking's turnover in the relevant market in Austria,[21] SMEs do, in general, profit from their lower turnover.
- Furthermore, an agreement covering the whole of Austria was considered as being aggravating,[22] while in *Printing Chemicals*[23] the regional character was taken into account as a mitigating factor.
- In *Europay*,[24] the Supreme Cartel Court, in increasing the fine of the Court of First Instance, referred to the profit achieved in the business concerned and the high economic power of the parent companies.
- At last, Section 30 Austrian Cartel Act, in listing the criteria for imposing a fine, also mentions "economic capacity". In *Chemical Industry Wholesale Cartel*,[25]

---

[20] Judgment of the Cartel Supreme Court of 25 March 2009, case number 16 Ok 4/09, *Chemical Industry Wholesale Cartel.*

[21] See, e.g., judgment of the Cartel Supreme Court of 25 March 2009, case number 16 Ok 4/09, *Chemical Industry Wholesale Cartel.*

[22] See, e.g., judgment of the Cartel Supreme Court of 8 October 2008, case number 16 Ok 5/08, *Elevator Cartel.*

[23] Judgment of the Cartel Supreme Court of 4 October 2010, case number 16 Ok 5/10, *Printing Chemicals.*

[24] Judgment of the Cartel Supreme Court of 12 September 2007, case number 16 Ok 4/07, *Europay.*

[25] Judgment of the Cartel Supreme Court of 25 March 2009, case number 16 Ok 4/09, *Chemical Industry Wholesale Cartel.*

the Supreme Cartel Court, in referring to the undertaking's turnover, rejected the argument that the criterion "economic capacity" implies that the fine imposed must be in a certain relation to the missing profit achieved. Whether SMEs, in referring to their small turnover, could apply for a lower fine due to their limited economic capacity seems, to the author's knowledge, so far not issued in Austrian jurisprudence.

2.2.5 Recommendations

In the author's view, every natural and legal person, regardless of economic size, should be confronted with the same substantive and procedural rules of public antitrust enforcement.

2.3 Private Antitrust Enforcement and SMEs

2.3.1 Substantive Rules, Procedural Aspects for SMEs in Civil Suits

Austrian national legislation does not contain any specific rule to protect SMEs in civil suits for anticompetitive conducts.

So far, there had been uncertainty in Austria as to whether members of a cartel can be held liable in joint severability in compensation for damages proceedings. However, recently, the Austrian Supreme Cartel Court clearly stated that cartel members in general can be held liable for each other.[26]

Furthermore, the Supreme Cartel Court confirmed in the same decision that based on Art 6 Z 1 Brussels Regulation,[27] also 100 % foreign parent companies of cartel members can be sued in the place of jurisdiction of the subsidiary if there is a strong relation between the respective causes of action for damages.

Last, the Supreme Cartel Court also confirmed that a natural person who was, at the time of the cartel, CEO of one of the cartel members can be held jointly and severally liable based on his intentional and tortious behaviour as a CEO within the cartel.

One general procedural difficulty that affects SMEs, in particular, in damage proceedings is the extreme high court fees. In Austria, the fees are determined as a percentage of the amount in dispute, without any cap. Furthermore, following Section 40 Austrian Code of Civil Procedure, it is the defeated party in the procedure that has to bear all costs of the proceedings, including the costs of the lawyers of the winning party. This principle is reasoned by principle of justice; however, this also hinders SMEs to file suits against big market players.

[26] Judgment of the Supreme Court of 14 February 2012, case number 5 Ob 39/11p.

[27] Council Regulation (EC) No 44/2001 of 22 December 2000 on jurisdiction and the recognition and enforcement of judgments in civil and commercial matters.

2.3.2 Collective Redress

2.3.2.1 Current Situation

With regard to the Austrian Cartel Act, SMEs do not have legal standing to bring collective legal actions based on anticompetitive conducts.[28]

Explicitly, the Austrian legislator only provides collective redress mechanisms within the field of consumer protection.[29] However, it is accepted that Section 227 Austrian Code of Civil Procedure ("ZPO") provides an indirect possibility to connect not only different claims but also different claimants under certain circumstances.[30]

Furthermore, it is also possible and common practice to assign the claims.

2.3.2.2 Policy Recommendations

A possibility of collective redress that is directly stated in the law would surely improve the rights of SMEs. However, as outlined above, the current Austrian law provides SMEs some mechanisms that can be used to act in collective redress.

2.3.3 The Role of Trade Associations

Trade associations do not have any special status in Austrian procedural competition law. In the view of an SME, which is member of an industrial association, a direct collective redress scheme, which could be applied by the association, would be surely appreciated. However, due to the legal standard in Austria, associations can interact for its members by assignments of claims or support in collective redress claims according to Section 227 ZPO.

2.3.4 Policy Recommendations

In the author's view, every natural and legal person, regardless of economic size, should be confronted with the same substantive and procedural rules of private antitrust enforcement.

---

[28] E.g., in relation to requests for remedy of cartel behaviour according to Section 26 in connection with Section 36 Austrian Cartel Act.

[29] See Section 29 Austrian consumer protection act ('Konsumentenschutzgesetz').

[30] See, e.g., the judgment of the Supreme Court of 31 March 2005, case number 3 Ob 275/04v, according to which different claimants can act within one proceeding if the respective claims issue the same factual or legal issues, which have an effect on the subject (or an essential preliminary question) of the proceedings.

2.4 Conclusions and Policy Recommendations

As outlined above, in the author's view, SMEs should not have any special rights in Austrian competition law.

An effective coverage of SMEs based on actual legal statutes such as appreciability of the restriction of competition, *de minimis* in the current form, collective redress is sufficient. An additional national regulation as it had been in force with regard to former versions of the Austrian Cartel Act or a notice drafted by the national competition authorities, illustrating cooperation between SMEs that are exempted from the scope of competition law (e.g., common market strategies, etc.), will increase legal certainty for SMEs. Such measures are therefore requested.

Belgium

3

Norman Neyrinck

3.1 Introduction

Small and medium enterprises occupy a place of utmost importance in the Belgian economy: 92.5 % of the Belgian enterprises employ less than 10 workers, and 98.8 % of them employ less than 50 workers.[1] Convinced that SMEs play a major role in the Belgian economy and that SMEs are key to national economic growth, the current Belgian government is willing to increase SMEs' competitiveness and alleviate the administrative burden that weighs on them.[2] In order to achieve these objectives, a clear and comprehensive framework on the application of antitrust law to SMEs should be drawn up and made easily available to the stakeholders, which are SMEs, and also to practitioners and scholars.

Along this line, the present report aims at gathering data and legal analysis to contribute to the delineation of Belgian antitrust law for SMEs. Hence, in accordance with the general directives provided in the LIDC questionnaire, this report studies whether Belgian SMEs are subject to different rules from those applicable to other economic operators and what rationales support possible differences of treatment. In so doing, we take into account the economic context under which

The original version of this paper was submitted in September 2012 for the LIDC Prague Congress; minor editorial changes were made in June 2013 for publication purpose only.

[1] Eurostat, *Key figures on European business with a special feature on SMEs*, Luxembourg, Publications Office of the European Union, 2011, p. 12, table 1.2 (2008).

[2] Accord de Gouvernement, 1 December 2011, p. 120, available at http://premier.be/files/20111206/Accord_de_Gouvernement_1er_decembre_2011.pdf.

N. Neyrinck (✉)
University of Liège, Liège, Belgium

Dehin and Brüls, Liège Bar, Belgium
e-mail: norman.neyrinck@ulg.ac.be; n.neyrinck@avocat.be

P. Këllezi et al. (eds.), *Antitrust for Small and Middle Size Undertakings and Image Protection from Non-Competitors*, LIDC Contributions on Antitrust Law, Intellectual Property and Unfair Competition, DOI 10.1007/978-3-642-54000-4_3, © Springer-Verlag Berlin Heidelberg 2014

SMEs struggle: the minimal anticompetitive impact of SMEs' practices, the difficulties there are for SMEs to deal with the complex economic issues that may arise in antitrust litigations, etc. Prior to this, however, we first provide guidance on the legal definition given to the notion of SMEs in Belgian law.

3.2 SMEs in Context

3.2.1 Legal Definition

The legal definition of SMEs in Belgian antitrust law is a complex, unresolved issue. Several definitions are available for consideration. Amongst these,[3] we introduce what we consider as the three main contenders.

Article 2 of the Belgian Competition Act (hereafter referred to as "BCA")[4] explicitly refers to the notion of SMEs. Yet, no clear definition is given to this notion. Article 5 of a prior version[5] of that same law expressly referred to the definition given in Article 12 §2 of the Accounting Law.[6] The relevance of this definition[7] is dubious though as (1) reference to the Accounting Law has now totally disappeared from the BCA and (2) Article 12 §2 has been abrogated.[8]

[3] We set aside several competition-law-related definitions that have been adopted by the various Belgian legislators to frame the grant of state aid measures for SMEs. See, for instance, Decreet betreffende een waarborgregeling voor kleine, middelgrote en grote ondernemingen, 6 February 2004, *M.B.*, 20 February 2004, art. 2; Ordonnance organique relative aux aides pour la promotion de l'expansion économique, 13 December 2007, *M.B.*, 10 January 2007, art. 2; Décret relatif aux incitants régionaux en faveur des petites ou moyennes entreprises, 11 March 2004, *M.B.*, 8 April 2004, art. 3. Those norms enacted by the Flemish, Brussels, and Walloon legislative authorities, respectively, directly refer to the SME definition provided in Annex I of EU Regulation No 800/2008 of 6 August 2008 declaring certain categories of aid compatible with the common market in application of Articles 87 and 88 of the Treaty (General block exemption Regulation), OJ 2008, L 214/3.

[4] Loi sur la protection de la concurrence économique, 15 September 2006, *M.B.*, 29 September 2006.

[5] Loi sur la protection de la concurrence économique, 5 August 1991, *M.B.*, 11 October 1991.

[6] Loi relative à la comptabilité et aux comptes annuels des entreprises, *M.B.*, 4 September 1975, Article 12 § 2: "Paragraph 1 applies to enterprises that do not exceed more than one of the following thresholds:

50 employees, on an annual average;
annual turnover (excluding VAT) of 6,250,000 €;
balance sheet total of 3,125,000 €;
except where the number of employees excesses 100 on an annual average."

[7] The relevance of this definition was once supported by M. Waelbroeck and J. Brouckaert in "La loi sur la protection de la concurrence économique", *J.T.*, 1992, p. 285.

[8] Furthermore, several commentators voiced doubts from the very beginning that the definition provided in Article 5 BCA for notification thresholds might not be relevant for Article 2 BCA, which relates to illegal agreements. See S. Plingers, De verhouding tussen Belgisch en Europees kartelrecht, *Jura Falconis*, 1997–1998, n°4, p. 585.

The second best contender is Article 2(1) of the Law for the Promotion of Independent Enterprise,[9] the purpose of which is to provide a workable definition of the notion of SMEs.[10] No reference is made to this status in antitrust law, though.

Finally, the definition provided in Article 15 of the Code of Companies[11] is also sometimes elicited in the legal literature.[12] Considering that the Code contributes to define what is Belgian common business law, it is not unreasonable to support that Article 15 should be the reference definition for antitrust law as well. Two objections to the prevalence of this definition must be mentioned though: (1) the Code only applies to legal companies, while the scope of antitrust law encompasses

---

[9] Loi-programme pour la promotion de l'entreprise indépendante, 10 February 1998, *M.B.*, 21 février 1998, Article 2: "For the purpose of the present law:

1° S.M.E.: shall mean enterprises which:

do not employ more than 50 workers on an annual average;

do not have more than 25 % of their stocks or shares in the capital or related voting rights that are owned by one or more enterprises others than SMEs;

and which have an annual turnover not exceeding ECU 7 million, and/or an annual balance sheet total not exceeding ECU 5 million.

The average number of employed workers on an annual basis is calculated in annual working units, i.e. the number of full-time workers employed during one year, with part-time workers and seasonal workers being counted in fractions of annual working units.

The reference year to take into account is, like for thresholds for annual turnover and balance sheet total, the latest complete approved accounting period.

An enterprise loses its status of S.M.E. when it does not meet the employment criterion, the annual turnover or the balance-sheet total during two successive accounting periods.

Unless the contrary is proved, evidence that the enterprise meets this definition is supposed to be brought by a sworn statement".

[10] Chambre des Représentants, Projet de loi pour la promotion de l'entreprise indépendante, Exposé des motifs, Ordinary session 1996–1997, 24 September 1997, - 1206 / 1–96 / 97, p. 2.

[11] Code des sociétés, 7 May 1999, M.B., 6 August 1999, Art. 15 § 1er:

"§1 Small companies are companies with a legal personality which, during the last and second-to-last approved accounting periods, do not exceed one of the following thresholds:

50 employees, on an annual average;

annual turnover (excluding VAT) of EUR 7,300,000;

balance-sheet total of EUR 3,650,000;

except where the number of employed workers, on an annual average, exceeds 100.

§ 2. The application of the criterions listed at § 1 to companies that start their activities is assessed in good faith at the beginning of the accounting period (...)

§ 5. Where a company is linked to one or more others, in the meaning of Article 11, turnover and balance sheet total criterions, as set at §1, are determined on a consolidated basis. Regarding the employed workers criterion, the number of employed workers on an annual average is the addition of the workers employed by each linked company".

[12] G. Zonnekeyn and D. Smeets, "De hervorming van de Belgische mededingingswet: een nieuwe start of een gemiste kans", *RDC-TBH*, 2006/9, November 2009, p. 909, footnote 51.

any entity providing goods and services on the market, private individuals included and (2) the Code only defines what small enterprises are but neglects medium ones.

The difficulties arising from the absence of any clear definition for SMEs in competition law are directly attributable to the Belgian legislator. The preparatory documents reveal that from the very first drafts of the BCA the Belgian Council of State had drawn the attention of the Parliament on this lack of definition.[13] Unfortunately, the calls of the Council of State for more precisions remained without answer. The three above-mentioned definitions provide altogether only a blurred impression of what are SMEs in competition law: if these three provisions define SMEs according to the number of workers and the annual turnover/annual total of the balance sheet of the undertaking, the convergence is only limited[14] as the financial thresholds differ from one statute to another. Moreover, where two provisions state that the SME status is barred for those entities that are part of a bigger group, the third one remains silent on the impact of the existence of a holding company. Only the 50-worker threshold is common to the three above-mentioned definitions.

In practice, Belgian courts never ruled on the question of the relevant definition for SMEs in antitrust law. In the sole two rulings that dealt with the matter, the courts expressly referred to the appearances of the case and admitted[15] or rejected[16] the SME status of the involved firms on this sole basis. The courts' disinterest for this issue can be criticised since firms' accounts are easily available online with all the relevant information related to staff and financial results.[17] At least, this approach corresponds to two of the above-mentioned provisions that state that the size of the firm may be judged on the basis of a good faith assessment of the firm or that proof of the SME status may be made by sworn statement.

[13] Chambre des Représentants, Projet de loi sur la protection de la concurrence économique, Avis du Conseil d'Etat, Ordinary session 1989–1990, 10 September 1990, 1282/1 - 89/90, p. 63: "In our legislation "small and mediums entreprises" has, besides, diverse meanings and, since then, does not provide legal certainty".

[14] The EU Recommendation on the definition of SMEs clearly states that the thresholds it defines should be regarded as maximum values and that Member States may fix lower ceilings. See Recommendation 2003/361, Article 2.

[15] Voorz. Kh. Brussel, 15 February 1995, Jaarboek Handelspraktijken & Mededinging, 1995, p. 744: "Whereas, pursuant to Art. 5 of the Competition Act of 5 August 1991, legal provisions on restrictive practices do not apply to small and medium enterprises unless the contrary is proved; that the defendant appears to be such company".

[16] Hof van Beroep te Antwerpen, 27 October 2008, Jaarboek Handelspraktijken & Mededinging, 2008, p. 891: "Finally, the reference made by the respondent to Article 5 of the BCA is not relevant. Under this article SMEs are conditionally exempted from notification. First, it does not appear that *in casu* the conditions of Article 5 BCA are met".

[17] See the National Bank of Belgium's website: http://www.nbb.be.

Hence, to date, the definition remains an open issue. Should the debates focus on that specific question in a future case, we believe that the staff criterion should be central in the analysis of the courts. Once this criterion is fulfilled, courts should show flexibility regarding the financial criterions. Because of the plurality of financial thresholds available and because of the changing nature of financial results, short-term overcrossings of the financial thresholds should not deprive the firm from possible benefits linked to the SME status. Conversely, we believe that the existence of a parent company exercising a decisive influence on the main decisions[18] of the entity at stake should in any event disqualify the latter as an SME where the group is itself out of the SME's scope. To decide otherwise would incentivise big firms to split their activities into several legal persons to conclude antitrust-sensitive operations.

3.2.2 Treatment of SMEs Under Competition Law

3.2.2.1 Overview

The enforcement record of the Belgian competition authority is notably weak.[19] The lack of financial means and the shortage of human resources from which the NCA suffers[20] are responsible for long waiting periods before decisions are delivered[21] and for a very significant number of closing or limitation decisions. Amongst the rulings that have been issued in the last 5 years, not one decision identifies the presence of an SME on the basis of the three factors listed in the law (number of employees, financial results, and integration in a group). The same is true with court rulings that, to our best knowledge, never followed the three-step test legally set by the law to identify SMEs. Only incidentally do these decisions refer to one of these three criterions: out of the 153 decisions issued by the NCA between 2006 and

[18] In substance, the *Viho* ruling states that where an entity exercises a decisive influence on the main decisions of its subsidiary, the two entities should be regarded as one undertaking under antitrust law. See ECJ, case C-73/95 P, *Viho Europe BV v Commission of the European Communities*, ECR 1996 I-5457, para. 51.

[19] E. Provost, *Which, if any, agreements, practices or information exchanges about prices should be prohibited in vertical relationships?*, Report of the AEDC (Association pour l'étude du droit de la concurrence – Belgium), LIDC Bordeaux 2010, p. 1, available at http://www.concurrences.com/IMG/2010rapportAbelge.pdf.

[20] L. Parret, "La perspective du Conseil de la concurrence", in N. Petit (dir.), *Le Nouveau droit belge de la concurrence. Bilan et perspectives après quatre années d'application*, CUP vol. 124, Liège, Anthémis, 2010, p. 293.

[21] SPF Economie, Direction Générale de la concurrence, *Rapport annuel (2007 à 2010)*, available at http://economie.fgov.be/fr/entreprises/concurrence/Autorite_belge_concurrence_Introduction/Directon_generale_concurrence/.

2011, 9 % mention that they relate to self-employed people, 12 % refer to the existence of bigger, holding companies, and 1 % relate to the annual turnover of the firm—a turnover that is usually kept confidential.[22]

Hence, in order to track those antitrust decisions that are indirectly or tacitly influenced by the small size of the undertakings implicated, we sorted the NCA decisions according to the likelihood they involve SMEs. The results are categorised under three groups according to our own assessment of the size of the firms. We used proxies to sort the decisions. For instance, we assume that the various trade associations that were the target of the NCA are SMEs, regarding that most of them have an activity limited to the defense of their members—what usually do not require more than a fistful of administrative assistants and lobbyists—and have a turnover limited to the subscription fee paid by their members.[23] Likewise, it is reasonable to assume that firms active in the telecom markets are big-sized undertakings, while local butcheries qualify as SMEs.[24] We find that out of the 153 decisions issued by the NCA between 2006 and 2011, 20 % involved no SMEs, 51 % possibly involved an SME, and 29 % involved at least one SME. These data tend to indicate that a significant proportion of cases already deal with SMEs and confirm that SMEs are a relevant field of study for antitrust law.

The review of the cases involving SMEs shows that most of them deal with fee coordination scheme or opening day/hour regulation imposed by professional associations. Several discrimination and boycott cases are also identified.

3.2.2.2 Specific Programmes Addressed to SMEs

No specific programme and no specific policy have been adopted by the legislator or the NCA regarding SMEs. In contrast, the NCA recently realised a sectorial report on price levels in the supermarket sector.[25] This tends to indicate that big firms are a priority issue for the competition authority, while SMEs are not a primary matter of interest.

---

[22] An Annex table was drafted for the realisation of this paper with a detailed report of the cases issued by the NCA. We did not list judicial case law because of the significant grey number unpublished decisions represent.

[23] See, for example, Raad van Mededinging, Decision nr. 2008-I/O-04, 25 January 2008, MEDE-I/O-04/0045, *Vlaamse federatie van verenigingen van Brood- en Banketbakkers, Ijsbereiders en Chocoladebewerkers* (*VEBIC*), para. 66: "In the present case, where it comes to behaviors that can be attributed to the association, the Council takes into account the statutory maximum, [. . .] % of the turnover of the association, which mainly results from of the membership fees of the bakers".

[24] A similar methodology was used for a similar review. See M. Baillat, "Appendice. L'examen des décisions du Conseil de la concurrence révèle-t-il une influence de la petite taille des entreprises sur la mise en œuvre des règles? Dépouillement des décisions rendues de 1987 à 2006", in Y. Chaput (dir.) *Les PME et le droit de la concurrence. Analyse critique, comparative et perspective*, Paris, LexisNexis, 2009, p. 46.

[25] SPF Economie, DG Concurrence, *Niveaux de prix dans les supermarchés*, 13 February 2012, 128 p., available at http://economie.fgov.be/fr/binaries/etude_niveaux_prix_supermarches_tcm326-163021.pdf.

3.3 Public Antitrust Enforcement and SMEs

3.3.1 Substantive and Procedural Rules Applicable to SMEs

3.3.1.1 Introduction: Article 2 §1 BCA

Article 2 BCA prohibits anticompetitive coordination to the extent that they "significantly distort[s] competition on the Belgian market or on a substantial part of it".[26] This requirement makes size matters in Belgian competition law.

It is well-known and well-accepted EU policy that agreements that have "only an insignificant effect on the markets, taking into account the weak position which the persons concerned have on the market of the product in question"[27] fall short of the prohibition of anticompetitive coordination of Article 101(1) TFEU. This so-called *de minimis* doctrine, once focused on the market share and market position of the firms under investigations, was progressively extended to include agreements involving enterprises of a limited size.[28]

Belgian law followed a similar path, with rulings taking the size of the firms into account—and not their market shares—to decide whether or not the agreement at stake should be held illegal. For instance, in a case related to the legality of an exclusive distribution scheme, the Court of Commerce of Brussels held that an important turnover may, under all circumstances, bar the benefits of the *de minimis* rule.[29] According to the Court, the agreement could not fall under the *de minimis* principle because the common turnover of the two contracting parties was superior to ECU 200 million,[30] whatever their market shares are.

In the same vein, the NCA stated that the importance of the turnover was a relevant criterion to assess whether an agreement could cause a significant

[26] Loi sur la protection de la concurrence économique, 15 September 2006, Article 2 §1: "Without the need for a prior decision to that effect, all agreements between undertakings, all decisions by associations of undertakings and all concerted practices, the aim or consequence of which is to prevent, restrict or distort significantly competition in the Belgian market concerned or in a substantial part of that market are prohibited (. . .)".

[27] ECJ, case C-5/69, *Franz Völk v SPRL Ets J Vervaecke*, ECR 1969, p. 295, para. 7.

[28] In the *Ventouris v Commission* case, the General Court held that agreements "to which all the parties are SMEs" fall out of the scope of the prohibition of Article 101 TFEU. CFI, case T-59/99, *Ventouris Group Enterprises SA v. Commission*, ECR 2003, II-5257. The 1986 version of the *de minimis* Notice equally assimilated unsignificant market shares with SMEs. See Commission Notice of 3 September 1986 on agreements of minor importance which do not fall under Article 85(1) of the Treaty Establishing the European Economic Community, *OJ*, 1986, C-231/2, para. 1: "The Commission considers that it is important to facilitate cooperation between firms as long as it is economically desirable and does not raise objections with regard to competition policy, what is specifically of application for small and medium undertakings".

[29] Comm. Bruxelles, 28 January 1994, *J.L.M.B.*, 1994, p. 1262: "Moreover, whatever the market shares held by APT-B and A.M.C., the agreement at stake could not be considered as of minor importance and fall out of the scope of Article [101] since the total turnover of the participating undertakings exceeds ECU 2 hundred million".

[30] European Currency Unit or EUR 200,000.

distortion of competition. Echoing the *Société technique minière* decision,[31] the NCA held that the economic and legal context of the agreement had to be considered to determine whether competition is significantly hampered by the agreement under review. In order to do so, several factors have to be taken into account and, among those, the turnover of the firms.[32]

Conversely, in the *Professional Association* of *Pharmacists* cases involving small, independent undertakings part to an anticompetitive coordination on a limited portion of the Belgian territory, the NCA ruled that the conditions of Article 2 §1 BCA were not met. In the case at hand, several pharmacists had introduced complaints against the national and local professional associations for imposing regulated opening hours to their members. The NCA held illegal the decision of the national association but rejected the complaints targeted at the local associations. Because the decisions of the local associations produced effects on the territory of a small number of municipalities only,[33] the NCA judged that no significant restriction of competition on a substantial part of the Belgian market could be established—or in other words: *de minimis non curat praetor*. Quite remarkably, the NCA also stated that the relevant markets were local and matched the territory of the local associations.[34] The fact that a whole market was crippled by an anticompetitive practice was not held illegal because of the small-sized features of the case.[35]

The size of the enterprises may thus have an impact on the likelihood of an agreement to fall under Article 2 §1 BCA[36]: big-sized firms have a higher

[31] ECJ, case 56/65, *Société Technique Minière v Maschinenbau Ulm GmbH*, ECR 1966, p. 235.

[32] Raad voor de mededinging, *N.V. L.-D.*, 25 March 1997, *Rechtskundig Weekblad*, 1997–1998, n°2, 13 September 1997, p. 53: "Moreover, in accordance with the minimum rule one should not lose sight that the agreement must still be considered in its economic and legal context; it may indeed be part of a network of agreements, so that in the present case the competition may be appreciably reduced.

To assess whether competition is substantially impacted, different criteria can be taken into account, including the turnover criterion, the market shares and the very nature of the anticompetitive agreement itself."

[33] Conseil de la concurrence, Decision n° 2007-I/O-27, 26 October 2007, CONC-I/O-98/0004, *E. S./Ordre des pharmaciens*; CONC-I/O-98/0024, *L.P.D./Ordre des pharmaciens*; CONC-I/O-98/0032, *Groupe Multipharma/Ordre des pharmaciens*, para. 75 and ff.

[34] Conseil de la concurrence, Decision n° 2007-P/K-35, 20 December 2007, CONC-P/K-05/0026, *F.N.H. / Ordre des pharmaciens - GLEP 30*, para. 21.

[35] According to us, the limited territory on which the anticompetitive restraint took place cannot in itself explain the rejection of the complaint; the limited size of the undertakings also played a decisive role. In the *Canal+* case, a refusal to supply related to a territory of a similar size than the one of the *Professional Association of Pharmacists* case was said to take place on a substantial part of the Belgian market. True enough, the players here involved were the local incumbent for TV services and Canal+, the main EU pay TV supplier, while pharmacists are more often than not small, independent retailers. Compare Conseil de la concurrence, Decisions n° 2007-I/O-27, n° 2007-P/K-35, and Bruxelles, 18 juin 2004, *Canal+ Velgique c. WoluTV et United Pan European Communications Belgium*, *A&M*, 2004/4, p. 357.

[36] It is worth noting that the prohibition of abuses of dominance is also limited to those behaviour that take place "on the Belgian market or on a substantial part of it" (Art. 3 BCA).

probability to be punished for the agreements they conclude, while SMEs may avoid a similar fate despite the fact that their respective market positions would have indicated the contrary. If the regime applied to big firms may be explained by the fact that those are often in a strong enough financial position to quickly increase their market shares,[37] the very favourable regime applied to SMEs is less acceptable. If one may understand that SMEs may fall out of the scope of Article 101 (1) TFEU for jurisdictional purposes,[38] such outcome at the national level equals to a denial of justice for consumers that are confronted to an agreement that cripples the geographical market[39] they live in.[40]

3.3.1.2 Infringement Scenarios

We have not identified any specific infringement scenario that would apply differently to SMEs. Non-compete clauses may be seen as an exception to this statement, though, as prohibition decisions applicable to non-compete clauses are influenced by the size of the undertakings. For instance, in the construction sector, small undertakings with a small staff can answer to a limited number of contracts only that, in most cases, will be executed in the close vicinity of the location of the

---

[37] "Even if they have a small market share, undertakings can still appreciably affect competition if, in the light of a number of other elements such as their turnover, production, financial power, technical capacity, etc. they cannot be considered as unimportant undertakings on the relevant market. This may be the case where an undertaking with a small market share belongs to a large group of undertakings that is able to increase its market share in the relatively short term through financial and economic power." P. Maes, "*De minimis non curat praetor en de toepassing van de Wet Bescherming Economische Mededinging. Belgische variaties op een Europees thema?*", note after Raad voor de mededinging, *N.V. L.-D.*, p. 56.

[38] From the beginning, the Commission Notice on agreements of minor importance made clear that agreements that are not prohibited under EU law because they do not affect interstate trade may nonetheless be caught under national law. Commission Notice of 3 September 1986 on agreements of minor importance which do not fall under Article 85 paragraph 3 of the Treaty Establishing the European Economic Community, *OJ*, 12 September 1986, C 231/2: "The Commission considers it is important to facilitate cooperation between undertakings to the extent it is economically desirable and that it does not raise objections regarding competition policy, what is particularly true for cooperation between small and medium undertakings." (no official translation available); J. Bocken and K. De Corte, "La communication du 22 décembre 2011 concernant les accords d'importance mineure qui ne restreignent pas sensiblement le jeu de la concurrence au sens de l'article 81, paragraphe 1, du traité CE", *RDC*, 2002, p. 239.

[39] The dismissing of a claim on the basis that the anticompetitive behaviour does not affect a substantial part of the Belgian market is less controversial when the geographical portion of the market that is crippled by that conduct represents only a tiny share of the whole, relevant, geographical market. In such a case, consumers still have the opportunity to move towards other suppliers. See, for instance, Prés. Comm. Bruxelles, 30 May 1994, *Annuaire Pratiques du commerce & Concurrence*, 1994, p. 186, where the anticompetitive conduct took place on the territory of a few municipalities only while the total relevant market was said to be national.

[40] To this denial of justice, one might also add the existence of an obvious discrimination between consumers.

firm.[41] Hence, under such circumstances, the boundaries of a non-compete clause related to the market for roof repairs must be limited to a 30-km circle.[42]

3.3.1.3 Safe Harbours for SMEs

Without speaking of a true safe harbour regime, Article 2 §3 BCA provides a specific exemption for SMEs.[43] According to the preparatory documents, the aim of this regime is twofold: (1) to help SMEs to strengthen their competitive position and (2) to favour the dispersion of economic operators.[44]

Quite disturbingly, this regime is rarely evoked by litigants and is often seen as an oddity by the doctrine,[45] as well as the NCA.[46] A relatively recent piece even stated that the exemption regime for SMEs had never been applied so far.[47]

Contrary to the previous statement, a few decisions deal with the SME exemption regime. These few decisions fail to provide all the necessary directions for use, though, considering the various questions the application of this provision raises.

First, Article 2 §3 BCA does not allow litigants to clearly determine what conditions must be met to claim the benefit of the SME exemption. Most unfortunately, the wording of Article 2 §3 BCA intertwines the SME regime with the four conditions of the general exemption—that same four conditions listed under

---

[41] Gent, 25 May 2005, *DAOR*, 2005, liv. 76, p. 33.

[42] Voorz. Kh. Hasselt, 16 February 2004, *RABG*, 2004, liv. 11, p. 685.

[43] Loi sur la protection de la concurrence économique, 15 September 2006, Article 2 § 3: "The provisions of § 1 may however be declared inapplicable in the case of:

1° any agreement or category of agreements between undertakings,

2° any decision or category of decisions of associations of undertakings, and

3° any concerted practice or category of concerted practices which contribute to improving production or distribution or to promoting technical or economic progress or which enable small and medium-sized undertakings to assert their competitive position in the market concerned or internationally, while enabling users to benefit from a fair share of the resulting benefits, without however:

a) imposing on the undertakings concerned restrictions which are not indispensable to the attainment of these objectives;

b) giving the undertaking the possibility to eliminate competition for a substantial part of the affected products."

[44] "However, it appeared opportune to add an exemption motive for allowing the confirmation of competition agreements such as those that are concluded between small and medium enterprises – in order to allow them to strengthen their competitive position on the Belgian concerned market – and to favour a dispersion of economic operators. This is all the more justified in a national context where the role of small and medium enterprises is relatively more important than in intracommunity trade." Chambre des Représentants, Projet de loi sur la protection de la concurrence économique, Exposé des motifs, Ordinary Session 1989–1990, 10 September 1990, 1282/1 - 89/90, p. 18.

[45] G. Zonnekeyn, "De hervorming van de Belgische mededingingswet: een stille (r)evolutie?", *C.J.*, n° 4/2005, p 72, footnote 15.

[46] Conseil de la Concurrence, *Avis du Conseil de la concurrence relatif à l'avant-projet de loi sur la protection de la concurrence économique (art. 78 de la Constitution)*, 29 June 2005, p. 2, available at http://economie.fgov.be/fr/binaries/Advice_art78_fr_tcm326-43331.pdf.

[47] J. Stuyck "Restrictieve Mededingingspraktijken", in J. Stuyck, W. Devroe and P. Wytinck (dir), *De nieuwe Belgische Mededingingswet 2006*, Mechelen, Kluwer 2007, p. 32.

Article 101(3) TFEU. Hence, some commentators held that *five* conditions have to be cumulatively met for an illegal agreement to fall under the SME exemption provision or, in other words, that Article 2 §3 BCA was stricter than Article 101 (3) TFEU.[48] However, most voices consider that an *effet utile* must be provided to the SMEs' exemption so that not all four conditions of the general exemption regime should be fulfilled in addition to the SME requirement.[49] Those support the view that the SME status should exempt firms from demonstrating that the agreement improves welfare,[50] with the three other general conditions left unchanged.[51]

One may however wonder whether SMEs should prove that consumers receive a fair share of the benefits generated by the anticompetitive agreement—second condition of the general exemption regime—if the agreement is not welfare enhancing. To apply, the SME exemption requires that the anticompetitive agreement "allows small and medium enterprises to strengthen their competitive position on the relevant market or on the international market". True enough, an agreement that contributes to the growth of the market shares of an SME should logically imply an increase of its benefits that could be passed on to consumers. However, the wording of Article 2 §3 BCA does not require an "increase" of the market shares of the SME. The "strengthening of the SMEs' competitive position" may as well imply a mere consolidation of the SMEs' situation with the creation of new barriers to entry. No direct, economic benefit being generated from such a kind of agreement, no passing on to consumers could be required. From a policy standpoint, the dismissal of the two first conditions would present the advantage to significantly alleviate the burden of proof that lies on SMEs, providing a true advantage to these when embarked in the vicissitudes of a trial.

Another debate related to the application of Article 2 §3 BCA refers to the number of SMEs the agreement should involve. Should all the contracting parties be SMEs, or is only one enough for the SME exemption to apply? According to several commentators, because Article 5 of the first version of the BCA imposed the presence of two SMEs for an agreement to be exonerated from the obligation of

---

[48] D. Szafran, "La loi sur la protection de la concurrence économique réforme de 1999", *J.T.*, 2002, n°23, p. 475.

[49] Chambre des Représentants, Projet de loi sur la protection de la concurrence économique, *Avis du Conseil d'Etat*, p. 63.

[50] The "*welfare improvement condition*" refers to the need for the agreement to contribute "to improve[e] production or distribution or promoting technical or economic progress". See D. Gerardin, A. Layne-farrar and N. Petit, *EU Competition Law and Economics*, Oxford, Oxford University Press, 2012, p. 165.

[51] S. Plingers, *De verhouding tussen Belgisch en Europees kartelrecht*, *Jura Falconis*, *1997–1998*, *n°4*, p. 585 and ff.; Answer of the Minister for Economy to the question of I. Van Belle, "Concurrence économique. - PME. - Exemption de l'interdiction de cartel", *Q.R.*, 14 April 1997, B77, p. 10455: "In any event, agreements cannot enclose restrictions that are not indispensable to reach the objectives and cannot allow these undertakings to eradicate competition for a substantial part of the concerned products. Moreover, these agreements must reserve a fair share of profits to users".

notification while Article 2 §3 BCA did not mention such requirement, a different regime should be applied to the SME exemption. This past discrepancy would then justify that one SME suffices to validate the entire agreement.[52]

In practice, Article 2 §3 BCA was relied on in a case dealing with the organisation of a distribution scheme. Most unfortunately, no directive regarding the implementation of the SME exemption may be deduced from this ruling. The judge contented himself with an invocation of Article 2 §3 BCA in a host of considerations that led to the validation of the distribution agreement.[53]

More interestingly, a recent decision of the Court of Appeal of Antwerp imposed limitations to the SME exemption regime.[54] According to the Court, the SMEs' exemption does not release SMEs from their duty to comply with competition law obligations "in particular regarding hardcore restrictions of competition". In the case at hand, the Court refused to exempt a resale price maintenance clause ("RPM") on the basis of the SME exemption. We understand this ruling as an application of the principles set for the application of Article 101 TFEU. According to these, "In principle, all restrictive agreements which cumulatively met the four conditions of Article [101(3)] are covered by the exemption rule. However severe restrictions of competition are unlikely to fulfill the conditions of Article [101 (3)]".[55] The conditions for the application of Article 2 §3 BCA slightly differ from the ones of Article 101(3) TFEU, though. The policy line established for the application of Article 101(3) TFEU is generally justified by the fact that hard-core restrictions "neither create objective economic benefits, nor do they benefit consumers (. . .) and generally also fail the indispensability test under the third criterion".[56] However, regarding hard-core restrictions of which SMEs are part, the nonfulfillment of the first (two) general condition(s) cannot explain an *a priori* exclusion from exemption; only the last two conditions may justify the inapplicability of the SME exemption to those restrictions that are not indispensable or that are so severe that they eliminate competition for a substantial part of the product in question. Hence, price-fixing cartels or regulated opening hours that totally eliminate rivalry on one aspect of competition should not be exempted. The same conclusion should be reached for boycott practices that prevent the apparition of

---

[52] S. Plingers, De verhouding tussen Belgisch en Europees kartelrecht, *Jura Falconis*, 1997–1998, n°4, p. 585 and ff.; P. Eeckman, "Kartelpraktijken", in P. de Vroede (ed.), *Bescherming van de economische mededinging. Wet van 5 augustus 1991*, Brugge, Die Keure, 1993, pp. 52–53.

[53] Voorz. Kh. Brussel 15 February 1995, Jaarboek Handelspraktijken & Mededinging, 1995, p. 744.

[54] Hof van Beroep te Antwerpen, 27 October 2008, *Jaarboek Handelspraktijken & Mededinging*, 2008, p. 891: "Furthermore, Article 5 BCA holds that small and medium-sized enterprises are not free from the obligation to comply with the legislation on competition, this is especially true concerning the prohibition of "hardcore" cartels agreements".

[55] *Ibidem.*

[56] *Ibidem.*

competitors relying on new technologies.[57] On the other hand, RPM clauses do not inevitably eliminate all competition and should be thoroughly assessed.

The opportunities opened by the SME exemption should not be exaggerated though. In many cases, national courts will have no other choices than to limit themselves to the general exemption of Article 101(3) TFEU as the primacy principle of EU law and Regulation 1/2003 require full compliance with Article 101 TFUE when national courts deal with agreements that affect interstate trade.[58] Under such circumstances, national courts would have no other choice than to set aside the SME exemption.

3.3.1.4 Remedies

No case issued by the NCA[59] deals with the issue of access to remedies for SMEs.[60] In our opinion, facilitated access to remedies for SMEs should be taken into consideration in two kinds of situations: (1) on markets where an unlimited number of competitors may enter and (2) on markets where tacit collusion concerns may appear.

The first hypothesis may be illustrated by the *Microsoft I* case, where Microsoft was obliged to make interoperability information available for competitors active on the market for work group server operating systems.[61] Information being a nonexclusive good, the Commission's decision could theoretically benefit an unlimited number of licensees. In practice though, the communication of the interoperability required Microsoft to adapt its interoperability package to the particular needs of different licensees.[62] We believe that in such kind of situation where any kind of firm could equally pretend to enter the market, SMEs should serve as the "least common multiple" for the definition of the remedy, so that the remedy is tailored in an easy-to-use fashion.

---

[57] See for instance: Liège, 5 February 2009, *Annuaire Pratiques du commerce & Concurrence*, 2009, p. 955, note A. Vanderelst, where according to the number of workers and the annual turnover/annual total of the balance sheet that has been published, apparently all companies involved on the oxygenotherapy market have SMEs profiles. According to EU Commission Decision No COMP/M.6504, *LINDE / AIR PRODUCTS HOMECARE* of 18 April 2012, most of these companies seem to be linked to firms active in other states, though.

[58] Regulation 1/2003, Article 3(1).

[59] Judicial decisions are of no use here as they only grant or reject the claims of the applicants but do not adapt remedies according to the vicissitudes of the market.

[60] Access to the remedy was discussed in access to telephony network cases, what is of little insight for SMEs cases. See for instance: Conseil de la concurrence, Decision n° 2010-L/G-27, 22 July 2010, L/G-07/0015, *Mobistar / Belgacom*.

[61] EU Commission Press Release, "Antitrust: Commission ensures compliance with 2004 Decision against Microsoft", 22 October 2007, IP/07/1567.

[62] Hence, concerning the licensing of interoperability information to an open-source developer (Samba), weeks of negotiations were needed only to determine the exact protocol information that would be included in the license. A. Tridgell, *The PFIF Agreement*, 20 December 2007, available at http://www.samba.org/samba/PFIF/PFIF_agreement.html.

Second, where a market is between the hands of an oligopoly of big-sized firms, a reserved access to the remedy could be offered to SMEs. In such kind of market configuration, SMEs should be used as mavericks, to thwart the tacitly collusive equilibrium. For instance, where docking slots have to be freed in order to open sailing lines to competition,[63] a quota of these slots should be allocated in priority to SMEs in order to bring in contact different-sized firms so that their different profiles make coordination between them more difficult.

3.3.2 Procedural and Fundamental Rights of SMEs

Belgian antitrust procedure does not differ according to the size of the undertaking. The procedure set in the BCA is neutral with regard to the size of the undertaking involved. Admittedly, differences of treatment may be deduced from the case law of the European Court of Human Rights when it comes to the rights of legal companies in comparison to the rights of private individuals.[64] However, we emphasise that this case law (1) is not specific to antitrust and (2) does not distinguish on the basis of the *size* of the operator but on the basis of its kind (natural or legal person).

The sole procedural peculiarity that may be mentioned in relation to SMEs is that investigations may be launched not only at the initiative of the Minister for Economy but also at the initiative of the Minister for SMEs,[65] who may not always be the same occupant. Now that the two portfolios are split,[66] one might expect that the Minister for SMEs will take the initiative to launch investigations tailored at the redress of anticompetitive conducts that specifically impact SMEs.

3.3.3 Leniency for SMEs

Because of their small size and limited financial means, one may fear that SMEs are easy targets for retaliatory measures after leniency applications. However, no specific rule exists under Belgian Antitrust Law to protect SMEs against big undertakings after denunciation. Regarding possible *commercial retaliation*,

---

[63] See, for instance, Commission Decision of 21 December 1993, *Holyhead*, 94/19, *OJ*, 18 January 1994, L 15/8; Commission decision, 21 December 1993, *Rødby*, 94/119, *OJ*, 26 February 1994, L 55/52.

[64] See for instance: ECHR, 16 December 1992, No13710/88, *Niemietz v. Allemagne*, stating that the entitlement of Contracting States to interfere with situations where professional or business activities or premises are involved is more far-reaching than in situations where the domicile of a private individual is involved.

[65] Loi sur la protection de la concurrence économique, 15 September 2006, Article 44.

[66] The two portfolios have often been in the hands of the same man. Currently, Vice-Minister Johan VANDE LANOTTE is in charge of the Economy, and Minister Sabine LARUELLE is in charge of SMEs.

denunciating firms may benefit from the protection of unfair competition law provisions.[67] Regarding possible *judicial retaliation*, Belgian law provides protection against *temerarious and vexatious* proceedings[68] that any person might introduce and, among those, proceedings that could be launched by big-sized undertakings willing to retaliate.

On this point, we favour the status quo as, to our best knowledge, no retaliation attempt after denunciation has been reported in Belgium so far.[69] Additionally, one may wonder what *kind* of protection mechanism could effectively (1) induce denunciation and (2) protect SMEs from retaliation (3) without impairing the normal course of business activities. Hence, no specific rules should be enacted to facilitate the participation of SMEs to leniency proceedings. A priori, SMEs and big-sized undertakings have all an equal and fair chance to apply for a first-rank leniency once they have made the decision to do so.

Moreover, economic theory teaches that collusion is all the more sustainable when firms are symmetric and have similar profiles (with regard to size, cost structure, etc.).[70] As detection of deviation is more difficult where firms of dissimilar proportions are active on the same market, the most durable cartels gather undertakings of similar sizes. Hence, the adoption of specific rules to deal with small versus big issues in this area should not be a priority in Belgium; instead, efforts should be made to popularise the knowledge of the existence of a leniency programme.

3.3.4 Sanctions: Different Penalties for Different Size?

The Belgian guidelines for setting fines[71] do not establish any specific rule for SMEs. However, the guidelines indirectly take into account the size of the infringer for the calculation of the sanction as they define the basic amount of the fine

[67] Loi relative aux pratiques du marché et à la protection du consommateur, 6 April 2010, *M.B.*, 12 April 2010.

[68] Cass. 31 October 2003, RG C.02.0602.F, *J.T.*, 2004, liv. 6127, p. 135.

[69] True enough, leniency applications before the NCA are uncommon under Belgian law. For some examples of cartel cases initiated following a leniency applications, see Council Press Release, "Le Conseil de la concurrence impose des amendes pour un cartel dans le secteur chimique", 4 avril 2008; "Le Conseil de la Concurrence impose des amendes pour un cartel dans le secteur des radiateurs", 20 mai 2010; "Ententes sur les prix entre les entreprises de manutention dans les ports belges", 26 avril 2012, available at http://economie.fgov.be/fr/entreprises/concurrence/Activites/Actualites_communiques_presse/. Because leniency applications remain unfrequent, no relevant analysis of the order of application according to the size of the applicant is feasible, though.

[70] M. Motta, *Competition Policy. Theory and Practice*, Cambridge, Cambridge University Press, 2004, p. 147.

[71] Communication du Conseil de la concurrence, Lignes directrices sur le calcul des amendes imposées en matière de pratiques restrictives de concurrence en application de l'article 63 de la Loi sur la protection de la concurrence économique, 19 Décembre 2011, para. 21, available at http://economie.fgov.be/fr/binaries/Communication_Lignes_directrices_amendes_tcm326-158194.pdf.

according to the concerned turnover—i.e., the value of the sales of goods or services made by the infringer and to which the infringement relates—or, if unavailable, according to a percentage of the total turnover of the infringer. In the same vein, the fact that the fine is capped to 10 % of the total turnover of all the undertakings that are part of the same group[72] indirectly takes into account the size of the undertakings. As an SME is not supposed to be part of a group whose global size would exceed the financial thresholds set in the law, the maximum fine will be lower for SMEs than for other undertakings.

Beyond these preliminary remarks, sanctions for SMEs have also been partially adapted out of the scope of the Guidelines for setting fines. In practice, here and there, the case law of the BCA has adjusted the repressive regime to the small size and small means of the infringers.

It is noteworthy that in the first times of enforcement of the Belgian Competition Act, no fine could be imposed on SMEs. According to the first version of the BCA, SMEs were immune from fines[73] with the consequence that, even where competition law breaches were found by the public authority, infringers were left with a mere prohibition decision.[74]

The abrogation of the immunity system with the 2006 reform of the BCA may be seen as a step towards more severity against SMEs. The case law of the NCA reveals that this reform has only mild effects on the fine SMEs incur. Admittedly, the Belgian competition authority is not in a position to exhibit any kind of convincible track record on fines, whatever the size of the infringer is.[75] Still, the NCA shows substantial punitive moderation when it comes to setting fines for SMEs.

We have already mentioned the strong proclivity of the NCA to bring proceedings against associations of undertakings. This may be seen as an adaptation technique to the fact that otherwise the NCA would have to bring proceedings against a myriad of SMEs with the negative consequences it may have on the investigation resources of the competition authority. Moreover, the imposition of a

[72] Loi sur la protection de la concurrence économique, 15 September 2006, Articles 63 and 86.

[73] Loi sur la protection de la concurrence économique, 5 August 1991, Articles 31 and 36 of the coordinated version of 1st July 1999.

[74] Raad van Mededinging, Decision n°2007-I_O-05, 29 January 2007, MEDE-I/O-04/0072, *Fedoba*; Raad van Mededinging, Decision n°2007-I/O-19, 21 August 2007, MEDE-I/O-00/0027, *Orde der Dierenartsen*; Raad van Mededinging, Decision n°2008-I/O-04, 25 January 2008, *MEDE-I/O-04/0045*, *Vlaamse federatie van verenigingen van Brood- en Banketbakkers, Ijsbereiders en Chocoladebewerkers* (*VEBIC*); Conseil de la concurrence, Decision, n°2008-P/K-43, 7 July 2008, CONC-I/O-98/0031, *ISC c/ FAB et ses membres*, CONC-P/K-05/0023, *Test-Achats c/ auto-écoles de Belgique*.

[75] See the stats we publish in L. de Muyter and N. Neyrinck, "Une transaction en droit belge de la concurrence? Approche critique de la proposition de la Direction Générale de la Concurrence", *Revue de droit de la concurrence belge*, 2012, n°2-3, pp. 106–118.

fine to an association of undertakings presents the advantage that the fine will, in principle, be passed on to its members.[76] The fining of professional associations may thus be used as a convenient mean to discipline SMEs.

Such policy is not without consequences on the level of fine, though. First, the turnover of an association that has for sole object the defense of the interests of a profession is often limited and is in all cases inferior to the sum of the turnovers of its members. Hence, the maximum possible fine—and its deterrent effect—is lower than the total amount that could be imposed on the members of the association.

Considerations inherent in the punishment of associations of undertakings may also lead the NCA to limit the level of its fines. For instance, in the *Belgian driving schools* case, the competition authority limited the amount of the fine because the membership of the professional association had evolved between the period of infringement and the date of the ruling. Because it would have been unfair to impose a too heavy fine on the new members, the NCA limited the fine to its most basic amount.[77] This was the case, notwithstanding the fact that the infringement related to price coordination and was said to be serious.

Likewise, in several cases (*Interior Architects*,[78] *Real Estate Agents' Institute*[79]), the NCA ruled that it would be more efficient to condemn the professional associations to the publication of its decision on their website and to inform their members of the state of the law rather than to impose a fine.[80] The fining policy of the NCA is thus affected by the capacity of the association to reach its members, what could not be required from a mere SME.

Speculatively, one may finally add that the targeting of professional associations is also likely to dissuade the competition authority from charging heavy fines. Considering that the association's members could prefer to declare the association

---

[76] Whether it is via an express requirement to pay the fine or via an increase of the subscription fees, the sole exception being the situation where the association has sufficient cash reserves to pay the fine.

[77] "Moreover, when a fine is inflicted to an association, members may be held liable by the association for the payment of the fine. Yet, in the case at hand, the current number of members is only a tiny proportion of the number of members at the beginning of the instruction. It does not seem justified that current members suffer disproportionate consequences." Conseil de la concurrence, Decision, n°2008-P/K-43, *Test-Achats c/ auto-écoles de Belgique*, para. 81.

[78] Raad voor de Mededinging, Decision n° 2008-P/K-45, 25 July 2008, MEDE-P/K-06/0006: *Review BVBA/Associatie van Interieurarchitecten van België vzw* – [...], para. 61 and ff.

[79] Raad voor de Mededinging, Decision n° 2010-I/O-30, 26 August 2010, CONC – I/O-01/0042: *Beroepsinstituut van Vastgoedmakelaars*.

[80] Formally, NCA decisions *first* rule out the imposition of a fine because of the unreasonable duration of the investigations and *then* separately decide to impose publication duties. However, the discretion the NCA enjoys regarding the consequences to give to any kind of breach of Article 6 ECHR may perfectly be instrumentalised to make a trade-off between a fine and a publication decision.

bankrupt and set up a new one rather than make the effort to clear the debts, the NCA could be more receptive to inability to pay allegations.[81]

3.4 Private Antitrust Enforcement and SMEs

3.4.1 Substantive Rules, Procedural Aspects for SMEs in Civil Suits

3.4.1.1 Obstacles

To our best knowledge, no final decision[82] has been published[83] on private damages for victims of cartels in Belgium so far.[84] In our opinion, the main possible reasons for this are threefold. First, victims of cartel damages often ignore that a possibility is open to them to claim money back in cartel cases. As shows the great number of cases dealing with work associations in Belgium, even the most respectable professionals act in breach of competition law, partly because they disregard the gravity of their coalition, partly out of blunt ignorance of competition law.[85] Along the same line, victims of antitrust breaches may simply ignore that they can mobilise the law for violations of antitrust.

[81] Interestingly, much like Regulation 1/2003 (Art. 23(2) and Art. 23(4)4), the Belgian Guidelines for setting fines state that in case of insolvency, associations could be obliged to request the contribution of their members. However, one may question the legality of a rule that would inflict to several undertakings the sanction pronounced against another, distinct legal person. Communication du Conseil de la concurrence, Lignes directrices sur le calcul des amendes imposées en matière de pratiques restrictives de concurrence en application de l'article 63 de la Loi sur la protection de la concurrence économique, *19 Décembre 2011, para. 21, available at* http://economie.fgov.be/fr/binaries/Communication_Lignes_directrices_amendes_tcm326-158194.pdf, para. 40.

[82] Following its fining decision in the elevator cartel case, the Commission sued the cartelists for private damages before Belgian civil courts. To date, this case only led to an interlocutory judgment with several questions asked to the EU Court of Justice. Kh. Brussel, 18 April 2011, *RCB*, 2011–2, p. 156.

[83] One decision was identified as dealing with private damages in Belgium in a 2004 EU survey. This decision does not deal with a cartel case though but with a distribution agreement subsequently declared void. The decision is not published but kept in the NCA's library. Ashurst, EU DG Competition, Study on the conditions of claims for damages in case of infringement of EC competition rules, Report for Belgium, August 2004, p. 1, available at http://ec.europa.eu/competition/antitrust/actionsdamages/study.html.

[84] This statement should not lead to a too negative view regarding private antitrust enforcement in Belgium. An upsurge of cases may be observed since 2004, with several rulings being issued each year on claims for annulment of anticompetitive contracts or cease and desist orders, if not on cartel damages.

[85] As already mentioned above, the track record of the NCA is not tremendous (L. de Muyter and N. Neyrinck, "*Une transaction en droit belge de la concurrence ? Approche critique de la proposition de la Direction Générale de la Concurrence*", *Revue de droit de la concurrence belge, 2012, n°2-3*). Only five cartels have been detected and condemned by the NCA between 2007 and 2011. Thus, in order to encourage private action from SMEs, the NCA should not only communicate more on its results but also investigate and condemn more.

Second, potential litigants may ignore the existence of the specific cartel that affected their business. Despite the efforts made by the EU Commission[86] to report and disseminate news of cartel infringements, the visibility of such information is often short-lived. Hence, it is very likely that many SMEs ignore having been victim of a cartel and do not consider to act against the detrimental consequences of a conspiracy they are not aware of.

Third, the difficulties inherent to the quantification of damages—amply illustrated by the Commission's Draft Guidance Paper[87]—may also play a role in the decision of potential litigants not to act for the reimbursement of their losses. Thus, while extra efforts should be made towards a more efficient communication on the availability of civil recourses against cartels, clear proxies to assess cartel damages[88] should simultaneously be adopted in order to develop private enforcement.

3.4.1.2 Best Practices

In spite of taking specific, tailored measures to protect SMEs' ability to take legal action against anticompetitive practices, diverse soft measures could be adopted to prioritise the action of the investigation authority in a way that is favourable to SMEs.

Belgian case law shows that SMEs that are party to antitrust proceedings may have utmost difficulties to use economic tools to articulate a convincing market definition before the courts. Not surprisingly, this weakness is particularly pregnant in abuses of dominance cases where—contrary to illegal coordination cases—the boundaries of the relevant market must be precisely defined before any condemnation.[89] Here, small versus big issues are most relevant as big undertakings may use

[86] Disregard towards market discipline and competition law are often stressed in continental Europe, especially when the introduction of criminal sanctions against antitrust infringement is discussed, with some groups pleading that public moral condemnation is not strong enough to justify such kind of penalties. M. Zuleeg, "Criminal Sanctions to Be Imposed on Individuals as Enforcement Instruments in European Competition law", 2001 EU Competition Law and Policy Workshop/Proceedings, EUIRSCAS, p. 8 (available at http://www.eui.eu/).

[87] EU Commission, DG Competition, *Draft Guidance Paper – Quantifying harm in actions for damages based on breaches of Article 101 or 102 of the Treaty*, June 2011, 69 p.

[88] *Ibidem*, para. 5: Some legislators have established presumptions regarding the amount of the damages and allowed a shift of the burden of proof. Another solution could be for the investigation authority to provide an estimation of the cartel's surplus with the condemnation decision.

[89] Compare: Conseil de Concurrence, Décision n'2008-P/K-43, 7 July 2008, aff. CONC-I/O-98/0031, *I.S.C./F.A.B. et ses membres* ("regarding agreements (...) the obligation to thoroughly delimitate the market at stake does exist only to the extent that this exercise is necessary to determine if the agreement or the decision fulfills the conditions of Article 2 BCA or of Article [101 TFEU]") and Conseil de la Concurrence, Décision n°2009-P/K-10, 26 May 2009, CONC-P/K-05/0065, Base/ BMB ("In the framework of Article 3 BCA and of Article [102 TFUE], it is essential to define the relevant market to be able to conclude to the existence of a possible dominant position").

superior financial means to look for—or even order—the market analysis needed to counter allegations of dominance. The *Vlan* case is a textbook example of the struggle SMEs are sometimes confronted with when dealing with market definition.[90] In the case at hand, a small entrepreneur willing to create a website for online classified ads decided to challenge the bundle offered by Vlan, a highly well-known ads publisher that offered to its advertisers free publication on its website for any paid publication in its paper. Debates on the relevant market raised a whole host of sophisticated issues with discussions related to (1) the existence of separate markets for the diffusion of online and physical ads, (2) the existence of separate market for free and paying papers and (3) the boundaries of the different product markets. On multiple occasions, the Court's ruling stresses that the claimant failed to provide any relevant price analysis (SNIPP test, price elasticity) or any market study to support its allegations of dominance. Logically, the Court rebutted the claims brought by the applicant.

Yet, beyond the complications SMEs may encounter when dealing with economic analysis and market definition,[91] what strikes us is that on top of all these troubles, heavy legal costs may fall on the failing applicant. In the *Vlan* case, the applicant had to pay EUR 10,000 to compensate the legal costs of the winning party.[92] The Court's ruling does not state the reasons for the level of these costs. However, it is very likely that these were requested by the winning party to compensate the efforts made to bring economic evidence of its non-dominance.[93]

In order to compensate this asymmetry of means, SMEs could prefer to introduce a complaint before the BCA to benefit from the economic expertise of the Prosecutor's Office instead of applying before a civil court where they would be on their own. This supposes however that the Prosecutor's Office welcomes such complaints and do not dismiss them on the basis of a non-priority assessment. The adoption of an SME agenda at the Prosecutor's Office level could thus induce small and medium undertakings to show more activism in the fight against

---

[90] Bruxelles, 24 April 2009, *Les Editions Urbaines SA / F. Peters*, *Annuaire Pratiques du commerce & Concurrence*, 2009, p. 928.

[91] Market definition issues also appeared in *'t Winkelke* case, where a small café-bookshop failed to prove the dominance of its press supplier that had terminated its supplies. The court stressed that the burden of proof lied on the applicant before rebutting its claim of abuse for refusal to supply. Voorz. Kh. Kortrijk, 6 February 1995, *Jaarboek Handelspraktijken & Mededinging*, 1995, p. 722.

[92] Bruxelles, 24 April 2009, *Les Editions Urbaines SA / F. Peters*, *Annuaire Pratiques du commerce & Concurrence*, 2009.

[93] Article 1022 of the Code judiciaire allows courts to correlate the amount of the legal costs with the complexity of the case. See Loi relative à la répétibilité des honoraires et des frais d'avocat, 21 April 2007, *M.B.*, 31 May 2007; Arrêté royal du 26 octobre 2007 fixant le tarif des indemnités de procédure visées à l'article 1022 du Code judiciaire et fixant la date d'entrée en vigueur des articles 1er à 13 de la loi du 21 avril 2007 relative à la répétibilité des honoraires et des frais d'avocat, *M.B.*, 9 November 2007.

anticompetitive practices. Voices here retort that SMEs should not be treated as an enforcement priority as it would produce under optimal social results.[94] One must however distinguish the complaints that are targeted by SMEs towards bigger undertakings and those aimed at other SMEs' adversaries. Undoubtedly, the former would present the double advantage to compensate asymmetry of means between players and to help to discipline important market operators in a way satisfactory for taxpayers.[95]

In the course of judicial proceedings, SMEs could also (1) bring to the attention of the court that it may ask to the Commission its opinion on questions related to the application of EU law or (2) directly alert the NCA or the Commission of their situation and prompt the sending of an amicus curiae letter.[96]

Another solution could be to exonerate SMEs from all or part of the legal costs due in case of rejection of an action introduced against a bigger undertaking. In this scenario, the respective size of the undertakings would affect the allocation of the proceeding indemnities linked to economic analysis. The sharing of these costs between the two parties could reduce the risks of litigation and induce SMEs to act.[97]

3.4.2 Collective Redress

Third parties are in principle prevented from bringing an action before civil courts if SMEs do not take action. Under Belgian law, applicants need to have a personal, direct and immediate interest to fill a claim: only if the claim can result in a patrimonial or moral benefit for the applicant will its action be admissible.[98]

This requirement is strict and in principle impairs the intervention of third parties. Exceptionally, consumers' associations and professional associations having specific provisions in their articles of associations for the defense of their members are allowed to bring cease and desist actions with respect to antitrust

---

[94] Cases against SMEs should not be treated as an enforcement priority as it would produce below optimal results regarding the minimal prejudice SMEs are likely to cause to consumers. F. LÉVÊQUE, "Caractéristique des PME et droit de la concurrence: le regard de l'économiste", in Y. CHAPUT (dir.), *Les PME et le droit de la concurrence. Analyse critique, comparative et perspective*, Paris, LexisNexis, 2009, p. 46.

[95] The spoiling of public money in SMEs v SMEs cases could be minimised though, with public investigations against SMEs targeted to those markets where support for economic analysis is the most needed, in opposition to easy cases – i.e., where prior market definition is provided by past case law, in after-market cases, etc.

[96] Regulation 1/2003, Article 15.

[97] Interestingly, Article 1022 of the Code judiciaire already authorises courts to take into account the financial capacity of the defeated party to modulate the amount of the indemnity allowed; however, this criterion may be counterbalanced by the complexity of the case, another factor that courts must consider to allocate compensations for legal costs.

[98] Code judiciaire, Articles 17 and 18.

breaches.[99,100] The Belgian legislator did not allow them to bring action before civil courts on damages, though.

The obligation for litigants to exhibit legal interest to act also prevents collective action. However, natural or legal persons who have individually suffered damage can regroup themselves and file a single claim as a closed group of applicants.[101] In such a case, damages are awarded to each person individually and not to the group as a whole.

This kind of arrangement offers the advantage to allow claimants to share the risks and mutualise lawyers' fees. Hence, while the introduction of a collective redress mechanism would require a substantial reform of Belgian judicial law,[102] the organisation of industrial associations of SMEs could provide an efficient palliative to class action. In order to best defend the interests of their members, industrial organisations could then embrace the mission to survey cartel decisions and communicate to their members the possible opportunities to act collectively against antitrust infringers. Along this line, the Prosecutors' Office could take the initiative to directly communicate cartel condemnation decisions to those industrial organisations that are the most likely hit by the antitrust infringement.

3.4.3 Additional Substantive Rules

Most antitrust litigations involving SMEs relate to vertical relationships.[103] The proportion of cases dealing with refusal to supply or, conversely, with attempts to prevent the distribution of products by undesirable retailers is substantial.

---

[99] Loi relative aux pratiques du marché et à la protection du consommateur, 6 April 2010, *M.B.*, 12 April 2010, Article 113; Loi concernant le règlement de certaines procédures dans le cadre de la loi du 6 avril 2010 relative aux pratiques du marché et à la protection du consommateur, 6 April 2010, *M.B.*, 12 April 2010, Article 2. The cease and desist action available under unfair competition law may be invoked to bring cease and desist proceedings against anticompetitive behaviour. D. Gérard, "Le droit belge des pratiques restrictives de concurrence" in N. Petit (dir.), *Le nouveau droit belge de la concurrence. Bilan et perspectives après quatre années d'application*, CUP n°124, Liège, Anthémis, 2010, p. 30.

[100] The procedure before the NCA being an objective procedure, complaints before the NCA are open for any natural or legal person. Hence, contrary to the limitations they know before civil courts, consumer's associations may introduce a complaint before the NCA without having to demonstrate any kind of personal interest. See Conseil de la concurrence, Decision, n°2008-P/K-43, *Test-Achats c/ auto-écoles de Belgique*.

[101] Ashurst, EU DG Competition, EU DG Competition, Study on the conditions of claims for damages in case of infringement of EC competition rules, Report for Belgium, August 2004, p. 3.

[102] M. Piers, "Class actions", *Nieuwe Juridische Weekblad*, 2007, pp. 825 et s.

[103] We observe that, while NCA case law primarily focuses on the decisions of professional associations, judicial case law mainly deals with supplier–buyer issues. This observation is also made by D. Gérard, "Le droit belge des pratiques restrictives de concurrence", in N. Petit (dir.), *Le nouveau droit belge de la concurrence. Bilan et perspectives après quatre années d'application*, CUP n°124, Liège, Anthémis, 2010, p. 66.

In order to somehow police supplier–retailer relationships, the Belgian legislator enacted two laws whose objective is to curb the commercial freedom of the one undertaking that is perceived to be the strongest party—i.e., the supplier. The first statute[104] deals with exclusive concession agreements in cases where the supplier imposes on its distributor obligations such that the latter would suffer serious damages in the event the supplier should terminate the contract—e.g., where specific investments were made by the distributor for the sale of the supplier's products. Under such circumstances, the law subordinates the termination of the agreement to (1) the sending of a significant advance warning and (2) the payment of an additional indemnity, two obligations that are supposed to secure the supplying of the concessionaire. The second status[105] imposes a 1-month cooling-off period before the signature of franchise agreements. It requires precise information on the duration of the contract, prorogation opportunities, termination conditions, and non-compete clauses with the objective to anticipate and diffuse possible future conflicts in the supply relationship.

The two mentioned statuses are not limited to any sector but apply transversally. The notoriety of the first legal instrument and the fact that it has not been amended since 1971 demonstrate that it efficiently protects small and medium operators against abrupt termination of supply.

Acknowledgement The author would like to thank Nicolas Petit, Marc Abenhaim, Laurent Demuyter, Charlotte Lousberg, and Elise Provost for their insights and remarks. The author is especially indebted to Pierre Sabbadini, who provided great research assistance in the early preparation of this paper. Translations of Belgian legal texts and case law are mine, with any error that may come with it.

[104] Loi relative à la résiliation unilatérale des concessions de vente exclusive à durée indéterminée, 27 July 1961, *M.B.*, 5 October 1961.

[105] Loi relative à l'information précontractuelle dans le cadre d'accords de partenariat commercial, 19 December 2005, *M.B.*, 18 January 2006.

Croatia

4

Boris Andrejaš

4.1 SMEs in Context

4.1.1 SMEs' Economic Context and Legal Definition

4.1.1.1 Legal Definitions of SMEs

Croatian competition law[1] does not include a separate legal definition of SME. However, several Croatian laws include provisions that could serve as a definition of SME. First, the Croatian Act on Development Incentives for Small Economy[2] defines that an undertaking belongs to the "small economy" if the following criteria are met: (1) the average annual number of employees is less than 250, (2) the undertaking is independent (i.e., generally there is no single or joint shareholding exceeding 25 % from the entities that do not meet the criteria for "small economy"), and (3) its aggregate annual turnover is less than EUR 50,000,000.00 or the value of the aggregate assets is less than EUR 43,000,000.00.

The Act on Development Incentives for Small Economy[3] also clarifies the difference between (1) micro entities, (2) small entities, and (3) medium entities falling within the "small economy". The criteria for the micro entities are as follows: (1) the average annual number of employees is less than ten and (2) the aggregate annual turnover is less than EUR 2,000,000.00 or the value of the aggregate assets is less than EUR 2,000,000.00. Small entities are defined according to the following criteria: (1) the average annual number of employees is less than

[1] Competition Act, Official gazette, nos. 79/2009, 80/2013.

[2] Act on Development Incentives for Small Economy, Official gazette, nos. 29/2002, 63/2007, 53/2012 and 56/2013, Article 2.

[3] Act on Development Incentives for Small Economy, Official gazette, nos. 29/2002, 63/2007, 53/2012 and 56/2013, Article 3.

B. Andrejaš (✉)
Babić & Partners, Zagreb, Croatia
e-mail: boris.andrejas@babic-partners.hr

P. Këllezi et al. (eds.), *Antitrust for Small and Middle Size Undertakings and Image Protection from Non-Competitors*, LIDC Contributions on Antitrust Law, Intellectual Property and Unfair Competition, DOI 10.1007/978-3-642-54000-4_4, © Springer-Verlag Berlin Heidelberg 2014

50 and (2) the aggregate annual turnover is less than EUR 10,000,000.00 or the value of the aggregate assets is less than EUR 10,000,000.00. The medium entities exceed criteria for small entities but are still within the general ambit of the "small economy".

In addition, the Croatian Accountancy Act[4] distinguishes its addressees (i.e., business undertakings) as (1) small, (2) medium, or (3) large. A "small" undertaking is a company that does not exceed two of the following thresholds: (1) aggregate assets of HRK 32,500,000.00 (approximately EUR 4.3 million), (2) gross income of HRK 65,000,000.00 (approximately EUR 8.6 million), and (3) average annual number of employees of 50. A "medium" undertaking is a company that exceeds two thresholds for the "small" undertaking but does not exceed two of the following thresholds: (1) aggregate assets of HRK 130,000,000.00 (approximately EUR 17.3 million), (2) gross income of HRK 260,000,000.00 (approximately EUR 34.6 million), and (3) average annual number of employees of 250.

Obviously, the definitions from the Act on Development Incentives for Small Economy and from the Accountancy Act are not harmonised and may well serve only for application of the respective statutory rules. However, they may provide guidance on qualification of SMEs for purposes of competition law.

4.1.1.2 The Economic Perspective

According to data published by the Croatian Ministry of Entrepreneurship and Crafts, SMEs constitute about 99.5 % of total economic activity and provide for about 63 % of the employment in the Republic of Croatia.[5]

4.1.1.3 Relevant Cases

As indicated above,[6] there is no definition of SME for purposes of application of Croatian competition law. In addition, since there are no specific rules for SMEs, the Croatian Competition Agency (hereafter referred to as "CCA" or "Competition Agency")[7] does not indicate in its rulings whether (1) it takes into consideration the size of the entities involved and (2) whether it considers that the parties to the proceedings enjoy a special status due to their size. Consequently, the track record of the Croatian Competition Agency cannot be properly analysed. In addition, it should be noted that CCA has only recently been granted authority to levy fines for violations of the competition law.[8]

On the other hand, there is no available case law on private antitrust enforcement before Croatian courts.

---

[4] Accountancy Act, Official gazette, no. 109/2007, 125/2011 and 54/2013, Article 3.

[5] Program of Incentives to Small and Medium Size Entrepreneurs 2008-2012, Ministry of Entrepreneurship and Craft; available at http://eobrazovanje.mingorp.hr.

[6] See Sect. 4.1.1.1.

[7] Agencija za Zaštitu Tržišnog Natjecanja (AZTN), available at http://www.aztn.hr/.

[8] See Sect. 4.2.3.

In this context, Table 4.1 below contains the decisions of the CCA in the proceedings against the companies that could possibly qualify as "small economy" within the meaning of the Act on Development Incentives for Small Economy.[9] Based on the available data, we believe that the legal assessment of the Competition Agency has not been influenced by the economic dimension of SMEs.

4.1.2 Specific Treatment of SMEs Under Competition Law

4.1.2.1 The Nature and Scope of Specific Treatment for SMEs

Croatian Competition Law does not differentiate between undertakings based on their size, and SMEs do not enjoy any special treatment. In addition, there are no programs of the CCA specifically addressed to SMEs. However, the Competition Agency is extensively engaged in advocacy efforts targeting, e.g., central and regional Chambers of Economy, special subdivisions of the Chamber of Economy (for instance the automotive industry). Bearing in mind various elements, such as the size of Croatian economy and the prevailing size of the business undertakings, we believe that these advocacy programmes are actually mostly used by the SMEs.

4.1.2.2 Substantive and Procedural Rules

SMEs do not enjoy any specific treatment under substantive or procedural rules of Croatian competition law.

4.1.2.3 Influence of Size and Economic Power in Decisions of the National Competition Authorities and Courts

Available practice of the Competition Agency and competent courts does not reveal that size and economic power influence their decisions. The situation is of course different when substantive law provisions specifically refer to market (economic) power of the undertakings (e.g., provisions on abuse of dominant position or application of the block exemption regulations).

4.1.2.4 Specific Programmes Addressed to SMEs

To the best of the author's knowledge, there are no programmes of the Croatian Competition Agency, such as compliance, information policies, enhancement of competition enforcement programmes, that are specifically addressed to SMEs.

---

[9] It should be noted that based on the publicly accessible data, it is not possible to conclusively establish that a certain company qualifies as "small economy" within the meaning of the Act on Development Incentives for Small Economy. Consequently, we have prepared Table 4.1 based on our reasonable assessment, and it is illustrative only.

Table 4.1 Cases involving SMEs

Subject matter	Parties	Date	Decision no. (class)
Procedural order on dismissal of the complaint (prohibited agreement/abuse of a dominant position)	CCA v Consortium of the transport operators in the area of Međimurje county and its municipalities	27 February 2012	UP/I 030-02/ 11-01/050
Procedural order on dismissal of the initiative (prohibited agreement—cartel)	CCA v Media d.o.o., Zagreb and Medical Intertrade d.o.o., Sveta Nedjelja	26 January 2012	UP/I 030-02/ 2011-01/021
Procedural order on dismissal of the initiative (abuse of a dominant position)	CCA v Inel – medicinske tehnike d.o.o., Zagreb and Croatian National Institute for Public Health, Zagreb	15 December 2011	UP/I 030-02/ 2011-01/048
Procedural order on dismissal of the initiative (abuse of a dominant position)	CCA v Discovery d.o.o.	15 December 2011	UP/I 030-02/ 2011-01/022
Procedural order on dismissal of the initiative (abuse of a dominant position)	CCA v Blitz d.o.o., Zagreb, Blitz-Cinestar d.o.o., Zagreb, Blitz-Cinestar Adria d.o.o., Zagreb and Duplicato media d.o. o., Zagreb	01 December 2011	UP/I 030-02/ 2011-01/007
Ruling on a prohibited agreement	Auto Teskera d.o.o., Velika Mlaka, Autokuća Horvat, Zagreb and Morić d.o.o., Velika Mlaka v Euro rent sport d.o.o., Zagreb	13 October 2011	UP/I 030-02/ 2010-01/024
Ruling on a prohibited agreement—cartel	CCA v the Office Products Retailers' Association and its members	21 July 2011	UP/I 030-02/ 2010-01/018
Ruling on termination of the proceedings (prohibited agreement)	CCA v TM ZAGREB d.o.o., Zagreb	16 June 2011	UP/I 030-02/ 2010-01/017
Procedural order on dismissal of the initiative (abuse of a dominant position)	CCA v DDL d.o.o., Zagreb	19 May 2011	UP/I 030-02/ 2011-01/001
Procedural order on dismissal of the initiative (abuse of a dominant position)	CCA v I.S. d.o.o. and MEDIKAL INTERTRADE d.o.o.	07 April 2011	UP/I 030-02/ 2010-01/035
Ruling on dismissal of the request (abuse of a dominant position)	Hosni-compitel d.o.o, Sveti Ivan Žabno v Nikola Andričić, owner of the craft "Andričić", Bjelovar	24 March 2011	UP/I 030-02/ 2011-01/009
Ruling on rejection of the request (abuse of a dominant position)	KINO ZADAR FILM d.d., Zadar v BLITZ d.o.o., Zagreb and DUPLICATO MEDIA d.o.o., Zagreb	24 February 2011	UP/I 030-02/ 2008-01/080
Ruling on a prohibited agreement	Rivulus d.o.o., Odra and M SAN Grupa d.d., Zagreb	07 October 2010	UP/I 030-02/ 2008-01/061
Ruling on a prohibited agreement	Monte d.o.o., Pula v Hyundai auto Zagreb d.o.o., Zagreb	08 April 2010	UP/I 030-02/ 2008-01/036

(continued)

Table 4.1 (continued)

Subject matter	Parties	Date	Decision no. (class)
Ruling on a prohibited agreement	CCA v Kmag d.o.o., Gornji Stupnik	02 December 2010	UP/I 030-02/ 2010-01/015
Ruling on a prohibited agreement—cartel	CCA v EKI-inžinjering d.o.o., Pula, Uljanik upravljanje stambeno – poslovnim zgradama d.o.o., Pula, Stambeni inženjering d.o.o., Pula and Kany d.o.o., Pula	23 December 2009	UP/I 030-02/ 2008-01/078
Ruling on a prohibited agreement—cartel	CCA v Managers of residential buildings in Split (TEHNOPLAST d.o.o., JAMB-TUKIĆ d.o.o., DUB-INŽENJERING d.o.o., STANO-UPRAVA d.o.o., NOVI DANI d.o.o., UPRAVITELJ d.o. o., DIKA d.o.o.)	24 November 2009	UP/I 030-02/ 2008-01/003
Ruling on a prohibited agreement	Šimatić d.o.o., Osijek and Tomić & Co. d.o.o., Zagreb	03 November 2009	UP/I 030-02/ 2008-01/052
Ruling on a prohibited agreement	CCA v Adria Lada d.o.o., Zagreb	24 September 2009	UP/I 030-01/ 2008-01/067
Ruling on a prohibited agreement—cartel	CCA v sixteen Driving schools from Rijeka and Matulji	30 July 2009	UP/I 030-02/ 2008-01/068
Ruling on rejection of the request (prohibited agreement)	Sanabilis d.o.o., Šibenik v Citroen Hrvatska d.o.o., Zagreb	17 December 2008	UP/I 030-02/ 2006-01/080
Ruling on a prohibited agreement—cartel	CCA v Bus transport operators	24 September 2007	UP/I 030-02/ 2006-01/039

4.1.3 The Role of Trade Associations

Considering the structure of the Croatian economy,[10] the overwhelming majority of members of Croatian trade associations (e.g., members of Croatian Chamber of Economy) are SMEs. Although there are specific policies targeting SMEs in the context of development incentives, there are no particular competition law instruments or programmes that are designed for SMEs specifically.

However, trade associations sometimes appear as complainants in cases before the Croatian Competition Agency.[11] It is safe to assume that in such cases the complaint originated from SME members of the trade association, which in turn serve to provide more credibility in the proceedings before the Competition Agency.

[10] See Sect. 4.1.1.2.

[11] Croatian Chamber of Economy (Sector for Industry) v Prirodni Plin Ltd (*Natural Gas LLC*) of 5 April 2012, class: UP/I 030-02/2011-01/038, no. 580-05/63-2012-131.

4.1.4 Policy Recommendations

Bearing in mind the structure of the Croatian economy, it might be worthwhile to establish special competition law rules, particularly at a substantive level, for SMEs.[12] Introduction of such rules should be accompanied with broad advocacy programmes implemented by the Croatian Competition Agency, specifically targeting SMEs.

4.2 Public Antitrust Enforcement and SMEs

4.2.1 Substantive and Procedural Rules Applicable to SMEs

4.2.1.1 Introduction

Croatian competition law does not differentiate between SMEs and other undertakings. Consequently, there are no specific, different, administrative substantive rules and judicial substantive rules applicable or applied in relation to SMEs.

This also holds true for (1) the general rules on administrative procedure, applicable in proceedings before Croatian Competition Agency and (2) the general litigation rules applicable in proceedings before ordinary courts.

4.2.1.2 Safe Harbours for SMEs

There are no safe harbours designed specifically for SMEs under Croatian competition law. However, certain standard instruments such as *de minimis* rules[13] or block exemption regulations[14] take into account the "size" of the entities concerned. These instruments are predominantly market share based rather than turnover based.

4.2.1.3 Access to Justice

SMEs enjoy all procedural rights under Croatian law, and there are no specific obstacles for use of these rights by SMEs. In our opinion, access of the SMEs to justice, including remedies, does not need to be specially facilitated. Special

---

[12] See Sect. 4.2.4.

[13] Regulation on Agreements of Minor Importance, Official gazette, no. 9/2011, available at http://www.aztn.hr/trzisno-natjecanje/29/croatian-legislation/.

[14] Regulation on Block Exemption for Agreements in Transport Sector, Official gazette, no. 78/2011; Regulation on Block Exemption for Insurance Agreements, Official gazette, no. 78/2011; Regulation on Block Exemption for Horizontal Agreements between Undertakings, Official gazette, no. 72/2011; Regulation on Block Exemption for Agreements on Distribution and Servicing of Motor Vehicles, Official gazette, no. 37/2011; Regulation on Block Exemption for Vertical Agreements between Undertakings, Official gazette, no. 37/2011; and Regulation on Block Exemption for Technology Transfer Agreements, Official gazette, no. 9/2011, available at http://www.aztn.hr/trzisno-natjecanje/29/croatian-legislation/.

position of SMEs should be rather emphasised in the context of the substantive provisions rather than in the context of the access to justice.[15]

This being said, there are instances in both administrative and judicial procedure that take into account the legal nature of the entities involved rather than their size (e.g., with respect to the delivery of court orders and other decisions or with respect to representation). In addition, it may be that natural persons would more easily claim benefits of certain protective mechanisms available both under administrative and judicial rules, which oblige the competent court or the administrative body to provide additional protection to unknowledgeable parties.

Bearing in mind the current state of development of Croatian competition law and related procedures, there might be no immediate reasons for differentiation between SMEs and other entities on the procedural level. Nevertheless, opening up the possibility of collective redress in the context of private enforcement might facilitate the procedural position of SMEs.[16]

On the other hand, access to justice in Croatia may be generally impeded due to various factual (e.g., rather ineffective judicial control over the CCA decisions) and legal reasons (e.g., complainants do not enjoy a standing in the proceedings before Competition Agency). However, these impediments do not target SMEs specifically and should not be remedied with "SMEs specific" actions.

4.2.2 Fundamental Rights of SMEs as Infringers and Victims

Under Croatian law, differences in relation to fundamental rights arise solely from different legal nature of the undertakings (legal entity v natural person) and should be so maintained. It would be even worthwhile to expand efforts to alleviate these differences to the extent possible rather than to introduce new grounds for differences (e.g., based on size in relation to SMEs). By way of example, Croatian law[17] affords certain personality rights (e.g., right to free market activity) to legal entities and recognises the right of the legal entities to compensation for violations of such personality rights.[18] Introduction of new differences in relation to the fundamental rights would not be feasible approach, especially if the basis for differences is "fluid" category such as size, and would be questionable from the perspective of certain constitutional guarantees, such as the principle of non-discrimination.

4.2.2.1 Complaints

Croatian competition law does not differentiate between SMEs and other undertakings either as infringers or as victims. In this context, all fundamental

[15] See Sect. 4.2.4.

[16] See Sect. 4.3.2.

[17] Act on Obligations, Official gazette nos. 35/2005 and 41/2008, Article 19.

[18] Act on Obligations, Official gazette nos. 35/2005 and 41/2008, Article 1100.

and other procedural rights are equally afforded (or denied) to the SMEs. In the author's opinion, any deficiency in this respect should not be remedied by actions specifically addressing SMEs' concerns but rather by broad legislative action that should equally benefit SMEs and all other undertakings. In this context, it would be worthwhile to amend the procedural rules on initiation of the proceedings, party status, down raids, judicial control, which are included in the Croatian Competition Act.

4.2.2.2 Access to the File

The Croatian Competition Act[19] provides that only parties to the proceedings may access the file of the CCA. It should be noted that the complainant is not a party to the proceedings before the CCA and can access the file only in very limited circumstances. Although we believe that such solution is deficient and should be amended, this deficiency does not impact specifically SMEs and therefore should not be addressed through measures emphasising the difference between the SMEs and other entities.

4.2.2.3 Leniency, Settlements, and Commitment Decisions for SMEs

Croatian competition law does not contain provisions that regulate the position of SMEs in relation to leniency arrangements, settlements, and commitment decisions.

However, all these instruments have been introduced in Croatian competition law only recently,[20] and enforcement practice based on them is virtually nonexistent.[21] Consequently, it remains to be seen whether their application by the Competition Agency might necessitate special provisions or mechanics for SMEs.

In addition, general rules of the Croatian Competition Act on initiation of the proceedings[22] may indeed require improvement with respect to anonymous complaints, as well as to procedural rights of the complainants. However, these issues are not SME specific. Consequently, at this stage, it might be advisable to proceed with limited reform of the Croatian Competition Act rather than with the introduction of specific provisions dealing with the position of SMEs.

4.2.3 Sanctions: Different Penalties for Different Sizes?

The Competition Agency has only recently been granted authority to levy fines for violations of the competition law.[23] Under the previously applicable Competition

[19] Competition Act, Official gazette, nos. 79/2009 and 80/2013, Article 47.

[20] Competition Act, Official gazette, nos. 79/2009 and 80/2013, in force as of 1 October 2010 and Regulation on Immunity from Fines and Reduction of Fines, Official gazette, no. 129/2010, available in English at http://www.aztn.hr/trzisno-natjecanje/29/croatian-legislation/.

[21] There are no reported leniency decisions and only few report commitment decisions.

[22] Competition Act, Official gazette, nos. 79/2009 and 80/2013, Article 37 ff.

[23] The Competition Act, Official gazette, nos. 79/09 and 80/2013, entered into force on 1 October 2010.

Act,[24] the Competition Agency would only determine that certain entity has violated competition law, while the sanctioning phase would be delegated to the competent misdemeanour court. There have been only very few sanctions imposed by the misdemeanour courts, mainly due to the operation of the statute of limitations and the reported sanctions have been fairly low. In addition, the case law of misdemeanour courts is not readily accessible, and therefore it is difficult to assess to which extent, if at all, has the courts taken into account differences between SMEs and other economic operators.

However, it is interesting to note that the largest reported fine was imposed by the misdemeanour court on the entity that might be considered as SME (the fine amounted to HRK 550,000, approximately EUR 73,000).[25]

4.2.4 Policy Recommendations

The Competition Act does not include any specific provisions addressed to SMEs or protecting SMEs. However, it might be worthwhile to introduce the rules protecting SMEs in specific circumstances. By way of example, the rules of the Croatian Competition Act[26] are drafted along the lines of Article 102 TFEU, and there is no available practice on the application of this provision on entities with substantial buyer power. Introduction of such specific rules, particularly in the retail sector, would draw attention of the Competition Agency to these issues and could benefit small and medium undertakings.[27] Although such rules should not specifically protect SMEs, we believe that SME producers and suppliers would benefit the most from their introduction.

On the other hand, bearing in mind the structure of Croatian economy and the difficulties faced by SME businesses, as well as proclaimed governmental support for SME entities, it might be worthwhile to consider the introduction of a more lenient approach toward allegedly anticompetitive behaviour of the SME entities. By way of example, it is doubtful whether even price-fixing arrangement between SMEs, especially when they are faced with significant competitive pressure from larger entity, has any adverse effects on the economy. Rather, it appears that such conduct may be even pro-competitive and certainly does not warrant investment of efforts and resources of the Competition Agency. One may even consider that comparison with merger control proceedings warrants such conclusion. On one hand, price-fixing agreement between SMEs is strictly prohibited by competition law, and the Competition Agency vigorously pursues enforcement in such cases. On the other hand, merger between SMEs would not be even considered by the

[24] Competition Act, Official gazette, no. 122/203.

[25] Decision of the Misdemeanour Court in Zagreb no. XX-G-12118-05 of 30 November 2007.

[26] Competition Act, Official gazette, nos. 79/2009 and 80/2013, Article 13.

[27] It is often reported in the media that various suppliers, not only SME suppliers, face significant obstacles with access to larger retail chains.

Competition Agency (due to the lack of significant turnover). Such different approaches seem difficult to reconciliate since both price-fixing agreement and merger in economic terms have the same result: single-pricing policies implemented by (former) competitors. In addition, fines for such behaviour may have significant anticompetitive effects and cause even bankruptcy of businesses and therefore a relaxation of competitive pressures. Therefore, in the author's opinion, certain SME protective rules should be introduced into the Croatian Competition Act.[28]

4.3 Private Antitrust Enforcement and SMEs

4.3.1 Substantive Rules, Procedural Aspects for SMEs in Civil Suits

The Competition Act[29] and the Civil Procedure Act[30] do not contain any rules designed specifically to protect SMEs in private antitrust enforcement. The Competition Act[31] includes only a short reference that the competent commercial courts are empowered to hear claims for damages arising out of a breach of the Competition Act. Croatian rules of civil procedure do not contain any specific provisions dealing with private antitrust enforcement.

Due to these and other reasons, jurisprudence on private antitrust enforcement in Croatia is virtually nonexistent.

Furthermore, there are no specific rules in the context of private antitrust enforcement addressing the possibility for a third party to bring an action before civil courts in the name or on behalf of an SME if the SME fails to bring the action itself. However, we do not believe that such a solution would be feasible under general rules governing civil procedures.

Of course, an SME could generally transfer its claim against the tortfeasor (entity violating competition law) to a third party. Under rules of Croatian contract law, any claim (including claims based on tort) could be transferred from the creditor to the third person based on a simple assignment agreement. The debtor (i.e., tortfeasor) should be simply notified of the assignment.[32] The third party would then have an autonomous right to institute proceedings against the tortfeasor.

[28] E.g., along the lines of Article 3, German Act Against Restraints of Competition (*Gesetz gegen Wettbewerbsbeschränkungen*), available at http://www.gesetze-im-internet.de/gwb/index.html.

[29] Competition Act, Official gazette, nos. 79/2009 and 80/2013.

[30] Civil Procedure Act, Official gazette, nos. 4/1977, 36/1977, 6/1980, 36/1980, 43/1982, 69/1982, 58/1984, 74/1987, 57/1989, 20/1990, 27/1990, 35/1991, 53/1991, 91/1992, 112/1999, 88/2001, 84/2008, 123/2008, 57/2011, 148/2011 and 25/2013.

[31] Competition Act, Official gazette, nos. 79/2009 and 80/2013, Article 69.

[32] Act on Obligations, Official gazette, nos. 35/2005, 41/2008 and 25/2011, Article 80 ff.

4.3.1.1 Obstacles

In the author's opinion, a claimant bringing before Croatian ordinary courts a claim for damages arising from violations of the competition law would have to overcome various procedural and substantive obstacles, as illustrated below.

First, the rules of Croatian law on the standing of the claimant might pose challenges in a competition law setting. More specifically, while rules on tortuous liability do not specifically exclude different types of claimants (e.g., direct purchasers, competitors, and indirect purchasers),[33] it may be difficult for at least certain of these categories to show all elements required for a successful claim. By way of example, it may be difficult for indirect purchasers to prove causality and quantum of damages due to the fact that they will not have a direct business relationship with the infringer.

In addition, the interests of direct and indirect purchasers may be in conflict where they claim damages for the same infringement. Such claims will normally be mutually exclusive—the direct purchaser is not harmed if the overcharge was passed on to the indirect purchaser and *vice versa.*

The claims of direct and indirect purchasers may be brought in independent actions, which may result in irreconcilable judgments. Purchasers may theoretically decide to cooperate and submit their claims as alternatives in a single action on the basis of Article 196(1) Civil Procedure Act, which provides possibility for independent litigants to participate in the same proceedings. Also, if an action by one purchaser is pending against the infringer, it is conceivable that another purchaser intervenes in support of the infringer in order to prove that the damage was not caused to the plaintiff.[34]

Second, the general rules on damages have not as yet been tested by the courts in the context of antitrust violations, and there are no antitrust-specific rules in the relevant legal provisions. It still remains to be seen what difficulties the claimants might face while proving all necessary legal requirements for an award of damages in the context of private antitrust enforcement and how such obstacles will be overcome. By way of example, as the exact quantum of damage suffered may be difficult, if not impossible, to establish, the effectiveness of the remedy will depend on the margin of discretion attributed to the first instance courts and, particularly, tolerance of this margin by higher courts.

Third, it remains to be seen to what extent will the courts accept certain types of defences specific for private antitrust enforcement. General rules of Croatian law appear adequate to support at least some of these defences. By way of example, in an action for damages the defendant may claim that, even if any damage has occurred, it was passed on to the plaintiff's customers (the passing-on defence). The essence of this defence is that any award on damages would result in unlawful

[33] Generally, any natural person or legal entity has standing to sue or be sued before the Croatian courts. In specific circumstances, standing is given even to groups or associations that do not have legal personality (Civil Procedure Act, Official gazette, nos. 4/1977, etc., Article 77).

[34] Civil Procedure Act, Official gazette, nos. 4/1977, etc., Article 206 ff.

enrichment of the plaintiff.[35] Since passing on is an independent defence made in response to a claim for damages, the burden of proof that passing on has occurred is on the defendant. Also, if the plaintiff has contributed to the damage or the extent of damage, the damages are reduced in proportion to the contribution. If such proportion cannot be established, the court is to award damages taking into account the overall circumstances of each individual case.[36]

Fourth, it appears that the standard rules on burden of proof may provide another layer of challenges for the claimant. Croatian civil procedure is, for the most part, adversarial in style. According to the Civil Procedure Act, each party has the burden of supplying facts and evidence that form the bases of their claims or objections.[37] The court may remind the parties of the burden of proof, when it deems appropriate.

Since the primary aim of litigation proceedings is to establish whether or not the claimant's statement of claim is founded, the burden of proof in litigation rests mainly on the claimant. To the extent that the defendant has made objections or allegations to support his defence, it is for the defendant to prove the facts on which he relies.

Fifth, it appears that the claimant may face additional challenges in producing sufficient evidence. The parties have a duty to state all facts supporting their claims and indicate the relevant evidence before the first substantive hearing. The court may order a party to the proceedings or a third party to produce a specific document requested by the other party.[38] If either party refuses to produce the requested document or alleges that it is not in the possession of the document, the court may draw negative inferences from such behaviour.[39] In Croatian civil procedure, the courts do not have the authority to order wide, American-style discovery.

Sixth, even in case of follow-on actions, the reliance on the decisions of the Competition Agency may be rather limited. Courts are generally bound by final and not-subject-to-appeal decisions of the competent authorities. However, this binding effect is limited to the operative (dispositive) part of the administrative ruling. The rest of the ruling, such as the statement of reasons, has only persuasive effect. Therefore, it will depend on particular circumstances if and to what extent previous administrative ruling may be used in the subsequent litigation. In the context of private actions, the Competition Agency's decisions would have the status as described above. Obviously, numerous issues of relevance for the private action would be contained only in the statement of reasons of the Competition Agency's decision (i.e., in its nonbinding part that may be reassessed by the court). It remains to be seen to what extent the competent courts will rely on persuasiveness of the

[35] Bukovac Puvača M, Butorac V (2008) Izvanugovorna odgovornost za štetu prouzročenu povredom pravila tržišnog natjecanja. *Hrvatska pravna revija* 12:32-54 (in English: Liability in Tort for Infringements of Competition Law).

[36] Act on Obligations, Official gazette, nos. 35/2005, 41/2008 and 125/2011, Article 1092.

[37] Civil Procedure Act, Official gazette, nos. 4/1977, etc., Article 7.

[38] Civil Procedure Act, Official gazette, nos. 4/1977, etc., Articles 233 and 234.

[39] Civil Procedure Act, Official gazette, nos. 4/1977, etc., Article 233(5).

nonbinding parts of the Competition Agency's administrative rulings, including the underlying economic and legal analysis.

Lastly, different evidentiary rules are applied in administrative proceedings before the Competition Agency and private actions proceedings. Therefore, evidence invoked by the parties would have to be produced anew before the litigation court, irrespective of whether such evidence has been already produced in the proceedings before the Competition Agency. By way of example, an ordinary court generally could not rely on the minutes of the witness' testimony occurred during the administrative proceedings before the Competition Agency but would have to examine the witness.

4.3.1.2 Best Practices

Due to the overall lack of case law and appropriate legislative solutions, there is no best practice addressing private antitrust enforcement in general or in specific SME setting.

4.3.2 Collective Redress

Various types of collective actions as known in different jurisdictions are not available under Croatian procedural rules. This holds true also for competition cases.[40]

On the other hand, it would be possible for numerous claimants to appear in the same private action as co-litigants provided that they satisfy the requirements set by the Civil Procedure Act. In this context, they would generally have to prove that their claims arose from substantially the same factual and legal background and that the same court is competent for their claims, for instance that they are customers of the same dominant undertaking. However, they would be treated as separate parties to the same proceedings, which may result in some of them succeeding in proving all requirements for the tortfeasor's liability, while others not.

Right to collective redress could help to improve the rights of the SMEs. Such a collective approach might mitigate typical obstacles that are faced by SMEs, such as underfunding or access to top legal advice, and might increase the occurrence of private enforcement actions.

[40] Consumer Protection Act, Official gazette nos. 79/2007, 125/2007, 79/2009, 89/2009, 78/2012 and 56/2013, opens a possibility for collective redress for violations of consumer's rights (Article 131). The authority to institute appropriate proceedings is awarded to, *inter alia*, consumer's association. However, it appears that this mechanism would not cover competition cases and certainly could not result in award of damages.

4.3.3 Standing of Trade Associations

Trade associations do not enjoy any special position under Croatian competition law. However, they do appear as complainants in the proceedings before the Competition Agency[41] and thus arguably facilitate the position of their SME members.

In addition, Croatian litigation rules that would be applicable in cases of private antitrust enforcement do not specifically address standing of the trade associations. Provided that the trade associations could show sufficient legal interest on the basis of assignment of the victims' claims or otherwise, they could support their members in private antitrust enforcement proceedings.

4.3.4 Policy Recommendations

Specific rules should be introduced to address the possible challenges on private antitrust enforcement. The purpose of these rules would be to facilitate the position of claimants in such actions, for instance by reversing or relaxing the burden of proof, by using appropriate presumptions regarding quantum of damages, or by providing clear rules on (1) claimants and their standing, and (2) defences allowed to the defendants. However, these rules should address the issues common to all possible claimants and not specifically SMEs.

Conclusions and Policy Recommendations

The structure of the Croatian economy[42] might warrant special treatment of the SMEs under competition law. However, in the author's opinion, this special treatment could be emphasised solely in specific substantive law rules. As to the other possible areas of reform (e.g., procedure before the Croatian Competition Agency, fundamental rights, etc.), introduction of special provisions addressing the position of the SMEs in these other areas might be counterproductive since described deficiencies should be addressed by broader reform (i.e., problems are not SME specific). In addition, at this stage these reforms may be even premature since the relevant practice is virtually nonexistent (e.g., in leniency programmes).

[41] Croatian Chamber of Economy (Sector for Industry) v Prirodni Plin Ltd (*Natural Gas LLC*) of 5 April 2012, class: UP/I 030-02/2011-01/038, no. 580-05/63-2012-131.

[42] See Sect. 4.1.1.2.

Czech Republic

5

Lenka Čížková

5.1 Introduction

The purpose of this report is to summarise the legal regime of SMEs in the Czech Republic and to point out any potential deficiencies in their regulation. The regulation of SMEs in the Czech Republic is particularly important as they constitute the backbone of the economy, amounting to 99.84 % of all enterprises in the Czech Republic and providing for 60.88 %[1] of employment in the Czech Republic. Firstly, the definition of SMEs is being discussed, together with the relevant case law. Secondly, it is being elaborated on whether a special regulation is provided for SMEs under competition law and any differences in substantive and procedural rules in public and private enforcement. Finally, all conclusions are being summed up and assessed.

5.2 SMEs in Context

5.2.1 SMEs' Economic Context and Legal Definition

5.2.1.1 Legal Definition of SMEs

The legal definition of SMEs is set out in Section 2 of Act No. 47/2002 Coll., on the support of small and medium-sized enterprises, and Act No. 2/1969 Coll., on the establishment of ministries and other central institutions of state administration in the Czech Republic, as amended (hereafter referred to as "**Act 47/2002**"), and reads as follows: "For the purposes of this Act (meaning Act 47/2002), an enterprise shall

[1] Source: Ministry of Industry and Trade – Information for 2010.

L. Čížková (✉)
Associated Law Offices Všetečka Zelený Švorčík Kalenský and Partners, Prague, Czech Republic
e-mail: lenka.cizkova@sak-alo.cz

P. Këllezi et al. (eds.), *Antitrust for Small and Middle Size Undertakings and Image Protection from Non-Competitors*, LIDC Contributions on Antitrust Law, Intellectual Property and Unfair Competition, DOI 10.1007/978-3-642-54000-4_5, © Springer-Verlag Berlin Heidelberg 2014

be considered small or medium-sized enterprise provided that it fulfils the criteria laid down in the directly applicable regulation of the European Communities."[2]

Furthermore, an Interpretation Notice (*soft law*) on the definition of SMEs (described as Application Manual) has been prepared by the Czech Competition Authority, in cooperation with the Ministry of Industry and Trade of the Czech Republic.[3] This Interpretation Notice elaborates on the definition of an autonomous enterprise and partner enterprises.

5.2.1.2 Context

As already outlined in the Introduction, SMEs in the Czech Republic constitute 99.84 % of all enterprises and provide for 60.88 % of employment in the Czech Republic.

The relevant cases under European State aid law regarding SMEs are as follows.[4]

Case No. (EC)	Subject Matter	Conduct	Outcome	Relation to SMEs
N32/ 2007	Insurance of short-term export credits of SMEs against the risk of non-payment	The measure was intended for SMEs having a total annual turnover not exceeding EUR 2 million	The notification was withdrawn by the Czech Republic	The addressees of the grant
N497/ 2006	Prerov Municipal Hall	A subsidy to a small undertaking IMIT s.r.o. in order to run the cultural activities of Prerov Municipal Hall	A subsidy shall supposedly not be considered as state aid because it most probably has no impact on trade between the member states	IMIT s.r.o. considered as small undertaking under the legal definition of SMEs

[2] The bottom line reference refers to Annex I of the Commission Regulation (EC) No 70/2001 of 12 January 2001 on the application of Articles 87 and 88 of the EC Treaty to State Aid to small and middle-sized enterprises. Such reference is obviously outdated, and Annex I of the Commission Regulation (EC) No. 88/2008 of 6 August 2008 declaring certain categories of aid compatible with the common market in application of Articles 87 and 88 of the Treaty (the "General Block Exemption Regulation") shall apply.

[3] The Interpretation Notice came into effect on 1 March 2012.

[4] Other state aid cases regarding the Czech Republic, e.g. Bus transport CAS Services (C3/2008), Green Knowledge Centre/Open-air museum, Town of Bystřice nad Pernštejnem (SA.33.433), Reconstruction of Funicular at Mt Snežka (N702/2009), do not concern SMEs.

5.2.2 Specific Treatment of SMEs Under Competition Law

5.2.2.1 The Nature and Scope of Specific Treatment for SMEs

There is no specific treatment for SMEs under Czech competition regulations. Act 47/2002, which is specifically dedicated for the support of SMEs, states the rules for the granting of state aid in case of a business start-up, as well as during the strengthening of the economic position of SMEs, and determines the areas eligible for state aid for SMEs. State aid can be grated for projects aimed at investment programmes, instruction, and education in the training programmes of secondary schools that end with the issue of a certificate of apprenticeship; for the improvement of the professional skills of adults; for economic and technical counselling; for projects of associations to develop SMEs and reinforce the market position of SMEs; for the acquisition of information about business activities; for research and development projects, the results of which are used by SMEs; for projects in regions with concentrated state aid and in other regions where state aid is desirable for other reasons; for the creation of new job; for contact networking and cooperation with foreign business partners and participation at domestic and international expositions, as well as trade fairs; for the establishment of systems ensuring an improvement in the quality of the production and management of enterprises and the use of services supporting an increase in competitiveness; and for projects focused on investments connected with environmental protection, the provision of technical information and consulting services, or selected operating costs intended for activities connected with environmental protection.

Public aid is provided in the form of a repayable loan, a grant, a financial donation, a guarantee, or a credit with a reduced interest rate. The granting of state aid resources shall comply with the rules for the provision of state aid. To this end, CzechInvest Agency for the Promotion of Business and Investments (the "**CzechInvest**") is being set up as a state contributory organisation, aiming at providing support to SMEs.[5]

5.2.2.2 Substantive and Procedural Rules

There are no specific substantive and administrative rules applicable for SMEs; the general rules for the provision of state aid provided by Act 215/2004 shall apply. In case of a state aid provided to SMEs, it has to be evidenced that the applicant falls under the category of micro, small, or medium-sized enterprise, which evidence may be in the form of, e.g., a tax declaration, an annual report, or a commercial register excerpt.

---

[5] Other agencies are the Ministry of Industry and Trade of the Czech Republic, the Czech Agency for the Promotion of Trade and the Design Centre of the Czech Republic and the Czech-Moravian Guarantee and Development Bank.

5.2.2.3 Influence of Size and Economic Power in Decisions of the National Competition Authorities and Courts

As can be seen in the list of case laws above, case law regarding SMEs has not developed much so far. In case N497/2006, the court has classified the relevant undertaking as a small undertaking without, however, providing any special (different) treatment for such undertaking.

5.2.2.4 Specific Programmes Addressed to SMEs

The government has introduced the Operational Programme on the Enterprise and Innovation, which is mainly dedicated to support SMEs; the programme applies partially to large enterprises. This programme has seven priority areas, namely the establishment and development of firms, fostering of innovation and effective energy, protection and improvement of the environment for entrepreneurship, innovation, and business development services, as well as technical assistance.

The programme was approved by the European Commission on 3 December 2007 for the period 2007–2013.

5.2.3 The Role of Trade Associations

Trade associations generally bring together SMEs from around the Czech Republic and cooperate with the government, individual ministries, and other relevant bodies to improve and further develop the business environment of the SMEs on the Czech market by employing and using statutory and non-statutory measures.

In the Czech Republic, there is a non-political platform, Association of Small and Medium-Sized Enterprises and Crafts CZ, established in 2001 that promotes as its priorities the enforceability of the law, the statutory responsibility of the state for the decisions reached by its civil servants, the simplification of taxes, state support for employment, and easier access to loans.

The association[6] promotes members' interests regarding current economic and social problems that are further being debated with the administrative and legislative bodies, and thus the association aims to assist in the creation of a favourable framework and climate for business.

[6] The association is a legal entity established in accordance with Act 83/1990 Coll., on federations of citizens, as amended. It is registered with the Ministry of the Interior of the CR under ref. no. VS/1-1/48 640/01-R.

5.3 Public Antitrust Enforcement and SMEs

5.3.1 Substantive and Procedural Rules Applicable to SMEs

5.3.1.1 Introduction

The substantive and procedural rules are not different in the case of SMEs. In particular, there are no safe harbours or any exemptions applicable to SMEs.

The special regulations for SMEs are the following:

- *Section 369a of the Commercial Code.* A legal person which was established for the purpose to protect the rights and interests of SMEs may file a claim that the terms and conditions for general usage regarding the delayed payment may be probably abusive[7]; no establishment of legal person for the purpose to protect the rights and interests of large undertakings is expected[8];
- *Drug Control Regulation.* Pursuant to Section 3, letter b) Decree No. 427/2008 Coll., on reimbursement of expert activities conducted by the State Institute for Drug Control and the Institute for the State Control of Veterinary Biological and Medicaments, the applicant shall reimburse as much as 50 % of the amount of costs established by the Pricelist for the requested expert activity conducted on the basis of an application where the applicant meets the conditions for the classification as a micro, small or medium-sized entèrprise and has not been contracted or otherwise engaged by any other entity which does not meet the criteria of a micro, small or medium company, to conduct an activity associated with the requested activity, hereto in compliance with a directly applicable regulation of the European Communities;
- *Employment Encouragement.* Section 2(3) of the Government Order No. 515/2004 Coll., on material support for creation of new work places and material support of retraining or training of employees regarding investment encouragements states that in case of retraining or training of employees with health inability or disadvantaged employees according to the Regulation of the Commission (EC) No. 800/2008 of 6 August 2008, the material support shall be in the areas of unemployment higher of 50 % than the average amount of unemployment 55 % from the costs for retraining or training of such employees by small enterprises; 45 % from the costs for retraining or training of such employees by small enterprises by middle-sized enterprises and 35 % from the costs for retraining or training of such employees by small enterprises by large enterprises.

According to Act No. 89/2012 Coll., the Civil Code, which shall become effective as of 1.1.2014 ("**Act No. 89/2012**"), there is a special regulation regarding pledges in Section 1315 (2), whereby in case the pledger or a bailor is an SME, any

---

[7] The legal basis therefore was set by the Directive 2000/35/EC of the European Parliament and of the Council of 29 June 2000 on combating late payment in commercial transactions.

[8] Similar regulation was adopted in Section 1964 (2) and 1972 (2) of the Act No. 89/2012, the Civil Code, effective as of 1 January 2014.

provision stipulating that the creditor may convert the pledge into money by any means or may retain it for any, or previously agreed, price shall be invalid.

5.3.1.2 Access to Justice

There is no facilitated access to justice in favour of SMEs. Act No. 155/2010 Coll., on change of several Acts in order to improve the quality of their application and lower the administrative burden of businessmen, was accepted on 21 April 2010 in order to ease certain procedures for businessmen[9]; however, this Act applies to all businessmen, not only SMEs.

5.3.2 Fundamental Rights of SMEs

5.3.2.1 Complaints

There are no particular rules in handling the complaints of SMEs and other undertakings. However, there is a special Act No. 395/2009 Coll., on Significant Market Power in the Sale of Agricultural and Food products and Abuse thereof ("**Act 395/2009**"), which relates only to agricultural and food products and any potential abuse of significant market power by buyers. The buyers are deemed to have significant market power in case their net turnover exceeds CZK 5 billion. For buyers who have significant market power, Act 395/2009 in its Annexes specifies practices listed as abusive and are prohibited and, e.g., stipulates a maximum maturity date for invoices of 30 days, etc. Currently in the Chamber of Deputies is being discussed the proposal to cancel the validity of Act 395/2009 and introduce a new regulation into Act No. 143/2001 Coll., on protection of competition, as amended (the "**Act 143/2001**"), called as "significant economic position of the competitor". According to the proposal, no competitor in significant economic position shall abuse its position. In the proposal, there are listed examples of abusive practices that are prohibited. This proposal applies to all areas of production and services, not only to agricultural and food products as regulated in the original Act 395/2009.

Further, Act No. 89/2012 specifies a so-called protection of a weaker party, whereby an entrepreneur may not abuse its quality as a professional or its economic position in order to create or make use of a dependent weaker party and to achieve obvious and unjustified imbalance in the mutual rights and obligations of the parties. This provision may apply even in case both parties are entrepreneurs.

5.3.2.2 Access to the File

Section 38 of Act No. 500/2004 Coll., the Code of Administrative Procedure, states that the participators and their representatives may inspect the file even in case the

[9] E.g., registration in the Trade Register, introduction of "all in one" Czech point places, i.e. a network of assisted public administration centres where every citizen can obtain all the information on the data kept on him by the state in its central register, etc.

decision comes into force. Other persons may inspect the file in case they show legal or other serious interest and the right of other participants or third persons or the public interest will not be breached, as the case may be. From the inspection of the files are excluded such parts of the documentation that contain confidential information or other data, to which the confidentiality obligation relates by either imposition or recognition by law; this shall not relate to such parts of the documentation that shall be used when carrying out a proof, which parts of the documentation may be viewed only by the participant or his representative, provided he is aware of any consequences regarding the breach of confidentiality obligation and signs a protocol in this respect.

Further, Act No. 106/1999 Coll., on free access to information, regulates general obligation of the state authorities to provide information, save for certain exceptions.

5.3.3 Leniency, Settlements, and Commitment Decisions for SMEs

No specific leniency programmes, settlements, and commitment decisions apply in relation to SMEs.

5.3.4 Sanctions: Different Penalties for Different Sizes?

There is no difference in penalties for SMEs.

5.3.5 Policy Recommendations

In our opinion, the leniency and agreement system should include specific rules for SMEs in order to ease the sanctioning procedure in case the infringer is an SME. It would be also certainly beneficial to introduce a protection mechanism in order to enhance SMEs to inform about anticompetitive practices.

5.4 Private Antitrust Enforcement and SMEs

5.4.1 Substantive Rules, Procedural Aspects for SMEs in Civil Suits

5.4.1.1 Obstacles

There are no specific rules to protect SMEs confronted by large undertakings for anticompetitive conducts.

To our knowledge, there are no procedural difficulties for victims of cartel damage; however, it is being criticised for lack of foreknowledge towards the competitors to claim damages for anticompetitive behaviour against other competitors before the courts.

5.4.2 Collective Redress and the Role of Trade Associations

Czech law does not allow the bringing of collective legal action in general. Therefore, SMEs do not have any legal standing to bring collective legal actions based on anticompetitive conducts.

Under Section 369a(5) of the Commercial Code, it is "allowed" that a legal person that was established for the purpose of protecting the rights and interests of SMEs may file a claim that the terms and conditions for general usage regarding the delayed payment may be probably abusive (see paragraph 5.1). Such claim is not dependent on the fact of whether other SMEs have or have not taken action for that purpose.

Conclusions

Although SMEs constitute the vast majority of undertakings in the Czech Republic, there are no relevant specific rules for SMEs which would enable their protection. Such legislation framework seems insufficient as the SMEs do not receive any protection to enhance their position and further develop. Regarding granting of state aid, there is one specific Operational programme called Enterprise and Innovation dedicated to improve the activity SMEs in specified areas, but further initiatives in this respect shall be supported by the state. As to the private enforcement, currently is being formed the legal initiative to introduce the "prohibition to abuse the significant economic position" with the aim to protect undertakings without any significant market power. The outcome of the legal initiative shall be further awaited, whether it shall provide for any protection of *primarily* SMEs.

Denmark 6

Sune Troels Poulsen

6.1 Introduction

This report sets out how SMEs are treated under the Danish Competition Act. Due to their limited turnover and market share, SMEs might be exempted from the prohibition in accordance with Section 6 of the Danish Competition Act on agreements restrictive of competition,[1] and SMEs are most often not covered by the provision on abuse of a dominant position on a market or the rules on merger control.

The exemption from the prohibition on agreements restrictive of competition is not applicable in case of participation in hard-core cartels. The implication of this is that also cartels commanding only a very limited market share and local cartels with a limited geographical coverage have been subjected to fines under the Danish Competition Act.

In Denmark, there is very little activity concerning private antitrust enforcement and almost no final judgments. For this reason, we will only briefly mention a judgment and a case pending before the Danish Courts.

6.2 SMEs in Context

6.2.1 SMEs' Economic Context and Legal Definition

6.2.1.1 Legal Definitions of SMEs

Under Danish law, there is no special definition of which companies are considered to be SMEs.

[1] Consolidated Act no 972 of 13 August 2010 of the Danish Competition Act.

S.T. Poulsen (✉)
Centre for European Studies of Economic Law, University of Copenhagen, Copenhagen, Denmark
e-mail: supou@jur.ku.dk

P. Këllezi et al. (eds.), *Antitrust for Small and Middle Size Undertakings and Image Protection from Non-Competitors*, LIDC Contributions on Antitrust Law, Intellectual Property and Unfair Competition, DOI 10.1007/978-3-642-54000-4_6, © Springer-Verlag Berlin Heidelberg 2014

According to Section 6 of the Danish Competition Act, it is prohibited for companies to enter into agreements that restrict competition. This provision is identical to Article 101 (1) TFEU. According to Section 7 of the Danish Competition Act, agreements of minor importance (*de minimis* agreements) are exempted from such prohibition.[2]

As stated above, in case of hard-core cartels the exemption from the prohibition is not applicable.[3]

The exemption under Section 7 of the Danish Competition Act includes some of the elements of the EU *de minimis* notice, although differences can also be observed. The provision has also some of the elements that are contained in the EU definition on SMEs from 2003[4]:

- The exemption in Section 7 is only applicable if the undertakings have a combined market share not exceeding 10 % (for companies with turnover less than DKK 150 million [EUR 20 million], there is no market share threshold).
- The exemption in Section 7 is not applicable where the undertakings have entered into hard-core cartels.
- Section 7 sets out a threshold on turnover where the EU *de minimis* notice has no such threshold.
- The threshold for turnover in the Danish Competition Act is lower compared to the EU definition on SMEs.

6.2.1.2 The Economic Perspective

In 2009, a number of 299,248 undertakings was registered in Denmark, including limited liability companies and personal companies. A major part of these undertakings (297,305) had fewer than 100 employees, and the average turnover for undertakings with less than 100 employees did not exceed EUR 50 million.

---

[2] Section 7 reads as follows: "The prohibition set out in Section 6(1) above shall not apply to agreements between undertakings, decisions made by an association of undertakings or concerted practices between undertakings, in case the undertakings involved have

i) an aggregate annual turnover of less than DKK 1 billion [EUR 133 million] and an aggregate share of less than 10 per cent of the product or service market concerned, cf. however subsections (2) – (4); or

ii) an aggregate annual turnover of less than DKK 150 million [EUR 20 million], cf. subsections (2)–(4)." Under this part of the provision, there is no limitation on the market share.

[3] According to Section 7(2): "The exceptions in subsection (1) above shall not apply in cases where undertakings or an association of undertakings agree, coordinate or decide on

i) prices, profits etc. for the sale or resale of goods or services,

ii) restrictions on production or sales,

iii) sharing of markets or customers, or

iv) fixing bids prior to their tendering, fixing conditions for the opening of bids, deferring bids, prior notification of bids, or any other form of bid rigging."

[4] An undertaking is considered an SME if it has less than 250 employees and a turnover not exceeding EUR 50 million (DKK 375 million).

A total of 1,943 undertakings had more than 100 employees, and the average turnover of these undertakings was approximately EUR 180 million (DKK 135 billion).

As it can be observed from these figures, the structure of the Danish business environment is composed of SMEs, and approximately 99 % of all Danish undertakings are considered as SMEs under the EU definition on SMEs; although in Denmark, there are also important undertakings with internationally known trademarks such as Arla (a dairy), Carlsberg (a brewer), Danish Crown (a slaughter house), Lego (a toy factory), Maersk (a container shipping line), Oticon (a hearing aid producer).

6.2.1.3 Relevant Cases

In a number of court cases, SMEs have been prosecuted and convicted for breaking the prohibition in Section 6 of the Danish Competition Act on agreements restrictive of competition. The judgments include agreements between hostels and hotels on minimum prices,[5] agreements between veterinary doctors in a local area (part of a town) on a common basis for setting their fees,[6] agreements on bid rigging,[7] and agreements on resale price maintenance.[8]

6.2.2 Specific Treatment of SMEs Under Competition Law

6.2.2.1 The Nature and Scope of Specific Treatment for SMEs

Section 7 of the Danish Competition Act has a *de minimis* rule from which SMEs might benefit (see Sect. 6.2.1.1).

SMEs also benefit from the fact that other provisions of the Danish Competition Act have thresholds for the turnover of undertakings and for their market share (see Sect. 6.2.2.2).

6.2.2.2 Substantive and Procedural Rules

The Danish Competition Act and SMEs

As of 1997, the Danish Competition Act was founded on a principle of prohibition. This amendment was, to a large extent, motivated by an intention to harmonise the Danish Competition Act with the competition rules of the EU. The Danish

---

[5] Judgment of the City Court of Horsens of 4 October 2007 in case no SS 785/2007.

[6] Judgment of the High court of Western Denmark of 19 May 2010 in department 8, case no. S-0513-10, where the high court upheld a judgment given by the City Court of Aarhus of 24 February 2010 in case no 10-2233/2009.

[7] Judgment of the High Court of Eastern Denmark of 4 April 2012 in department 15, case no S-2637-11 and more, where the high court upheld a judgment given by the City Court of Glostrup of 25 March 2011 in case no 954/2011.

[8] Judgment of the High Court of Eastern Denmark of 17 January 2012 in department 16, case no S-1656-11, where the high court upheld a judgment given by the City Court of Svendborg of 18 May 2011 in case no R2-2234/2010.

Competition Act now has provisions corresponding to Articles 101 and 102 TFEU, and it also has provisions corresponding to the EU's Regulation 139/2004 on merger control.

The Danish Competition Act was amended in 2000, 2002, 2005, 2007, 2008, and 2010. In 2012, the Danish Competition Act was amended with the aim of strengthening the enforcement of the Act and criminal sanctions, and jail sentences of up to 18 months for breaking the prohibition in Section 6 on agreements restrictive of competition (cartels) are now part of the Danish Competition Act.

In 1997, when introducing the prohibition principle in the Danish Competition Act, a special rule was set out for dominant undertakings, according to which a fine could not be imposed unless the dominant undertaking previously had been warned that its behaviour constituted an infringement of the Danish Competition Act. The political reasoning for this provision was that dominant undertakings should have a grace period where they could adapt to the new rules. This rule obviously did not benefit SMEs as they most often would be targets of an abuse. This provision was abolished in 2000 with effect as from 2002.

The *de minimis* rules set out in Section 7 of the Danish Competition Act also has its origin in the 1997 amendment of the Danish Competition Act (see Sect. 6.2.1.1).

The rules on merger control became part of the Danish Competition Act of 2000. Until then, it was believed that as Denmark is a society with an open economy and considerable cross-border trade, there was not any need for controlling mergers. A couple of mergers in Denmark leading to both near monopoly and the strengthening of a dominant position without the Danish Competition Authority having the powers to intervene led to a change in the view on the need for merger control. In 2010, the thresholds for turnover were lowered considerably and mergers are now subject to merger control and should be notified to the Danish Competition Authority if the participating undertakings has a combined turnover exceeding EUR 120 million [DKK 900 million] and at least two of the participating undertakings each has a turnover exceeding EUR 13 million [DKK 100 million].

Consequently, SMEs benefit from the provisions of the Danish Competition Act in several ways:

- Agreements that restrict competition entered into by SMEs are exempted from the prohibition of Section 6 of the Danish Competition Act on the basis of their turnover and the market share of the SMEs, unless the subject matter of the agreements deals with prices, restrictions on production, market sharing, or bid rigging (hard-core restraints).
- The prohibition on abuse of a dominant position on a market will usually not be applicable to SMEs as they normally do not possess any significant market share and therefore not have a dominant position.
- Mergers between two SMEs will normally not be subject to merger control under the Danish Competition Act due to the size of the turnover thresholds in the Danish Competition Act.

The Organisation of the Competition Authority and SMEs

The Danish Competition Act is distinct from EU competition law in at least two respects:

- Business and consumers representatives sit in the Competition Council, the body deciding whether an infringement of the Competition Act has taken place or not.
- The Competition Council does not have power to impose fines or other sentences for breach of the Danish Competition Act; only the ordinary courts have this power.

Competition cases are initiated and investigated by the Competition Authority—a department of the Ministry of Business and Growth—but it is the Competition Council, which has a chairman and 17 members,[9] that is the decision-making body. The chairman of the Competition Council and eight of its members must be independent of business and consumer interests; seven members are appointed after consultation with business organisations, one member is appointed after consultation with consumer organisations, and one member is appointed after consultation with the organisation of municipalities. The representation of business, consumers, and municipalities in the Competition Council has the advantage that their views on competition issues are balanced towards the views of the administration, but it cannot be seen as being especially advantageous for SMEs.

Decisions taken by the Competition Council may be reviewed by the Competition Appeals Board, which consists of five members: A Supreme Court judge, two members having economic expertise, and two members having legal expertise.[10] The decisions of the Competition Appeals Board may be reviewed by ordinary courts. Decisions of the Competition Council cannot be reviewed by ordinary courts before the Competition Appeals Board has taken a decision in the case.[11]

Neither the Competition Council nor the Competition Authority has the power to impose sanctions for breach of the Danish Competition Act as this power is reserved to ordinary courts. Fines can therefore only be imposed on an undertaking as part of a penal case. On the basis of Section 23b of the Danish Competition Act, the Competition Authority is authorised to settle a case if the undertaking acknowledges to have breached the Danish Competition Act.

In most cases, there will be a duplication of the investigation as the Competition Authority will investigate and the Competition Council will take a decision in the case. And if the Council decides that there has been a breach of the Danish Competition Act, then the director of the Competition Authority will send the case to the police and suggest that the case be investigated as a criminal case with the aim of having a fine imposed. This duplication of the investigation is time consuming and can be seen as having the consequence that fewer fines are imposed, which will be an advantage for business and undertaking but cannot be seen as something that is especially advantageous to SMEs .

[9] Section 14 of the Danish Competition Act.

[10] Section 21 of the Danish Competition Act.

[11] Section 20 of the Danish Competition Act.

The Danish Competition and Consumer Authority (the Danish Competition Authority) is the authority overseeing competition in Denmark. The Competition Authority initiates cases and conducts the necessary investigations and issues draft decisions, which it presents to the Competition Council. The Competition Authority also has activities concerned with the provision of information and advice on the Danish Competition Act, which can be seen as especially targeting the needs of SMEs that rarely have legal experts employed.

6.2.2.3 Influence of Size and Economic Power in Decisions of the National Competition Authorities and Courts

Fines can be imposed for breach of the Danish Competition Act on both limited liability companies and personal undertakings. The management of an undertaking can also be subjected to a fine. Section 23 of the Danish Competition Act sets out that when deciding on the amount of the fine, the turnover of a limited liability company will be among the criteria providing the basis for setting the amount of the fine.

In the preparatory works to the Danish Competition Act, it is stated that when a breach of the act is considered very serious, a fine amounting to at least EUR 2 million (DKK 15 million) should be imposed on the undertaking:

> A breach of the Danish Competition Act will normally cover Denmark or part hereof. On this basis the basic amount for a breach of the Danish Competition Act will have to be lower when compared with a breach of the EU competition rules. The aim of harmonisation with the EU competition rules necessitates, that the basic amount for a less serious breach of the Danish Competition Act will be from DKK 10,000 [EUR 1,300] to DKK 400,000 [EUR 53,000] When deciding on a serious breach the basic amount will be from DKK 400,000 [EUR 53,000] to DKK 15 million DKK [EUR 2 million] and a fine for a very serious breach should be DKK 15 million [EUR 2 million] and more.[12]

In the preparatory works to the Danish Competition Act, it was stated that price fixing, market sharing, and serious abuses of a dominant position on a market should be considered very serious breaches.[13]

The Danish Courts have, until this date, only considered breaches of the Danish Competition Act to be either less serious or serious and not very serious. The amount of a typical fine for breach of the Danish Competition Act is for an undertaking approximately EUR 66,000 [DKK 500,000], and a typical fine for the management of the undertaking is approximately EUR 3,300 [DKK 25,000]. This level of fines has been set out by the Danish Supreme Court in 2010, and later court judgments have been in line with this level. Fines of this amount have been imposed for agreements on resale price maintenance, bid rigging, trade associations

[12] Preparatory act no L 171 for an amendment to the Danish Competition Act, presented by the Minister to the Parliament on the 20 March 2002. FT 2001-2002, 2. setting, comments to no 13 (unofficial translation).

[13] The preparatory works of 2000 for an amendment of the Danish Competition Act.

activities with harmonising prices among their members. These agreements have all been classified as serious breaches of the Danish Competition Act.

When the courts set the fine for a breach of the Danish Competition Act, they will in most cases take the turnover of the undertakings into consideration. On the other hand, it cannot be observed from the published judgments that differences in turnover have had any effect on the size of the fine (see Sect. 6.3.3).

The largest fine was imposed in 2006 on Arla (a dairy) for breach of Section 11 of the Danish Competition Act on abuse of a dominant position on a market.[14] The abuse consisted in Arla attracting the customer (a super market chain) of a smaller competitor by offering a very low price conditional upon the customer instantly severing its commercial relations with the competitor. The fine was set by the court to approximately EUR 670,000 (DKK 5 million),[15] which according to information provided by the Danish Competition Authority corresponds to 0.06 % of Arla's turnover.

6.2.2.4 Specific Programmes Addressed to SMEs (Compliance, Information Policies, Enhancement of Competition Enforcement)

The Danish Competition Act has in Section 7a *de minimis* rules, which SMEs might benefit from.[16]

The activities of the Competition Authority related to the provision of information on the Danish Competition Act can be seen as benefitting especially SMEs.

6.2.3 The Role of Trade Associations

In Denmark, trade associations are important for SMEs, as they assemble and distribute information on business opportunities and markets to their members. Trade associations do also provide legal expertise to their members.

In recent years, the Competition Council has decided in several cases that a trade organisation has breached Section 6 of the Danish Competition Act on the prohibition against agreements restrictive of competition, and on this basis either a court has imposed a fine on the trade association or the case has been settled by the association agreeing to a fine. Amongst the cases are the following:

- Danish Christmas Tree Growers.[17] The association had distributed a recommendation to its members on minimum prices. It was sentenced with a fine of EUR 66,000 [DKK 500,000].

[14] Public prosecutor v Arla Foods Amba, judgment of the City Court of Aarhus of 10 February 2006 in case SS 8.1420/205.

[15] In a follow-on case, damages were awarded to the competitor that was the target of Arla's abuse. The amount of the damage is not published.

[16] See Sect. 6.2.1.1.

[17] Judgment of the Supreme Court of 30 August 2010 in case no 319/2009.

- Danish Tourist Buses.[18] The association had distributed a recommendation to its members on raising their prices by 4 % due to increased fuel costs. It was sentenced to a fine of EUR 66,000 [DKK 500,000].
- Danish Undertakers.[19] In its code of conduct, the association had stated that it was reserved for the association to advertise in radio and TV and that it was illegal for the members of the association to state anything with respect to prices, free services, etc., when advertising in other media. The case was settled with the association agreeing to a fine of DKK 400,000.
- Danish Potato Growers.[20] The association had issued a recommendation to its members on minimum prices and limits on production. It was sentenced to a fine of EUR 66,000 [DKK 500,000].

There seems to be a fine line for a trade association between providing its members with information on business opportunities and markets, on the one hand, and coordinating the market activities of its members, on the other hand, which the trade associations sometimes find hard not to overstep.

6.2.4 Policy Recommendations

6.2.4.1 Enforcement

Being a small country like Denmark, the question can be raised as to whether the competition rules should be stricter or more lenient when compared to larger countries.

It is probably a consequence of Denmark being a small country with its own language and there also being other barriers to entry for foreign undertakings such as toll bridges that the Danish business environment to a very large extent, consists of SMEs.

Exploitation of consumers can take place on both large and small markets, and whether the market is large or small makes no difference for the consumer that feels the effect of an increase in prices due to a cartel agreement or an agreement on resale price maintenance. Based on this observation, it could be argued that enforcement of the competition rules in Denmark should reflect the Danish business environment as it is in the interest of the consumers that enforcement action should be taken against any restriction of competition that has a substantial negative effect on competition on the market. For this reason, the important issue should be whether the undertakings in question have market power and therefore are able to restrict competition and raise prices, and the EU definition of SMEs might therefore not be relevant in a Danish context, as it is in the interest of the consumers also to enforce the competition rules against cartels entered into by SMEs. It follows from this that also restrictions of competition taking place in a geographical small area

---

[18] Judgment of the Supreme Court of 30 August 2010 in case no 320/2009.

[19] Decision of the Competition Council of 22 December 2010.

[20] Judgment of the City Court of Kolding of 6 September 2011 in case no 1-4944/2010.

(local area) should be enforced if this area can be delimited to be a separate geographical market, no matter whether the turnover of the undertakings involved is below the *de minimis* thresholds in the Danish Competition Act or the undertakings are defined as SMEs under the EU definition.

On the other hand, it could be argued that industrial policy considerations should lead to rules that are more lenient for SMEs as they usually are facing obstacles in competition due to their limited size. This fact is reflected in the rules on merger control in the Danish Competition Act as the thresholds for notification of a merger are set at such a level that mergers between two undertakings that are both SMEs according to the EU definition are not covered by merger control. With respect to agreements that are in breach of the prohibition in Section 6 of the Danish Competition Act, it is not as obvious that enforcement should be more lenient based on industrial policy considerations as fierce competition among SMEs is a useful tool for strengthening their competitiveness, which also will benefit an SME when trying to compete in other parts of the EU. If SMEs were allowed to enter into cartels, agree on their bidding activities, etc., this could lead to them being less competitive. Setting up a joint venture might, on the other hand, be something that should be looked upon more favourably in a small economy in order for the joint venture to be able to compete on the EU's internal market.

6.2.4.2 SMEs' Market Problems

The obstacles for SMEs when competing with larger undertakings are, to a large extent, connected with SMEs having fewer resources. Amongst other things, SMEs face difficulties with access to risk capital as a basis for making investments as an SME does not itself have accumulated such capital. And due to this fact, it will have to convince a bank or another investor that the SME or its project is a good business opportunity for the investor, which due to information asymmetry might be difficult. Also, information on markets or technologies is more limited for SMEs when compared to larger undertakings due to the fact that SMEs have less experience with respect to development of new technology, marketing of new products, or entering new markets.

With respect to breaches of the Danish Competition Act, a number of issues special for SMEs that are related to their limited size and resources can be identified. As the capital base on SMEs is smaller, they have accordingly less strength when taking up a fight with larger undertakings on prices, legal battles, etc. Also, legal expertise on competition rules is very often not something that an SME has taken effort in investing in. For this reason, SMEs might be ignorant as to when their agreements or other activities are in conflict with the competition rules.

These types of problems of SMEs mentioned above are related to their size and lack of experience and are not issues that can easily be dealt with by amending the competition rules.

6.3 Public Antitrust Enforcement and SMES

6.3.1 Substantive and Procedural Rules Applicable to SMEs

6.3.1.1 Introduction

Due to their limited size and market share, SMEs are in many circumstances exempted from the Danish Competition Act, but an exemption is not applicable if SMEs enter into hard-core cartels. The implication of this is that also cartels commanding only very limited market share and local cartels with a limited geographical coverage have been subjected to fines under the Danish Competition Act.

6.3.1.2 Safe Harbours for SMEs

As mentioned in section "The Danish Competition Act and SMEs", SMEs fall to a large extent outside the prohibitions of the Danish Competition Act.

SMEs Are Often Not Covered by the Competition Act

Agreements among SMEs are due to their limited turnover and limited market share exempted from the prohibition in Section 6 of the Danish Competition Act, unless the subject matter of the agreement is related to price fixing, limiting of production, market sharing, or bid rigging (hard-core restraints).

SMEs will most often not have any significant market share and accordingly not have a dominant position on a market, and the conduct of an SME will therefore normally not be covered by the prohibition in Section 11 of the Danish Competition Act on abuse of a dominant position on a market.

Mergers between two undertakings that are both SMEs under the EU definition are, according to Section 12 of the Danish Competition Act, not subject to merger control in Denmark as the thresholds are set at such a level that the participating undertakings should have a combined turnover of at least EUR 120 million [DKK 900 million] and at least two of the participating undertakings should have a turnover of EUR 13 million [DKK 100 million] or more.

SMEs and the *De Minimis* Rule in Section 7 of the Competition Act

SMEs can take advantage of the *de minimis* rule in Section 7 of the Danish Competition Act, unless the subject matter of the agreement is related to price fixing, limiting of production, market sharing or bid rigging (hard-core restraints).

The case on local banks involving market sharing and information exchange is an example demonstrating that SMEs can take advantage of the *de minimis* rule in Section 7 of the Danish Competition Act.[21] Seven local banks had divided the market between themselves as they agreed on (1) not setting up a branch in a city where another bank had its main branch and (2) not attracting each other's

---

[21] Decision of the Danish Competition Council of 28 March 2007 on Cooperation between Local Banks, upheld by order of the Danish Competition Appeals Board of 2 October 2007.

customers. Furthermore, the seven banks had shared information on their prices and fees. The Competition Council decided that the agreement amounted to a cartel in breach of Section 6 of the Danish Competition Act and that there had been a substantial effect of the agreement. The basis of this assessment was that the agreement was considered to be a hard-core breach of the Competition Act and that the banks had a market share of 3–6 %. The breach was considered serious as it was concerned with market division, thereby limiting the possibilities of banks for competition for new customers.

The product market in the case was defined as the market for private customers and smaller business, and the large banks of Denmark had on this market approximately a market share of 80 %. Over 120 local or regional banks were active on this market, and all of these banks had a combined market share of less than 10 %. The geographic market was split between Eastern and Western Denmark, and the Council was of the opinion that the market most likely was even narrower and could be defined as smaller regions or local areas as having a branch or an office in an area was vital for the possibilities to compete in an area.

The *de minimis* rule in Section 7 of the Danish Competition Act was relevant in this case as the agreement did not include price fixing, limiting of production, market sharing, or bid rigging. In 2002 and 2003, the turnover of the seven banks were below the threshold in Section 7; their combined market share was also below the 10 % market share threshold, and based on this the agreement fell outside of the prohibition of Section 6 of the Danish Competition Act. As for the period 2004–2006, the combined turnover of the seven banks exceeded the threshold set out in Section 7 of the Danish Competition Act and accordingly the agreement was not exempted from the prohibition in Section 6 of the Danish Competition Act.

The case Milana og Miljølaboratoriet (bid rigging) is an example demonstrating that SMEs cannot benefit from the *de minimis* rule of Section 7 of the Danish Competition Act as the agreement was concerned with bid rigging.[22] In 2009, Milana had a turnover of approximately EUR 6 million [DKK 44 million], and Miljølaboratoriet had in 2009 a turnover of approximately EUR 6.5 million [DKK 49 million]. On this basis, both undertakings qualify as SMEs under the EU definition. Milana and Miljølaboratoriet had coordinated their bidding, and bid rigging is explicitly mentioned in Section 7 of the Danish Competition Act as one of the types of agreements that hinder the application of the *de minimis* rule set out in Section 7. The fines were set to EUR 66,000 [DKK 500,000] for each of the undertakings and EUR 3,300 [DKK 25,000] for each of the CEOs.

The Danish Competition Council has, in a number of cases, decided that SMEs breached the Danish Competition Act by setting and enforcing resale price maintenance. The judgment in Lise Aaagaard Copenhagen case demonstrates that an undertaking enforcing resale price maintenance is not in a position to benefit

[22] Judgment of the High Court of Eastern Denmark of 4 April 2012 in department 15, case no S-2637-11 and more, where the high court upheld a judgment given by the City Court of Glostrup of 25 March 2011 in case no 954/2011.

from the exemption in Section 7 of the Danish Competition Act.[23] The undertaking had obliged its dealers to uphold a minimum level of prices. The producer had a market share of 1–2 % in a product market defined as jewellery, accessories, etc. No information on the turnover of the undertaking was published. When setting the fine, the breach of the Danish Competition Act was classified as serious, but it was also considered mitigating factors that only two dealers were involved and that the breach of the competition rules only lasted for a very short time. The fine for the undertaking was set to 600,000 DKK, and the fine for the CEO was set to EUR 3,300 [DKK 25,000].

The case of Danish Hostels and Hotels (limitations on the use of prices in the marketing) demonstrates that undertakings could not benefit from the exemption in Section 7 of the Danish Competition Act when a trade association coordinates the marketing activities of its members.[24] The trade association had stated in its statutes that members were not entitled to advertise prices below a certain level, but besides this restriction on advertising there were no restrictions on the prices or discounts that the members could negotiate with their customers for rent of rooms or other services. The prohibition in Section 6 of the Danish Competition Act was breached, and the exemption in Section 7 was not applicable as the internal rule of the association restricted the advertising of prices. The members of the trade association had a combined market share of 3.7 %, and the trade association itself had a turnover of approximately DKK 10 million. When setting the fine, the limited turnover of the trade association and the limited market share of its members were taken into account. The fine was set to DKK 400,000, and the fine for the CEO was set to DKK 10,000.

6.3.1.3 Access to Justice

There does not seem to be any rules special for SMEs with respect to access to justice or court fees.

6.3.2 Fundamental Rights of SMEs

6.3.2.1 Complaints, Access to Files, and Leniency Regulations

There are no particular rules for SMEs with respect to complaints, access to file, or leniency regulations.

[23] Judgment of 26 November 2010.

[24] Danish Hostels and Hotels, judgment of the City Court of Horsens of 4 October 2007 in case no SS 785/2007.

6.3.3 Sanctions: Different Penalties for Different Size?

It can be observed from the published judgments that the size of an undertaking's turnover is taken into account as one element when setting the amount of the fine, although it is not possible to determine the relative weight of this factor. And in most judgments, the fine is set approximately to EUR 66,000 [DKK 500,000].

In two judgments concerning Milana A/S and Miljølaboratoriet I/S,[25] Milana had in 2009 a turnover of approximately EUR million [DKK 44 million] and Miljølaboratoriet had in 2009 a turnover of EUR 5.5 million [DKK 49 million]. When setting the fine, the court explicitly took the subject matter of the case (bid rigging) and the market shares of the undertakings into account, whereas it did not mention the turnover of the undertakings:

> When setting the fine, the starting point will have to be the principles stated in the preparatory works to the Danish Competition Act of 2002. Furthermore the market share of the undertakings and their very limited profit earned on the contracts in question should be taken into account. On the basis of all elements of the case the fine should be set to DKK 500,000 [EUR 66,000] for each of the undertakings.[26]

The fine for the CEOs of the two undertakings was set to EUR 3,300 [DKK 25,000], and the court did not find it relevant to take the relative size of the income of the CEOs into account when setting the fine.

In a judgment from 2011 concerning Erik Jørgensen Furniture Factory,[27] the subject matter of the case was resale price maintenance. The turnover of Erik Jørgensen Furniture Factory in 2003 (the time when the breach of the Danish Competition Act took place) was EUR 5.5 million [DKK 49 million]. When setting the fine, the court did not mention the turnover of the undertaking as it only took into account that the breach was classified as serious and had lasted for a while. And as a mitigating factor, it was taken into account that the activity apparently had not had any effect on competition on the market.

The judgment of the Danish Supreme Court from 2010 concerns the Danish Christmas Tree Growers,[28] an association that had encouraged its members to keep a certain minimum price level for the sale of Christmas trees. The Supreme Court took the relatively limited turnover of the members of the association into account when setting the fine to EUR 66,000 [DKK 500,000]:

---

[25] Judgment of the High Court of Eastern Denmark of 4 April 2012 in department 15, case no S-2637-11 and more, where the high court upheld a judgment given by the City Court of Glostrup of 25 March 2011 in case no 954/2011.

[26] Unofficial translation.

[27] Judgment of the High Court of Eastern Denmark of 17 January 2012 in department 16, case no S-1656-11, where the high court upheld a judgment given by the City Court of Svendborg of 18 May 2011 in case no R2-2234/2010.

[28] Judgment of the Supreme Court of 30 August 2010 in case no 319/2009, which increased the fine set by the High Court of Eastern Denmark in a judgment of 24 September 2009 in department 10, case no S-1011-09.

> When assessing the encouragements of the Danish Christmas Tree Growers association in the time period lasting from December 2002 until August 2006 on the minimum price level of the sale of Christmas trees it will have to be taken into account that the members of the association have a relatively limited turnover and a limited market share. On the other hand emphasis must also be put on the type of the breach and the time period it has lasted – we are concerned with encouragements concerning prices during a period lasting 3–4 years.[29]

In a judgment of the Danish Supreme Court given on the same date concerning Danish Tourist buses,[30] a trade association had distributed a recommendation to its member on raising their prices by 4 % due to increased fuel costs. When setting the fine to EUR 66,000 [DKK 500,000], the Supreme Court, amongst other elements, put emphasis on the following:

> . . . it must be taken into account that the members of the association had a considerable turnover and a large combined market share. On the other hand it will also have to be taken into account that the breach of the competition rules only lasted for a short period and that the competitive conditions in the transport sector made it likely that the encouragement only would have a limited effect.[31]

As it can be seen from the judgments referred above, the turnover of an undertaking will normally be taken into account as an element when setting the amount of the fine. On the basis of these judgments, it is on the other hand not possible to determine the relative weight of the turnover when setting the amount of the fine, and in most cases the fine is set to EUR 66,000 [DKK 500,000].

6.3.4 Policy Recommendations

As long as the level of fines for breaches of the prohibition in Section 6 of the Danish Competition Act on agreements restrictive of competition is as low as EUR 66,000 [DKK 500,000], it is in our opinion not necessary to differentiate between SMEs and large undertakings when setting the amount of the fine.

6.4 Private Antitrust Enforcement and SMES

6.4.1 Substantive Rules, Procedural Aspects for SMEs in Civil Suits

In Danish Law, there are not any special rules set out for SMEs in relation to private antitrust enforcement.

---

[29] Unofficial translation.

[30] Judgment of the Supreme Court of 30 August 2010 in case no 320/2009, which increased the fine set by the High Court of Eastern Denmark in a judgment of 3 September 2009 in department 10, case no S-971-09.

[31] Unofficial translation.

Under Section 26 of the Danish Competition Act, there is a possibility for class actions:

> In case several persons have raised claims for damages due to infringements of this Act or Articles 101 and 102 TFEU, the Consumer Ombudsman may be appointed as a representative for the class for the purpose of the class action to recover these damages, cf. Part 23a of the Administration of Justice Act.

At our best knowledge, there has been no final judgment under this provision.

One case involving more than 1,000 plaintiffs is pending before the Commercial and Maritime Court of Denmark. The Danish Competition Council has, in several decisions, concluded that the dominant Danish electricity company (DONG and its predecessor, Elsam) has abused its dominant position by charging excessive prices for electricity. The complainants sued in 2008 for damages amounting to more than EUR 500 million. The case has not yet been decided by the court.

Another case has, in 2013, been decided by the Supreme Court of Denmark concerning a possible abuse of a dominant position on the market. The Danish Competition Council decided in 2004 that Post Denmark (the former Danish postal monopoly) had tried to exclude its only competitor by offering very low prices to one of the large supermarket chains in Denmark for the distribution of commercials. In 2009, the High Court of Eastern Denmark awarded the plaintiff damages amounting to EUR 10 million [DKK 75 million]. After a preliminary reference to the Court of Justice of the European Union, the Supreme Court ruled that there had not been a breach of the Danish Competition Act.[32]

A plaintiff in Denmark must have a sufficient interest in the case before it can bring it before the courts, and this rule applies as well to trade associations when bringing cases on behalf of their members.

Conclusions and Policy Recommendations

The important aspect for SMEs with respect to competition rules is, in our opinion, that the competition rules should not be a limitation for the possibilities for SMEs to enter into agreements unless such agreements might have an effect on competition on a market, and this is dependent on the market share of the undertakings and not their size or the size of their turnover.

There cannot be seen to be a "one size fits all" with respect to a relation between the size of an undertaking and the size of its market share as this is dependent on the size of the relevant product and geographical market as for instance producers of medicine might have a turnover on several billion euros but only command a limited market share on a market, whereas producers of specialised machinery might have a large market share although they do only have a relatively limited turnover, and suppliers of services will often provide their services within a geographically limited (local) area and on this market will often have a substantial market share.

[32] Judgment of Danish Supreme Court of 15 February 2013 in case 2/2008, Post Danmark A/S vs the Competition Council.

The *de minimis* rule in Section 7 of the Danish Competition Act exempts certain agreements from the prohibition in Section 6 on agreements restrictive of competition, unless the subject matter of the agreements is price fixing, limitation on production, market sharing, or bid rigging. The *de minimis* rule is based on the turnover of the undertakings, but turnover will not always be linked to the effect that an agreement will have on a market, and turnover will neither be determinative of whether or not an undertaking has a dominant position on a market.

There might be seen to be a need for more information for SMEs on the rules of the Danish Competition Act in order for them to avoid entering into agreements that are in breach of the prohibition in Section 6. The Danish Competition Authority conducts a number of activities with respect to providing SMEs with information on the Danish Competition Act, although undertakings should be cautious when making contact with the Competition Authority as it has been seen that an enforcement action has been initiated after an undertaking sought advice from the Competition Authority.

France

7

Mathilde Boudou, Laurence Charvoz, Jean-Patrice de La Laurencie, Olivier Sautel, and Véronique Sélinsky

7.1 General Background

As is the case in most countries, the approach adopted in France is that of market power rather than size, given that, with a few rare exceptions (niche market for instance), a small size entails small market power.

The issue of principle to be discussed will thus be to determine whether or not size alone justifies specific provisions. Overall, the French Competition Authority (hereafter referred to as "FCA") does not have a general policy of treating SMEs specifically, except under exceptional circumstances, to take account of their size, at least in theory, with regard to sanctions.

French competition law includes several texts specifically covering SMEs, namely (1) the law governing individual restrictive competition practices, (2) the concept of abuse of economic dependence, (3) "small thresholds" in terms of merger control, and (4) most importantly, the existence of a specific regime of "local" anticompetitive practices whose treatment is related to the size of the companies in question.

State aids and public procurements are outside the scope of this contribution, as is merger control. This contribution covers vertical restraints where relevant to SMEs.

M. Boudou (✉)
Cabinet Jean-Claude Coulon et Associés, Paris, France
e-mail: m.boudou@pragma-fr.com

L. Charvoz
Cabinet Charvoz, Angers, France

J.-P. de La Laurencie
Independent Lawyer, Paris, France

O. Sautel
Microeconomix, Paris, France

V. Sélinsky
Independent Lawyer, Montpellier, France

P. Këllezi et al. (eds.), *Antitrust for Small and Middle Size Undertakings and Image Protection from Non-Competitors*, LIDC Contributions on Antitrust Law, Intellectual Property and Unfair Competition, DOI 10.1007/978-3-642-54000-4_7, © Springer-Verlag Berlin Heidelberg 2014

7.2 Definition of SMEs

French competition law does not expressly define SMEs.

However, French competition law includes provisions regarding anticompetitive practices that apply specifically to SMEs, since they specifically target companies above or below thresholds distinguishing the company's size. This is the case of Article L. 464-9 of the Commercial Code targeting anticompetitive practices with a local scope, which does not involve deeds pertaining to European law: the turnover made by each of the parties in France over the previously ended financial year must not exceed EUR 50 million, and the total turnover must not exceed EUR 100 million.

French legislation includes other rules that distinguish the companies according to the turnover and the number of employees.

Decree no. 2008-1354 of 18 December 2008, relating to criteria enabling the membership category of a company to be determined for the purposes of statistical and economic analysis, distinguishes between four categories of companies according to their size. Two criteria are combined: the number of people employed, on the one hand, and the turnover or annual balance sheet total, on the other.

SMEs themselves contain two subcategories. (1) The microenterprise category, which covers companies employing less than ten persons and with an annual turnover or balance sheet not exceeding EUR 2 million; and (2) the small and medium-sized enterprise category, which includes companies with fewer than 250 employees and an annual turnover not exceeding EUR 50 million or balance sheet total of under EUR 43 million.

The definition of SMEs refers expressly to Recommendation no. 2003/361/EC from the European Commission of 6 May 2003.[1]

In 2008, the SME Minister noted that "[t]here is no single definition for an SME. The criteria selected differ according to the regulatory or legislative enactments instituting assistance schemes aimed at SMEs".[2]

The labour legislation takes account of the size of staff representation only based on the criterion of the number of employees: in companies having less than 11 employees, their representation is not compulsory; in companies of more than 11 and fewer than 50 employees, the staff is only represented by shop stewards[3]; companies with over 50 employees has a Works Council.[4]

[1] Article 2 of the annex to the Commission's recommendation, OJ L. 124 of 20.05.2003: "To gain a better understanding of the real economic position of SMEs and to remove from that category groups of enterprises whose economic power may exceed that of genuine SMEs, a distinction should be made between various types of enterprises, depending on whether they are autonomous, whether they have holdings which do not entail a controlling position (partner enterprises), or whether they are linked to other enterprises."

[2] See the Law on the self-employed, law no. 2008-776 of 4 August 2008, Chapter 1.

[3] French Labour Code, Art. L.2312-1.

[4] French Labour Code, Art. L.2312-1.

Lastly, in companies employing more than 50 but fewer than 200 persons, the employer may decide to set up a single staff representative delegation.[5]

There are no specific programmes or National Competition Authority policies addressed to SMEs in France. However, in practice, such authorities adapt the application of certain rules to SMEs, taking account of the size at the implementation stage for these rules.[6] We consider that National Competition Authorities should establish specific programmes addressed to SMEs.

We recommend concrete measures be put forward below, both in terms of procedure and in terms of substance. To start with, it would be desirable to ensure that a general definition of SMEs, applicable without the specific need to continuously state that a given text targets SMEs, appears in national competition law. In our view, French legislation should adopt the definition of Recommendation 2003/361/EC of 6 May 2003, relating to the definition of micro, small and medium-sized companies.[7]

7.3 SMEs as Infringers

7.3.1 Statistical Analysis

At our request, Microeconomix[8] has performed a statistical analysis of the relevant case law of the FCA with the scope of showing the involvement of SMEs in anticompetitive practices and in the outcome of proceedings.

7.3.1.1 Data Used

The statistical analysis is carried out using a database made available by Microeconomix, which lists all the decisions of the French Competition Authority between 2005 and 2010. The decisions considered include rejections and nonsuits. The database relies solely on information contained in those decisions relating to the originators of said practices (sector, turnover, group turnover, profitability), the practices themselves (duration, value of sales affected, types of practice, complaints upheld), the behaviours of said originators relating to the practice (leader, repeat offence, leniency application), the procedure (appeal, judicial review proceedings), and the sanction (basic sanction, modulation, final sanction).

For the specific purposes of this survey concerning SMEs, the originators of practices are identified as SMEs on the sole basis of a revenue criterion, with the threshold set at EUR 50 million, which is in line with the European definition. Furthermore, two subcategories have been created that identify SMEs belonging to

[5] French Labour Code, Art. L.2312-1.

[6] For instance rules relating to compliance programmes and sanctions, see Sect. 7.3.4 of this contribution.

[7] OJ L. 124 of 21 May 2003.

[8] www.microeconomix.com.

Table 7.1 Decision and SMEs occurrences

Data type	Number of observations in the database
Decisions	291
Company-decision couplings	1,462

Source: Microeconomix FCA decisions database

a group (when a "group" revenue figure is explicitly given) and various professional organisations whose turnover is very low but that are not companies per se (for instance, professional organisations or national bodies).[9]

The database includes the following items (Table 7.1).

7.3.1.2 Involvement of SMEs in Litigation for Anticompetitive Practices

Tables 7.2 and 7.3 show the presence of SMEs in litigation undertaken by the Competition Authority between 2005 and 2010 in all practices combined, taking into account the number of decisions in which at least one SME is involved as an originator of the practice, then the number of "company-decision" couplings where the company is an SME.

We can see equivalence between these two measures, with a level of SME involvement of 30 % in relation to the total number of decisions. Figure 7.1 shows that this SME involvement is stable over time, varying between 22 and 38 %.

Consequently, SMEs are not an epiphenomenon in respect of the Competition Authority's activity. Their small size does not prevent SMEs from being regularly confronted with competition law, which underlines the interest of the question at the centre of the LIDC's work.

The study of Microeconomix examined the distribution according to the type of practices. Figure 7.2 compares the distribution of types of practice according to the classification used by the Competition Authority in its annual reports (which is cartel, abuse, vertical), depending on whether or not the company is an SME.

As expected, in relative terms, SMEs are more often involved in cartel cases and less often involved in other antitrust cases. However, a significant number of SMEs are prosecuted for abuse of dominant position practices, bearing in mind that a proportion of these abuses may have been committed by a professional organisation with very modest turnover.

The study focused also on SMEs and the outcome of proceedings.

Table 7.4 shows the outcome of proceedings and the reaction of the company regarding said outcome, irrespective of whether or not it is an SME.

The results for SMEs appear here to be in rather sharp contrast to those of the general diagnostic. SMEs are found guilty by the Competition Authority almost systematically (in 96 % of cases), while three-quarters of major companies avoid all

[9] It should be noted that different levels of statistics are possible, since several companies are associated with each decision and each company can be the source of several complaints. Statistics can thus be created by decision, by "company-decision" coupling, or by "company-complaint" coupling. The preferred level for an SME study seems to be the "company-decision" coupling.

Table 7.2 Involvement of SMEs (as a percentage of decisions)

	Freq.	Percent
No SME involvement	204	70
Involvement of at least one SME	87	30
Total	291	100

Source: Microeconomix FCA decisions database

Table 7.3 Involvement of SMEs (as a percentage of "Company-decision" couplings)

	Freq.	Percent
Major company (> EUR 50 m)	1,020	70
SME (< EUR 50 m)	442	30
Total	1,462	100

Source: Microeconomix FCA decisions database

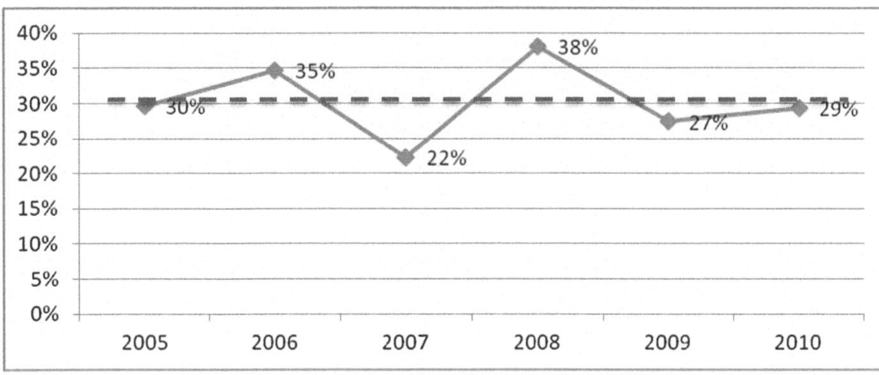

Fig. 7.1 Evolution of the relative involvement in SMEs in decisions made by the French Competition Authority (2005–2010, as a percentage of company-decision couplings). *Source*: Microeconomix FCA decisions database

sentences. This variation is not due to the prevalence of cartels among SMEs, which, it may be considered, lead to a higher conviction rate. In fact, the same very unfavourable result for SMEs is confirmed if only decisions relating to cartels are examined. In relative terms, SMEs that originate practices are thus more often found guilty than major companies, with equivalent types of practice. This correlation is confirmed by various statistical (Chi-square test) and econometrical tests.

This interpretation is not unequivocal. It may of course be possible that SMEs are more often involved in cases that have clearer anticompetitive effects and/or for which the Competition Authority has more material evidence. It could also be suggested that because SMEs are, on average, subject to less monitoring, the cases that do appear before the Competition Authority are the most flagrant, and thus systematically end in a sentence. However, the systematically unfavourable nature of the case results for SMEs could also be explained by the limited legal resources available to them—they may not be able to find the necessary funds for an effective

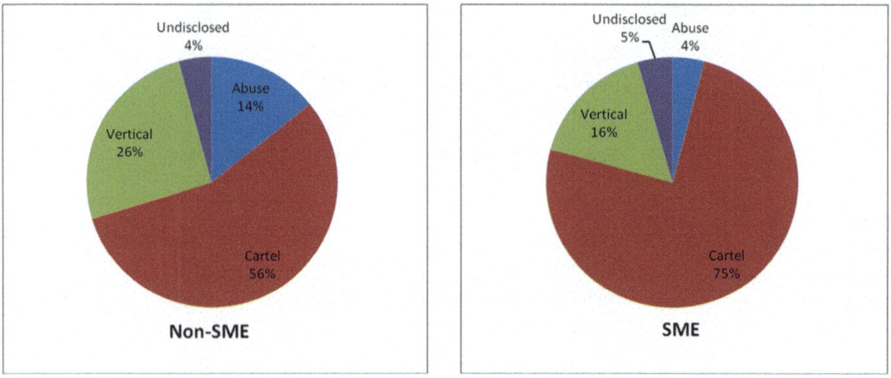

Fig. 7.2 Distribution of companies by type of practice. *Source*: Microeconomix FCA decisions database

Table 7.4 Outcome of proceedings and decision to appeal

SME	Rate of confirmation of at least one complaint (all practices combined) (%)	Rate of confirmation of at least one complaint (cartel) (%)	Appeal rate when at least one complaint is upheld (%)
Non-SME	24	27	63
SME	96	97	29
Total	51	54	41

Source: Microeconomix FCA decisions database

defence (including the most skilful lawyers, setting up of a dedicated internal team, or support from economists). This result would then show an asymmetry between SMEs and major companies in respect of means of defence.

Furthermore, once they have been found guilty, SMEs are much less inclined to appeal against the FCA's decision, since just 20 % of them do so, compared to 63 % of major companies. Here again, the two interpretations of increased flagrancy or of a lack of legal means are possible. The second interpretation of asymmetry in terms of legal resources does however seem preferred. In fact, more extensive econometric tests[10] show that even when controlling the sanction level, the fact of being an SME decreases the probability of the convicted company appealing. Since the decision to appeal is based on the choice of a legal strategy, the very clear divergence on this point between SMEs and major companies seems to confirm a divergence in legal strategies, where an asymmetry of means constitutes the most obvious explanation.

[10] A simple probit model that tests the probability of appeal according to practice, sanction level, and the fact of being an SME shows a significant effect of 1 % due to being an SME.

Lastly, it should be noted that it is difficult to express any specific features of SMEs in terms of their conduct within the practice. The number of successful requests for leniency is too small (only six cases) to draw any statistical conclusions. However, it is noted that though two out of the six cases are triggered by SMEs, in line with their overall weight in terms of decisions, both these SMEs belong to a group, which would tend to support the hypothesis whereby the weight of a group behind its SMEs' legal strategy is decisive.

7.3.2 Substantive Rules

7.3.2.1 Existing Rules

The provisions expressly targeting SMEs are very limited. There are three relevant sets of provisions.

First, Article L. 420-4-II of the Commercial Code exempts from prohibition in respect of anticompetitive practices "certain categories of agreement, or certain agreements, in particular when their purpose is to improve the management of small or medium-sized enterprises". In practice, the agreements covered by this text are extremely limited.[11]

Second, rules specific to local anticompetitive practices schedule for their part specific jurisdiction of the Minister of the Economy for practices involving companies where "turnover achieved by each of them in France over the previous financial year does not exceed EUR 50 million and where the total turnover does not exceed EUR 100 million.[12] Because of these thresholds, these rules can be considered as specifically targeting SMEs.

Last, Title 4 of Volume IV of the Commercial Code can be considered as designed to protect SMEs. Indeed, these provisions concern transparency and restrictive practices. The rules in question are not governed by competition regulations as such, but they nonetheless target organisation of the market and, more specifically, relationships between economic operators.

These restrictive practices, for the most part, are covered by Article L. 442-6 of the Commercial Code, which has seen many additions over the years. The complexity of the rules it lays out and the myriad of cases scheduled make it very difficult for SMEs to implement. Even so, the general nature of these provisions make them applicable to all economic relationships, and jurisprudence has shown

[11] Competition Council, Decision no. 96-499 of 7 June 1996 relating to agreements between producers benefiting from signs of quality in the agricultural sector (OJ 11 June); Decree no. 96-500 of 7 June 1996 relating to agreements between agricultural producers or between agricultural producers and companies regarding adaptation measures for crisis situations (OJ 11 June); Decree no. 2007-1884 of 26 December 2007 regarding an agreement relating to payment periods in motor vehicle subsidiaries (OJ 30 December); Opinion no. 07-03 given by the ECCP (BOCC 31 July 2007) and no. 07-A-14 of 9 November 2007 of the Competition Council (BOCC 4 March 2008).

[12] See Article L 494-9 of the Commercial Code.

that it has been implemented regardless of the size of the economic operator subject to investigation.

The development of specific provisions has been particularly notable in France, but its effectiveness seems limited, especially in terms of protecting SMEs. The complexity of the rules is rather a source of difficulty for SMEs[13] which do not schedule the legal services required for their implementation. The origin of these provisions can be traced back to the existence of a *per se* prohibition on resale at a loss.[14] However, though these provisions could be explained as a means of ensuring respect for this prohibition when the legal resale at a loss threshold was independent of economic resale at a loss threshold, the utility of said measure disappeared once the legislator reduced the resale at a loss threshold in the sense of Article L. 442-2 of the Commercial Code to the level of the actual price, after consideration of all financial advantages provided, regardless of their form (net triple price). The upholding of a per se prohibition on resale at a loss is even called into question, including in respect of SMEs, since these regulations appear to be a source of legal insecurity that may even put SMEs in a situation of dependence in respect of their more powerful partners, which are better able to manage the formalisation of these monitoring tools and remain within the law.

We may also mention the existence of rules indirectly covering SMEs: those regarding the applicable thresholds in respect of market share at European and French levels and the concept of abuse of economic dependence.

In France, there are no specific safe harbours for SMEs, but their smaller size means that they naturally benefit from the safe harbours that exist for all companies (market share thresholds for the *de minimis* rule and vertical restraint rules).

The existence of a *de minimis* threshold in competition law in the absence of any hard-core restriction[15] allows the FCA to end the proceedings regarding antitrust practices if certain thresholds are not reached, which benefits SMEs.

The exclusion of independent SMEs does not cause difficulties. However, as regards the application of thresholds to SMEs that are subsidiaries of a group, the issue must be distinguished according to whether or not the SME retains its autonomy on the market.

Indeed, regarding subsidiaries that do retain such autonomy, the lack of effect on the market justifying the exclusion of independent SMEs is identical. These subsidiaries must thus be treated as independent SMEs and benefit from the application of thresholds.

In practice, the exception scheduled under Article L. 464-6-1 of the Commercial Code was found not to apply when it was invoked, since the practices in question are most often considered as *per se* restrictive of competition practices, and can thus

---

[13] See, for instance, rules governing billing, Article L.441-3 of the Commercial Code, rules governing the formalisation of commercial negotiation, Article L.441-7.

[14] Article L. 442-2 of the Commercial Code.

[15] Article L. 464-6-1 of the Commercial Code.

not benefit from the presumption of safety outlined in this text or from an exemption.[16]

7.3.2.2 Possible Changes in Favour of a Specific Treatment of SMEs

Differential treatment of SMEs in relation to anticompetitive practices occurs mostly via the differential application of rules according to size. Due to their size, SMEs that commit infringements are more often involved in practices causing little damage to the economy, on markets where barriers to entry are lower and competition is stiffer. This may lead the competition authorities to monitor these markets less closely and not to prioritise those cases involving SMEs that commit offences. However, once the case has been investigated, the following question arises: is there sufficient reason to allow the rules and their application to differ?

From the standpoint of economic theory, there would be no obvious reason to make things easier for SMEs when they commit anticompetitive practices. However, it is advisable to differentiate between types of practice: abuse of dominance and anticompetitive agreements. In relation to abuse of dominance, SMEs act in this case in a situation of favourable asymmetry in relation to other companies that are larger than them. As such, there is no reason why different rules should apply to them.

Regarding anticompetitive agreements and in the absence of vertical links with other members of the cartel, the argument of coercion is difficult to prove, since it is always possible not to follow an agreement, regardless of its size.

Nor is the argument for a defensive cartel an easy one: any price freezing to cope with downward pressure harms the consumer. If the defensive cartel is designed to save jobs, then the challenge is no longer the rules of competition law as such but their use in connection with other objectives, e.g. employment policy.

In vertical restraint practices (vertical agreements), both partners involved in an agreement can be considered as at fault. We consider below two cases.

In the first case, the SME is the originator of the agreement in question (for instance, RPM (resale price maintenance) practice when it is the supplier). If the SME originates a practice on a market where large competitors are also present, there is very little chance that the agreement will generate substantial anticompetitive effects. An effect-based approach will thus conclude in the harmless nature of the practice without the need to specify immunity for SMEs. If the SME originates a practice on a small-scale market, it may then be the case that the practice has anticompetitive effects. But in this case, it is difficult to legitimise differentiated treatment from an economic perspective. The SME must show that the pro-competitive effects supplant the anticompetitive effects, with no a priori justification of the practice due to its size.

In a second case, the agreement is made by a major company that has significant negotiating power.

[16] Article L. 420-4 I of the Commercial Code.

It is highly unlikely that a very powerful player on a large market would implement a vertical agreement that gives benefits to a distributor SME. For instance, a powerful supplier on a large-scale market will not choose to give exclusive distribution to an SME. However, it may negotiate with said SME in relation to being the exclusive supplier. But in this case, the SME does not gain any competitive advantage and thus should not be convicted.

On the balance sheet, it is difficult to see how their size can legitimise differential treatment of SMEs with regard to justifying practices and prohibiting them in the event of anticompetitive effects. But from a practical and social point of view (which is difficult to quantify), and thus in terms of legal purpose (SMEs' access to justice), we consider that it does seem necessary.

We suggest in relation to procedural aspects that specific attention can be drawn by also applying here the suggestions outlined at point 7.3.3.2 below.

As regards content, the ambiguities relating to specific handling of the company's size, as indicated above, explain legitimate hesitation to adopt special substantial provisions on SMEs.

We suggest also an improvement to the existing legislation aimed at taking better account of the absence of any competitive effect—thus, measures indirectly favourable to SMEs since these make up the vast majority of companies that do not have market power and, additionally from a more focused perspective, measures that are directly favourable to SMEs, since they deliberately take account of the size of said companies.[17]

Other indirect measures may be, in our view, favourable to SMEs. One is modification of existing thresholds in competition law, from both a Community perspective and a national perspective, in various legislative texts that lay down below market share thresholds, which companies can benefit from a presumption of absence of anticompetitive effects or an exemption by category. It is suggested to both slightly raise (for some thresholds) and simplify the vast number of different thresholds in terms of community law, retaining a "general" threshold of 30 % and a "subsidiary" threshold of 15 % for agreements of minor importance, horizontal guidelines, and purchasing and marketing agreements. In French law, a switch is to be made from two thresholds to a single threshold for the *de minimis* system—to be set at 15 %, as in the United Kingdom.[18]

Lifting of the prohibition on minimum resale prices is a French specificity featured in Article L. 442-5 of the Commercial Code. Currently, SMEs can be sanctioned in the same way as major companies, according to a formal approach that economists are right to decry, since it takes no account of impact on competition—this *per se* prohibition is not found in European legislative texts (it is simply a

[17] These proposals are taken from the CREDA report, *SMEs and competition law*, LexisNexis LITEC, November 2009, which readers are invited to read for a more detailed introduction (pp. 211–255).

[18] http://www.oft.gov.uk/shared_oft/business_leaflets/ca98_guidelines/oft.pdf.

presumption of anticompetitive nature); moreover, in the United States, it is replaced by the application of the 'rule of reason' to Restrictive Price Maintenance.

Lessening of restrictions and prohibitions appearing under Heading 4 of Volume IV of the Commercial Code, another French specificity—SMEs suffer more than other companies from restrictions imposed in terms of billing rules,[19] "single agreement",[20] or resale below cost.[21] One might even wonder—as the FCA did during the latest reforms to French competition law—if SMEs, in whose favour these provisions were in principle drawn up, would not be better off without the provisions of Article L. 442-6 or at least with a single global definition of the prohibited practice.

A simplification of Article L. 442-6, or even its removal, actually seems necessary in order for it to function effectively within the scope of protecting SMEs. Its key provision—sanctioning the "actual or attempted submission of a business partner to obligations that create a significant imbalance in the rights and obligations of the parties" and sanctioning the abrupt termination of business relations—could be reused in an amalgamated article establishing the guiding principles of abuse in relations between economic operators. Even so, the implementation of common obligations law and its general principles such as good faith could justify the removal of these special provisions, but jurisprudence prior to these specific provisions did not provide complete satisfaction on this point. In this respect, the adverse effects and difficulties of application caused by the provision, scheduling the intervention of the Minister of the Economy, on his own initiative, in this type of practice, suggest at the very least that companies falling victim to the decried restrictive practices are automatically called into question, if said provision is retained.

In terms of case law, a more generous approach is awaited, both from Community and national authorities around the concept of "hard-core restrictions", applied until now in a most formalistic way. All that is needed is the presence of a "blacklist clause" interpreted in the broadest sense of the term to ensure that an anticompetitive practice without the slightest scope, due to the absence of market power, leads either to the non-application of the *de minimis* rule or the disappearance of the favourable presumption existing below certain market share thresholds in respect of both horizontal and vertical relations. SMEs would of course be the first beneficiaries of any interpretation that takes more account of economic reality.

Another set of measures targeting directly and deliberately SMEs in view of favouring them can be envisaged. It would be possible and desirable, for instance, to adopt a provision that, currently in Europe, does not exist anywhere except in British law: the granting of specific immunity from fines relating to "small agreements" when applying the *de minimis* rule. The UK Competition Act of 1998 grants this immunity to companies with turnover of under GBP 20 million,

[19] See Article L. 441-3 of the Commercial Code.

[20] Article L. 441-7 of the Commercial Code.

[21] Article L. 442-2 of the Commercial Code.

provided that certain practices are not used (resale price maintenance, applicable community law).

An SME-specific approach in terms of 'crisis agreement' may be also envisaged, in the same vein as the *Stichting Baksteen*[22] decision adopted by the European Commission—legal precedent that has remained isolated until now.[23] This case concerned the acceptance by the Commission of a concerted reduction in production capacities between 17 manufacturers—all SMEs, with a limited market share.

There are but a few cases in which this kind of horizontal agreement—a cartel—can be *in fine* favourable to the company, in the first instance. It is useful to recall that in economic terms, a cartel always has two effects: a transfer of wealth from consumers to companies and a net loss of wealth due to the fact that consumers stop purchasing.

Regardless of the background (SME or non-SME, crisis or no crisis), the second effect is necessarily harmful to consumers and producers alike (and it may specifically aggravate the effect of lower demand observed in times of crisis). The thinking behind the legitimisation of the crisis agreement is that, in some cases, the first effect (transfer of wealth from consumers to companies) is positive. This is particularly the case if the companies are fragile SMEs that need to preserve their margin levels in crisis periods in order to subsist. The effect on jobs or the long-term effect on the competition (they are shielded from competition in the short term, so they can be competitive in the future) could more than offset the negative effect of consumers' loss of wealth. However, it should be noted that the wealth lost by consumers will be reflected by a drop in consumer spending on another market, which transfers part of the crisis from one sector to another.

Cases where the company may work better with a crisis agreement than without one can appear very limited and difficult to determine (there is a balance to be struck between positive and negative effects of the transfer of wealth), but it seemed possible to avoid the adverse effects of accepting the concept of crisis agreements by restricting them to SMEs and by recalling the restrictive conditions chosen by the Commission in the *Stichting Baksteen* case (specifically the absence of market power and the medium-term efficiencies resulting from the rationalisation of intended production).

It should also be noted, to strengthen the economic analysis, that the competition authorities could explicitly take into account, as a mitigating circumstance, the fact that companies' margins would have, to all intents and purposes, been negative in the absence of a cartel. This is considered at the sanction stage but not when appraising the practice itself. This boils down to distinguishing security-providing cartels from wealth-making cartels. This position is not easy to justify

[22] Decision EC-IV/34 of 29 April 1994, OJEC L. 131/15 of 26 May 1994.

[23] In the more recent case, *Irish beef*, the European Court of Justice was more restrictive than the Commission's decision in *Stichting Baksteen*, ECJ, case C-209/07, *Competition Authority v Beef Industry Development Society Ltd and Barry Brothers (Carrigmore) Meats Ltd ("BIDS")*, ECR 2008 I-8637.

economically, but it would be favourable by far to a total exemption of crisis agreements and would be in addition to the account taken of SMEs and to the required conditions outlined above.

7.3.3 Procedural Aspects

7.3.3.1 Specific Existing Rules

Strictly speaking, only the legal provisions regarding local anticompetitive practices[24] resent procedural specificities: these appear subsequent to the enquiry phase and on the condition that the Competition Authority has not sought legal approval.[25]

If the Competition Authority does not intend to initiate proceedings, then companies benefit from a simpler, less contradictory procedure, directly implemented by management, which results in a settlement.

The specific local anticompetitive practice system that covers SMEs is supposed to allow faster processing of local cases for which the solution seems obvious.

The Competition Council, consulted about this project, considered that the turnover of companies that could benefit from this faster processing to be very high. The law has established a bridge with the FCA by providing an option open to the Competition Authority to process such a case if it seems significant, despite the relatively small size of the companies in question. This was the case of the previously outlined case relating to anticompetitive practices in Saint-Pierre-et-

[24] Article L. 464-9 of the Commercial Code: The Minister of the Economy can order companies to terminate the practices outlined in Articles L. 420-1, L. 420-2 and L. 420-5 which they originated, when these practices affect a local-sized market, and do not concern deeds relating to Articles 81 and 82 of the treaty instituting the European Community, subject to the condition that the turnover of each of the companies achieved in France over the previous financial year does not exceed EUR 50 million and that their total turnover does not exceed EUR 100 million.

The Minister of the Economy can also, under the same conditions, offer a compromise, or settlement. The value of the settlement can exceed EUR 75,000 or 5 % of the last known turnover figure in France if this value is lower. The procedures of the settlement are set down by decree by the Council of State. Performance within the stipulated timeframes of the obligations resulting from the injunction and acceptance of the settlement terminates all actions before the Competition Authority for the same deeds. The Minister of the Economy notifies the Competition Authority of any settlement concluded.

He or she cannot offer a settlement or impose an injunction when the same deeds have previously been subject to a referral to the Competition Authority by a company or a body outlined in the second paragraph of Article L. 462-1.

In the event of a refusal to reach a settlement, the Minister of the Economy refers the matter to the Competition Authority. He or she also refers the matter to the Competition Authority in the event of non-performance of the injunctions scheduled in the first paragraph resulting from the acceptance of the settlement.

[25] See, for a recent example, Decision no. 12-D-06 of 26 January 2012 relating to practices implemented in the aggregates sector and downstream markets in Saint-Pierre-et-Miquelon.

Miquelon. The procedure is wholly confidential, and the fines are moderate, which represents a major incentive to companies not to refuse it.

7.3.3.2 Suggested Specific Procedural Measures in Favour of SMEs

SMEs are subject to several procedural difficulties.

First of all is asymmetry of information. When facing a large (or indeed very large) company, SMEs have difficulty finding the relevant information for their defence (market shares, size of the market, cost and margin of main firms, etc.). For this reason, it should be possible to improve the situation by relaxing certain rules, specifically in terms of evidence or protection of business confidentiality, when the SME is the distraining party in a procedure aimed at sanctioning anticompetitive practices. Conversely, when an SME is prosecuted for anticompetitive practices, it is important to check whether its legal representative is fully aware of its rights of defence in order that these be exercised effectively: assistance from a lawyer, the prohibition of any questions leading the party to accuse themselves.

Second, SMEs face a lack of human and financial resources. SMEs face a series of difficulties owing to a lack of human and financial resources, which weakens them. Most SMEs do not have an in-house legal department. It is difficult therefore for them to find adequate financing to complete particularly complex procedures, particularly when they face powerful opponents that can call on substantial resources.

This imbalance is corrected, but only in part, by the opportunity to refer the matter to the Competition Authority, which for its part has sufficient resources to gather evidence of anticompetitive behaviour.

Consequently, as regards traditional litigation proceedings, the Competition Authority is obliged to pursue the matter. However, the SME still has to get over the hurdle of the admissibility of the referral, which obliges it to sustain its complaint by providing evidence that, though perhaps not complete, must be at least sufficient to establish the "probability" of the alleged deeds. If this is the case, the Competition Authority can then make enquiries to flesh out said evidence.

In connection with advisory procedures, on the other hand, the situation has been more awkward since the Competition Authority has had the option of dealing with competition issues immediately. The possibility of referring the matter to the Competition Authority for an opinion has all but dried up, whereas for professional organisations comprising SMEs, it was once a most appreciable way to have legislation applied and rules laid down in situations where they risked disappearing: thus, the association supporting continued competition on the motorway network (AMCRA) (an SME association), decrying the expected consequences of the announced privatisation of motorways, obtained Opinion no. 05-A-22 of 2 December 2005, subsequent to which the State obliged all motorway companies, even those that were privatised, to continue to provide calls for tenders for all contracts greater than EUR 2 million.

Given the above, we suggest the following improvements—in order to offset the asymmetry of information and the lack of human resources, it seems necessary for the competition authorities to take specific measures to assist SMEs, as has already been suggested in France[26]:

- drafting of a guide outlining SME procedures and law in terms of competition, with the initiative possibly taken via joint action by the Competition Authority and the DGCCRF (Directorate-General for Competition, Consumption and the Fight against Fraud) in France;
- institution of an "SME office" within these two authorities, which could be used as an information office, and an assistance office in terms of how the law is applied to SMEs and how they use competition law.

As regards local anticompetitive practices, it would be desirable to (1) give a more civil than repressive character to the ad hoc settlement procedure on the same template as the Competition Authority's own procedure for "standard anticompetitive practices"; (2) formally entrust the creation of the settlement project to a DGCCRF agent other than the one investigating the case; (3) institute more explicit rules to guarantee the respect of the principle that both parties should be heard; (4) extend the response time given to an SME (currently this stands at two months) due to the draft settlement decision put forward by the DGCCRF, to take into account the SMEs' restricted resources and longer response time; (5) provide an internal redress mechanism.

In relation to the right to have access to the file, due account shall be taken of the position of SMEs.

Within the framework of litigation proceedings brought before the Competition Authority, investigation is confidential: as a result, disclosure by one of the parties of information concerning another party or a third party of which the disclosing party could only have become aware during communications or consultations that were undertaken is punished by the sanctions laid down at Article 226-13 of the Criminal Code.[27]

Parties have full access to the file, with no distinction made according to their position. They can however be faced with rules regarding the protection of business confidentiality that allow some data to be classified as confidential. Declassification is performed at the initiative of the Reporter alone. With regard to commitment procedure, which allows a company to stop a procedure that has been started by offering—before any notification of a Statement of Objections—to correct its behaviour, the Court of Cassation criticised the limitation of access to the full file afforded to the distraining party (which may be an SME falling victim to anticompetitive behaviour)[28]. Parties involved in the proceedings (both the distraining party and the company in question) now have access to all the documents that the Reporter used in order to draw up the preliminary assessment and to all those documents submitted to the Authority to rule on the commitments, that is to say, at least the preliminary assessment and third-party observations included in the file in

[26] SMEs and competition law, CREDA – LexisNexis LITEC, November 2009.

[27] See Article L.463-6 of the Commercial Code.

[28] Cass. Com. (French Supreme Court), 4 November 2008, Canal 9 P 07-21.275, Bull. IV n° 188.

response to the market test.[29] Evidence is thus made easier to peruse for the distraining party, which can, if need be, show that the commitment procedure is not appropriate.

Third parties, whether interested or not, do not have any access to the litigious file sent to the Competition Authority. At the very most, they can informally register their interest with the investigation department and be received by it, which is what effectively happens, especially when it is a matter of providing information useful to the Reporter—but this is not an acquired right. However, the right of notification of third parties does exist, in limited form, with regard to merger control investigation in phase 2.

The confidentiality of the investigation is designed to prevent any actions for damages made by victims who are obliged to demonstrate a fault, the evidence for which can be found in the documents held in the Competition Authority's file. However, it is felt that the principle of respecting the rights of the defence justifies disclosure, in a civil trial, of information covered by the confidentiality of the investigation before the Competition Authority, if said disclosure is necessary to the performance of these rights.[30]

In broad application of this case law, the Commercial Court in Paris deemed it "legitimate", in its ruling of 11 April 2012, to authorise the members of an alleged cartel denounced on the basis of a request for leniency that resulted in a nonsuit decision being given by the Competition Authority,[31] to produce documents from the file held by the Authority, though they would be "made anonymous."

In opinion, it is necessary to facilitate or accelerate the access to SMEs if they prove to have an objective interest: in litigation procedures, relating to the anti-competitive practices processed by the Authority, it is advisable to explicitly introduce the possibility of interested SMEs being heard when they can assert a legitimate interest.

In "local" anticompetitive practices, by also including the possibility of intervention in the event of legitimate interest (although the procedure is today not public, a third-party SME may be notified of it).

In order for a third-party SME to engage a damages action following a settlement, it would be desirable if the confidential nature of said procedure were to disappear, as has occurred in equivalent procedures in the USA or in Europe (where settlement procedures apply to SMEs as they do to others).

More generally, specific notification tools for SMEs, as suggested previously, would be valuable for third-party interested SMEs and for SMEs presumed to have been behind an offence or for SMEs that are victims, for instance, in the form of an "SME office".

[29] Notice on Competition Commitments, 2nd of March 2009 http://www.autoritedelaconcurrence.fr/doc/cpro_autorite_2mars2009_engagements_antitrust.pdf.

[30] Cass com.(French Supreme Court), 19 January 2010 P 08-19.761, Bull. IV n°8.

[31] Decision 10-D-36, 17 December 2010, relating to practices applied in the sector of Liquefied Petroleum Gas (LPG) packaged.

7.3.4 Sanctions and Leniency Programme

7.3.4.1 Sanctions

The fact of being an SME is taken into account in sanctions: firstly, in an indirect way, via the volume of sales affected by the practice, which will be lower for an SME than for a major company in the case of a cartel, and secondly, directly, when the ability to pay is taken into account. A single-product company (as a large number of SMEs are) will be given a lower sanction (relative to its size) than that of a multi-product company.

Economically, it is not always easy to justify this difference: deterrence is based on the comparison of the sanction and the illicit profit, which depends on the value of sales affected and not by the total value of the company's sales. But this difference can still be justified if we suggest that money has a different value in multi-product companies, given their easier access to credit and their pooling of the legal risks over several entities.

The first observation that can be made based on statistical studies regarding SMEs and sanctions is that SMEs are more often subject to financial sanctions than major companies. A total of 90 % of the SMEs involved are sanctioned as a result of the procedure, while only 20 % of major companies are. This gap is obviously linked to the fact that complaints are upheld against major companies in only 25 % of cases, compared to 96 % for SMEs. But this gap persists if we look only at the percentage of financial sanctions imposed for anticompetitive agreements in which a complaint is upheld: 17 % of major companies escape any financial sanction whatsoever, compared to only 7 % of SMEs in the same situation.

The second observation is that the sanctions imposed on SMEs are lower than those imposed on major companies, obviously in absolute terms, but also relative to their turnover. Table 7.5 shows the levels of absolute sanction, reduced to turnover in the event of at least one complaint upheld, distinguishing major companies, SMEs affiliated to a group, company collectives, and finally SMEs where no group affiliation is mentioned.

We can thus observe that despite a higher rate of non-sanction, major companies are, on average, sanctioned more harshly than SMEs, since their level of sanction is 1.5 times higher than that for SMEs. The very high amounts observed for collectives and affiliated SMEs result from the fact that the Competition Authority does not use the turnover figure for players within the organisation itself, rather that of its members (in the case of a collective) or of the group (in the case of an affiliated SME).

Economic theory offers interesting observations for optimal sanctions.

Classically, economic theory considers that the optimal sanction that deters against practices is independent of the size of the company. The sanction must offset the illicit gains linked to the practice, while taking into account the probability of detection of the cartel. The sanction must thus be equal to the excess anticompetitive profit divided by the probability of detection: a company faced with the choice of implementing an anticompetitive practice thus expects that the desired gain of this practice is null and chooses not to implement it. In this case, for

Table 7.5 Fine amount depending on type of company

Type of company	Number of cases (at least one complaint upheld)	Fine (in EUR k)	Fine (as % of turnover)
Collective	36	120	37.5 %
Major company	240	9,263	1.8 %
SME	368	96	1.2 %
Affiliated SME	27	4,489	94.6 %

Source: Microeconomix FCA decisions database

a given excess price, the only variable to take into account is the value of sales affected by the practice for the company in question, as well as the size of the excess price. The sanction for SMEs expressed as a percentage of sales or turnover should be equal to that for other companies.

However, three arguments can be put forward to call this result of optimal sanction equivalence into question, which actually stem from three information-based imperfections.

The first argument consists of highlighting the differentiated valuation of sanctions due to a different capital access cost (due in fine to the information-based imperfections on the credit/capital market). Sanction equivalence can be called into question if we consider that not all companies value an identical sanction in the same way and, more specifically, whether or not an SME assigns a higher weight to a sanction than a major company. If a fine representing 3 % of turnover is considered as a higher sanction by one company than another, it will not have the same deterrent effect: it would then be legitimate to differentiate the sanction according to the valuation of the sanction by the company.

To justify a lower sanction for SMEs, it must thus be proved that the same sanction will weigh down more heavily on SMEs compared to larger companies. This can be the case if we include the cost of capital in the optimal calculation made by the company and the cost of capital is higher for SMEs. For instance, let us imagine that companies have two ways of paying their fine, e.g. their cash reserves and debt.

If their cash reserves are lower than the amount of the fine, then they will be obliged to use debt. If the interest rate is higher for SMEs, in like-for-like cash terms, then an equivalent sanction in turnover points will represent a higher discounted net loss for an SME, which could thus be deterred using a lower fine. It should be noted that this result is further accentuated if we consider that cash reserves are proportionally lower for SMEs, and thus their use of debt will not only be more costly but also bigger.

A second argument for calling into question the assumption of equivalent sanctions is consideration of the risk of false positives on the part of the Competition Authority. It may be legitimate to weigh the sanction if we consider that there is a risk that it will be imposed wrongly. This risk is of course valid for all companies, but it may justify a lower sanction if we consider that it is higher in the case of an

SME than in the case of larger companies. This may be the case if we take into account the smaller resources that SMEs have to defend themselves. The number of elements provided by SMEs in their defence will be relatively fewer or less convincing, which increases the risk of a false positive on the part of the Competition Authority. In addition, statistics show in a most unambiguous way that the fact of being an SME significantly reduces the probability of appeal, in terms of equivalent practices and levels of sanction. The absence of an appeal procedure increases the risk that the fine effectively paid is wrongly imposed. Given this higher risk of false positive, it is thus rational in connection with calculating the optimal sanction to proportionally reduce the amount of the fine imposed on SMEs.

The third argument justifying differentiated treatment is consideration of practices committed through negligence. A competition authority may wish to take into account in its analysis the fact that a practice breaching competition law may have been instigated by a form of negligence or without awareness of its effects on the competition or of its illegal nature. This argument is specifically used in literature to justify an increased sanction in the case of a repeat offence.[32] The higher the risk is of negligent practice, the more rational it is to sanction a second offence more harshly, in relative terms. The thinking behind this is simple: the company could be negligent when committing the first offence but not the second. The first sanction is thus diminished in relation to the optimal sanction, to take account of the probability of negligence, while the second is set at the optimal level in a situation where the party is fully informed. This reasoning, valid for all companies, can be extended to SMEs to justify a relatively lower sanction solely in the event of a first offence.

This is a strong argument for an adaptation of the sanctions: for instance, we can imagine not issuing a fine for an SME offending for the first time in an area, or else issuing a suspended fine or a conditional fine (a fine or obligation to organise or take a training session in competition law).

7.3.4.2 SMEs and Leniency

There is no exact precedent that demonstrates that large companies have more chances than SMEs to "win the race" to file a leniency application, but the cases examined by the Competition Authority show that those requesting leniency are generally part of the larger companies in a given sector; they have a spill-over effect on SMEs that rally to the cartel. Thus, leniency does not benefit them, except to implement a "two-tier" procedure or one where complaints are not disputed. Nevertheless, sanctions remain proportionately high.[33]

---

[32] Rubinstein, A. "An optimal conviction policy for offences that may have been committed by accident", in *Applied game theory*, published by S. Brahms, A. Schotter, and G. Schwödiauer. Würzburg: Physica-Verlag, 1979, 406-413, as well as in a different setting, Emons, W. "Escalating sanctions for repeat offenders", *International Review of Law and Economics*, 27, 2007, 170–178.

[33] See Cons. Conc., dec. n° 06-D-09 of 11 April 2006 relating to practices implemented in the door manufacturing sector, dec. n° 07-D-48 of 18 December 2007 relating to practices implemented in the national and international relocation sector.

In addition, we can note that in a case concerning the plywood sector,[34] "implementation of the leniency procedure, at the initiative of the market leader, a subsidiary of a worldwide operator, ended in the disappearance from the market of several small operators" involved in the denounced cartel.[35]

Conversely, any proceedings for damages caused by anticompetitive practices are more difficult to bring against a company that has requested and obtained leniency: in fact, if the Competition Authority only commits to conserve the confidential nature of some information for the duration of the proceedings[36] and if it confirms that "full or partial immunity from fines granted by the Authority to an undertaking does not protect it from any civil law consequences that may result from its participation in an infringement under the provisions of article L. 420-1 of the Commercial Code and/or Article 81 of the EC treaty" (ditto point 47), the fact still remains that the Competition Authority cannot run the risk of discouraging requests for leniency by facilitating their access to the evidence. Though this difficulty is real for all companies, it can have an even bigger impact on an SME.

We may assume that the lower resources of SMEs prevent them from creating leniency files as well constructed as those submitted by major companies. It may thus be envisaged that the requirements in terms of evidence could be lower for SMEs so as to ensure the same gain-risk arbitration when the decision to denounce a cartel is taken. It would also be advisable to accept a file that may be slightly incomplete in order to allow an SME to be included.

It would be possible to justify establishing protection mechanisms in order to enhance SMEs to inform about anticompetitive practices, using an argument based on SMEs' asymmetric power of negotiation, which would modify their arbitration when denouncing an anticompetitive practice. But we are talking here about SMEs as originators of such practices, thus those denouncing cartels. As such, it is not easy to assess the risks that cartel partners would then take retaliatory trade action (except perhaps via a price war on local markets where the SME operates); above all, it is not easy to imagine the protection mechanisms.

---

[34] Cons. conc., dec. n° 12 of 21 May 2008 relating to practices implemented in the plywood production sector.

[35] Comment by Alain Ronzano, SMEs and competition law, op. cit., p. 260.

[36] Procedural Notice of 2 March 2009 relating to the French leniency programme, point 44, http://www.autoritedelaconcurrence.fr/doc/cpro_autorite_2mars2009_engagements_antitrust.pdf.

7.4 SMEs as Victims

7.4.1 Private Antitrust Enforcement

7.4.1.1 French Antitrust Legislation Does Not Contain Any Specific Provisions in This Area in Order to Protect SMEs Confronted to Large Undertakings in Civil Suits for Anticompetitive Conducts, but Some Provisions in the Commercial Code Relating to Vertical Restrictive Practices Are Aimed at Specifically Protecting SMEs

In connection with sanctioning restrictive practices,[37] the Minister of the Economy is given the power to instruct specifically competent civil court of law when dealing with a practice he sees as contrary to this legislation. This action is considered as an autonomous act undertaken by the Minister, independently of any action or lack thereof taken by parties to the agreement.[38] This qualification circumvents any intervention of the other party. This solution is however disputed, particularly in the name of respecting contractual freedom. The Constitutional Council has however validated this action, subject to the parties being informed of the Minister's action (Const. Counc. 13 May 2011). For its part, the ECHR considered that the autonomous nature of the Minister's action is based on the defence of economic public order and does not represent damage for the defender, given that this party is able to sue the other contracting parties at the proceedings instigated by the Minister (ECHR 17 I 2012, Galec/France).

In practice, the Minister's action is taken with a view to targeting market organisation, and the control of some practices considered as harmful per se, independently of the size of the contracting party.

In order to reconcile the utility of a ministerial action when the economic operators are unable to intervene, and the respect of the parties' rights, a compulsory intervention by all parties to the agreement in question, with regard to the action in respect of one of the parties to said agreements, may limit the adverse effects of any autonomous action.

7.4.1.2 There Are Procedural Difficulties for Victims of Anticompetitive Practices

It is clear that SMEs are in a weak situation to denounce anticompetitive practices. If we consider their motivations, we will doubtlessly have to distinguish between antitrust practices and vertical restraint practices.

As regards exclusionary practices, SMEs are in the first instance encouraged to lodge a complaint anyway, since the counterfactual scenario is their disappearance. However, in some case, if the practice is irreversible, they may prefer to exit the market without incurring the costs of a procedure. But in this case, they do still have the incentive to request a decision by the FCA and then seek damages. However, the

---

[37] Article L. 442-6 of the Commercial Code.

[38] Cass. com, 8 dec. 2008, Bull IV n° 143.

possibility could be envisaged of pooling complaints from various players more easily.

In relation to vertical restrictive practices, a contract may be imposed upon them that harm both the company and consumers without being threatened with exclusion. Their incentive to lodge a complaint is thus weaker, since they may fear trade retaliatory measures. Heading 4 of the Commercial Code may be considered a protection mechanism for SMEs in this respect, but experience in France tends to show that this reflects more a pious wish on the part of the legislator than actual reality on the ground.

In both types of situation, SMEs may prefer to go directly before a judge to obtain damages, rather than contacting a Competition Authority. In France, the procedures engaged for the purpose of compensation must be brought before specialised tribunals when the invoked damage is a result of the violation of rules forbidding anticompetitive practices or "restrictive competition" practices. This specialisation makes it easier for the victims of such practices to take action, particularly SMEs.[39] Nevertheless, the fact that the specialisation is also geographical, with only eight specialised jurisdictions for the whole of France and her overseas dependencies, means that any litigant SME is further away from the judge, and this makes the procedure more complex and more expensive. A good corrective measure would be not to oblige the litigant to act before the specialised tribunal and to waive said specialisation if the litigant deems this is in its interest.

7.4.1.3 Third Party's Right to Bring an Action Before Civil Courts if Some SMEs Do Not Take Action

The specific role of the Minister and the DGCCRF is used mainly in connection with applying Title 4 of the Commercial Code. The DGCCRF exercises its power of investigation in order to denounce restrictive practices that are subject to criminal sanction.[40]

In addition, the Minister has the right to instigate an autonomous action in respect of Article L. 442-6 III of the Commercial Code (see above). However, in practice, this action is used with regard to practices implemented regardless of the respective size of the parties taking part in the practice;[41] see above for the boundaries of this action.

---

[39] For a recent application, cf. Paris com. Tribunal, 31 Jan 2012, RG 2009061231, conviction of Google France and its parent company for antitrust, RLC no. 31.

[40] See the billing rules, Article L. 441-3 of the Commercial Code; "single agreement", Article 441-7 on resale below cost, Article L. 442-2.

[41] For instance: Angers Court of Appeal, 29 V 2007, Ch. Com. *Finamo/Minister of the Economy*, Juris-Data n° 2007 -342249, Dalloz 2007, Jur. 2433 note M.BANDRAC; Créteil com. Tribunal, 24 X 2006, *Minister of the Economy/Système U*, RG 2005 F 00025, RLC April-June 2007 87, obs. M. Chagny.

7.4.2 Collective Redress

In France, there is no collective legal action available to SMEs, nor is any class action available to consumers. But the recent change of government in France has led to the adoption of a bill on class action in favour of consumers, including victims of antitrust practices, currently under examination before the Parliament. The extension of this mechanism to include SMEs is an interesting way and one that is consistent from an economic standpoint. The problem faced by SMEs when applying for compensation is actually the same one faced by end consumers (fragmentation of damages and high individual cost of applying for compensation). In addition, a class action could limit the risks of retaliatory trade measures.

7.4.3 Substantive Rules

7.4.3.1 Existing Rules

There are no rules aiming at protecting specifically SMEs by trying to prevent business to operate or larger undertaking to act in a way that is harmful to them. But several types of rule, in practice, aim at preventing major companies from taking advantage of their structural asymmetry in respect of SMEs, all derived from well-established case law on the basis of the prohibition of abuse of dominant position appearing in French law under Article L. 420-2, paragraph 1 of the Commercial Code: (1) prohibition of predatory pricing, which protects SMEs that would structurally have more difficulty in accessing credit; (2) prohibition of loyalty discounts (under certain conditions), which protects SMEs that would be just as effective at meeting a small part of the order but would not be able to meet the entire order; (3) prohibition of conditional sales (under certain conditions), which protects SMEs that would not be able to develop their business quickly in a second market to offer the same bundle of products.

Nevertheless, this protection of an economic model specific to small companies goes against the economic principle whereby only an equally efficient competitor must be protected.

In order to be exhaustive, we must also mention the existence of a provision prohibiting the abuse of economic dependence,[42] which can in fact only work in favour of SMEs but which up to now has been used very little.

7.4.3.2 The Opportunity to Introduce in the Legislation Specific Rules Protecting SMEs

The answer to the question of the opportunity to introduce in the legislation specific rules protecting SMEs depends crucially on whether or not we accept the assumption whereby competition law can only protect competitors on the condition that

[42] Article L. 420-2, 2nd paragraph of the Commercial Code.

they are as efficient as the dominant player. In respect of SMEs, this is saying that they must be as efficient as other companies in terms of the goods they produce.

In our view, there should not be different rules for SMEs if we uphold the assumption of equivalent efficiency.

If we accept the assumption, it follows that the substantive rules do not have to be different for SMEs but that the common rules naturally protect SMEs against asymmetries they face in comparison with major companies. Competition law will naturally protect them against the risk of exclusion due to asymmetries linked directly or indirectly to size but not against asymmetry of efficiency due to size.

SMEs may fall victim to anticompetitive practices linked directly to their size when they produce as efficiently but at a lesser volume. They cannot thus compete for the entire deal. A dominant player can attempt to exploit this asymmetry of size (though not of efficacy as such) by transforming competition into a competition for all the volumes purchased, via loyalty discounts that oblige an SME either to fulfil all requirements in their entirety or to set a price that is lower than that set by the firm in the dominant position. By prohibiting loyalty discounts, competition law prevents the SME from being marginalised or ousted.

SMEs can also fall victim to anticompetitive practices that are indirectly linked to their size. Thus, given its size, an SME does not generally have a substantial base of liquidity and/or more difficult access to credit. By prohibiting predatory pricing, competition law prevents the SME from being ousted.

In our opinion, it seems particularly difficult to give up the assumption of an equally efficient competitor.

Currently, competition law does not protect an SME that may, due to its size, be less efficient than the dominant company. Can we still foresee exceptions to this rule (which would come down to calling into question the assumption whereby the exclusion of a less efficient competitor is not a problem)?

In the first analysis, two cases can be put forward, but though it is possible to show that this protection can in the long term be useful to consumers, it is difficult to find implementation methods.

The first case is when the size differential is due to past asymmetry, independent of merit.

This is, for instance, the case of a historical monopoly of a dominant company that has been able to garner an established customer base before any possibility of market entry is given to competitors and that uses its size to oust new entrants when the market is opened up.

In this case, competition law faces a dilemma. Forcing the dominant company not to use its size benefits means to reduce efficiency and penalise consumers in the short term. But this could preserve the growth opportunity of an efficient (except size) competitor and lead to a long-term competition, which would be beneficial to consumers.

Consequently, it may be efficient to apply different rules restricting dominant operators' ability to oust new entrants due solely to their large size. Such a policy would actually act as a counterweight to asymmetrical regulation in terms of competition law. But the actual methods of implementing such protection for new-entrant SMEs are difficult to establish.

Two practical problems are in fact apparent.

On the one hand, how can a competitor who is as efficient as the dominant operator—excluding size effects—be distinguished from a competitor that is inefficient in any case and would be even if it were of a comparable size? This question is a central one, since a policy that was aimed at protecting all new entrants would obviously be very disputable. In other words, a Competition Authority that may accept to protect a new entrant SME facing a historical operator must ensure that this new entrant is at least as efficient as the other firms of a comparable size.

On the other hand, how can the size effect be countered in real terms? Preventing a historical operator from benefiting from these size effects actually boils down to asking it to not express in its prices any efficiency gains that are specifically attributable to its historical position. The first difficulty is that this comes down to penalising the consumer, at least in the short term. The second difficulty is a methodological one: it implies being able to distinguish, in terms of efficiency of the dominant operator, which part is due to its historical size. Such an estimation should be difficult and disputable.

The second case is when the presence of significant barriers to entry arouses fear that the disappearance of competitors also signals the disappearance of competition for a long time.

In other words, even a competitor that is less efficient than the dominant operator would socially be more useful than a "dead" competitor when barriers to entry actually prevent competitors that are equally efficient from entering. However, here again, the application of such protection is problematic.

It creates a problem of predictability for the dominant operator, which will be obliged to moderate its aggressive commercial behaviour solely in the event that barriers to entry are significant. But it is difficult for an operator to evaluate the barriers to entry on its own market and to assess cases where it as an operator is restricted by the competition exercised in respect of its rivals.

Furthermore, this difficulty in assessing the critical level of barriers to entry also holds true for the competition authority. However, we can suppose that smaller competitor companies are protected as such when they are the only competitors of a major company. But the problem of knowing how to restrict price competition from the most efficient company would continue to arise.

It seems particularly difficult to give up the assumption of an equally efficient competitor, especially because this implies actively restricting the commercial aggression of the dominant operator. It would be rather difficult to find tools that would restrict said efficacy without harming consumers too much. However, the discussion remains open.

Germany

8

Meinrad Dreher and Julia Körner

8.1 SMEs in the Economic and Political Context

The German "Mittelstand" is known to be the "engine" of the German economy. SMEs—here, for the purpose of the economic context, defined as enterprises with less than 500 employees and annual sales of less than EUR 50 million—represent more than 99 % of all German firms and account for about 60 % of all employees being subject to social insurance contribution. SMEs generate roughly 36 % of all sales.[1] These numbers show the economic significance of SMEs. Consequently, they play an important role in securing competitiveness.[2] Naturally, it is in the interest of politics to support the variety and survival of SMEs.[3]

Recently, the Third Act to Alleviate the Burdens for SMEs ("Drittes Mittelstands-entlastungsgesetz")[4] was passed in 2009 in order to reduce bureaucratic constraints.[5] It shows that SMEs are permanently on the legislative agenda.

[1] See, for the exact numbers, the market study issued by the Institut für Mittelstandsforschung, Bonn, http://www.ifm-bonn.org/statistiken/mittelstand-im-ueberblick/#accordion=0&tab=1. The definition of SMEs used is taken from this market study.

[2] See *Heitzer*, Der Mittelstand als Garant der Wettbewerbsordnung, FIW Heft 239, Mittelstand im globalen Wettbewerb, p. 45 ff.

[3] See Federal Ministry of Economics and Technology, http://www.bmwi.de/DE/Mediathek/publikationen,did=506316.html.

[4] BGBl. 2009 I 550.

[5] The Act added a second domestic turnover threshold to Sec. 35 (1) No. 2 ARC; see under point 8.2.5.

M. Dreher (✉) • J. Körner
Johannes Gutenberg-University of Mainz, Mainz, Germany
e-mail: m.dreher@uni-mainz.de

P. Këllezi et al. (eds.), *Antitrust for Small and Middle Size Undertakings and Image Protection from Non-Competitors*, LIDC Contributions on Antitrust Law, Intellectual Property and Unfair Competition, DOI 10.1007/978-3-642-54000-4_8, © Springer-Verlag Berlin Heidelberg 2014

8.2 SMEs in the Legal Context

8.2.1 General Remarks

Against this background, the question arises as to how competition law treats SMEs.[6] In Germany, effective competition is safeguarded by the German Act against Restraints of Competition[7] (hereafter referred to as "ARC"). The ARC is primarily enforced by the Federal Cartel Office[8] (hereafter referred to as "FCO") and by the state cartel offices[9] in the 16 "German Länder" (together with the FCO, hereafter referred to as "NCA"). There is no special regime in place in order to protect SMEs. However, a number of provisions exist that aim at improving the competitive situation of SMEs. It would be one-sided though to see SMEs as victims only. As infringers, they are caught by the German competition law.

8.2.2 Legal Definition

SMEs are explicitly mentioned in Sec. 3 ARC and Sec. 20 (1) and (3) ARC. German competition law does not provide for a legal definition of SMEs. Whether an enterprise is small or medium sized within the meaning of Sec. 3 ARC is determined in relation to the other enterprises active on the relevant market.[10] Undertakings benefit from the provisions applying to SMEs if they are relatively small compared to their competitors. In principle, the horizontal comparison also applies in the Sec. 20 ARC cases.[11] However, the German Federal Court of Justice ("BGH") held that with regard to a business-induced dependence ("unternehmensbedingte Abhängigkeit"), also the vertical relationship vis-à-vis the addressee of Sec. 20 (1) ARC has to be taken into account.[12]

In order to determine the relative size, all structural criteria such as sales, production capacities, number of employees, etc. have to be considered.[13] Some voices in the literature suggest as a thumb rule sales less than 50 % of the sales generated by the strongest undertaking on the market in order to qualify as a

---

[6] Procurement law is not dealt with in this questionnaire; see on this topic *Dreher*, NZBau 2005, 427 ff.

[7] Gesetz gegen Wettbewerbsbeschränkungen – GWB, version of June 26, 2013 (BGBl. I 1750). The new law (eighth amendment) entered into force on June 30, 2013.

[8] Bundeskartellamt.

[9] Landeskartellbehörden.

[10] See *Fuchs*, Immenga/Mestmäcker (Eds.), GWB, 4th ed., 2007, § 3 note 35; *Rittner/Dreher*, Europäisches und deutsches Wirtschaftsrecht, 3rd ed., 2008, § 15 note 39, § 17 note 62.

[11] See the legislative history, WuW 1990, 332, 345, 346; see also BGH WuW 2003, 56, 59 = WuW/E DE-R 984, 987 - Konditionenanpassung.

[12] BGH WuW 1993, 941, 944, 945 = WuW/E BGH 2875, 2878, 2879 – Herstellerleasing.

[13] Cf. *Dittrich*, WuW 2009, 1006, 1010; *Fuchs* in: Immenga/Mestmäcker (Eds.), GWB, 4th ed., 2007, § 3 Rn. 38.

medium-sized enterprise.[14] Others want to use absolute figures such as the thresholds of merger control as an indication, i.e. 10–25 million for a small enterprise.[15] In a recent court decision, the qualification as an SME was based on the fact that the undertaking generated significantly less than EUR 250 million sales.[16] The wide range shows that absolute numbers are not feasible. Also, Sec. 3 ARC intends to level competitive disadvantages but not to allow structural policy.

8.2.3 Cartel Enforcement

8.2.3.1 Prohibition

The prohibition of agreements restricting competition pursuant to Sec. 1 ARC applies to all undertakings, irrespective of size. In many cases, SMEs are participating together with larger companies in cartels fined by the FCO.[17] Fewer cases concerning cooperation among SMEs only ("Mittelstandskartelle") were investigated by the FCO in the past years.[18] As a general rule, the FCO refrains from initiating a proceeding if the agreement is of minor importance to competition within the meaning of its *de minimis* notice[19] (e.g., in horizontal cases the combined market share of the undertakings involved in an agreement does not exceed 10 % in any one of the relevant markets covered by the agreement and no hard-core restrictions are agreed upon).

8.2.3.2 Exemption

However, SMEs benefit from a special exemption governed by Sec. 3 ARC. Its significance is limited to national cases that do not affect trade between member states. The provision reads as follows:

> **§ 3 Cartels of Small or Medium-Sized Enterprises**
>
> (1) Agreements between competing undertakings and decisions by associations of undertakings, whose subject matter is the rationalization of economic activities through cooperation among enterprises, fulfil the conditions of § 2(1) if:

---

[14] *Nordemann*, Loewenheim (ed.)/Meessen/Riesenkampff, GWB, 2009, § 3 Rn. 15; *Dittrich*, WuW 2009, 1006, 1010.

[15] *Bechtold* (ed.), GWB, 7th ed., 2013, § 3 note 11.

[16] LG Nürnberg-Fürth, decision dated April 16, 2010, WuW 2010, 1272, 1275 = WuW/E DE-R 3078, 3081 – JPG "Le Male", obviously understood as a rebuttable presumption.

[17] See only press release dated 10 February 2011, http://www.bundeskartellamt.de/SharedDocs/Meldung/DE/Pressemitteilungen/2011/10_02_2011_Feuerwehrfahrzeuge.html and press release dated 10 August 2011, http://www.bundeskartellamt.de/SharedDocs/Meldung/DE/Pressemitteilungen/2011/10_08_2011_Betonrohre.html.

[18] New proceedings initiated by the FCO in 2005: 4, 2006: 4, 2007: 5, 2008: 3, 2009: 2, and 2010: 0; see activity reports of the Federal Cartel Office (Bundeskartellamt), Drcks. 16/5710, p. 230; Drcks. 16/13500, p. 184; Drcks. 17/6640, p. 164.

[19] Bundeskartellamt, Bagatellbekanntmachung, 2007, http://www.bundeskartellamt.de/SharedDocs/Publikation/DE/Bekanntmachungen/Bekanntmachung%20-%20Bagatellbekanntmachung.html?nn=3590970.

1. competition on the market is not significantly affected thereby, and
2. the agreement or the decision serves to improve the competitiveness of small or medium-sized enterprises.

Addressees of Sec. 3 ARC are small or medium-sized enterprises.[20] The legal form is not relevant. Cooperation may concern, *inter alia*, joint research and development, joint purchasing, production, logistics and joint advertising, or joint customer and repair service. Cooperation among large firms is not captured by Sec. 3 ARC. However, large firms may, under certain circumstances, be part of a cooperation exempted under Sec. 3 ARC,[21] e.g. if the purpose of the cooperation cannot be realised without the contribution of a large firm.[22]

The provision only applies to horizontal agreements between SMEs. Sec. 3 ARC is a legal fiction in nature. If all the conditions are met, the agreement is deemed to fulfil the conditions of the general exemption rule of Sec. 2 (1) ARC. As said above, Sec. 3 ARC constitutes a special, more favourable rule for SMEs. The provision aims at improving the competitiveness of SMEs and facilitating cooperation among them. It can be conceived as a "structural compensation" to SMEs.[23] Even if cooperation among SMEs is not exempted under Sec. 3 ARC, it can still be exempted under the general provision of Sec. 2 ARC applying to any undertaking, irrespective of size.

One major condition set out in Sec. 3 ARC requires that the subject matter of the cooperation is the rationalisation of economic activities, rationalisation meaning "measures which improve the ratio of the operational input for economic activities to the output (calculated per unit of production) for every participating SME".[24] Even hard-core restrictions such as the restriction of prices may be covered by the exemption.[25] However, the Higher Regional Court Düsseldorf stated that agreements regarding prices or price components are only exempted if they are closely linked to the aimed rationalisation.[26]

Another prerequisite of Sec. 3 ARC is that the competition on the market is not significantly affected by the agreement. The FCO states that competition may be affected already in case of market shares between 10 and 15 % but acknowledges

[20] Addressees are also associations of SMEs, regarding so-called recommendations to SMEs (Mittelstandsempfehlungen) see *Fuchs*, Immenga/Mestmäcker (Eds.), GWB, 4th ed., 2007, § 3 note 28.

[21] BGH WuW/E 2321, 2325 – Mischguthersteller; BGH WuW/E DE-R 1087, 1090 – Ausrüstungsgegenstände für Löschfahrzüge.

[22] Bundeskartellamt, Information leaflet on cooperation possibilities for small and medium-sized enterprises, 2007, note 37.

[23] Cf. *Fuchs*, Immenga/Mestmäcker (Eds.), GWB, 4th ed., 2007, § 3 note 2, 3.

[24] Bundeskartellamt, Information leaflet on cooperation possibilities for small and medium-sized enterprises, 2007, note 28.

[25] Cf. *Fuchs*, Immenga/Mestmäcker (Eds.), GWB, 4th ed., 2007, § 3 note 50; *Rittner/Dreher*, Europäisches und deutsches Wirtschaftsrecht, 3rd ed., 2008, § 17 note 61.

[26] OLG Düsseldorf, decision dated June 20, 2007, WuW 2008, 70, 74 = WuW/E DE-R 2146, 2150 – Nord-KS/Xella.

that market shares may be above 15 % if less significant parameters than price, discounts, etc. are concerned.[27]

The once special exemption rule relating to purchasing cooperation was abandoned with the seventh amendment of the ARC in 2005. Today, the FCO considers purchasing agreements among SMEs to be likely exempted if the market shares are below a 15 % threshold.[28] The Regional Court Hannover—when dealing with a purchasing pool of SMEs—held that Sec. 3 ARC is most likely to be applicable if the market share is below 15 % since the purchasing pool had no market power.[29]

8.2.3.3 Assessment

Undertakings have to assess themselves whether the agreement in question is permitted under the antitrust laws (system of legal exception). Information leaflets issued by the cartel authorities may serve as guidance. The German Federal Cartel Office published a leaflet on cooperation between SMEs,[30] informing on the FCO's standpoint regarding the evaluation of SMEs. Also, the state cartel office of Bavaria issued a brochure on cooperation among SMEs.[31]

Until 30 June 2009, SMEs were entitled to a decision pursuant to Sec. 32 c ARC by the FCO, finding about the legality of the cooperation provided a substantial legal or economic interest was demonstrated. Today, SMEs may still approach the FCO informally and ask for a competitive assessment of the cooperation. In this case, it may make sense to provide a self-assessment. A decision pursuant to Sec. 32 c ARC is, in any case, up to the discretion of the FCO.

8.2.3.4 Sanctions, Leniency, Settlements, and Commitment Decisions for SMEs

No special rules for SMEs exist regarding sanctions, leniency, settlements, or commitments. We think that there is no need for a special treatment of SMEs because either the size does not matter—in case of leniency and commitments—or

[27] See Bundeskartellamt, Information leaflet on cooperation possibilities for small and medium-sized enterprises, 2007, note 35.

[28] Bundeskartellamt, Information leaflet on cooperation possibilities for small and medium-sized enterprises, 2007, note 38.

[29] LG Hannover, decision dated June 15, 2011, WRP 2012, 99.

[30] Bundeskartellamt, Information leaflet on cooperation possibilities for small and medium- sized enterprises (Merkblatt des Bundeskartellamts über Kooperationsmöglichkeiten für kleinere und mittlere Unternehmen), March 2007, available in English at FCO's website.

[31] Landeskartellbehörde Bayern, Information leaflet on Cooperation and Competition – a guide to SMEs (Kooperation und Wettbewerb – Ein Ratgeber für kleine und mittlere Unternehmen, 6th ed., 2006.

the rules already recognise the individual situation of the undertakings. The fining guidelines (foreseeing a multiplier based on the size of the firm),[32] the 10 % maximum fine,[33] as well as the possibility to invoke "inability to pay" all take into account the sales and economic ability of the undertaking. Furthermore, a recent decision by the Federal Court of Justice interpreting the 10 % maximum fine rule as an upper limit of the fining range and not as a cap (understanding of European law), followed by the new fining guidelines of the FCO, will likely lead to lower fines in the future for small companies that sell one product only.[34] The settlement before the FCO is an informal procedure; undertakings may be granted a reduction of up to 10 %. It is also conceivable that deferred payment is agreed upon.

8.2.4 Abuse

8.2.4.1 General Remarks

Apart from being infringers, SMEs can be victims of anticompetitive behaviour. German competition law—its rules relating to unilateral conduct being stricter than Article 102 TFEU—protects SMEs not only from abusive conduct by dominant undertakings but also from abusive conduct by undertakings with market power below dominance.

The eighth amendment of the ARC changed the systematic of the provisions relating to abusive behaviour. However, the legislator did not intend any substantive changes. Sec. 19 ARC now governs all behaviour by dominant undertakings.[35] Sec. 20 ARC concerns undertakings with relative market power in relation to small and medium-sized suppliers and purchasers and undertakings with superior market power in relation to competing of small and medium-sized undertakings. In case Sec. 20 ARC is infringed, SMEs may claim remediation (e.g., supply), an order to refrain, or even damages (see Sec. 33 (1), (3) ARC).

8.2.4.2 Sec. 20 (1) ARC

Section 20 (1) ARC, in connection with Sec. 19 (1) in connection with (2) No. 1, protects SMEs being economically dependent on larger companies with relative market power, e.g. retailers in relation to brand manufacturers, retailers in relation to warehouses, suppliers in relation to final production companies such as car manufacturers. Prohibited are discriminatory practices and unfair hindrance. The

---

[32] See fining guidelines by the FCO, http://www.bundeskartellamt.de/wDeutsch/download/pdf/Merkblaetter/Merkblaetter_deutsch/Bekanntmachung-_Bu__geldleitlinien-Juni_2013.pdf.

[33] Sec. 81 (4) ARC.

[34] BGH, decision dated 26 February 2013, WuW 2013, 609 = WuW/E DE-R 3861 - Grauzementkartell; commented by *Meinhold-Heerlein/Engelhoven*, EWiR 2013, 349, 350. SMEs with one product often reach 10 %, unlike larger companies with multiple products.

[35] Please note that the eighth amendment lifted the presumption for dominance in Sec. 19 (4) ARC from previously one-third to 40 % market shares.

concept of relative dominance means alleviation for SMEs, especially in civil matters, as they do not have to prove dominance.

Relative dominance is legally defined in Sec. 20 (1) 1 ARC aiming at undertakings "insofar as small or medium-sized enterprises as suppliers or purchasers of certain kinds of goods or commercial services depend on them in such a way that sufficient and reasonable possibilities of resorting to other undertakings do not exist (relative dominance)". Furthermore, Sec. 20 (1) 2 ARC foresees a presumption that "a supplier of a certain kind of goods or commercial services shall be presumed to depend on a purchaser within the meaning of sentence 1 if this purchaser regularly obtains from this supplier, in addition to discounts customary in the trade or other remuneration, special benefits which are not granted to similar purchasers".

Whether *sufficient* possibilities within the meaning of sentence 1 exist has to be assessed from an objective point of view. The mere fact that a number of competitors are active on the market does not in itself equal sufficient possibilities.[36] The question is whether substitution of the products or services offered by the undertaking with relative market power entails competitive disadvantages or not.[37] In order to find out whether *reasonable* possibilities exist, the individual situation of the SME has to be taken into account.

Several categories of economic dependence can be distinguished. First, an undertaking may be dependent on a range of products or one specific brand in a way that it would have to fear losing customers if these products are not part of its offer (sortimentsbedingte Abhängigkeit/product-line-induced dependence). Second, the dependence can arise from a business decision to closely link the business to the products of another company (unternehmensbedingte Abhängigkeit/business-induced dependence). Third, dependence may result from a situation of shortage, e.g. in the event of war or strike (mangelbedingte Abhängigkeit/shortage-induced dependence). Fourth, dependence may follow from the decision of a supplier to concentrate on few or only one buyer (nachfragebedingte Abhängigkeit/demand-induced dependence).[38]

Most relevant in the context of Sec. 20 (1) ARC are the cases of product-line-induced dependence.[39] Whether dependence on a product line or specific brand is

---

[36] See BGH WuW 1976, 249, 251 = WuW/E BGH 1391, 1393 – Rossignol.

[37] *Markert*, Immenga/Mestmäcker (Ed.), GWB, 4th ed., 2007, § 20 note 51.

[38] For example, in the food sector, see KG WuW 1987, 531 = WuW/E OLG 3917 – Coop/Wandmaker.

[39] See BGH WuW 1976, 249 = WuW/E BGH 1391 – Rossignol; BGH WuW 1976, 777 = WuW/E BGH 1429 – Asbach-Fachgroßhändlervertrag; BGH WuW 1979, 772 = WuW/E BGH 1620 – Revell Plastics; BGH WuW 1980, 127 = WuW/E BGH 1629 – Modellbauartikel II; BGH WuW 1980, 133 = WuW/E BGH 1635 – Plaza SB-Warenhaus; BGH WuW 1980, 415 = WuW/E BGH 1671 – robbe-Modellsport; BGH WuW 1982, 458 = WuW/E BGH 1885, 1886 – adidas; BGH WuW 1981, 722, 725 = WuW/E BGH 1814, 1817 – Allkauf-Saba; BGHZ 81, 322, 329, 331 – Original-VW-Ersatzteile; BGH WuW/E DE-R 481, 482 – Designer-Polstermöbel.

given has to be assessed taking into account the position and the prestige of the product on the market. The latter is made up of price, quality, and advertisement.[40] High market shares may be an indication for economic dependence; however, they are not a prerequisite.[41]

Dependence was found with regard to a sport shop on the delivery of Rossignol skis, although the market share of Rossignol skis was only 8 % and the sales with Rossignol skis made up only DM 100,000 of the sport shop's total turnover in the amount of DM 3 million.[42] Dependence was also found in the famous spirit brand Asbach Uralt, which was said to be a prerequisite for competitiveness (Konkurrenzvoraussetzung) for a wholesaler of spirits.[43] Another example is the delivery of original spare parts, on which repair shops are dependent.[44]

In a recent case,[45] the Regional Court Nürnberg denied economic dependence with regard to a parfum shop requesting supply of parfums of JPG brand from a manufacturer of various beauty products. The court denied both dependence due to a leading position (Spitzenstellungsabhängigkeit), in which case the retailer must stock a particular brand in order to be competitive, as well as dependence due to a leading group (Spitzengruppenabhängigkeit), in which case the retailer must stock a certain range of recognised brands in order to be competitive, whereas the stocking of one particular brand is not required.

The court based its decision on the facts that the supplier's market shares between 4 and 5 % on the market for male fragrance are not to be considered as high and that the buyer was able to make gains even without the product in question, although the overall market was stagnating. Lastly, sales with JPG Le Male products only stood for about 1 % of the parfum shop's total turnover. In general, the Regional Court Nürnberg stated that dependence due to a leading group depends on the market shares (5–10 % may suffice) and the selection of goods by comparable purchasers.

8.2.4.3 Sec. 20 (2) ARC

Section 20 (2), in connection with Sec. 19 (1) in connection with (2) No. 5 ARC, pursuant to which an undertaking with relative market power shall not use its market position to invite or to cause other undertakings to grant advantages without any objective justification (so-called passive discrimination), is seldom applied.

[40] LG Nürnberg-Fürth, decision dated April 16, 2010, WuW 2010, 1272, 1276 = WuW/E DE-R 3078, 3082 – JPG "Le Male".

[41] LG Nürnberg-Fürth, decision dated April 16, 2010, WuW 2010, 1272, 1276 = WuW/E DE-R 3078, 3082 – JPG "Le Male".

[42] BGH WuW 1976, 249 = WuW/E BGH 1391 – Rossignol.

[43] BGH WuW 1976, 777, 778, 779 = WuW/E BGH 1429, 1430, 1431 – Asbach-Fachgroßhändlervertrag.

[44] BGH WuW 1999, 1111 = WuW/E DE-R 357 – Feuerwehrgeräte.

[45] LG Nürnberg-Fürth, decision dated April 16, 2010, WuW 2010, 1272 = WuW/E DE-R 3078 – JPG "Le Male".

However, the FCO learned from the market that the provision has a signalling effect.[46]

8.2.4.4 Sec. 20 (3) and (4) ARC

While Sec. 20 (1) ARC prohibits unfair hindrance and discrimination by companies with relative vertical market power, Sec. 20 (3) ARC prohibits unfair hindrance by companies with superior market power towards their competitors (horizontal relationship). Section 20 (3) ARC intends the protection of SMEs from being squeezed out of the market and thereby safeguarding variety on the market.[47] Section 20 (3) No. 1–3 ARC prohibits certain competition practices, such as an offer below cost price and margin squeeze. Section 20 (4) ARC contains a reversal of the burden of proof.

8.2.5 Merger Control

The provisions of the ARC relating to merger control do not explicitly mention SMEs. However, a number of provisions take the interests of SMEs into account. For example, the Third Act to Alleviate the Burdens for SMEs added a second domestic turnover threshold to Sec. 35 (1) No. 2 ARC in order to reduce the cases subject to German merger control.[48]

Furthermore, Sec. 35 (2) ARC contains a so-called affiliation clause (Anschlussklausel), providing that notification is not required if one party to the merger achieved less than EUR 10 million turnover. This provision now also applies to the press sector. Besides, the situation of the press sector—mostly SMEs—was improved by no longer taking into account the 20-fold amount of the turnover when calculating the threshold for notification but only the eighth-fold amount of the turnover; see Sec. 38 (3) ARC. Consequently, fewer mergers between press undertakings will be subject to German merger control in the future.

Section 36 (1) No. 2 ARC (Bagatellmarktklausel) concerns *de minimis* markets and sets out that a proposed merger must not be prohibited if the relevant market in existence for at least 5 years had a total sales volume of less than EUR 15 million in the last calendar year.

---

[46] *Mundt*, in: FIW, Heft 239, Mittelstand im globalen Wettbewerb, 2012, p. 3, 8.

[47] *Mundt*, FIW, Heft 239, Mittelstand im globalen Wettbewerb, 2012, pp. 3, 9.

[48] Sec. 35 (1) ARC reads as follows: "Scope of Application of the Control of Concentrations

(1) The provisions on the control of concentrations shall apply if in the last business year preceding the concentration:

1. the combined aggregate worldwide turnover of all the undertakings concerned was more than EUR 500 million, and

2. the domestic turnover of at least one undertaking concerned was more than EUR 25 million and that of another undertaking concerned was more than EUR 5 million."

8.2.6 Certain Sectors of the Economy

The fifth chapter of the ARC includes specific rules for certain sectors of the economy. Especially, Sec. 28 ARC (agriculture) and 30 ARC (newspaper and magazines) mostly concern SMEs. Nonetheless, the rules apply to all businesses irrespective of size insofar as they are active in the relevant sector.

8.2.7 Procedural Rules

German competition law recognises the fact that, typically, SMEs may hesitate to file a complaint with the NCA because they fear to lose their business partner, on whom they are economically dependent.

Therefore, Sec. 54 ARC allows the NCA to initiate a proceeding *ex officio* at the complainant's request in order not to reveal the identity of the complainant. In such case, the burden of proof is alleviated pursuant to Sec. 70 (4) ARC insofar as the NCA has to substantiate factual aspects only in case the request for information is challenged by the alleged infringer. At this stage, i.e. only with regard to the request for information proceeding, the NCA is exempted from substantiating the economic dependence of SMEs within the meaning of Sec. 20 ARC; the alleviation does, however, not apply in the main proceeding.[49] Furthermore, in 2012, the FCO installed a website where anonymous complaints can be submitted.[50]

8.2.8 Private Enforcement

According to Sec. 33 (3) ARC, victims of anticompetitive conduct can claim damages. Damages may arise on different levels of the market chain. Direct purchasers of goods or services from cartel members may be able to increase prices and pass on damages to the next level. In a landmark decision, the German Federal Court of Justice held that indirect purchasers—for example, SMEs that acquired goods from wholesalers at overcharged prices—are entitled to claim damages directly from the members of the cartel.[51] At the same time, direct customers are not prevented from bringing an action even if they resold the goods or services onto further downstream markets. However, the infringer may raise a passing-on defence, for which he carries the burden of proof. That means that the infringer can defend himself by proving that the direct purchaser passed on the overcharge to the indirect purchaser. In order to avoid multiple liabilities, the infringer shall, in

[49] See *Schmidt*, Immenga/Mestmäcker, (Eds.), GWB, 4th ed., 2007, § 70 note 16; *Bechtold* (ed.), 7th ed., GWB, 2013, § 70 note 11.

[50] See https://www.bkms-system.net/bkwebanon/report/clientInfo?cin=2bkarta151&language=ger.

[51] BGH, decision dated June 28, 2011, WuW 2012, 57 = WuW/E DE-R 3431 - ORWI.

the court's opinion, make use of the procedural third party notice vis-à-vis all purchasers.

The burden of proof regarding the causation and the amount of the damages lies with the victim who claims damages. The standard of proof is the same for the direct and indirect customers. Nevertheless, indirect purchasers may face more practical problems due to information deficiencies resulting from their likely position on a remote level in the market chain.

Follow-on actions benefit from the provision in Sec. 33 (4) ARC, pursuant to which the finding of infringement by the commission or a national competition authority is binding. Direct and indirect purchasers are confronted with the difficulty to demonstrate the overcharge. Section 33 (3) ARC refers to Sec. 287 Code of Civil Procedure, enabling the judge to estimate the amount of damage. The party that has not prevailed in the dispute has to bear the costs of the legal dispute (Sec. 91 Code of Civil Procedure).

In this context, third-party access to documents is crucial. The rules apply to SMEs and other firms without distinction. Neither size nor legal form requires any special rights.

In principle, claimants for damages can demand access pursuant to Sec. 406e of the German Code of Criminal Procedure. However, access can be denied under certain circumstances. With regard to leniency applications, German courts have been restrictive and denied access in two recent cases. Following the Pfleiderer decision by the ECJ, the national courts have to weigh on a case-by case basis the respective interests in favour of disclosure of the information and in favour of the protection of the information provided voluntarily by the applicant for leniency.[52]

After the referral decision of the ECJ, the local court Bonn[53] denied Pfleiderer access to the leniency applications of the participants in the decor paper cartel on the grounds of jeopardising the purpose of the investigation; see Sec. 406e (2) of the German Code of Criminal Procedure. The court argued that potential infringers may be prevented from filing leniency applications, if access is granted. The court therefore found that the interests of effective cartel prosecution prevail.

The Higher Regional Court Düsseldorf also denied third-party access to the leniency applications in a case concerning a cartel agreement between coffee roasters. The court held that the claimant's interests in the case were satisfied by granting access to the prohibition decision only.[54]

[52] ECJ, case C-360/09, *Pfleiderer AG v Bundeskartellamt*, ECR 2011 I-5161 = WuW/E EU-R 1976 = WuW 2011, 769 – Pfleiderer.

[53] LG Bonn, decision dated January 18, 2012, WuW 2012, 275 = WuW/E DE-R 3497 – Pfleiderer II.

[54] OLG Düsseldorf, decision dated August 22, 2012, WuW 2012, 962 = WuW/E De-R 3662 – Kafferöster; commented by *Meinhold-Heerlein/Engelhoven*, EWiR 2013, 29.

8.2.9 Third Party Actions

Section 33(2) No. 1 ARC allows industrial associations to bring an action for remediation or an order to refrain in front of civil courts. It is not required that one of their members is affected by the anticompetitive conduct. This right was already included in the original version of the ARC from 1957. It was however never used much.[55] The eighth amendment of the ARC expanded that right to consumer organisations; see Sec 33 (2) No. 2.

No special rules exist relating to collective redress. However, several lawsuits are pending, where the claimant is a company called Cartel Damages Claims that bundled claims of multiple alleged victims.[56]

Conclusions

German competition law takes the interests of SMEs into account. As regards public enforcement and SMEs as infringers, their situation is considered at several levels, from the evaluation of the infringement to the fining. As victims, SMEs are protected from abusive behaviour to a wider extent than under European Law. Finally, procedural rules in favour of SMEs secure the enforcement of rights. Therefore, there is no need for a special regime for SMEs. Also with regard to merger control, the interests of SMEs seem to be addressed.

Concerning private enforcement, SMEs face difficulties of proof due to information deficiencies resulting from their likely position on a remote level in the market chain. Collective redress is often said to be the solution. However, while collective redress may help to bring more cases of scattered damages to court, the main obstacle still lies in the burden of proof.[57]

---

[55] Cf. e.g. *Kling/Thomas*, Kartellrecht, 2007, § 21 note 33; *Rehbinder*, Loewenheim (Ed.)/ Meessen/Riesenkampf, Kartellrecht, 2nd ed., 2009, § 33 note 5; *Rittner/Dreher*, Europäisches und deutsches Wirtschaftsrecht, 3rd ed., 2008, § 23 note 135 and 144.

[56] See the overview on the website of Cartel Damage Claims, http://www.carteldamageclaims.com/Cases.shtml. The bundling model of CDC was declined by the LG Düsseldorf on legal grounds, see LG Düsseldorf, WuW 2014, 183 = WuW/E DE-R 4087-Zementkartell II.

[57] In its new initiative regarding collective redress, the commission recommends the member states to foresee collective redress also in competition cases, see COM (2013) 401, p. 4; in addition, the commission intends to remove existing obstacles to a successful private enforcement with its proposal for a directive on certain rules governing actions for damages; see http://ec.europa.eu/competition/antitrust/actionsdamages/proposal_directive_en.pdf.

Hungary

9

Álmos Papp, Kinga Bölcskei, Gábor Fejes, Zoltán Hegymegi Barakonyi, Márton Horányi, Márton Kocsis, Zoltán Marosi, Tamás Riba, Pál Szilágyi, and Péter Virág

9.1 SMEs in Context

9.1.1 SMEs' Economic Context and Legal Definition

9.1.1.1 Legal Definitions of SMEs

The Hungarian competition legislation does not provide for any specific legal definition for SMEs. As a matter of general level, Act XXXIV of 2004 on the Definition of, and Aids to, Small and Medium-sized Enterprises substantially transposes into the Hungarian legislation the principles set forth in Commission Recommendation 96/280 on the definition of small and medium-sized enterprises

Álmos Papp: Coordinator of the working group; Márton Kocsis: This contribution expresses the personal views of the authors and under no circumstances can be treated as the official opinion of the Hungarian Competition Office; Péter Virág: This contribution expresses the personal views of the authors and under no circumstances can be treated as the official opinion of the Hungarian Competition Office.

Á. Papp (✉) • K. Bölcskei
Bán, S. Szabó & Partners, Budapest, Hungary
e-mail: apapp@bansszabo.hu

G. Fejes • M. Kocsis • Z. Marosi
Oppenheim, Budapest, Hungary

Z.H. Barakonyi • M. Horányi
Baker & McKenzie, Budapest, Hungary

T. Riba
Bozzay & Partners Law Office, Budapest, Hungary

P. Szilágyi
Pázmány Péter Catholic University, Budapest, Hungary

P. Virág
Hungarian Competition Authority, Budapest, Hungary

P. Këllezi et al. (eds.), *Antitrust for Small and Middle Size Undertakings and Image Protection from Non-Competitors*, LIDC Contributions on Antitrust Law, Intellectual Property and Unfair Competition, DOI 10.1007/978-3-642-54000-4_9, © Springer-Verlag Berlin Heidelberg 2014

and Commission Recommendation 2003/361 on the definition of micro, small, and medium-sized enterprises.

9.1.1.2 The Economic Perspective

SMEs play an important role in the Hungarian economy as 99.9 % of the Hungarian undertakings qualify as SMEs (based on the definition set forth in Commission Recommendation 96/280 and Commission Recommendation 2003/361). SMEs employ nearly 71 % of the total employees in Hungary and, in aggregate, account for 55 % of the total Hungarian GDP.[1]

9.1.1.3 Relevant Cases

No statistics are available in Hungary regarding court decisions of cases initiated directly before courts (i.e., enforcement of damage claims). Public access is available only to anonymous judgments selected by the courts on the basis of their importance and/or unique features. Therefore, we will provide under Annex 1 the excerpts of some of the recent cases conducted by the Hungarian Competition Authority (*Gazdasági Versenyhivatal*, hereafter referred to as "HCA") against SMEs.

The excerpts demonstrate that the HCA, in principle, does not take the economic dimension of the SMEs into account as a general mitigating circumstance of the infringements. Nevertheless, the financial situation and/or the low market shares of the SMEs and, in some particular cases, the economic difficulties of the industry in which they are engaged were taken into consideration by the HCA as reasons justifying lower fines.

9.1.2 Specific Treatment of SMEs Under Competition Law

There are no specific substantive rules for SMEs under the Hungarian competition law. The substantive competition rules are also applied uniformly to SMEs and to larger undertakings.

Nonetheless, the market share and market power of an undertaking are important factors that influence the application of the substantive rules of competition law. Therefore, the fact that SMEs are small-sized undertakings with typically low market shares leads to certain practical considerations regarding the impact of the competition rules on the behaviour of SMEs.

The HCA has not issued programmes or policies specifically for SMEs that are available in Hungary.

Also, no specific administrative rules apply to SMEs.[2] As far as the substantive rules are concerned, we believe that appropriately designed *de minimis* rules would sufficiently address the issue.[3]

---

[1] SBA Fact Sheet Hungary 2010–2011, available at http://ec.europa.eu/enterprise/policies/sme/facts-figures-analysis/performance-review/files/countries-sheets/2010-2011/hungary_en.pdf.

[2] Please see the detailed description under Sect. 9.2.1.

[3] Act LVII of 1996 on the Prohibition of Unfair Trading Practices and Unfair Competition, Section 13.

9.1.3 The Standing of Trade Associations

Trade associations have the same rights as other persons, who become aware of an anticompetitive behaviour. They are entitled to file a notification or a complaint with the HCA as described in detail in Sect. 9.2.2.2 of this Report. Accordingly, there is no need to create special legal institutions, as *actio popularis*, to act against anticompetitive conduct as anyone is entitled to initiate an investigation with regard to the alleged anticompetitive behaviour. Consequently, there is no specific role of the trade association in connection with SMEs.

9.1.4 Policy Recommendations

As later described, we are of the opinion that maintaining the absolute prohibition of hard-core horizontal infringements (meaning that the prohibition applies irrespective of size/market share) is important. However, we could imagine the HCA to *express its intent* not to investigate arrangements between SMEs due to the lack of public interest in such investigations. This would allow the Competition Authority to set enforcement priorities and allocate its scarce resources to investigations with a greater market impact.

9.2 Public Antitrust Enforcement and SMEs

9.2.1 Substantive and Procedural Rules Applicable to SMEs

9.2.1.1 Substantive Rules

The general rules of the Competition Act[4] apply without any specific difference to the SMEs. These general rules are applied uniformly irrespective of the size of the undertakings concerned. This is true both for the substantive prohibitions contained in the Competition Act (prohibition of restrictive agreements and the abuse of a dominant position) and also for the (substantive) rules governing fines.

Notwithstanding the above, there are some sensible considerations, primarily related to the size and market position or power of the SMEs, that in practice substantiates different application of the competition rules in relation to SMEs.

First, although the size of an undertaking is unrelated to its market share, SMEs typically have negligible market shares. This means, on the one hand, that most SMEs are unlikely to hold a dominant position within the meaning of Section 22 of the Competition Act and therefore the prohibition of an abuse of a dominant position[5] does not bear much relevance for most SMEs (even though there are

[4] Act LVII of 1996 on the Prohibition of Unfair and Restrictive Market Practices.

[5] Section 21 of the Competition Act.

some atypical precedents—such as in the case of funeral services[6]—where the Competition Office established that an SME was in a dominant position). On the other hand, given the typically small market share of SMEs, most agreements between SMEs would fall under the *de minimis* rules laid down in Section 13 of the Competition Act. The safe harbour contained in Section 13 applies—with the exception of horizontal price-fixing and market-sharing agreements—if the joint market share of the parties to the agreement does not exceed 10 % on the relevant market.

Second, the size of the undertaking concerned may also influence the amount of the fine imposed in case of infringement. This is so for two reasons.

On the one hand, Section 78(3) of the Competition Act and also the Notice on fines of the Competition Authority[7] expressly mention the market position (market share) of the undertaking concerned as a factor to be taken into account when establishing the amount of the fine. Infringements by undertakings with high market shares and strong market power will likely result in a more serious impact on competition, and therefore in higher fines. As discussed above, SMEs typically have lower market shares. Therefore, in case of an infringement by an SME, the market impact of the infringement is unlikely to warrant a higher fine.

Moreover, the size of the group of undertaking(s) concerned also influences the maximum fine the Competition Authority may impose. Pursuant to Section 78(1) of the Competition Act, the maximum amount of the fine is capped in 10 % of the turnover of the undertaking concerned. However, if the Competition Authority identifies the group of undertakings to which the company committing the infringement belongs, the turnover of the whole group is taken into account for the application of the 10 % cap. This may significantly increase the maximum amount of the fine that the Competition Authority can impose. SMEs, however, do not belong by definition to large groups with significant turnover. This means that in the case of SMEs, there is no risk that the Competition Authority would impose in the pursuit of deterrence a significantly higher fine that is to reflect the high turnover realised by group companies other than the company involved in the infringement.

9.2.1.2 Procedural Aspects

Legally speaking, within the meaning of Hungarian administrative procedural law,[8] undertakings are all clients before the HCA, who are to be treated equally. As a result, small and large firms enjoy the same procedural rights and obligations in such procedures. We are also not aware of a case where the HCA would have

[6] See cases Vj-118/2004, Vj-136/2002, Vj-108/2001, Vj-153/2010, Vj-219/2000, Vj-10/2000, Vj-174/1999.

[7] Notice no 1/2012 of the president of the Hungarian Competition Authority and the chair of the Competition Council of the Hungarian Competition Authority on the method of the setting of fines, available at http://www.gvh.hu/domain2/files/modules/module25/19939E3741DB36983.pdf).

[8] Act CXL of 2004 on the General Rules of Administrative Proceedings and Services.

treated SMEs and large undertakings differently from the perspective of their procedural rights.

The situation is the same in case of judicial proceedings: there are no differences in the legal treatment of SMEs and larger undertakings.

The only aspect where a difference may be found is the way in which the maximum level of the procedural fines is set in the Competition Act. Under Section 61(3) of the Competition Act, the HCA may impose a procedural fine of up to 1 % of the net turnover of the given undertaking, while in case of a delay in a procedural obligation, the HCA may impose a fine of up to 1 % of the daily ratio of the annual net turnover of the given undertaking for any day of delay. In such a case, the maximum is clearly higher for larger undertakings and lower for SMEs.

For private antitrust litigation, the procedural rules for claims based on civil law are applicable. There are no rules that would make it more difficult to litigate antitrust claims than any other claim based on civil law. However, in practice, Hungarian civil procedural law is not well suited for antitrust claims. There are no rules in antitrust cases that would help the collection of evidence (e.g., discovery), and the burden of proof is completely on the plaintiff in stand-alone actions, except for the enforcement of damage claims, which is facilitated by a presumption that a hard-core cartel results in damages of 10 % of the contract price offered by the infringer.[9]

9.2.1.3 Safe Harbours for SMEs

There are no specific safe harbours in relation to SMEs. The *de minimis* rules of the Competition Act would apply to agreements entered into between SMEs, with the exception of horizontal price fixing and market sharing.

Contrary to the European Commission's *de minimis* Notice, under the *de minimis* rules of the Competition Act all types of vertical restrictions, including vertical price fixing and market sharing, may benefit from the *de minimis* safe harbour, as only hard-core horizontal agreements are excluded from this benefit. As EU competition law is unlikely to apply to the behaviour of SMEs active on local markets, this is an important difference between EU and Hungarian competition law, as it allows SMEs to apply vertical price-fixing arrangements.[10]

However, the Hungarian *de minimis* exemption poses certain interpretation issues.[11]

The issue is that the Hungarian rules set the same market share threshold and calculation method for *vertical* and *horizontal* agreements. This simpler approach poses not much interpretation problem when applied to agreements among

[9] See Sect. 9.3.1.

[10] For instance, in the agricultural sector.

[11] The rule literally reads as follows: "an agreement is deemed to fall outside of the application of the competition if it is of minor importance. The agreement is deemed to be of minor importance if the aggregate market share held by the parties to the agreement (together with their related parties) is less than 10 % on the relevant market, unless the agreement is aimed at fixing prices and/or market partitioning among competitors".

competitors; it is quite easy and obvious to aggregate market shares of the competitors on the same horizontal market. However, it has significant drawback when we try to measure the potential *de minimis* exemption of a vertical agreement. Not surprisingly, it is difficult to calculate aggregate market share of the supplier and its reseller in the absence of a horizontally affected market where they simultaneously operate. This manifest uncertainty in the practical application of the *de minimis* exemption in vertical cases poses major difficulties primarily for SMEs as usually they fit in the definition of the *de minimis* rules.

In addition, we note that under EU competition law, there is "safe harbour" for most SMEs under the so-called NAAT ("no appreciable affectation of trade") rule. Pursuant to the Commission's Guidelines on the effect on trade concept,[12] agreements are in principle not capable of appreciably affecting trade between Member States (and therefore EU competition law is not applicable to them) if two cumulative conditions are met:

(a) the aggregate market share of the parties on any relevant market within the Community affected by the agreement does not exceed 5 %; and
(b) in case of *horizontal agreements*, the aggregate annual Community turnover of the undertakings concerned in the products covered by the agreement does not exceed EUR 40 million or, in case of *vertical agreements*, the aggregate annual Community turnover of the supplier in the products covered by the agreement does not exceed EUR 40 million.

If the above two cumulative conditions are met, EU competition law does not apply to the agreement due to the absence of an appreciable effect on trade between Member States. This is so even if the agreement contains hard-core restrictions such as price fixing and/or market sharing.

However, it has to be mentioned that the NAAT rule is not a true safe harbour that would directly acknowledge that certain anticompetitive conducts, due to their limited size and effects, are automatically exempted from the general cartel prohibition. Rather, the NAAT rule delineates the boundaries of the application and scope of the Community competition rules. Accordingly, it seems to be impossible to set a similar rule in the Hungarian competition law as it would interfere with the already existing *de minimis* rules.

Nevertheless, we have to mention the legal grounds along which the HCA opens an investigation as they, to some extent, resemble to the principles of the NAAT rule in the domestic competition law. Accordingly, under Hungarian law, the HCA has the right and duty to open an investigation (a) if it is likely that competition rules are infringed, (b) provided that the conduct falls within the competency of the HCA, and (c) so far as the protection of public interest requires so.

While this seems to be a pure procedural issue, it has certain substantive implications as potentially anticompetitive behaviour of SMEs, owing to their limited market impacts, may not be sufficient to give rise to any harm of public

[12] Commission Notice – Guidelines on the effect on trade concept contained in Articles 81 and 82 of the Treaty, OJ 2004C 101, p. 81, point 50*ff*.

interest, in the absence of which the HCA would and should not investigate. The assessment as to whether the protection of the public interest justifies the investigation in each given case is in the sole discretion of the HCA. It is sensible to presume that potentially anticompetitive market conducts of SMEs are presumably more likely to stay below the level that would endanger the public interest.

9.2.1.4 Access to Justice

As to the question regarding facilitated access to justice or remedies in case of SMEs as victims, see Sect. 9.2.2.1. In case of SMEs as infringers, we are of the view that "policing the markets" does not, and should not, justify SMEs (or any other undertaking) to engage in anticompetitive behaviour.

In our view, with due respect to the administrative law principle of equal treatment of clients, no difference should be made between SMEs and larger firms from a procedural perspective, with the exception of obviously necessary differences due to the different maximums of fines.

9.2.2 Fundamental Rights of SMEs as Infringers and Victims

9.2.2.1 Introduction

In our view, it is questionable as to what extent there is indeed a differentiation between legal entities and individuals within the framework of the rights encapsulated in the ECHR (or, respectively, the CFREU). For instance, under the practice of the European Court of Human Rights, the protection encapsulated in Article 8 of the ECHR (right to respect one's home) was applied in respect of undertakings.[13] In our view, there should be no difference in terms of the procedural rights enjoyed either by an undertaking or an individual in competition proceedings. It is to be noted in this respect that it would be difficult to argue that a wealthy individual exercising direct control over companies operating in several countries, which individual can thus be considered as an undertaking from the perspective of competition law, should be treated more favourably than a newly established local company operating a barber shop.

There are, however, under the Hungarian procedural rules some natural differences between an individual and a company: these include the obligation of the authority to inform an individual that legal aid could be available to it in proceedings, the possibility to use regional languages, the taking of different data for identification, and the possibility to act as a witness. These differences, however, are not in any way special to competition law proceedings but rather are issues being of general relevance to administrative procedure. The only rule that could be regarded as slightly special in this respect is the extent of the maximum procedural fine that can be imposed by the HCA on a natural person: here, the maximum is

---

[13] See also cases Colas Est v France (37971/97), Niemetz v Germany (13710/88), Funke v France (10828/84).

defined in a nominal value as opposed to undertakings, where the maximum is defined in a percentage of turnover.[14]

9.2.2.2 Notifications, Complaints

No special rules apply to SMEs with regard to notifications and complaints. Any person or undertaking that believes to become a victim of an anticompetitive behaviour or only becomes aware of such conduct has the right to file a notification or a complaint with the HCA and request that its identity remain undisclosed throughout the entire proceedings and in the potential follow-up litigation before the court. Notifications should be filed by way of a predefined form, available at the HCA website, while complaints can be submitted also by virtue of a simple letter or notice. However, in the latter case, the complainant has fewer rights in connection with the proceeding than a person who files a formal notification.[15] Accordingly, the complainant is neither entitled to be informed of the conducted investigation or the decisions of the HCA nor has the right to appeal if the HCA refuses to initiate a formal competition proceeding on the basis of the investigation introduced by the complaint, while the person who filed a formal notification has all these rights.

However, in both cases the HCA may request more data in connection with the notification or complaint and may conduct a hearing for the parties concerned. Nevertheless, it has no legal consequences if the requested party refuses to cooperate with the authority. The investigation introduced on the basis of a notification or complaint does not form part of the formal competition proceeding, and its costs are covered by the state, which may be a relief for SMEs when filing a notification or a complaint.

9.2.2.3 Specific Protection for SMEs Against Larger Undertakings

There are no specific rules protecting SMEs as competitors. SMEs may rely on the general rules of unfair competition and on the general competition law (antitrust) rules,[16] which are both contained in the Competition Act.

Notwithstanding the above, there are specific rules protecting, amongst others, SMEs as business partners. These are laid down, on the one hand, in Section 7 of the Trade Act,[17] which prohibits the abuse of significant market power (hereafter referred to as "SMP") by traders *vis-à-vis* suppliers, and in the Retailer-Supplier Act,[18] which protects the suppliers of agricultural and food products against a wide range of unfair practices by traders.

The Trade Act applies to relations between suppliers and traders. A supplier is any person who provides goods or services to a trader for the purpose of resale. A

---

[14] See Section 61(3) and (4) of the Competition Act.

[15] See Section 43/G-43/I of the Competition Act.

[16] See Sections 2–7 of the Competition Act.

[17] Act CLXIV of 2005 on Trade,

[18] Act XCV of 2009 on the prohibition of unfair distributor practices against the suppliers of agricultural and food products.

trader is a person engaged in trading activities (retail and/or wholesale). The SMP prohibitions of the Trade Act only apply to traders who are considered to hold significant market power *vis-à-vis* suppliers. Pursuant to Section 7(3)–(4) of the Trade Act, a trader is considered to possess significant market power *vis-à-vis* suppliers if its consolidated net group turnover (or in case of purchasing organizations, the members' aggregate) from trading activities exceeded HUF 100 billion (EUR 0.33 billion) in the previous business year or if the trader is in a unilaterally favourable bargaining position *vis-à-vis* suppliers (due to the structure of the market, barriers to entry, the market share of the trader, its financial strength, the scope of its trading network, the size of outlets, etc.). Section 7 of the Trade Act contains a general prohibition of the abuse of significant market power, what includes among other practices (1) unjustifiedly discriminating suppliers, (2) restricting suppliers' access to sales opportunities, (2) requesting unfair conditions from suppliers that are unilaterally favourable to traders, (4) unilaterally amending contractual terms to the detriment of suppliers, (5) using other unjustified and unfair conditions, such as MFN clauses, exclusivity requirements for promotions, or listing fees. With certain narrow exceptions, below cost selling is also considered to constitute an abuse of significant market power.

The prohibitions of the Trade Act are enforced by the Competition Authority under the procedural rules of the Competition Act. The Competition Authority may impose fines in case of violations. Similarly, as in the case of antitrust infringements, the 10 % cap applies for the maximum amount of the fine.

The Retailer-Supplier Act protects the interest of the suppliers of agricultural and food products. It prohibits traders, defined as any person who sells to end consumers products purchased directly or indirectly from the supplier or resells such products without transformation/processing, to enter into unfair distributor practices.

The Retailer-Supplier Act defines unfair distributor practices by providing a blacklist of prohibited conduct; the Act does not contain a general clause. The blacklist provided for in Section 3 of the Retailer- Supplier Act is similar to the exemplary list of prohibited conduct contained in Section 7 of the Trade Act, although the blacklist of the Retailer-Supplier Act is broader. The prohibitions of the Retailer-Supplier Act are enforced by the Central Agricultural Office,[19] which may impose an administrative fine on retailers violating the provisions of the Act. The maximum fine is HUF 500 million (EUR 1.67 million); in case of repeat infringements, this may be higher (minimum of 1.5 times the previous fine, maximum of two billion HUF) but in any case a maximum of 10 % of the trader's net turnover. The prohibitions of the Retailer -Supplier Act and the Trade Act show a considerable overlap. Therefore, in order to avoid conflicting and parallel decisions, the Retailer-Supplier Act provides that the Central Agricultural Office may not initiate proceedings, must suspend or terminate proceedings, and must even withdraw its decision if the Competition Office starts an investigation or

[19] *Nemzeti Élelmiszerlánc-biztonsági Hivatal.*

adopts a decision under the Trade Act. As of August 1, 2012, this "order in proceeding" has been amended.[20] According to the amended Section 1(4) of the Retailer-Supplier Act and Section 7 of the Trade Act, the HCA no longer enjoys a "leader" position in investigations conducted under the Trade Act before investigations carried out by the Central Agricultural Office, except abuse of dominance cases under the Competition Act. This practically indicates a change in the ranking between the proceeding authorities.

On the basis of the foregoing, we are of the view that the specific rules of the Trade Act and the Retailer-Supplier Act grant sufficient protection to SMEs as suppliers.

It should be noted that the Trade Act is not sector specific (although it is not applicable to health care services and certain metal trade activities); its provisions generally protect suppliers against traders with significant market power (who are mainly large retailers).

The Retailer-Supplier Act is sector specific; it only protects the suppliers of agricultural and food products against the unfair practices of traders (again, mainly large retailers, although the definition includes a broader range of market players, such as wholesalers).

As already mentioned above, SMEs acting as competitors of larger enterprises may seek protection under the general unfair competition rules and the general competition law prohibitions of the Competition Act.

9.2.2.4 Need for Improvement

The prohibitions of the Trade Act and the Retailer-Supplier Act show a considerable overlap. Given that two different authorities are responsible for their enforcement, there is a high risk of diverging interpretations of the same or similar prohibitions.

Moreover, given the rather vague wording of the legislation, it is also difficult to establish the exact content of the prohibitions. These uncertainties relating to the exact content of the applicable norms may undermine their efficiency, as market players may find it difficult to align their behaviour with the applicable rules. Moreover, if market players experience that they are randomly fined for their behaviour despite their commitment to comply with the applicable rules, the incentives to strictly follow the rules could be weakened.

9.2.2.5 Access to the File

Regarding access to files, no special rules apply to SMEs. The investigated undertakings have access to the files of the case only when the "preliminary opinion"[21] of the Competition Council[22] is prepared.

[20] Act No. LXXXIX of 2012 on the Amendment of the Retailer-Supplier Act.

[21] Similar to the Statement of Objections issued by the Commission of the EU.

[22] The ultimate decision-making body of the HCA.

However, it must be noted that if the complainant files a notification (as opposed to a simple complaint, see Sect. 9.2.2.2), it shall have access to the files[23] if the HCA decides to refuse the complaint and not to launch a formal investigation (the complainant may seek legal remedy against the refusal of the HCA). However, should the HCA decide to initiate the formal investigation against the complained undertaking based on the complaint, the complainant loses its right to access the file.

9.2.3 Leniency, Settlements, and Commitment Decisions for SMEs

No special rules apply to SMEs in the fields of settlements and commitment decisions. Furthermore, we are not aware of any cases where the large multinational enterprises applied for leniency and received full immunity from fines for disclosing the details of a restrictive arrangement, while heavy fines were imposed on SMEs for participating in the same cartel. To date, there is no indication that SMEs, due to their limited resources, are somewhat less efficient in putting together a complete leniency application, while larger companies with sufficient background are more prepared to do this.

However, as a matter of substantial help for undertakings that have fewer resources to employ professional outside counsel for the preparation of a full leniency application with all required details and attachments, the Hungarian Competition Act permits "marker" applications.[24] Marker application, in broad terms, is an incomplete leniency application that contains only the very basic information of a possible infringement: the name of the applicant, the known facts on the alleged infringement, and information on the evidence.

The HCA, after the receipt of the marker application, sets a deadline for the marker applicant to complete the marker application. Until the expiry of the deadline, the marker applicant reserves its position in the possible sequence of further lenience applications. The marker application thus primarily is in the benefit of undertakings that have fewer resources to come up with a complete leniency application within a relatively short period of time. However, it can be argued that SMEs, due to their limited size and simpler operating mechanisms, can react faster than large undertakings with complex decision-making competences and levels.

9.2.4 Sanctions: Different Penalties for Different Size?

No different sanctions or severity levels are specified in relation to SMEs under Hungarian competition law. However, the rules on setting the fines for

[23] Except to those the confidential treatment of which is granted by the HCA.

[24] Section 78/B of the Competition Act.

infringements indirectly permit the HCA to reflect the economic dimension of the SMEs in the level of the fine, as follows.

First, the HCA, in imposing fine for any competition infringement, is required to take into account *all* mitigating and aggravating circumstances of the given case. As already explained, Section 78(3) of the Competition Act and also the Notice on fines of the Competition Authority specifically mention the market position (market share) of the infringer as a factor to be taken into account when setting the amount of the fine. These considerations technically enable the HCA to treat SMEs differently and to take all the mitigating circumstances of the infringement if the violation is committed by SMEs. The rationale behind this concept is that infringements of SMEs, due to their limited size and resources and ultimately limited market power, are not capable of causing significant harm or market failure comparable to that of the infringements committed by large undertakings.

Second, as referenced earlier, Section 78(1) of the Hungarian Competition Act sets the ultimate ceiling of the fine to be imposed by the HCA for an infringement at 10 % of the net turnover of the group of undertaking to which the infringer belongs. In the course of the calculations, the same rule in the Hungarian Competition Act permits the HCA to take into consideration the group's foreign turnover, in addition to the Hungarian, especially if the proceeds from the infringement were realised predominantly by foreign members of the corporate group. As SMEs do not belong to large multinational groups, the limit of the fine to be imposed upon them is usually calculated on a smaller base amount, i.e. on the basis of a single company turnover, which predominantly originated from Hungary. This ultimately may lead to lower fines imposed on SMEs compared to those applied against the members of large multinational groups for similar infringements; however, regarding SMEs, it must be stated that the appropriate level of deterrence may be achieved through lower fines as well.

9.2.5 Policy Recommendations

We are of the opinion that for policy reasons, it would be inappropriate under national competition law to create an absolute *de minimis* exception from the prohibition of restrictive agreements covering hard-core horizontal market sharing and price fixing. However, it would be a major help from the legislator transposing the principles of the EU *de minimis* regulations into the Hungarian competition law so that different market share tests would apply to horizontal and vertical arrangements.

Nonetheless, while maintaining the absolute prohibition of hard-core horizontal infringements, irrespective of the size or the market share, it may be conceivable in the future for the HCA to *express its intent* not to investigate arrangements between SMEs or potential abuses by SMEs due to the lack of public interest in such investigations. This would allow the HCA to set enforcement priorities and allocate its scarce resources to investigations with a greater market impact. Potential victims of such anticompetitive practices that would then fall outside the scope of public antitrust enforcement (but would fall under the prohibition of restrictive agreements) would still be able to initiate private actions before civil courts.

9.3 Private Antitrust Enforcement and SMEs

9.3.1 Substantive Rules, Procedural Aspects for SMEs in Civil Suits

In private antitrust litigation, no special rules apply to SMEs. However, it must be noted that in 2009 the automatic presumption was introduced in the Competition Act,[25] according to which, unless otherwise proved, horizontal price-fixing and/or market-sharing arrangements, including fixing of sale or purchase quotas, are automatically implied to result in 10 % increase in the contract prices. This presumption is intended to facilitate the enforcement of cartel damage claims, whereas plaintiffs in civil lawsuits are released from the necessity of affirmatively proving the level of the damages they have suffered by virtue of the cartel. Therefore, the undertakings participating in the cartel (i.e., the defendants in the private enforcement litigation cases) are required to prove before the court that the contract prices would have been the same in the absence of the cartel arrangement. Undertakings that receive full immunity from the fines under the leniency rules may refuse to indemnify the injured parties as long as the final judgment can be enforced against other undertakings that participated in the same cartel. This latter conditional immunity from damage claims might primarily be in the interest of the SMEs and facilitate that SMEs more frequently apply for leniency as they are usually more vulnerable, and have lower liquidity, to withstand follow-up damage claims. Also, the legal presumption as to the amount of damages suffered as a result of a cartel might be in the interest of and prove to be a major help for SMEs in enforcing their damage claims.

9.3.2 Collective Redress

The HCA is authorised to file a "public petition" on behalf and in the interest of consumers that are (potential) victims of anticompetitive practices. However, this public petition is permitted only if the harmed consumers, as a distinct group, are easy to identify and if the HCA already initiated investigation upon the undertaking against whom the petition is filed. The court must suspend the litigation so long as the investigation of the HCA in the same matter is pending. If the HCA is able to prove to the requisite standard of proof the amount of the damage caused by the infringement to the affected consumers, the HCA may request the court to require the infringer to indemnify all consumers eligible for the indemnity, even if some of the consumers did not participate in the litigation. If the HCA fails to prove the

[25] See Section 88/C of the Competition Act.

exact amount of the damages, it may ask the court to conclude in its judgment that the infringement is committed. Thereafter, any consumer affected by the infringement is allowed to launch individual claim against the infringer where it has to prove only the level of damages it suffered. The HCA recently filed a successful "public petition" claim against some online real estate advertisement websites.[26]

As far as SMEs are concerned, no similar enforcement arrangement exists. Nevertheless, the Hungarian civil procedure permits that two or more plaintiffs launch a single lawsuit against a defendant if they have a joint claim or their claims originate from the same or closely connected legal basis. This rule technically makes it possible to launch collectively private enforcement claims by two or more injured parties against the same infringer, either as a follow-on litigation after the HCA concluded that the infringement is committed or as a stand-alone action. However, if the plaintiffs win the case, third parties who suffered damages from the same infringement will not be eligible to enforce their claims against the infringer.

Nevertheless, it must be noted that the Hungarian Parliament, in December 2009, adopted an amendment to Hungarian law in an attempt to introduce "class actions" in the field of competition law enforcement (Amendment no. T/11332). In particular, according to the amendment, any injured party had the possibility to launch a class action against an alleged infringer and simultaneously ask the court to require the infringer to indemnify all parties that suffered damages by virtue of the same infringement, regardless of whether they participated in the litigation or not. The amendment finally did not enter into force due to a veto by the President of the Republic of Hungary.

9.3.3 Policy Recommendations

We do not generally believe that the introduction of general protective mechanisms should be necessary in respect of the SMEs. In our view, "soft measures" such as the raising of competition law awareness by competition authorities and governmental organs are sufficient for this purpose. Nevertheless, if private enforcement of competition law by SMEs is regarded as a priority by a government, possible measures to enhance such enforcement actions could include:

- a waiver (or reduction) of stamp duties payable for statements of claim for SMEs,
- a waiver (or reduction) of expert fees payable during the court proceedings, or
- availability of legal aid/assistance to SMEs either by the government or by the bar association to provide free or reduced charge advice on such matters.

We would welcome an amendment of the Competition Act along the basic principles of the one explained in the foregoing that would create the true collective redress mechanism in the Hungarian law. However, we do not support that the

[26] The case is still pending before the Court of Appeal due to a legal remedy sought by the defendant.

collective redress, as a joint enforcement mechanism, should be designed exclusively to the SMEs, as in our view it should be available to everybody regardless of size and nature.

Further, as the Hungarian legislation currently does not authorise the chambers or other trade associations with any power to enforce collective redress claims on behalf or in the protection of SMEs, we would welcome the authorisation of the trade associations to launch "public petition" on substantially similar grounds in the interest and on behalf of their members, including SMEs.

9.4 Annex 1

VJ-26/2006, Navi-Gate Kft (agreement). The resale agreements of Navi-Gate Kft. and its navigation device distributors were found to infringe the Hungarian cartel prohibition rules. The challenged agreements fixed the retail prices of certain navigation tools and navigation software. Navi-Gate Kft. was ordered to pay a fine of HUF 43 million (approximately EUR 169,000). All the affected undertakings were Hungarian SMEs; however, they were considered by the HCA as significant players on the Hungarian market.

VJ-80/2006 (agreement). The HCA investigated the activities of Synergon Informatikai Rt., Humansoft Kft., Getronics Kft., KFKI Direkt Kft., Delta Elektronik Kft., ICON Számítástechnikai Zrt., Systrend Zrt. (all are Hungarian SMEs) on grounds of possible bid rigging infringement related to public procurements for the purchase of server, IT support, and other IT-related services by the Hungarian State Treasury and the Hungarian State Railways. The HCA terminated the proceeding without finding any infringement on the ground that the evidence obtained did not prove any violation.

VJ-81/2006 (agreement). The HCA concluded that the exclusivity provisions in the agreement of Kortex Mérnöki Iroda Kft. (Kortex, a Hungarian SME) and Olympus Hungária Kft. (Olympus) concluded with a major Hungarian hospital for the supply of various medical devices were in conflict with Article 11 of the Competition Act (the prohibition of agreements in restraint of trade). Kortex, as a result of the infringement, was ordered to pay a fine of HUF 77 million (approx. EUR 260 thousand). It is a particularly unique feature of the case that Olympus, the Hungarian member of the multinational Olympus electronic device manufacturer, received full immunity as a result of the acceptance of its leniency application filed against Kortex.

VJ-164/2006 (agreement). The HCA investigated Büki Ásványvíz- és Üdítőital Kereskedelmi Kft. ("BÜKI") on the ground of possible restrictive practices in conflict with Article 11 of Competition Act and Article 81 (current 101 TFEU) of the EC Treaty. BÜKI, the producer of a Hungarian energy drink under the brand "Bomba!", entered into substantially uniform supply agreements with hotels, restaurants, and cafes throughout the country (700 agreements), which fixed the resale price of the "Bomba!" drinks. The agreements also involved exclusivity provisions that prohibited the distribution of any competing energy drink by the resellers. The HCA finally concluded that BÜKI's agreements were not capable of substantially restricting the competition. The main reason underlying the HCA's conclusion was that BÜKI's distribution agreements, irrespective of their large number, were of relatively minor importance in view of the total volume of supply agreements entered into in the Hungarian HORECA sector. The HCA specifically referenced that the low market share of BÜKI (its market share on the energy drink market was between 2 % and 3 %) was far insufficient to confer any market power capable of restricting the competition to an appreciable extent.

VJ-166/2006 (agreement). The HCA imposed a fine in an aggregate amount of HUF 103 million (approx. EUR 350,000) on four Hungarian SMEs (MITAC International Corporation, LCP Systems Kft., HAMEX Zrt. and RRC Hungary Kft.,) that were manufacturing and distributing car navigation products. The undertakings fixed the retail prices of their vehicle navigation products between 2005 and 2006. Although not specifically referenced in the decision, the relatively low level of the fine, in aggregate, shows that the HCA took into consideration the size of the infringers as a mitigating factor.

VJ-57/2007 (agreement). The HCA imposed a total fine of 73 million HUF (approximately EUR 245,000) on several Hungarian SMEs engaged in the Hungarian bakery industry. According to the HCA, the undertakings, through the Hungarian Bakery Association, fixed the resale prices of the white bread products (and also coordinated to uniformly increase the prices). In addition, the members were found to share strategic information on their pricing policies. The undertakings were Hungarian SMEs; however, this characteristic was apparently ignored by the HCA when setting the fines.

Vj-157/2007 (abuse of dominant position). The HCA initiated an investigation against "N&P KEGYELET 2006" Temetkezési, Kereskedelmi és Szolgáltató Kft ("N&P Kft.") based on an alleged abuse of a dominant position on the local funeral services market by way of discriminating in prices for the same services based on the nationality of the deceased person. N&P Kft. offered commitments and undertook to refrain from its discriminatory pricing practices. As a result, the HCA terminated the case against N&P Kft. We note that there are a number of similar HCA decisions in respect of funeral service providers, which undertakings are generally treated by the HCA as holding a "natural" dominance on the local funeral markets surrounding the municipalities in the country. Nevertheless, all these market players are typically SMEs, which is an interesting example that in certain niche markets SMEs can indeed hold dominant positions.

VJ-29/2008 (agreement). The HCA established that seven taxi companies (all Hungarian SMEs) concluded restrictive agreements in order to exclude one of their major competitors, Rádió Taxi Kft from the market. The HCA found that the taxi companies had colluded in advance and agreed on the winners of the public procurements tenders and regular taxi services (i.e., bid rigging). The HCA also investigated the coordination of taxi fare increases in 2006. On the basis of the foregoing, the HCA imposed a total fine of HUF 34 million (approximately EUR 113,000) on the seven taxi companies, which is still a relatively low amount.

Vj-69/2008 Mill-cartel 1 (*agreement*). The HCA imposed a fine of HUF 2,3 billion (approximately EUR 8,4 million) in aggregate on 16 undertakings for illegal market-sharing arrangements on the Hungarian grain processing and mill markets between February 2005 and April 2008. In particular, the mills coordinated the prices of whole-grain products and also maintained territorial market sharing arrangements to protect each other's "home" market from any competition. The HCA took into consideration as a mitigating circumstance the particular economic situation of the given sector. Therefore, the fines were lower for those justified serious financial difficulties that would have led to inability to pay higher fines. In addition, the HCA allowed five infringers (Cerbona Zrt., Első Pesti Malom- és Sütıipari Zrt., Gyermely Zrt., Hajdúsági Gabonaipari Zrt., ABO MILL Zrt.) to pay the fines in instalments on the same grounds. However, all these measures were allowed by the HCA in view of the general financial difficulties of the Hungarian mill industry rather than on the basis of the general acceptance of the lower economic dimension of the SMEs.

Vj-134/2008 Mill-cartel 2 – (*agreement*). As a sequel to the previous case, the HCA investigated a number of Hungarian SMEs engaged in grain-processing activities based on potential market-sharing and horizontal price-fixing arrangements in respect of the Hungarian flour market. The investigation also covered the possible bid rigging related to the public procurement tenders issued by the Agricultural and Rural Development Agency for agricultural products. The HCA imposed a total fine of HUF 50 million (approx. EUR 166,000) on three undertakings (while released all other mills from the case). The HCA took into consideration as a mitigating circumstance the particular economic situation of the given sector and undertakings. However, just like in the foregoing case, all these preferential measures were approved by the HCA in view of the general financial difficulties of the Hungarian mill industry rather than the economic dimension of the SMEs.

Vj-60/2009 (*agreement*). The franchise agreements of GEKKO Garden Kft. (GEKKO, a Hungarian undertaking engaged in licensing special education techniques for children) were found by the HCA to be anticompetitive as they included vertical price-fixing and non-compete clauses between 2001 and 2008. Nevertheless, the HCA applied no fine against GEKKO on the ground of its rather insignificant market share.

Italy

10

Clare Zammit

10.1 Introduction

This Report provides an overview of the Italian small-medium enterprises scenario, including the most relevant legislation. Small-medium, and especially micro-, enterprises are a cornerstone of the Italian economy. In fact, according to some estimates for 2010[1], the Italian economy is characterised by an extremely high number of microenterprises, amounting to 94.5 % of enterprises in Italy. According to the European Commission's Fact Sheet on Italy, this does not seem to constitute a disadvantage for the Italian economy as a whole.

In 2010, the Italian Government adopted a series of measures to improve the business environment in Italy. More specifically, some of these measures included the establishment of the *Tavolo Permanente PMI*, which encompasses a number of professional organisations; local and regional authorities; chambers of commerce; the National Institute of Industrial Promotion; and national experts. This technical committee monitors and identifies the needs and critical aspects faced by small-medium enterprises. Moreover, fiscal incentives were also introduced in relation to the *reti di impresa* or companies' networks. This mechanism was launched by the Italian Government in order to provide incentives to companies and, specifically, SMEs, to cooperate, allowing them to carry out activities in common. Companies forming part of this network benefit from a tax deferral.[2]

[1] European Commission SBA Fact Sheet on Italy, available at http://ec.europa.eu/enterprise/policies/sme/facts-figures-analysis/performance-review/files/countries-sheets/2010-2011/italy_en.pdf. As acknowledged by the European Commission itself in relation to the 2010–2011 statistics on SMEs, the number of microenterprises in Italy exceeds the average number of the said enterprises in other EU Member States.

[2] A more detailed explanation of companies' networks will be provided in this report under the description of substantive rules.

C. Zammit (✉)
Independent Lawyer, Milan, Italy

P. Këllezi et al. (eds.), *Antitrust for Small and Middle Size Undertakings and Image Protection from Non-Competitors*, LIDC Contributions on Antitrust Law, Intellectual Property and Unfair Competition, DOI 10.1007/978-3-642-54000-4_10,

As will be seen, the legislative scenario of SMEs in Italy is a rather fragmented one, in that there are different laws that impact these types of enterprises in some way or another.

10.2 SMEs in Context

10.2.1 SMEs' Economic Context and Legal Definition

10.2.1.1 Legal Definitions of SMEs

It must be pointed out at the outset that the Italian legal system is characterised by an extensive amount of primary and secondary legislation affecting small-medium enterprises. The entire system is however extremely fragmented, and one does not find a single corpus of rules relating to these types of enterprises.

The concept of "small-medium enterprise" does not figure, either at Constitutional level or under the Italian Civil Code. The Italian Civil Code provides a generic definition of "trader",[3] and another provision distinguishes between the "small" trader ("piccolo" imprenditore) and the "not (so) small" trader ("non piccolo"), whereas the aforesaid Civil Code does not distinguish between "medium" and "large" enterprises.

One of the Italian laws that, though not defining small-medium enterprises, is closely related to these types of enterprises, and is worth mentioning, is the Law on Subcontracting in Manufacturing (hereafter referred to as "Subcontracting Law"),[4] which was enacted following intensive lobbying by associations of small-medium undertakings, who advocated specific regulation that would safeguard their contractual position *vis-à-vis* the large undertakings. In particular, the Subcontracting Law contains a provision on abuse of economic dependence, aiming at "safeguarding" small-medium undertakings in their commercial relationships with "larger market players". This law does not however define small-medium enterprises as such.

Although the Italian legislator has, over the years, attempted to provide a definition of small-medium enterprises,[5] reference will here be made to the more recent legislative definitions set forth under the Italian system.

One of the Italian laws that has sought to provide a definition of small-medium enterprises is the Ministerial Decree of 18th April, 2005 (hereafter referred to as "2005 Ministerial Decree").[6] The said Decree sets forth the criteria for

[3] Article 2082, Italian Civil Code, Codice civile, Libro V, Titolo II,, R.D. 16 marzo 1942, n. 262 Approvazione del testo del Codice Civile -*Gazzetta Ufficiale, n. 79 del 4 aprile 1942.*

[4] Law no. 192/1998, on the *Disciplina della subfornitura nelle attività produttive,* as subsequently amended by Law no. 57 of 5th March, 2001, Italian Official Gazette no. 143, 22 June1998.

[5] For an outline of the various definitions of SMEs under Italian laws, see Stefanelli M. A., (2011) Il Riconoscimento Normativo delle Piccole e Medie Imprese – Regole e realtà produttiva, CEDAM, Milano.

[6] Decreto del Ministero delle Attività Produttive 18 aprile 2005, Italian Official Gazette, 12 October 2005, no. 238.

identification of micro-, small, and medium enterprises, in accordance with Commission Recommendation 2003/361 concerning the definition of micro-, small and medium-sized enterprises, which superseded Commission Recommendation of 3 April 1996 concerning the definition of small and medium-sized enterprises (hereafter referred to as the "1996 Recommendation"). The 2005 Ministerial Decree provides criteria for determination of the dimension of a company for the purposes of granting of aid to production activities and applies to all enterprises of the production industry.

The 2005 Ministerial Decree contains both a generic definition of SMEs, wherein the general category of "small", "medium", and "micro" enterprises includes those enterprises that, first, have less than 250 employees and, second, have a total annual turnover not exceeding EUR 50 million or an annual balance sheet total not exceeding EUR 43 million.

The 2005 Ministerial Decree also however contains a specific definition of small enterprises, which includes enterprises having (1) less than 50 employees and (2) having an annual turnover or a total annual balance not exceeding EUR 10 million. Microenterprises include those enterprises having (1) less than 10 employees and (2) an annual turnover or an annual balance sheet total not exceeding EUR 2 million. As specifically provided by the 2005 Ministerial Decree, the aforesaid requisites (1) and (2) are cumulative. Therefore, for an enterprise within the production sector to fall within the purview of these definitions, it would have to satisfy both requisites.

It is worth pointing out that in Italy, the European Small Business Act[7] (hereafter referred to as "SBA"), which acknowledges the central role of SMEs in the European economy and, as known, sets forth ten best practices for the formulation and implementation of policy both at EU level and at Member State level, was implemented through the 2010 Presidential Directive.[8] Italy was among the first European countries that implemented the SBA through the 2010 Presidential Directive[9]. One of the most recent Italian laws that specifically refer to SMEs, and to a definition of the same, is the PFEL. In its definition provision, the PFEL specifically refers to the SBA, stating, under Article 5, that "micro", "small", and

[7] Communication from the Commission to the Council, the European Parliament, the European Economic and Social Committee and the Committee Of The Regions "Think Small First" "Small Business Act" for Europe, Brussels, 25 June 2008 COM(2008) 394 final.

[8] Direttiva del Presidente del Consiglio dei Ministri 4 maggio 2010, *Attuazione della comunicazione della Commissione UE del 25 giugno 2008, recante: "Pensare anzitutto in piccolo" Uno "Small Business Act per l'Europa*, Italian Official Gazette no.144, 23 June 2010.

[9] For a detailed assessment of the implementation of the European Small Business Act in Italy and the 27 EU Member States, reference may be made to the 2010 Report of the Italian Ministry for Economic Development 2010 Report "Small Business Act – Le Iniziative a Sostegno delle PMI in Italia e Nell'Europa a 27", available on the Ministry for Economic Development's website: http://www.sviluppoeconomico.gov.it/index.php?option=com_content&view=article&viewType=0&id=2015901&idarea1=576&idarea2=0&idarea3=0&idarea4=0&andor=AND&sectionid=2&andorcat=AND&partebassaType=0&idareaCalendario1=0&MvediT=1&showMenu=1&showCat=1&showArchiveNewsBotton=0&idmenu=2705&directionidUser=0.

"medium-sized" enterprises are "those enterprises falling within the definitions under the recommendation of the Commission 2003/361/EC, published in the Official Journal of the European Union n. L. 124 of 20th May, 2003", and the subsequent Communication From the Commission to the Council, the European Parliament, the European Economic and Social Committee and the Committee of the Regions—Review of the "Small Business Act" for Europe[10] (the "2011 Communication"). The PFEL contains some key provisions on SMEs in Italy.

Essentially, it aims to ensure the full application of the principles of the SBA and the conformity of rules adopted by the Italian State and various Italian regions with the relative EU framework implementing the SBA. The general principles underlying the PFEL include, *inter alia,* the participation and access of undertakings, and specifically micro-, small, and medium enterprises, to public policy, through innovation, an instrument to be used for greater transparency of the public administration, as well as public support of micro-, small, and medium enterprises.

Moreover, the PFEL also advocates, through specific amendments to other relevant laws, due consideration of the impact of laws and regulations, including those of a fiscal nature, on undertakings, prior to the enactment of the PFEL. Due consideration is also afforded by the PFEL to the administrative burdens and costs on citizens and undertakings.

It is pertinent to point out that pursuant to the PFEL, as regards the rules on late payments in commercial transactions for provision of goods and services, both among private undertakings and between a private undertaking and the public administration, the Italian government must implement the relative EU late payments directive by November 2012.

The PFEL[11] establishes the role of the "Garante per le micro, piccole e medie imprese" (hereafter referred to as "GMPM"), an authority with the role of, *inter alia*, monitoring implementation of the SBA and the 2011 Communication; carrying out a pre- and post- analysis of the impact of regulation on micro-, small, and medium enterprises; come up with proposals aimed towards the development of micro-, small, and medium enterprises; annually submit a report to the Italian President of the Council of Ministers on the activities it has carried out. The said report is then addressed to the Italian Parliament.

According to the PFEL, the report will feature a pre- and post-analysis of public policy on micro-, small, and medium enterprises and will identify measures to increase their competitiveness. The GMPM will also play the role of monitoring regional laws that are of interest to micro-, small, and medium enterprises and promote spreading of best practices, as well as coordinating the different authorities entrusted with safeguarding the interests of micro-, small, and medium enterprises. Thus, micro-, small, and medium enterprises will have their interests safeguarded by a special authority, specifically entrusted with the aforementioned tasks.

[10] Brussels, 23 February 2011, COM (2011) 78 final.

[11] Article 17.

Pursuant to the PFEL, the GMPM will not function in isolation, but it will make use of analyses carried out by, *inter alia*, the Central Bank of Italy, the national statistics office, and the collaboration of the competent Ministers and chambers of commerce. The chambers of commerce may assume an active role by proposing measures for simplification of the regulatory framework on start-up and operation of enterprises.

Another significant provision of the PFEL[12] lays an obligation on the Italian Government to annually submit a draft law on micro-, small and medium enterprises to the Chamber of Deputies. The PFEL articulates the various provisions of the said draft law, which include, *inter alia,* rules promoting micro-, small, and medium enterprises; reduction of bureaucratic hurdles; and introduction of measures for simplification of administration, also in relation to proceedings for sanctions linked to the fulfilment of obligations by micro-, small, and medium enterprises with respect to the public administration. The PFEL prescribes that apart from any other relevant reports required by other laws, a report is to be annexed, which will evidence, *inter alia*, compliance of the Italian legal framework to the principles and aims of the SBA; the status of implementation of the measures foreseen by the previous annual laws for the protection and development of micro-, small, and medium enterprises; and so forth.

Finally, it is pertinent to point out that the recent Decree-Law 1/2012[13] (hereafter referred to as "Liberalisation Law"), which, *inter alia,* amends the Italian Consumer Code, defines a microenterprise as "an entity, company or association which, independently of its juridical form, carries out an economic activity, even on an individual or family basis, employing less than ten persons and attaining an annual turnover or an annual balance not exceeding EUR 2 million, pursuant to article 2, paragraph 3 of the annex to Commission Recommendation n. 2003/361/EC of 6th May, 2003". It is important to point out that the Liberalisation Law extends protection of the Italian Consumer Code[14] from unfair commercial practices to microenterprises.

In order to understand the implications of the extension of protection to microenterprises, it is useful to provide a brief outlook on the relative provisions of the Italian Consumer Code on unfair commercial practices.

The said Code prohibits unfair commercial practices, that is, practices that are contrary to the requirements of professional diligence and materially distort or are likely to materially distort the economic behaviour with regard to the product of the average consumer whom it reaches or to whom it is addressed or of the average member of the group when a commercial practice is directed to a particular group of consumers.

More specifically, under the Italian Consumer Code, unfair commercial practices may be "misleading" commercial practices or "aggressive".

---

[12] Article 18.

[13] Italian Official Gazette no. 19, 24 January 2012.

[14] Legislative Decree no. 206 of 6.09.2005, as subsequently amended.

According to the aforesaid Code,[15] a commercial practice shall be regarded as misleading if it contains false information and is therefore untruthful or in any way, including overall presentation, deceives or is likely to deceive the average consumer, even if the information is factually correct, in relation to one or more elements related to the product, traders commitments, or the price, and in either case causes or is likely to cause him to take a transactional decision that he would not have otherwise taken.

The consequences of misleading conduct are regulated by Article 21(2) of the aforesaid Code[16], and misleading omissions are covered by the Italian Consumer Code.[17]

---

[15] Article 21: "(a) the existence or nature of the product;

(b) the main characteristics of the product, such as its availability, benefits, risks, execution, composition, accessories, aftersale customer assistance and complaint handling, method and date of manufacture or provision, delivery, fitness for purpose, usage, quantity, specification, geographical or commercial origin or the results to be expected from its use, or the results and material features of tests or checks carried out on the product;

(c) the extent of the trader's commitments, the motives for the commercial practice and the nature of the sales process, any statement or symbol in relation to direct or indirect sponsorship or approval of the trader or the product;

(d) the price or the manner in which the price is calculated, or the existence of a specific price advantage;

(e) the need for a service, part, replacement or repair;

(f) the nature, attributes and rights of the trader or his agent, such as his identity and assets, his qualifications, status, approval, affiliation or connection and ownership of industrial, commercial or intellectual property rights or his awards and distinctions;

(g) the consumer's rights, including the right to replacement or reimbursement under Article 130 of this Code."

[16] Article 21(2), introduced by Article 36 of Decree Law 201/2011, which was converted with modifications from Law no. 214 of 22 December 2011 - Conversion to law, with modifications, of Decree Law no. 201 of 6 December 2011 on urgent measures for the growth, equity and consolidation of public finances, reads as follows: "A commercial practice shall also be regarded as misleading if, in its factual context, taking account of all its features and circumstances, it causes or is likely to cause the average consumer to take a transactional decision that he would not have taken otherwise, and it involves:

(a) any marketing of a product, including comparative advertising, which creates confusion with any products, trade marks, trade names or other distinguishing marks of a competitor;

(b) non-compliance by the trader with commitments contained in codes of conduct by which the trader has undertaken to be bound, where the commitment is firm and capable of being verified, and the trader indicates in a commercial practice the binding nature of the code.

3. It is considered to be an unfair commercial practice, in relation to products likely to harm the health and safety of consumers, to fail to state this likelihood such that consumers are induced to neglect to observe the normal standards of prudence and vigilance.

3-bis. It is considered to be an unfair commercial practice when a bank, credit institution or financial agency makes the stipulation of a loan contract conditional on the stipulation of an insurance policy supplied by the same bank, institution or intermediary."

[17] Article 22 of the Consumer Code reads as follows: "1. A commercial practice shall be regarded as misleading if, in its factual context, taking account of all its features and circumstances and the limitations of the communication medium, it omits material information that the average consumer needs, according to the context, to take an informed transactional decision, thereby causing or

Furthermore, pursuant to Article 24 of the Italian Consumer Code, an aggressive commercial practice shall be regarded as aggressive if, "in its factual context, taking account of all its features and circumstances, by harassment, coercion, including the use of physical force, or undue influence, it significantly impairs or is likely to significantly impair the average consumer's freedom of choice or conduct with regard to the product and thereby causes him or is likely to cause him to take a transactional decision that he would not have taken otherwise".

In summary, microenterprises will now enjoy the safeguards provided by the aforesaid provisions on unfair commercial practices, at par with consumers and users. This may be considered an extremely important legislative step forward, not only in view of the very high percentage of microenterprises in Italy[18] but also in view of the fact that these new safeguards are very welcome by microenterprises, in that their position is strengthened at a time of economic crisis.

---

being likely to cause the average consumer to take a transactional decision that they would not have taken otherwise.

2. It shall also be regarded as a misleading omission when, taking account of the matters described in paragraph 1, a trader hides or provides in an unclear, unintelligible, ambiguous or untimely manner such material information as referred to in that paragraph or fails to identify the commercial intent of the commercial practice if not already apparent from the context, and where, in either case, this causes or is likely to cause the average consumer to take a transactional decision that they would not have taken otherwise.

3. Where the medium used to communicate the commercial practice imposes limitations of space or time, these limitations and any measures taken by the trader to make the information available to consumers by other means shall be taken into account in deciding whether information has been omitted.

4. In the case of an invitation to purchase, the following information shall be regarded as material, within the meaning of paragraph (1), if not already apparent from the context:

(a) the main characteristics of the product, to an extent appropriate to the medium and the product;

(b) the geographical address and the identity of the trader, such as his trading name and, where applicable, the geographical address and the identity of the trader on whose behalf he is acting;

(c) the price inclusive of taxes, or where the nature of the product means that the price cannot reasonably be calculated in advance, the manner in which the price is calculated, as well as, where appropriate, all additional freight, delivery or postal charges or, where these charges cannot reasonably be calculated in advance, the fact that such additional charges may be payable by the consumer;

(d) the arrangements for payment, delivery, performance and the complaints handling policy, if they depart from the requirements of professional diligence;

(e) for products and transactions involving a right of withdrawal or cancellation, the existence of such a right.

5. Information requirements established by Community law in relation to commercial communication including advertising or marketing, shall be regarded as material within the meaning of paragraph (1)."

[18] As seen in the General Introduction, microenterprises in Italy amount to 94.5 % of total enterprises.

10.2.1.2 The Economic Perspective

As seen, SMEs, and, in particular, microenterprises, form a cornerstone of the Italian economy (amounting to 94.5 % of total enterprises).

10.2.1.3 Relevant Cases

As a preliminary remark, it is necessary to point out that the IAA itself has attested that it has not dealt with a high number of cases involving small-medium enterprises.[19]

In this section, the general definition of SMEs provided by the PFEL (which, as seen, adopts the definition of Recommendation 2003/361, that is, "enterprises which employ fewer than 250 persons and which have an annual turnover not exceeding EUR 50 million, and/or an annual balance sheet total not exceeding EUR 43 million") will be taken into consideration.

As regards number of employees, it must firstly be pointed that the IAA's decisions do not indicate this specific data, since it is not normally pertinent to antitrust proceedings.

For instance, to cite but a few examples, in the *Logistica Internazionale* case,[20] a number of parties to the proceedings had, in 2010, according to the IAA, a total turnover not exceeding EUR 50 million. However, the IAA decision does not specify the number of employees of the undertakings at stake, and consequently it is not possible, from the IAA decision alone, to ascertain whether the aforementioned undertakings satisfy the cumulative requirements of the relevant definition that is being taken into consideration for purposes of this Report. It may very well be the case therefore that, with respect to undertakings having a turnover not exceeding EUR 50 million, the number of employees does not exceed 250 and that consequently they fall within the definition taken into consideration in this Report.

In *Retail sale of cosmetics* case,[21] a number of undertakings had a turnover not exceeding EUR 50 million, yet the number of employees was not specified in the decision, and thus it is not possible to ascertain whether they fall within the definition being taken into consideration in this Report.

Similarly, in the *Riciclaggio delle batterie* case,[22] a number of undertakings had a turnover not exceeding EUR 50 million, but the number of employees was not specified by the decision.

Moreover, as for the turnover of undertakings involved in antitrust proceedings, it is worth pointing out that this usually features in the part of the IAA's decision on calculation of fines imposed on infringing undertakings, if any. Moreover, the IAA

[19] See former President Catricalà's speech, delivered on 8 June 2011, on http://www.agcm.it/stampa/news/5575-audizione-del-presidente-catricala-sul-disegno-di-legge-sullo-statuto-delle-imprese.html.

[20] IAA, 2011, Decision no. 22521, I722 - *Logistica Internazionale.*

[21] IAA, 2010, Decision no. 21924, I701 - *Vendita al dettaglio di prodotti cosmetici.*

[22] IAA, 2009, Decision no. 19814, I697 - *Riciclaggio delle batterie esauste.*

Table 10.1 Relevant cases in Italy

Year	Case reference/comment/description	Type of conduct
2011	–	–
2010	–	–
2009	I694 – *Listino prezzi della pasta* ("Pasta Price List" case) decision No. 19562. In this case, Unionalimentari, an association of SMEs in the Food Industry, having around 2,000 members (some active in the pasta manufacturing sector), was fined by the IAA for collusive practices in the pasta production sector[a]. The said decision was affirmed on appeal by the Tribunale Amministrativo Regionale del Lazio ("TAR Lazio"), at first instance, and subsequently by the Consiglio di Stato (CdS) (the Italian Supreme Administrative Court).	Article 101 TFEU (ex Article 81 EC)
2008	By way of example, it may be pointed out that one of the IAA's 2008 decisions related to a small bakers' association in Rome, which had engaged in collusive practices under article 2 of the ICL (article 2 is the "national" equivalent of Article 101 TFEU). Although the said decision does not specify details that enable one to classify the association's members as SMEs or otherwise, it may be assumed, given the description of the characteristics of the relevant market provided by the IAA, wherein the latter refers to, *inter alia*, numerous "small" undertakings as *numerose piccole imprese artigianali*, that (at least) some of the addressees of this decision would fall under the definition of SMEs adopted for the purposes of the present Report (IAA, 2008, Decision no. 18443, – I695 – *Listino prezzi del pane* – "Bread Price List case"). The same reasoning may be applied to the I684 – *Federfarma Teramo-sconti sui prezzi al pubblico* case, "Federfarma Teramo case" (IAA, 2008, Decision no. 18421), which related to an association of undertakings whose members were pharmacies in the province of Teramo, which is located in the central Italian region of Abruzzo. It may be assumed that some of the 82 members of the association at stake (i.e., pharmacies in the province of Teramo) would fall within the definition of SME adopted for the purposes of this Report, but the IAA decision does not specify the necessary details that would enable inclusion of the enterprises to the aforementioned category.	Article 2 of ICL ("national" equivalent of Article 101 TFEU)
2007	Also in 2007, some IAA decisions related to undertakings having a turnover of less than EUR 50 million. However, the said decisions did not specify whether the number of employees of the undertakings concerned was less than 250. By way of example, reference may be made to the I646 – *Produttori vernici marine* case (IAA, 2007, Decision n. 16404), which related to collusive practices under Article 101 TFEU (then article 81EC), among a number of undertakings in the marine paint sector.	Article 101 TFEU (ex Article 81 EC)

[a]This association is classified as an association of small-medium undertakings

often uses turnover ranges rather than indicating the precise turnover, in order to protect commercially sensitive information. Thus, the IAA does not always indicate precise turnover value.

In view of the foregoing, it is difficult to assess the IAA's decisions on SMEs using the definition of SME provided by the PFEL and adopted for the purposes of this Report. This section will therefore take account of those decisions that dealt with undertakings having a "smaller" dimension.

Moreover, as regards the national courts, these also do not usually contain the necessary information for classification of the undertakings involved as SMEs for the purposes of this Report, so that it is not possible to come up with precise data on the number of cases before the national courts regarding SMEs (as defined above).

In the light of the foregoing, Table 10.1 and its relative footnotes illustrate the most relevant case law before the IAA and the competent Italian Courts on SMEs' anticompetitive conduct in Italy between 2007 and 2011.

10.2.2 Specific Treatment of SMEs Under Competition Law

Law 287/1990, i.e. the Italian Competition Law (hereafter referred to as "ICL"), does not set forth a definition of SME.

In the Italian competition law field, application of competition law rules to an entity depends on whether that entity falls within the definition of "undertaking" as applied under EU and Italian competition laws and practices.[23]

In the absence of a legal definition of SMEs under the ICL, when assessing whether an undertaking falls under competition law rules, as seen, reference is made to the concept of "undertaking" endorsed at EU and national levels. Consequently, an individual business may very well fall under the definition of "undertaking" if it engages in an economic activity, "regardless of the legal status of the entity and the way in which it is financed".[24] In line with EU case law and practice, the IAA has classified even non-profit-making entities as undertakings for the purposes of antitrust law.[25]

10.2.2.1 Substantive and Procedural Rules

Although Italian antitrust law does not contain substantive and procedural rules specifically aimed at SMEs, it is worth mentioning that under the Italian legal

[23] Pursuant to Article 1(4) of the ICL, antitrust provisions in Italy must be interpreted in accordance with the principles of EU antitrust law. Thus, the IAA and the Italian courts have largely followed EU principles and practices when applying antitrust law.

[24] As known, this is the definition of undertaking adopted by EU case law and practice; see for instance, ECJ, case C- 41/90 *Hofner and Elser v Macrotron*, ECR 1991 I-1979).

[25] See, for instance, A378C – FEDERITALIA/Federazione italiana sport equestri (FISE).

IAA, 2011, Decision n. 22503, wherein FISE, a non-profit organisation was considered to be an association of undertakings for the purposes of antitrust law (Section II of the IAA decision).

system, as for administrative rules, these do not generally distinguish between SMEs and other parties.

Moreover, from an administrative law point of view, the PFEL contains some provisions on public tenders. More specifically, according to Article 13 of the PFEL, the State, the regions, and local entities must provide information on public tenders involving awards that do not exceed the thresholds established by the EU, as well as tenders for access to incentives by micro-, small, and medium enterprises.

In compliance with the relative EU public procurement rules, in order to facilitate access of micro-, small, and medium enterprises, the public administration and the competent authorities are obliged (as long as this does not entail any new or more "onerous" financial implications) to, *inter alia*, facilitate access to tenders by micro-, small, and medium enterprises, favouring temporary associations of undertakings, consortia, and *reti di impresa* (companies' networks),[26] in the area of public contracts and to facilitate access of micro-, small, and medium enterprises to public tenders for provision of local public services, issued by countries having a population of less than 5,000 inhabitants and for sums that do not exceed the prescribed EU public procurement thresholds.[27] On a practical note, the PFEL ensures that, in their participation in tenders for works, services, or supplies, SMEs are not unduly burdened with obligations to provide documents or certificates that are already in possession of the public administration or additional documentation that is not provided for in the relevant administrative law.[28]

[26] The *reti d'impresa* (or companies' networks) are dealt with in Law 33/2009, as subsequently amended by Law 122/2010, providing for the *contratto di rete* and the *reti d'impresa*. The "contratto di rete" enables companies to cooperate in their area of activity, to exchange relevant information or services (commercial/technical/technological), or to exercise in common one/more of their activities. This mechanism was introduced by the Italian Government in order to provide incentives to companies and, specifically, SMEs, to cooperate, allowing them to carry out activities in common. The companies forming part of the network remain autonomous and independent, and the contract provides for a flexible form of association among companies forming part of the relative network. Although the *contratto di rete* is not limited to SMEs, but may also be entered into by larger enterprises, this type of cooperation was strongly advocated by SMEs, which, as seen, are a cornerstone of the Italian economy. For completeness' sake, it is pointed out that by Decision N343/2010 – Italy (Support to set up companies' networks (reti di impresa), the European Commission authorised the Italian Government to provide financial support in the form of a tax deferral to companies willing to form a network (rete d'impresa). The Commission concluded that the notified measure did not constitute state aid in accordance with Article 107 TFEU. Although, as outlined in the said decision, the measure was addressed to all enterprises, SMEs may be said to draw significant benefits from this measure. Of course, one cannot fail to mention the antitrust concerns raised by the IAA on the *contratti di rete* (see, in this respect, IAA Bulletin n. 17, 16 May 2011). However, the antitrust implications of this mechanism go beyond the scope of this Report.

[27] Article 13, PFEL.

[28] Decreto Legislativo 12 aprile 2006, n. 163 "Codice dei contratti pubblici relativi a lavori, servizi e forniture in attuazione delle direttive 2004/17/CE e 2004/18/CE" (Code on Public Contracts of works, services and supplies, implementing directives 2004/17/EC and 2004/18/EC) published in the Italian Official Gazette n. 100, 2 May 2006 – Ordinary Supplement n. 107.

As for judicial rules, there are no differences between rules applicable to SMEs and those applicable to other (larger) undertakings.

From a procedural point of view, it must be pointed out that as far as the Italian Code of Civil Procedure is concerned, the latter Code does not differentiate between applicable procedural rules to small-medium enterprises and those applicable to larger undertakings. Thus, from this standpoint, the procedural rights of SMEs and those of larger undertakings are the same.

Neither does administrative law distinguish between procedural rights accorded to SMEs and larger undertakings.

As for procedural rights in antitrust enforcement, SMEs are treated in the same way as other undertakings. For instance, pursuant to Presidential Decree no. 217/98 ("Antitrust Procedural Law"), the right to access to file is granted on equal terms to all types of undertakings.

Furthermore, it is worth mentioning some particular substantive rules that, though not specifically "protecting" SMEs, may be deemed beneficial to the same.

Firstly, reference is made to the Subcontracting Law. In Italy, abuse of economic dependence is specifically regulated by the aforesaid law, which contains provisions on abuse of economic dependence and may hence end up safeguarding "smaller" undertakings when "larger" undertakings violate the provisions of the Subcontracting Law. One of the primary aims of the Subcontracting Law is that of remedying the contractual imbalance deriving from disparities in economic and negotiating powers. More specifically, Article 9 of the Subcontracting Law prohibits the abuse by one or more undertakings of economic dependence of a *client or supplier*. In summary, Article 9:

- prohibits the abuse by one or more undertakings of economic dependence of a client or supplier;
- specifies that economic dependence is a situation whereby an undertaking is capable of maintaining an excessive imbalance of rights and obligations, stating that economic dependence must be assessed also on the basis of a real possibility of the party that suffered the abuse to find a plausible alternative on the market;
- specifies that the abuse may also consist in the refusal to sell or acquire, in the imposition of unduly onerous or discriminatory conditions, in the arbitrary interruption of commercial relations at stake;
- states that the agreement that constitutes an abuse of economic dependence is null; attributes competence to decide on actions on abuse of economic dependence to the ordinary judge, including interim measures and compensation for damages; and
- also attributes competence to the Italian Antitrust Authority but only where the abusive conduct "is relevant from a competition law perspective".

Although a livened doctrinal debate has centred on the Subcontracting Law[29] and, more specifically, on the aforesaid Article 9, this debate has not been reflected

[29] See, for instance, Alpa G and Clarizia A (1999) La Subfornitura, Giuffre Editore; Alberto Musso (2003) La Subfornitura, Zanichelli Editore.

in case law, which is rather scarce in this respect. This scarcity in case law may be attributed to the fact that undertakings, which, in this case would be the weaker party to a contractual relationship (which could also be SMEs), would on the one hand have an interest to safeguard their rights at law, but their interest in amicably preserving their commercial relationship with (the) other larger undertaking (s) would prevail, thus "dissuading" "weaker" or "smaller" undertakings from taking legal action.

Agreements that constitute an abuse of economic dependence are null.

It should be noted that although the Subcontracting Law relates to manufacturing, the above-mentioned provisions are nevertheless extensively applied. This "general" applicability may also be inferred from the wording of Article 9 itself, which indeed generically refers to "undertakings, clients and suppliers", and therefore is not restricted to contractors and subcontractors. This extensive applicability was also affirmed by the Italian Courts, which reiterated that the rules on abuse of economic dependence also extend to contractual relationships other than subcontracting relationships and more specifically apply to distribution agreements.[30]

Thus, it may be said that the Subcontracting Law might very well afford SMEs with protection from the conduct of larger undertakings on which they are "economically dependent" pursuant to the aforesaid law.

To conclude on the Subcontracting Law, it is worth pointing out that the said law was recently amended by the PFEL, and it now provides that in case of repeated violation of Legislative Decree no. 231/2002 on late payments in commercial transactions (hereafter referred to as "Late Payments Law"), to the prejudice of companies, and particularly SMEs, abusive conduct would subsist independently of the ascertainment of the economic dependence or otherwise.

Secondly, another specific provision that may be deemed beneficial to SMEs is Article 62 of the Liberalisation Law. This provision is a novelty worth mentioning. It governs commercial relationships concerning sale of agricultural and food processing products and prohibits, *inter alia*, clauses that directly/indirectly impose purchase, sales, or other contractual conditions that are unusually onerous, as well as extra-contractual or retroactive conditions; applying objectively dissimilar conditions to equivalent transactions, making the conclusion of contracts subject to acceptance by the other parties of supplementary obligations that, by their nature or according to commercial usage, have no connection with the subject of such contracts; requiring performance of unilateral obligations that are not justified by the nature or content of the commercial relations; undertaking any other unfair commercial behaviour in commercial relations that characterise supply conditions. Moreover, Article 62 of the Liberalisation Law stipulates a maximum payment term of 60 days for transfer of non-perishable food products and 30 days for perishable food items. The IAA is the competent authority with respect to this

---

[30] See, for instance, *Wind v Arama* S.r.l., Court of Rome, 17 March 2009; *Autofur v Renault S.p.A.*, Court of Rome, 5 November 2003.

provision, and administrative penalties amounting to a maximum of EUR 500,000 may be imposed in case of violation. The IAA may act both upon complaint and *ex officio*.

It may be said that this provision will help to safeguard SMEs from any of the above-described types of conduct by "larger" undertakings.

Thirdly, one could mention Article 10(1)(b) of the PFEL. The PFEL also seeks to broaden the IAA's competence in the area of late payments in commercial transactions, wherein Article 10(1)(b) of the PFEL obliges the Italian Government to promulgate a law (by November 2012) enabling the IAA to carry out investigations, send warning letters, and impose fines on large undertakings for their unlawful conduct. This broadening of the IAA's competence is expected to contribute towards alleviating the problems faced by SMEs in late payment by "larger" undertakings and also the public administration.[31]

10.2.2.2 Influence of Size and Economic Power in Decisions of the National Competition Authorities and Courts

This section will briefly assess whether the antitrust legal assessment in the above-mentioned IAA/Court decisions were influenced by the economic dimension of SMEs (i.e., SMEs as defined for the purposes of this Report).

In compliance with EU and national consolidated principles on methods for calculation of antitrust fines, in the Pasta Price List case, the IAA, albeit recognising the serious nature of the antitrust infringement at stake, in setting fines for the said infringements and, in particular, in assessing the gravity of the same, considered the dimension of each party to the infringement.[32]

In the Bread Price List case,[33] the IAA, applying, as it normally does, EU and national consolidated principles on methods for calculation of antitrust fines, in considering the deterrent effect of the fine it was imposing in its decision, took into account the fact that, also in the light of the relevant EU Guidelines on setting fines, on the one hand, the association at stake was an association of undertakings having

[31] The importance of this provision of the PFEL is even clearer, if one were to take a cursory look at some recent Italian statistics on late payments by the public administration to its suppliers. According to a recent study by an Italian trade association, Confartigianato, even the richest Italian regions, i.e. Friuli Venezia Giulia and Trentino Alto Adige, do not abide by the 30-day payment term provided by the relative EU Directive on late payments in commercial transactions but in practice respectively effect payment within an average term of 87 to 96 days. On a general note, the average payment term in Italy, according to these statistics, is 135 days (as cited in Spoto G., (2012) La Nuova Direttiva contro i ritardi di pagamento della P.A., Contratto e impresa, Pubblicazione Bimestrale Anno XXVIII N.2 March-April.

[32] Paragraph 320 of the IAA decision, previously quoted. It should be recalled that, as seen earlier in the section on legal definitions, pursuant to Article 1(4) of the ICL, in its application of antitrust law, the IAA refers to principles of EU antitrust law. Consequently, in this decision, as it usually does, the IAA referred to the European Commission's Guidelines on setting fines (Guidelines on the method of setting fines imposed pursuant to Article 23(2)(a) of Regulation No 1/2003 (2006/C 210/02) ("EU Guidelines on setting fines").

[33] Previously quoted.

a "local" dimension, with an extremely limited turnover, and, on the other hand, that the fine had to be set in the light of the gravity of the antitrust infringement.[34]

Similar considerations were also made by the IAA in the Federfarma Teramo case,[35] always in line with EU and national consolidated principles on methods for calculation of antitrust fines.

10.2.2.3 Specific Programmes Addressed to SMEs

A brief overview will here be provided on the line of thought of the IAA as regards SMEs.

The IAA has, on several occasions, recognised the key role played by small-medium enterprises in the Italian economy, also advocating, as regards companies in general, the reduction of administrative burdens and simplified processes linked to communication of undertakings with public entities, in line with international best practices, such as those outlined in the SBA, and reaffirmed by the 2011 Communication.

To cite but one example of the IAA's line of thought on SMEs, one could mention last year's hearing of the former IAA President, Antonio Catricalà, before the Italian Senate, wherein the IAA presented its views on the draft version of the PFEL.[36]

For an illustration of the IAA's line of thought with respect to SMEs, though unlinked to a specific "programme" in the strict sense of the word, reference may be made, for instance, to the IAA's 2006 extension of the pre-notification procedure also to transactions involving undertakings of a smaller dimension. This measure was adopted by the IAA with a view to facilitating matters for SMEs, which would benefit from collaboration with the IAA at the pre-notification stage of a transaction.[37] As from 25 September 2006, even undertakings obliged to notify due to attainment of only the "second turnover threshold"[38] would be able to benefit from the pre-notification procedure. Prior to the IAA's decision to extend the pre-notification threshold, SMEs would not have benefited from this useful interaction with the IAA at pre-notification stage, since pre-notification was limited to transactions that exceeded both of the prescribed thresholds for notification of concentrations.

For completeness' sake, it is worth mentioning that following the recent amendments of the Liberalisation Law, for the obligation to notify to arise, *both* of the prescribed thresholds will have to be reached, as opposed to the current

[34] See § 75 IAA decision.

[35] Previously quoted, see § 69 of IAA decision.

[36] See former President Catricalà's speech, delivered on 8 June 2011, previously quoted.

[37] See IAA Press Release, "Operativa dal 25 Settembre Prenotifica per le Operazioni di Concentrazione delle PMI", 19 September 2006, http://www.agcm.it/stampa/news/4122-operativa-dal-25-settembre-prenotifica-per-le-operazioni-di-concentrazione-delle-pmi.html.

[38] At the time of publication of the IAA Press Release, the second turnover threshold was EUR 43 million turnover of the target undertaking at national level.

situation, which requires notification of transactions even if only one of the prescribed thresholds is reached. This amendment to the Liberalisation Law will, in practice, reduce the number of concentrations that will need to be notified, and more specifically the "smaller" transactions will not be subject to the notification requirement.

Nevertheless, the fact that in 2006 the IAA extended the pre-notification procedure to favour matters for SMEs indicates its willingness to facilitate matters for these types of enterprises.

10.2.3 Policy Recommendations

Given the fundamental role of small-medium enterprises in the economy, national competition authorities could implement specific awareness programmes in order to enhance and spread general knowledge of antitrust rules and the importance of compliance with the said rules for small and large undertakings alike. From a practical point of view, this could be done, for instance, by publication of guidelines containing the "dos and don'ts of antitrust law", which clearly indicate that anticompetitive conduct remains such even if committed by an undertaking/s having a small(er) dimension.

10.3 Public Antitrust Enforcement and SMEs

10.3.1 Substantive and Procedural Rules Applicable to SMEs

10.3.1.1 Introduction

There are no specific substantive and procedural rules applicable to SMEs within the ambit of public antitrust enforcement.

10.3.1.2 Safe Harbours for SMEs

Considering that, as seen, antitrust provisions in Italy must be interpreted in accordance with the principles of EU antitrust law (pursuant to article 1(4) of the ICL), the principles of the Commission Notice on agreements of minor importance which do not appreciably restrict competition under Article 81(1) of the Treaty establishing the European Community (de minimis) (hereafter referred to as "*de minimis* Notice") would also be applicable to the Italian legal context. As known, pursuant to the *de minimis* Notice, an agreement is presumed to fall outside the scope of Article 101(1) TFEU if it fulfils two conditions: firstly, it falls within the "safe harbour thresholds" of the Notice; secondly there is absence of hard-core restrictions.

If an agreement falls within the scope of the safe harbour of the aforesaid Notice and the individual market share of each party to the agreement at stake does not exceed 15 %, in case of non-competitors, the agreement would not fall within the purview of Article 101(1) TFEU. In case of competing undertakings, the individual market share of each party to the agreement must not exceed 10 %.

Therefore, in the light of the foregoing, although it must be pointed out that there are no specific safe harbours in relation to SMEs under Italian antitrust law, it may be said that, further to the *de minimis* Notice, Article 101(1) TFEU is not applicable where the impact of an agreement on intra-EU trade or on competition is not appreciable.

Furthermore, as known, the *de minimis* Notice acknowledges that "agreements between small and medium-sized undertakings, as defined in the Annex to Commission Recommendation 96/280/EC (3), are rarely capable of appreciably affecting trade between Member States."[39]. Thus, the principles and thresholds set forth by the *de minimis* Notice are to be taken into account when assessing agreements between SMEs.

10.3.1.3 Access to Justice

Access to justice and remedies should be facilitated for all types of undertakings, independently of their size. In view of the key role that SMEs play in many markets, the said undertakings will surely benefit if access to justice and remedies are open and transparent for all.

10.3.2 Fundamental Rights of SMEs

From a more general perspective, as regards fundamental rights, the Italian legal system distinguishes, in certain aspects, between legal entities and individuals. For instance, as regards data privacy provisions, pursuant to the Italian Personal Data Protection Code[40] (hereafter referred to as "Data Protection Code"), the "data subject" is defined as "any natural person that is the subject of the personal data", whereas "personal data" "shall mean any information relating to natural persons that are or can be identified, even indirectly, by reference to any other information including a personal identification number".[41] Legal entities are not accorded the right to privacy.

The definition of "personal data" was only recently amended by Decree Law 201/2011.[42] Prior to this amendment, the definition of "personal data" included also legal persons within its purview. The new definition of "personal data" may be

---

[39] Para 3 of the *de minimis* Notice.

[40] Legislative Decree 196/2003, *Codice in materia di protezione dei dati personali,* (Data Protection Code), Published in Italian Official Gazette, n. 174, 29.07.2003, Ordinary Supplement no. 123.

See Article 4 of the Data Protection Code.

[41] This definition was amended by Article 40(2)a of decree no. 201, dated 6 December 2011, subsequently converted, with amendments, into Act no. 214 dated 22 December 2011.

[42] Decree Law 201/2011 (s.c. "Salva Italia"), *Disposizioni Urgenti per la crescita, l'equità e il consolidamento dei conti pubblici*, published in the Italian Official Gazette no. 300, 27.12.2011.

considered to be an important innovation, since it totally excludes data relative to legal persons, undertakings, associations and entities from the ambit of the Data Privacy Code, limiting the protection of "personal data" to natural persons. Following the recent amendment to the definition of "personal data" therefore, data pertaining to legal persons may be freely processed, without prejudice, of course, to any confidential agreements in force.

Moreover, the amendment to the definition of "data subject" also entails similar implications. Notably, legal persons, entities, or associations will not be able to invoke their rights to access personal data and other rights pursuant to Article 7 of the Data Privacy Code in potential judicial proceedings or use the mechanisms to exercise rights set forth by Article 9 of the aforesaid Code. Legal persons, entities, or associations would only therefore be able to assume the role of defendant in possible proceedings, as "Data Controller"[43] or "Data Processor",[44] being unable to actively safeguard their rights.

In a nutshell, rules on data privacy will no longer apply to data of legal entities but will continue to apply to legal entities when they handle "personal data" (as per the new definition), in that they will have to do so in line with the Data Privacy Code provisions.

From an antitrust point of view, as seen commenting the legal definition of small-medium enterprises, the definition of "undertaking" adopted by the Italian system is the same as that adopted at EU level. Thus, both individuals as well as legal entities could fall under the definition of undertaking for the purposes of antitrust law, as long as they engage in an economic activity. Therefore, if an undertaking falls within this definition, it will consequently benefit from procedural rights (such as access to file), just like a larger undertaking would. This reasoning would also apply even if the "undertaking" were an individual.

As a concluding note to this introduction, in the author's view, as regards the "general" differences between legal entities and individuals, these differences should be maintained as a result of the different nature of physical and legal persons.

10.3.2.1 Complaints

The ICL does not contain any specific protection mechanism for SMEs following a complaint before the NCA, in the sense that it does not attribute the IAA with specific "powers" in this respect.

However, "protection" is generally afforded to undertakings' confidential data, which is usually redacted from the case file.

---

[43] Pursuant to the Data Privacy Code, the "data controller" "shall mean any natural or legal person, public administration, body, association or other entity that is competent, also jointly with another data controller, to determine purposes and methods of the processing of personal data and the relevant means, including security matters" (Article 4 (1) (f)).

[44] Pursuant to the Data Privacy Code, the "data processor" "shall mean any natural or legal person, public administration, body, association or other agency that processes personal data on the controller's behalf" (Article 4 (1) (g)).

Indeed, all information communicated to the IAA regarding the undertakings involved is wholly confidential and may not be divulged even to other government departments and other authorities.[45] This information is exclusively used for the purposes for which it was collected or requested, except for the obligation to report any matters governed by Article 331 of the Italian Code of Criminal Procedure and to cooperate with EU institutions. Nevertheless, confidentiality granted by the above-mentioned provisions must be balanced with third parties' right of access to the IAA's file, as well as the publicity requirements of the IAA's decisions.

In view of the right of access of all parties participating in investigations to the IAA's file,[46] undertakings shall indicate documents or parts thereof that contain business secrets or personal, commercial, industrial, and financial information of a confidential nature, specifying reasons why such information should not be disclosed or published. The final decision on these requests is up to the IAA.

The IAA has, on several occasions, showed how it seeks to safeguard undertakings' confidential information. To cite but one example, reference may be made to the previously mentioned Retail sale of cosmetics case, wherein the IAA denied full access to file due to confidentiality of leniency applicant documents. The IAA's line of thought in this case was also subsequently affirmed by the Italian administrative courts.

This "protection" of confidential information is of course not limited to SMEs but covers *all* undertakings involved in proceedings before the IAA.

Moreover, case law of the Italian courts has affirmed the lawfulness of the IAA's decision to deny the right to access to file as regards the identity of undertakings that had filed an antitrust complaint to companies challenged with anticompetitive conduct, also to avoid "retaliation" to the detriment of complainants.[47] Thus, although there do not seem to be "specific" rules in the ICL or Italian legislation, "protecting" SMEs when filing a complaint to the IAA, the line of thought followed by the Italian administrative courts, seems to have moved in this direction.

10.3.2.2 Access to the File

As regards access to file in antitrust proceedings, the relative rules are essentially found in the Antitrust Procedural Law under Article 13, which grants parties who are directly involved in procedures concerning agreements, abuses of a dominant position, and concentrations the right of access to any documents produced or permanently retained by the IAA in antitrust proceedings whilst providing for necessary safeguards in relation to information of a confidential nature, in that access to documents containing commercial secrets is not allowed.

Moreover, there are certain internal documents, such as notes made by the IAA case handlers or even correspondence between the IAA and other national competition authorities or the European Commission, that the parties having a right to

[45] Article 14(3), ICL and Article 12 of the Antitrust Procedural Law.

[46] Article 13, Antitrust Procedural Law.

[47] See, for instance, Consiglio di Stato, Sez. IV, 17.1.2008, judgment no. 102.

access to file are not entitled to access. Article 13 of the Antitrust Procedural Law does not specifically refer to these internal documents. Concerning, for instance, relations between the IAA and EU institutions, case law has affirmed that the IAA does not enjoy any discretionary power in granting access to such internal documents.[48]

Pursuant to Article 13, right of access shall be exercised by submitting a reasoned request in writing, which the official responsible for the case shall act upon within 30 days.

The IAA's Board resolves on the procedures for exercising the right of access and on the costs of reproducing the documentation, and the relative resolution is published in the IAA's bulletin.

Under the Italian system, in line with the EU and other Member States' system, a balance is sought between, on the one hand, the right of access to file of the parties and, on the other hand, the protection of business secrets.

10.3.3 Leniency, Settlements, and Commitment Decisions for SMEs

Reference may be made to the Italian Leniency Notice[49] (hereafter referred to as "Leniency Notice"), which contains provisions that limit access to material submitted by the leniency applicant. Under paragraph 10 *bis* of the Leniency Notice,[50] access to oral or written leniency declarations made by leniency applicants is deferred[51] until the Statement of Objections is notified to the parties concerned.

Once the statement of objections is received by its addressees, the latter are entitled to access the leniency declarations, on condition that the information contained therein shall not be copied by any means, whether mechanical or electronic, and that none of the information shall be used for any purpose other than the application of laws on competition in the context of legal or administrative proceedings.

Furthermore, pursuant to the Leniency Notice, whenever measures for initiating proceedings are issued for alleged violations of Article 2 of the ICL or Article 101TFEU, access to any annexed documentation or other supplements to the disclosure statement presented by the leniency applicant may be deferred pursuant to and in accordance with Article 13 of the Antitrust Procedural Law.

---

[48] See, for instance, T.A.R. Lazio, Sez. I, n. 191., 17.1.2000.

[49] Comunicazione Sulla Non Imposizione e Sulla Riduzione delle Sanzioni ai sensi dell'Articolo 15 della Legge 10 Ottobre 1990, n. 287, available at http://www.agcm.it/trasp-statistiche/doc_download/2881-comunicazione-programma-di-clemenza-mod-2010.html.

[50] Paragraph 10 *bis* was introduced by introduced by IAA resolution No. 21092 of 6 May 2010, published in the IAA's Bulletin 18/2010.

[51] Pursuant to Article13 of the Antitrust Procedural Law, which governs access to documents and confidentiality of information.

Furthermore, third parties, including other participants of the antitrust proceedings before the IAA, do not have access to disclosure statements and any annexed documentation.

The Leniency Notice thus provides for a general protection mechanism of leniency applicants, available to all types of undertakings, whether SMEs or larger undertakings, by limiting the right to access leniency documents. This mechanism may be said to enhance undertakings to inform the IAA about anticompetitive practices.

Furthermore, a cursory look at the IAA's case law reveals that in many cases, it was the "larger" undertakings that benefited from the leniency procedure.[52] For instance, in the Retail sale of cosmetics case,[53] the whistleblower was a well-known multinational. It should be noted, however, that the relative antitrust proceedings also involved "smaller" undertakings, which were also ultimately condemned to pay a fine for the antitrust breach (although pursuant to EU and Italian antitrust case laws and practices, this fine was lower than that to be paid by the "larger" undertakings that had taken part in the infringement).

The fact that, in assessing the seriousness of antitrust infringements, as seen, the IAA refers to a number of factors, such as economic strength of the undertaking/s that took part in the infringement, implies that if SMEs are found to be involved in anticompetitive practices, the IAA will take their economic dimension into account.

In conclusion, it is submitted that the fact that leniency applications in Italy have normally been filed by "larger" undertakings might be due to a lack of " awareness" among "smaller" undertakings on the importance of compliance with antitrust rules of small and larger undertakings alike. Hence, it would certainly help if, as outlined in Sect. 10.3.5 on policy recommendations, awareness programmes be put into place by national competition authorities, aiming to increase consciousness among larger and smaller undertakings about the importance of compliance to antitrust rules.

10.3.4 Sanctions: Different Penalties for Different Size?

Pursuant to the ICL,[54] when the IAA ascertains serious infringement of antitrust rules, it imposes a fine not exceeding 10 % of the turnover of each undertaking/entity concerned in the last-closed financial year preceding the issuing of the decision to cease and desist from the anticompetitive behaviour.

---

[52] See, for instance, the Retail sale of cosmetics case, where the whistleblower was a well-known multinational. See also the more recent I733 - *Servizi di agenzia marittima* case ("Maritime Agency Services case") (IAA, 2012, Decision n. 23338), wherein a larger undertaking was the whistleblower.

[53] Previously quoted.

[54] Article 15.

As seen above,[55] in imposing fines on undertakings that have committed antitrust infringements, the IAA takes into account the EU Guidelines on setting fines.

As regards the seriousness of antitrust infringements, the IAA usually ascertains this by referring to a number of factors, such as, *inter alia,* the context in which the challenged conduct took place and the importance and economic strength of the undertakings that committed the infringement.

Thus, although there is no explicit difference in the ICL as regards imposition of sanctions on SMEs and larger undertakings, in practice, it may be submitted that, in quantifying fines for antitrust infringements, the IAL would take into account the economic dimension of an SME.

10.3.5 Policy Recommendations

As regards access to justice and remedies, these should be facilitated for all types of undertakings, independently of their size. In view of the key role that SMEs play in many markets, the said undertakings will surely benefit if access to justice and remedies are open and transparent for all. In the author's view, there should be no differences in procedural rights of small-medium undertakings and larger enterprises. Indeed, facilitating, for instance, access to file solely for small-medium undertakings might end up prejudicing the rights of other (larger) undertakings.

10.4 Private Antitrust Enforcement and SMEs

10.4.1 Substantive Rules, Procedural Aspects for SMEs in Civil Suits

By way of providing a general background to the private enforcement scenario in Italy, it would be useful to briefly touch upon the courts having jurisdiction in civil law suits relative to anticompetitive conduct.

Prior to the Liberalisation Law, the Italian Courts of Appeal had jurisdiction on the merits, at first and last instance, over national antitrust law infringements, whereas lower civil Courts (*Giudici di Pace/Tribunali*), at first instance, and the Courts of Appeal, at second instance, had jurisdiction on the merits with respect to EU antitrust law infringements. The "Specialised Divisions in industrial and intellectual property rights", instituted within the framework of 12 civil Courts and the respective Courts of Appeal, were called to rule on antitrust infringements connected to the exercise of industrial property rights.

Pursuant to the recently promulgated Liberalisation Law, the *Tribunale delle Imprese* (hereafter referred to as "Specialised Courts") are competent to decide upon civil suits for anticompetitive conduct.

[55] See Sects. 10.3.3 and 10.3.4.

As regards SMEs, neither the ICL nor the Liberalisation Law contains specific provisions "protecting" them from large undertakings in civil suits for anticompetitive conduct.

10.4.1.1 Obstacles

In Italy, private actions are brought before the Italian judicial authorities. Private actions may either be *follow-on actions*, following a decision by the IAA or the European Commission, or *stand-alone actions*, i.e. actions that are not preceded by a previous decision ascertaining the antitrust infringement.

Private enforcement has unfortunately not yet really taken root in Italy and is certainly not as widespread as some other EU countries such as the UK. Moreover, victims of cartel damages do face certain procedural difficulties in private enforcement, some of which are common to those encountered in other EU Member States.

On a general note, prior to the promulgation of the Liberalisation Law, it is worth noting that, the Italian private enforcement system was complex.[56] Following the enactment of the Liberalisation Law, which has set up the Specialised Courts, the aforesaid courts will be competent to decide upon, *inter alia*, claims for damages for breaches of antitrust rules, as well as disputes on violations of EU antitrust rules. Thus, the Liberalisation Law seems to have addressed this competence problem, which had, for many years, created difficulties as to the right choice of forum for claiming damages suffered for breaches of antitrust rules. It may therefore be said that victims of cartel damages had encountered this procedural hurdle prior to the enactment of the Liberalisation Law.

Moreover, as regards the burden of proof in an action for damages, in Italy, the victim of a cartel who sues the infringer for the breach of antitrust rules would have to prove

- the subsistence of the damage,
- the amount of damages suffered,
- the defendant's fault,
- the causal link between the defendant's conduct and the damage.

The known financial difficulties that an SME would encounter throughout the private enforcement procedural *iter* in Italy may certainly be considered a dissuasive factor in instituting private litigation for breaches of antitrust rules.

To mention one concrete example, reference may be made to the Liberalisation Law, which has increased financial burdens in private enforcement, in that the fixed court fee ("contributo unificato") to be paid to the Specialised Courts has doubled.

[56] For an overview of the antitrust problems and issues arising from this complex structure prior to the amendments introduced by the Liberalisation Law, see Raffaelli E.A., (2012) The Jurisdiction of Italian Judges in Enforcing Antitrust Law: Problems and Solutions, in Competition Law and Intellectual Property: a European Perspective, edited by Caggiano G., Muscolo G. and Tavassi M., Wolters Kluwer, Kluwer Law International B.V., The Netherlands.

10.4.1.2 Best Practices

On a general note, in order to encourage undertakings to act against anticompetitive practices, costs and duration of proceedings should be reduced as much as possible.

10.4.2 Collective Redress

In Italy, collective redress is primarily regulated by Article 140 *bis* of the Italian Consumer Code ("Consumer Code"). Pursuant to the aforesaid code, consumers and users, also through consumer associations, may institute a collective action for redress, *inter alia*, against anticompetitive conduct. Undertakings are therefore not entitled to institute an action pursuant to Article 140 *bis* of the Consumer Code.

Thus, according to the Consumer Code, SMEs would not have standing to bring a collective action. Collective redress rules are exclusively applicable to actions instituted by consumers and not on behalf of individuals acting within the scope of their trade, business, and profession.

10.4.3 The Role of Trade Associations (Standing)

It is worth mentioning that, as regards Italy, the PFEL grants standing to industrial associations that are represented in at least five different chambers of commerce, or in the *Consiglio nazionale dell'economia e del lavoro*, to institute actions both in the interests of the general category of businesses they represent and in the case of specific interests of some of the members of the said associations. Moreover, industrial associations that are more "representative" of their sector at national, regional, or provincial levels ("maggiormente rappresentative a livello nazionale, regionale e provinciale") may challenge administrative acts that are in breach of their interests.

10.4.4 Policy Recommendations

Cost reduction and limiting duration of proceedings as much as possible would, in the author's view, be all the more beneficial to SMEs, which might be dissuaded from taking action if they do not have the necessary financial resources to do so.

Conclusions and Policy Recommendations

Establishing specific protection mechanisms for SMEs does not, in the author's view, seem to be necessary. As highlighted above, access to justice and remedies should be facilitated for all undertakings alike, independently of their dimension. SMEs will then ultimately benefit if procedures and processes are simplified.

Furthermore, as said, attributing procedural rights to particular undertakings might work to the detriment of others. It would therefore be preferable to apply rules to all undertakings alike, at a level playing field.

Awareness programmes by antitrust authorities should, in particular, seek to encourage leniency applications by all undertakings, independently of their dimension.

As for leniency procedures, establishing further specific protection mechanisms apart from those already contained in leniency programmes, thus "favouring" SMEs, might unfairly "tip the balance" and prejudice rights of other parties.

11 Luxembourg

Gabriel Bleser

11.1 General Background in Luxembourg

It is important to mention that it was only in 2004 when Luxembourg adopted a law[1] on competition and two competition authorities were created. On 23 October 2011, a new law[2] on competition was introduced. The substantial rules have not been changed by the new law. The main objective was to merge the two competition authorities into a new competition authority with new powers and to enhance an efficient application of the law.

Unfortunately, since 2004, only a few infringement decisions have been adopted by the Luxembourg competition council,[3] and no specific rules and no case law exist in relation to specific treatment of SMEs.

11.2 Legal Definitions

Domestic competition law does not provide a definition for an SME.

Other Luxembourg rules (labour law and state aid legislation, for example) provide for a definition of SMEs. National Competition Authorities should establish specific programmes addressed to SMEs, and it would make sense to have a definition of an SME.

It would be helpful to have a general applicable definition of SMEs. Such a definition could be inspired by Recommendation 2003/361, relating to the definition of micro-, small, and medium-sized companies.

[1] Law of 17 May 2004, published in Mémorial A, n. 76 of 26 May 2004.

[2] Law of 23 October 2011, published in Mémorial A, n. 218, of 28 October 2011.

[3] www.concurrence.lu.

G. Bleser (✉)
Kleyr Grasso Associés, Luxembourg, Luxembourg
e-mail: gabriel.bleser@kckg.com

P. Këllezi et al. (eds.), *Antitrust for Small and Middle Size Undertakings and Image Protection from Non-Competitors*, LIDC Contributions on Antitrust Law, Intellectual Property and Unfair Competition, DOI 10.1007/978-3-642-54000-4_11, © Springer-Verlag Berlin Heidelberg 2014

The new law on competition introduced the possibility for the Luxembourg competition council to issue opinion letters. This new instrument is not specific to SMEs, but there is a risk that this new instrument will be used by Luxembourg SMEs to get a preliminary view on agreements that they want to adopt.

Taking into account the small size of the Luxembourg domestic market, it would make sense to have a domestic *de minimis* rule. Unfortunately, when the new law was introduced, the introduction of specific rules applicable to SMEs was not discussed.

11.3 Procedural Aspects

No specific procedural rules exist in Luxembourg. We consider that it would make sense to have specific procedural rules in favour of SME's for the following reasons:

- Small companies, in principle, lack human and financial resources and very often do not have a legal department.
- Small companies have difficulties finding adequate financing to defend themselves in complicated and lengthy competition procedures when facing large and international companies.
- Small companies have difficulties finding relevant information.

Concerning local anticompetitive practices, it would be desirable to extend the response time given to an SME to reply to a statement of objections and questionnaires sent out by the competition council. We also believe that it is necessary to facilitate or accelerate the access to SMEs if they prove to have an objective interest.

11.4 Sanctions and Leniency Programme

No specific rules exist in Luxembourg. However, the fact of being an SME is taken into account when sanctions are calculated. Firstly, the volume of sales affected by the anticompetitive practice is in principle lower for an SME than for a larger company. Second, the ability to pay a fine is also taken into account. A multinational company will be given a higher fine than an SME.

In the first ever leniency case, it is worth mentioning that one of the largest companies was among the first to apply for leniency.

We believe that the leniency and agreement systems should include specific rules for SMEs in order to facilitate their participation during a sanctioning proceeding. Luxembourg law does not provide any specific rules to protect SMEs before big undertakings after a complaint before the NCA. We believe that it is necessary to establish protection mechanisms in order to enhance SMEs to inform about anticompetitive practices.

11.5 Private Antitrust Enforcement

Luxembourg legislation does not provide for any specific rules in order to protect SMEs facing larger companies in civil claims for anticompetitive behaviour. We believe it is necessary to establish protection mechanisms in order to enhance SMEs' ability to take legal action against anticompetitive practices. Luxembourg legislation does not allow a third party to bring an action before civil courts if some SMEs do not take action. In Luxembourg, there are no collective legal actions available to SMEs, nor is any collective action available to consumers.

We do not believe that there should be specific collective actions available to industrial associations as long as there do not exist specific collective actions available to consumers. In Luxembourg, any specific rules that aim at protecting SMEs as competitors or as partners by trying to prevent business to operate or larger undertaking to act in a way that is harmful to them do not exist.

Sweden 12

Robert Moldén

12.1 Introduction to the Legal Framework of Swedish Competition Law

This contribution deals with the treatment of small and medium-sized undertakings under Swedish competition law. Before analysing the specific issues, a short introduction to the legal framework of Swedish competition law may be appropriate.

The new Swedish Competition Act of 2008[1] contains provisions prohibiting anticompetitive agreements and abuse of a dominant position, which constitute copies of Articles 101 and 102 TFEU.[2] According to the *travaux préparatoires*

[1] Konkurrenslagen (2008:579).

[2] Articles 1, 2, 6, and 7 of the Swedish Competition Act read as follows:

"*Article 1:* Agreements between undertakings shall be prohibited if they have as their object or effect, the prevention, restriction or distortion of competition in the market to an appreciable extent, if not otherwise regulated in this act. This shall apply, in particular, to agreements which:

1. directly or indirectly fix purchase or selling prices or any other trading conditions; [...]

Article 2: The prohibition in Article 1 does not apply to agreements which

1. contributes to improving the production or distribution or to promoting technical or economic progress;
2. allows consumers a fair share of the resulting benefit;
3. only imposes on the undertakings concerned restrictions which are indispensable to the attainment of the objective referred to in paragraph 1, and
4. does not afford such undertakings the possibility of eliminating competition in respect of a substantial part of the utilities in question.

Article 6: Any agreements or provisions included in agreements that are prohibited under Article 1 shall be void. The relevant provision of the Swedish Competition Act prohibiting abuse of a dominant position is the following.

Article 7: Any abuse by one or more undertakings of a dominant position on the market shall be prohibited.

R. Moldén (✉)
Gärde Wesslau, Göteborg, Sweden
e-mail: robert.molden@garde.se

P. Këllezi et al. (eds.), *Antitrust for Small and Middle Size Undertakings and Image Protection from Non-Competitors*, LIDC Contributions on Antitrust Law, Intellectual Property and Unfair Competition, DOI 10.1007/978-3-642-54000-4_12,

behind the preceding Competition Act,[3] the fact that the substantive provisions of the Swedish Competition Act are in line with those of EU competition law means that the Commission's practice and jurisprudence of the Court of Justice can serve as guidance when interpreting the Swedish Competition Act.[4]

The Swedish Supreme Court has, in a case concerning the existence of a dominant position,[5] concluded that the substantive provisions of Swedish competition law are in line with the corresponding provisions of EU competition law to such a degree that it in fact does not matter whether Swedish or EU competition law is applied; in practice, the analysis to be effected is the same.

Public enforcement of Swedish competition law is entrusted to the Swedish Competition Authority[6] and its approximately 140 employees. In the majority of cases handled by the Swedish Competition Authority, the procedure is very similar to that of the Commission's DG Competition and to that of most other national competition authorities in the EU. The Swedish Competition Authority is entitled to take both final and interim injunction decisions on its own,[7] ordering an ongoing violation of Swedish or EU competition law to be terminated; such decisions can be combined with a penalty to be paid in case the antitrust offender would not comply with the injunction decision.[8] Moreover, the Swedish Competition Authority is entitled to take decisions making voluntary commitments mandatory, under threat of penalty payments.[9] The Authority is also entitled to issue non-mandatory fine orders.[10]

Such abuse may, in particular, consist in

1. directly or indirectly imposing unfair purchase or selling prices or other unfair trading conditions,
2. limiting production, markets or technical development to the prejudice of consumers,
3. applying dissimilar conditions to equivalent transactions with other trading parties, thereby placing them at a competitive disadvantage, or
4. making the conclusion of contracts subject to acceptance by the other parties of supplementary obligations, which by their nature or according to commercial usage have no connection with the subject of such contracts."

[3] The Swedish Competition Act of 1993, Konkurrenslagen (1993:20), available in English at http://www.kkv.se/upload/Filer/ENG/Publications/The_Swedish_Competition_Act.pdf.

[4] See Government Bill 1992/93:56, p. 21.

[5] Judgment of the Swedish Supreme Court in case T 2808–05 of 19 February 2008, *The Ystad Harbour Case*.

[6] Konkurrensverket.

[7] Chapter 3, Articles 1 and 3 of the Swedish Competition Act.

[8] Chapter 3, Article 1, and Chapter 6, Article 1 of the Swedish Competition Act.

[9] Chapter 3, Article 4 and Chapter 6, Article 1 (2) of the Swedish Competition Act.

[10] Chapter 3, Article 17 of the Swedish Competition Act; if the undertaking to which the fine order is addressed does not consent to the order within the time specified, the Swedish Competition Authority may initiate court proceedings concerning fines instead.

These decisions by the Swedish Competition Authority can be appealed to the Swedish Market Court.[11] An appeal against the judgment of the Swedish Market Court to the Swedish Supreme Court is not permitted; the Swedish Market Court is thus first and last instance court in the majority of cases when Swedish competition law is enforced by the Swedish Competition Authority.

However, a peculiarity of Swedish procedural competition law consists in the fact that the Swedish Competition Authority may not take any mandatory decision on its own to impose fines for breaches of Swedish or EU competition law. In these cases, the Swedish Competition Authority has to sue the undertakings involved before the District Court of Stockholm. It is thus the District Court of Stockholm that, if the Swedish Competition Authority wins its case, imposes fines at first instance. Also in these cases, there is only one more instance, as the judgments of the Stockholm District Court can be appealed to the Swedish Market Court only, without any appeal to the Swedish Supreme Court being possible.

Another peculiarity of Swedish competition procedural law is that private injunction claims to cease any ongoing infringement of Swedish or EU competition law may not be brought directly to court. First, a complaint has to be made to the Swedish Competition Authority. If the Swedish Competition Authority decides to pick up the case, the Authority would take an injunction decision, which then could be appealed to the Swedish Market Court; in these proceedings, the complainant does not enjoy any standing as a party. If, however, the Swedish Competition Authority decides not to pursue the case and the complainant obtains a so-called subsidiary right of action, the complainant can directly lodge her case at the Swedish Market Court, which may then, as first and last instance, take an injunction decision.[12]

12.2 Legal Definitions

12.2.1 Legal Definition of SME

There is no specific legal definition of SMEs as such used in the context of Swedish competition law. The Swedish Competition Authority refers to the definition of SMEs provided by the Commission. Recommendation 2003/361 issued by the Commission aims at improving the consistency and effectiveness of the policies targeting SMEs, and the Recommendation provides provisions regarding the number of employees, turnover, or annual balance sheet (see Article 2 of the Recommendation).

[11] Marknadsdomstolen, www.marknadsdomstolen.se; see Chapter 7, Article 1 of the Swedish Competition Act.

[12] Chapter 3, Article 2 of the Swedish Competition Act.

Table 12.1 SME categories

Company category	Employees	Turnover or Balance sheet total
Medium size	< 250	≤ EUR 50 m or ≤ EUR 43 m
Small	< 50	≤ EUR 10 m or ≤ EUR 10 m
Micro	< 10	≤ EUR 2 m or ≤ EUR 2 m

These provisions are summarised in Table 12.1.

As Table 12.1 shows, the SME category of enterprises is made up of enterprises falling within the above-mentioned scopes regarding number of employees (less than 250) and that have an annual turnover of less than EUR 50 million *or* a balance sheet total of less than EUR 43 million. Within this category, enterprises are divided into the categories regarding small or microenterprises according to the figures indicated.

12.2.2 Specific National Rules to Be Considered in the Definition of SMEs

In Sweden, the term "small enterprises" is widely used in a number of different areas. The term is defined in many different ways, often relating to the number of employees, the total annual net turnover, or whether the owner is working within the enterprise, just to list a few variables.

One interesting example of a definition of small enterprise is found in Swedish law applicable to annual reports and limited companies. These rules provide information on when small enterprises are governed or not by certain provisions provided in these acts. Significant reduction as to the regulatory burden is accorded to small enterprises, e.g., regarding the rules on when a limited company is obliged to assign an authorised public accountant. *The Swedish Act on Annual Reports*[13] defines small enterprises in Chapter 1, Article 3, as "enterprises not included in the definition of large enterprises". Large enterprises are defined as enterprises that fulfil at least two of the following conditions:

1. The average number of employees in the company has, for each of the two most recent fiscal years, amounted to more than 50.
2. The company's reported balance sheet total has, for each of the two most recent fiscal years, amounted to more than SEK 40 million.
3. The company's reported net turnover amounts to more than SEK 80 million.

Another interesting example of legal area where significant reduction of regulatory burden is accorded to small enterprises is the *Swedish Act on Employment Protection*,[14] Article 22. This provision defines small enterprises as those with no more than ten employees, and such small enterprises are exempted from the

[13] Årsredovisningslagen (1995:1554).

[14] Lag (1982:80) om anställningsskydd.

obligation to apply a strict seniority *last-in, first-out* principle when reducing the number of employees due to redundancies.

12.2.3 Specific Programmes or Policies Addressed to SMEs

The Swedish Competition Authority has, since 2007, also been the competent supervisory authority in the field of public procurement. The Swedish Competition has an explicit mission to take measures increasing the possibilities of SMEs to take part in public procurement proceedings.[15]

The Swedish Competition Authority has pointed out that to uphold an effective competition, it is of utmost importance that SMEs are allowed to take part on fair terms in public procurement proceeding. In a report published in 2009[16] on the possibilities of an increased participation in public procurement proceedings by SMEs, the Swedish Competition Authority states that the average number of tenders received in a given public procurement proceeding can be used as an indication of the level of competition and that this number had decreased in Sweden in the years prior to 2009. This development is considered problematic by the Swedish Competition Authority. The report states that the basic principle of equal treatment prohibits special considerations related to, in this case, the size of the enterprise but that there are some measures that could be taken to increase the possibilities of SMEs to participate in public procurements proceedings.

12.3 SMEs as Infringers

12.3.1 Case Law

Swedish case law as to SMEs as infringers will be presented below in the following order. Firstly, relevant cases concerning vertical agreements will be presented. Secondly, relevant cases concerning horizontal agreements will be presented. Finally, a number of cases concerning bid rigging will be set out. To the author's knowledge, the Swedish Competition Authority has so far not taken any case concerning abuse of a dominant position committed by an SME to court.

12.3.1.1 Prohibition Against Vertical Agreements

There are not many interventions by the Swedish Competition Authority against cases of purely vertical constraints since 2004, when the earlier notification system

[15] See, e.g., Swedish Competition Authority: http://www.kkv.se/t/Page____4337.aspx, 4 April 2012.

[16] PM Upphandling och mindre företag- öka SME:s deltagande och dra nytta av konkurrensen, 14 January 2009, file ref. 385/2008.

was scrapped as part of the modernisation of EU competition law procedure. However, there are two interesting cases relating to SMEs to be reported.

In the *Eco-Boråstapeter* case,[17] the Swedish Competition Authority actively intervened. In its Statement of Objections, the Swedish Competition Authority found that Eco-Boråstapeter applied anticompetitive selection criteria for admittance to a selective distribution system. The company then offered voluntarily commitments not to apply any quantitative selection criteria. The Swedish Competition Authority accepted these commitments. The economic dimension of the company is mentioned in the decision by the Swedish Competition Authority as well in the background (where total turnover for 2004 was SEK 263 million and the number of resellers was 230) as in their assessment of the relevant market, which led to the preliminary conclusion of an anticompetitive conduct. The SME status is not mentioned, but the Swedish Competition Authority considers the company's distribution system to lead to a significant anticompetitive effect on the relevant market.

In the *Make Up Store* case,[18] the Swedish Competition Authority actively intervened and started an investigation of Make Up Store's control of prices set by their franchisees. The company used a cashier system called Navision, which it recommended to its franchisees. This system provided fixed prices for all products, and only Make Up Store was enabled to change prices in the system, thus making it technically impossible for franchisees to set their own prices. Make Up Store also provided the franchisees with shelve-top product information with printed prices, as well as an internal order list with fixed prices. The Swedish Competition Authority's preliminary view was that this kind of resale price maintenance infringed Chapter 2, Article 1 of the Swedish Competition Act. The company offered voluntary commitments that, in short, consisted of changing Navision so that the franchisees were enabled to change prices, change order lists from fixed to recommended prices, and also change routines for the shelve-top product information. The Swedish Competition Authority accepted these commitments. The economic dimension of this SME is mentioned in the case, both in the general background (annual turnover for 2008/2009 was SEK 128.4 million) and in the reasons for the commitments suggested by the Swedish Competition Authority. There is, however, no mentioning of any particular considerations due to the company's SME status. The Swedish Competition Authority expressly stated that the extent of the company's and their franchisees' business leads to the preliminary conclusion of an anticompetitive conduct.

[17] Decision of the Swedish Competition Authority of 13 December 2005, File ref. 532/2004.

[18] Decision of the Swedish Competition Authority of 15 December 2010, File ref. 402/2010. The author of this contribution worked at that time as Senior Case Officer for the Swedish Competition Authority and served as senior advisor ("projektråd") to the case team handling the Make Up Store case.

12.3.1.2 Prohibition Against Horizontal Agreements

In the *Swedish plumbers case*,[19] the Swedish Competition Authority intervened against an organisation of enterprises within the ventilation and sanitation business. The organisation provided a subscription service to a price list, the so-called Large R-List offered to both members and nonmembers of the organisation. This subscription listed all the most frequent sought-after products within the business and contained information on many factors—including prices. The Swedish Competition Authority found in its decision[20] this distribution of the lists to constitute an anticompetitive cooperation and took an injunction decision obliging VVS-Installatörerna to cease distribution of the "Large R-List". The economic dimension of the VVS-Installatörerna is mentioned in the background, and the total annual turnover for the part of VVS-Installatörerna providing the subscription service amounted to SEK 31 million during the year 2002. The Swedish Competition Authority focuses instead on the total turnover for the members of the organisation, which for 2002 was estimated to be SEK 14 billion (70 % of the turnover in that market in Sweden). The decision by the Swedish Competition Authority was upheld by the Swedish Market Court in its judgment of 9 February 2005.[21]

In the *Volvo dealers case*,[22] the Swedish Competition Authority found that a number of Volvo car dealers in the south of Sweden had engaged in horizontal price fixing. The dealers argued that they were so much integrated in the Volvo vertical distribution chain that the cooperation should be seen as part of the vertical relationship. The Stockholm District Court shared this view.[23] However, on appeal, the Swedish Market Court fined the car dealers for horizontal price fixing. The economic dimension of the individual dealers involved in this cartel is not in focus in the Judgment of the Swedish Market Court. The focus is instead on the collective impact on the relevant market. In total, the cumulative level of fines was set at approximately SEK 21 million. These fines were divided among the eight car dealers, out of which most were SMEs. The smaller car dealers were subject to considerably lower fines than the larger car dealers.

In the *Svenska Bilsportförbundet case*,[24] the Swedish Competition Authority investigated the Federation's rules regarding licenses for both those who compete and those who work at automobile sports competitions. These rules forbid those who were licensed under the Federation to compete or work at other commercial competitions held by any association other than the Swedish Automobile Sports Federation. The Swedish Competition Authority found these rules to be in breach of the Swedish Competition Act (Chapter 2, Article 1 of the Act) and took an injunction decision obliging the federation to revise the rules so that they no longer

[19] Judgment of the Swedish Market Court of 9 February 2005, 2005:5.

[20] Decision of the Swedish Competition Authority of 2 March 2004, file ref. 498/2002.

[21] Judgment of the Swedish Market Court of 9 February 2005, 2005:5.

[22] Judgment of the Swedish Market Court of 10 September 2008, 2008:12.

[23] Judgment of the Stockholm District Court of 7 June 2006 (T 4231–04).

[24] Decision of the Swedish Competition Authority of 13 May 2011, file ref. 709/2009.

would constitute an anticompetitive conduct. The Federation is a nonprofit organisation with approximately 104,000 members. The total annual turnover for 2010 amounted to SEK 32.4 million. The economic dimension of the Federation is mentioned by the Swedish Competition Authority, but of relevance to the legal assessment in the case is not the SME status but the impact on the relevant market where the majority of events and competitions were held by the Federation. This decision has been appealed to by the Swedish Automobile Sports Federation.

In the *bus travelling case* of 2012, two SMEs, Scandorama AB and Ölvemarks Holiday AB, were during 2006/2007 discussing a possible merger.[25] The transaction should, according to a contract signed in July 2007, be carried out gradually over a period of 3 years. However, the financial situation of Scandorama deteriorated to such a critical point that the third and final stage was not completed. In April 2009, the two parties agreed to abandon the deal. Instead, Ölvemarks acquired Scandorama in June 2009. During the period from April 2007 until March 2009, the two enterprises were engaged in extensive cooperation regarding prices, discounts, costs, as well as destinations. The court ruled that the case did not concern a "classic" secret cartel and that the non-concealed way of coordinating business between the two enterprises at hand entailed less anticompetitive effects than would otherwise have been the case. Another mitigating factor was that the breach of competition law was not malicious. The Stockholm District Court found that the fine should be set at SEK 4.6 million for Ölvemarks Holiday AB and SEK 6,790,000 for Scandorama AB after having taken into consideration the value of sales in the relevant market and the duration of the breach of competition law.

12.3.1.3 Prohibition Against Bid Rigging

In the *power supply poles case* of 2009, the Swedish Competition Authority investigated a bid-rigging cartel between the SMEs ScanPole Sverige AB and Rundvirke Poles AB.[26] ScanPole submitted a leniency application and provided information on the cartel, which led to a dawn raid carried out by the Swedish Competition Authority on Rundvirke Poles. The two enterprises had cooperated in seven different public procurement proceedings regarding power supply poles made of wood. This price-related cooperation was found to infringe competition law and a non-mandatory fine order was proposed to Rundvirke Poles at the amount of SEK 2 million. Rundvirke Poles accepted this fine and thus avoided court proceedings. This case was the first time a non-mandatory fine order was taken by the Swedish Competition Authority. The fines proposed to the enterprise were considerably reduced due to its active cooperation in the investigation.

In the *transport of deceased case* of 2010, three Swedish funeral parlours, out of which two were SMEs, made voluntary commitments to pay the administrative fine set by the Swedish Competition Authority after having participated in illegal cooperation concerning a bid-rigging cartel in public procurement proceedings.[27]

[25] Judgment of the Stockholm District Court of 24 February 2012 (T 19974–10).

[26] Fine order by the Swedish Competition Authority of 30 June 2009, file ref. 237/2007.

[27] Decision of the Swedish Competition Authority of June 2010.

The three enterprises chose to make a voluntary commitment and thus avoided court proceedings. The fines set by the Swedish Competition Authority varied, and the two SMEs' fines were set to approximately SEK 40,000 and SEK 140,000—to be compared to the fine set to the large enterprise, which was set at approximately SEK 300,000.

In the *burnt waste transport case* of 2011, the Swedish Competition Authority proposed a non-mandatory fine order to ASFAB—a Swedish SME.[28] The enterprise had participated in a bid-rigging cartel in a public procurement proceeding regarding transport of burnt waste products from combined power and heating plants in two Swedish cities, together with Björn Hägglunds Maskiner AB. The Swedish Competition Authority used its Guidelines on methods of setting administrative fines and, after taking the different aspects under consideration, decided that the infringement of competition law was to be considered very serious and that such bid-rigging horizontal agreements typically constitute very serious restrictions of competition and, hence, for the public economy and consumers. The total value of sales in the relevant market for the enterprise was approximately SEK 587,000, and the fine was set at SEK 293,000. As to Björn Hägglunds Maskiner AB,[29] the same considerations were made regarding the setting of the fine, as when setting the fine for ASFAB. The value of sales on the relevant market for this enterprise was approximately SEK 351,000, and the fine for Björn Hägglunds Maskiner AB was set at SEK 175,000. In this case, no mitigating factors were found by the Swedish Competition Authority.

12.3.2 Substantive Rules

There is no direct differentiated application as to the substantive rules. However, there is an indirect differentiated application in that small and medium-sized enterprises normally have low market shares and therefore normally have considerably less market power than large enterprises. The degree of market power held by an undertaking is a very important criterion of substantive Swedish competition law analysis.

12.3.2.1 Safe Harbours in Relation to SMEs

Swedish Provisions on Safe Harbours in Line with the EU De Minimis Notice

As a complement to the Swedish Competition Act of 2008,[30] the Swedish Competition Authority provides guidelines on how to interpret Swedish competition law.

---

[28] Fine order by the Swedish Competition Authority, 2011-12-01, file ref. 327/2010.

[29] Fine order by the Swedish Competition Authority, 2011-12-01, file ref. 327/2010.

[30] Konkurrenslagen (2008:579).

In 2009, the Swedish Competition Authority published its present Guidelines on agreements of minor importance,[31] which are of particular interest for SMEs.

These provisions are in most aspects identical to those provided by the EU Notice on agreements of minor importance (*de minimis* Notice), which quantifies what is not an appreciable restriction of competition under Article 101 TFEU. The main principle of the *de minimis* Notice is the same, i.e. that an agreement that would otherwise be caught by Article 101 TFEU and Chapter 2, Article 1 of the Swedish Competition Act falls outside the scope of the above-mentioned Articles as long as the aggregate market share held by the parties to the agreement does not exceed 10 %, in case of horizontal agreements, and 15 %, in case of vertical agreements. As under EU law, hard-core restrictions are explicitly not covered by the Swedish *de minimis* provisions. The provisions regarding hard-core restrictions are thus the same in the Swedish guidelines as in the *de minimis* Notice.

Swedish Provisions on Safe Harbours Differing from the EU Notice

The Swedish Guidelines do, however, differ from the *de minimis* Notice in one important aspect. The Swedish Guidelines contain provisions that are more generous as to the possibility of SMEs to enter into non-hard-core horizontal agreements. Pursuant to the Swedish Guidelines' Article 7, cooperation between enterprises does not fall under the prohibition of chapter 2, Article 1 of the Swedish Competition Act as long as the annual net turnover of each of the contracting parties does not exceed SEK 30 million and their joint market share is less than 15 %, compared to the 10 % market share threshold applicable to horizontal cooperation agreements under the *de minimis* Notice.

12.3.3 Procedural Aspects

There are no situations under Swedish competition law where procedural rights are explicitly different between SMEs and larger undertakings.

The Swedish Competition Authority has issued a priority policy document stating the factors taken into consideration regarding prioritisation of the matters dealt with by the Swedish Competition Authority in competition law and public procurement.[32] The relevant part of the priority policy document reads as follows:

> The aim of this policy is to clarify how the Swedish Competition Authority should generally prioritise the problems that ought to be investigated.
>
> The Swedish Competition Authority must be selective when choosing which matters to pursue. The Authority must focus on investigating matters that are of general interest and that will produce clear results. The aim must always be to promote effective competition.

[31] Konkurrensverkets allmänna råd om avtal av mindre betydelse (bagatellavtal) som inte omfattas av förbudet i 2 kap. 1 § Konkurrenslagen (2008:579), KKVFS 2009:1.

[32] The Swedish Competition Authority's policy for prioritising competition and procurement issues of 5 October 2010, ref 675/2010, it can be downloaded in English language from http://www.kkv.se/upload/Filer/ENG/About/Prioriteringspolicy_eng.pdf.

> Even though priority has been given to a matter, the Authority may limit the issues in the matter to be investigated. The Authority must consider the following factors when prioritising matters:
> 1. the gravity of the problem or occurrence.
> 2. the importance of getting a ruling to provide guidance
> 3. whether it would be more appropriate for another authority or stakeholder to take action regarding the matter or whether it would be more suitable for it to be dealt with by applying a different system of rules.
>
> Priority will be given to matters involving serious problems or occurrences. The gravity of a matter depends on the negative effects that may arise for competition, and thereby for consumers and public bodies. The Swedish Competition Authority considers that certain behaviour is particularly serious, such as agreements on prices, limiting markets, market sharing, exclusionary abuse of a dominant position, illegal direct procurement and, as regards public sales operations that restrict competition, operations that may be prohibited when they conflict with both the Competition Act and other statutes and involve the combined conduct of official operations and sales operations. Of course, this does not prevent the need for other kinds of violation to be given priority.
>
> A repetition of behaviour that has previously been considered to constitute a violation or has been prohibited is regarded as a serious problem, and is normally given priority. One example in the area of procurement is that there are organisations and authorities subject to the procurement rules, and which should consequently apply them yet never do so.
>
> Another important factor to take into account is whether the problem or occurrence bears on the entire Swedish market or a significant part of this market, or whether it is wide-ranging in some other way. A further factor is whether the problem applies to sectors of importance to the national economy that may be deemed to be of public interest; for example, that affect a large consumer collective. There is a risk that behaviour restricting competition in a market characterised by few stakeholders and weak competition will have a significant negative impact on competition in such a market. This may, for example, occur in markets that have recently been re-regulated.

In regards to the first factor (gravity of the problem), the Swedish Competition Authority, in its policy document, clarifies that the gravity of a matter depends on the negative effects on competition and thereby for consumers and public bodies. It is interesting to note that the document does not contain any direct reference to the effects of an antitrust infringement on those companies adversely affected by the infringement.

In the author's view, an updated version of the priority policy document should also explicitly mention the negative effects of the antitrust infringement in question on the enterprise having made the original complaint, possibly with an explicit mentioning of the perspective of SMEs put under financial stress and threatened by market exit because of an anticompetitive conduct committed by large enterprises. This would make the protection of SMEs a higher priority—particularly when SMEs are victims of an abuse of a dominant position committed by a large company. Moreover, the incentives of SMEs and other enterprises to inform the Swedish Competition Authority of ongoing competition law infringements would be enhanced.

As the Swedish system stands today, an SME faces particular difficulties in case the Swedish Competition Authority decides not to give priority to its complaint, which means that the SME would need to use its subsidiary right to initiate legal action before the Swedish Market Court. Large companies often have both the financial and legal resources to make use of this right—SMEs often do not. In particular, the obligation to pay for the large enterprise's potentially very high legal costs should the SME lose its case before the Swedish Market Court often constitutes a de facto barrier for an SME, making it financially too risky to initiate such legal action. For many SMEs therefore, the only financially viable option is to hope that the Swedish Competition Authority will give priority to its complaint and undertake an investigation that then may lead to an injunction decision forbidding the large company in question to abuse its dominant position.

12.3.3.1 Sanctions and Leniency Programme

The Swedish Competition Authority has issued Guidelines on methods of setting administrative fines[33] to clarify the ways in which the Swedish Competition Authority will interpret and apply the rules in the Swedish Competition Act relating to administrative fines. Pursuant to Article 6 of the Guidelines, "a sanction value will be set *by reference to the value of sales in the relevant market*, the gravity of the infringement and its duration" (emphasis added by the author). As the value of sales in the relevant market being one of the relevant factors for determining the level of fines, SMEs will typically be liable to pay lower fines than a large firm would have to do for the same kind of infringement.

To the author's knowledge, there has not been any case so far in Sweden where large enterprises won the race to file a leniency application, while small and medium-sized enterprises ended up paying hefty fines.

Swedish legislation does not contain any specific rules to protect SMEs from a large undertaking's retaliatory measures after a complaint has been lodged at the Swedish Competition Authority. However, if the large undertaking in question holds a dominant position, retaliatory measures may constitute an abuse of a dominant position.

In the author's view, no additional protection mechanisms for SMEs are required. However, the Swedish Competition Authority should continue to inform, in particular, small and medium-sized enterprises of its leniency programme. A very good example of such information is the film "Be the first to tell – a film about leniency" produced by the Swedish Competition Authority.[34]

---

[33] Swedish Competition Authority, Method of setting administrative fines, file ref. 394/2009, of 19 November 2009; the guidelines can be downloaded in English language here: http://www.kkv.se/upload/Filer/ENG/Competition/Metod_fastställa_konkskadeavgift_%20eng.pdf.

[34] The film is published on Youtube and can be downloaded from http://www.kkv.se/t/Page____5767.aspx.

12.4 SMEs as Victims

12.4.1 Private Antitrust Enforcement

One of the most interesting cases is the *Arlanda Taxi case* of 2010,[35] which was investigated by the Swedish Competition Authority upon complaint by a number of small taxi enterprises. The case concerned the planned change of structure regarding taxi lanes at Sweden's largest airport, the Stockholm Arlanda Airport. The three largest taxi companies in Stockholm would—after the planned change outside Terminal 5—have four out of five taxi lanes, and the other smaller companies would have to share only one lane between them. The Swedish Competition Authority issued an interim injunction decision against Luftfartsverket (the Swedish Aviation Authority) obliging the latter not to go ahead with these changes as the Authority's preliminary investigation indicated that the effect of the planned changes would amount to an abuse of a dominant position by means of discrimination.[36] The Swedish Market Court upheld the interim decision taken by the Swedish Competition Authority. This case constitutes a rare example of the Swedish Competition Authority intervening to protect SMEs from abuse of a dominant position by a large undertaking.

In the *Uppsala Taxi case*,[37] Uppsala Taxi 100 000 AB lodged a complaint concerning abuse of a dominant position before the Swedish Competition Authority. After the Swedish Competition Authority had decided not to intervene, Uppsala Taxi 100 000 used its subsidiary right of action and initiated injunction proceedings before the Swedish Market Court. The case before the Swedish Market Court concerned a system imposed by Swedavia and EuroPark at the Stockholm Arlanda Airport with additional fees for "extra service" provided by Taxi companies (e.g., preordered taxis). The Court found the "normal service" fee not to be an abuse of dominant position but found the "high-service" fee to constitute an abuse of dominant position, and Swedavia and EuroPark were obliged to stop the practice in question. As in the above cases, no explicit references were made to the economic dimensions of the SME.

12.4.1.1 Specific Rules to Protect SMEs

There are no explicit provisions in Swedish competition law that protect SMEs confronted with large undertakings in civil suits for anticompetitive conducts. However, if the large undertaking in question holds a dominant position, retaliatory measures may constitute an abuse of a dominant position. Swedish national

[35] Decision of the Swedish Market Court of 5 February 2010, MD 2010:5.

[36] Decision of the Swedish Competition Authority of 23 October 2009, file ref. 542/2009. The Swedish Competition Authority's investigation in this case was led by the author of this National Report, at that time Senior Case Officer at the Swedish Competition Authority. The views here are of the author alone and not of the Competition Authority.

[37] Judgment of the Swedish Market Court of 23 November 2011, 2011:28.

legislation allows a third party to bring an action before civil courts but only if the SME in question assigns its claims to the third party.

One major obstacle for SMEs derives from the principle in civil litigation that the defeated party has to reimburse the legal cost of the winning party. High legal costs may deter, in particular, SMEs from taking legal action for damages against larger enterprises.

12.4.1.2 Collective Redress

A procedural framework enabling class actions has been in force in Sweden since 1 January 2003 through the Group Proceedings Act. Class actions may, theoretically, be brought with respect to all claims where the applicants otherwise, according to the general procedural civil law framework in Sweden,[38] would have been permitted to bring an action (e.g., standing). The Act provides a possibility of bringing group proceedings when a plurality of claims against the same defendant is based on the same or similar circumstances (commonality) and when the claims cannot be equally well pursued through other procedural forms (superiority).

There are three types of group actions. Group actions can be initiated (1) by an individual member of a group that can in itself be a natural person or a legal entity (private group action); (2) by an association of, for example, consumers (organisational group action); and (3) by a designated public authority (public group action). Only private group actions and organisational group actions are available in the context of antitrust law.

It is possible for ad hoc organisations to bring private group actions. In this regard, the right of standing may be achieved by setting up an organisation merely created for the purpose of bringing an action as well as by transferring the right to present a claim from the private undertakings to the organisation. The organisation thus gains standing by means of acquiring a claim of its own.

The Swedish Competition Authority is currently not allowed to bring public group actions in the field of antitrust law. This topic has been discussed on various occasions in connection to the passing/evaluation of the Act.[39] To the author's knowledge, there are currently no legislative reforms planned in this respect.

To the author's knowledge, there have not yet been any judgments rendered as to group proceedings for damages related to an infringement of the Swedish Competition Act.

---

[38] The Swedish Code of Judicial Procedure (Rättegångsbalken).

[39] E.g., prop. 2004/05:117 and Ds 2008:74.

12.4.2 Substantive Rules: New Legislation Against Anticompetitive Sales Activities by Public Entities

The provisions regarding anticompetitive sales activities by public entities are embodied in the Swedish Competition Act, Chapter 3, Articles 27–32, and apply as of 1 January 2010.[40] In short, they provide a new procedural framework with regard to reviewing the legality of sales activities carried out by public entities in competition with private undertakings.

Given that many SMEs in Sweden compete with public entities in small, local markets (e.g., limited liability companies owned by Swedish municipalities), one may argue that the new framework is of particular value for SMEs. This view is also reflected in the *travaux préparatoires*, which state that it is expected that SMEs in particular will (indirectly) benefit from the provisions.[41] According to the industry organisation for privately owned businesses, Företagarna, 18 % of all SMEs are competing with public entities.[42]

Legal actions are primarily to be initiated directly by the Swedish Competition Authority, which may file an application to the Stockholm District Court requesting a certain activity or conduct to be prohibited. Should, however, the Swedish Competition Authority decide not to bring such an action, a private undertaking is allowed to proceed with a private complaint to the court (i.e., subsidiary right of action).

A court decision prohibiting a certain activity/conduct has only legal effects for the future (*ex nunc*). Hence, no fine or penalty whatsoever may be imposed on the public entity if it decides to fully comply with the court order.

Four of the pending cases concerning anticompetitive sales activities by public entities are briefly described below.

In the *Räddningstjänsten Dala Mitt case*,[43] the Swedish Competition Authority has sought an injunction to prohibit the public entity in question from refusing

---

[40] Chapter 3, Article 27 of the Swedish Competition Act stipulates:

"A certain conduct by the State, a municipality or a county council within a sales activity covered by Chapter 1, Article 5, first paragraph, may be prohibited through an injunction, if such conduct

1. distorts, by object or effect, the conditions for effective competition in the market, or

2. impedes, by object or effect, the occurrence or the development of such competition. An injunction may not be imposed in relation to conduct that can be justified by public interest considerations. A certain sales activity by a municipality or a county council may also be prohibited in cases referred to in the first paragraph. However, such a sales activity may not be prohibited if it is compatible with law. An injunction shall take effect immediately, unless decided otherwise."

[41] Government Bill 2008/09:231, p. 55.

[42] Government Bill 2008/09:231, p. 28.

[43] Reference number at the Swedish Competition Authority: Dnr 304/2010. The author of this contribution worked at that time as Senior Case Officer for the Swedish Competition Authority and served as the first senior advisor ("projektråd") to the case team handling the Räddningstjänsten Dala Mitt case.

private competitors' access to certain key infrastructure facilities (a safety training area) under public control.

In the *Skelleftebuss AB case*,[44] the Swedish Competition Authority has brought an action to prohibit a company owned by a Swedish municipality from running business towards other municipalities than the owner (i.e., to limit its sales activities to the very area of that municipality).

In the *Mälarenergi Stadsnät AB case*,[45] the Swedish Competition Authority has requested the court to prohibit a company from offering its services outside the area of the municipality controlling it.

In the *Borås kommun case*,[46] The Swedish Competition Authority has sought an injunction to prohibit a municipality from offering certain services, which allegedly lack the required general interest, to private undertakings, to consumers, and to other municipalities. The Director General of the Swedish Competition Authority, Dan Sjöblom, has stated that the purpose of the Authority's action was not only to clarify the rules and to protect competition and consumers but also to protect SMEs.[47]

Conclusions

While the Swedish Competition Authority has an explicit mission to enhance the possibilities of SMEs to take part in public procurement proceedings, the Swedish Competition Authority makes no explicit reference to SMEs in its policy document concerning the application of competition law. In the author's view, there may be good reasons for the Swedish Competition Authority to attribute a higher level of priority to situations where SMEs are victims of competition law infringements by larger firms.

The new provisions concerning anticompetitive sales activities by public entities that were added to the Swedish Competition Act in 2010 may prove particularly beneficial to SMEs as they often are particularly vulnerable to anticompetitive sales activities performed by publicly owned enterprises. The provisions make it considerably easier for SMEs to act against unilateral anti-competitive behaviour by publicly owned enterprises as no dominance in the conventional sense needs to be proven for the provisions to be applicable.

A particular difficulty for SMEs that consider taking legal action against abuse of a dominant position by a large enterprise is generally the difficulty to prove that the large enterprise actually has a dominant position. Such a finding often involves complicated—and costly—economic analysis, which combined with a high burden of proof may deter SMEs from taking legal action against abuse of a dominant position committed by a large and normally much more financially strong enterprise. This problem could be addressed by changes in

[44] Reference number at the Swedish Competition Authority: Dnr 391/2011.

[45] Reference number at the Swedish Competition Authority: Dnr 438/2011.

[46] Reference number at the Swedish Competition Authority: Dnr 45/2012.

[47] Swedish Competition Authority, http://www.kkv.se/t/NewsPage____7916.aspx, 7 April 2012.

either procedural or substantive Swedish competition law. Procedural law could be amended by explicitly lowering the burden of proof imposed to prove dominance. Alternatively, substantive law may be amended by extending the protection against abuse of a dominant position also to include protection from abusive unilateral conduct by large enterprises whose market power does not reach the high level required for dominance but still have such a high level of significant market power that SMEs are prevented from competing on the merits on a level playing field.

Acknowledgement The author is grateful for the valuable comments and advice of the supervisors of his doctoral thesis, Prof. Hans Henrik Lidgard and Prof. Mats Bergman. The author is also grateful for comments from the members of the Nordic Section of the LIDC present at the meeting of 18 June 2012 in Stockholm, where an earlier draft of this contribution was discussed, and in particular for comments received from Prof. Ulf Bernitz, Giovanni Gozzo, Cecilia Torelm Tornberg, and Richard Jacobsson. Moreover, the author wants to thank his colleagues at the Gärde Wesslau Competition Law Practice Group for their valuable comments and support, in particular Roland Adrell, Karl-Arne Olsson, Johan Lidén, and Sara Karlsson.

13 Switzerland

Nicolas Birkhäuser

13.1 General Background

13.1.1 General

The question posed at the outset concerns an issue that in Switzerland is again and again the subject of mainly political and also cartel law debates. Following the amendment of the Swiss Cartel Act (hereafter referred to as SCA[1]) in 2003, a new provision was introduced that focuses on the "improvement of the competitiveness of small and medium-sized enterprises" [Article 6 para 1(e) SCA]. Previously in the public debate, the criticism was that the competition authorities were focusing their attention too much on small and medium-sized enterprises and too little on large market players.[2]

Article 6 para 1 SCA stipulates that the conditions under which individual types of agreements are, as a general rule, deemed justified on grounds of economic efficiency may be set out in ordinances or general notices. According to Article 6 para 1(e) SCA, in particular, agreements that have the purpose of "improving the competitiveness of small and medium-sized enterprises provided their effect on the market is limited" should be considered. The Swiss Competition Commission (Competition Commission) has met this requirement and in December 2005 published the Notice Regarding Agreements with Limited Effects on the Market dated 19 December 2005 (SME Notice). This is to be seen mainly in the context of the background of political pressure and the introduction of direct sanctions in the event of specific agreements

[1] RS 251, available at http://www.weko.admin.ch/dokumentation/00160/index.html?lang=en.

[2] Notice regarding the amendment of the Swiss Cartel Act of 7 November 2001, BBl 2002 2022, p. 2025; Ducrey Patrik/Tagmann Christoph, Die Anwendung des Kartellrechts auf KMU [Applying Cartel Law to SMEs], in: ZBJV 143/2007, p. 70 ff.

N. Birkhäuser (✉)
Niederer Kraft & Frey Ltd, Zurich, Switzerland
e-mail: nicolas.birkhaeuser@nkf.ch

P. Këllezi et al. (eds.), *Antitrust for Small and Middle Size Undertakings and Image Protection from Non-Competitors*, LIDC Contributions on Antitrust Law, Intellectual Property and Unfair Competition, DOI 10.1007/978-3-642-54000-4_13, © Springer-Verlag Berlin Heidelberg 2014

(Article 49a SCA).[3] In the considerations of the SME Notice, the Competition Commission holds, amongst other things, that agreements between SMEs and also microenterprises are justified above all if they serve to improve competitiveness. Hence, the Competition Commission wants to take into account the specific competitive position of SMEs in the domestic market and also in the macroeconomic and international environment while simultaneously specifically considering the starting point of microenterprises.

Indeed, the view does seem to prevail that SMEs are in a different position regarding competition in comparison to large enterprises. For this reason, they should be subject to special rules. It seems that, in the political discussion, the need for a higher level of legal certainty is allocated above all with regard to SMEs.[4] Trade groups even appear to have demanded to exclude SMEs completely from the application of cartel law or at least to significantly water down its application regarding SMEs in the context of the macroeconomic significance.[5] But what is this view based on? In order to be able to answer this question, one must first of all establish what is meant by an SME.

13.1.2 What Are SMEs?

The term SME for small and medium-sized enterprises is a collective term for companies that do not exceed a certain limit with regard to their staff number, turnover, or balance sheet. The company census delivered by the Federal Office of Statistics subdivides private companies in terms of the number of their employees, with a company being regarded as an SME if it has less than 250 staff.

13.1.3 SME Environment in Switzerland

Following the current company census carried out by the Federal Office of Statistics, there are in Switzerland some 313,000 companies. Of these, 311,707 are regarded as SMEs due to their staff number, while 1,154 are considered large enterprises. The corporate environment in Switzerland consists therefore of 99.6 % SMEs with less than 250 full-time staff and only 0.4 % large enterprises with over 250 full-time staff. What is also interesting is that the 99.6 % of the SMEs employ in total 2,327,802 people. In the 0.4 % of large enterprises, on the other hand, 1,166,269 employees have a job. A total of 33.4 % of employees work therefore at 0.4 % of Swiss companies, which represents a remarkable ratio. Finally,

[3] Ducrey Patrik/Tagmann Christoph, Die Anwendung des Kartellrechts auf KMU [Applying Cartel Law to SMEs], in: ZBJV 143/2007, pp. 71 and 77 ff.

[4] Neff Klaus, in: Basler Kommentar KG, Article 6 para 1(e) N 2.

[5] Ammann Martin/Strebel Mario, Die KMU-Bekanntmachung der WEKO [The WEKO SME notice], in: sic! 2007, p. 229 ff.

one should add that approximately 2/3 of companies in Switzerland are either individual enterprises (one-man companies) or limited liability companies, whereby the most common legal form by far being that of the individual enterprise numbering 142,546: almost half of all companies in Switzerland act in legal terms as an individual enterprise.[6]

13.1.4 SMEs as an Object for Cartel Law?

Switzerland consists therefore mostly of SMEs. This is significant for the question posed at the outset. A law should be made to cover the widest possible number of cases. In other words, it does not appear sensible to make a law solely for the exceptions. However, that would mean that the SCA, as it stands, *would have to be* focused on SMEs already. To this extent, with this background, the answer to the question as to whether SMEs should be the object of particular norms of cartel law would have to be "no", as SMEs (in Switzerland) would already have to be the object of the actual cartel law norms.

The question arises, however, as to whether that is in fact the case. In order to answer this question, one first has to examine what the nature and essence of SMEs are and then go into the currently enacted cartel law stipulations afterwards.

13.1.5 The Nature of SMEs

The need to subject SMEs to different rules under certain circumstances is of special significance in relation to cartel law. Cartel law essentially exists to promote effective competition (Article 1 SCA). Against this background, it is legitimate to ask whether the actions of SMEs restrict competition less than those of large enterprises and, as such, whether they should be treated differently. In fact, it might be argued that the behaviour of SMEs in competition in most cases, due to their smaller size and therefore lower level of economic influence, is less relevant than that of larger companies.[7]

In this context, the numbers produced by the Federal Office of Statistics demonstrate something surprising: in sector two and sector three, both SMEs and large enterprises are present. The only exception is the sector "mining, stones and soils", in which 246 companies are to be found, all having fewer than 250 full-time staff. In

---

[6] Cf., in general, also Ammann Martin/Strebel Mario, Die KMU-Bekanntmachung der WEKO [The WEKO SME notice], in: sic! 2007, p. 233; Ducrey Patrik/Tagmann Christoph, Die Anwendung des Kartellrechts auf KMU [Applying Cartel Law to SMEs], in: ZBJV 143/2007, p. 82.

[7] Klotz Robert/Zurkinden Philippe, Die Anwendung des Kartellrechts auf kleine und mittlere Unternehmen, Ein Vergleich zwischen der EU und der Schweiz [Applying Cartel law to small and medium-sized enterprises, a comparison between the EU and Switzerland], in: WuW 2/1999, p.120 ff.

addition, however, the number of large enterprises is in most cases in the double digit, while the number for SMEs is in the triple, quadruple, or even quintuple digits. That means therefore that there are hardly any SMEs that are monopolistic, but these often face many other SMEs, and these SMEs are in most cases competing in the market with large enterprises.

Can therefore a law that is made to promote effective competition be customised to the corporate reality in Switzerland as described? Can the more than 140,000 individual enterprises exercise significant influence in the market? Is competition fostered if SMEs and large enterprises are treated in the same way from a cartel law point of view although the starting point for an SME in competition with a large enterprise is presented in a completely different way than in the reverse case? In the parliamentary discussion, opinions were indeed presented that the competition authorities should focus on the important competition-limiting circumstances and not get involved with minor cases involving the many agreements between SMEs.[8]

Despite these justified questions and statements, one must still consider that the number of employees alone does not permit any form of conclusion to be drawn regarding the existing competition position. For example, it is quite possible for an SME with only few staff members to have a market share allowing that company to have a significant influence in the market and therefore also upon competition, for example, in niche markets. Conversely, the influence of an SME with a large number of employees can be marginalised in some circumstances if, in addition to that SME, there are further SMEs and, in particular, several large enterprises that are active in a particular market. Just concentrating on the number of staff would appear to achieve little. The EU therefore focuses on additional features regarding the definition of an SME. In its recommendation regarding the definition of micro-companies and of small and medium-sized companies dated 5 May 2003, it states that the number of staff is the most significant and therefore the main criterion. In addition, however, it also wants to have a financial criterion as a necessary addition in order to assess the real importance of a company, its performance, and competition position. The EU describes turnover and balance sheet as financial criteria.[9]

As will be shown, Swiss Cartel law does not have a definition for SMEs.[10] The state company census does take into account the number of employees, but this number, as demonstrated, only has a limited significance in terms of cartel law. What is more decisive, in addition to the number of employees, is a financial criterion such as, for example, turnover and market share. This makes it possible to correctly assess specific circumstances under cartel law even if niche or other special markets are to be assessed. This is an approach similar to the one used, for example, in the area of Swiss merger law (Merger Act[11]; cf. Article 2 e FusG). On

[8] Ammann Martin/Strebel Mario, Die KMU-Bekanntmachung der WEKO [The WEKO SME notice], in: sic! 2007, p. 230.

[9] Cf. Official Journal of the European Union dated 20 May 2003, p. 36 ff.; 2003/361/EG.

[10] Cf. also Ducrey Patrik/Tagmann Christoph, Die Anwendung des Kartellrechts auf KMU [Applying Cartel Law to SMEs], in: ZBJV 143/2007, p. 80 ff.

[11] RS 221.301.

the other hand, it is understandable that the Competition Commission has dispensed with a definition if almost all Swiss companies are accordingly to be included.[12] However, this is no argument against using market shares as a way of differentiating.

13.2 SMEs as Infringers

13.2.1 Substantive Rules

13.2.1.1 General

Swiss cartel law is based on three pillars. Competition is protected through a ban of agreements restricting competition, through a ban on abusive behaviour of companies that dominate the market, and finally through the control of the concentration (merger) of undertakings. Cartel law fundamentally is administrative law and therefore public law. The substantive legal provisions of the SCA are therefore applied by the Competition Commission as the first instance authority and reviewed by the Federal Administrative Court as the second instance authority. However, private individuals too can take legal action before the civil courts to have substantive legal provisions assessed and to assert claims arising from their breach. For this purpose, SCA has in its Article 12–15 provisions relating to civil law procedure. Civil cartel law is therefore in Switzerland primarily procedural law and has so far been of secondary importance.[13]

13.2.1.2 Merger Control

Both merger control and also the assessment of the behaviour of companies having a dominant position on the market do not have any explicit rules for SMEs. However, in order for a concentration (merger) of companies to be subject to a notification duty, certain criteria have to be fulfilled. Planned concentrations of companies must be notified to the Competition Commission before their implementation if in the financial year preceding the concentration (1) the companies concerned together reported a turnover of at least CHF 2 billion or a turnover in Switzerland of at least CHF 500 million, and (2) cumulatively, at least two of the companies concerned each reported a turnover in Switzerland of at least CHF 100 million (Article 9 para 1 SCA). At least the 140,000 individual enterprises in Switzerland are not caught by this provision. It is at least theoretically possible for a micro-company to produce a higher turnover than that of an SME or even a large enterprise. This would, however, be an exception and would not in principle justify setting up special cartel law rules. The control of company mergers differentiates

[12] Ammann Martin/Strebel Mario, Die KMU-Bekanntmachung der WEKO [The WEKO SME notice], in: sic! 2007, p. 233; Ducrey Patrik/Tagmann Christoph, Die Anwendung des Kartellrechts auf KMU [Applying Cartel Law to SMEs], in: ZBJV 143/2007, p. 82.

[13] Basler Kommentar KG-Jacobs Reto/Gion Giger, before Articles 12–17 N 5 and 10.

therefore according to turnover generated, which in most cases is sufficient to exclude SMEs from merger control (whereby it is questionable whether they generally or in a majority of the cases do have less influence on the market than large enterprises).

13.2.1.3 Dominant Companies

Dominant companies are one or more companies in a specific market that are able, as suppliers or consumers, to behave, to an appreciable extent, independently of the other participants (competitors, suppliers, or consumers) in the market (Article 4 para 2 SCA). Describing a company as market dominant always requires an examination of the market and of the position of one company in this market. Market definition serves in this regard to determine the forces of competition that have an effect on the potentially dominant company. It consequently focuses on measuring the competitive pressure. In this regard, any peculiarities of SMEs can be considered, for instance the fact that, in competition, these cannot have the same effect as that of large enterprises. However, there will also be exceptions: an SME in Switzerland is as a rule subject to a certain level of competitive pressure because, often, other SMEs and, in particular, large enterprises are also active in the market. To that extent, they cannot, in many cases, act independently to a material extent. For this reason, they cannot be described as dominant on the relevant market. But the starting point is different, for example, if a medium-sized company only has to compete with one or just a few microenterprises. Then it is absolutely possible that the medium-sized company could be termed dominant on the relevant market. In this case, however, it is hardly justifiable to have other or special rules. Things look different, however, with regard to the ban on agreements restricting effective competition. This requires more detailed analysis.

13.2.1.4 Unlawful Agreements

Structure of the Legal Provisions

Article 5 para 1 SCA holds that agreements that significantly restrict competition in a market for specific goods or services and are not justified on grounds of economic efficiency and also agreements that result in the elimination of effective competition are unlawful. This provision differentiates accordingly between two different types of agreements, namely those that eliminate effective competition and those that significantly restrict it. Both agreements are basically unlawful, but those that "only" significantly restrict effective competition can be justified on grounds of economic efficiency, which would mean that such agreements are lawful.

Article 5 paras 3 and 4 SCA provides a list of such agreements in which the elimination of competition is assumed, which would mean that they are unlawful.[14]

[14] Para 3 lists agreements between companies at the same market level (horizontal agreements), while in para 4 agreements are listed between companies at different market levels (vertical agreements).

The qualification of an agreement as falling under Article 5 paras 3 and 4 SCA is significant because, according to the interpretation of the Competition Commission (which is disputed), such agreements, even if the assumption can be rebutted, can be subject to sanctions.[15] Article 49a para 1 SCA provides, amongst other things, that a company that is party to an unlawful agreement or that is acting in an unlawful manner based on Article 7 SCA can be subject to fines.

Grounds of Economic Efficiency

According to Article 5 para 2 SCA, agreements are deemed to be justified on grounds of economic efficiency if (1) they are necessary in order to reduce production or distribution costs, improve products or production processes, promote research into or dissemination of technical or professional know-how, or exploit resources more rationally, and (2) they will under no circumstances enable the parties involved to eliminate effective competition.

Article 6 para 1 SCA provides, as already mentioned, that the conditions under which agreements are as a general rule deemed justified on grounds of economic efficiency may be set out in ordinances or general notices. One should however note that such a notice has no binding legal effect. What is required in each case is a subsumption in Article 5 para 1 and 2 SCA. If an agreement is not covered by a notice, then an independent justification is still possible according to Article 5 para 2 SCA.

13.2.1.5 SME Notice

Overview of the Principal Stipulations in the SME Notice

Article 6 para 1 SCA also contains, in addition to the basic possibility of issuing ordinances or general notices, a listing of possible agreements to be considered for such ordinances or notices. In this regard, in particular, agreements are mentioned that serve to improve competitiveness of SMEs insofar as they only have a limited effect on the market [Article 6 para 1(e) SCA].

The Competition Commission has made use of this possibility and on 19 December 2005 issued a notice regarding agreements with limited effect on the market (SME Notice). According to Section 1 para 1 of the SME Notice, agreements are justified on grounds of economic efficiency if they (1) serve to enhance the competitiveness of the companies involved and (2) only have limited market influence. An agreement serves, as a rule, to improve competitiveness if it makes possible size or association advantages through actions that enhance performance or promote innovation or if it creates sales incentives at this level and is necessary for this purpose (Section 2 para 1 of the SME Notice). Such improvements of competitiveness, according to Section 2 para 2 of the SME Notice, are conceivable above all in production, research and development, administration,

[15] This view however is not uncontroversial in literature.

advertising and marketing, purchasing, sales and logistics, and also in sales circumstances (market entry for products or companies).

Agreements between companies having a limited effect on the market according to Section 3 of the SME Notice are generally those where the companies together do not exceed a certain market share on the relevant market affected by the joint agreement. The Competition Commission regards this market share to be 10 % in the case of horizontal agreements and 15 % in the case of vertical agreements (Section 3a and b of the SME Notice).

This provision confirms, at least at first glance, that not all agreements are automatically the same. If the companies involved only have limited impact on the market and if the agreement serves to improve competitiveness, then other rules apply. One wonders however whether this conclusion also applies at second glance.

It should however be noted that, in addition to the SME Notice, other Competition Commission's notices also exist, such as the Notice on the Treatment of Vertical Agreements dated 28 June 2010 (Vertical Notice). Of course, SMEs can form agreements with companies at different market levels (vertical agreements). One wonders therefore what the relation between the SME Notice and the Vertical Notice is above all because the latter also contains market share thresholds. According to the Competition Commission practice, the Vertical Notice takes precedence over the SME Notice. This is stated explicitly in Section 9 para 2 of the Vertical Notice. The exception to this is merely the Section 5b of the SME Notice regarding the vertical agreements of microenterprises.[16]

Considerations Regarding the SME Notice

To begin, the relationship between the SME Notice and Article 5 para 1 and 2 and Article 6 SCA should be assessed in more detail: Article 5 para 1 SCA holds that agreements are unlawful if they (1) eliminate effective competition or (2) significantly restrict competition. The consequence of this is that agreements that do not significantly restrict competition are lawful.

Section 1 of the SME Notice stipulates, however, that agreements are *lawful* (1) if they improve the competitiveness of the companies that are parties to such agreements and (2) if they have only limited impact on the market. However, as shown, according to Article 5 para 1 and 2 SCA, "only" agreements that are either not significant *or* can be justified on grounds of economic efficiency are lawful. The Competition Commission does not have the requisite authority to stipulate a third category. For this reason, the two above criteria according to the Competition Commission would have to have an influence either on the assessment of significant impact on competition or on the opportunity of a justification on grounds of economic efficiency.

However, Article 5 para 2 SCA holds that significant restrictions of competition can be justified on grounds of economic efficiency. According to Article 6 SCA the

[16] RPW/DPC 2010/4, p. 669, para 154 (RPW/DPC, the publication of the Swiss Competition Commission is available at http://www.weko.admin.ch/.

Competition Commission has the power to delineate these circumstances in more detail. This means that the Competition Commission can therefore in notices delineate the conditions in which certain *significant* agreements affecting competition could be justified. This means that the Competition Commission should not be issuing notices regarding the question as to when agreements are to be deemed as having a significant impact on competition. Article 6 SCA gives to the Competition Commission, in other words, only the right to delineate significant but justified agreements, but not to completely dispute the significance in a notice. One should however point out that, irrespective of Article 6 SCA, the Competition Commission is basically free to publish its practice or understanding of the law. This means however that the criteria listed in the SME Notice would have to be either a concrete representation of Article 5 para 2 SCA (i.e., of the opportunity for justification based on the statutory requirement according to Article 6 SCA) or an intended practice of the Competition Commission regarding significance according to Article 5 para 1 SCA. In this sense, an alignment of the criteria with the content of Article 5 SCA follows below.

The criterion of improving competitiveness according to the SME Notice appears at first sight to be a concretisation of Article 5 para 2 SCA (concerning the justification on grounds of economic efficiency). However this is different with regard to the criterion of limited market impact, which can be assumed to be related to significance at least in terms of wording. However, if it is assumed that the terms "significance" and "limited market impact" have the same meaning, that is to say that "limited market impact" means "insignificance", then agreements between companies with limited market impact, based on the statutory regulation previously described, would always be lawful. That would then mean however that the criterion of improving competitiveness would be meaningless. If, on the other hand, limited market impact is to be in addition to significance, then its integration in Article 5 para 1 and 2 SCA is unclear.

On the other hand, it can also not be assumed that the criterion of limited market impact is a concretisation of the justification according to Article 5 para 2 SCA. If a limited market impact were necessary for justification, then there would be a contradiction with the statutory stipulation, since precisely those agreements that have a corresponding market impact can be justified. In this sense, it can hardly be the opinion of the Competition Commission that agreements, which do not have a limited market impact, are not justifiable in the sense of Article 5 para 2 SCA. For even hard-core restrictions in the sense of Article 5 paras 3 and 4 SCA can be justified, provided that the assumption of the elimination of competition can be rebutted. If the criterion of limited market impact is treated in connection with the justification according to Article 5 para 2 SCA, then this would contradict Article 5 para 1 and 2 SCA.[17] Therefore, the criterion of limited market impact can hardly apply in connection with the justification but rather (as the wording already infers)

[17] Cf. also Ducrey Patrik/Tagmann Christoph, Die Anwendung des Kartellrechts auf KMU [Applying Cartel Law to SMEs], in: ZBJV 143/2007, p. 79 ff.

in connection with significance. However, the function of this criterion remains to be clarified.[18]

It is also significant that the term "improvement of competitiveness", as has already been intimated, can hardly have anything to do with significance.[19] Nor, however, can it be found in Article 5 para 2 SCA. This is unproblematic if this improvement goes hand in hand with economic efficiency, i.e. if it is the reason for efficiency in terms of Article 5 para 2 SCA.[20] In this case, the criterion of improving competitiveness can be considered a concretisation of Article 5 para 2 SCA. If this, however, is not possible, the question is what significance can be attributed to this criterion. In any event, it is not within the competence of the Competition Commission to introduce further requirements for justification, in addition to the preconditions in Article 5 para 2 SCA.[21] It can, furthermore, hardly be in the interest of the Competition Commission to make it even more difficult to achieve justification by introducing a new criterion specifically for SMEs.

It follows therefore that integrating the criteria of the SME Notice into the system of Article 5 SCA is extremely difficult. This lack of clarity is made even more difficult in that the SME Notice dispenses with the definition of the term "SME", although the draft version had originally intended to include such a definition (albeit a limited one).[22] The SME Notice therefore does not show which companies are to be regarded as SMEs. It does however contain in Sections 4 and 5 special rules for microenterprises. Companies are regarded as such if they have less than ten staff and if their annual turnover in Switzerland does not exceed CHF 2 million. The Competition Commission regards, as a rule, agreements in which only microenterprises are involved as *insignificant*. It is easier therefore to separate microenterprises, which effectively leads to the SME Notice differentiating between microenterprises and other companies.[23] To this extent, it can be ascertained that at least for those companies a guideline exists such that the Competition Commission does not assume significance insofar as the preconditions for the number of staff and the annual turnover are fulfilled. Microenterprises are

[18] Different view, clearly, Ducrey Patrik/Tagmann Christoph, Die Anwendung des Kartellrechts auf KMU [Applying Cartel Law to SMEs], in: ZBJV 143/2007, p. 84 ff.

[19] Also Ducrey Patrik/Tagmann Christoph, Die Anwendung des Kartellrechts auf KMU [Applying Cartel Law to SMEs], in: ZBJV 143/2007, p. 83, dispute this.

[20] Cf. also Basler Kommentar KG-Neff Klaus, Article 6 para 1 e N 9; Ducrey Patrik/Tagmann Christoph, Die Anwendung des Kartellrechts auf KMU [Applying Cartel Law to SMEs], in: ZBJV 143/2007, p. 83 ff.

[21] The listing in Article 5 para 2 SCA is exhaustive, cf. Zäch Roger, Schweizerisches Kartellgesetz [The Swiss Cartel Act], 2nd edition, Bern 2005, p. 196; Ducrey Patrik/Tagmann Christoph, Die Anwendung des Kartellrechts auf KMU [Applying Cartel Law to SMEs], in: ZBJV 143/2007, p. 83 ff.

[22] Ducrey Patrik/Tagmann Christoph, Die Anwendung des Kartellrechts auf KMU [Applying Cartel Law to SMEs], in: ZBJV 143/2007, p. 81.

[23] Ammann Martin/Strebel Mario, Die KMU-Bekanntmachung der WEKO [The WEKO SME notice], in: sic! 2007, p. 233; Ducrey Patrik/Tagmann Christoph, Die Anwendung des Kartellrechts auf KMU [Applying Cartel Law to SMEs], in: ZBJV 143/2007, p. 82 ff.

therefore not required to conform to the unclear preconditions for the improvement of competitiveness and limited market impact. The Competition Commission therefore clarifies that the notion that SCA generally does not apply to agreements between microenterprises is, as a rule, not applicable.[24]

However, then, there is still the question regarding the relationship between the SME Notice and Article 5 paras 1 and 2 SCA. One welcome clarification is the fact that for microenterprises significance is not given. Apart from this, following a detailed assessment of the SME Notice, the conclusion must be that agreements between SMEs and/or other companies are, due to the unclear meaning of the two criteria "limited market impact" and "improvement of competitiveness", to be assessed in all cases based on significance according to Article 5 para 1 SCA. However, it will be shown below to which extent the Competition Commission's findings regarding limited market impact might be integrated into the assessment of significance according to Article 5 para 1 SCA.[25]

The stipulations of the SME Notice are therefore not particularly well thought through as they do not strictly follow the criteria contained in Article 5 SCA (the Competition Commission's hands must have effectively been tied as the preliminary legal work regarding terminology was already found wanting[26]). As the form in which the SME Notice is issued is not defined in Swiss law and in any event is binding for neither courts nor companies subject to the SCA, the conceptual lack of clarity must be the reason that the SME Notice, as far as can be seen, has so far only been applied in a very limited manner.

It follows from the above that Switzerland does not have its own (cartel) law for SMEs but that the practice of the Competition Commission provides, at least for microenterprises, a significant exception from cartel law.[27] There are, however, exceptions. Neither microenterprises nor other companies in general are permitted to make so-called hard-core restrictions, i.e. agreements according to Article 5 paras 3 and 4 SCA, that is to say horizontal agreements on prices, quantities or territories, and vertical agreements regarding minimum or fixed prices or absolute territorial protection (i.e., the foreclosure of territories). With regard to microenterprises, Section 5 of the SME Notice stipulates that for such agreements insignificance may not be assumed.[28] Furthermore, Section 3 stipulates with regard to other companies that for these agreements limited market impact may not be

[24] Cf. also Basler Kommentar KG-Neff Klaus, Article 6 N 23 ff. and fig. 4 ff. KMU-BM N 1 ff.

[25] Following on this Sect. 13.2.1.7

[26] Cf. the notes in Ducrey Patrik/Tagmann Christoph, Die Anwendung des Kartellrechts auf KMU [Applying Cartel Law to SMEs], in: ZBJV 143/2007, p. 83 ff.

[27] Ammann Martin/Strebel Mario, Die KMU-Bekanntmachung der WEKO [The WEKO SME notice], in: sic! 2007, p. 233.

[28] What is notable however is that Ducrey Patrik/Tagmann Christoph, Die Anwendung des Kartellrechts auf KMU [Applying Cartel Law to SMEs], in: ZBJV 143/2007, p. 92, interpret the word "insignificant" differently from the meaning in the sense of "to want to understand as justified" – which, as shown, would not correlate with the system in Article 5 Para. 2 and Article 6 SCA; what however hardly makes sense is that competition agreements are not economically

assumed. Agreements in the sense of Article 5 paras 3 and 4 SCA can therefore not be concluded by small or microenterprises either.[29] In general, it must be noted however that an agreement cannot be regarded as unlawful in the sense of Article 5 para 1 and Article 5 paras 3 or 4 SCA only because an agreement does not fulfil the preconditions of a notice. Instead, an agreement is only to be deemed unlawful based on the particular circumstances of the individual case, i.e. following an independent subsumption under Article 5 SCA, irrespective of the SME Notice (which is not binding for the courts).

This shows that, apart from microenterprises, SMEs are not subject to any special rules. The lawfulness of particular agreements under cartel law between SMEs is therefore, as for all other companies, dependent on the assessment based on Article 5 SCA. The requirement of significance according to Article 5 para 1 SCA is therefore of particular importance.

13.2.1.6 Significance of Agreements Affecting Competition Based on Article 5 Para 1 SCA

Practice of the Swiss Competition Commission

As mentioned, according to Article 5 para 1 SCA, agreements are only unlawful if they significantly restrict competition and are not justified on grounds of economic efficiency (or if they eliminate effective competition). The practice of the Competition Commission assesses the significance of agreements through a holistic assessment of the individual case, with both qualitative and quantitative aspects being considered. With regard to the qualitative significance, the relevance of the competition parameter affected by the agreement in the relevant market and also the type and extent of the intervention in this competition parameter must be assessed. With regard to the quantitative significance, it has to be assessed how comprehensively the relevant market is affected by the agreement, in other words what weight or what importance the agreement and the companies that are parties to the agreement have in the relevant market (number, market share, turnover, etc.).[30] What is important is that the overall assessment can lead to the conclusion that a qualitatively significant restriction is compensated by the fact that the restriction is quantitatively insignificant and the restriction on competition caused by the agreement is deemed to be insignificant. Conversely, however, it is also possible that a qualitatively significant restriction (due to a restriction of a key competition parameter) is assessed as significant even if there is merely a minimal quantitative restriction.[31] The Competition Commission increasingly takes the view that certain

---

efficient because microenterprises are part of them. "Insignificant" is to be understood based on the view here indeed in the sense of "insignificant".

[29] Cf. also Zäch Roger, Schweizerisches Kartellgesetz [The Swiss Cartel Act], 2nd edition, Bern 2005, para 511.

[30] Cf. on the whole issue recently RPW/DPC 2012/1, p. 105, para 175.

[31] Basler Kommentar KG-Krauskopf Patrick L./Schaller Olivier, Article 5 N 176 ff.

hard-core restrictions, i.e. qualitatively significant restrictions, are per se unlawful, in other words they lead to an all-over significant restriction of competition in the sense of Article 5 para 1 SCA even if they have no or only a minimal effect on competition. This approach of the Competition Commission is widely disputed but may become the law following the ongoing revision of the SCA (see also below, in particular Sect. 13.4, para 5).

Thus yet again the discrepancy with the SME Notice becomes clear. The (limited) market impact according to Section 3 of the SME Notice can refer at best (or at least) to the quantitative significance. In addition, however, the practice of the Competition Commission is also always to consider qualitative significance. This is indirectly confirmed through para 2 of Section 3 of the SME Notice in that in the event of hard-core restrictions (i.e., certain types of agreements irrespective of the concrete market impact), it is not assumed that limited market impact applies. Even if the preconditions described in Section 3 para 1 of the SME Notice were fulfilled, qualitative significance would still have to be considered (even a restriction that is not a hard-core restriction in the sense of Article 5 paras 3 and 4 SCA and Section 3 para 2 of the SME Notice can be qualitatively significant). The consequence of this is that Section 3 of the SME Notice does not replace the assessment of the (qualitative) significance, and the actual meaning of the criterion of limited market impact still remains unclear beyond quantitative significance.[32]

Problem

Imagine the situation in which two bakers, each having minimal market share in a (large) town in which there are countless other bakers and, above all, several large retailers or big distributors, agree for whatever reason to charge the same price for their bread. The restriction of the freedom to act on the part of both bakers with regard to the "price" competition parameter is doubtlessly qualitatively significant. In the view of the Competition Commission, this starting position could already suffice for the assumption of a significant restriction of competition insofar as the definition of the relevant market does not lead to the result that the two bakers are not active at all in the same market. Such an agreement would, according to the practice of the Competition Commission, have to be sanctioned contrary to all reason (Article 49a SCA)[33] as the two bakers will, with regard to the pricing agreement, hardly be able to claim justification on grounds of economic efficiency according to Article 5 para 2 SCA.

The practice whereby in certain circumstances qualitative significance suffices to qualify agreements as unlawful therefore has far-reaching consequences, especially for micro- or small companies in which quantitative significance can normally not be assumed because microenterprises or small companies often hardly have any impact on the market as would be the case in the example of the two bakers. With this assertion, at least the term "market impact" is brought into relation

[32] Cf. on this, however, section "Problem", para 3.

[33] Probably against RPW/DPC/DPC 2008/1, p. 214, para 11, second example.

with the SME Notice, but it is in reality of hardly any use for SMEs due to the various uncertainties.

Nothing would change either if the SME Notice were taken into consideration with regard to the assessment of significance. If the criteria of limited market impact were, according to Section 3 of the SME Notice, applied with regard to significance, which however only makes sense with regard to *quantitative* significance, then the market share thresholds at least provide a guideline. However, this does not help the SME much with regard to legal certainty if the Competition Commission, despite a market share of under 10 %, regards an agreement as significant just because a central competition parameter is restricted, and therefore qualitative significance has to be assumed. The Competition Commission regards so-called hard-core restrictions as unlawful anyway (cf. Section 3 para 2 in conjunction with Section 1 para 1 of the SME Notice). This applies, as shown, even if microenterprises are involved (Section 5 of the SME Notice). This means, in effect, that the Competition Commission regards pricing agreements as significant, irrespective of their effect on the market (i.e., irrespective of the "quantity"). But because SMEs as a rule are only distinguished from larger companies based on the number of their staff or the level of their turnover (and therefore indirectly in most cases also by their market share) but not based on the type of agreements they make, this leads, in Swiss cartel law, to the result that all companies are effectively treated equally, irrespective of their impact on the market. Market impact as a criterion only becomes significant if the agreement is not *qualitatively* significant. In this case, companies that are party to an agreement can probably assume that significance is denied if their total market share does not exceed 10 % in any of the relevant markets affected by the agreement.

The conflict between quality and quantity in Swiss cartel law is related to the conflict that has existed for years between the principle of *protecting competition as an institution*, according to which the significance of an agreement is to be determined solely and objectively through its effects on the relevant market, and the principle of *individual protection*, which ultimately only has as a precondition pure qualitative significance. The latter principle only assesses a restriction of competition based on a specific restriction of a competitor or of such competitor's commercial freedom.[34] The Swiss Federal Court, which has not often been able to pass judgements regarding this issue, seems to have adopted a conciliatory view. In the judgement regarding fixed book prices, it held that "in addition to protecting the personality of individual competitors (individual protection) [. . .] the SCA should also protect competition as such (protection of competition as an institution)". It therefore held that significance is to be assessed not just from the point of view of individual companies but in connection with the operation of effective competition itself. The Swiss Federal Court concluded from this that a significant restriction of competition should at least be assumed if the agreement affects a relevant

[34] Basler Kommentar KG-Krauskopf Patrick L./Schaller Olivier, Article 5 N 155 ff.

competition parameter in the market concerned *whereby* the parties involved would have a significant market share.[35]

At least based on this ruling of the Swiss Federal Court, it is not possible to regard an agreement as significant when solely basing it on qualitative elements, particularly as the Swiss Federal Court expressly refers to legal opinions that even require certain quantitative thresholds.[36] On the other hand, the law does not permit an assessment of significance based on purely quantitative criteria.[37] Contrary to an opinion in the doctrine,[38] the Swiss Federal Court did not hold that the parties to an agreement should have a "not insignificant market share" but that they should have "a significant market share".[39] Whether a market player has a not insignificant or a significant market share is relevant insofar as one can assume that the quantitative significance does not consist of black-and-white but of grey areas.

Conclusion

As demonstrated, the Competition Commission has, in the SME Notice, held that companies that are party to an agreement may only have limited market impact. If this element specified in Section 3 of the SME Notice is not used for the justification but for the assessment of significance based on Article 5 para 1 SCA, then one could at least draw conclusions regarding quantitative significance (at least the wording of Section 1 of the SME Notice would permit such an interpretation as it does not talk of "justification" but of "lawful according to Article 5 SCA"). SMEs could therefore assess quantitative significance based on their market share. However, even here uncertainty remains as to qualitative significance.

As far as can be seen, the practice of the Competition Commission, in which the mere presence of a qualitatively significant restriction of competition (e.g., in the event of a restriction of the "price" competition parameter) would suffice for the qualification of significance according to Article 5 para 1 SCA, has not yet been judicially reviewed by the Swiss Federal Court. In view of the decision regarding fixed book prices, doubt would rightly prevail whether this practice, partly stated by the Competition Commission in notices, would stand up to judicial review.

13.2.1.7 Consequences for SMEs

Based on the descriptions above, it follows that there is no particular cartel law for SMEs in Switzerland. The only statutory regulation is to be found in Article 6 para

[35] BGE 129 II 18, para 5.2.1.

[36] BGE 129 II 18, para 5.2.1, with other refs.

[37] Borer Jürg, Schweizerisches Kartellgesetz, Wettbewerbsrecht I [Swiss Cartel Act, Competition Law I], 3rd edition, Zürich 2011, Article 5 N 19.

[38] Borer Jürg, Schweizerisches Kartellgesetz, Wettbewerbsrecht I [Swiss Cartel Act, Competition Law I], 3rd edition, Zürich 2011, cf. footnote 37; Ammann Martin/Strebel Mario, Die KMU-Bekanntmachung der WEKO [The WEKO SME notice], in: sic! 2007, p. 233; Ducrey Patrik/Tagmann Christoph, Die Anwendung des Kartellrechts auf KMU [Applying Cartel Law to SMEs], in: ZBJV 143/2007, p. 82.

[39] BGE 129 II 18, para 5.2.1.

1. e SCA, which is however only a competence norm for the issuing of notices. Such a notice for SMEs (namely the SME Notice) has indeed been published, but it is "merely" a notice regarding the practice of the Competition Commission and not actual law. As such, the SME Notice, to the extent it can be used for this purpose, is only a guideline as to how the Competition Commission intends to apply the term of "quantitative significance" according to Article 5 Abs. 1 SCA (with regard to SMEs). However, the cartel law situation of SMEs would appear to have been clarified in that the Competition Commission expressly stated that hard-core restrictions (Article 5 paras 3 and 4 SCA) are *significant* or *not justified* irrespective of market share. Furthermore, agreements on the part of microenterprises, insofar as they do not concern hard-core restrictions, are generally insignificant. That means therefore that, in terms of the "status quo", SMEs in particular cannot rely on not being caught by cartel law just because they have limited impact on the market.[40]

13.2.2 Statistics

The case that possibly caused the issuance of Article 6 para 1 e SCA and subsequently also the SME Notice is probably the one known as "Des tarifs conseillés de l'Association fribourgeoise des écoles de circulation (AFEC)".[41] In this case, the Association of driving instructors in Freiburg issued recommendations for individual categories of driving lessons, which were almost adhered to. Even nonmembers were stated to have followed them. Based on this background, the Competition Commission decided that price recommendations would be regarded as price agreements in the sense of Article 4 para 1 in conjunction with Article 5 para 3 a SCA, insofar as they were followed. Due to the lack of external and internal competition, the assumption of the elimination of competition according to Article 5 para 3 SCA could not be rebutted, which is why the price recommendations were held to be unlawful. Issuing them on the part of the Association was therefore forbidden.[42]

In view of the fact that the corporate environment in Switzerland comprises more than 99 % SMEs, there are many cases in the practice of the Competition Commission that concern SMEs.[43] However, as far as can be ascertained, no decisions have been made based on the application of the SME Notice.[44] Not

[40] Cf. also Ducrey Patrik/Tagmann Christoph, Die Anwendung des Kartellrechts auf KMU [Applying Cartel Law to SMEs], in: ZBJV 143/2007, pp. 85 ff. and 101 ff.

[41] Ducrey Patrik/Tagmann Christoph, Die Anwendung des Kartellrechts auf KMU [Applying Cartel Law to SMEs], in: ZBJV 143/2007, p. 70, footnote 2.

[42] RPW/DPC 2000/2, p. 167 ff.

[43] Cf., e.g., RPW/DPC 2009/3, p. 196 f. (fitting companies); RPW/DPC 2012/2, p. 270 ff. (road construction and civil engineering in the Canton Aargau).

[44] Cf. Basler Kommentar KG-Neff Klaus, Article 6 para 1(e) N 20; in 2008, WEKO held in a report that the SME Notice had proved itself since coming into force. "Consequently with regard to the interpretation of the SME notice only few enquiries came in. Most of these enquiries related to the

until 2010 at the level of the Federal Administrative Court (which is the appellate court against the Competition Commission orders) was an order regarding a sanction issued following a refusal to provide information, the object of a proceeding in which the SME Notice was taken into consideration primarily with regard to calculating the sanction.[45] Therefore, there is no case law that would enable the formulation of guidelines for the application of cartel law to SMEs.

13.2.3 Procedural Aspects

13.2.3.1 In General: Basic Principles

As mentioned at the outset, cartel law is basically public law, although the substantive law provisions can also be enforced in the civil courts[46]. For this reason, administrative proceedings must be distinguished from civil proceedings. The civil proceedings are governed in a rudimentary fashion in Article 12–17 SCA, but mainly in the Swiss Code of Civil Procedure (CCP).[47] Provisions on administrative proceedings, on the other hand, are also to be found in the SCA (Article 18 f. SCA) and in the Administrative Procedure Act (APA),[48] as well as further Acts.

These procedural orders basically have no special rules in relation to SMEs. Two points at most might be emphasised under this heading. First, in administrative proceedings (though not in civil proceedings), the discretionary principle[49] applies, i.e. the Competition Commission must in its duty-bound discretion decide whether or not it intends to open proceedings. This also means that any affected party has no entitlement to proceedings being initiated. The Competition Commission can therefore in its discretion decide independently on whether to open proceedings. If large enterprises or enterprises with market power are targeted, the exercise of discretion should scarcely ever result in a decision not to open proceedings. Things could look different, on the other hand, in the case of very small SMEs, which are economically (or regarding competition on the relevant market) of little significance. The Competition Commission would accordingly have the possibility of not dealing with minor cases due to the discretionary principle. In this regard, the position of an SME might be distinguished from that of a large enterprise at the beginning of a proceeding. However, as mentioned, there are no real rules in this

question regarding the application of SCA in terms of hardcore restrictions between SMEs, a question which the SME Notice clearly answers"; cf. RPW/DPC 2008/1, p. 213 ff. para 7. Reference to rulings is however not to be found, and therefore "having stood the test of time" can only relate to the application by companies (which is why enquiries came in) and not to WEKO.

45 RPW/DPC 2010/1, p. 196, para 6.4.3 (judgment B-8115/2008; 7x2 AG v WEKO); RPW/DPC 2009/4, p. 465, in particular para 35.

46 Cf. Sect. 13.2.1.

47 RS 272.

48 RS 172.021.

49 Ammann Martin/Strebel Mario, Die KMU-Bekanntmachung der WEKO [The WEKO SME notice], in: sic! 2007, p. 236.

regard. Instead, reference must also be made again in this connection to the practice of the Competition Commission, although no figures are available in this regard.

Moreover, Article 49a para 1 SCA, as mentioned, provides that certain types of agreements can be sanctioned. The fine amounts to up to 10 % of the turnover generated in the last three financial years in Switzerland. The amount is calculated by the duration and gravity of the illegal conduct. The alleged profit generated by the enterprise as a result must be considered reasonable. This provision too does not, at first sight, differentiate between SMEs and large enterprises. At second glance, however, there is here too the possibility when calculating the sanction of considering the special situation of SMEs, and in this the Competition Commission has discretionary latitude. This will be gone into in more detail later in Section 3.2.4. Other procedural aspects in the broadest sense of the word are, on the other hand, not evident, with this conclusion applying equally to civil proceedings.

13.2.3.2 In Detail: Constitutional Principles

Also in relation to the constitutional principles, SMEs are treated under Swiss cartel law practice not differently from large enterprises. The type or economic significance or size of the SMEs plays no role in the legal reasoning.[50] Notwithstanding this, two points should be mentioned at this stage, which are of significance regardless of the SME question in Swiss cartel law: the question about the criminal charge as defined in Article 6 of the European Convention on Human Rights (ECHR) and the principle of legality. Both points are significant primarily in connection with sanctions, namely the sanction provision in Article 49a SCA.

The question about the criminal charge as defined in Article 6 ECHR concerns the legal nature of Article 49a SCA or the threat that is specified there of sanction in the sense of a penalty and, in the broader sense therefore, the delineation between administrative law and criminal law. Prevailing legal opinion and the judicial decisions issued in the interim qualify the sanction designated in the statute as "amount" as a criminal law charge, which is why it is criminal in character within the meaning of Article 6 ECHR. For this reason, in proceedings to impose sanctions, criminal law aspects, including the procedural safeguards of the Federal Constitution (Cst.) and the ECHR, would have to be considered.[51] This qualification is associated with crucial consequences, for example the question of whether the imposition of sanctions is predicated upon fault or the principles "*ne bis in*

[50] It should moreover be noted that in Switzerland, for example, not just individuals but – as a matter of principle – legal entities too have a right to privacy; Cf. Article 13 Federal Constitution and Article 2 para 1 of the Data Protection Act (DSG).

[51] BGE 135 II 60, para 3.2.3; RPW/DPC 2010/2, p. 358, para 8.1.3; Borer Jürg, Schweizerisches Kartellgesetz, Wettbewerbsrecht I [Swiss Cartel Act, Competition Law I], 3rd edition, Zürich 2011, Article 49a N 2; Basler Kommentar KG-Niggli Marcel A./Riedo Christof, before Articles 49a–53 N 43 a.

idem" and "*nemo tenetur*" (see, however, Article 159 CPC).[52] At this point, however, this aspect cannot be gone into more detail or else the scope of this paper would be inordinate. We would simply comment that the sanction in Article 49a SCA constitutes a punishment as defined in Article 6 ECHR.

The principle of legality, in connection with Article 49a SCA, is also a much-debated problem. The principle of legality must be respected in all administrative actions. In this sense, the Competition Commission's activity is also bound by the statute, which applies in particular to the imposition of direct sanctions under Article 49a SCA. The requirement of certainty derives from the principle of legality. This requires that a statutory rule (both the legal elements and legal consequence), upon which an order is based, must be sufficiently defined. Only then is the action of the authority foreseeable and predictable. Legal opinion is split as to whether Article 49a SCA fulfils the precondition of sufficient certainty.[53] It will be for practice to create clarity here. Recently, the Federal Court analysed the question and considered the rule to be sufficiently defined.[54]

In summary, there is a lively debate about various problems in connection with procedural safeguards in Switzerland. This debate, however, has no impact on the position of SMEs in the proceedings.

13.2.3.3 Right of Access to the File

General

The initial position is exactly the same regarding the right of access to the file. The right of access to the file touches on a whole series of legal bases and spheres of interest. Given this, the problem cannot be gone into detail at this point. However, here is a brief summary of the current status of the debate.

The focus is on the balance between the public interest in the proceedings; the interests of any aggrieved parties (claimants); the interests of the potential parties filing leniency applications and parties cooperating with the Competition Commission, who deliver or have delivered information or documents to the Competition Commission in the context of Article 8 ff. of the Ordinance regarding the Sanctions for Unlawful Restrictions of Competition (OS SCA); and, in general, the interests and the procedural rights of the parties being affected by an investigation of the Competition Commission. In addition to the constitutional bases in Article 29 para 2 Cst. or Article 6 para 1 and Article 13 ECHR, the following come into play in the delicate balance: the procedural law regulations of SCA (Article 39 ff. SCA) and, based on the reference in Article 39 SCA, in particular Article 26–28 APA; further,

[52] Cf. the references in Borer Jürg, Schweizerisches Kartellgesetz, Wettbewerbsrecht I [Swiss Cartel Act, Competition Law I], 3rd edition, Zürich 2011, Article 49a N 3, and Basler Kommentar KG-Tagmann Christoph/Zirlick Beat, Article 49a N 10.

[53] Cf, instead of many others, Basler Kommentar KG- Niggli Marcel A./Riedo Christof, before Article 49a–53 N 70 ff. und Basler Kommentar KG- Tagmann Christoph/Zirlick Beat, Article 49a N 19 ff.

[54] The Swiss Federal Court decided accordingly in a case concerning PubliGroupe on 29 June 2012; the written decision had not yet been published on 16 September 2012.

the Criminal Procedure Act (CPA),[55] Federal Civil Procedure Act (FCPA); and, finally, the Freedom of Information Act (AIA),[56] the Data Protection Act (DPA),[57] and the Code of Civil Procedure (CCP) in the civil law area.

We would single out the currently most debated situations, namely (1) inspection by parties to proceedings of documents belonging to other parties to these proceedings, including parties filing leniency applications and cooperating with the Competition Commission, and (2) inspection by aggrieved parties (claimants) of the case files, although it is already clear now that no established practice yet exists in respect of either of the points. Instead, the assumption is one of legal uncertainty since the concrete scope of the right of access to the file is not evident either from the wording of the Cst. or the ECHR or from that of the APA and the other applicable acts. However, it follows that the right of access to the file is a constitutional entitlement. This entitlement is at least embodied by Article 26 ff. APA. Pursuant to Article 26 para 1 APA, documents can be inspected at the premises of the authority. However, the right of access to the file can be refused or simply restricted due to overriding public or private interests (Article 27 para 1 APA). The limitation to be adhered to, however, in any case guarantees an effective defence of the parties to proceedings, namely, if they are incriminated based on documents being part of the file, they must know the relevant content of the file.[58]

Access to the File by Parties to Proceedings

Regarding this latter point, the Competition Commission is interested primarily in not jeopardising the incentive effect of the bonus leniency programme since pursuant to Article 49a para 2 SCA the sanction can be waived in whole or in part if the enterprise collaborates in uncovering and eliminating the restriction on competition. However, it will not do this if it must then fear reprisals of other incriminated companies. Nevertheless, as against this interest, there is the right of the incriminated parties to the proceedings to effectively address the matter and state their defence. For this reason, the Competition Commission, like other competition authorities, has developed various special procedural law aspects for parties filing leniency applications. These primarily help to ensure that the information that it has received in the context of the leniency application cannot be used in other proceedings. The Competition Commission has developed this practice, in particular, with regard to American civil trials, yet they also apply equally to Swiss or European civil proceedings.

If the Competition Commission were to permit the information of the parties filing leniency applications to be inspected without restriction and used in other proceedings, the leniency application would obviously lose its appeal. For this reason, Article 9 para 1 OS SCA also provides that the parties making leniency applications can give their testimony orally. The Competition Commission now

[55] RS 312.

[56] RS 152.3.

[57] RS 235.1.

[58] RPW/DPC 2012/2, S. 269, para 40.

connects this procedure to the rule that, during the proceeding, the documents of parties filing leniency applications can only be inspected by parties to the proceeding at the offices of the authority in situ. In addition, no reproductions, particularly photocopies, may be made.

The other documents that may, in some circumstances, preexist are provided to the other parties (parties to proceedings) as part of the inspection of documents, which can also be done electronically. However, they have been asked in certain proceedings to undertake by their signature that they will only use these documents for the purpose of a defence in the Competition Commission proceedings. In other proceedings, there have been no restrictions on, and no commitments by, the parties to the proceeding. The practice of the Swiss Competition Commission has been inconsistent so far.

The result is that parties to proceedings are granted access to the documents directly submitted by a party filing leniency application only in situ and with a ban on reproducing them (in particular, oral statements placed on record or statements in writing). The other preexisting documents can be inspected fully, but the parties must undertake to use the information acquired only for the purpose of a defence in the Competition Commission proceedings. However, the practice of the Competition Commission has been inconsistent so far, as there have been various proceedings with no restrictions on the parties with regard to preexisting documents at all. In the view of the Competition Commission, in part of the proceedings, these principles only apply in case of effective leniency application but not in case of mere cooperation with the Competition Commission. In other proceedings, the Competition Commission has also, in case of cooperation outside leniency application, enhanced the protection of the cooperating parties by requesting the parties to undertake to use the information acquired only for the purpose of defence in the Competition Commission proceedings.

Access to the File by Aggrieved Parties

In relation to the inspection of documents by aggrieved parties (claimants), a distinction must first be made: to the extent that claimants participate or were involved in the proceedings, they are deemed as a matter of principle to be "parties to proceedings". In this case, the above also applies to claimants. It should, however, be noted that the possibilities of limiting the document inspection right should go further in the case of claimants than in the case of parties to proceedings, who are also incriminated at the same time and would therefore be targets of the order, but these are the very ones who must be guaranteed the right to an effective defence (see Article 27 APA). In other words, a restriction on inspection in the case of claimants should probably be more proportionate than in the case of "accused parties".[59]

[59] See, in this regard, also Brunner Stephan C, in: Auer Christoph/Müller Markus/Schindler Benjamin (Hrsg.), Kommentar zum Bundesgesetz über das Verwaltungsverfahren (VwVG), Zürich/St. Gallen 2008, Article 26 N 12.

Given this, two crucial questions must be asked now. If a claimant (originally) participating in the proceedings wishes, however, to use in subsequent civil proceedings the information and documents obtained by the inspection: how is the obligation to use the documents or information merely in the context of the Competition Commission proceedings to be assessed in civil procedural terms? And how does a claimant access the documents of the Competition Commission proceedings if he was not party to the proceedings and now wishes to lodge an action for damages in a civil court or such proceedings are already underway?

As far as can be seen, with regard to the first question, so far there are no precedents. It therefore remains to be seen whether such a case will even crop up at all and, if so, how the civil court assesses the specified obligation.[60] As regards the second question, the situation is as follows: the parties or their representatives are the first ones with entitlement to inspect documents. The legal standing of parties derives here from Article 6 APA. Pursuant to this provision, "parties" are persons whose rights or obligations will be affected by the order and other persons, organisations or authorities who have a legal remedy against the order, which is the case if they will be—adversely—affected by an administrative act that is being considered.[61] Purchasers (in the sense of consumers) cannot, pursuant to Article 43 para 1 SCA, participate in the proceedings and should as a rule not be affected by the Competition Commission order. This means they can hardly be parties to the proceedings. This in turn means that pursuant to APA they would enjoy no right to inspect the documents. Whether and to what extent outside parties/third parties (even as claimants) may have access to completed proceedings before the Competition Commission has still not been clarified.

13.2.4 Sanctions and Leniency Programme

As already described, in the context of the sanctions under cartel law only isolated aspects can be made out that might have a special influence on SMEs. The word is "might" because even in the case of the sanctions there is no independent SME law. In each case, however, it follows that the difficulty for SMEs in organising their behaviour so that it is in accordance with competition law results either in a considerable risk or in a consultancy expense. For financial reasons, not every SME can afford to obtain corresponding advice. To this extent, there are differences

[60] One possibility, for example, might be that the granting of the right to access to the file subject to the obligation mentioned constituted an order, so that a contravention of it could be sanctioned. The construction of a contract could also be considered. However, the consequences of breaching it are unclear. The other question was who the parties to this contract would be. Lastly, another option might be a procedurally justified right that, in the event of breach of the obligation referred to in the documents (in the rule), would be excluded from evidence.

[61] Brunner Stephan C., in: Auer Christoph/Müller Markus/Schindler Benjamin (Hrsg.), Kommentar zum Bundesgesetz über das Verwaltungsverfahren (VwVG), Zürich/St. Gallen 2008, Article 26 N 10.

between SMEs and large enterprises, but these differences are not attributable to the cartel law stipulations but to the economic performance of many SMEs.

Also, leniency applications can generate considerable expense. This is recently strengthened by the so-called *Ascopa practice* of the Competition Commission, according to which in the case of leniency applications it proceeds on the basis that the parties (parties filing leniency application) at least admit they were involved in an unlawful and sanctionable restriction on competition. The leniency application is therefore similar to an admission in a criminal trial. In both cases, there is an admission of participation in a situation (i.e., in facts) which the party making the admission or party filing leniency application would acknowledge was not in statutory compliance. For this reason, according to the Competition Commission, it is not possible to submit a leniency application with the reservation that the submitting party was not involved in a restriction on competition. The Competition Commission is further of the view that in principle a company making a leniency application must be requested to be in a position to assess whether and how the agreement impacted the market, i.e. it must also admit to the effects on the market.[62]

SMEs therefore are faced with the following problem: leniency application is, according to the Competition Commission's practice, associated with various consequences regarding the facts of the case. Assessing the consequences of a leniency application generally requires legal advice, yet SMEs can often not afford this. SMEs might, because of this practice and because of circumstances, be inclined to dispense with leniency application, although this would be the "better" way. In this sense, certain less performing SMEs are disadvantaged in relation to the more powerful large enterprises. The Competition Commission should probably review its practice in this regard. This is all the more true since only the company that files leniency application first benefits from the (complete) exemption from sanctions (Article 8 Abs. 1 OS SCA). The time pressure accordingly accentuates the aforementioned problem.

Nor, finally, do any special rules for SMEs apply in relation to their protection following a leniency application (or general cooperation) from possible reprisals from competitors, especially from large enterprises. There is only reference to the (not SME-related) possibility of enacting preliminary measures. After the official opening of the investigation, the Competition Commission can enact preliminary measures. During the preliminary investigation, on the other hand, this is not possible, but in practice it happens that when the investigation is opened a simultaneous decision is made about the preliminary measure.[63] The enactment of preliminary measures is in principle also possible in the civil courts (Article 261 ff. ZPO), but the petitioner is then set a period to initiate legal action (Article 263 ZPO) to the extent that these are preliminary measures before the legal action is pending

[62] RPW/DPC 2011/4, p. 576, recital 326.

[63] Basler Kommentar KG-Zirlick Beat/Tagmann Christoph, Article 26 N 49 ff. and Basler Kommentar KG, Bilger Stefan, Article 39 N 92 ff.

(prosecution burden). If the petitioner does not in any case initiate civil proceedings, it will hardly ever try to take "civil law" preliminary measures based on this regulation. It must also be assumed that the preconditions of legal protection in clear cases (Article 257 CCP) will generally not exist.

Two Competition Commission decisions from the year 2009 must be mentioned precisely in this connection: the "Hors-Liste"[64] and "Gaba/Gebro".[65] In the first case, dealing with the issue of public price recommendations (and finally a resulting price agreement) for non-reimbursable drugs, the Competition Commission fined only the three large pharmaceutical companies involved in the agreement. The not-completely-known pharmacies also involved in it (1,672 in all) and self-dispensing doctors (SD-doctors, totalling 3,693), on the other hand, were not incriminated, primarily because of practical considerations. The Competition Commission opined: "Even if a list could be drawn up of those points of sale which have breached the SCA the sanction amount for each enterprise would have to be calculated separately. The fact that this would be disproportionate is evident from the very fact that numerous points of sale sold only a few boxes of erectile dysfunction drugs and the sanction that would have to be calculated at some expense would therefore in each case only amount to a few Swiss francs". The Competition Commission further held that it "[would] in the end be totally unreasonable to determine, in a legally satisfactory way and giving actual names, which points of sale [would have] followed price recommendation and which did not and to impose individualised sanctions on almost 5,000 parties. The average amount of the fines to be imposed [was] disproportionate to the expense necessary to do this".[66] In actual fact, the points of sale that were not sanctioned will have been SMEs, yet in our view discretionary considerations are at the forefront, not the type of companies involved (even if a similar situation in which merely large enterprises were involved is scarcely conceivable simply due to the number of active large enterprises in Switzerland).

In the second case, Gaba/Gebro, it is true that the Competition Commission was able to establish an alleged unlawful agreement (obstruction of parallel imports) between both these companies, and at least Gaba was accordingly also fined. The Competition Commission, however, decided not to impose more than a symbolic amount on Gebro. This approach was based on a "thorough consideration" of Gebro's participation in the agreement. The Competition Commission compared the economic interests of the parties with each other and essentially came to the conclusion that Gebro had been the weaker contractual party, which is why Gaba was able to enforce certain contractual terms unilaterally against Gebro. In addition, Gaba had a greater interest in enforcing the agreement. And based on the longstanding contractual relationship, together with corresponding investments, Gebro had not wanted to risk termination of the contract. Given this background,

[64] RPW/DPC 2010/4 p. 649 ff.

[65] RPW/DPC 2010/1 p. 65 ff.

[66] RPW/DPC 2010/4 p. 699, para 382 ff.

the Competition Commission held that "The overall assessment of the arguments listed above therefore leads to the conclusion that both Gaba and Gebro deliberately enforced the territorial protection agreement in question, but this must be viewed in relative terms [...]. As a result it was possible for Gaba to enforce its contractual terms in relation to Gebro". Based on these considerations, the sanction against Gebro was to be limited to a symbolic amount. In assessing the circumstances specified and considering the seriousness of the conduct condemned and the proportionality principle, a symbolic administrative sanction was justified under Article 49a para 1 SCA in the amount of CHF 10,000—for Gebro.[67] These statements by the Competition Commission seem to fundamentally support the theory that the mostly smaller economic significance of an individual SME can be taken into account when calculating the sanctions (in contrast to large enterprises). In the case in question, it seems in our view, however, to be questionable whether this was actually the motivation of the Competition Commission—even if the considerations generally help to support it. It is also conceivable that the Competition Commission had to resort to this "gimmick" since Gebro had generated no (appreciable or not easily verifiable) turnover in Switzerland, and turnover forms the basis for calculating the sanction. If, however, this were actually to have been the case, then the Competition Commission should not even have imposed a symbolic fine on Gebro.

13.3 SMEs as Victims

13.3.1 Private Antitrust Enforcement

Private enforcement of cartel law claims plays hardly any role in Switzerland, even if in judicial practice, however, cartel law circumstances played a role sporadically.[68] The reasons are probably manifold. First, just based on the investigative rule of thumb that applies at the Competition Commission, it should be simpler to notify an allegedly unlawful conduct of a company than to bring a case oneself. The latter involves not only considerable expense but also a significant cost risk. In the civil proceedings, the onus is on the plaintiff to assert and prove the elements constituting the offence (Article 8 Civil Code and Article 150 CCP). If he is unsuccessful, he loses and he must pay not only the judicial costs but also the counterparty's costs (Article 106 CCP). Just proving loss or damage probably stops many private plaintiffs from bringing a civil case. The restriction on the capacity to bring an action should also be noted: it is true that every individual or legal entity or group of individuals has capacity to bring an action. However, it is necessary that the party is impeded in commencing or exercising competition as a result of an

[67] RPW/DPC 2010/1 p. 113 ff. recital 374 ff.

[68] See, e.g., BGE 134 III 438, especially para 2; RPW/DPC 2003/2, p. 451 ff.; RPW/DPC 2010/4, p. 793 ff.

unlawful restriction on competition pursuant to Article 5–7 SCA. A direct competitive relationship is not necessary here, and it is sufficient that the party bringing the action is indirectly affected. With these preconditions, however, economic and professional associations or consumers generally bow out.[69]

However, the SCA seems to contain a full range of tools for civil cases. A plaintiff who has been adversely affected by a competition agreement or by an abusive conduct can not only file a petition for the issuance of an order to cease or desist from restraint but also demand damages and satisfaction in accordance with the Code of Obligations (CO). The same applies to the surrender of unjustly generated profits (Article 12 para 1 SCA). For the purpose of enforcing the claim for a cease and desist order, the court can, upon motion of the plaintiff, also declare the contracts to be invalid in whole or in part or order the perpetrators of the restriction on competition to enter into fair market contracts or standard industry contracts with the party impacted by the restraint (Article 13 SCA). In addition, since the prosecution burden is not a problem here, preliminary measures may be applied for (Article 261 ff. CCP).

It cannot be predicted whether in future anything will change regarding the minimal importance of civil cartel law in Switzerland. At least, the legislator originally intended at any rate with the deterrent effect of civil actions to beef up compliance with cartel law rules. It should be added, however, that the lack of appeal of civil cartel law (except for the cost point) has nothing to do with who the party bringing the action is. Here too there are therefore no differences between SMEs and large enterprises. Nor does it appear sensible, given the large number of SMEs in Switzerland, to create special SME rules. The same applies to class actions, which anyway are hardly in line with Swiss legal tradition. One thought that might be considered, however, would be to give consumers the capacity to bring actions, yet there is no direct connection to SMEs here.

13.4 Is There a Need for Regulation?

Now that the *status quo* has been described, we can return to the question posted at the outset. The Swiss corporate environment consists mainly of SMEs. If a statute aims to cover as many applicable cases as possible, it must be tailored to the majority. A Swiss cartel law must accordingly be geared not to large companies but to SMEs. The fact that no special cartel law rules apply for SMEs is actually logical, given this background. And yet the question is whether it is sensible to make all enterprises that are active on Swiss markets subject to the SCA. In particular, however, the other question that would have to be asked is whether it is justified to declare certain agreements generally unlawful regardless of their effect on the market based on qualitative significance. Would it not be better to

[69] Borer Jürg, Schweizerisches Kartellgesetz, Wettbewerbsrecht I [Swiss Cartel Act, Competition Law I], 3rd edition, Zürich 2011, Article 12 N 3 ff.

exclude actual minor or *bagatelle* cases totally from the SCA—irrespective of whether or not they are so-called hard-core restrictions?

As shown, the SME Notice for microenterprises is basically trending in this direction, since in Section 5 it explicitly mentions "insignificant". However, the SME Notice is, as mentioned, not binding on the courts, and the so-called hard-core restrictions are not permitted even if they emanate from microenterprises. Furthermore, even there the Competition Commission is leaving a back door open for itself, in that it merely "as a rule" assumes that the agreement has an insignificant impact. Uncertainty is therefore always present. This is also strengthened by the fact that the consequences of the overall consideration[70] conducted by the Competition Commission in the context of assessing significance is hard to predict unless a qualitatively significant restriction on the competitive freedom of action is being discussed. In the latter case, the Competition Commission's practice results in a de facto per se ban on qualitatively significant agreements (in the view of the Competition Commission, in particular, hard-core restrictions).

These comments make it clear that SMEs, in particular, have to struggle with uncertainties regarding their conduct's compliance with cartel law. These uncertainties cause costs, whether it is because a consultancy-related expense arises or because favourable conduct due to an alleged illegality is superseded by a less favourable alternative. What SMEs need is legal certainty. The answer to the question would therefore have to be that SMEs initially need, above all, legal certainty so that they can plan investments and through cost savings be able to actively enter in competition with other SMEs or with large enterprises. It should further be noted that the discretionary principle has been anchored in Article 27 SCA. In the case of obvious *bagatelle* cases, the Competition Commission does not, therefore, have to intervene—however, it can. Legal certainty is therefore not even achieved by the discretionary principle.

It would therefore be apposite here to say what clearly does not fall within the scope of application of the SCA. The fundamental concept of a statute will be addressed. While in European law all competition agreements are, in principle, unlawful unless they have been individually or collectively held to be lawful, in Swiss law anything that is not (often after the event) found to be unlawful is permitted. This concept in Swiss cartel law seems, at first sight, to be more liberal than the European concept. Appearances however can be deceptive. It cannot be estimated how many resources are squandered merely in order to determine whether a competition agreement is admissible. The best help for SMEs competing with large enterprises is, however, to provide them with resources to be used efficiently in competition and not for reviewing regulations.

This goal could be achieved by statutorily limiting the personal scope of application of the SCA. Agreements of companies that have no effect or scarcely any effect on the market could be completely excluded from the SCA. The guide for this should, however, be not the number of employees but, as already mentioned,

---

[70] RPW/DPC 2012/1, p. 105, para 175.

the market share. Such a view is supported by the fact that any state intervention in a basic right, namely economic freedom pursuant to Article 27 Cst., must be proportionate (Article 36 para 3 Cst.). Here, a distinction is made between the *appropriateness* of the measure to achieve the intended purpose, the *necessity*, according to which the measure has to be the least stringent remedy and *proportionality in the narrower sense*, which is done by weighing up the affected public and private interests. The proportionality principle is met by excluding pure bagatelle cases from the SCA. Nor would this kind of approach conflict with the statutory provision in Article 5 para 1 SCA or the assessment of the significance and the constitutional requirement—quite the contrary. There would instead be clarification that significance must be there both in qualitative and quantitative terms, with the possibility of lesser quality being offset by greater quantity. Quality or quantity alone is not, however, enough to say there is significance.[71] There could be a statutory provision therefore saying up to what market share there is *no* quantitative significance, which is why even a qualitatively significant agreement (such as a hard-core restriction) might not result in the application of Article 5 para 1 SCA. This result would, as shown, also be in line with previous Federal Court case law relating to significance.

Against the background of the Swiss corporate environment, the response to the question posted at the outset must be answered as follows: yes, SMEs *should* be subject to special cartel law rules in so far as legal certainty requires this. This can be achieved as follows:

- By a restriction of the personal scope of application of the SCA: bagatelle cases must be excluded completely, with the bagatelle limit being based on the market shares of the companies involved in the agreement. Hard-core restrictions could also be termed bagatelle circumstances. Under Article 5 para 1 SCA, they even would *have to* be termed bagatelle circumstances if they do not significantly restrict competition.
- It should be noted, however, that this request might not find any support in today's political environment. The trend instead seems to be in the opposite direction.[72] Still, it would be desirable to move closer to EU law, which says SMEs below a certain market share threshold (if need be, combined with a financial criterion such as turnover) are not caught by cartel law unless there are so-called hard-core restrictions (Article 5 paras 3 and 4 SCA).
- In the case of both options, explicit statutory rules would have to be created (by a partial revision of the SCA) to strengthen the legal certainty of SMEs.
- On the other hand, the criteria of "limited market effect" and "improvement of competitiveness" need to be abandoned, since, as shown, they cannot provide any particular insight or significance anyway in the statutory regulation in Article 5 SCA.

---

[71] BGE 129 II 18, paras 5.2.1 and 5.2.2.

[72] Cf, instead of many others, Ammann Martin/Strebel Mario, Die KMU-Bekanntmachung der WEKO [The WEKO SME notice], in: sic! 2007, p. 235 ff. und Ducrey Patrik/Tagmann Christoph, Die Anwendung des Kartellrechts auf KMU [Applying Cartel Law to SMEs], in: ZBJV 143/2007, p. 85 ff.

United Kingdom 14

David Bailey

14.1 Introduction

This contribution discusses the domestic competition law, policy, and practice towards small and medium-sized enterprises in the United Kingdom. A draft version of the report was circulated to members of the UK Competition Law Association ("CLA") in March 2012 to seek the views of members on its content. The final version of this report incorporates the views expressed by CLA members at a meeting held in May 2012.

14.2 SMEs in Context

14.2.1 SMEs' Economic Context and Legal Definition

14.2.1.1 Legal Definitions of SMEs

There is no standard definition of an SME in the UK. The Competition Act 1998[1] does not itself contain a definition of an SME for the purposes of applying the EU and/or UK competition rules in the UK. Frequently used definitions are based on the number of employees (less than 250) and/or annual turnover (less than GBP 25 million).[2]

[1] Available at http://www.legislation.gov.uk/ukpga/1998/41/contents.

[2] BIS Economics Paper No 16, *SME Access to External Finance*, January 2012, available at www.bis.gov.uk.

D. Bailey (✉)
Brick Court Chambers, London, UK
e-mail: davidbailey@brickcourt.co.uk

P. Këllezi et al. (eds.), *Antitrust for Small and Middle Size Undertakings and Image Protection from Non-Competitors*, LIDC Contributions on Antitrust Law, Intellectual Property and Unfair Competition, DOI 10.1007/978-3-642-54000-4_14, © Springer-Verlag Berlin Heidelberg 2014

14.2.1.2 The Economic Perspective

There are approximately 4.8 million SME businesses in the UK, comprising 99.9 % of all businesses.[3] The UK Government has acknowledged that SMEs have a crucial importance for the UK economy and has introduced various policies to support the financing and growth of SMEs.[4] In parallel to this domestic agenda, the European Commission is committed to promoting the growth of SMEs. In June 2008, the Commission adopted the 'Small Business Act' for Europe,[5] which applies to all independent companies that have fewer than 250 employees, seeking to reduce the 'red tape', at EU and national levels, on SMEs. In November 2011, the Commission published a report entitled *Minimizing regulatory burden for small and medium sized enterprises (SMEs) Adapting EU regulation to the needs of micro-enterprises*,[6] which sets out how the Commission intends to strengthen the use of exemptions or specific, 'lighter' legislative regimes for SMEs or micro-companies.[7]

14.2.2 Specific Treatment of SMEs Under Competition Law

14.2.2.1 The Nature and Scope of Specific Treatment for SMEs

Recital 8 of Regulation 1/2003[8] mentions provisions of national law that prohibit or impose sanctions on abusive behaviour toward economically dependent undertakings. It is understood that other Member States of the EU have provisions concerning the abuse of economic dependence or superior bargaining power.[9] The aim of such rules is, essentially, to control disparities of bargaining power in the supply chain.

There do not appear to be any rules in English law that seek specifically protect SMEs,[10] either as competitors or as trading partners, from abuse of a

---

[3] Department for Business, Innovation & Skills/HM Treasury, *Financing a private sector recovery*, Cm 7923, July 2010, para 3.5.

[4] See, e.g., the Department for Business, Innovation & Skills initiative, *Business Coaching for Growth programme*, available at www.businessgrowth.uk.com; HM Treasury *Accelerating the SME economic engine: through transparent, simple and strategic procurement*, available at www.hm-treasury.gov.uk.

[5] COM(2008) 394, final, 25 June 2008. See Commission Press Release IP/11/218, 23 February 2011.

[6] COM (2011) 803, 23 November 2011.

[7] See similarly the OECD Best Practices Roundtable, *General Cartel Bans: Criteria for Exemption for Small and Medium-sized Enterprises* (1996), available at www.oced.org.

[8] OJ 2003 L 1, p. 1.

[9] Staff Working Paper accompanying the Report on the functioning of Regulation 1/2003, SEC (2009) 574 final, paras 162–169 (describing the domestic provisions on economic dependence in France, Germany, Italy, Portugal, Spain, Greece, Latvia, and Hungary).

[10] Cf Sections 140A-D of the Consumer Credit Act 1974, inserted by Section 19 of the Consumer Credit Act 2006, which enables a court to make an order if it finds that the relationship between a creditor and the debtor arising out of a consumer credit agreement is unfair because of the terms of

superior bargaining position.[11] Certain sectors in the UK, however, have been subject to intense political and industrial pressure for the competition authorities or the Government to provide redress for smaller operators.[12]

The CLA members were unanimously of the view that there is no need to enact legislation specifically to protect SMEs as competition or trading partners in the UK. Where particular instances of market failure arise, these can be adequately addressed by using one or more of the instruments of domestic competition law.

14.2.2.2 Substantive and Procedural Rules

Competition Act 1998

Sections 39 and 40 of the Competition Act provide small companies with immunity from the imposition of financial penalties for breach of the Chapter I and/or the Chapter II prohibitions.[13] Section 39(3) of the Competition Act provides that a party to a "small agreement" is immune from the imposition of a penalty in respect of an infringement of the Chapter I prohibition. Small agreements are those between undertakings whose combined turnover in the business year preceding the infringement does not exceed GBP 20 million.[14] Section 40(3) of the Act provides that a person is immune from the imposition of a penalty in respect of an infringement of the Chapter II prohibition if its "conduct is of minor significance". Conduct of minor significance is defined as conduct by an undertaking whose turnover in the business year preceding the infringement does not exceed GBP 50 million.[15]

The limited immunity conferred by Sections 39 and 40 is subject to certain qualifications[16] but has been of some significance in practice. In *Cardiff Bus*,[17] the OFT found that Cardiff City Transport Services Limited (trading as 'Cardiff Bus') contravened the Chapter II prohibition by engaging in predatory conduct in order to exclude its principal competitor from the local bus services market. The OFT decided, however, that, given that its applicable turnover did not exceed GBP 50 million, Cardiff Bus benefited from the immunity conferred by Section 40

the agreement, the way in which it has been applied by the creditor, or any other thing done or not done by the creditor.

[11] *Report on Abuse of Superior Bargaining Position* (ICN, April 2008), p. 5, n 7, and p. 10.

[12] See, e.g., the Milk (Pricing) Bill, which was introduced in the House of Commons in July 2007 with the intention to confer further powers on the OFT and the CC to investigate the prices of milk paid by retailers to producers. The Bill was introduced, but not enacted, following concern about the low prices that farmers were paid for producing milk that is sold in supermarkets.

[13] There is no equivalent provision of domestic law purporting to confer immunity from the imposition of fines for infringements of Articles 101 and/or 102 TFEU.

[14] SI 2000/262, Reg 3.

[15] Ibid, Reg 4.

[16] E.g., price-fixing agreements are excluded from partial immunity under Sections 39(1)(b) and 39(9) of the Act, and the OFT may withdraw the benefit of immunity in an individual case, and immunity does not extend to transgressions of Article 101 TFEU (Section 39(4)).

[17] OFT Decision of 18 November 2008, available at www.oft.gov.uk.

(3) of the Competition Act.[18] The OFT declined to withdraw the immunity from a financial penalty in the circumstances of that case but provided no explanation for that decision. Another undertaking, W Austin and Sons (Stevenage) Limited,[19] a funeral director, was found guilty of a breach of the Chapter II prohibition by the CAT but benefited from the limited immunity under Section 40(3) of the Act.

The Enterprise Act 2002

Under Sections 22(1) and 33(1) of the Enterprise Act 2002,[20] it is for the OFT to conduct a preliminary assessment of anticipated or completed mergers; broadly speaking, if it considers that a merger may be expected substantially to lessen competition, it must refer the case to the CC for a second stage investigation. The duties imposed by Sections 22(1) and 33(1) are in each case subject to subsection (2), which entitles the OFT not to make a reference if it believes that the relevant markets are not sufficiently important to justify making a reference to the CC. This exception refers, of course, to the value of the market and not to the size of the companies concerned. Moreover, it is not limited to SMEs. It is clear, however, that this exception to the OFT's duty to refer may be important in practice for acquisitions by or involving SMEs.

The OFT's most recent guidance[21] on the so-called *de minimis* exception explains that where the annual value in the UK of the market(s) concerned is, in aggregate, less than GBP 3 million, the OFT will generally not consider a merger reference to the CC justified, provided that there is in principle not a clear-cut remedy available. Where the annual value in the UK, in aggregate, of the market (s) concerned is between GBP 3 million and GBP 10 million, the OFT will consider whether the expected customer harm resulting from the merger is materially greater than the average public cost of a CC reference (said to be around GBP 400,000). Where the annual value in the UK of the market is more than GBP 10 million, the OFT considers that it will generally be of sufficient importance to justify a reference. The OFT applied the *de minimis* exception in July 2011 in relation to the acquisition by Rentokil Initial of the pest control, fire and water businesses of Connaught.[22]

Market Studies

Section 5 of the Enterprise Act 2002 provides that one of the general functions of the OFT is to obtain, compile, and keep under review information about matters relating to the carrying out of its functions. One of the ways in which the OFT

[18] Ibid, paras 8.5–8.7.

[19] Case No 1044/2/1/04 *JJ Burgess & Sons v OFT* [2005] CAT 25.

[20] Available at http://www.legislation.gov.uk/ukpga/2002/40/contents.

[21] OFT1122, December 2004, available at www.oft.gov.uk.

[22] www.oft.gov.uk/shared_oft/mergers_ea02/2011/rentokil.pdf; see also *Sports Universal Process SAS/Prozone Group Limited*, 4 October 2011, www.oft.gov.uk/shared_oft/mergers_ea02/2011/sports-universal.pdf.

carries out this general function is by conducting 'market studies' of markets that appear not to be working well for consumers but where enforcement action under competition or consumer law does not, at first sight, appear to be the most appropriate response.

In its market study into *Homebuilding in the UK*,[23] the OFT noted the importance of small homebuilders (and individuals building their own homes) for building on smaller sites, which larger homebuilders would leave undeveloped. The OFT found that the homebuilding industry was broadly competitive but recommended that the Government alleviate certain regulatory requirements for smaller homebuilders that might otherwise hinder the building of new homes in the UK.[24]

In March 2011, the OFT published the findings of its market study into *Commissioning and competition in the public sector*.[25] The study looked at procuring a wide range of public services, including health, education, social welfare, and the administration of justice. The OFT considered the role of SMEs and made recommendations to commissioners of public services in local, central, and devolved government on how to devise procurement procedures that do not discriminate against smaller suppliers. To address its concerns, the OFT proposed that procurers encourage SMEs to form consortia, either between themselves or with larger suppliers, to overcome barriers to entry associated with aggregating contracts or joint procurement.

14.2.2.3 Influence of Size and Economic Power in Decisions of the National Competition Authorities and Courts

The possible relevance of the size and economic power of parties under investigation (in the case of competition authorities) or litigants (in the case of the courts and tribunals) will be discussed in Sects. 14.3 and 14.4.

14.2.2.4 Specific Programmes Addressed to SMEs

The OFT's Championing Competition Campaign

The calendar year 2005 was a prominent year for promoting UK competition policy to SMEs. In May 2005, the OFT launched a 'Championing Competition' campaign to highlight the positive aspects of competition for business and to demonstrate to SMEs that competition should be embraced rather than feared.[26] This campaign was a response to a research commissioned by the OFT that showed that 49 % of respondents from organisations employing between 10 and 19 individuals claimed to be aware of the Competition Act.[27] This figure contrasted with 80 % of those

---

[23] OFT 1020, September 2008, available at www.oft.gov.uk.

[24] Ibid, paras 1.9, 7.25, 7.28, and 7.32. The Government's response to the OFT market study is available on the BIS website, www.bis.gov.uk.

[25] OFT 1314.

[26] OFT Press Release 92/05, available at www.oft.gov.uk.

[27] Synovate, *Competition Act and Consumer Rights*, OFT 799, April 2005, available at www.oft.gov.uk.

from organisations with more than 200 employees that claimed to have an understanding and knowledge of competition law. The OFT considered it was important for SMEs to be aware of their rights and responsibilities under competition law 'so that they can take best advantage from competitive markets'.

The OFT has tried to promote awareness of competition law by liaising with UK business organisations such as the Confederation of Business Industry ("CBI") and the Federation of Small Businesses. It sought to focus, in particular, on SMEs in sectors such as healthcare markets and construction and housing markets, which were identified as priority sectors for the OFT at the time.[28] A crucial element of the campaign—forming part of its wider efforts to detect and prohibit cartels—was the OFT's policy of actively encouraging SMEs to approach it with information about cartels in return for immunity from any penalty that might otherwise have been imposed.[29]

The OFT's "Come Clean on Cartels" Campaign

In July 2005, the OFT published further research showing that one in three of the 500 SMEs surveyed said that they were aware of anticompetitive practices in their sector and one in five SMEs felt they had been the victim of such practices.[30] The OFT research also showed, however, that SMEs understood and acknowledged the benefits of the competitive process and a market economy: 75 % of SMEs agreed that competition is a driver for innovation and economic growth. This research was followed on November 2005 by the OFT's "Come Clean on Cartels" month, which urged businesses, and in particular SMEs, to make a 'clean break' with any subsisting anticompetitive agreements.[31] The Come Clean on Cartels month was part of the Championing Competition campaign to promote competition to SMEs. Its purpose was to encourage SMEs to approach the OFT with information about cartels and avail themselves of the leniency programme.

Initiatives to Improve Compliance with Competition Law

In June 2011, the OFT published guidance on *How your business can achieve compliance*.[32] So far as SMEs are concerned, the OFT explains that its risk-based,

[28] The OFT Annual Plan 2005–06, HC461, March 2005, p. 6, available at www.oft.gov.uk.

[29] *Guidance as to the appropriate amount of a penalty* (OFT 423, December 2004), Part 3.

[30] OFT Press Release 129/05, 21 July 2005, available at www.oft.gov.uk. For the purposes of NOP World research, SMEs were defined as a business employing between 10 and 250 employees, with a turnover under EUR 50 million for medium-sized companies and under EUR 10 million for small companies. See further Storey 'The Competitive Experience of UK SMEs: Fair and Unfair' (2009–2010) 17(1) Small Enterprise Research Journal 19.

[31] OFT Press Release 206/05, 2 November 2005, available at www.oft.gov.uk.

[32] *How your business can achieve compliance* OFT1341, June 2011, available at www.oft.gov.uk; on the motivation for compliance and non-compliance with competition law generally see *Drivers of Compliance and Non-compliance with Competition Law* (OFT 1227, May 2010) (excluding SMEs: ibid, paras 3.4 and 6.26).

four-step approach[33] is intended to help all businesses, regardless of their size. The OFT emphasises that smaller businesses must not ignore competition law and should take appropriate compliance measures that are proportionate to their degree of risk. The OFT guidance notes that the size and structure of small businesses are likely to mean that practical methods by which they ensure competition law compliance are likely to be different from those of larger businesses. For example, the necessary compliance efforts of SMEs might be less formalised and structured than that of larger businesses. Separate, but related, initiatives include a film on competition law compliance and a *Quick Guide to Competition Law Compliance* specifically aimed at small businesses, both of which accompany and complement the guidance,[34] and guidance on *Company directors and competition law*.[35]

Survey of Businesses' Awareness of Competition Law

At the same time as the above initiatives on encouraging competition compliance, the OFT commissioned a *Competition Law Compliance Survey*.[36] Of 2,000 businesses (of all sizes) surveyed, 95 % were aware of the OFT, 71 % claimed to know something about competition law, and 25 % claimed to know a lot or a fair amount. The research categorised businesses according to the number of employees: up to 9 (micro-business), 10–19 (small business), and 20–249 (medium-sized business). Micro- and small businesses were found to be much more likely to lack knowledge of competition law: three in ten businesses with up to four employees claim to "know nothing" about competition law.[37] A total of 40 % of medium-sized and large businesses claim to know a "fair amount" or "a lot" about competition law, whereas only 20 % of small businesses claimed to have this level of familiarity. In light of these findings, the OFT stated that it would work with business groups, including the CBI, Institute of Directors, and the Trade Association Forum, in order to raise awareness of its new guidance and to disseminate the Quick Guide and the film on competition compliance.[38] As recently as December 2011, the OFT published a research by London Economics, which indicated that SMEs are still less likely to state that they were knowledgeable about competition law.[39]

[33] The first step is to identify the key competition law risks faced by the business. The second step is to assess how serious the identified risks are. The third step involves risk mitigation in the form of establishing policies, procedures, and training to prevent the risks identified from occurring or adequately dealing with them if they do arise. The fourth step is regularly reviewing the first three steps to ensure that the business has 'an effective compliance culture'.

[34] www.oft.gov.uk/OFTwork/competition-act-and-cartels/competition-law-compliance.

[35] OFT 1340, June 2011, available at www.oft.gov.uk.

[36] OFT 1270, June 2011.

[37] Ibid, para 4.3.

[38] OFT Press Release 74/11, 27 June 2011.

[39] *Assessing the Impact of Competition Intervention on Compliance and Deterrence* (OFT 1391), available at www.oft.gov.uk.

14.3 Public Antitrust Enforcement and SMEs

14.3.1 Substantive and Procedural Rules Applicable to SMEs

The UK competition authorities have applied the Competition Act across a number of sectors, ranging from local bus services to distribution of tobacco products to companies of all sizes, including SMEs.

14.3.1.1 Introduction

The OFT's decision that Cardiff Bus infringed the Chapter II prohibition by intentionally sustaining losses in the short term in order to eliminate competition is an example of the Competition Act being applied to an SME without "uncritical sentimentality" in favour of small business.[40] An earlier high-profile case in UK competition law involved the OFT fining ten undertakings of various sizes for fixing the retail prices of replica football kits manufactured by Umbro.[41] One of the infringing retailers fined by the OFT was an SME, Sportsetail Ltd, which, in its first 15 months of trading up to 31 December 2000, had a total UK turnover of GBP 174,576. Sportsetail Ltd received immunity from the fine of GBP 4,000, which would otherwise have been imposed as it had provided the OFT with crucial information about the agreements.[42]

Collusive Tendering Involving SMEs

An important illustration of the OFT's determination to apply the Competition Act to SMEs just as much as to larger companies are its five decisions fining a total of 39 contractors for collusion in relation to the making of tender bids in flat roofing contracts.[43] A number of the contractors were SMEs, and some of them were parties to one or more of the decisions.[44] The OFT's first decision in March 2004 in *West Midlands Roofing* is, perhaps, the most notable because it clarified the law in relation to collusive tendering and was appealed by two contractors.

[40] See, e.g., Bork "Vertical Restraints: Schwinn Overruled" (1977) *The Supreme Court Review* 171, at 189; see also Bork *The Antitrust Paradox* (Free Press, 1978), 54.

[41] OFT Decision of 1 August 2003.

[42] On appeal by another retailer, JJB Sports, Case No 1021/1/1/03 *JJB Sports plc v OFT* [2004] CAT 17, the CAT upheld most of the OFT's findings of infringement but held that JJB had not been a party to an agreement with Sportsetail and others in relation to prices charged on the England Direct website from spring 2000 to autumn 2001: ibid, paras 990–1053 (appeal on other grounds dismissed, [2006] EWCA Civ 1318).

[43] OFT Decisions of 17 March 2004 (*West Midlands Roofing*), 18 March 2005 (*Scotland Roofing*), 18 March 2005 (*North East England Roofing*), 12 July 2005 (*Western-Central Scotland Roofing*), 23 February 2006 (*England and Scotland Roofing*), upheld on appeal, Case No 1061/1/1/06 *Makers UK Ltd v OFT* [2007] CAT 11.

[44] See, e.g., Briggs Roofing & Cladding Ltd, Pirie Group Ltd, Rio Asphalt & Paving Company Ltd and WG Walker Ltd.

The OFT decision in *Construction Bid-rigging* is a further indication of its resolve to apply the Competition Act to companies irrespective of their size. Following the largest ever investigation under the Act, lasting a total of 5 years and involving over 1,000 parties at one stage, the OFT decided that 103 construction firms had infringed the Chapter I prohibition and imposed fines totalling GBP 129.2 million. A number of SMEs were found to have engaged in illegal bid-rigging activities in relation to a wide range of tendered construction projects, including tenders for schools, universities, and hospitals. The OFT found, in particular, that companies had engaged in cover pricing, that is to say, collusion by one or more bidders during a competitive tender process in order to obtain a price from a competitor that is not intended to win the bid but only to give the appearance of competition. A number of companies appealed to the CAT.

The CAT ultimately handed down nine judgments disposing of the 25 admissible appeals.[45] In each case (save in those cases where an appeal against a finding of infringement was successful), the Tribunal substantially reduced the penalties imposed by the OFT in the decision. Putting the matter very broadly, the CAT concluded that the fines imposed by the OFT were excessive, given the nature of infringements and the mitigating factors arising from the fact that cover pricing was a long-standing practice in the construction industry and was widely regarded as legitimate at the time.[46] The penalties were not reduced specifically on account of the small size of any infringing company, although the CAT did adjust some of the penalties on grounds of financial hardship.[47]

14.3.1.2 Safe Harbours for SMEs

There are no safe harbours for SMEs from liability under the Competition Act.

Sector-Specific Guidance

The OFT has, however, published sector-specific guidance on how competition law applies to cooperation between farming businesses,[48] to the exchange of

[45] Case Nos 1114/1/1/09, etc, *Kier Group plc & Ors v OFT* [2011] CAT 3; Case No 1121/1/1/09 *Durkan Holdings Ltd v OFT* [2011] CAT 6; Case Nos 1117/1/1/10, etc, *GF Tomlinson Building Ltd & Ors v OFT* [2011] CAT 7 (the Court of Appeal allowed an appeal by Interclass Holdings Ltd on the ground that the CAT had given no reasons for doubling the provisional penalty imposed on Interclass to secure deterrence: [2012] EWCA Civ 1056, paras 49–72); Case Nos 1125/1/1/09, etc, *Barrett Estate Services Ltd v OFT* [2011] CAT 9; Case No 1126/1/1/09 *ISG Pearce Ltd v OFT* [2011] CAT 10; Case No 1120/1/1/09 *Quarmby Construction Company Ltd v OFT* [2011] CAT 11; Case No 1118/1/1/09 *GMI Construction Holdings plc v OFT* [2011] CAT 12; Case No 1124/1/1/09 *North Midland Construction plc v OFT* [2011] CAT 14; Case No 1122/1/1/09 *AH Willis & Sons Ltd v OFT* [2011] CAT 13.

[46] See, e.g., Case Nos, etc, 1114/1/1/09 *Kier Group plc & Ors v OFT* [2011] CAT 3, para 78 *et seq.*

[47] See, e.g., Case Nos, etc, 1117/1/1/09 *GF Tomlinson Group Ltd Ors v OFT* [2011] CAT 7, paras 222–237; the Court of Appeal dismissed Interclass' appeal on the ground of financial hardship: [2012] EWCA Civ 1056, paras 73–82.

[48] OFT 740rev, November 2011.

information between independent schools,[49] and to the bus sector.[50] The guidance refers to circumstances in which agreements may fall outside the Competition Act if the parties have an insignificant share of the market.

De Minimis Effect on Competition and on Trade Between Member States

The European Commission has published a Notice on agreements of minor importance which do not appreciably restrict competition under Article 101(1) TFEU[51] ("*De Minimis* Notice") and Guidelines on the effect on trade concept contained in Articles 101 and 102 TFEU[52] ("Effect on Trade Guidelines"), both of which refer to SMEs as defined in the Annex to Commission Recommendation 2003/361/EC.[53] Both Notices state that agreements between small and medium-sized undertakings are rarely capable of appreciably affecting trade between Member States. The Commission has explained that the reason for this view is the fact that the activities of SMEs are normally local or, at most, regional in nature.[54] It is, of course, a matter of EU law whether this view is correct. When applying Articles 101 and 102 TFEU in the UK, it is likely that the domestic competition authorities and courts will adhere to the Commission's considered view that the conduct of SMEs is unlikely to affect interstate trade.

De Minimis Effect on Competition and Trade Within the UK

A material difference between Articles 101 and 102 TFEU and their UK equivalents is that the latter do not require an effect on trade between Member States; they apply when an agreement and/or conduct affects trade within the UK. Section 60 of the Competition Act contains provisions designed to maintain consistency between EU competition law and decisions adopted under the Act. Section 60(3) provides that the domestic competition authorities and courts must 'have regard to' any relevant 'decision or statement' of the European Commission.[55] The *De Minimis* Notice and Effect on Trade Guidelines both carry the authority of the Commission and therefore qualify as 'statements' for the purposes of Section 60(3). The domestic competition authorities and courts will 'have regard

[49] OFT 444, June 2004.

[50] OFT 452, March 2009, paras 4.14–4.15.

[51] OJ 2001C 368/13, para 3.

[52] OJ 2004 C 101/81, para 50.

[53] OJ 2003 L 124/36: Small undertakings are defined in that recommendation as undertakings that have fewer than 50 employees and have either an annual turnover not exceeding EUR 10 million or an annual balance sheet total not exceeding EUR 10 million. Medium-sized undertakings are defined as those that have fewer than 250 employees and have either an annual turnover not exceeding EUR 50 million or an annual balance sheet total not exceeding EUR 43 million.

[54] OJ 2004 C 101/81, para 50.

[55] Note that Section 60(2) imposes a stronger obligation to maintain consistency between the principles applied and the decision reached by the domestic authority and the principles laid down by the Treaty and the EU Courts and any decisions of the EU Courts in determining corresponding questions of competition law.

to' the Commission's views when determining whether the conduct of SMEs 'may affect trade' within the UK.

In *Aberdeen Journals Limited v Office of Fair Trading*,[56] the CAT held that there was no requirement to show that the impugned conduct has an appreciable effect on trade within the UK. The requirement of appreciability is understood in EU law as a jurisdictional requirement that demarcated the boundary line between the application of EU competition law and national competition law, a demarcation unnecessary under the Chapter II prohibition.[57] This could lead to some divergence in the way in which the Chapter I and II prohibitions and Articles 101 and 102 are applied. The Tribunal's decision extends the territorial scope of the Competition Act to the activities of smaller operators in local markets. Two Judges of the Chancery Division of the High Court have expressed doubt about the correctness of the Tribunal's decision, at least in the context of Chapter I prohibition cases.[58] The High Court Judges have stated that the Chapter I prohibition necessarily requires it to be shown that the relevant agreement had more than a *de minimis* effect on trade within the UK.[59] The High Court's approach would mean that fewer SMEs in local markets would be caught by the Competition Act. There is therefore a conflict of authority on whether it is necessary to prove that an appreciable effect on trade within the UK and thus the extent to which the local activities of SMEs are subject to the Competition Act.

14.3.1.3 Access to Justice

A number of appeals to the UK Competition Appeal Tribunal have been brought by SMEs.[60]

Judicial Application of Substantive Rules to SMEs

The Tribunal's early case law under the Chapter II prohibition, for example, was concerned with smaller firms in the pharmaceutical sector who were seeking to bring new products to the market for benefits to the consumers in the face of allegedly abusive practices of dominant firms. In *Napp Pharmaceutical Holdings Ltd v Director General of Fair Trading*,[61] the CAT upheld the OFT's decision that

---

[56] Case No 1009/1/1/02 [2003] CAT 11.

[57] Ibid, paras 459–460.

[58] *P&S Amusements Ltd v Valley House Leisure Ltd* [2006] EWHC 1510, para 22 per Sir Andrew Morritt (formerly the Chancellor of the High Court) and in *Pirtek (UK) Ltd v Joinplace Ltd (t/a Pirtek Darlington)* [2010] EWHC 1641, paras 61–62 per Briggs J.

[59] Ibid. Cf. Case No 1124/1/1/09 *North Midland v OFT* [2011] CAT 14, para 49 (the reasoning in *Aberdeen Journals* applies equally to the effect on trade requirement in the Chapter I prohibition).

[60] In addition to the *Burgess*, *Albion Water*, *Brannigan* and *Cityhook* cases discussed in the text below, see also Case No 1006/2/1/01 *BetterCare Group Ltd v Director General of Fair Trading* [2002] CAT 7; Case No 1024/2/3/04 *Floe Telecom Ltd v Director General of Telecommunications* [2004] CAT 18; Case No 1068/2/1/06 *Casting Book Ltd v OFT* [2006] CAT 35; Case No 1027/2/3/04 *VIP Communications Ltd v OFCOM* [2009] CAT 28.

[61] Case No 1001/1/1/01 [2002] CAT 1.

Napp, a virtual monopolist, had infringed the Chapter II prohibition by offering below-cost prices to UK hospitals and doing so selectively on those drugs where it faced competition from smaller competitors.[62] The CAT found that the effect of Napp's pricing policy in foreclosing competition in the hospital segment was significant.[63]

In *Genzyme Ltd v Office of Fair Trading*,[64] another Chapter II case involving protection of an SME from an abuse of dominance in the pharmaceutical sector, the CAT held that Genzyme had abused its dominant position by supplying a drug to a small provider of home care services at a price that did not allow it to trade profitably regardless of how efficient it may be; a practice known as an abusive "margin squeeze".[65] The CAT concluded that the effect, or potential effect, of Genzyme's pricing policy was to foreclose the market for the supply of home care services to patients.[66] The CAT rejected Genzyme's justification for its conduct—that it could provide home care services more efficiently itself—and preferred the evidence of doctors and patients to the effect that they wished the smaller provider of home care services to continue.[67] In *Napp* and *Genzyme*, the CAT clearly considered that the Chapter II prohibition should be applied to maintain an effective competitive structure in the market, including, where appropriate, the protection of smaller competitors.

Two further appeals involving Chapter II are of particular interest: the first concerned an SME as a defendant (*Burgess v OFT*[68]), and the second involved an SME as a third party appellant (*Albion Water*[69]). In *Burgess*, the case concerned a dispute between two family-owned funeral directors. The CAT set aside the OFT's decision rejecting the complaint of unlawfully refused access to crematoria services. The CAT was clearly influenced by the facts of this case concerning SMEs serving a vulnerable class of consumer, and which had been subject to a long running administrative procedure.[70] In *Albion Water*, a new entrant sought access to distribute water over a pipeline belonging to another water company. The CAT found OFWAT had provided inadequate and erroneous reasons for reaching its non-infringement decision. While the CAT's judgment was specific to the water

---

[62] Ibid, para 228.

[63] During the period of infringement, there was only one other competitor, Link, an SME with an annual turnover of £6.7 million, who had managed to acquire and maintain a "toehold" in the market (4 per cent of the total market): see paras 16 and 284.

[64] Case No 1016/1/1/03 [2004] CAT 4.

[65] Ibid, para 552.

[66] Ibid, paras 555 and 575.

[67] Ibid, paras 584–585.

[68] Case No 1044/2/1/04 [2005] CAT 25.

[69] Case No 1046/2/4/04 [2006] CAT 23 and [2006] CAT 36, upheld on appeal, *Dŵr Cymru Cyfyngedig v Albion Water Ltd* [2008] EWCA Civ 536. The CAT awarded Albion Water approximately £1.8 million in damages to compensate Albion for the harm it had suffered as a result of the infringement found by the CAT: Case No 1166/5/7/10 [2013] CAT 6.

[70] Case No 1046/2/4/04 [2006] CAT 23, para 139.

industry in general, it is not unreasonable to suppose that the CAT considered that there are markets in which a new SME may add to the total cost of supply in the short run but should be protected by the Chapter II prohibition on the basis of their potential contribution to effective competition in the long run.

Judicial Application of Procedural Rules to SMEs

The CAT has interpreted its rules and procedures in order to ensure that smaller companies may have recourse to the Tribunal in appropriate circumstances. This approach appears to have influenced the CAT's rather expansive approach to its jurisdiction to hear appeals against implicit non-infringement decisions under the Competition Act. For example, in *BetterCare*,[71] the CAT disagreed with the OFT's finding that a health care trust was not acting as an undertaking when it provided and outsourced the provision of social care services for the elderly in Belfast. Had these activities fallen outside the scope of the Act, the CAT was concerned that BetterCare would not have had an adequate legal remedy.[72] Similarly, in its judgments in *Burgess* and *Albion*, discussed above, the Tribunal was concerned that a small company had failed to obtain redress from the relevant competition authority and decided to make its own infringement decision.

The importance of procedural flexibility for SMEs can also be seen in the CAT's handling of an appeal by a sole trader against an implicit non-infringement decision of the OFT in *Brannigan v OFT*.[73] The CAT held that the trader (who represented himself) should be permitted to challenge a decision of the OFT and also should be given an opportunity to clarify his grounds of appeal.[74] It was, of course, subsequently up to the appellant to formulate his case, but the Tribunal expressed the hope that he might be assisted by the Competition Pro Bono Service.[75] The CAT ultimately dismissed the trader's appeal, but the way in which it managed the appeal shows its willingness to enable SMEs and individuals to have access to the Tribunal.

14.3.2 Fundamental Rights of SMEs (as Infringers and Victims)

14.3.2.1 Complaints

The provisions of the Competition Act are virtually silent on the procedure for dealing with complaints. It is generally accepted, however, that complaints have an important role to play in bringing matters to the attention of the OFT, in leading to investigations under the Competition Act, and in helping to secure the effective enforcement of the Chapter I and Chapter II prohibitions.

---

[71] Case No 1006/2/1/01 *BetterCare Group Ltd v Director General of Fair Trading* [2002] CAT 7.

[72] Ibid, para 261.

[73] Case No 1073/2/1/06 *Brannigan v Office of Fair Trading* [2006] CAT 28.

[74] Ibid, para 82.

[75] www.probonogroup.org.uk/competition/index.php.

Complainants Before the OFT

The OFT has stated that "In order to exercise its powers under the Act effectively, the OFT places significant reliance on third parties drawing to its attention suspected competition law infringements through the submission of well-informed complaints".[76] The OFT has published guidance on the type of information that it expects to be contained in a written, reasoned complaint and also on its practice and procedure in handling complaints.[77] It has also indicated that when setting a time limit for the submission of documents or information during an investigation under the Competition Act, the OFT will consider, amongst other matters, the resources available to the individual or undertaking.[78]

In October 2008, the OFT adopted its *OFT Prioritisation Principles*,[79] which are used to decide which projects and cases it will take on across all of its functions. In particular, it will consider the direct and indirect effect on consumer welfare that intervention in a particular case is likely to have, its strategic significance, the risks and the resources involved.[80] The principles do not distinguish between allegations made by, or against, large or small companies. Their application has, however, affected the investigation of certain SMEs under the Competition Act. The OFT applied the principles in *Tobacco* when it excluded companies with a small presence in the UK tobacco sector.[81] The OFT said that it wanted to concentrate its limited resources on those parties whose activities would be most likely to cause detriment to consumers. A corollary of this administrative decision was, of course, that small and medium-sized retailers were excluded from the streamlined investigation.

Anonymity of Complainants

In some cases, an aggrieved SME might have no qualms about having its identity disclosed when it reports anticompetitive behaviour.[82] There may be cases, however, in which a complainant, whether an SME or a larger company, may be legitimately concerned about the risk of reprisals for divulging anticompetitive behaviour. Whether there will be such a risk will naturally depend on the nature of the industry in question and the type of infringement being alleged and will

[76] *Involving third parties in Competition Act investigations*, OFT 451, April 2006, para A.1.

[77] OFT 451, April 2006.

[78] OFT 404, December 2004, para 3.11.

[79] OFT 953, October 2008.

[80] Para 4.2 of the draft Prioritisation Principles (OFT 953con, September 2007) said that: "increased competition in a market serving small or medium-sized business consumers would also be considered as a positive direct impact". This was amended in the final version to say that: "the effects of increased competition in a market serving businesses would therefore also be considered as a positive direct impact": OFT 953, para 4.2.

[81] OFT Decision of 15 April 2010, para 2.100.

[82] See, e.g., the complaint made by Cityhook Ltd to the OFT about an alleged collective boycott in *R (Cityhook Ltd and Cityhook (Cornwall) Ltd) v Office of Fair Trading* [2009] EWHC 57.

ultimately be a question of fact to be determined in the particular circumstances of each case.

In *Lladró Comercial*,[83] the OFT held that Lladró, a Spanish porcelain producer, had entered into unlawful distribution agreements that prevented retailers from selling below the recommended resale price. The OFT rejected Lladro's argument that it had been contrary to Article 6 of the European Convention on Human Rights and to its rights of defence for the OFT to rely on evidence from complainants whose identity had not been disclosed. In the OFT's view, it was entitled to rely on anonymous evidence in circumstances where it considered that Lladro's rights of defence had been respected and the legitimate commercial interests of the complainants would be harmed by disclosing their identity.

Interestingly, in 2012, the CAT refused an application by a claimant to anonymise witness evidence in the context of a private action for damages because it was not satisfied that the subjective concerns of the individual witness outweighed the objective considerations of open justice.[84]

Complainants Before the CAT

Section 47 of the Competition Act provides for appeals to the CAT by third parties who have 'a sufficient interest'. The Tribunal has said that the persons who seek to appeal under Section 47 are very often complainants, who are competitors of another undertaking, and that most of them have 'a sufficient interest' for the purposes of Section 47.[85] The CAT has repeatedly emphasised the role that third party complainants, which have often been SMEs, play in the enforcement of the Act.[86] In *Freeserve.com v Director General of Telecommunications*,[87] the Tribunal acknowledged that many SMEs lack sufficient resources to deal with the complex issues of competition law.[88] The CAT has therefore been willing to adapt its procedures and practice to accommodate the limited resources of SMEs. This 'procedural flexibility' can be seen in rulings on matters involving applications to amend a notice of appeal,[89] to award costs,[90] and to obtain security for costs in a damages claim.[91]

---

[83] OFT Decision of 31 March 2003, available at www.oft.gov.uk.

[84] Case 1178/5/7/11 *2 Travel Group plc (In liquidation) v Cardiff City Transport Services Limited* [2012] CAT 7.

[85] Case No 1017/2/1/03 [2004] CAT 10, para 196.

[86] See, e.g., Case No 1017/2/1/03 *Pernod Ricard v OFT* [2004] CAT 10, paras 197 and 229, and Case 1071/2/1/06 *Cityhook Ltd v OFT* [2007] CAT 18, para 203.

[87] Case No 1007/2/3/02 [2003] CAT 5.

[88] Ibid, paras 114–115.

[89] Case No 1024/2/3/04 *Floe Telecom Ltd v Office of Communications* [2004] CAT 7, para 43, noting that appeals are brought by well-funded major companies and 'by small companies, or even sole traders, and with few resources, little or no access to legal advice, but having a genuine sense of grievance' and emphasising the need to manage cases appropriately; see also para 50.

[90] Case No 1032/1/1/04 *Apex Asphalt and Paving Co Ltd v OFT (costs)* [2005] CAT 11, para 25.

[91] Case No 1028/5/7/04 *BCL Old Co Ltd v Aventis SA* [2005] CAT 2 (declining the defendants' request that the claimants should be required to give security for costs).

In the early days of the Competition Act, the CAT declined to apply a general or rigid rule to the effect that unsuccessful appellants should be liable to pay the OFT's costs, as well as their own, as such a rule might deter some appeals, in particular, brought by SMEs.[92] The CAT held that such a rule would be "seriously counter-productive from the point of view of achieving the objectives of the Act, particular as regards smaller companies, representative bodies and consumers".[93] The CAT maintained this SME-friendly approach to the issue of costs in the *West Midlands Roofing* appeals in 2005.[94] In 2011, however, the CAT indicated that the 'starting point' in all types of appeals under the Competition Act[95] is that the successful party should obtain a costs award in its favour.[96]

14.3.2.2 Access to the File

The UK competition authorities apply the same procedures to SMEs as they do to other entities when investigating suspected infringements of the Competition Act. In March 2011, the OFT published *A guide to the OFT's investigation procedures in competition cases*[97] ("the Investigation Procedures Guide") as part of a series of initiatives to improve the transparency and efficiency of its investigations under the Competition Act.[98] The Investigation Procedures Guide discusses the OFT's approach to the major steps in any investigation under the Act, including the handling of third party complaints,[99] access to file,[100] and possible outcomes of an investigation.[101] The Investigation Procedures Guide does not distinguish SMEs from other entities that may be the subject of, or involved in, an investigation. If an SME were to be a third party complainant, then OFT has stated that it will generally not be given access to documents other than the non-confidential version of a statement of objections.[102]

[92] Case No 1002-4/2/1/01 *Institute of Independent Insurance Brokers v Director General of Fair Trading* (costs) [2002] CAT 2, para 54.

[93] Ibid.

[94] Case No 1032/1/1/04 *Apex Asphalt and Paving Co Ltd v OFT* (*costs*) [2005] CAT 11, para 25.

[95] This applies both to penalty-only appeals and appeals against liability for an infringement of the Act.

[96] Case Nos 1140 and 1142/1/1/09 *Eden Brown Ltd v OFT* (costs) [2011] CAT 29, paras 3–18, in particular para 18.

[97] OFT 1263, March 2011.

[98] See, e.g., *Transparency: A Statement on the OFT's Approach* OFT 1234, June 2010.

[99] OFT 1263, March 2011, para 3.11 *et seq.* See also *Involving third parties in Competition Act investigations*, OFT 451, April 2006, Annexe A (guidance on making complaints).

[100] OFT 1263, March 2011, paras 11.19–11.21.

[101] OFT 1263, March 2011, Chap. 10.

[102] *Involving third parties in Competition Act investigations*, OFT 451, April 2006, para 3.22.

14.3.3 Leniency, Settlements, and Commitments Decisions Involving SMEs

There are no SME-specific procedures for the application of the leniency programme,[103] settlements (more commonly referred to as "early resolution agreements"[104]), and/or commitments[105] in the UK. The CLA members did not consider that any of these procedures should be amended to include SME-specific provisions. As regards leniency, in particular, the CLA members acknowledged that certain SMEs may well be disadvantaged in the race to 'blow the whistle' on a cartel to the extent that they have limited resources and/or lack knowledge of competition law. Certain CLA members pointed out, however, that as and when an SME does become aware that it has been involved in cartel activity, it might actually be easier and quicker for it to seek a marker for leniency than a large, possibly bureaucratic, multinational firm.

14.3.4 Sanctions: Different Penalties for Different Sized Companies?

Section 36 of the Competition Act provides that the OFT (or a sectoral regulator) may impose a financial penalty on an undertaking where either intentionally or negligently it has infringed Articles 101 and/or 102 TFEU and/or the prohibitions in the Act. The financial penalties that may be imposed do not formally differ for SMEs as opposed to other entities. Any penalty imposed by the OFT must not exceed 10 % of the worldwide turnover of the undertaking in the business year preceding the OFT's decision.[106]

In one of the appeals against the OFT decision in *Construction bid-rigging*,[107] it was argued that the OFT had discriminated against SMEs by increasing the fine on the ground that directors had been involved as SME directors are more likely than larger companies to be involved directly in cover pricing. The CAT rejected this argument and held that directors of companies of any size must be aware of their

[103] On leniency, see *OFT's guidance as to the appropriate amount of a penalty*, OFT 423, paras 3.1–3.18. The OFT has consulted on revising its guidance: see *OFT's guidance as to the appropriate amount of a penalty: A consultation on OFT guidance*, OFT 423con, October 2011, paras 3.1–3.24, and also *Applications for leniency and no-action in cartel cases: OFT's detailed guidance on the principles and process*, OFT803con, October 2011.

[104] On early resolution agreements, see Case Nos 1160-5/1/1/10 *Imperial Tobacco Group plc v OFT* [2011] CAT 41, paras 5 and 89.

[105] On commitments, see Competition Act, s 31A and *Enforcement*, OFT 407, December 2004, Part 4 and Annexe A.

[106] Competition Act 1998, s 36(8).

[107] Case Nos, etc, 1125/1/1/09 *Barrett Estate Services Ltd & Ors v OFT* [2011] CAT 8.

obligations to compete lawfully as "it would plainly be inappropriate for the OFT to hold directors of smaller companies to a lower standard of compliance".[108]

Separately, as noted in section "Competition Act 1998", the Competition Act provides for limited immunity for SMEs from the imposition of financial penalties for infringements of the Chapter I and II prohibitions [but not Articles 101(1) and 102 TFEU]. It should be noted that, even where limited immunity from fines is applicable, the OFT has reserved the right to apply to the court for an order disqualifying a company director from office for up to 15 years.[109]

14.4 Private Antitrust Enforcement and SMEs

By 16 June 2013, there had been two awards of final damages and one award of interim damages in the UK. In *2 Travel Group plc (in liquidation) v Cardiff City Transport Services Ltd*,[110] the CAT awarded compensatory damages of GBP 33,818.79 to 2 Travel, plus interest, and exemplary damages in the sum of GBP 60,000. This was an action that followed on from a decision of the OFT that Cardiff Bus had engaged in predatory conduct contrary to the Chapter II prohibition, discussed in section "Complainants Before the OFT". 2 Travel, the claimant, was awarded compensation for the profits it had lost as a result of the infringement. It was awarded exemplary damages because Cardiff Bus had deliberately decided to disregard the law, and this conduct was done in cynical disregard of the claimant's rights; this is the first time that such an award has made in a competition case in the UK. In *Albion Water Limited v Dŵr Cymru Cyfyngedig*,[111] the CAT held that Dŵr Cymru was liable for damages of GBP 1,694,343.5 (plus interest) in relation to Albion's claim that, but for Dŵr Cymru's abuse of dominance, Albion could have supplied water to a customer more profitably. The CAT further held that Dŵr Cymru was liable for damages of GBP 160,149.66 (plus interest) for Albion's lost opportunity to supply another customer. On this occasion, however, the CAT dismissed the claim for exemplary damages because Dŵr Cymru had not been shown to have intended to issue an abusively high price or that it was reckless as to whether the price was abusive. Separately, in *Healthcare at Home v Genzyme Limited*,[112] the CAT made an interim award of damages of GBP 2 million, after which the case was settled out of court. Indeed, many private actions in the UK have been settled, and the details of the settlements have been kept confidential.

[108] Ibid, para 95.

[109] *Director disqualification orders in competition cases*, OFT 510, June 2010, para 4.11.

[110] Case No 1178/5/7/11 [2012] CAT 19.

[111] [2013] CAT 6.

[112] Case No 1060/5/7/06 [2006] CAT 29.

14.4.1 Substantive Rules, Procedural Aspects for SMEs in Civil Litigation

There are currently no specific rules of civil procedure that apply solely to SMEs in the UK.

14.4.1.1 Obstacles to Private Enforcement by SMEs

The typical difficulties for victims of anticompetitive behaviour are well known and include, for example, the difficulties for claimants to prove to the satisfaction of the court the facts necessary to substantiate their claim and the costs, delays, and burdens of court proceedings. The risk of having to pay the defendant's costs (in some cases, as well as the claimant's own costs) if an action is unsuccessful can be a particularly significant deterrent. A further obstacle to private enforcement in some cases can be that the immediate customers of a cartel (or a dominant undertaking) will have passed on the cartelised (or monopolised) price to its own customers, in which case the defendant may have a defence that the claimant has suffered no harm and can recover nothing. It should be noted, however, that the existence of a passing-on defence has yet to be decided in English law.

14.4.1.2 Best Practices

There do not appear to be any "best practices" as such for handling private litigation involving SMEs in the UK. The overriding objective of the procedural rules of the High Court[113] and the CAT[114] is to secure the just, timely, and effective disposal of proceedings. And in order to further that objective, the High Court[115] and the CAT[116] may give directions that manage the conduct of the proceedings.

14.4.2 Collective Redress

Multiparty litigation in England and Wales is typically managed by the High Court using two main procedures: representative actions[117] and group litigation orders[118] ('GLOs').[119]

[113] CPR, r 1.1.

[114] Competition Appeal Tribunal Rules 2003, SI 2003/1372, r 19(1).

[115] CPR, r 1.2.

[116] Competition Appeal Tribunal Rules 2003, SI 2003/1372, r 19(2).

[117] A named claimant or defendant may act on his or her own behalf and also on behalf of a class of individuals under CPR, r 19.6.

[118] Multiple actions based on the same or similar facts can be bought. Under rules 19.10–15, GLOs are 'opt in' in nature so all claimants must be identified and parties to the proceedings.

[119] It is also possible to apply to the court to consolidate multiple actions into a single case with multiple parties under CPR, r 3.1(2)(g).

14.4.2.1 Representative Actions in the High Court

Representative actions are ones in which a named claimant or defendant may act on his or her own behalf and also on behalf of a class of individuals under rule 19.6 of the Civil Procedure Rules ("CPR"). This procedure can only be used when the class sought to be represented has a common interest and a common grievance and the relief sought must, in its nature, be beneficial to all of them. In *Emerald Supplies v British Airways*, the claimants, importers of cut flowers, wanted to bring a representative action, on behalf of themselves and on behalf of all other direct or indirect purchasers, to recover damages from BA for losses caused by the Air Cargo price fixing cartel.[120] This was a way of funding the litigation, as the more claimants involved, the more there is to be distributed at the end of the case. However, the Chancellor of the High Court,[121] with whom the Court of Appeal agreed,[122] held that the claimants and the 178 additional claimants they purported to represent did not share 'the same interest' required by rule 19.6. It was not possible at the time the claim was issued to say of any individual whether he or she was a member of the (putative) class, as the individuals' inclusion in the class would depend upon the outcome of the action itself. A further difficulty was that the members of the class that Emerald purported to represent did not have the same interest in recovering damages where, for example, the 'passing on defence' was available in answer to the claims of direct purchasers but not those of indirect purchasers. The Chancellor suggested that it would have been more appropriate for multiple actions to be dealt with by using the GLO procedure.[123]

14.4.2.2 Group Litigation Orders

The GLO procedure provides another way of handling multiple actions based on the same or similar facts. GLOs are governed by rules 19.10–15 of the CPR and are 'opt in' in nature, so that all claimants must be identified and be parties to the proceedings. A GLO enables the court to manage multiple claims by, for example, issuing stays of related claims, appointing a managing judge and a lead solicitor, identifying common issues and test claims, and delivering binding judgments. It is understood that the High Court has ordered a GLO in one competition law case: *Prentice v DaimlerChrysler UK Ltd*. Prentice was one of a number of car dealers in the DaimlerChrysler network and alleged that DaimlerChrysler's reorganisation of its distribution network infringed Article 101(1) TFEU.[124] A GLO was ordered by Cresswell J because there was a single issue pervading all of the claims brought

---

[120] Commission Decision of 9 November 2010, on appeal to the General Court, Cases T-9/11, etc, *Air Canada v Commission*, not yet decided.

[121] [2009] EWHC 741.

[122] [2010] EWCA Civ 1284.

[123] [2009] EWHC 741, para 38.

[124] See www.justice.gov.uk/guidance/courts-and-tribunals/courts/group-litigation-orders.htm.

by the dealers, all of whom were represented by the same law firm.[125] The claim was settled, however, before it could proceed to trial.

14.4.3 The Role of Trade Associations

A trade association could, in principle, apply to the High Court to bring a representative action or to seek a GLO; both procedures were discussed in Sects. 14.4.2.1 and 14.4.2.2.

As at 10 July 2012, however, trade associations may not bring claims on behalf of their members in the CAT. Claims may be brought by specified consumer bodies on behalf of affected individuals pursuant to Section 47B of the Competition Act. Which?[126] (formerly known as the Consumers' Association) is the only consumer body to have been specified by the Secretary of State for this purpose.[127] SME organisations are not eligible for designation. There has been to date only one claim for damages under Section 47B arising from the OFT's infringement decision in the *Football Shirts* case.[128] The claim was brought on behalf of 130 individual consumers seeking compensatory damages of such sum as the Tribunal considered appropriate. The case was settled before the CAT had given a final judgment; however, in a judgment on the assessment of costs, the CAT observed that 'the fullness or otherwise of Section 47B as a vessel for consumer class claims remains a matter of debate'.[129]

Some commentators have called for Section 47B to be amended so as to enable single, collective claims to be brought on behalf of all customers, whether consumers or businesses, who have suffered harm as a result of anticompetitive behaviour.[130]

14.4.4 Policy Recommendations and the Draft Consumers Rights Bill

In 2007, the OFT made recommendations to the Government as to how to improve the effectiveness of the private enforcement of competition law in the UK. In particular, the OFT recommended that the Government should consult on whether, and how, to allow representative bodies to bring stand-alone and follow-on

[125] Further details of the action are available at www.concurrences.com/article.php3?id_article=36187&lang=en.

[126] http://www.which.co.uk/.

[127] See The Specified Body (Consumer Claims) Order 2005 SI 2365/2005.

[128] OFT Decision of 1 August 2003, substantially upheld on appeal Case Nos 1021/1/1/03-1022/1/1/03 *JJB Sports Plc v Office of Fair Trading* [2004] CAT 17, upheld on appeal [2006] EWCA Civ 1318, permission to appeal to the House of Lords (now the UK Supreme Court) refused on 5 February 2007.

[129] Case No 1078/7/9/07 *The Consumers Association v JJB Sports plc* [2009] CAT 2, para 8.

[130] See, e.g., Wells 'Collective Actions in the United Kingdom' [2008] Competition Law Journal 57.

representative actions for damages and injunctions on behalf of small businesses in competition law cases. The OFT noted some of the evidential and cost-related difficulties encountered by SMEs seeking private redress. In the OFT's view, SMEs should be on an equal footing with consumers and big business in relation to their ability to seek redress for anticompetitive conduct.

Following an 8-month public consultation in 2012, the UK Government decided, in January 2013, to reform the law governing private actions in competition law.[131] The objective of the draft Consumers Rights Bill is to increase the ability of consumers and businesses that have suffered loss as a result of anticompetitive behaviour to obtain redress. Schedule 7 to the draft Consumers Rights Bill proposes to extend the jurisdiction of the CAT so that it can hear actions for damages, whether they are brought in reliance on a prior infringement decision or not,[132] as well as applications for injunctions. The Government's policy objective is to establish the CAT "as a major venue for competition actions in the UK, to make it easier for businesses, especially SMEs, to challenge anticompetitive behaviour that is harming them".[133] If enacted, the draft Consumers Rights Bill will enable the CAT Rules to provide for a "fast track" procedure for SMEs to bring actions before the CAT. In particular, such a procedure is intended to help SMEs to apply to the CAT in order to obtain injunctive relief, a speedy trial on the merits, and a cap on their cost liabilities.[134] This process, it is hoped, will make it cheaper, quicker, and simpler for SMEs to have access to courts in order to challenge anticompetitive behaviour.

The draft Consumer Rights Bill also proposes to introduce a collective action in the CAT for competition law claims[135] affecting multiple SMEs (as well as consumers), on an "opt-out" basis, and subject to a certification procedure and enhanced case management by the CAT. A corollary of this proposal is the possibility of aggregate damages, which would involve the CAT being enabled to give judgment in an aggregate sum, without proof by individual class members of their loss, if the defendant's aggregate liability to all or some of the members of the class can reasonably be determined. Unclaimed damages in opt-out collective proceedings would be paid the charity for the time being prescribed by order of the Lord Chancellor, currently the Access to Justice Foundation, a charity that facilitates access to pro-bono legal assistance.

Acknowledgement The author gratefully acknowledges the editorial assistance of Sarah Long of the OECD. All views expressed in this paper are those of certain members of the UK Competition Law Association.

---

[131] Private actions in competition law: a consultation on options for reform, April 2012.

[132] Available at https://www.gov.uk/government/publications/draft-consumer-rights-bill.

[133] Ibid, para 3.20.

[134] Ibid, paras 4.24–4.35.

[135] It is proposed that SMEs should be able to bring collective actions in both 'follow-on' actions, which follow on from that preexisting infringement finding and 'standalone' claims, where there is no pre-existing infringement finding by a competition authority.

United States of America 15

Emilio Varanini

15.1 Introduction and Findings

The objective of this contribution is to address the question of whether small and middle-sized undertakings should be subject to other or specific competition rules and to explore the extent to which SMEs are subject to the same treatment, or to differing treatment, *vis-à-vis* other economic operators, as well as the justifications for such treatment. In this regard, the international reporter has specifically asked the national reporter for the United States to explore differences or similarities between the treatment of SMEs and other economic operators as to (1) liability for violations of competition law; (2) procedures, including the existence of safe harbours from liability for SMEs, the facilitation of complaints and civil lawsuits from SMEs *vis-à-vis* their competitors, and the extension of special due process rights to SMEs; and (3) punishment, including fines and damages. Finally, the international reporter has also asked the national reporter to explore whether reforms are required to the existing procedural and substantive structures of competition law *vis-à-vis* SMEs, specifically referencing (1) whether additional substantive or procedural protections are required for SMEs and (2) whether additional measures need to be taken to facilitate further the ability of SMEs to file civil lawsuits for redress—including conferring standing on SME associations.[1]

The views herein are those of the author and should not be ascribed to the California Office of the Attorney General or the National Association of Attorneys General.

[1] We assume mergers of SMEs are not intended to be covered. However, as set out in the recent 2010 merger guidelines in the United States, horizontal mergers involving SMEs are largely shielded from government enforcement actions unless an SME were to have turnover sufficient to require its merger to be reported and an SME were an important maverick in the market (meaning its status is far more important than its market shares would indicate) or a direct effect

E. Varanini (✉)
Antitrust Section, California Office of the Attorney General, San Francisco, CA, USA
e-mail: Emilio.Varanini@doj.ca.gov

P. Këllezi et al. (eds.), *Antitrust for Small and Middle Size Undertakings and Image Protection from Non-Competitors*, LIDC Contributions on Antitrust Law, Intellectual Property and Unfair Competition, DOI 10.1007/978-3-642-54000-4_15,

While there are definitions of SMEs that are used for purposes of analysing their role in the national economy, providing aid, or even giving them certain advantages in procurement rules,[2] SMEs are defined only with respect to their market share insofar as American competition law is concerned.

Because SMEs are highly unlikely to have a monopoly-level share of any relevant market, they are not civilly liable for unilateral conduct. This substantive difference is uncontroversial and finds no reason for altering the state of affairs to place greater liability on *all non-monopolies*, even large economic actors, for unilateral conduct, at least as an American matter.

Because joint, conspiratorial, or collaborative conduct (hereinafter "joint conduct") violating competition norms constitutes a more serious threat to the free market, any economic operator engaging in such conduct could in theory find itself subject to liability notwithstanding its size. Nonetheless, there is recognition in the law and in prosecutorial guidelines that the employment of restraints by small to medium-sized enterprises with a 20–30 % market share or less poses little threat to competition norms where the restraint in question has pro-competitive effects when used by such SMEs. We find this recognition, however necessarily imprecise as discussed *infra*, to be an important one that should be affirmed by the international reporter.

In encapsulating this key principle differentiating SMEs even from other large economic operators in engaging in joint conduct, it is important to note its broad limitations: (1) it does not apply to hard-core conduct, (2) it does not apply if direct negative effects can be established from the restraint, and (3) it does not apply if the restraint in question has been adopted market-wide. However, these limitations all make empirical sense: consequently, we find all three of these limitations to be the important ones that should be affirmed by the international reporter as well.

Under the laws of several individual states such as California, though not federal law, hard-core violations also include resale price maintenance (hereinafter "RPM"). In our opinion, the only justification that may exist for manufacturer-SMEs to employ manufacturer-initiated vertical RPMs is as a "new entry" tool for a reasonably limited period of time in order to break into a market.

Regarding procedural rules, though SMEs in the United States have the same rights of access to evidence against them as individuals, they only receive enhanced due process rights to the extent that said enterprises are *unincorporated* sole proprietorships that are owned and ran by individuals. Drawing a distinction

---

analysis of some kind were to yield a negative impact (meaning again that an SME's status in the market is more important than its market shares would indicate). *See*, *e.g.*, United States Department of Justice & Federal Trade Commission, Horizontal Merger Guidelines (Aug. 19, 2010), available at http://ftc.gov/os/2010/08/100819hmg.pdf (hereinafter "2010 Horizontal Merger Guidelines").

[2] See, e.g., Small Business Association, Office of Advocacy, Frequently Answered Questions, *available at* http://www.sba.gov/sites/default/files/sbfaq.pdf (in 2008, there were 5.9 million businesses with employees of which 99.9 % are small businesses—defined as 500 employees or fewer—and 21.4 million businesses without employees; in comparison, there were only 18,469 large businesses).

based on corporate form rather than corporate size, a distinction with a long history in the United States satisfies the key principles of *fairness, administrability, and proportionality.*

Insofar as standing is concerned, the key distinction for SMEs (or indeed for any economic enterprise) is whether the lawsuit is to be filed against *competitors* or against *upstream or downstream economic actors* who violate the law. The current—and appropriate—state of law makes it more difficult for SMEs to file lawsuits against competitors (absent foreclosure effects) than against upstream or downstream economic actors. Aside from that important point, however, American jurisprudence contains a number of flexible and powerful tools that enhance the ability of SMEs to file lawsuits to go after other economic actors who violate antitrust laws, including associational standing and, of special importance here, class actions.

Here, the national reporter respectfully urges the international reporter to look to these findings as a possible model for the Congress in enhancing in an appropriate manner the rights of SMEs, with the significant exception of state-owned enterprises (hereinafter "SOEs"). Though the matter of SOEs' liability under American competition law as market participants is in flux, it would be appropriate, in the view of the national reporter, for the international reporter to recommend a rebuttable presumption of SOEs having a dominant position in the market in allowing SMEs to have a right of action even against an SOE competitor.

Finally, the international reporter asks the national reporter to examine the punishment imposed on SMEs. In that respect, on the one hand, the national reporter finds that the status of SMEs as such may be taken into account in imposing civil fines (criminal fines remain a special issue) both as a matter of prosecutorial discretion and by the courts—an appropriate state of affairs.

On the other hand, the national reporter finds that SMEs remain jointly and severally liable for *all* damages they cause to their victims. Moreover, because the United States does not recognise a right of contribution or indemnity, SMEs cannot argue that larger economic enterprises, even those that may have initiated the offence or played a leading role in its commission, should pay a greater proportionate share of damages.

When an SME is involved in joint activities with more than one other entity, e.g. it is a participant in an international price-fixing conspiracy, then it may end up paying far more than its market share of damages. However, to the extent that another jurisdiction or the international reporter should decide to consider whether these principles of joint and several liabilities, along with no right of contribution or indemnity, should be imported into other jurisdictions, the national reporter finds these principles to be appropriate in balancing concerns of *fairness, administrability, and proportionality*.

This does, however, raise the final question of whether damages should be trebled automatically, as they are now, where SMEs are involved. The national reporter finds that trebling should remain for now, given the policy reasons that motivate trebling in the United States (and may motivate its similar use elsewhere). However, we are mindful that trebling, especially when coupled with joint and several liabilities and no right of contribution, could remove a competitor from the marketplace—a result antithetical to competition laws. Accordingly, we recommend that, to protect the ability of SMEs to act as a competitive counterweight in the marketplace, they be allowed to invoke a failing firm defence post-trial if faced with such trebled damages.

15.1.1 Basis for Findings of National Report as to Substantive Standards Applicable to SMEs

15.1.1.1 Unilateral Conduct Versus Joint Conduct

In understanding the liability of SMEs for violations of competition law, it is first important to understand that SMEs are not liable for unilateral acts in contrast to joint conduct. In the case of *American Needle v. Nat'l Football League*, the United States Supreme Court explained that Congress restricted liability for unilateral conduct to those enterprises with a monopoly share—as opposed to joint conduct where a non-monopolistic market share may suffice for liability—precisely in order to "[avoid] chilling vigorous competition" and "avoid [...] judicial scrutiny of routine, internal business decisions".[3]

For these reasons, the wisdom of limiting liability for unilateral acts to economic enterprises that have monopoly power, or a dangerous probability of acquiring it,[4] is manifest. While the determination of an economic enterprise's market share in a relevant market is one of fact,[5] the repeated dictum of Judge Learned Hand holds here as a shorthand reference as to when an economic enterprise has a monopoly market share: a market share of 90 % "is enough to constitute monopoly; it is doubtful whether sixty or sixty-four percent would be enough; and certainly thirty-three is not."[6] Correspondingly, whatever imprecision may exist in defining what market shares or other criteria constitute an SME, an SME is not a monopoly by any analytical stretch under American law and thus not subject to liability for the commission of unilateral acts. We thus agree that SMEs should not be liable for the commission of unilateral conduct under federal and state antitrust laws.[7]

[3] 130 S. Ct. 2201 (2011) at 2208–09. *See* Annex II for full quotation.

[4] *Spectrum Sports, Inc. v. McQuillan*, 506 U.S. 447, 456 (1993).

[5] See, e.g., *United States v. Microsoft*, 253 F.3d 34, 81–82 (D.C. Cir. 2001) (determination of a relevant market is a factual question to be resolved by the district court) (citations omitted); Federal Trade Commission, *Opinion of the Commission in In the Matter of Evanston Northwestern Healthcare Corporation*, 57 n. 67 (Docket No. 9315) (Aug. 6, 2007), available at www.ftc.gov/os/adjpro/d9315/070806opinion.pdf ("However, market definition is a question of fact."). The principles that underlay determining a relevant market, and the defendant's market share in that market, can be found in numerous cases and treatises. and so will not be discussed here.

[6] *United States v. Aluminum Co. of Am.*, 148 F.2d 416, 424 (2d Cir. 1945).

[7] Although Section 5 of the Federal Trade Commission (hereinafter "FTC") Act can, in theory, be used by the FTC to hold any SME liable for unilateral conduct, it is not covered in this contribution because it can only be implemented by the FTC, its traditional contours of application exclude

15.1.1.2 General Rules Exempting or Limiting SME Liability for Joint Conduct

The General, Albeit Imprecise, Exemption of SMEs from Liability for Joint Conduct

An enterprise may be liable for joint conduct with other companies that violate the antitrust laws where it has a large enough share of the relevant market that it can be inferred it has market power and where the conduct itself is likely to lead to anticompetitive effects.[8] That market share of a relevant market is smaller than the share required to label an enterprise a monopolist[9] but still must be substantial enough that the enterprise in question can exercise market power, meaning that it can raise market-wide prices profitably by restricting output.[10] And though there is imprecision in the market shares that suffices to show market power as such a determination is a question of fact, it is fair to say that SMEs, generally speaking, lack a sufficient share of the market for liability to be imposed.[11]

most unilateral conduct by SMEs, it historically has not been applied to SMEs outside of two very limited arenas in any event, and the remedies involved are extremely limited. See Annex I for fuller discussion of Section 5.

[8] See, e.g., *Realcomp II, Ltd. v. FTC*, 635 F.3d 815, 827(6th Cir. 2011), *cert. den.* 132 S. Ct. 400 (Oct. 11, 2011) (rejecting assertions that the FTC must show actual adverse anticompetitive effects of the restraint: "Applying the rule of reason, we first look to see 'whether [the] FTC has demonstrated actual detrimental effects or the potential for genuine adverse effects on competition.' Market power and the anticompetitive nature of the restraint are sufficient to show the potential for anticompetitive effects under a rule-of-reason analysis, and once this showing has been made, Realcomp must offer pro-competitive justifications." (citation and internal quotation marks omitted)).

[9] See, e.g., *Eastman Kodak Co. v. Image Technical Services, Inc.*, 504 U.S. 451, 481 (1992).

[10] *NCAA v. Bd. of Regents*, 468 U.S. 85, 109 (1984); see *Realcomp II*, 653 F.3d at 827–29 & n. 6; ABA Section of Antitrust Law (2007) Antitrust Law Developments (Sixth), p. 65 & n. 351 (citing cases); Areeda, P, Hovenkamp, H & Solow, J, Antitrust Law, 3rd ed. 2007, p. 109, para 501 at 109 ("Market power is the ability to raise prices profitably by restricting output"); see *Leegin Creative Leather Prods., Inc. v. PSKS, Inc.*, 551 U.S. 877, 898 (2007) ("As a final matter, that a dominant manufacturer or retailer can abuse resale price maintenance for anticompetitive purposes may not be a serious concern unless the relevant entity has market power. If a retailer lacks market power, manufacturers likely can sell their goods through rival retailers").

[11] ABA Section of Antitrust Law (2007), p. 66 (citing cases) (suggesting that 30 % market share is minimum, below which market power will rarely be found); Areeda, P, Hovenkamp, H & Solow, J, Antitrust Law, 3rd ed. 2007, pp. 249–250, para 532c (although some courts have found that less than 50–60 % market shares can still create a jury question as to market power, commentators recommend that "[b]ecause it would be rare indeed to find that a firm with half a market could individually control price over any significant period, we would presume that market shares below 50 or 60 percent do not confer [market] power"). The market shares required to show market power may, as a practical matter, depend upon the degree of confidence that a market has been properly defined: "If the court's confidence is high that a relevant market has been identified that properly groups close substitutes, excludes non substitutes, and is protected by high entry barriers, then market shares along the lower range of acceptability are permissible." Areeda, P, Hovenkamp, H & Solow, J, Antitrust Law, 3rd ed. 2007, p. 243, para 532.

The requirement of showing that a restraint is likely to lead to anticompetitive effects does add a layer of additional protection for SMEs.[12] In determining whether a restraint can be deemed to be likely to lead to anticompetitive effects, such an effect cannot be presumed as a general matter so long as those effects may be even somewhat complex, but rather must be found to be present based on a judicial evaluation of the specific factual circumstances in a case.[13]

Government Safe Harbours Exempting SMEs That Engage in Specific Pro-Competitive Conduct

Nonetheless, American courts and government enforcers have employed market screens to shield SMEs when specific conduct is viewed as being pro-competitive when practised by economic enterprises with a relatively small market share.[14] The reason for government enforcers doing so is readily apparent:

> Market definition plays an important role in organizing and shaping investigations and enforcement recommendations. If putative market definitions do not yield a credible risk of market power, an investigation may be framed differently, competitive harm may seem unlikely, and it is possible that any entry analysis may not be fully developed.[15]

Accordingly, if there is specific joint conduct that on its face is manifestly pro-competitive absent *further circumstances* such as high market shares or additional anticompetitive restraints, the federal government will set out safe harbours, often involving a market share of 20–30 %, which only contain a limited caveat for

---

[12] *E.g., K.M.B. Warehouse Distributors, Inc. v. Walker Mfg. Co.*, 61 F.3d 123, 129–130 (2d Cir. 1995) (allegation of defendant's market power not enough where plaintiff failed to meet burden under rule of reason of showing that restraint was likely to lead to anticompetitive effects); ABA Section of Antitrust Law 2007 Antitrust Law Developments (Sixth), p. 67 (citing and quoting General Leaseways, *Inc. v. National Truck Leasing Ass'n*, 744 F.2d 588, 596 (7*th* Cir. 1984) ("[I]f it seems that the defendant does have the power to restrain trade substantially, then inquiry proceeds to the question whether the challenged practice was likely . . .to help rather than hurt competition")). Anticompetitive intent on the part of a defendant is not a substitute for this requirement, *K.M.B. Warehouse Distributors*, 61 F.3d at 130, though it can corroborate an inference of anticompetitive effects from other evidence; see, e.g., *General Leaseways*, 744 F.2d at 591–596.

[13] See, e.g., *Realcomp II*, 635 F.3d at 826–827 (quoting Cal Dental Ass'n v. FTC, 526 U.S. 756, 775 n. 12 (1999): "[T]here must be some indication that the court making the decision has properly identified the theoretical basis for the anticompetitive effects and considered whether the effects actually are anticompetitive. Where ... the circumstances of the restriction are somewhat complex, assumption alone will not do." (Internal quotation marks omitted.)). A comparison of the *Realcomp II* decision with State of California ex. rel. *Harris v. Safeway, Inc. et al.*, 651 F.3d 1118 (9th Cir. 2011) (*en banc*) (the latter being ostensibly a "quick look" case) illustrates what is required to show a restraint's likelihood of having an actual anticompetitive effect.

[14] See, e.g., Areeda, P, Hovenkamp, H & Solow, J, Antitrust Law, 3rd ed. 2007, pp. 235–236, para 531e (an analysis of market power can involve a screening function such as determining whether predatory pricing is a risk in a monopoly case or the foreclosure threat is real in vertical cases such as tying or exclusive dealing).

[15] Harbour, P & Koslov, T, Section 2 in a Web 2.0 World: An Expanded Vision of Relevant Markets. 76 Antitrust L.J. 2010 769:76, p. 775.

"exceptional circumstances".[16] In contrast, in more general, uncertain, or novel situations, the government has avoided imposing market screens with such limited screens that may, for example, preclude a direct effect analysis.[17]

Specific Court Decisions Exempting SMEs from Liability for Joint Conduct That Meets Certain Prerequisites

Apropos of SMEs, the courts themselves have employed such market screens while disfavouring (though not precluding altogether) direct effect analysis in circumstances where (1) there is pro-competitive activity, (2) that pro-competitive activity has negative foreclosure effects if the market shares of the participants are sufficiently high so as to confer market power, and (3) any actual anticompetitive effects (e.g., price increases) most likely arise from those foreclosure effects. This use of market screens, requiring a market share of anywhere between 20 and 40 % as a minimum, has been seen in three instances: (1) "group boycott" activity that is ancillary to legitimate cooperative activity,[18] (2) tying,[19] and (3) exclusive dealing.[20]

The Continuing Development of Market Screens

Generally speaking, efforts by courts and government authorities to develop market screens, however imprecise or cabined, should be encouraged. Though this involves some discretionary calls (or imprecision), that is necessary in trying to carefully balance competition norms and concerns as to when liability should be imposed for joint conduct.

Consequently, efforts by courts and government authorities to develop market screens, however imprecise or cabined, should be encouraged. However, there are broader exceptions here that also need to be addressed. We turn to those broader exceptions.

15.1.1.3 General Exceptions Imposing Liability on SMEs for Joint Conduct

As noted in the introduction to this report, there are three general exceptions under which SMEs can be held liable for joint conduct: (1) direct effect analysis, (2) the

---

[16] See, e.g., United States Department of Justice & Federal Trade Commission, Antitrust Guidelines for the Licensing of Intellectual Property, § 4.3 (Apr. 6, 1995), available at http://www.justice.gov/atr/public/guidelines/0558.htm#N_31_.

[17] See, e.g., United States Department of Justice & Federal Trade Commission, Antitrust Guidelines for Collaborations among Competitors, § 4.2 (Apr. 2000), available at http://www.ftc.gov/os/2000/04/ftcdojguidelines.pdf. For a fuller discussion of federal antitrust guidelines, see Annex III.

[18] *Northwest Whole Stationers v. Pacific Stationary & Printing Co.*, 472 U.S. 284, 294–98 (1985).

[19] *Jefferson Parish v. Hyde*, 466 U.S. 2, 15–17 (1984).

[20] See, e.g., *Jefferson Parish*, 466 U.S. at 45 (O'Connor, J., concurring); *Sterling Merchandising, Inc. v. Nestle, S.A.*, 656 F.3d 112, 123–24 (1st Cir. 2011). For a fuller discussion of group boycotts, tying, and exclusive dealing, see Annex III.

market-wide use of an illegal restraint, and (3) hard-core conduct such as price-fixing, market allocation, or bid-rigging. This contribution discusses all three of these exceptions and finds them all to be appropriate.

Direct Effect Analysis as Applicable to SMEs

It is sufficient under the rule of reason for a plaintiff to show direct anticompetitive effects, such as a reduction in output, arising from an allegedly illegal restraint.[21] In this regard, the determination of a defendant's market power through its share of a relevant market, along with the potential for a restraint to have anticompetitive effects, is supposed to be nothing more than a surrogate or alternative for the use of direct effects.[22] Accordingly, a direct effect analysis allows plaintiffs to determine when an ostensible SME is in fact an economic enterprise with market power, given that market power is nothing more than the ability of an enterprise to raise market-wide prices profitably by restricting output.[23] And an economic enterprise with market power should not be allowed to engage in anticompetitive conduct that can, by definition, cement or enhance its market power to the detriment of free markets.[24]

At the same time, however, we find supporting that the use of direct effect analysis does not unduly create a great zone of uncertain liability under the antitrust

---

[21] See, e.g., *NCAA*, 468 U.S. at 109–10; *FTC v. Indiana Fed'n of Dentists*, 476 U.S. 447, 460–61 (1986) (direct effects evidence enough under rule of reason); Toys-R-Us v. FTC, 221 F.3d 928, 937 (7th Cir. 2000) (same); *cf. Opinion of the Commission in In the Matter of Evanston Northwestern Healthcare Corporation* at 78 (actual price increase by merged entity in *post hoc* merger analysis enough to demonstrate anticompetitive analysis where regression analysis, pre- and post-merger documents of the merged entity, and testimony from insurers all supported the conclusion that the price increase arose from the market power of the combined entity and not from any competitively benign factors).

[22] See, e.g., Hovenkamp, H, Federal Antitrust Policy, 3rd ed. 2005, p. 550, §12.8; see also, e.g., *Indiana Fed'n of Dentists*, 476 U.S. at 460 ("[T]he purpose of the inquiries into market definition and market power is to determine whether an arrangement has the potential for genuine adverse effects on competition. . .."); *Tops Market, Inc. v. Quality Market, Inc.*, 142 F.3d 90, 98 (2d Cir. 1998) (finding that market power "may be proven directly by evidence of the control of prices or the exclusion of competition, or it may be inferred from one large firm's percentage share of the relevant market"); *K.M.B. Warehouse Distributors*, 61 F.3d at 129 ("If a plaintiff can show an actual adverse effect on competition, such as reduced output[,]. . . we do not require a further showing of market power") (citation omitted); *Capital Imaging Assoc. v. Mohawk Valley Med. Assocs.*, 996 F.3d 537, 546 (2d Cir. 1993) (explaining that plaintiffs may avoid a "'detailed market analysis' by offering 'proof of actual detrimental effects such as a reduction in output'" (citation omitted)).

[23] *NCAA*, 468 U.S. at 109; see *Realcomp II*, 653 F.3d at 827–29 & n. 6; ABA Section of Antitrust Law 2007, Antitrust Law Developments (Sixth), p. 65 & n. 351 (citing cases); Areeda, P, Hovenkamp, H & Solow, J, Antitrust Law, 3rd ed. 2007, p. 109, para 501 ("Market power is the ability to raise prices profitably by restricting output").

[24] See, e.g., *Copperweld Corp. v. Independent Tube Co.*, 467 U.S. 752, 768 (2007); accord, e.g., *Leegin*, 551 U.S. at 885–86; see also, e.g., *id.* at 893–94 (discussing how powerful or dominant manufacturer or retailer can abuse RPM to support its market power). Direct effect analysis has now become important to the merger analysis of the federal antitrust authorities as well. See 2010 Horizontal Merger Guidelines, §§ 2.1.1, 4, 5.3.

laws for true SMEs. Historically, it has been difficult for the government and the courts to determine the direct effects of joint restraints in a given market;[25] as this report observed *infra*, such difficulties may still exist today as to certain kinds of restraints and, should they be overcome, may be insufficient to confer standing.[26] Even today, it can be costly and difficult for private plaintiffs to obtain the data required to perform the analysis,[27] and such an analysis can be prone to second-guessing thereafter.[28] Moreover, although it is possible to "back in" to a relevant market by looking at direct effects first,[29] typically the federal government will still look into defining a relevant market—and then determining the economic enterprise's share of that market—to determine if there is a credible risk of market power that warrants a more in-depth investigation of that restraint.[30] Accordingly, a direct effect analysis utilises the latest economic analytical techniques, coupled with (at least for the government) unparalleled access to electronic data, to *supplement* the more traditional inference of market power analysis where, for example, markets may be difficult to define or subject to dispute.[31]

Market-Wide Use of an Illegal Restraint

A plaintiff may also choose to sue multiple enterprises, some of which may be SMEs, that all employ the same restraint where, in the aggregate, that restraint has anticompetitive effect on the market as a whole.[32] The multiple enterprises need not be working in concert together to institute this restraint for plaintiffs to have the

[25] See Areeda, P, Hovenkamp, H & Solow, J, Antitrust Law, 3rd ed. 2007, p. 233, para 531a ("Because they so often lack such data [for a direct effect analysis], antitrust courts traditionally define a market and examine the firms' marker shares").

[26] The national reporter cautions that difficult does not mean impossible. See, e.g., *Fleischmann v. Albany Medical Ctr.*, 728 F. Supp. 2d 130, 163–64 (N.D.N.Y. 2010) (exchange of nurse compensation data presents triable issue of fact under rule of reason because plaintiffs presented evidence of actual anticompetitive effects, including persistent shortage of nurses and depressed wages).

[27] Reeves, A & Stucke, M, Behavioral Antitrust. Ind. L. J. 2011 1527:86, pp. 1582–83.

[28] The potential second-guessing by courts of a direct effect analysis as opposed to an inference of market power analysis (though the direct effect analysis was ultimately upheld) is set out in the *Realcomp II* decision, 635 F.3d at 819, 828–34.

[29] Harbour, P & Koslov, T, Section 2 in a Web 2.0 World: An Expanded Vision of Relevant Markets. 76 Antitrust L.J. 2010 769:76, p. 774; *see, e.g.*, 2010 Horizontal Merger Guidelines, §§ 2.1.1, 4, 5.3.

[30] See, e.g., Harbour, P & Koslov, T, Section 2 in a Web 2.0 World: An Expanded Vision of Relevant Markets. 76 Antitrust L.J. 2010 769:76, p. 775.

[31] See, e.g., Werden, G (2012) Why (Ever) Define Markets: An Answer to Professor Kaplow. Available at SSRN: http://ssrn.com/abstract=2004655 or http://dx.doi.org/10.2139/ssrn.2004655.

[32] See, e.g., *Leegin*, 551 U.S. at 897 (citing various treatises and discussing the imposition of RPM by manufacturers market-wide); Elhauge, E, Tying, Bundled Discounts, and the Death of the Single Monopoly Profit Theory, Harv. L. Rev. 2009 397:123, pp. 470, 475–77 (discussing cumulative foreclosure by different companies engaged in tying or exclusive dealing, as well as multiple companies engaged in bundling).

authority to sue all of them.[33] And because the anticompetitive dangers of such restraints are greater if they are adopted market-wide,[34] it makes no sense to exempt SMEs in circumstances where such restraints have in fact multiplied across the entire market.

Hard-Core Conduct

Per se illegal or hard-core offences are punishable under federal and state antitrust laws without any inquiry into their market effects or pro-competitive justifications.[35] This is because these offences are conclusively presumed to be unreasonable and therefore illegal because of "their pernicious effect on competition" and "lack of any redeeming virtue".[36] Such offences include price fixing,[37] output limitation,[38] profit sharing,[39] market allocation,[40] and bid rigging.[41]

In the first instance, holding SMEs, like any other economic enterprise, liable for such offences is appropriate because "[t]he public interest requires free competition so that prices be not dependent upon an understanding among suppliers of any given commodity, but upon the interplay of the economic forces of supply and demand".[42] Furthermore, holding SMEs liable for such offences is appropriate because the participation of SMEs is as important as that of larger economic enterprises to prevent cheating on, or the undercutting of, the conspiracy or cartel committing such offences.[43] Accordingly, in our opinion, there should be no

[33] Elhauge, E, Tying, Bundled Discounts, and the Death of the Single Monopoly Profit Theory, Harv. L. Rev. 2009 397:123, pp. 476–77 & fns. 248–250 (citing and discussing cases and treatises).

[34] See, e.g., *Leegin*, 551 U.S. at 897; Elhauge, E, Tying, Bundled Discounts, and the Death of the Single Monopoly Profit Theory, Harv. L. Rev. 2009 397:123, pp. 470, 475–77.

[35] See, e.g., *Aguilar v. Atl. Richfield Co.*, 25 Cal. 4th 826, 851(2001).

[36] See, e.g., *Leegin*, 551 U.S. at 886; *N. Pac. R. Co. v. United States*, 356 U.S. 1, 5 (1958); *United States v. Socony-Vacuum Oil Co.*, 310 U.S. 150, 218 (1940); *Marin County Bd. of Realtors v. Palsson*, 16 Cal. 3d 920, 931 (1976); *Oakland-Alameda County Builders Exch. v. F.P. Lathrop Constr. Co.*, 4 Cal. 3d 354, 363 (1971).

[37] See, e.g., *Leegin*, 551 U.S. at 886; *Arizona v. Maricopa County Med. Serv.*, 457 U.S. 332, 347–50 & n. 18 (1982); *Costco Wholesale Co. v. Maleng*, 522 F.3d 874, 897 n. 19 (9th Cir. 2008).

[38] *E.g.*, *Westinghouse Elec. Co. v. Gulf Oil Corp.*, 588 F.2d 221, 226 (7th Cir. 1978).

[39] See, e.g., *Standard Oil Co. v. United States*, 283 U.S. 163, 169–71 (1931).

[40] *E.g.*, *Leegin*, 551 U.S. at 886; *United States v. Andreas*, 216 F.3d 645, 666–67 (7th Cir. 2000).

[41] See, e.g., *JTC Petroleum v. Piasa Motor Fuels*, 190 F.3d 775, 777 (7th Cir. 1999).

[42] *Speegle v. Bd. of Fire Underwriters*, 29 Cal. 2d 34, 44 (1946). The same is true even when an SME solicits other companies to commit such offenses – a violation of Section 5 of the FTC Act and its state analogues. *See* Areeda, P & Hovenkamp, H (2nd ed. 2003) Antitrust Law, p. 131, para 1419e2.

[43] See *United States v. Columbia Pictures Industries, Inc.*, 507 F. Supp. 412, 429 n. 47 (S.D.N.Y. 1980); see also, e.g., *Andreas*, 216 F.3d at 652 (discussing the need of price-fixing cartels to prevent cheating); *Vogel v. Am. Soc. of Appraisers*, 744 F.2d 598, 601 (7th Cir. 1984) (same). The national reporter has litigated international price-fixing cases in which SMEs were "recruited" into a price-fixing conspiracy by its participants in order to prevent the undermining of the conspiracy.

liability exceptions for SMEs insofar as hard-core offences are concerned, although, as discussed *post*, there should be a limited failing firm defence to the civil assessment of trebled damages.[44]

15.1.1.4 Proposal Regarding Resale Price Maintenance

Resale price maintenance or RPM involves an agreement between a manufacturer and one or more of its retailers to fix the prices of that manufacturer's goods. As noted above, federal antitrust law now views RPM as being a non-hard-core offence as the result of a majority decision of five justices of the United States Supreme Court in 2007 in the *Leegin* case.[45] However, the laws of several American States continue to view RPM as being a hard-core offence.[46] And in spite of *Leegin*, many other jurisdictions continue to view RPM as being a hard-core offence.[47]

We recommend that, insofar as SMEs are concerned, an exception to the application of RPM need only be created for new entry of manufacturer SMEs. However, conscious that the 2010 LIDC Congress approved a wider exception to RPM that would encompass this more narrow proposed exception of benefit to SMEs,[48] the national reporter believes that any re-examination of RPM should await future discussion. Accordingly, we discuss this proposed exception more fully only in the Annex IV to this report.

---

[44] This report will not address the unique American doctrine known as quick look because its impact on SMEs is, at this point in time, slight, given the extremely serious doubts that exist as to its application to enterprises. See Annex I.

[45] *Leegin Creative Leather Prods., Inc. v. PSKS, Inc.*, 551 U.S. 877 (2007).

[46] See, e.g., *O'Brien v. Leegin Creative Prods.*, Inc., No. 101,000, slip. op. (Kansas Supreme Ct. May 4, 2012); *People v. Bioelements, Inc.*, No. ING 10011659 (Cal. Super. Ct. Jan. 11, 2011) (California Attorney General—via consent decree—imposed fine of $51,000 and enjoining defendant from entering into retail price maintenance agreements with its distributors in the future); The State Bar of California Antitrust and Unfair Competition Law Section (2009 ed.) California State Antitrust Law and Unfair Competition Law, § 3, § 3; see also, e.g., Duncan, A & Guernsey, A, Waiting for the Other Shoe to Drop. Will State Courts Follow Leegin? Franchise L.J. 2008 173:27, p. 178 (noting that, in the wake of *Leegin*, because there are 13 to 17 States that likely will not follow that decision, "franchisors and other suppliers of goods will still have to exercise caution in implementing national account programmes or other programmes controlling the price at which franchisees and distributors resell goods").

[47] OECD, OECD Competition Committee Policy Roundtable, resale Price Maintenance, DAF/Comp (2008) 37 at 48, 53–55, available at http://www.oecd.org/dataoecd/39/63/43835526.pdf.

[48] LIDC Congress Bordeaux, Resolution (Oct. 2, 2010), available at http://www.ligue.org/documents/resolutionAanglais.pdf.

15.2 Basis for Findings of National Report as to Procedural Standards Applicable to SMEs

15.2.1 Due Process Rights Only for Unincorporated Solo Proprietorships

Though corporations have the same right to access to information against them as do individuals, any corporation, including any incorporated SME such as an S corporation,[49] or any officer of the corporation insofar as he is acting on its behalf, cannot invoke its Fifth Amendments right under the U.S. Constitution to refuse to produce documents or to testify.[50] Nor can that corporation or any officer of the corporation, insofar as he is acting on its behalf, invoke its rights under the Fourth Amendment of the U.S. Constitution and refuse to produce documents on the ground that compelling such a production constitutes an unreasonable search and seizure.[51] In comparison to incorporated entities, an individual (or a solo proprietorship that is an unincorporated business run by that individual) does have such rights.[52]

Leaving aside their foundation in the principles, and limits to those principles, of the United States Constitution,[53] those rules make empirical sense when the

---

[49] For federal tax purposes, individuals can form a C corporation or a S corporation; a S corporation form can be used by small businesses. See http://en.wikipedia.org/wiki/S_corporation.

[50] See, e.g., *Wilson v. United States*, 221 U.S. 361, 374–75 (1911); *United States v. Richardson*, 469 F.2d 349, 350 (10th Cir. 1972) ("privilege against self-incrimination cannot be invoked by a [Subchapter S] corporate officer to prevent disclosure of corporate records which might incriminate him even though the corporation is a mere alter ego of its owner"); *United States v. Mid-West Business Forms, Inc.*,474 F.2d 722, 723 (8th Cir. 1973) (privilege against self-incrimination not available to officer of Subchapter S corporation to prevent disclosure of corporate records); *United States v. Silverman*, 359 F. Supp. 1113, 1114 (N.D. Ill. 1973) (officer-shareholder of subchapter S corporation could not invoke constitutional privilege against self-incrimination as bar to compliance with IRS subpoena directing him to appear before special agent and produce corporate records and documents); *Naporano v. United States*, 834 F. Supp. 694, 701 n. 12 (D.N.J. 1993) ("Corporations are prohibited from invoking the Fifth Amendment privilege against self-incrimination to prevent the disclosure of corporate records which might incriminate a shareholder"). There is one limit here: an individual who is a corporate officer cannot be compelled to produce his private papers. See, e.g., *Wilson*, 221 U.S. at 377.

[51] See, e.g., *Wilson*, 221 U.S. at 375–76.

[52] See, e.g., *Braswell v. United States*, 487 U.S. 99, 104–05 (1988). Partnerships fall into the category of corporations, however, and not sole proprietorships. *Id.* at 107–08 (explaining "The test … is whether one can fairly say under all the circumstances that a particular type of organization has a character so impersonal in the scope of its membership and activities that it cannot be said to embody or represent the purely private or personal interests of its constituents, but rather to embody their common or group interests only" (internal citations and quotation marks omitted)).

[53] See, e.g., *Braswell*, 487 U.S. at 119 (dissenting op. of Kennedy, J., joined by Brennan, Marshall, & Scalia J.J.) ("Our long course of decisions concerning artificial entities and the Fifth Amendment served us well. It illuminated two of the critical foundations for the constitutional guarantee

artificial nature of corporations are concerned as entities chartered by law with resulting duties to the public absent insofar as individuals are concerned.[54]

15.2.2 Standing Regarding Lawsuits Against Competitors as Opposed to Lawsuits Against Upstream or Downstream Economic Actors

There are a variety of judicial doctrines and legislative enactments in the United States that are all designed, in one way or another, to ensure that cases are brought that involve injuries of the type that competition laws were designed to redress for conduct that constitutes a violation of those laws.[55] Here, we point out how SMEs, like other economic enterprises, are more likely to be found lacking a valid claim if they are suing competitors—rather than upstream or downstream economic enterprises—absent market foreclosure concerns.[56] The most powerful illustration of this point is *Weyerhaeuser Co. v. Ross-Simmons Hardwood Lumber Co., Inc.*,[57] in which the United States Supreme Court distinguished in determining liability for predatory bidding (i.e., bidding up input costs)[58] between a lawsuit from a competitor and a lawsuit from an upstream supplier of the input or the downstream purchaser of the input-containing product—holding the competitor-lawsuit to a higher standard.[59] This is not the only such case: in *Brunswick Corp. v. Pueblo-O-Mat*,[60] the Court held that, because the antitrust laws were enacted for the benefit of competition, not competitors, a plaintiff bowling company could not sue its competitor for causing it to lose profits when it acquired unprofitable bowling

---

against self-incrimination: first, that it is an explicit right of a natural person, protecting the realm of human thought and expression; second, that it is confined to governmental compulsion").

[54] See *Citizens United v. Federal Elec. Comm'n*, 130 S. Ct. 876, 949–50 (2010) (dissenting op.). For a more elaborate discussion of this point, *see* Annex V.

[55] See, e.g., Varanini, E, Exiting the Fun House of Mirrors: Clayworth v Pfizer and the Handling of Pass-On in Post-Trial Proceedings in Federal and State Courts, Competition 2011 28:20 (discussing California legislative enactment allowing for indirect purchaser lawsuits, federal judicial ruling allowing only for direct purchaser lawsuits, and federal standing and injury doctrines).

[56] For one example of a foreclosure case involving a competitor lawsuit and two highly related (in fact double-sided) high-technology markets, one for operating systems and the other for browsers, see, e.g., *Novell v. Microsoft*, 505 F.3d 302, 315–17 (4th Cir. 2007).

[57] 549 U.S. 312 (2007).

[58] *Id.* at 316, 320.

[59] See *id.* at 321 & n. 2, 324 n. 5. More specifically, a competitor lawsuit alleging predatory bidding must satisfy the same difficult-to-meet standard applicable to predatory pricing. See *id.* at 323–26; *see also, e.g.*, In re Dairy Farmers of America Cheese Antitrust Litig., 767 F. Supp. 2d 880, 905–06 (N.D. Ill. 2011) (distinguishing *Weyerhaeuser* on this ground).

[60] 429 U.S. 477 (1977).

centres.[61] And, in *Atlantic Richfield Co. v. USA Petroleum Co.*,[62] the Court held that a plaintiff gas station could not sue its competitor for fixing maximum or minimum prices, conduct which was then *per se* illegal, because its injury did not reflect the kind of injuries to *consumers* that had motivated the *per se* rule.[63] While the national reporter recognises, in reviewing these cases, that SMEs particularly may be disadvantaged when competitor claims are more often discouraged, we support the existing prudential rules that bar claims that are ill-suited for resolution under the antitrust laws.[64]

15.2.3 Lawsuits Through Associations or Class Action Device

In the United States, SMEs, like other economic enterprises, can bring collective antitrust lawsuits through an association in federal court so long as at least one member of that association can satisfy the federal constitutional requirements for standing.[65] In the context of the antitrust laws, this would require such an association to make a showing that at least one of its members suffered an economic injury (e.g., an injury to property or money) causally connected to the illegal actions of defendants.[66] Via well-funded small business professional associations, SMEs could in theory file lawsuits on their own, much as their larger brethren are doing already, when they find themselves the victims of illegal acts such as price fixing.[67] However, insofar as we are aware, SMEs have not, in fact, used professional associations in this manner in the United States—apparently because such associations either do not exist or do not have sufficient resources to fund antitrust lawsuits from the incredibly large number of SMEs that exist, even if they were interested in doing so[68]—but instead have primarily resorted to class certification.

"A class action, no less than traditional joinder (of which it is a species), merely enables a federal court to adjudicate claims of multiple parties at once, instead of in

---

[61] *Id.* at 488.

[62] 495 U.S. 328 (1990).

[63] *Id.* at 335–39.

[64] See, e.g., Varanini, E, Exiting the Fun House of Mirrors: Clayworth v Pfizer and the Handling of Pass-On in Post-Trial Proceedings in Federal and State Courts, Competition 2011 28:20, pp. 49–50 & n. 92.

[65] See *Northeastern Florida Chapter of the Associated General Contractors of America v. City of Jacksonville*, Florida et. al., 508 U.S. 656, 664–69 (1993).

[66] See, e.g., *Degelmann v. Advanced Medical Optics, Inc.*, 659 F.3d 835, 839–40 (9th Cir. 2011); *Gerlinger v. Amazon Co., Inc. et. al.*, 526 F.3d 1253, 1255–56 (9th Cir. 2008).

[67] Professional associations for small businesses do exist in the United States. See, e.g., http://www.nfib.com/.

[68] See Small Business Association, Office of Advocacy, Frequently Answered Questions, *available at* http://www.sba.gov/sites/default/files/sbfaq.pdf.

separate suits."[69] Class actions can also be brought on behalf of SMEs and other economic enterprises, either as a class of direct purchasers of products under federal law or as a class of indirect purchasers of products under state law, where those SMEs paid too much for those products because of the illegal actions of defendants.[70] Though large enterprises can just as easily be part of these classes as SMEs, large economic enterprises anecdotally have, over time, increasingly chosen to file their own cases seeking damages in lieu of participating in class actions.[71] Class actions have a long history in common law systems like the United States and also have important prerequisites that must be satisfied, namely that every certified class must share common questions of law or fact, common questions must predominate over individual questions, claims of the class representatives must be typical of the class, and the class action device must be superior to other available methods for fairly and efficiently adjudicating the controversy.[72]

Class actions can be used to enable defendants to obtain a global release of claims from millions of small (and large) businesses and consumers nationwide in exchange for giving those businesses and consumers hundreds of millions of dollars as part of a settlement.[73] Classes can also be certified as part of litigation to facilitate the trial of claims brought by millions of SMEs—and natural persons—but there are additional requirements that must be met in cases involving state antitrust claims: (1) manageability, i.e., showing that these claims can be sorted into a small number of groups with materially identical legal standards,[74] and (2) the merits of the claims of plaintiffs must be examined "rigorously" to determine that, in fact, those antitrust claims can be proved as to liability and damages through evidence common to the class as a whole and using methods common to the class as a whole rather than evidence individual to each member of the class.[75] The national report respectfully commends the class action device as an appropriate means by which SMEs can bring collective actions for redress of their damages for violations of competition law.

---

[69] *Shady Grove Orthopedic Assocs., P.A. v. Allstate Ins. Co.*, 130 S. Ct. 1431, 1443 (2010) (plurality op. of Scalia, J.).

[70] See, e.g., *Sullivan v. DB Investments, Inc.*, 667 F.3d 273 (3rd Cir. 2011) (*en banc*) (approving certification of a class for settlement of direct and indirect purchasers where many of those purchasers were small businesses and paid overcharges for diamonds because of the illegal acts of defendant).

[71] The national reporter participates in several international price-fixing cases in federal and state courts in Northern California and bases this conclusion on his own personal experience.

[72] See, e.g., *Sullivan*, 667 F.3d at 334–35 & n. 1 (conc. op. of Scirica, J.).

[73] See, e.g., *id.* at 289–90, 299–300, 310–11 (maj. op.).

[74] See, e.g., *id.* at 301–03 (maj. op.) (discussing cases).

[75] See, e.g., *id.* at 305–06 (maj. op.) (discussing cases); *see also id.* at 334–35 (conc. op. of Scirica, J.).

15.2.4 Proposal Regarding Exception for Lawsuits Against State-Owned Enterprises

As discussed above, it is more difficult for SMEs to sue competitors than it is for them to sue downstream or upstream defendants. We respectfully submit that, insofar as competitors are concerned, a special exception should be made for state-owned enterprises or SOEs.

SOEs claim some of the biggest companies in the world, overflow with cash, and account for over one-third of the emerging world's direct foreign investment between 2003 and 2010, as well as having made an even higher proportion of the emerging world's most spectacular acquisitions.[76] The ability of SOEs to call on huge strategic investments from their governments puts private companies at a severe disadvantage.[77]

The national reporter recognises that, insofar as American law is concerned, it is still an open question as to whether SOEs should be protected from antitrust lawsuits under applicable sovereign immunity doctrines.[78] However, we respectfully submit that such doctrines should not shield SOEs when they participate in the market as if they were private companies.[79]

15.3 Basis for Findings of National Reporter on Remedies Vis-à-Vis SMEs

15.3.1 Civil or Criminal Fines

The existing state of affairs on state civil fines provides appropriate treatment for SMEs in balancing their status (and financial condition) against the degree of responsibility that they bear for their actions. In the United States, civil fines can be assessed by such American States as California for antitrust violations, whereas the federal government assesses criminal fines. A court can, in its discretion, take into account the status of an economic enterprise as an SME in California for

---

[76] *Special Report*: *State Capitalism*, The Economist, at 4 (Jan. 21, 2012).

[77] *Id.* at 17.

[78] See *In re Vitamin C Antitrust Litig.*, 810 F. Supp. 2d 522 (E.D.N.Y. 2011) (rejecting foreign sovereign compulsion defence, comity, and act of state defences to price-fixing cartel). The national reporter is not taking a position on the extent to which immunity is appropriate for acts of state such as foreign government-required cartels or American state and local regulations.

[79] Whether there is currently such a market participation exception for SOEs to the general rule of immunity is a matter of dispute in federal law. The United States Supreme Court hinted in *City of Columbia v. Omni Outdoor Advertising*, 499 U.S. 365 (1991), at the possibility of a market participation exception when it stated in dicta that immunity does not necessarily apply "where the State acts not in a regulatory capacity but as a commercial participant in a given market". *Id.* at 374–375, 379 (referring to a "possible market participation exception"). Subsequently, the lower courts have divided on whether commercial activity should be treated differently from regulatory/ governmental activity.

purposes of determining its ability to pay state civil fines as one of many factors, including the degree of responsibility that the SME has for its actions.[80]

As to federal *criminal* fines, the situation is more complex. On the one hand, the United States Sentencing Guidelines Commission has taken the position in the first instance that "most defendants" have the "resources and earning capacity" to pay these fines "at least over time on an installment basis".[81] For SMEs and other economic enterprises, federal civil fines can add up, running as high as USD 100 million, or twice the gross gain or twice the gross loss resulting from the offence, whichever is greater.[82] And it does not appear as if the courts are constrained by any principle other than the need to avoid any gross disproportionality of these fines to the seriousness of the offence *vis-à-vis* SMEs,[83] if even that.[84]

On the other hand, an SME, like any other economic enterprise, can avoid such fines altogether by being the first-in applicant for amnesty in exchange for cooperation; a second-in-time enterprise can still obtain a quite substantial discount in exchange for cooperation.[85] And we believe that the size of an economic enterprise may be a factor that the federal government can take into account in its discretion in making appropriate prosecutorial decisions and sentencing recommendations.

The national reporter points out that criminal fines involve a set of circumstances particular to, if not unique to, the United States. Not only has there been a legislative judgment that the nature of criminal antitrust offences (e.g., price fixing) is serious enough to warrant the imposition of expansive fines that are tied to two times the gross gains or losses flowing from the offence,[86] but also there are strict requirements that must be met as a precursor to a criminal conviction by a jury at trial even for an SME, such as proving an SME committed the requisite elements of those offences beyond a reasonable doubt.[87] To date, almost all criminal fines

[80] E.g., Cal. Bus. & Prof. Code §17206; the State Bar of California Antitrust and Unfair Competition Law Section 2009, § 23.

[81] United States Sentencing Guidelines, § 2R1.1, Commentary (2011).

[82] 15 U.S.C. § 1 (2006); 18 U.S.C. § 3571(d) (2006); see *Exxon Shipping Co. v. Baker*, 554 U.S. 471, 511–12 (2008).

[83] *United States v. Bajakajian*, 524 U.S. 321, 328, 334–37 (1998). Proportionality can be assessed by examining the degree of harm committed by a defendant, the seriousness of the offense itself, and the seriousness of the defendant's involvement in that offense. *Id.*

[84] The Excessive Fines provision of the U.S. Constitution has never been found to apply to corporations. See *United States v. Chaplin's, Inc.*, 646 F.3d 846, 851 n. 15 (11th Cir. 2011).

[85] Taurn, R & Tomczak, P, Introductory Essay: A Proposal For A United States Department Of Justice Foreign Corrupt Practices Act Leniency Policy. American Criminal Law Review 2010 117:47, pp. 141–50.

[86] See *Bajakajian*, 524 U.S. at 336 (noting the need to defer to judgments of Congress in this area).

[87] See, e.g., *United States v. Socony-Vacuum Co.*, 310 U.S. 150, 251–53 (1940). In the price-fixing context, this does not just include the elements of conspiring with others for the purpose of fixing prices (see *id.*) but may also include the element of showing the exact gains or losses from the conspiracy for the purpose of imposing fines (see *O'Brien v. United States*, 130 S. Ct 2169, 2174–76 (2010); *Apprendi v. New Jersey*, 530 U.S. 466, 490 (2000)).

imposed in the antitrust arena have occurred by way of settlement, thus avoiding the issue of whether circumstances involving those fines are so distinct that ability to pay should not be taken into account by courts. Because of this state of affairs, and because the national reporter anecdotally has reason to believe that ability to pay issues involved with the imposition of criminal fines for a criminal conviction for price fixing will soon be teed up in a federal district court, the national reporter would respectfully submit that it is premature for himself to address this issue at this point in time.

15.3.2 Civil Damages

Damages rules are not different for SMEs than for larger economic enterprises. Of particular relevance, however, to SMEs in the United States, they are jointly and severally liable under federal and state antitrust law for *the entire amount of* damages committed by a conspiracy in which they participated.[88] If overcharges from a price-fixing conspiracy are one billion U.S. dollars, a conspiracy participant with only a two-percent market share could be liable for the full amount of damages.

Moreover, any amount of damages assessed against a defendant, SME or otherwise, is trebled *automatically* under state and federal antitrust law.[89] This means an SME with a two-percent market share that participated in a price-fixing conspiracy that inflicted overcharges in the amount of USD 1 billion could end up owing USD 3 billion with trebling.

Of course, the SME's fellow participants in any such anticompetitive conduct would equally be liable for the full amount of damages—unless they settled before trial. If such settlements do occur, the amount of such settlements is subtracted, but only *after* trebling has been carried out on any previous damage award.[90] So if damages arising from overcharges from a price-fixing conspiracy are USD 1 billion, and there are settlements with some of the participants amounting to USD 300 million, those damages must first be trebled to USD 3 billion before the USD 300 million in settlements may be subtracted. This means that an SME with a market share

[88] See, e.g., *In re Cement & Concrete Antitrust Litig.*, 817 F.2d 1435, 1439 (9th Cir. 1987), *rev'd on other grounds sub nom. California v. ARC America Corp.*, 490 U.S. 93 (1990); *In re Uranium Antitrust Litig.*, 552 F. Supp. 518, 521–22 (N.D. Ill. 1982); *Roth v. Rhodes*, 25 Cal. App. 4th 530, 544 (1994). In American law, this principle derives from the common law rule that tortfeasors who act in concert to commit a wrong are jointly and severally liable for the entire amount of the resulting damage. *Burlington Indus. v. Milliken & Co.*, 690 F.2d 380, 391 (4th Cir. 1982); *Classen v. Weller*, 145 Cal. App. 3d 27, 48 (1983); Order Denying Summary Judgment, *Fisherman's Wharf Bay Cruise Corp. v. Blue & Gold Fleet*, Pier 39, et. al. (Cal. Super. Ct. San Francisco, Dec. 5, 2002).

[89] See, e.g., 15 U.S.C. §15; *Turnbull & Turnbull v. ARA Transp., Inc.*, 219 Cal. App. 3d 811, 826–27 (1990); *Uneedus v. Calif. Shoppers, Inc.*, 86 Cal. App. 3d 932, 942 (1978).

[90] *Newby v. Vrowman*, 11 Cal. App. 4th 283, 289 (1992) (discussing federal and state laws).

of only 2 %, faced with this scenario, could owe USD 2.7 billion instead of USD 2.1 billion.

Finally, there is no right of contribution under federal antitrust law and, most likely, state antitrust law.[91] This means that an SME with a market share of 2 %, owing USD 2.7 billion for trebled overcharges due to the price-fixing conspiracy in which it participated, cannot argue that it should only pay 2 % of that amount or USD 54 million and its co-conspirators should pay the rest.[92]

There is a unique exception of relevance to SMEs. A successful applicant for amnesty from the federal government for committing antitrust criminal offences, whether an SME or a larger economic enterprise, is only required to pay single damages in any subsequent state or federal lawsuit (except for a lawsuit by a state government for damages to government entitles) so long as that applicant cooperates with civil plaintiffs.[93]

Though this interplay of damage rules may seem to be unfair to SMEs who committed illegal acts violating federal and state antitrust laws, especially when one sees how they may operate in conjunction with the hypothetical SME discussed in this section of the report, these rules do meet the criteria of *fairness, proportionality, and administrability*. For both joint and several liability, as well as the rule against contribution, given that economic operators must combine together in order to commit illegal offences, such as price fixing, it is fair and proportional to require each of these operators, even those that are SMEs, to owe the total amount of damages that they cause by acting together.[94] And it has a further benefit from both the perspective of both fairness and proportionality insofar as SMEs are concerned: it ensures that the largest economic operators, e.g. the ones with the deepest pockets, will pay all of the damages such that plaintiffs are not required to have to collect part of those damages from a financially weaker operator.[95]

In fact, requiring each operator to be liable for the total amount of damages they cause by acting together is an easier rule to administer than trying to divide up damages based on some other metric–whether it be each market share in a relevant

---

[91] *Texas Indus. Inc. v. Radcliffe Materials, Inc.*, 451 U.S. 630, 634–39 (1981) (common law did not provide for right of contribution among tortfeasors; nothing in the Sherman and Clayton Acts provide for it, and the policy interests involved in recognising it would add new complexities to damage awards).

[92] See *Browning-Ferris Industries of Vermont, Inc. v. Kelco Disposal, Inc.*, 492 U.S. 257, 263–64, 274 (1989) (ban on excessive fines in United States Constitution does not apply to award of civil damages, including trebled damages).

[93] Randall J, Does De-Trebling Sacrifice Recoverability of Antitrust Awards? Yale J. on Reg. 2006 311:23, pp. 312–13.

[94] See Cavanaugh, E Contribution, Claim Reduction, And Individual Treble Damage Responsibility: Which Path To Reform Of Antitrust Remedies? Vand. L. Rev. 1987 1277:40, pp. 1296–97, 1323; see *also Clayworth v. Pfizer*, 49 Cal. 4th 758, 783 (2010).

[95] Randall J, Does De-Trebling Sacrifice Recoverability of Antitrust Awards? Yale J. on Reg. 2006 311:23, pp. 314, 317.

market of each participant or the degree of responsibility of each economic operator involved in the joint conduct.[96] And mandatory trebling is a fair and administrable rule if not proportional: it provides important compensation for the extraordinary degree of difficulty involved in bringing and winning antitrust cases and serves as an important deterrent to the commission of illegal offences under the antitrust laws that threaten the free market.[97] These rules not only are important to a credible right of private action in common law countries such as the United States but also could play a similar role in other jurisdictions where the creation of such a right is being considered but where additional difficulties may exist such as limitations on the right of discovery or on attorneys' fees.[98]

We thus support these rules in spite of the impact that they have on SMEs. However, we realise that the cumulative effect of these rules could be to drive SMEs into bankruptcy[99] and so turns to that subject.

15.3.3 Proposal Regarding Creation of Limited Failing Firm Defence

SMEs that face such large judgments may have to declare bankruptcy; in so doing, they would remove themselves from the market, thereby inhibiting competition. To avoid such a result counter to antitrust policy, the national reporter suggests that SMEs faced with trebled damages be allowed to raise a failing firm defence similar to that allowed in the merger context. In particular, the defence would require an SME to prove the following: (1) the allegedly failing firm would be unable to meet its financial obligations in the near future because of the damage award, (2) it would not be able to reorganise successfully under federal bankruptcy laws *and* pay the damages award, and (3) it has made unsuccessful good-faith efforts to elicit additional financing that would keep its tangible and intangible assets in the relevant market while paying the damages award.[100]

[96] See Cavanaugh, E Contribution, Claim Reduction, And Individual Treble Damage Responsibility: Which Path To Reform Of Antitrust Remedies? Vand. L. Rev. 1987 1277:40, pp. 1298–99, 1316–21, 1334–35; ABA Section of Antitrust Law (1986), Contribution and Claim Reduction in Antitrust Litigation, MONOGRAPH NO. 11, p. 33.

[97] See *Reiter v. Sonotone Corp.*, 442 U.S. 330, 344–45 (1979); *Zenith Radio Co. v. Hazeltine Research*, 395 U.S. 100, 130–31 (1969); *Clayworth*, 49 Cal. 4th at 783; see also Cavanaugh, E Contribution, Claim Reduction, And Individual Treble Damage Responsibility: Which Path To Reform Of Antitrust Remedies? Vand. L. Rev. 1987 1277:40, p. 1311.

[98] See Rajabiun, R, Private Enforcement And Judicial Discretion In The Evolution Of Antitrust In The United States. J. Comp. Law & Econ. 2012 187:8, pp. 187–90 (discussing importance of private right of action); see also *Clayworth*, 49 Cal. 4th at 783.

[99] See, e.g., Randall J, Does De-Trebling Sacrifice Recoverability of Antitrust Awards? Yale J. on Reg. 2006 311:23, pp. 311, 316; Cavanaugh, E Contribution, Claim Reduction, And Individual Treble Damage Responsibility: Which Path To Reform Of Antitrust Remedies? Vand. L. Rev. 1987 1277:40, pp. 1290–91.

[100] See 2010 Horizontal Merger Guidelines, §11. If an SME is merely a division of a conglomerate, it would need to show that (i) applying cost allocation rules that reflect true economic costs, the

The court could exercise its discretion in such circumstances in reducing trebled damages, thereby enabling the SME to remain in the market. Providing for such a limited defence has a dual advantage when viewing it through the prism of fairness and administrability: it enables SMEs, and the wider marketplace, the worst excesses of the combination of the rules of joint and several liability, the lack of a right to contribution, and trebling *without* the complexities of determining market share or the degree of responsibility that would otherwise be required. And by allowing such a limited exception, courts in the United States (as those elsewhere contemplating mandatory trebling) may even choose to relax otherwise stringent limitations on liability imposed in order to balance out the perceived harshness of mandatory trebling.[101]

15.4 Conclusion

The answer to the question of whether SMEs should be subject to specific or other competition rules is (mostly) no. The reason why the answer is mostly no is that, to the extent that SMEs warrant special treatment, existing competition rules in the United States mostly ensure that they will receive it. The national reporter does make recommendations to the international reporter both as to those aspects of those rules worth following in other jurisdictions and as to limited reform of some of those rules. These constructive proposals will benefit SMEs worldwide in a manner that will not undermine the competitive nature of a free market.

15.5 Annexes

15.5.1 Annex I: Section 5 and Quick Look

This contribution does not discuss Section 5 of the Federal Trade Commission Act and the quick look doctrine because both doctrines, which are very peculiar artefacts of American competition law, have very limited application to SMEs.

Section 5 of the Federal Trade Commission (hereinafter "FTC") Act and its state analogues give the FTC and state antitrust enforcers additional powers to act against economic enterprises that violate federal or, in the case of state analogues, state

---

division will now have a persistently negative cash flow on an operating basis because of the damages award and (ii) the owner of the failing division has made unsuccessful good-faith efforts to obtain additional financing that would prevent it from declaring bankruptcy because of the damages award. See *id.*

[101] See, e.g., *Reiter*, 442 U.S. at 345; Kovacic, W, The Institutions of Antitrust Law: How Structure Shapes Substance. Mich. L. Rev. 2012 1019:110, pp. 1026, 1041 (noting that courts have increased requirements on the liability side to compensate for the harshness of mandatory trebling). Insofar as the United States is concerned, such an exception would have to be enacted by Congress. See *Reiter*, 442 U.S. at 345.

antitrust law. However, there is a separate strand or component of Section 5 of the FTC Act, known as a "pure" Section 5 case, a strand that has also made its way into at least one state analogue. The FTC can use the "pure" strand of Section 5 to hold any economic enterprise lacking a monopoly share of the relevant market liable for unilateral conduct if that enterprise commits either (1) anticompetitive conduct, without sufficient redeeming qualities, that would, if unchecked, lead to hard-core violation (e.g., one economic enterprise soliciting another economic enterprise to commit a hard-core violation) or (2) anticompetitive conduct, without sufficient redeeming qualities, that would, if left unchecked, cause a market itself to become fundamentally anticompetitive (e.g., facilitating practices in oligopolistic markets, technological tying and related bundling conduct in high-tech industries by large economic firms, or pirating intellectual property, as well as other "hold up" conduct involving intellectual property). In effect, Section 5 provides a tool by which the FTC can proscribe unilateral conduct that operates in a functionally equivalent manner or effect either to hard-core conduct or to illegal monopolistic conduct while that conduct is in its incipiency in a flexible and targeted way that does not treble damages: this use of Section 5 serves its purpose as proscribing conduct that constitutes an incipient violation of competition principles or violates the spirit or policies behind competition laws.

In Section 5, there is no exception for SMEs as such. Apparently, however, it has not been applied by the FTC (or by courts applying its state analogues) to SMEs except insofar as patent hold-up conduct and solicitation to commit hard-core offences may be concerned. Although patent hold-up conduct is more complex and beyond the scope of this report, it is otherwise appropriate to hold SMEs liable for solicitation to commit a hard-core offence for the same reasons discussed elsewhere in this report as to hard-core offences.

As importantly from the perspective of an SME, a pure Section 5 case is limited in its reach to injunctive relief and (in theory) to disgorgement of illegal profits obtained directly from the restraint. State analogues incorporating Section 5 are similarly limited; though civil fines are also possible, such fines have been imposed to date only for violations of antitrust law that are also treated as violations of those analogues and for solicitation to commit hard-core offences. And state analogues at least cannot be applied if there is a legal safe harbour that would otherwise shield the conduct of the economic enterprise.[102]

[102] For legal sources that discuss these principles, see, e.g., Thomas Dahdouh, *Section 5 and its Critics: Just Who Are the Radicals Here*?, 20 Competition 1 (2011); William Kovacic & Marc Winerman, *Competition Policy and the Application of Section 5 of the Federal Trade Commission Act*, 76 Antitrust L.J. 929 (2010); The State Bar of California Antitrust and Unfair Competition Law Section, California State Antitrust Law and Unfair Competition Law, §§10, 14, 16, 23 (2009 ed.); Einer Elhauge, *Disgorgement as an Antitrust Remedy*, 76 Antitrust L.J. 79 (2009); Susan Creighton & Thomas Krattenmaker, *Some Thoughts about the Scope of Section 5*, Workshop on Section 5 of the FTC Act (Oct 17, 2008) (unpublished manuscript), available at http://www.ftc.gov/bc/workshops/section5/index.shtml.

There is also a unique American doctrine known as quick look. In principle, that doctrine could expose SMEs, as well as larger enterprises, to liability for employing hard-core-like restraints under the rule of reason either (1) where these restraints do not appear on their face plausibly necessary to otherwise legitimate joint activity[103] or (2) where these restraints otherwise in and of themselves have such an immediately obvious anticompetitive potential on their face that the law would shift the relevant burdens to SMEs to justify such conduct.[104] Recent developments in the case law in the United States have placed into quite serious doubt whether courts will ever find a restraint, even one that is hard core like, to have such an apparent anticompetitive potential on their face that the law would shift the relevant burden to SMEs or larger enterprises to justify such conduct.[105] The current crabbed application of quick look means that it does not appreciably affect the legal environment for SMEs at this time; however, any future expansion of quick look would equally affect SMEs and larger economic enterprises in any event. And insofar as it may be expanded in the future to encompass restraints with an immediately obvious anticompetitive effect on the market—the ostensible quick look standard—it is appropriate to require SMEs to avoid such restraints to the same extent as their larger counterparts for the same reasons set out in the report itself as to actual hard-core offences.

15.5.2 Annex II: Unilateral Conduct Versus Joint Conduct

The passage from *American Needle* mentioned in the report is quoted in full here:

> "Taken literally, the applicability of §1 to "every contract, combination . . . or conspiracy" could be understood to cover every conceivable agreement, whether it be a group of competing firms fixing prices or a single firm's chief executive telling her subordinate how to price their company's product. But even though, "read literally," § 1 would address "the entire body of private contract," that is not what the statute means. *National Soc. of Professional Engineers v. United States*,435 U.S. 679, 688, 98 S.Ct. 1355, 55 L.Ed.2d 637 (1978); see also *Texaco Inc. v. Dagher*, 547 U.S. 1, 5, 126 S.Ct. 1276, 164 L.Ed.2d 1 (2006) ("This Court has not taken a literal approach to this language"); cf. *Board of Trade of Chicago v. United States*, 246 U.S. 231, 238, 38 S.Ct. 242, 62 L.Ed. 683 (1918) (reasoning that the term "restraint of trade" in § 1 cannot possibly refer to any restraint

[103] See, e.g., *Nat'l Soc. of Prof. Engineers v. United States*, 435 U.S. 679 (1978); *NCAA v. Bd. of Regents*, 468 U.S. 85 (1984); FTC v. Indiana Fed'n of Dentists, 476 U.S. 447 (1986).

[104] *Cal. Dental Ass'n v. FTC*, 526 U.S. 756 (1999) (summarizing concept)); *State of California ex. rel. Harris v. Safeway, Inc. et. al.*, 651 F.3d 1118 (9th Cir. 2011) (en banc) (same).

[105] See, e.g., *Cal. Dental Ass'n*, 526 U.S. 756 (rejecting application of doctrine to the dental association's restricting price advertising, particularly discount fees, and quality of service advertising because such a restriction could have a plausible pro-competitive effect or no competitive effect at all); *Safeway*, 651 F.3d 1118 (rejecting application of doctrine to an agreement among competitors to share revenues during the term of a labour strike); see also, e.g., Realcomp II, Ltd. v. FTC, 635 F.3d 815 (6th Cir. 2011), *cert. den.* 132 S. Ct. 400 (Oct. 11, 2011) (refusing to address question of whether quick look applied to the website policy of realtors' association that limited the access of the public to listings by limited service brokers who exerted price pressure on, and competed with, full-service traditional brokers).

on competition because "[e]very agreement concerning trade, every regulation of trade, restrains. To bind, to restrain, is of their very essence"). Not every instance of cooperation between two people is a potential "contract, combination ..., or conspiracy, in restraint of trade." 15 U.S.C. § 1.

The meaning of the term "contract, combination ... or conspiracy" is informed by the "'basic distinction'" in the Sherman Act "'between concerted and independent action'" that distinguishes § 1 of the Sherman Act from § 2.*Copperweld*, 467 U.S., at 767, 104 S.Ct. 2731 (quoting *Monsanto Co. v. Spray–Rite Service Corp.*, 465 U.S. 752, 761, 104 S.Ct. 1464, 79 L.Ed.2d 775 (1984)). Section 1 applies only to concerted action that restrains trade. Section 2, by contrast, covers both concerted and independent action, but only if that action "monopolize[s]," 15 U.S.C. § 2, or "threatens actual monopolization," *Copperweld*, 467 U.S., at 767, 104 S.Ct. 2731, a category that is narrower than restraint of trade. Monopoly power may be equally harmful whether it is the product of joint action or individual action.

Congress used this distinction between concerted and independent action to deter anticompetitive conduct and compensate its victims, without chilling vigorous competition through ordinary business operations. The distinction also avoids judicial scrutiny of routine, internal business decisions.

Thus, in § 1 Congress "treated concerted behavior more strictly than unilateral behavior." *Id.*, at 768, 104 S.Ct. 2731. This is so because unlike independent action, "[c]oncerted activity inherently is fraught with anticompetitive risk" insofar as it "deprives the marketplace of independent centers of decisionmaking that competition assumes and demands." *Id.*, at 768–769, 104 S.Ct. 2731. And because concerted action is discrete and distinct, a limit on such activity leaves untouched a vast amount of business conduct. As a result, there is less risk of deterring a firm's necessary conduct; courts need only examine discrete agreements; and such conduct may be remedied simply through prohibition. See Areeda & Hovenkamp ¶ 1464c, at 206. Concerted activity is thus "judged more sternly than unilateral activity under § 2," *Copperweld*, 467 U.S., at 768, 104 S.Ct. 2731. For these reasons, § 1 prohibits any concerted action "in restraint of trade or commerce," even if the action does not "threate[n] monopolization," *Ibid.* And therefore, an arrangement must embody concerted action in order to be a "contract, combination ... or conspiracy" under § 1.[106]

The United States Supreme Court further explained in a footnote the wisdom of the U.S. Congress's decision to avoid imposing liability on economic enterprises absent situations involving monopolisation or attempted monopolisation:

If Congress prohibited independent action that merely restrains trade (even if it does not threaten monopolization), that prohibition could deter perfectly competitive conduct by firms that are fearful of litigation costs and judicial error. See *Copperweld*, 467 U.S., at 768, 104 S.Ct. 2731 ("Judging unilateral conduct in this manner reduces the risk that the antitrust laws will dampen the competitive zeal of a single aggressive competitor"); cf. *United States v. United States Gypsum Co.*,438 U.S. 422, 441, 98 S.Ct. 2864, 57 L. Ed.2d 854 (1978) ("[S]alutary and procompetitive conduct ... might be shunned by businessmen who chose to be excessively cautious in the face of uncertainty"). Moreover, if every unilateral action that restrained trade were subject to antitrust scrutiny, then courts would be forced to judge almost every internal business decision. See 7 P. Areeda & H. Hovenkamp, Antitrust Law ¶ 1464c, at 206 (2d ed.2003) (hereinafter Areeda & Hovenkamp) (unilateral behavior is "often difficult to evaluate or remedy").[107]

[106] 130 S. Ct. at 2208–09.

[107] *Id.* at 2209 n. 2.

15.5.3 Annex III: Joint Conduct and the Use of Market Screens in the Rule of Reason: Federal Government Guidelines and Court Decisions

For the benefit of the reader, a fuller discussion is set out in this Annex as to the use of market screens, in the context of joint conduct, insofar as federal government guidelines and court decisions are concerned.

15.5.3.1 Federal Government Guidelines

In 1995, the first declaration regarding the use of such screens appeared with the United States Department of Justice and the Federal Trade Commission issuing their Antitrust Guidelines for the Licensing of Intellectual Property.[108] In analysing licensing agreements that involve intellectual property, those Guidelines declared:

> *Because licensing arrangements often promote innovation and enhance competition, the Agencies believe that an antitrust "safety zone" is useful in order to provide some degree of certainty and this to encourage such activity.* Absent extraordinary circumstances, the Agencies will not challenge a restraint in an intellectual property licensing arrangement if (1) the restraint is not facially anticompetitive and (2) the licensor and its licensees collectively account no more than twenty percent of each relevant market significantly affected by the restraint.[109]

The federal antitrust authorities further observed that, if it were difficult to calculate market shares, e.g. in technology or research and development markets, then, absent extraordinary circumstances, the Agencies would not challenge a restraint in an intellectual property licensing arrangement where there are four or more independently controlled technologies, or research and development efforts, that are close substitutes.[110]

In 1996, the United States Department of Justice and the Federal Trade Commission issued the Statements of Antitrust Enforcement Policy in Health Care.[111] In these statements, the federal antitrust agencies carved out "safety zones" for different types of joint conduct.[112] For example, in Statement 8, the federal antitrust

[108] United States Department of Justice & Federal Trade Commission, Antitrust Guidelines for the Licensing of Intellectual Property (6 April 1995), available at http://www.justice.gov/atr/public/guidelines/0558.htm#N_31_.

[109] *Id.* §4.3 (*italics added*).

[110] *Id.*

[111] United States Department of Justice & Federal Trade Commission, Statements of Antitrust Enforcement Policy in Health Care (Aug. 1996), available at http://www.justice.gov/atr/public/guidelines/1791.htm.

[112] Other safe harbours involve conduct so narrowly defined that, as such, needs no market share limitation. See, e.g., *id.* Statement 2(A) (hospital high-technology joint ventures involving the joint purchase, or the shared ownership of, high-technology equipment or other expensive equipment if the joint venture includes only those hospitals necessary to support the equipment or if additional hospitals that are included could not have purchased that equipment either on their own or through forming competing joint ventures, absent extraordinary circumstances). The joint collection of

authorities note that physician network joint ventures[113] may be pro-competitive and lawful, that many of them have received favourable business review letters or advisory opinions, and that "the statement sets forth antitrust safety zones that describe physician network joint ventures unlikely to raise substantial competitive concerns, and therefore will not be challenged [ ] under the antitrust laws absent extraordinary circumstances".[114] They then set out a market-share based screen of 20 % for a safe harbour applicable to exclusive physician network joint ventures and a similar screen of 30 % for a safe harbour applicable to non-exclusive physician network joint ventures, the market shares for which are to be determined based on a speciality basis, e.g., the number of physicians from a given speciality who are participating in the venture versus the number of physicians in the market for that speciality as a whole.[115] Exceptions exist to both safe harbours only for "extraordinary circumstances".[116] However, for the safe harbours to apply, the joint venture in question should have physician participants who share substantial financial risk; failure to do so risks a judgment by the federal antitrust authorities that the venture is a sham designed only to fix prices, in which case the safe harbour (or any rule of reason treatment) would not apply.[117]

15.5.3.2 Court Decisions

Apropos of SMEs, the courts themselves have employed such market screens while disfavouring (though not precluding altogether) direct effect analysis in circumstances where (1) there is pro-competitive activity, (2) that pro-competitive activity has negative foreclosure effects if the market shares of the participants are sufficiently high so as to confer market power, and (3) any actual anticompetitive effects (e.g., price increases) most likely arise from those foreclosure effects. This use of market screens has been seen in three instances: (1) "group boycott" activity that is ancillary to legitimate cooperative activity, (2) tying, and (3) exclusive dealing. Although the first two of these three circumstances nominally involve the per se rule, both in fact have involved the application of truncated or structured rules of reason. The third involves an application of the full rule of reason. We believe a

---

fee-related information and the exchange of price and cost information are both special cases because, even though there is no market screen as such, the data supplied by any one provider cannot amount to more than twenty-five percent of the total. See *id.* Statements 5, 6.

[113] Physician network joint ventures consist of physicians who have banded together in associations, such as preferred provider organisations, to market jointly their services to commercial insurers. *Id.* Statement 8 (Introduction).

[114] *Id.*

[115] *Id.* Statement 8(A) (1), (2). If the market in question has four or fewer physicians for a given speciality, the venture may include a single physician from that speciality even though the inclusion of that physician increases the applicable market share for that venture above the 20 % (for exclusive) or 30 % (for non-exclusive) thresholds without losing safe harbour status. *Id.*

[116] *Id.*

[117] *Id.* Statement 8 (A)(1), (2), (B)(1). Though rule of reason treatment may still apply if the venture is clinically integrated, the safe harbours do not appear to apply in those circumstances. *Compare id. with id.* Statement 8(C)(1).

limited discussion of these restraints in this Annex would be helpful in understanding the liability of SMEs under the antitrust laws of the United States.

Group Boycotts

In horizontal cases such as *Klor's v. Broadway Hale Stores*,[118] the United States Supreme Court held that naked group boycotts, i.e. concerted refusals to deal by two or more horizontal competitors directed at a competitive rival, are per se illegal such that an analysis of market shares would not be required and excuses or justifications would not be allowed.[119] Later, in *Northwest Whole Stationers v. Pacific Stationary & Printing Co.*,[120] the Court applied a different rule in addressing the legality of a wholesale purchasing cooperative's expelling one of its members for reasons pertinent to this report.

Distinguishing per se group boycott cases as "generally involv[ing] joint efforts by a firm or firms to disadvantage competitors by 'either directly denying or persuading or coercing suppliers or customers to deny relationships the competitors need in the competitive struggle'",[121] the Court found that the per se rule may apply only when the association "possesses market power or exclusive access to an element essential to effective competition".[122] The Court observed that wholesale purchasing cooperatives can increase efficiencies, e.g., enabling smaller competitors to compete more effectively by allowing them to achieve economies of scale in purchasing and warehousing otherwise only available to large retailers.[123] Because "[w]holesale purchasing cooperatives must establish and enforce reasonable rules in order to function effectively[,]," the act of expulsion of a retail supply store from a wholesale cooperative "does not necessarily imply anticompetitive animus and thereby raise a probability of anticompetitive effect" unless the cooperative has "market power" or "exclusive access to an element essential to effective competition".[124] As neither

[118] 359 U.S. 207 (1959).

[119] *Klor's* involved a large department store that orchestrated a concerted refusal to deal among its suppliers of appliances to have them boycott a smaller rival or otherwise sell to that smaller rival at discriminatory prices. *Id.* at 208–09, 212–13 ("This is not a case of a single trader refusing to deal with another, or even of a manufacturer and a dealer agreeing to an exclusive distributorship. Alleged in this complaint is a wide combination consisting of manufacturers, distributors, and a retailer" (footnote omitted)).

[120] 472 U.S. 284 (1985).

[121] *Id.* at 294 (quoting Lawrence A. Sullivan, The Law of Antitrust 261–62 (1977)). In these cases, "the boycott often cut off access to a supply, facility or market necessary to enable the boycotted firm to compete, and frequently the boycotting firm possessed a dominant position to the relevant market. In addition, the practices were generally not justified by plausible arguments that they were intended to enhance overall efficiency and make markets more competitive". *Id.* at 294.

[122] *Id.* at 296, 298.

[123] *Id.* at 286–87, 295.

[124] *Id.* at 296.

condition was present in *Northwest Whole Stationers*, the "boycott" was subject to rule of reason analysis in lieu of *per se* treatment.[125]

Since *Northwest Whole Stationers* was handed down, the courts draw a distinction between cases factually similar to the *Klor's* group boycott scenario in which the *per se* rule continues to apply because such joint activity has no plausible efficiencies and cases involving "industry self-regulation, sports leagues, health care, noneconomic boycotts and access to joint venture facilities" that have plausible efficiencies and so are subject to this market screen.[126] Though *Northwest Whole Stationers* does not in principle preclude government or private antitrust plaintiffs from skipping the market power screen and relying on a direct effect analysis to show an actual anticompetitive effect under the rule of reason, private antitrust plaintiffs typically rest their case on whether they can make a sufficient showing to trigger the per se rule.[127]

Tying

Tying arrangements condition the sale of one distinct product or service (the "tying product") on the sale of another distinct product or service (the "tied product") or the agreement not to purchase the tied product or service from any other supplier.[128] The United States Supreme Court has held that tying is per se illegal only if the defendant has market power in the market for the tying product.[129] Noting that market power is the "ability of a single seller to raise price or restrict output",[130] the United States Supreme Court has held that market power in the tying product market will be inferred if the seller's market share is high.[131] In determining what market share of the tying product market is sufficiently high to infer market power, the Court has rejected a thirty-percent market share as being sufficient.[132] However,

[125] *Id.* at 297–98.

[126] See, e.g., *In re* Tableware Antitrust Litig., 484 F. Supp. 2d 1059, 1069–71 (N.D. Cal. 2007) (citing and discussing cases and other authorities).

[127] See, e.g., *id.* at 1071 ("But plaintiffs' decision to rely on *per se* scrutiny comes at a cost: it renders the existence of a horizontal agreement essential to their suit"). This is true for two reasons: (i) insofar as private antitrust plaintiffs are concerned, if those plaintiffs are competitors of the defendants, they typically cannot recover damages for group boycotts even if those boycotts raise the market price or limit output where those competitors may themselves potentially benefit from such effects, see, e.g., *Retina Assocs., P.A. v. Southern Baptists Hosp. of Florida, Inc.*, 105 F.3d 1376, 1383–84 (11th Cir. 1997) (*per curiam*) (citing *Matsushita Elec. Indus. Co. v. Zenith Radio Co. Ltd.*, 475 U.S. 574, 582–83 (1986)), and (ii) a use of the *Northwest Whole Stationers* market screen might well yield the same result as a direct effect analysis without the extensive data analysis, and potential for second-guessing, inherent in a direct effect analysis, a point illustrated by *Realcomp II*, 635 F.3d 815.

[128] See, e.g., *Illinois Tool Works, Inc. v. Independent Ink, Inc.*, 547 U.S. 28, 33–34 (2006); *Kodak*, 504 U.S. at 461–62; *IBM v. United States*, 298 U.S. 131, 135 (1936).

[129] *Jefferson Parish v. Hyde*, 466 U.S. 2, 15–17 (1984).

[130] *Kodak*, 504 U.S. at 464 (citations and internal quotation marks omitted).

[131] *Jefferson Parish*, 466 U.S. at 17.

[132] See *id.* at 26–27 (30 % not enough).

the Court has never defined a specific market share threshold for inferring market power[133] and has held that a firm need not have a monopoly or dominant position in the tying product market for it to have market power.[134]

This market screen reflects congressional intent as to not only when tying conduct should be per se illegal but also when tying conduct presents the potential for anticompetitive effects.[135] Those effects principally involve foreclosure in the *tied product* market, although as the tying firm obtains market share in the tied product market, those effects can include increased prices paid by consumers in the tying or tied product markets as well.[136]

---

[133] *Id.* at 38 n. 2 (concurring op.).

[134] *United States Steel Co. v. Fortner Corp.*, 429 U.S. 610, 620 (1977) ("...these decisions do not require that the defendant have a monopoly or even a dominant position throughout the market for a tying product").

[135] See, e.g., *Jefferson Parish*, 466 U.S. at 10–12 (majority op.) (refusing to reconsider modified *per se* rule against tying arrangements because rule reflected anticompetitive dangers of tying arrangements and fit congressional intent regarding the Clayton Act).

[136] See, e.g., *Jefferson Parish*, 466 U.S. at 10–11 & n. 15 (in passing the Clayton Act, Congress expressed great concern about the anticompetitive effects of tying, including the use of tying arrangements in different industries to build up and shut out competition); *id.*, at 14 (noting that a tying arrangement can be used to shield inferior products from competition); *id.*, at 36 (conc. op.) (acknowledging that tying arrangements may be anticompetitive because they can be used to create additional market power in the tied product market); *Northern Pac. R. Co. v. United States*, 356 U.S. 1, 6 (1958) (basis for rule on tying is to prevent foreclosure in the tied product market); European Commission Guidelines on Vertical Restraints, 2000 O.J. (C291) 42 ("The main negative effect of tying on competition is possible foreclosure on the market of the tied product"); Einer Elhauge, *Tying, Bundled Discounts, and the Death of the Single Monopoly Profit Theory*, 123 Harv. L. Rev. 2009 397, 400–02, 477–78.

As a caveat, it is noteworthy that the application of this market screen is not solely limited to market share: market power may be inferred from the unique characteristics of a tying product. See, e.g., *Jefferson Parish*, 466 U.S. at 17 & n. 32 (citing and discussing with approval United States Steel Co. v. Fortner Corp. (Fortner I), 394 U.S. 495, 504–506 & n. 2 (1969)) (unique credit terms offered by seller gave it sufficient economic power in tying product market that plaintiff could go to trial on challenge to tying arrangement) and *Northern Pacific R. Co. v. United States*, 356 U.S. 1, 7–8 (1956) (control over land by seller gave it sufficient economic power in tying product market that tie could be challenged as being *per se* illegal). See also *United States Steel Co. v. Fortner Corp.*, 429 U.S. 610, 617, 621–22 (1977) (Fortner II) (unique credit terms could satisfy uniqueness requirement for finding of economic power if the seller had a unique cost advantage over its competitors or if its competitors could not profitably offer the same kind of unique credit package that the seller could). The courts also have held that market power may be inferred in the tying product market, even as to a tie involving a single product, where post-purchase conditions or network effects lock customers into the tying product market. See, e.g., *Kodak*, 504 U.S. at 464–66; *Newcal Industries v. Ikon Office Solutions*, 513 F.3d 1038, 1044–51 (9th Cir. 2008); Statement of Decision at 13–14, People of the State of California v. Econolite Control Prods., No. BC314141 (Cal. Superior Court Los Angeles, Jul. 24, 2006) (citing *Jefferson Parish* for the proposition that network effects from a public standard can also cause such lock-in). However, both of these caveats involve firms that are not really SMEs as such when the market is properly defined: it is hard to imagine a true SME with such a unique, unmatchable product that it can punch over its weight and exercise market power versus larger firms in that same market; it is

If the conditions under which an inference of anticompetitive effect may be drawn are inapplicable, tying law does not preclude a showing of actual anticompetitive effects such as foreclosure as sufficing in the alternative.[137] Proving foreclosure effects—the main negative effect of a tie—typically the foreclosure of a high market share of the tied product market through a specific foreclosed rival loosing economies of scale may also suffice.[138] Insofar as the proof of foreclosure effects typically involves the foreclosure of a high market share of the tied product market, such an analysis also involves the application of a market screen in any event of 20–30 % in the tied product market before foreclosure effects may be inferred.[139]

Plaintiffs can avoid such market screens if they can extract, from a single price for the tying and tied products, the unbundled price of either the tying or tied products and then show a price increase in either of those prices that arose due to the tying arrangement itself as opposed to the prices that would have prevailed due to preexisting market power in the tying market.[140] But this extraction can be difficult as it involves the calculation of a hypothetical but-for price;[141] moreover, even if such a price effect can be shown, it is not enough for *standing* purposes to bring the lawsuit in the first instance.[142] It is thus no surprise that tying cases do not appear to exist that involve the calculation of actual price effects from the tie.

Exclusive Dealing

Exclusive dealing agreements, in which a distributor agrees to distribute only the goods of a certain manufacturer to the detriment of other manufacturers, are subject to full rule of reason treatment because these "agreements can achieve legitimate

equally hard to imagine a true SME with the kind of product so desired by consumers *vis-à-vis* its competitors that lock-in effects loom large.

[137] See *Illinois Tools*, 547 U.S. at 44–45 (price discrimination plus an above-market price for tied package can suffice to demonstrate market power); *Jefferson Parish*, 466 U.S. at 29–31 (maj. op.) (no showing of adverse effect on competition made under rule of reason); *id.*, at 45–46 (con. op.) (no showing that choices of consumers unreasonably narrowed under rule of reason).

[138] See, e.g., Elhauge, E, Tying, Bundled Discounts, and the Death of the Single Monopoly Profit Theory, Harv. L. Rev. 2009 397:123, at 469–70, 471, 473 (discussing bundled discounting, exclusionary conduct, and tying).

[139] See *id.* at 469–70 & n. 219 (discussing bundled discounting, tying, and exclusive dealing by reference to cases and treatises).

[140] See, e.g., *id.* at 417 (tying arrangement can lead to foreclosure in the tied product market and thus to price increases in that market); *id.* at 468–69 (discussing how to prove pricing effects arising from the tying arrangement as opposed to the "but-for" price that would arise from preexisting market power in the tying market).

[141] See *id.* at 468–69.

[142] By way of further explanation, a negative effect on prices from a tying arrangement may, in a rule of reason context, demonstrate harm to the plaintiff; such a negative effect may not suffice to demonstrate antitrust injury, e.g., an injury to competition. To demonstrate such an injury, the tying restraint must cause some sort of foreclosure effect, raise barriers to entry, or otherwise force consumers to forego available substitutes for the tied product. See *Brantley v. NBC Universal*, No. 09–56785, slip. op. 2012 WL 1071257, *6-9 (9th Cir. Mar. 30, 2012). This national report will return to this point in discussing the standing of SMEs to bring actions against their *competitors*.

economic benefits (reduced cost, stable long-term supply, predictable prices)".[143] To draw an inference of anticompetitive effects under this full rule of reason analysis, plaintiffs must show a significant enough foreclosure share in the relevant market, i. e., that the exclusive agreement covers a significant percentage of the relevant market for a sufficiently long enough a period of time that these agreements may give the defendants market power and drive rivals out of the market—all other factors being equal.[144] Generally speaking, the foreclosure market screen requires a minimum market share for these agreements of 20–40 %.[145] It is noteworthy that the use of this foreclosure market screen does not involve only the exclusive dealing agreement under consideration but also other exclusive dealing agreements in the relevant market,[146] as well as tying agreements (if any).[147] As with tying, nothing rules out a direct effect analysis of exclusive dealing arrangements as an alternative to foreclosure market screens.[148] Nonetheless, no case appears to exist where such a direct effect analysis was successfully used to challenge an exclusive dealing agreement—again, presumably for the reasons that such analyses appear to be more complex than the use of a foreclosure market screen[149] and that the presence of such direct effects may not suffice to confer standing on a plaintiff.[150]

[143] *Stop & Shop Supermarket Co. v. Blue Cross & Blue Shield of R.I.*, 373 F.3d 57, 65–66 (1st Cir. 2004).

[144] See, e.g., *Jefferson Parish*, 466 U.S. at 45 (O'Connor, J., concurring); *Sterling Merchandising, Inc. v. Nestle, S.A.*, 656 F.3d 112, 123–24 (1st Cir. 2011); *Stop & Shop Supermarket*, 373 F.3d at 66–68; *Eastern Food Serv. v. Pontifical Catholic University Services Ass'n*, 357 F.3d 1, 8–9 (1st Cir. 2004); *Omega Environmental, Inc. v. Gilbarco, Inc.*, 127 F.3d 1157, 1163–64 (9th Cir. 1997); *Twin City Sportservice, Inc. v. Charles O. Finley & Co., Inc.*, 676 F.2d 1291, 1301–02, 1304–05 (9th Cir. 1982); Elhauge, E, Tying, Bundled Discounts, and the Death of the Single Monopoly Profit Theory, Harv. L. Rev. 2009 397:123, at 469–70 & n. 219 (citing cases and commentators).

[145] See, e.g., *Stop & Shop Supermarket*, 373 F.3d at 68 (citing cases and commentators); *Twin City Sportservice*, 676 F.2d at 1301, 1304 (24 % foreclosure sufficient); Elhauge, E, Tying, Bundled Discounts, and the Death of the Single Monopoly Profit Theory, Harv. L. Rev. 2009 397:123, at 469–70 & n. 219 (citing cases and commentators).

[146] *Stop & Shop Supermarket*, 373 F.3d at 66; Elhauge, E, Tying, Bundled Discounts, and the Death of the Single Monopoly Profit Theory, Harv. L. Rev. 2009 397:123, at 469–70, 476–77 (citing and discussing cases).

[147] See *Twin City Sportservice*, 676 F.2d at 1303; Elhauge, E, Tying, Bundled Discounts, and the Death of the Single Monopoly Profit Theory, Harv. L. Rev. 2009 397:123, at 469–70.

[148] See Elhauge, E, Tying, Bundled Discounts, and the Death of the Single Monopoly Profit Theory, Harv. L. Rev. 2009 397:123, at 473 (speaking generally of alternatives to foreclosure market screens).

[149] See, e.g., *Roland Machinery Co. v. Dresser Indus. Co.*, 749 F.2d 380, 395 (7th Cir. 1984) (Posner, J.); David Balto & Ernest Nagata, *Proof of Competitive Effects in Monopolization Cases: A Response to Professor Muris*, 68 Antitrust L.J. 309, 323 (2000); Thomas Krattenmaker & Steven Salop, *Anticompetitive Exclusion: Raising Rivals' Costs to Achieve Power Over Price*, 96 Yale L. J. 209, 283 (1986).

[150] As noted *supra* in the discussion of tying, notions of antitrust injury may bar reliance on such direct effect to challenge an exclusive dealing arrangement. See *Brantley*, 2012 WL 1071257 at *6-9.

15.5.4 Annex IV: Resale Price Maintenance

Because a previous LIDC Congress passed a resolution allowing wider scope for resale price maintenance ("RPM") schemes than the national reporter believes is necessary (or appropriate, given the state of the law) for American SMEs, the national reporter respectfully states that it better respects the prior work of LIDC Congresses for him to set out the reasons for his more limited recommendation here in this Annex.

As noted above, federal antitrust law now views RPM as being a non-hard-core offence as the result of a majority decision of five justices of the United States Supreme Court in 2007 in the *Leegin* case.[151] However, the laws of several American States continue to view RPM as being a hard-core offence.[152] And, in spite of *Leegin*, many other jurisdictions continue to view RPM as being a hard-core offence.[153]

This raises the question for the national reporter, and for the international reporter, of whether there should be a specific rule on RPM applicable to SMEs. The national reporter respectfully submits that, whether the jurisdiction is one that views RPM as being a hard-core or a non-hard-core offence, an RPM strategy employed by an SME should be free from challenge *only* if it is a temporary strategy employed in aid of *new entry*.

Recognition of a limited and easily identifiable *new entry* exception fits *Leegin* itself. The majority opinion of *Leegin* itself notes the existence of a myriad of circumstances in which an RPM scheme should be carefully scrutinised even under *federal* law for anticompetitive effects, including circumstances in which many competing manufacturers adopt the practice, the practice is retailer initiated, the practice is initiated by a manufacturer with market power, or the practice is used in conjunction with other vertical restraints.[154] There is no reason to carve out an express exemption for SMEs insofar as any of these circumstances are concerned.

---

[151] *Leegin Creative Leather Prods., Inc. v. PSKS, Inc.*, 551 U.S. 877 (2007).

[152] See, e.g. *O'Brien v. Leegin Creative Prods.*, Inc., No. 101,000, slip. op. (Kansas Supreme Ct. May 4, 2012); *People v. Bioelements, Inc.*, No. ING 10011659 (Cal. Super. Ct. Jan. 11, 2011) (California Attorney General—via consent decree—imposed fine of $51,000 and enjoining defendant from entering into retail price maintenance agreements with its distributors in the future); The State Bar of California Antitrust and Unfair Competition Law Section, California State Antitrust Law and Unfair Competition Law, § 3 (2009 ed.); see also, e.g., Alan Duncan & Alison Guernsey, *Waiting for the Other Shoe to Drop. Will State Courts Follow Leegin*?, 27 Franchise L.J. 173, 178 (Winter 2008) (noting that, in the wake of *Leegin*, because there are 13 to 17 States that likely will not follow that decision, "franchisors and other suppliers of goods will still have to exercise caution in implementing national account programs or other programs controlling the price at which franchisees and distributors resell goods").

[153] OECD, OECD Competition Committee Policy Roundtable, resale Price Maintenance, DAF/Comp (2008) 37 at 48, 53–55, available at http://www.oecd.org/dataoecd/39/63/43835526.pdf.

[154] See, e.g., *Leegin*, 551 U.S. at 892–98; OECD Competition Committee Policy Roundtable, resale Price Maintenance, DAF/Comp (2008) 37 at 43–44, 47; accord, Brief of Amicus Curiae

Moreover, both state and federal laws allow manufacturers to announce their resale prices in advance and refuse to deal with those who fail to comply—the so-called *Colgate* exception; a distribution can, in turn, comply with the manufacturer's demand to follow its resale prices in order to avoid termination.[155] The existence of the so-called *Colgate* exception for SMEs, and larger enterprises, who manufacture goods allowing them to refuse to deal with discounting retailers further reduces the need for any further express exemption for SMEs insofar as the American market is concerned.[156]

There are principally two pro-competitive benefits to RPM schemes that have at least some credibility to them: (1) inducing promotional and service investments by retailers in the manufacturer's product if that manufacturer is a new entrant and (2) preventing freeriding by discount retailers off of the promotional and service efforts of other retailers.[157]

However, the *majority* opinion in *Leegin* noted that, even at the time of that decision, there was scepticism as to freeriding being a precompetitive reason for RPM.[158] In turn, the dissenting opinion in *Leegin* questioned why an *established* manufacturer in a market would ever need RPM to combat freeriding[159] and pointed out that if it felt free to reconsider what had been the rule that RPM was a hard-core offence, it would make an exception for the use of RPM *only* to effectuate *new entry* because it is an "easily identifiable" and "temporary" condition that did not "invite [] lengthy time-consuming argument among competing experts, as they seek to apply abstract, highly technical, criteria to often ill-defined markets".[160] Recognizing an exception allowing SMEs to engage in RPM where it is related to new entry thus fits both the majority and the dissenting opinions in *Leegin*.

Comanor and Scherer in Support of Neither Party at 9–10, Leegin Creative Leather Products, Inc. v. PSKS, Inc., 551 U.S. 877 (2007) (No. 06–480) (retailer-induced RPM should be subject to a rebuttable presumption of being anticompetitive as should manufacturer-induced RPM when 50 % or more of the market uses RPM or the market is oligopolistic).

[155] *United States v. Colgate & Co.*, 250 U.S. 300, 307 (1919); see also, e.g., *Monsanto Co. v. Spray-Rite Serv. Corp.*, 465 U.S. 752, 761 (1984) ("Under *Colgate*, the manufacturer can announce its resale prices in advance and refuse to deal with those who fail to comply. And a distributor is free to acquiesce in the manufacturer's demand in order to avoid termination"); *Chavez v. Whirlpool Corp.*, 93 Cal. App. 4th 363 (2001).

[156] The national reporter takes no position on whether a *Colgate* exemption (or, if so, to what extent) should be recognised in other jurisdictions where a forward-looking need to further integrate markets may be more of an imperative. The American market is by and large integrated on a national scale with constitutional rules that prevent commercial discrimination by public actors on the state and local level on an in-state versus out-of-state basis.

[157] *Leegin*, 551 U.S. at 889–90; *see* OECD Competition Committee Policy Roundtable, resale Price Maintenance, DAF/Comp (2008) 37 at 26, 29.

[158] *Id*; see also, e.g., Brief of Amicus Curiae Comanor and Scherer in Support of Neither Party at 6, *Leegin Creative Leather Products, Inc. v. PSKS, Inc.*, 551 U.S. 877 (2007) (No. 06–480) (noting scepticism about how often freeriding – a justification for minimum RPM – occurs but not ruling out that instances could occur in which such a justification may exist).

[159] *Leegin*, 551 U.S. at 921 (dissenting op.).

[160] *Id*. at 917–18.

It also serves the end of administrability. Administrability has two facets: the first facet is that "legal rules should be stated with sufficient clarity to permit sensible implementation, especially in private suits that are conducted before courts of general jurisdiction and often are tried before juries"; the second (and related) facet is that "the application of competition rules ought to account for the capability, including the relative capabilities, of the institutions responsible for their implementation".[161] Allowing RPM to be used as a strategy for new entry fits both facets as a consensus matter, a point on which there is still controversy and debate insofar as the federal rule on RPM, as set out in the majority opinion in *Leegin*, is concerned.[162]

In fact, recognising an exception to RPM only for new entry also fits studies subsequent to *Leegin* that have cast further doubt on freeriding being a sufficient justification for RPM even in the age of the Internet.[163] And as a limited exception, its adoption would not suggest that state legislatures should reverse themselves wholesale on RPM: that is important not only because many state legislatures repealed so-called fair trade legislation that legalised RPM after such legalised RPM led to industry-wide price increases[164] but also because state legislatures have

---

[161] Kovacic & Wineman, *supra*, 76 Antitrust L. J. at 938 (citing Philip Areeda & Donald Turner, *Predatory Pricing and Related Practices under Section 2 of the Sherman Act*, 88 Harv. L. Rev. 697, 699 (1975)).

[162] See, e.g., OECD Competition Committee Policy Roundtable, resale Price Maintenance, DAF/Comp (2008) 37 at 36–42 (discussing weaknesses of rule of reason regarding administrability, observing that *Leegin* has significant weaknesses in that regard, and, after discussing a variety of factors that should be looked at to determine if an RPM scheme is likely to be pro-competitive or anticompetitive (including new entry), proposing the Comanor-Scherer approach of rebuttable presumptions may be the best way to proceed); Ashley Doty, *Leegin v. PSKS: New Standard, New Challenges*, 23 Berk. Tech. L. J. __ (2008), available at http://papers.ssrn.com/sol3/papers.cfm?abstract_id=1124649 (agreeing with majority decision in *Leegin* as a matter of principle but then observing that the decision raises serious administrability issues and that the majority was too quick to disregard *stare decisis*). There is an important debate in the halls of Congress—to which it may return after the upcoming November elections—as to whether antitrust law generally should return to the per se illegality rule for RPM. *See, e.g.*, S. 148, 111th Cong. (2009), available at http://www.orrick.com/fileupload/2665.pdf. Calling for a very limited exception allowing for RPM as a means of new entry does not substantially undermine or preclude that debate no matter how it may turn out.

[163] See, e.g., Avisham Tor & William J. Rinner, *Behavioral Antitrust: A New Approach to the Rule of Reason After Leegin*, 2011 U. Ill. L. Rev. 805 (2011); Marina Lao, *Resale Price Maintenance: The Internet Phenomenon and "Free Rider" Issues*, 55 Antitrust Bulletin 473 (2010), available at http://papers.ssrn.com/sol3/papers.cfm?abstract_id=1562051; see also OECD Competition Committee Policy Roundtable, resale Price Maintenance, DAF/Comp (2008) 37 at 26–29.

[164] See, e.g., *O'Brien v. Leegin Creative Prods., Inc.*, No. 101,000, slip. op. at 35 (Kansas Supreme Ct. May 4, 2012); The State Bar of California Antitrust and Unfair Competition Law Section, California State Antitrust Law and Unfair Competition Law, § 3 (2009 ed.); see also OECD Competition Committee Policy Roundtable, resale Price Maintenance, DAF/Comp (2008) 37 at 34 (noting that the effects of RPM on consumer welfare, even where it is only being used to increase presale services and thus demand, can be negative); *id.* at 44 (agreeing with Comanor and Scherer that, under certain conditions, the effects of RPM can often be negative on consumer

made a policy choice in favour of *administrability* by an easy-to-understand and apply rule barring RPM schemes.[165]

15.5.5 Annex V: Fuller Justification for Treating Corporations Differently in Matters of Procedural Rights

Finally, the Annex sets out more fully the pragmatic, non-constitutional reasons for treating corporations (excepting certain civil and criminal rights such as access to the file or requiring proof beyond a reasonable doubt for criminal offences) differently insofar as procedural rights are concerned.

Corporations were and are created, supervised, and regulated as artificial, "quasi-public" entities that owe their existence to law or, put another way, were and are "legally privileged" organisations, set up by the laws of whatever state they are incorporated in, that serve "a social function for the state" and whose "'purposes ha[ve] to be made consistent with the public welfare".[166]

Although corporations are generally and properly thought of as "socially useful" actors today,[167] the genesis of the corporation as a creature of the state imbues in it a duty to the public welfare that a natural person does not have such that it should not be able to shield itself from liability for illegal acts by, for example, having a right to remain silent.[168] Put another way, corporations are different from natural persons (or sole proprietorships that are unincorporated businesses run by natural persons

---

welfare *even* if output has increased due to the RPM scheme); *id.* at 52–55 (discussing experience of United Kingdom in which a revocation of RPM on medicine lowered prices and in which RPM was used to facilitate retailer cartels).

[165] See, e.g., *O'Brien v. Leegin Creative Prods., Inc.*, No. 101,000, slip. op. at 31–34, 38 (Kansas Supreme Ct. May 4, 2012); The State Bar of California Antitrust and Unfair Competition Law Section, California State Antitrust Law and Unfair Competition Law, § 3 (2009 ed.); see also OECD Competition Committee Policy Roundtable, resale Price Maintenance, DAF/Comp (2008) 37at 44 (highlighting new entry as a particularly important factor to examine in the treatment of RPM). This national report expresses no opinion as to whether such a new entry exception can be recognised as a matter of law in a state that otherwise views RPM as being *per se* illegal.

[166] *Citizens United v. Federal Elec. Comm'n*, 130 S. Ct. 876, 949 (2010) (dissenting op.) (citing and quoting Handlin & Handling, *Origin of the American Business Corporation*, 5 J. Econ. His. 1, 22 (1945) and R. Seavoy, Origins of the American Business Corporation 1784–1855, p. 5 (1982)). The national reporter takes no position one way or the other on the *Citizens United* case itself, which concerns the completely different subject of the application of the First Amendment of the U.S. Constitution to corporations.

[167] *Citizens United*, 130 S. Ct. at 949 (dissenting op.) (citing Hansmann & Kraakman, *The End of History for Corporate Law*, 89 Geo. L. J. 439, 440 (2001)).

[168] *Cf. Citizens United*, 130 S. Ct. at 949–50 (dissenting op.) ("The Framers took it as a given that corporations could be comprehensively regulated in service of the public welfare"); *Trustees of Dartmouth College v. Woodward*, 4 Wheat. 518, 636, (1819) (Marshall, C.J.) ("A corporation is an artificial being, invisible, intangible, and existing only in contemplation of law. Being the mere creature of law, it possesses only those properties which the charter of its creation confers upon it").

wherein natural persons remain fully liable for the activities of those businesses) such that they need not be accorded the same procedural rights: they have "limited liability" for their owners and managers, "perpetual life," separation of ownership and control, "and favourable treatment of the accumulation and distribution of assets ... that enhance their ability to attract capital and to deploy their resources in ways that maximise the return on their shareholders' investments".[169] And in viewing these rules from that perspective, there is no rational principle that would distinguish between an SME that has taken corporate form and a large economic enterprise.

Indeed, to try to draw such a distinction here would violate the rule of *administrability*. As previously noted, administrability has two facets: the first facet is that "legal rules should be stated with sufficient clarity to permit sensible implementation, especially in private suits that are conducted before courts of general jurisdiction and often are tried before juries"; the second (and related) facet is that "the application of competition rules ought to account for the capability, including the relative capabilities, of the institutions responsible for their implementation".[170] An SME carve out, where the SME is incorporated, satisfies neither facet: any market share threshold for determining when enhanced procedural protections should come into play would be invariably arbitrary, and determining whether such a threshold has been met in a properly defined market *at the onset of an investigation* (when such rights would need to be accorded to an economic enterprise and evidence presumably has not yet even been gathered) is beyond the institutional competence of enforcers, let alone a court that would have to review such a determination well after the fact for abuse of discretion.

[169] See *Citizens United*, 130 S. Ct. at 971 & n. 72 (dissenting op.) (internal citations and quotation marks omitted).

[170] Kovacic & Wineman, *supra*, 76 Antitrust L. J. at 938 (citing Philip Areeda & Donald Turner, *Predatory Pricing and Related Practices under Section 2 of the Sherman Act*, 88 Harv. L. Rev. 697, 699 (1975)).

Part II

Image Protection from Non-competitors

International Report 16

Martine Karsenty-Ricard

16.1 Introduction

A company is traditionally identified by third parties, thanks to the trademark overlaying its products or services, its other intellectual property rights, along with its corporate name, its trade name or its signage, and sometimes its domain name.

All these identification elements work together to give a specific image of the company, and they may be of substantial economic value, especially if the company has made sizeable investments to promote and protect them and if they enjoy a level of awareness. Such values are necessarily coveted by competitor companies, but in practice, it has been noted that these identification elements can also be used by non-competitor companies.

These uses or impairments (the latter term already presupposing the introduction of a concept of misconduct) can take many forms and have varied consequences, as well as those resulting from the different systems described by the national reports examined: imitation, whether voluntary or involuntary; creation of a likelihood of confusion; usurpation of a reputation or awareness; debasement or trivialisation of the company's image.

We may already ponder the nature of the reality and/or quantification of the harm endured in relation to such acts.

The trademark infringement action is traditionally designed to respond to the use by a third party of the trademark's constitutive mark for identical (or similar) products or services to those for which the trademark is registered, whereby both companies are thus by hypothesis in a competitive situation.

This principle of speciality is also generally applied when the identification element used is a trade name, a corporate name, and even a domain name.

M. Karsenty-Ricard (✉)
J.P. Karsenty & Associés, Paris, France
e-mail: mkarsenty@jpkarsenty.com

P. Këllezi et al. (eds.), *Antitrust for Small and Middle Size Undertakings and Image Protection from Non-Competitors*, LIDC Contributions on Antitrust Law, Intellectual Property and Unfair Competition, DOI 10.1007/978-3-642-54000-4_16,

However, specific to trademark law, this principle of speciality is not found to apply in terms of drawings and models or copyright.

In the absence of distinctive marks or the like, an action for unfair competition allows a degree of protection of a company's identification elements to be afforded, falling within the scope of a competitive relationship.

But could or should it obtain protection in the event of use of the various components of its image or identity by companies that are not its competitors and, if so, on what grounds and under which circumstances?

In the event of a positive response, is the use of laws governing intellectual property (trademarks, designs and models, copyright, and even patents) or distinctive marks (such as domain name, corporate name, trade name, etc. where the system of protection is sometimes equated with that of intellectual property laws) useful, necessary, satisfactory?

The use of intellectual property or distinctive mark laws can constitute an acceptable response but one that is necessarily partial.

Can/must this use be combined with the action for unfair competition (understood in its broadest sense), or is it separate from this other basis?

It should be remembered that Article 10(b) of the Paris Convention of 1883[1] schedules the obligation on countries within the Union to ensure effective protection against unfair competition and gives a definition in paragraph 2, which can be seen as very broad:

> Any act of competition contrary to honest practices in industrial or commercial matters constitutes an act of unfair competition.

It is not immediately clear whether this paper does not target companies in a competitive situation, since "any act of competition" could be understood to be any act by an economic operator on the market.

Furthermore, although indents 1 and 2 of paragraph 3 target a competitor's acts so as to prohibit them, indent 3 no longer suggests this restriction by prohibiting "*indications or allegations the use of which in the course of trade is likely to mislead the public as to the nature, the manufacturing process, the characteristics, the suitability for their purpose, or the quantity, of the goods.*"

This being the case, the offending acts and their consequences are rather restricted.

[1] Paris Convention for the protection of industrial property of 20 March 1883, revised (available at http://www.wipo.int/treaties/en/ip/paris/trtdocs_wo020.html), Article 10(b):

1) The countries of the Union are bound to assure to nationals of such countries effective protection against unfair competition. 2) Any act of competition contrary to honest practices in industrial or commercial matters constitutes an act of unfair competition. 3) The following in particular shall be prohibited:

1. all acts of such a nature as to create confusion by any means whatever with the establishment, the goods, or the industrial or commercial activities, of a competitor; 2. false allegations in the course of trade of such a nature as to discredit the establishment, the goods, or the industrial or commercial activities, of a competitor; 3. indications or allegations the use of which in the course of trade is likely to mislead the public as to the nature, the manufacturing process, the characteristics, the suitability for their purpose, or the quantity, of the goods.

Use of the theory of free riding (created in the 1960s by Yves Saint GALL, founder and leader within the League for many years) offers, in many countries that have submitted national reports, an acceptable judicial solution, but it seems sometimes difficult to fully understand the sanctioning of free-riding behaviour between non-competitors.

Taken together, do these tools represent useful, effective, sufficient, and appropriate protection, given that the spectre immediately looms of obstructing freedom of trade, the necessity of conserving judicial safety in relations between the various economic players and behavioural loyalty on the markets?

It should be noted that the eleven national reports studied all come from European Union member states, with the exception of Switzerland, a country whose legal system is nonetheless rather similar to the others, such that many converging elements can be seen in the responses given by the various national reporters.

Having said that, even based on the unified legal system constituted by European Union law (we can specifically quote in this respect Directive 2005/29/EC[2] of 11 May 2005 concerning unfair business-to-consumer commercial practices whereby some countries, but not all, have admitted that it could target actions brought by companies against other companies), each country retains its national law, which may contain notable specific features, on occasion).

16.2 Brand Image and Defence of Brand Image

Brand image does not have a legal definition in the positive law of countries that answered the questionnaire.

In any case, it is made up of various elements: intellectual property rights, visual and/or verbal elements, etc.

Only the French report[3] contains a doctrinal definition: "*intangible property consisting of all representations tending to single out in the public's eyes those well-known marks – or anything else that may have economic value – resulting from many investments (including advertising and marketing).*"

Other reports highlight the existence of definitions of a commercial nature such as the following, for example:

- "*the psychological aspect of a brand experience, a symbolic construct created within the minds of people, consisting of all the information and expectations associated with a product, service or the company(ies) providing them*"[4];
- "*psychological aspects attributed to a product or service*"[5];

[2] OJ 2005 L 149, p. 22.

[3] See *Arcelin et al.*, France, Part II, Chap. 19, p. 2.

[4] See *Mosing & Handig*, Austria, Part II, Chap. 17, p. 2.

[5] See *Henning-Bodewig*, Germany, Part II, Chap. 20, p. 1.

- *"view of the customers about a brand"*[6];
- *"impression the public has of a product, firm or commercial trademark, and by extension, the collective impression of an institution, [or of] a person"*.[7]

In England,[8] the concept of "*brand image*" is more or less equivalent to the concept of "*goodwill*", defined as follows: "*It is the benefit and advantage of the good name, reputation and connection of a business. It is the attractive force which brings in custom.*"

All these definitions refer to the idea of the commercial reputation of a product, service, or company built up in the public's mind. It could be assimilated to a sort of positive emblematic sign that can be immediately perceived by the public, whatever the level of its distinctiveness or originality.

All reports point out that, even in the absence of competitive relationships, "*trademark image*" can be indirectly protected by various means resulting from intellectual property law, commercial law, competition law, and/or general principles of civil liability.

16.3 Trademark, Principle of Speciality, and Competitive Relationship

All reports consider that the principle of speciality in force in trademark law most often involves the existence of at least an indirect competitive relationship in practice, between the parties, insofar as an assessment of the likelihood of confusion requires an examination of the identity of, at the very least, the similarity between the products or services concerned.

In particular, the German, Swedish, and Swiss contributors[9] point out that even in the absence of a direct likelihood of confusion between the products or services, an indirect likelihood of confusion may exist in terms of consumers who may believe that products or services have a common origin or that the products and services are from economically linked companies. The risk of indirect likelihood may also be described as "likelihood of association".

In Belgium and France,[10] an extensive assessment of the similarity of products and services may be the initial means by which to protect a trademark against non-competitor companies.

Above all, however, all reports underline that trademark law can be used against a non-competitor in the following cases:

[6] See *Lukácsi et al.*, Hungary, Part II, Chap. 21, p. 1.

[7] See *Ghassemi*, Switzerland, Part II, Chap. 25, p. 1.

[8] See *Longstaff*, United Kingdom, Part II, Chap. 26, p. 3.

[9] See *Henning-Bodewig*, Germany, Part II, Chap. 20, p. 5; *Jute*, Sweden, Part II, Chap. 24, p. 5; *Ghassemi*, Switzerland, Part II, Chap. 25, p. 4.

[10] See *Arcelin et al.*, France, Part II, Chap. 19, p. 4. The Belgian report is not published in the present volume.

- well-known trademarks (Article 6(*b*)[11] of the Paris Convention),
- trademarks of wide repute (Article 5(2)[12] of Directive no. 2008/95/EC).

Provisions relating to well-known trademarks and trademarks of wide repute are very useful instruments when it comes to protecting against the likelihood of association.

Although the provisions relating to well-known trademarks and trademarks of wide repute cannot be applied, Luxembourg and Swiss reports[13] state that it is possible to act on the basis of the general principle of liability (for example, according to Swiss Law, it is possible to use the Code of Obligations), whereas the Czech report refers to a general clause prohibiting unfair competition that can also be applied to non-competitors.[14]

The Austrian, Belgian, German, and Italian reports[15] also point out that the specific provisions of unfair competition law can be invoked if the conditions are present (for instance, 'imitation marketing' practices resulting from Directive no. 2005/29/EC of 11 May 2005, disparagement or acts contrary to honest marketing practices), while the German report[16] highlights that unfair competition law must not undermine trademark law.

In Hungarian law,[17] sanctions for impairment and unfair competition are the result of objective liability, regardless of whether the infringing party is a

---

[11] Article 6(b) of the Paris Convention reads:

"1) The countries of the Union undertake, ex officio if their legislation so permits, or at the request of an interested party, to refuse or to cancel the registration, and to prohibit the use, of a trademark which constitutes a reproduction, an imitation, or a translation, liable to create confusion, of a mark considered by the competent authority of the country of registration or use to be well known in that country as being already the mark of a person entitled to the benefits of this Convention and used for identical or similar goods. These provisions shall also apply when the essential part of the mark constitutes a reproduction of any such well-known mark or an imitation liable to create confusion therewith.

A period of at least five years from the date of registration shall be allowed for requesting the cancellation of such a mark. The countries of the Union may provide for a period within which the prohibition of use must be requested.

No time limit shall be fixed for requesting the cancellation or the prohibition of the use of marks registered or used in bad faith."

[12] Article 5(2) of Directive 2008/95/EC reads: "Any member may also provide that the proprietor shall be entitled to prevent all third parties not having his consent from using in the course of trade any sign which is identical with, or comparable to, the trademark in relation to goods or services which are not comparable to those for which the trademark is registered, where the latter has a reputation in the Member State and where use of that sign without due cause takes unfair advantage of, or is detrimental to, the distinctive character or the repute of the trademark."

[13] See *Decker & Decker*, Luxembourg, Part II, Chap. 23, p. 3; *Ghassemi*, Switzerland, Part II, Chap. 25, p. 6.

[14] See *Hajn*, Czech Republic, Part II, Chap. 18, pp. 3–4.

[15] See *Mosing & Handig*, Austria, Part II, Chap. 17, pp. 3–8; *Henning-Bodewig*, Germany, Part II, Chap. 20, pp 10; *La Rocca*, Italy, Part II, Chap. 22, pp. 2–3.

[16] See *Henning-Bodewig*, Germany, Part II, Chap. 20, p. 10.

[17] See *Lukácsi et al.*, Hungary, Part II, Chap. 21, p. 6.

competitor, whereas the general civil liability clause involves a subjective assessment of the behaviour of the person who, by their deeds, commits harm.

French and English laws[18] also allow brand protection and civil liability to be invoked cumulatively, in France, on the condition that a separate deed exists. In English law, the offence is known as 'passing off'.

For its part, the Swedish report[19] points out that although an infringement action and an action for unfair competition (which are dealt with by different courts) concerning the same product can be brought at the same time, they may have different outcomes.

The more 'automatic' and regulated nature of infringement assessment and its sanctions does not exist in the event that a civil liability action is brought, and this no doubt allows for a more subjective assessment of the litigious behaviour.

It is certain that an action for unfair competition and/or free riding confers longer and broader protection, thanks to certain distinctive marks.

We must also ensure that the same harm is not compensated for twice owing to different bases.

16.4 Trademark, Trademark "Economy", and Competitive Relationship

In trademark law, the use of a mark that impairs a prior trademark is, in principle, only prohibited for third parties in the course of trade.

As the Hungarian contributors underline,[20] it is often difficult to distinguish between those activities falling within the course of trade and those falling outside it.

The application of trademark law thus depends on the assessment of this concept made by jurisprudence in each country.

As such, Austrian jurisprudence[21] considers that the use of a trademark like Adwords constitutes use in the course of trade, which can be sanctioned under trademark law, whereas in Switzerland,[22] the use of Adwords is a controversial topic.

On the other hand, according to French jurisprudence,[23] the use of a trademark for reasons of parody or artistry does not constitute use in the course of trade (for instance, use by a political association), insofar as it does not seek to obtain economic advantage.

[18] See *Arcelin et al.*, France, Part II, Chap. 19, p. 6–7; *Longstaff*, United Kingdom, Part II, Chap. 26, p. 12.

[19] *Jute*, Sweden, Part II, Chap. 24, pp. 5–6.

[20] See *Lukácsi et al.*, Hungary, Part II, Chap. 21, p. 7.

[21] See *Mosing & Handig*, Austria, Part II, Chap. 17, p. 9.

[22] See *Ghassemi*, Switzerland, Part II, Chap. 25, p. 7.

[23] See *Arcelin et al.*, France, Part II, Chap. 25, p. 8.

Likewise, in Germany,[24] purely private or political behaviour cannot be sanctioned on the basis of trademark law.

A company falling victim to the use of its trademark outside the course of trade may nevertheless act on another basis.

Specifically, French and Italian reports[25] state that the use of a trademark '*outside the course of trade*' can be sanctioned on the basis of civil liability.

In France,[26] the parodied use of a trademark can thus be sanctioned on this basis if the use appears disproportionate.

In Belgium, such use of a trademark may represent impairment of a well-known brand or reprehensible acts contrary to honest market practices, while in Hungary and Switzerland,[27] use of this type may be sanctioned in the event of disparagement of the competitor.

In Luxembourg,[28] the use of a trademark for a purpose other than distinguishing products and services can be prohibited when this use is not justified, when it gains unjustified advantage, or when it may be damaging to the distinctive character or repute of the prior trademark.

In the end, as the English report states,[29] it is essential that some trademark uses by a non-competitor 'outside the course of trade' can be sanctioned. This is possible in numerous countries, with varying levels of severity, and on different bases.

Furthermore, the vast majority of reports consider than the approach of the Court of Justice of the European Union whereby, in order to be deemed as an infringement, the use of a sign representing a trademark must impair one of the four functions it recognises in terms of the trademark (namely notification of origin, guarantee of quality, communication, investment, and advertising functions) has an impact or is likely to have an impact on the issue of infringement.[30]

In Austria,[31] the definition of these functions may enable a more predictable assessment of trademark infringement, while in the English report,[32] it remains to be seen whether the functions of the trademark will evolve to the point that any use outside the course of trade may be deemed an infringement.

Examples already exist showing that these new functions have been taken into account in Czech jurisprudence and in Italian jurisprudence.[33]

---

[24] See *Henning-Bodewig*, Germany, Part II, Chap. 20, p. 11.

[25] See *Arcelin et al.*, France, Part II, Chap. 19, pp. 9; *La Rocca*, Italy, Part II, Chap. 22, p. 4.

[26] See *Arcelin et al.*, France, Part II, Chap. 19, p. 9.

[27] See *Lukácsi et al.*, Hungary, Part II, Chap. 21, pp. 7; *Ghassemi*, Switzerland, Part II, Chap. 25, p.

[28] See *Decker & Decker*, Luxembourg, Part II, Chap. 23, pp. 2–3.

[29] See *Longstaff*, United Kingdom, Part II, Chap. 26, p. 13.

[30] ECJ, case C-323/09, *Interflora Inc. and Interflora British Unit v Marks & Spencer plc et Flowers Direct Online*, Rec. 2011 I-8625; ECJ, case C-487/07, *L'Oréal SA, Lancôme parfums et beauté & Cie SNC and Laboratoire Garnier & Cie v Bellure NV, Malaika Investments Ltd and Starion International Ltd.*, Rec. 2009 I-5185.

[31] See *Mosing & Handig*, Austria, Part II, Chap. 17, p. 10.

[32] See *Longstaff*, United Kingdom, Part II, Chap. 26, p. 13.

[33] See *Hajn*, Czech Republic, Part II, Chap. 18, p. 4–5; *La Rocca*, Italy, Part 2, Chap. 22, p. 5.

The Luxembourg report[34] adds that acknowledgement of these various functions of the trademark could also help to solve new problems created by the digital environment and Internet.

However, other reports do not believe in a renewal of the classic approach.

According to the Belgian report,[35] the main function of the trademark remains the notification of origin of products or services.

The German report[36] points out that the fourth function of the trademark remains disputed.

For the Hungarian report,[37] the affirmations of the Court of Justice of the European Union have a simple declaratory value rather than a constituent value.

Lastly, contrary to community jurisprudence, Swiss law[38] only recognises the function of notification of origin. The promotional function associated with a trademark's reputation is only protected in the presence of a well-known trademark.

We may ask questions about the opportunity to acknowledge several functions served by the trademark, insofar as, according to the Court of Justice of the European Union, the function of notification of origin remains the main function, while in many countries, means of protection already exist regarding impairments made to the guarantee of quality, communication, investment, and advertising functions, specifically based on unfair competition and/or free riding.

The use of these other functions is likely to increase the flexibility of the principle of speciality and could be viewed as a means to widen a trademark's protection, independently of its awareness.

Thus, in the l'Oréal case (aforementioned decree of 18 June 2009), provisions relating to misleading advertising and comparative advertising could perhaps have sufficed to sanction the unauthorised use of trademarks in scent correlation tables, without resorting to infringement.

16.5 Other Distinctive Marks

All reports highlight the possibility of defending other intellectual property rights, as well as the *company name*, the *trade name*, the *signage*, and the *domain name*, even in the absence of a competitive relationship.

However, in the Austrian, Czech, and Swiss reports,[39] such protection requires that a likelihood of confusion exists in some cases. Such a likelihood of confusion

---

[34] See *Decker & Decker*, Luxembourg, Part II, Chap. 23, p. 4.

[35] Belgian report, pp. 9–10, not published in the present volume.

[36] See *Henning-Bodewig*, Germany, Part II, Chap. 20, p. 11.

[37] See *Lukácsi et al.*, Hungary, Part II, Chap. 21, p. 7–8.

[38] See *Ghassemi*, Switzerland, Part II, Chap. 25, pp. 7.

[39] See *Mosing & Handig*, Austria, Part II, Chap. 17, p. 11, which refers readers to pp. 3 to 8; *Hajn*, Czech Republic, Part II, Chap. 18, pp. 5–6; *Ghassemi*, Switzerland, Part II, Chap. 25, p. 8.

will generally be less difficult to demonstrate if the parties in question are competitors.

Belgian and Hungarian laws[40] stipulate that the use of a disputed mark must mislead the consumer.

In French law,[41] marks must additionally possess a sufficient degree of distinctiveness. This concept applies to the trademark and not to other distinctive marks.

In Sweden,[42] the extent to which a company's distinctive marks are protected is assessed in the same way as for a trademark, insofar as trademark law schedules that the holder of a company name or other business mark has a trademark entitlement over said name.

In England,[43] the 'passing-off' law can be invoked if evidence of 'goodwill' is reported.

Most of the reports highlight that *domain names* do not require any specific treatment insofar as there are ways to prohibit them when they impair a prior trademark, even in the absence of competitive relationship between the parties.

When trademark law is applied, the principle of speciality is taken into consideration.

In all the countries where a report was written, there are also ways to sanction *meta-tags* and *sponsored links* based on unfair competition and/or trademark law.

Generally speaking, with the exception of Sweden, the reports do not highlight any specific interest in using *alternative modes to settle disputes online*, and thus their involvement in judicial systems seem restricted up to this point.

16.6 "Questionable" Acts and Absence of Competitive Relationship

Only Luxembourg[44] considers that rules relating to unfair competition apply solely between competitors.

In the majority of countries,[45] unfair competition can be sanctioned outside the scope of any competitive relationship or in terms of indirect competitors.

Other countries[46] make a distinction between acts of unfair competition, according to whether they are only applied to competitors or can also be applied to non-competitors.

[40] See *Lukácsi et al.*, Hungary, Part II, Chap. 21, pp. 8–10.

[41] See *Arcelin et al.*, France, Part II, Chap. 19, p. 13.

[42] *Jute*, Sweden, Part II, Chap. 24, p. 9.

[43] See *Longstaff*, United Kingdom, Part II, Chap. 26, p. 14.

[44] See *Decker & Decker*, Luxembourg, Part II, Chap. 23, p. 6.

[45] See *Mosing & Handig*, Austria, Part II, Chap. 17, pp. 13–14; *Arcelin et al.*, France, Part II, Chap. 19, pp. 19–21; *Hajn*, Czech Republic, Part II, Chap. 18, p. 6–7; *Henning-Bodewig*, Germany, Part II, Chap. 20, p. 12; *Jute*, Sweden, Part II, Chap. 24, p. 11–12; *Ghassemi*, Switzerland, Part II, Chap. 25, p. 11; *Longstaff*, United Kingdom, Part II, Chap. 26, pp. 18–19.

[46] See *Lukácsi et al.*, Hungary, Part II, Chap. 21, p. 12; *La Rocca*, Italy, Part II, Chap. 22, p. 6.

Most of the reports observe that unfair competition specifically enables them to sanction non-competitors when they create ambiguity regarding their identity.

Furthermore, all the reports outline the possibility of incriminating parasitic acts, but this term does not always exactly match the definition given by French jurisprudence, namely '*all behaviours by which an economic agent follows in the wake of another so as to take advantage of the former's efforts and knowledge at no expense.*'

As such, some countries such as Belgium, Italy, and Luxembourg[47] refer to a concept close to the French one, while others such as Austria, Czech Republic, and Switzerland[48] tend more, in this respect, to incriminate the use of a third party's repute, image, or products. In England,[49] no special principle exists for protection against parasitic acts, but this concept is clearly inherent to trademark law and 'passing off'.

Regardless of their definition, all these parasitic acts can be sanctioned as unfair behaviour, generally on the basis of unfair competition rules (for example, the Swiss LCD) such that in the majority of countries, non-competitors can be held to account for this type of behaviour.

Only the Luxembourg report[50] talks of the need for a competitive relationship in order to sanction unfair competition such as free riding.

Furthermore, the French and German reports[51] recall that free riding can also be based on provisions relating to trademarks of wide repute and well-known trademarks.

16.7 Infringement, Unfair Competition, and Free Riding

As outlined in the Czech Republic and Italian reports,[52] the choice of basis for the action depends on the circumstance in point.

Nevertheless, most reports outline the possibility for holders of an intellectual property right to base their action cumulatively in trademark law and unfair competition (or 'passing off' in England) when their trademark is at stake. In Sweden,[53] these two actions are brought before different courts.

[47] See *La Rocca*, Italy, Part II, Chap. 22, p. 6–7; *Decker & Decker*, Luxembourg, Part II, Chap. 23, pp. 7.

[48] See *Mosing & Handig*, Austria, Part II, Chap. 17, pp. 13–14; *Hajn*, Czech Republic, Part II, Chap. 18, p. 7; *Ghassemi*, Switzerland, Part II, Chap. 25, p. 7.

[49] See *Longstaff*, United Kingdom, Part II, Chap. 26, p. 17.

[50] See *Decker & Decker*, Luxembourg, Part II, Chap. 23, pp. 6–7.

[51] See *Arcelin et al.*, France, Part II, Chap. 19, p. 26; *Henning-Bodewig*, Germany, Part II, Chap. 20, p. 12.

[52] See *Hajn*, Czech Republic, Part II, Chap. 18, p. 7; *La Rocca*, Italy, Part II, Chap. 22, p. 7.

[53] See *Jute*, Sweden, Part II, Chap. 24, p. 12–13.

Only the Luxembourg report[54] clearly excludes the possibility of cumulative action on both these bases, recalling that in Luxembourg an action for unfair competition cannot be brought against a non-competitor.

Furthermore, under French law,[55] an infringement action and an action for unfair competition that fall within the jurisdiction of the same court when they are brought cumulatively, though they must not concern the same deeds.

Nevertheless, several contributors[56] highlight the fact that an action for unfair competition must not be considered as a substitute for an infringement action, which would enable a mark not protected by an intellectual property right to be afforded equivalent or greater protection than that afforded a protected mark.

In addition, the distinction between free riding, on the one hand, that solely sanctions behaviours between non-competitors and unfair competition, on the other, reserved for companies in a competitive situation, has yet to be made.

In France, the Commercial Chamber of the Court of Cassation does not apply it, and enables actions to be brought against non-competitors, and by extension any misconduct in the market, based on the general theory of unfair competition.

16.8 Conclusion and Policy Recommendations

After studying the national reports, it appears that even though conditions may vary by country, numerous ways exist to protect a company's identification elements from other companies that are not its competitors, whether via trademark law or other bases.

Thus, when the company holds a valid registered trademark, it may sometimes bring an infringement action against non-competitors, despite the principle of speciality, more particularly by taking into consideration some economical reality such as inter-brand partnerships, diversification of some company in the luxury area (for example, clothes and perfumes).

Furthermore, if the registered trademark enjoys sufficient repute, its holder may, as part of a specific liability action, incriminate the use without due cause in the course of trade of a mark that unduly takes advantage of the distinctive character or repute of the trademark or that damages these, for non-similar products or services.

In the event that the trademark has not been registered, the company may ask to benefit from the well-known trademark system in line with Article 6(b) of the Paris Convention, to counter the use of the same mark for similar products, provided that proof of a likelihood of confusion is shown.

[54] See *Decker & Decker*, Luxembourg, Part II, Chap. 23, p. 7.

[55] See *Arcelin et al.*, France, Part II, Chap. 19, pp. 25–26.

[56] See *Arcelin et al.*, France, Part II, Chap. 19, p. 27; *Decker & Decker*, Luxembourg, Part II, Chap. 23, p. 8; *Ghassemi*, Switzerland, Part II, Chap. 25, p. 13–14.

We have seen that the company's brand image, which is memorised by the public, is made up of various elements: if it is in respect of other intellectual property rights, the principle of speciality specific to trademark law does not apply.

However, is it possible to bring an action against a non-competitor company that reproduces a drawing or model or a creation covered by copyright?

We must overlook the existence of a likelihood of confusion, which in most cases is not required when assessing the infringement of these rights.

Such hypotheses are seldom, if ever, quoted in national reports. They seem to be rare, in actual fact.

Concerning a non-competitive situation, it seems that the application of the theory of unfair competition in its broadest sense, and more specifically that of free riding and/or civil liability according to country, is the most commonly used tool to protect against the unauthorised use of a trademark.

However, these concepts are very broad, and through the specific cases quoted by national reports, we can see that jurisdictions react differently according to the specific situations they face.

As long as a copy does not impair an exclusive right, it cannot be considered as improper in itself since freedom of trade must be preserved.

In this regard, we can quote Article 8.2 of the TRIPS[57] agreement, according to which:

> Appropriate measures, provided that they are consistent with the provisions of this Agreement, may be needed to prevent the abuse of intellectual property rights by right holders or the resort to practices which unreasonably restrain trade or adversely affect the international transfer of technology.

However, such copying becomes improper once fair trade use is no longer respected, once it is neither necessary nor accidental and thus results from a voluntary act or one that is indeed malicious.

Protection of brand image boils down to protecting an asset that is often essential to the company, that is to say the return that it is entitled to expect from often substantial and long-term investments it makes in order to build this image and then to promote it so that it symbolises a strong or visual identity that is spontaneously recognisable to consumers.

This undue misappropriation of other people's investment so as to take illegitimate advantage is one of the criteria of free riding.

In respect of non-competitor companies, it is essential that this strong identity exists and that, as part of judicial proceedings, proof of this is provided. Jurisdictions must be demanding as to the extent of this proof.

Without doubt, we will often be required to prove a level of awareness.

Next, the wrongdoing must be identified: as regards non-competitor companies, which we may say benefit from a sort of presumption of good faith, a degree of

[57] TRIPS agreement of 15 April 1994.

seriousness regarding this 'misappropriation' must be evident, and this must be demonstrably voluntary.

Returning to intellectual property rights, it is interesting to note that even in this area, Directive 2004/48/EC of 29 April 2004 on intellectual property rights seems to encourage Member States to take into account an act committed with full knowledge of the facts.

Thus, before widening the scope to compensation for damages though not punitive damages, Point 26[58] and Article 13[59] of the Directive go beyond strict reparable damage for harm effectively endured and refer to 'an infringer who engaged in an activity in the knowledge, or with reasonable grounds for knowing, that it would give rise to such an infringement'.

Illicit use should also be substantial in terms of the number of reproductions incriminated, the intensity of said uses, their visibility in the eyes of the public (websites, search engines, etc.), or their duration.

On such case, the injunction to stop these litigious acts should be obtained.

Next, we must attempt to characterise the harm endured by the company whose brand image has been misappropriated: as regards companies that are not in a competitive situation, quantifying this harm may be difficult or even impossible in the absence of a misappropriation of the customer base since there is no common customer base.

In that case however, should we thus require the presence of a likelihood of confusion or a likelihood of association, belief in the common origin of the products or services, or business links between the companies in question?

Even if the trend today is towards a diversification of activities, such a likelihood of confusion may seldom be proven or difficult to establish.

The current practices of sponsoring or partnership must be taken into account—for instance, a prêt-à-porter fashion company whose visual identity is strong accepts 'to fit out' a car with its identification elements, which are very well-known by the public.

Such a partnership, extolled to consumers, exists both because the public has knowledge of the company's image and because the company aims to further strengthen it.

This partnership has a certain economic interest since a common customer base exists: women who buy products by the prêt-à-porter company will also buy the city car fitted out in the colours of the initial company.

So what happens if a car manufacturer, which by hypothesis is a non-competitor of the prêt-à-porter company, reproduces the fashion company's image?

---

[58] Point 26 of Directive 2004/48/EC: With a view to compensating for the prejudice suffered as a result of an infringement committed by an infringer who engaged in an *activity in the knowledge, or with reasonable grounds for knowing, that it would give rise to such an infringement.*

[59] Article 13.1 of Directive 2004/48/EC: Member States shall ensure that the competent judicial authorities, on application of the injured party, order the infringer who knowingly, or with reasonable grounds to know, engaged in an infringing activity, to pay the rightholder damages appropriate to the actual prejudice suffered by him/her as a result of the infringement.

It would doubtlessly be specious to consider this use as purely accidental, because in reality, the car manufacturer most likely wants to take advantage of the partnership of which it is already aware.

However, is it reasonable to consider that the prêt-à-porter company would have grounds to act against the car manufacturer?

This is where other elements of harm can be brought into play: dilution of brand image, its debasement, trivialisation, loss of opportunity (denial of a possible partnership).

In other cases, impairment may occur to the reputation of the company whose brand image has been unduly reproduced.

In the first instance, in the absence of misappropriation of customer base, the harm endured by the holder of these rights must be characterised in another way.

As such, we could take as an example the car manufacturer using the brand image of the prêt-à-porter company without its authorisation, where the latter had not yet envisaged such a partnership.

In this case, harm could be seen to come from a loss of opportunity to be able to build such a partnership and a weakening of the attractive power of the brand image.

The reality of the injury could be challenged when the identification elements are reproduced together with the trademark of the car manufacturer, which is also often well-known.

We can also quote the example of 'ambush marketing', which can be defined as a business practice that aims to associate a company's trademark (or another distinctive mark) with an event (in most cases, a sporting event) without the consent of the organiser, so as to take advantage of the event's media impact.

In this case, we observe either use of a distinctive mark (for instance, the Olympic rings) or an image that is characteristic of the sporting event or reference to a non-existent partnership.

Such a practice is likely to harm the official sponsors of the event, who pay a license fee with a view to benefiting from rights of exclusivity.

The topic of ambush marketing was dealt with by the League in 2007, and further to his very exhaustive international report,[60] *Kobel* concluded that there was no need to enact specific legislation to sanction these practices, talking of the boundaries essential to freedom of trade and, more generally, fundamental freedoms.

At this time, regarding harm, we could also point out the introduction by Directive 2004/48/EC of 29 April 2004 on respecting intellectual property of the concept of "moral prejudice", which can be taken into account when compensating harm endured due to infringement.

[60] *Pierre Kobel*, ILCL International Report (2007): "Ambush Marketing too smart to be good? Should certain ambush practices be declared illegal and if so, which ones and under what conditions?".

Undeniably, this development must be considered insofar as the type of prejudice that may be compensated due to infringement is not just direct prejudice resulting purely from margin lost or profit forfeited.

As such, we can foresee consideration for prejudice that is no longer strictly based on financial impoverishment, as traditionally results from at least a potential loss of a customer base but now very clearly taking account of "prejudice to image", that is to say debasement, dilution or even trivialisation of the company's image.

However, even some of the elements that constitute a given prejudice that have just been evoked may be lacking.

In addition, it is perfectly conceivable that the non-competitor company may have unduly made gains by reproducing the brand image of another company, without ever observing any impoverishment whatsoever in the latter company.

In this case, it would be a matter of sanctioning a behaviour that is admittedly contrary to accepted business practice, by which its perpetrator can make undue gains though not actually causing harm to the initial company.

We may consider that it is competitors in the motor vehicle sector who endured harm: litigious actions have allowed an economic advantage to be built up based on an unfair act, since it was achieved not through investing but through copying others.

In tackling this issue, we touch on a broader question linked to the behaviour of economic players on the market: this is doubtlessly the point at which it becomes necessary to allow the initial company to act against a non-competitor company by acting as regulator, thus re-establishing equality of arms not on a given market but on the market in general.

These concepts must be able to be used in order to sanction the undue use or "theft" of a company's brand image by a non-competitor, under conditions that must be strictly assessed.

Ultimately, a company that has made substantial investments in order to build up a strong, identified brand image must be able to act against a non-competitor company that unduly misappropriates this image, if it appears that said misappropriation does not comply with fair trade uses, that is to say it does not appear to be accidental or necessary but rather voluntarily aims to achieve economic advantage without incurring the expenditure that it should have, if the initial company on the market did not have this well-known image, and this means that the image of said company is debased or diluted, its reputation or awareness is infringed upon, a likelihood of confusion as to the origin of the products or services is created, or the existence of economic links between the companies in question is inferred.

16.9 Resolution Adopted by LIDC

The brand image of an undertaking can comprise a variety of visual and/or verbal elements that may or may not be protected by specific intellectual property rights, such as trademarks, copyrights, industrial designs, identification of the company in the mind of the public, and representation of a substantial economic value, known in some jurisdictions as “goodwill”.

LIDC considers that such brand image generally deserves protection against misappropriation by a non-competitor.

A brand image may also be protected by other laws, such as laws against unfair competition (as provided for by the Paris Convention), passing off, or other torts, but specific regulation is neither necessary nor desirable.

The use of intellectual property rights may constitute a legal basis for this protection, and the current conditions for their implementation appear to be satisfactory both in terms of the right that may be invoked (for instance, well-known trademark or mark with a reputation) and evidence that must be produced to establish the nature and importance of the impairment and harm endured. Consequently, it does not appear necessary nor desirable to extend the scope of the protection of the trademark.

The protection of brand image against its use by a non-competitor undertaking should more generally be ensured when it becomes apparent that this use contravenes the principles of fair trade.

The undertaking that complains of such use should provide sufficient evidence of the existence of its brand image in the mind of consumers and the nature of the harm it suffers (for example, likelihood of confusion or of association, debasement, dilution), even if this is not quantifiable financially.

Remedies available should include injunctions and financial compensation, which may, in the absence of direct prejudice, take into account any undue gains made by the non-competitor undertaking.

Austria

17

Max W. Mosing and Christian Handig

17.1 Introduction

The legal action for trademark infringement is traditionally seen as a response to a third party's use of the sign that forms the trademark for goods or services that are identical (or similar) to those for which the trademark is registered, meaning for goods or services regarding which the two undertakings are, by definition, competing.

Similarly, unfair competition presupposes, *a priori*, as its name suggests (in the very text of the founding Treaty, the Paris Convention), a relation of competition.

However, although Article 10*bis* of the Paris Convention states that the following acts are to be prohibited, as constituting unfair competition, "all acts of such a nature as to create confusion by any means whatever the establishment, the goods, or the industrial or commercial activities, of *a competitor*", the following indent does not make any such requirement when it adds that "indications or allegations the use of which in the course of trade is liable to mislead the public as to the nature, the manufacturing process, the characteristics, the suitability for their purpose, or the quantity, of the goods" are to be prohibited.

Strikingly, in numerous continental European countries, case law has developed that condemns "parasitic acts", which do not necessarily imply competition between the person committing the parasitic practices and their victim or the existence of a risk of confusion.

In fact, while the regulation of competition has to be understood not only as a regulation of relations between competitors but as an element for the structuring of the market and while, significantly, the Court of Justice of the European Union sees the trademark as being an essential element of an undistorted system of

M.W. Mosing (✉)
Gassauer-Fleissner, Vienna, Austria
e-mail: m.mosing@gassauer.at

C. Handig
Chamber of Commerce, Vienna, Austria

P. Këllezi et al. (eds.), *Antitrust for Small and Middle Size Undertakings and Image Protection from Non-Competitors*, LIDC Contributions on Antitrust Law, Intellectual Property and Unfair Competition, DOI 10.1007/978-3-642-54000-4_17, © Springer-Verlag Berlin Heidelberg 2014

competition, it is perfectly legitimate to ask whether the undertaking should not seek protection, not only against its competitors that might use its trademark, distinctive signs, or other components of its image and identity but also against non-competing undertakings that act in a similar manner.

Recent decisions by the CJUE[1] seem to be oriented towards an extension of the scope of trademark rights, by enlarging the trademark's functions.

Thus, could or should an undertaking obtain such protection?

The question, as asked, requires a distinction between the protection of *distinctive signs* and the protection of *other elements* that are not covered by intellectual property rights.

17.2 The Status of the Brand Image

17.2.1 Legal Definition of the Brand Image

In Austria, the "brand image"[2] is not a legal notion. However, the "reputation of a trade mark" and its "image transfer" are legal notions in Austria.[3] Moreover, the "brand imitation marketing"[4] Article has recently become a legal notion in Austria.

17.2.2 The Notion of "Brand Image" Through Case Law or Academic Writing

There is no legal definition of "brand image". Neither the Austrian case law nor the Austrian legal academic writing developed a definition of the term.

However, the Austrian Business Administration/Marketing literature follows more or less *Kevin Lane Keller*'s term of "brand image", namely the psychological aspect of a brand experience, a symbolic construct created within the minds of people, consisting of all the information and expectations associated with a product, service, or the company(ies) providing them.[5]

[1] ECJ, case C-323/09, *Interflora Inc. and Interflora British Unit v Marks & Spencer plc et Flowers Direct Online Ltd.*, ECR 2011 I-8625 and ECJ, case C-487/07, *L'Oréal SA, Lancôme parfums et beauté & Cie SNC and Laboratoire Garnier & Cie v Bellure NV, Malaika Investments Ltd and Starion International Ltd.*, ECR 2009 I-5185.

[2] See definitions in Sect. 17.2.2.

[3] See Sect. 17.2.3.

[4] Cf. Article 6(2)(a) of Directive 2005/29/EC: "a commercial practice shall also be regarded as misleading if, in its factual context, taking account of all its features and circumstances, it causes or is likely to cause the average consumer to take a transactional decision that he would not have taken otherwise, and it involves: (a) any marketing of a product, including comparative advertising, which creates confusion with any products, trademarks, trade names or other distinguishing marks of a competitor."

[5] *Mayerhofer*, Markenimageforschung [2009].

17.2.3 The Legal Instruments Used to Defend the "Brand Image" and the Implementation of the Notion of the Competitive Relations

Although "brand image" is no legal notion and as such not protected under Austrian law, the "image transfer" of a brand (in the broadest sense, namely name, sign, trademark, etc) could be defended based on the following legal instruments, respectively Acts.

17.2.3.1 Protection of a Trademark—Sign: Slogan with Reputation

Section 10 of the Austrian Trade Mark Act[6] reads: "[…] (2) The proprietor of a registered trade mark shall also be entitled to prevent all third parties not having his consent from using in the course of trade any sign identical with, or similar to, the trade mark in relation to goods or services (Section 10a) which are not similar to those for which the trade mark is registered, where the latter has a reputation in Austria and where use of that sign without due cause takes unfair advantage of, or is detrimental to, the distinctive character or the repute of the trade mark. The reputation of the trade mark filed earlier shall be required to have existed at the latest on the day of the application for registration of the subsequent trade mark, or the date of priority or seniority claimed for the registration of the subsequent trade mark or at the time of creation of the other sign."

Consequently, the competitive relation between the involved undertakings is an aspect that could, but must not be, taken into consideration regarding the element of "unfair advantage": based on the Austrian case law, the use of an identical or similar sign as the one of a trade mark with reputation even for not identical or similar goods or services leads to the assumption of an unfair advantage, and the user has to show special circumstances that justify the use.[7] In other words, the user of a third party's trademark with reputation, who uses the sign only to focus the public's interest on his product or service, benefits from the reputation of that sign without having to make own efforts; consequently, the user takes unfair advantage of the reputation of another's trademark to promote the sale of own goods or services, whereas the competitive relation or the similarity of goods or services is of no relevance.

On the other hand, the reference to a third party product or sign and the use of its reputation is not always a violation of Sec 10(2) Austrian Trade Mark Act. Additional unfair elements are required, whereas—based on Austrian case law—indications are the use of an identical sign, the use in obstruction of the proprietor's marketing or exploitation of its trademark, and the obvious parasitism on the third party's reputation.[8]

---

[6] Austrian Trademark Act Federal Law Gazette 1970/260 as amended by Federal Law Gazette 2009/126.

[7] Austrian Supreme Court 17 Ob 28/08d.

[8] Austrian Supreme Court 4 Ob 110/10w.

Furthermore, the use of a third party's trademark with reputation in the form of a parody respectively in a humorous adoption can—in the light of the Austrian constitutional rights and freedoms—not be considered as an unfair exploitation if the conduct is an expression of artistic creativity or a contribution to a public discourse (trademark parody); however, this is not applicable if the use primarily serves the purpose to exploit the reputation of the trademark for marketing respectively to sell the own goods or services[9] or infringes the credit, the income, or the advancement of another person pursuant to Sec 1330 para 2 of the Austrian General Civil Code[10]: the use of well-known marketing slogans in parody against the dangers of tobacco products was considered to constitute an infringement of the trademark owner's credit, reputation, and commercial standing (here: "Nur ein Kamel geht meilenweit für eine Zigarette" ["Only a Camel goes for miles for a cigarette"]).

In balancing the interests in the context of a parody, it has to be considered, what the essential reason for the use is: the artistic or ironic contribution or, rather, commercial motives.[11] In our opinion, the case law applies too strict criteria in this context: pumpkin seeds were sold with blue icing under the sign "Styriagra" (a combination of "Styria"[12] and "Viagra"). The trademark Viagra is known as "the little blue pill". As the pumpkin seeds have no pharmaceutical implication and constitute simply "food", the reference to "Viagra" was intended to be witty. However, the Austrian Supreme Court was of the opinion that this reference was made primarily for commercial motives and thus a violation of the rights of the right holders.[13]

Please note that the Austrian Supreme Court issued a decision that, based on Section 1 of the Austrian Unfair Competition Act in combination with Sec 10 (2) Austrian Trade Mark Act, also non-registered marks with reputation are protected against the unfair exploitation of their distinctiveness and/or reputation,[14] whereas again the competitive relation is of no further relevance.

17.2.3.2 Protection from "Imitation Marketing"

Section 2(3) of the Austrian Unfair Competition Act[15] reads: "A commercial practice shall also be regarded as misleading if it is able to cause a market participant to take a transactional decision that he would not have taken otherwise, and which involves the following: 1. any marketing of a product, including

[9] Austrian Supreme Court 17 Ob 15/09v.

[10] Austrian Supreme Court 4 Ob 189/89.

[11] Austrian Supreme Court 4 Ob 119/10v.

[12] A federal state of the Republic of Austria.

[13] Austrian Supreme Court 17 Ob 15/09v.

[14] Austrian Supreme Court 4 Ob 212/11x.

[15] Austrian Unfair Competition Act Federal Law Gazette 1984/448 as last amended by Federal Law Gazette I 2007/79.

comparative advertising, which creates a danger of confusion with a product or sign of enterprise of a competitor. [. . .]"

The claimant must not be the holder or proprietor of the rights in the product or sign of enterprise: pursuant to Section 14 of the Austrian Unfair Competition Act, the following entities are entitled to raise an action in this regard[16]:

- any entrepreneur who manufactures or markets goods or services of the same or a similar kind (competitor);
- by associations to promote the economic interests of entrepreneurs, provided that such associations represent interests which are affected by the offence;
- the Federal Chamber of Labour;
- the Federal Economic Chamber;
- the Presidential Conference of the Austrian Chambers of Agriculture;
- the Austrian Trade Union Federation;
- the Feral Competition Authority; or
- the Society for Consumer Information[17]; or
- under specific circumstances, any of the bodies and organisations of another European Union Member State under Article 4(3) of Directive 98/27/EC.[18]

Consequently, the competitive relation between the undertakings involved in the proceeding might, but must not be, an aspect, which specially has to be taken into consideration. This is primarily the case if the claimant is a competitor basing its claim regarding a product or sign not on rights of its own.

On the other hand, as the "danger of confusion" refers to a product or sign of a competitor, a competitive relation between the proprietor or the holder of the rights in the product or sign and the one using those in marketing has to be given. Thus, the use by someone who is not a competitor does not fall under this provision. In this context, it is worth mentioning that the (older) Austrian case law provides for as so-called *ad hoc* competitive relation if non-competitors act in the course of business in a way to (unfairly) benefit from the other or harm the other, especially regarding the misuse of the good reputation of the other undertaking.[19] Nevertheless, we are of the opinion that the extension of the application of the prohibition of "Imitation Marketing" to non-competitors only via an "*ad hoc* competitive relation" does not meet the full harmonisation requirements of Directive 2005/29/EC.[20]

When assessing the likelihood of confusion in the field of "Imitation Marketing", it has to be asked whether the relevant average consumer might be of the

[16] Austrian Supreme Court 17 Ob 19/11k.

[17] *Verein für Konsumenteninformation.*

[18] Directive 98/27/EC of the European Parliament and of the Council of 19 May 1998 on injunctions for the protection of consumers' interests, OJ 1998 L 166, 51.

[19] Austrian Supreme Court 4 Ob 2200/96z.

[20] Directive 2005/29/EC of the European Parliament and of the Council of 11 May 2005 concerning unfair business-to-consumer commercial practices in the internal market and amending Council Directive 84/450/EEC, Directives 97/7/EC, 98/27/EC and 2002/65/EC of the European Parliament and of the Council and Regulation (EC) No 2006/2004 of the European Parliament and of the Council ('Unfair Commercial Practices Directive' OJ 2005 L 149, 22.

opinion that the product comes from a different company, which requires that the consumer is aware of the earlier sign of the competitor of the user.[21] Consequently, pursuant to recent Austrian case law, the earlier sign has to be a sign with reputation.[22] We are of the opinion that the requirement of reputation is too strict and not in line with the full harmonisation requirements of Directive 2005/29/EC and its approach towards consumer protection: in our opinion, there is no doubt that the sign/product has to have a certain standing on the market because otherwise there cannot be a factual likelihood of confusion on the market. The requirement of reputation however goes beyond such simple "awareness on the market". A consequence of such strict requirement, namely for reputation, could be that signs or products without such reputation, but that are still known by parts of the consumers, could be (mis)used for purposes of "Imitation Marketing". In the eyes of part of the consumers knowing that sign or product, a likelihood of confusion would exist, and still—because of the requested missing reputation on the (entire) market—Sec 2 (3) of the Austrian Unfair Competition Act would not be applicable. On the other hand, one has to note that the decision by the Austrian Supreme Court requiring reputation is consistent with the legal situation regarding trademarks or signs with reputation.

17.2.3.3 Misuse of Designations of an Enterprise

Section 9 of Austrian Unfair Competition Act reads: "(1) Any party who, in the course of business, uses any name, [registered] company name or special designation of an enterprise or publication not subject to Section 80 of the Copyright Act in a manner that it is likely to be confused with a name, [registered] company name or special designation rightfully used by another party, may be sued by the latter party to cease and desist [from such action].

(2) The user shall be liable to compensate the injured party for any damage if the user knew or was bound to know that the abusive use was likely to cause confusion.

(3) The special designation of an enterprise shall also include such business signs and other facilities designed to distinguish the enterprise from other enterprises, including but not limited to the presentation of goods, their packaging or enveloping and of stationery, which are by the market participants involved perceived as designations of the enterprise.

(4) Supplementary to any claims accruing from any violation of designation rights pursuant to Paras 1 and 3 above of this Federal Act, Section 150(1) and (2)b (reasonable consideration and surrender of profit) as well as Sections 151 (rendering of accounts) and Section 152(2) (entrepreneur's liability) of the Patent Act,[23] shall

---

[21] Austrian Supreme Court 17 Ob 26/11i.

[22] Austrian Supreme Court 17 Ob 22/11a; previous case law was of the opposite opinion: Austrian Supreme Court 7 Ob 14/10y.

[23] Austrian Patent Act, Federal Law Gazette 1970/259 as last amended by Federal Law Gazette 2009/135.

apply *mutatis mutandis*. Section 1489 of the General Civil Code[24] shall apply to all monetary claims and the claim for accounting. The limitation period for any and all such claims shall also be interrupted by an action for the rendering of accounts. [...]"

Section 9 of the Austrian Unfair Competition Act refers to "the course of business" but not to the competitive relation between the involved undertakings.[25] On the other hand, a likelihood of confusion is required to base claims on Section 9 of the Austrian Unfair Competition Act, which is more likely if the involved undertakings are active in the same or similar field of goods and services. Totally different fields of goods and services might be a reason for the exclusion of a likelihood of confusion.[26]

The injunctive relief requires that someone uses a corporate or trade name in a manner that is likely to cause confusion with the distinctive sign of another. However, Section 9 of the Austrian Unfair Competition Act is only applicable if the signs are used as marks or brands. Consequently, the use of other signs shall not be absolutely prohibited, but only under the named circumstances.[27]

The protection of special designations of an enterprise, including unique product features, etc, requires reputation of those special designations.[28]

17.2.3.4 Misuse of Names

Section 43 of the Austrian General Civil Code reads: "If a person's right to bear his/her name is denied or injured due to unauthorized use of his/her name (including assumed names and pseudonyms), this person may demand the omission and damages in case of culpability."

This provision does not apply to physically existing persons only but also to any legal entities like corporations or companies, which are seen to constitute the so-called "moral" persons according to Section 26 of the Austrian General Civil Code.

Pursuant to Austrian case law, the competitive relation is of no specific relevance when evaluating a violation of the right in names pursuant to Section 43 of the Austrian Civil Code. However, all circumstances have to be taken into account when evaluating the possible compromising of a name: Section 43 of the Austrian General Civil Code constitutes grounds for a defence claim if the legitimate interests of the name of the carrier are affected. Such an affection of interests is in place if there is a likelihood of confusion or if someone could have the (wrong) impression that there exist ideological or economic relations between the two identical or similar names used.[29]

[24] Austrian General Civil Code, JGS 1811/946 as last amended by Federal Law Gazette I 2012/68.

[25] Austrian Supreme Court 4 Ob 340/72; 4 Ob 341/81.

[26] Austrian Supreme Court 4 Ob 110/88.

[27] Austrian Supreme Court 4 Ob 290/98w.

[28] Austrian Supreme Court 17 Ob 28/11h.

[29] Austrian Supreme Court 17 Ob 44/08g.

17.2.3.5 Unauthorised Use of the Company Name ("*Firma*")

Section 37 of the Austrian Enterprise Book reads: "If a person's rights are injured by someone else's use of the company name without permission, this person may demand the omission of the use of this company name. Claims for damages under other provisions shall remain unaffected."

The violation of a Company Name is not bound to any competitive relation between the involved undertakings. However, again, a competitive relation makes it more likely to impinge upon the rights of the proprietor of the Company Name.

17.2.3.6 Protection of "Public Image" of a Natural Person

Section 16 of the Austrian General Civil Code reads: "Everyone has innate rights, based on rationality, and is therefore regarded as a person [. . .]"

In connection with Section 16 of the Austrian General Civil Code, the competitive relation between the involved undertakings is of no relevance.

17.2.3.7 Protection of "Title of a Work"

Section 80 of the Federal Act on Copyright of Works of Literature and Arts and Related Rights [Austrian Copyright Act][30] reads: "(1) In the course of business a title, a designation of a work of literature or art or a presentation of works must not be used for other works in a manner that is likely to cause confusion. (2) Paragraph 1 shall apply also to works of literature and art which do not enjoy copyright protection of this law."

In connection with Section 80 of the Austrian Copyright Act, the competitive relation between the involved undertakings is of no relevance. However, acting in the course of business is required.

17.3 The Link Between the Rule of Speciality Applicable in Trademarks Law and the Possibility to Act Against Non-Competitors

17.3.1 The Link Between the Rule of Speciality and Competitive Relations

As trademark rights can be enforced without actually having used the trademark for the respective goods or services, in practice the principle of speciality must not have a direct connection to a competitive relation. However, in practice, most trademark disputes—even based on non-used trademarks—are between competitors: the list of goods and services in the trademark application already implies at least a "potential completion" in the regarding field of goods and services. However,

[30] Federal Act on Copyright of Works of Literature and Arts and Related Rights, Federal Law Gazette 1936/111 as last amended by Federal Law Gazette I 2010/58.

after the grace period, it is likely that trademark rights can generally, in the light of the list of goods and services, only be enforced against competing undertakings.

Furthermore, as shown above, the competitive relation is (except regarding Section 2 para 3 of the Austrian Unfair Competition Act) actually of no necessity to enforce the rights in a trademark or sign with reputation, respectively the right in a name.

17.3.2 Influence on the Rules of Civil Liability

In Austria, registered trademark rights may be opposed to the use of the trademark by a non-competing undertaking in the following cases:

- enforcement of the rights in trademarks within the grace period,
- enforcement of the rights in trademarks with reputation,[31]
- claim by a proprietor based not on Section 10(2) of the Austrian Trade Mark Act but on "Imitation Marketing".[32]

Please note that pursuant to the Austrian case law, the "general (tort) clause" of the Austrian Unfair Competition Act shall not be used to overcome the limits of legal protection for trademarks with reputation.[33]

However, the Austrian Unfair Competition Act can—respectively shall—be applied to cases where special provisions of the Unfair Competition Act are violated regardless of a possible interference with trademark rights,[34] e.g. "Imitation Marketing" in terms of Section 2(3)(1) of the Austrian Unfair Competition Act.[35]

17.4 Trademark, "Economy" of the Trademark, and Relation of Competition

17.4.1 The Liability of a Non-Competitor Who Uses a Previous Trademark "Outside Business"

A trademark infringement requires the use of the sign in the course of trade (Section 52 *et seq.* in connection with Section 10 of the Austrian Trade Mark Act). Thus, the trademark has to be used in a "business context"; furthermore, the trademark has to be used as a trade sign. The Austrian case law sees both requirements fulfilled when using trademarks as *Adwords*.[36]

[31] See Section 10(2) of the Austrian Trade Mark Act in Sect. 17.2.3.1.

[32] Cf. Austrian Supreme Court 17 Ob 26/11i; see Section 2(3)(1) of the Austrian Unfair Competition Act in Sect. 17.2.3.2.

[33] Austrian Supreme Court, 4 Ob 38/08d.

[34] Austrian Supreme Court 17 Ob 25/08p.

[35] Austrian Supreme Court 17 Ob 26/11i.

[36] Austrian Supreme Court 17 Ob 3/10f.

As shown above, Section 43 and 16 of the Austrian Civil Code ("misuse of names" and "protection of 'public image' of a natural person") do not require any business context. Therefore, if a "brand" is also a name or part of the 'public image' of a natural person, the Austrian positive law provides for legal grounds to raise claims against the "unfair" use of such name, sign, or image, even "outside business".

On the other hand, as the above-named provisions of the Austrian Trade Mark Act, the Austrian Unfair Competition Act, and the Austrian Copyright Act require in any case acting in the course of business, those provisions are not applicable to cases being actually "outside business". However, the Austrian case law—especially regarding unfair competition—sees an acting "outside business" only in extraordinary cases: any activity, which intends to promote any business purpose, is considered to be acting in the course of trade/business,[37] also promoting the business of a third party[38] or acting to promote future activities in the course of business.[39] Consequently, in general, whenever an advantage or damage of an undertaking based on an unfair practice occurs, it is likely that the Austrian courts would consider an acting to be in course of business and not "outside business".

17.4.2 The Future of the Community Case Law Regarding the Grounds of Trademarks Infringement

As the trademark functions stated by the CJEU (identification of origin, guarantee of quality, communication, investment, and advertising) have not been completely defined, this approach seems like the renewal of the traditional problem of how to draw the borders of an infringement. However, we are of the opinion that such test of the undermining of one of the (hopefully in the future well-defined) trademark functions could lead to a more systematic and therefore more predictable assessment of trademark infringements.

17.5 Other Distinctive Signs

17.5.1 Examples of the Liability of a Non-Competitor Who Uses Other Signs as Company Names, Brand Names

As mentioned above, concrete examples of the liability of a non-competitor that uses other signs as company names are the following:
- brand names, Section 9 of the Austrian Unfair Competition Act;
- Section 43 of the General Civil Code;

[37] Austrian Supreme Court, 4 Ob 130/10m.

[38] Austrian Supreme Court, 4 Ob 105/99s.

[39] Austrian Supreme Court, 4 Ob 225/01v.

- Section 1330 of the General Civil Code;
- Section 37 of the Austrian Commercial Code, and
- Section 80 of the Austrian Copyright Act.

17.5.2 Examples of the Liability of a Non-Competitor That Uses Domain Names

It is worth mentioning that domain name disputes have had no influence on the content or interpretation of the law: as the relation of competition is generally not a requirement of an infringement of the above-named provisions [except Section 2 of the Austrian Unfair Competition Act ("Imitation Marketing")], the competitive relation is also in connection with domain names of no specific relevance. However, as a competitive relation was a necessary element to base claims on the (former) Austrian Unfair Competition Act, the Austrian case law referred in several domain name cases to a so called *ad hoc* competitive relation when there was no direct competitive relation between the domain grabber and the right holder in place.[40]

The Austrian case law regarding domain names has always taken the principle of specialty of trademark law into account: the mere registration or delegation of a trademark as a domain name cannot be evaluated as a trademark infringement. Relevant for assessing whether the use of a sign in terms of Section 10 of the Austrian Trade Mark Act is in place and whether this leads to a likelihood of confusion is the content of the websites that is provided under the website to be reached under the domain name.[41]

As due to the principle of speciality in (more and more) cases the Austrian Trade Mark Act is not applicable, the claims in those cases have been based on the above-named provisions regarding other distinctive signs, especially Section 43 of the Austrian Civil Code: the use of a name as a domain name by an unauthorised person generally violates the legitimate interest of the name holder, independent of the actual content of the website operated under the domain name.[42] On the other hand there has to be a balancing of interests, especially regarding the use of names for "criticising domains".[43]

As the (extensive) Austrian case law on domain name disputes shows, there is no (urgent) need for special treatments of such cases. However, on an international level, one specific issue remains: if the defendant is not under the jurisdiction of Austria and hence a(n Austrian) court decision cannot be enforced against the defendant, there should be possibilities to enforce the respective rights against infringers "hiding" in jurisdictions where the court decisions cannot be enforced.[44] However, also in those

[40] See, e.g., Austrian Supreme Court 4 Ob 139/01x.

[41] Austrian Supreme Court, 17 Ob 6/11y.

[42] Austrian Supreme Court 4 Ob 197/10i.

[43] Austrian Supreme Court 17 Ob 2/09g.

[44] See UDRP below.

cases and when .at-Domains are involved, the claimant may request from the .at-Registrar (www.nic.at) to cancel the delegation of an illegal domain name.[45]

17.5.3 Same Question Concerning Meta-Tags and Sponsored Links

Answers are the same as that in the domain name disputes. However, the Austrian case law stresses the balancing of interests in connection with the use of meta-tags: the use of a third party's trademark as a meta-tag does not violate the trademark rights if the user has a legitimate interest to use the trademark and if the use does not cause inaccurate impressions. Such legitimate interest is, for example, in place where the website with the meta-tag provides information in direct connection with the products marked with the trademark—here, information about the sale of patents of the user to the trademark holder.[46]

17.5.4 Possible Implication of Alternative Dispute Resolution Systems

Please note that the Austrian Alternative Dispute Resolution Centre for .at-domain names (.at-ADRC) stopped its work on October 31, 2008. Background was that—for several reasons—right holders preferred to raise actions with the Austrian courts than to file complaints with the .at-ADRC.

As the UDRP generally refers to trademarks or service marks (although case law extended it to names used like marks), we are of the opinion that domain name ADR has not had particular implications regarding the infringement of other distinctive signs in Austria. The Austrian case law also does, in any case, not even make reference to the evaluation under the UDRP as the necessary requirements are entirely different.[47] Consequently, the Austrian case law does not see any implication of the UDRP on the Austrian legal situation—not even for domain name disputes.

It is worth mentioning that the Austrian case law does not provide for the transfer of a disputed domain name to the claimant. Furthermore, the Dispute Notice with the National top level domain ".at" is deleted as soon as the domain name is cancelled, and thus everybody (and not only the claimant) can apply for the delegation of the then free domain name. Consequently, the claim for transfer under the UDRP is an advantage.

Finally, it is worth mentioning that the costs of a successful UDRP proceeding can be claimed and enforced by the right holder with the Austrian courts.[48]

---

[45] Cf. Austrian Supreme Court, 4 Ob 176/01p.

[46] Austrian Supreme Court 4 Ob 308/00y.

[47] Cf. regarding <schladming.com> the UDRP proceeding and Austrian Supreme Court, 17 Ob 16/10t.

[48] Austrian Supreme Court, 4Ob42/04m.

17.6 "Reprehensible" Conduct and Lack of Competitive Relations

17.6.1 Unfair Competition by Non-Competing Undertakings

Concerning the issue of competition, none but, besides the above-mentioned "Imitation Marketing" regarding a sign or product of a competitor, one regulation of the Austrian Unfair Competition Act includes the premise of "competitive purposes"; this one is Section 7 of the Austrian Unfair Competition Act, dealing with the "Degradation of an Enterprise".[49]

Firstly, if a non-competing undertaking or product creates doubts concerning its identity, the reason may well be an exploitation of a good reputation, which is a fact of the case of Unfair Commercial Practices.[50]

Secondly, it might also mislead some market participants, especially consumers. Thus, this could be subsumed as a fact of the case of a Misleading Commercial Practice.[51]

Thirdly, there might be a misuse of designations of an enterprise involved, which would constitute a violation of Section 9 of the Austrian Unfair Competition Act.

Austrian case law deems the exploitation of a good reputation as an unfair commercial practice, irrespective of the competing relation, e.g., this is the case if a person "exploits parasitic the good reputation of a famous and attractive designations, whose popularity has establish at considerable cost and effort of its right holder". Thereby, the offender "exploits the good reputation under circumstances which are exceptional and therefore unfair, if the offender does so for commercial purposes to promote his own products or uses the designation for his own products in a way which will damage the good reputation".[52]

[49] Section 7 of the Austrian Unfair Competition Act reads: "(1) Any party who for competitive purposes alleges or disseminates facts about the enterprise of another, about the person of the owner or manager of the enterprise or about the goods or services of another which may be detrimental to the business of the enterprise or the credit standing of its owner shall be liable [to pay] damages to the injured [party] unless such facts are demonstrably true. The injured [party] may file a claim to cease and desist from alleging or disseminating the facts. The injured [party] may furthermore demand retraction and publication of the retraction. (2) Where confidential information is concerned and the disclosing or receiving party has a legitimate interest in such information, any claim to cease and desist shall be permissible only when the facts have been alleged or disseminated contrary to the truth. Any claim for payment of damages may be asserted only when the disclosing party knew or was bound to know the untruthfulness of the facts."

[50] See Section 1 of the Austrian Unfair Competition Act.

[51] See Section 2 of the Austrian Unfair Competition Act.

[52] Austrian Supreme Court 4 Ob 212/11x.

Besides the rights conferred by the legal instruments of the European Union for trademarks (see Regulation 2009/207/EC[53] and Directive 2008/95/EC[54]), in Austria there are subsidiary remedies against unfair commercial practices. As mentioned, such practices may be

- a parasitic exploration of the good reputation[55];
- a misleading commercial practice, including "Imitation Marketing"[56];
- misuse of Designations of an Enterprise.[57]

The case law deems the exploitation of a good reputation as an unfair commercial practice, e.g. as indicated above the Austrian Supreme Court applies the provision concerning misleading commercial practice (Section 2 of the Austrian Unfair Competition Act) to cases of "Imitation Marketing", e.g. if a product packaging might mislead consumers about the product's origin.[58,59]

In cases dealing with the distribution of spare parts or accessory items for foreign products, the Austrian Supreme Court ruled that a reference to the main product is fair only if the impression of a common origin is not awakened. For this purpose, the original trademark or the original designation has to be used for information only; therefore, the graphic element of the original designation must not be used.[60]

By and large, the Austrian case law concerning unfair competition/unfair business practice is aligned with the case law applicable to trademarks. And this uniform Austrian case law makes results pretty predictable and is therefore appreciated.

17.7 The Links Between Infringement, Unfair Competition, and Parasitism in a Legal Action

Please note that pursuant to the Austrian Civil Procedural Law in one action, the respective claims can be based on any legal ground. Consequently, the claim for omission and damage for exploitation of a third party's sign or product can be based on all the above-named legal grounds at the same time—the court has to make its own legal evaluation if the claims can stand on one or even more of the grounds. Consequently, the claimant has the possibility to base its claim on trademark rights

[53] Council Regulation 207/2009/207/EC of 26 February 2009 on the Community trade mark (codified version) OJ 2009 L 78, p. 1.

[54] Directive 2008/95/EC of the European Parliament and of the Council of 22 October 2008 to approximate the laws of the Member States relating to trade marks (Codified version) OJ L 299, 25.

[55] Section 1(1)(1) of the Austrian Unfair Competition Act.

[56] Section 2 of the Austrian Unfair Competition Act.

[57] Section 9 of the Austrian Unfair Competition Act.

[58] Austrian Supreme Court 17 Ob 7/09t.

[59] See also Sect. 17.2.3.2.

[60] See, e.g., Austrian Supreme Court 17 Ob 28/08d.

and, alternatively, on unfair competition, including parasitic practices, especially "Imitation Marketing".

However, as mentioned above, generally the Austrian Unfair Competition Act is only applicable if the Austrian Trade Mark Act does not apply for whatever reason: the Austrian Unfair Competition Act shall not undermine the limits of legal protection for trademarks with reputation.[61] Nevertheless, the Austrian Unfair Competition Act can be applied to cases where special provisions of the Unfair Competition Act are violated, regardless of a possible interference with trademark rights,[62] e.g. "Imitation Marketing" in terms of Section 2(3)(1) of the Austrian Unfair Competition Act.[63]

Also regarding the competence of the courts, it makes in most cases no differences which of the above legal grounds the claimant chooses to base its claim regarding the exploitation of a sign or product by a non-competitor. Exceptions may be the claims exclusively based on Section 43 or 16 the Austrian Civil Code ("Misuse of Names" or "Protection of 'Public Image' of a natural person"). However, if claims are based on trademark rights, violation of unfair competition, or unfair trade practices, the same courts are competent to decide the case.

It is also worth mentioning that in Austria it has no effect on the court fees or on the compensation of legal costs if the claimant bases its claim on several legal grounds and the court decides that such a claim is only justified regarding one of the grounds. Consequently, also from this perspective, there is no need for the claimant to base claims only on one specific legal ground.

None of the provisions requires a direct-competitive relation.[64] However, generally it appears that the claim based on a trademark with reputation is the most adapted to apprehend offending behaviour of non-competitors.

Generally, for the above-mentioned reasons, there is no substitution from trademark law claims to unfair competition law claims for example.

Unfair competition and similar proceedings are mainly aimed to claim "cease and desist orders" from the court; such may also contain further claims like publication of the award, revocation of statements, damages etc. and are very often combined with applications for preliminary injunctions.

Conclusions and Policy Recommendations

The Austrian laws and the Austrian case law provide for protection of an undertaking against the use by non-competing undertakings of their trademark, distinctive signs, and other components of their image and identity, under certain circumstances.

[61] Austrian Supreme Court, 4 Ob 38/08d.

[62] Austrian Supreme Court, 17 Ob 25/08p.

[63] Austrian Supreme Court, 17 Ob 26/11i.

[64] Cf. regarding "Imitation Marketing".

Pursuant to the Austrian Trade Mark Act, a competitive relation, in the broadest sense, is not required within the grace period. Thereafter, it is likely that the proprietor of the trademark and the third party user are actually competitors. Due to the principle of specialty trademark, rights can only be enforced in situations of double identity (identical sign and identical goods or services) or in situations of similarity causing a likelihood of confusion (identical signs for similar goods or services, similar signs for identical goods or services, or similar signs for similar goods). An exception is the rights in a trademark with reputation pursuant to Section 10(2) of the Austrian Trade Mark Act,[65] in which case (a) no factual competitive relation and (b) no likelihood of confusion are required for a successful claim under this provision.

Except the fact that the Austrian case law is rather strict regarding "trademark parodies", we are of the opinion that regulations and case law are rather balanced, not to hinder the marketing of new trademarks on the one hand and not to create a situation where trademarks (with reputation) are unfairly exploited on the other hand.

We also agree with the approach that an actual competitive relation is not necessary regarding the exploitation of a trademark with reputation. However, we want to state that the scope of trademarks' protection with reputation should remain distinct and should not become excessive: if every use is considered to be an unfair advantage, the numerous—especially national—trademarks with reputation would cover nearly the entire possible scope of protection. Thus, every new sign is in (imminent) unpredictable danger of an alleged or possible infringement, especially as (especially internationally conducted) similarity search results are not in the position to show this specific "extensive protection" of numerous trademarks with reputation.

Inter alia, Section 9 of the Austrian Unfair Competition Act provides for the protection of unregistered signs against the use in the course of business if this leads to a likelihood of confusion. Also special designations of an enterprise—including unique product features—are subject to this protection, however, only if they have required secondary meaning.

We agree with the approach that the competitive relation is not necessary in connection with Section 9 of the Austrian Unfair Competition Act as otherwise its scope would be too limited. On the other hand (a) the likelihood of confusion and its application by the Austrian case law and (b) the requirement of a secondary meaning of unique product features set limits that the protection does not become too extensive.

In our opinion also regarding the protection (a) of Company Names pursuant to Section 37 of the Austrian Commercial Code and (b) of Title of Work pursuant to Section 80 of the Austrian Copyright Act, the Austrian case law provides for a good balance of interests involved.

[65] Cf. Article 5(2) Directive 2008/95/EC.

Neither the protection of names (Section 43 of the Austrian Civil Code) nor the "public image" of a (natural) person (Section 16 of the Austrian Civil Code) nor the credit of a person/commercial standing (Section 1330 of the Austrian Civil Code) requires competitive relations or the course of business. Consequently, those signs are protected against misuse by non-competitors. Again, a test has to be conducted on a case-by-case basis to balance the interest involved. By and large, we think that the Austrian case law usually achieves the right balance between protection and freedom.

Summarising, in Austria an undertaking can obtain protection against the use of its trademark, distinctive signs, and other components of its images and identities by non-competing undertakings, as a competing relation is not necessity for most of the relevant provisions. Furthermore, in Austria protection against the misuse of names and images/identities can be obtained regardless of whether it happens in the course of business. In our opinion, such protection is justified, but it must always be balanced against the interests of users, e.g. regarding the freedom of expression, especially in cases of parodies and regarding the freedom to market new signs and—last not least—regarding the predictability of the legal situation when using a sign.

Czech Republic 18

Petr Hajn

18.1 Status of Brand Image

The English-Czech dictionary offers the following Czech equivalents for the term "brand image": (1) image of a trademark (*image obchodní značky event. pověst obchodní značky*) (2) image of a product that is associated with the name of a trademark (*pověst výrobku, který je spojován s obchodní značkou*). (3) sound of trademark (*pověst obchodní značky event. renomé obchodní značky*). The first equivalent seems to be the best one. For the sake of simplification, the term "brand image" will be used in the text that follows.

18.1.1 The Legal Definition of Brand Image

Before examining whether the concept of "brand image" is a legal notion or not under Czech law, we need to see what can be understood under the term "legal notion". If we understand "legal notion" in our case as one of the aforementioned Czech equivalents of "brand image" contained in the wording of a specific statute, the answer will probably be negative. The term "trademark with good reputation in the Czech Republic" might be close to "brand image" within the Czech legal system: it is used in the Czech Act on Trademarks; however, in a more specific sense, it is understood as the repute or renown of a trademark. "Brand image" seems to have a slightly different content and, above all, a broader and more general scope.

Neither the case law nor academic authorities hint at a single, generally recognised definition of "brand image" or, as the case may be, its possible Czech translations. However, the case law and the academic writing do refer to a notion that can be labelled as "brand image", usually in relation to cases in which the rights

P. Hajn (✉)
Metropolitan University Prague, Brno, Czech Republic
e-mail: petr.hajn@law.muni.cz; petrhajn@volny.cz

P. Këllezi et al. (eds.), *Antitrust for Small and Middle Size Undertakings and Image Protection from Non-Competitors*, LIDC Contributions on Antitrust Law, Intellectual Property and Unfair Competition, DOI 10.1007/978-3-642-54000-4_18,

to a sign of a specific entity were violated and the administrative or court proceedings aim to draw the legal consequences of that violation (especially if the argument relies on the alleged disturbance of the distinctive capacity of a trademark, a phenomenon called "dilution" of a trademark).

Brand image is taken into consideration, expressly or implicitly, in unfair competition disputes, including, without limitation, disputes relating to rights to a sign. One of the features of unfair competition is its capacity to cause damage to competitors, consumers, and other customers. Damage is deemed to include potential infringement of immaterial values (repute or prestige) and, by extension, cases in which another entity's "brand image" is damaged or misused. The legal instruments to protect these values include cease and desist actions, claims for the remedy of a defective state, actions for adequate satisfaction (payable in kind and in monies) and for the surrender of unjust enrichment.

The competitive aspect of trademark disputes is touched upon under Sect. 18.2. The current wording of the law and the case law dictates that competitive aspects be taken more seriously in some trademark disputes, compared to the approach employed previously. The decision of the High Court in Prague file no. 7 A 4/2000[1] contained a general direction that the registration proceedings take some account of the requirements of unfair competition law. The reasoning of the decision made reference to the rules binding upon the accession to an international treaty, namely the Paris Convention. The court came to the conclusion that administrative authorities could not refuse to comply with these rules without special reasons, if only due to the obligation of the Czech Republic to ensure that other members of the union be effectively protected against unfair competition, as indicated in Article 10 of the Paris Convention. The reasoning of the decision followed up on this conclusion as follows: "*There is no doubt... that the cited Article 10 of the [Paris Convention] has been reflected in our legislation primarily through the provisions of the Commercial Code. On the other hand, we cannot ignore that the obligation ensuing from this article of the international treaty must be taken into account in trademark proceedings, too, namely as an interpretation rule when we consider whether the protection guaranteed by the convention is not denied by the registration of a sign or trademark that was "alienated", as asserted by the claimant*".

[1] Published in Horáček, R. et al. Zákon ochranných známkách. Zákon o ochraně označení původu a zeměpisných označení. Zákon o vymáhání práv z průmyslového vlastnictví. Komentář. [*Act on Trademarks. Act on the Protection of Designations of Origin and Geographic Signs. Act on Enforcement of Industrial Property Rights. Commentary*.] 2nd ed. Prague: C.H.Beck, 2004, p. 79. A decision of the Industrial Property Office dated 21 February 1996 (OZ 70130–92) already required that the Office take all the circumstances of the case into account within registration proceedings, including, without limitation, the provisions of international industrial property treaties signed by the Czech Republic. See Jakl, L., in Horáček, R. et al. Zákon ochranných známkách. Zákon o ochraně označení původu a zeměpisných označení. Zákon o vymáhání práv z průmyslového vlastnictví. Komentář, p. 52.

18.2 Trademark, Principle of Specialty, and Competitive Relationship

Czech law and Czech case law originally put an emphasis on differences between the criteria used in trademark law and in unfair competition law. The decisions made before the second world war stated that the "*registration of a trademark, although duly obtained, is of formal nature only, and decisions on rights to trademarks are formal only.... The person entitled to use a trademark may use its formal title in the interest of higher material justice only within the boundaries of fair competition and good morals; however, it may not misuse its right in order to pursue unfair conduct and to damage material rights*". *In addition to that, it was stated that "trademark law must be interpreted so as to never contradict the principle of good competitive morals*". These decisions and their heritage were relied upon in Decision of the High Court in Prague R 3 Cmo 1446/94, which was confirmed as a decision of essential importance when it was published as Decision No. 51 in the Collection of Decisions and Positions No. 8/1996, p. 278.[2] Under this decision, conduct against good competitive morals, and thus unfair competitive conduct, may include the use of a registered trademark.

A later decision of the High Court in Prague R 3 Cmo 109/96 stated the following: "*If, as asserted in the claim, the right of a trademark owner has been violated by another trademark holder using the trademark in compliance with its registration (in favour of the latter trademark holder), the claim, which invokes the applicable provision of the Trademark Act, cannot be satisfied. However, the foregoing does not rule out that the court may come to the conclusion that although the user uses a certain sign in full compliance with a registered trademark, this usage of the sign or, as the case may be, the conduct within which the sign is being used, constitutes unfair competitive conduct.*"

The current legislation and case law aims at minimising the frequency of cases in which various legal resolutions would coexist in trademark law and in unfair competition law, especially where a competitive aspect, which is however interpreted quite broadly (see below), may be at play.

If we accept a quite narrow definition of competitors as parties active in the same market segment that manufacture the same or substitutable goods, we have to define "non-competitors" quite broadly. These "non-competitors" are protected, in terms of their rights to signs and other titles, primarily under the institute of "opposition proceedings" under Section 7 of the Czech Act on Trademarks.[3] The grounds for objections defined therein are based on the EU trademark legislation, the Paris Convention, and the Agreement Establishing the WTO.

---

[2] Text of the decision in Macek, J. Rozhodnutí ve věcech obchodního jména a nekalé soutěže. [*Decisions in Maters Relating to Business Names and Unfair Competition.*] Prague: 2000, C.H. Beck, p. 78 ff.

[3] Act No. 441/2003 Coll., as amended.

We will now examine whether Czech law includes a provision protecting "well-known trademark" or "trademark with reputation" and, if so, the connection between such a rule, the competitive link between the undertakings at stake, and the usual condition that one undertaking takes undue advantage of the distinctive character or repute of the other's trademark or the damage caused to it.

The provisions for the opposition proceedings and the case law protect earlier trademarks with repute in the Czech Republic or in the EU and also protect earlier well-known trademarks even where they are not to be used for the same class of products or services, i.e. not in a relationship of immediate competition.

The meaning and importance of the opposition proceedings were described by the Municipal Court in Prague in is Decision file no. 8 Ca 58/2004, which concentrated on the purpose and the meaning of opposition proceedings and rejected their formalistic construction. The Decision understood the provisions on opposition as a "*rule that should serve primarily to avoid granting protection to signs that might benefit from the repute or the distinctive character of existing trademarks established on the market and that might dilute their protection and thus damage their proprietor, and not as a rule that should serve to assign a certain sign to a single entity that itself derives its title from earlier rights of someone else, and thus to create a monopoly position for that entity on the market.*"[4]

The general clause against unfair competition may also be used in relation to well-known trademarks where trademark law protection would be unavailable. This applies despite the language contained in the general clause against unfair competition that refers to "conduct in competition".[5] Indeed, that language only means the usage of typical competitive means (e.g., advertisement and signs) and not conduct aimed against an immediate competitor. Conduct in competition may also include conduct whereby a party typically aims to achieve a competitive goal (competitive advantage); this conduct may also cause harm to another competitor (i.e., another undertaking involved in a competitive process). For more information, one can refer to the 19 April 1995 Decision of the High Court in Prague, file no. 3 Cmo 3287/94, which states that *competition cannot be restricted to rivalry between directly competing manufacturers or service providers.*

18.3 Trademark, Trademark "Economy", and Competitive Relationship

In many cases, the distinction between business activities and activities "outside business" is very difficult. Section 41 of the Czech Commercial Code, which expressly stipulates that competitors do not have to be necessarily entrepreneurs, is the essential provision of Czech unfair competition law. Similarly, one can point attention to the term "competition", which has a broader meaning than "business",

[4] See Horáček, R., work cited above, p. 113.

[5] See Section 44(1) of the Commercial Code.

as the latter is understood in Czech (e.g., charity organisations may compete for donations, and their competition may be based on unfair practices with which the trademark proprietor would not want to be associated).

Decision O-198168 of the Czech Industrial Property Office dated 6 March 2006 rejected an application for a trademark entitled POST COITUM (applied for in numerous classes including, without limitation, toys and games, food and beverages, cosmetic products etc.). In the first instance proceedings, the application was rejected as it was found to contradict public order and good morals. The body of appeal did confirm the rejection, albeit on other grounds: it came to the conclusion that the "sign that is the subject-matter of the application may not be registered in the trademarks registry because it is in its nature incapable of distinguishing between the registered products and services originating from other undertakings, as assumed by the provision of Section 1 of Act No. 441/2003 Coll., on Trademarks, and thus this sign alone cannot achieve the fundamental function of a trademark".[6]

18.4 Other Distinctive Signs

Section 19b of the Czech Civil Code grants general protection to the names of legal entities. These names also enjoy protection against unauthorised infringements of their repute under the same provision.

Section 8 f. of the Czech Commercial Code covers the "business name", the name given to businesses registered with the Commercial Register. Section 10 stipulates that the business name may not be interchangeable with the name of another business and may not cause confusion. Within its provisions for unfair competition, Section 47 of the Commercial Code condemns "causing a risk of confusion", which may consist in the use of the business name or name of an individual or a special sign, which has already been rightfully used by another competitor, or the use of special signs of an undertaking or a special sign of products, performances, or business materials of an undertaking that are deemed characteristic for a specific undertaking or enterprise.

For legal consideration purposes, domain names can be deemed to constitute a "special sign" under the aforementioned provision of Section 47 of the Czech Commercial Code that condemns causing a risk of confusion. It may collide with other signs (typically trademarks or business names), and disputes relating to unfair competition take account of all the criteria for the legal qualification of "unfair competition". One can imagine that the domain name may infringe public or public interests without the case having competitive aspects.

[6] Published in Horáček, R. Macek, J. Sbírka správních a soudních rozhodnutí ve věcech průmyslového vlastnictví. [*Collection of Administrative and Court Decisions Relating to Industrial Property.*] Prague: C.H.Beck, 2007, p. 122.

The consideration of domain names is guided by the fundamental postulate of unfair competition law and perhaps law in general—"all depends on the circumstances of the specific case". In this respect, Czech courts state—in line with Directive of European Parliament and Council 2005/29/EC and with the case law of the Court of Justice—that "*the average internet user … can be seen as an informed "consumer" who is, based on his or her experience, well aware of the importance of every character, number, symbol in any internet address*." However, this does not mean that even this Internet user could not be confused by specific conduct or, as the case may be, that he or she can dare to do everything on the Internet.[7]

Disputes pertaining to meta tags or sponsored links are governed by similar principles.

Alternative systems of resolution of domain name disputes have been adopted, and decisions made thereon, by the Arbitration Court of the Economic Chamber and the Agrarian Chamber of the Czech Republic. The weight, if any, given to competitive relationships in these disputes will primarily depend on the facts of the case and the legal grounds relied upon by the statement of claim. We must stress again that the notion of competitive relationship is approached quite broadly in the Czech legal provisions for unfair competition and in Czech case law. The outcome of decisions may sometimes be affected by the individual arbitrators and their awareness of unfair competition law.

18.5 "Reprehensible" Conduct and Lack of a Relation of Competition

The answer to the question of whether unfair competition principles may apply in the absence of competitive relationship really depends on our understanding of "competitive relationship" or "competitive conduct" as used in Czech legislation,[8] which is closely related to the definition of a "competitor" as a participant to competition. As already mentioned above, certain conducts of a competitive nature, in which a participant to competition uses competitive methods (solicitation, adequate degree of competitive assertiveness), can be contested by legal action on the grounds of unfair competitive conduct. The legal action will be brought by another participant to competition who may be damaged by the asserted conduct. The claimant and the respondent do not need to be in direct competitive relationship.

For example, a writer, acting in concert with his publisher, used the title "Viagra is out, the time has come for Cialis" (a text used in an advertisement) for his book of

[7] See Decision of the High Court in Prague 3 Cmo 404/10. in Macek, J. Rozhodnutí ve věcech nekalé soutěže a obchodní firmy (2000–2010). [*Decisions on Unfair Competition and Business Names* (*2000–2010*).] Prague: C.H.Beck, 2011, p. 536.

[8] See Section 44(1) of the Commercial Code.

fiction. The title of the book (as acknowledged by the author and the publisher) also had a promotional function, and the title was used in the advertisement for the book (as part of competitive conduct). The publishing house clearly was a participant to competition. Another participant to competition (but not a direct competitor to the publisher), the manufacturer of Viagra, Pfizer, was successful in objecting to this conduct on the grounds of unfair competitive conduct.

The concept of parasitic practices is often referred to in case law: the described conduct is characterised as "free riding" or "boarding a train in motion". It can be condemned as a special case (facts of the case) of unfair competition under Section 48 of the Czech Commercial Code (reputational parasitism) or, as the case may be, under the general clause condemning unfair competition ("other expressions of economic parasitism"). This case law has its source in the traditional case law existing before the Second World War.

This case law deserves support. A specific problem has come to light recently: in addition to, or in parallel with, intensely parasitic relationships, economic and other societal relationships may also entail symbiotic relationships in which the parties benefit from each other and provide each other with mutual benefits by taking advantage of the reputation of the other while allowing the other party to take advantage of their own reputation.

18.6 Infringement, Unfair Competition, and Parasitism

The common and usual answer to the interplay between infringement proceedings, claims for unfair competition, and/or parasitic practices is that all will depend on the circumstances of the specific case. A recent case from the Czech Republic can be deemed instructive: a tabloid newspaper repeatedly used photographs of a famous popular singer on its title page over a relatively short period of time—the action was brought on the grounds of unjust enrichment. The singer did not object to her photographs being published *per se*, acknowledging that she voluntarily agreed to appear in advertisements; nevertheless, she expected to receive the consideration standard in the artistic circles for her "involuntary advertising engagement". Courts of various instances considered whether the action should have been brought on the grounds of unfair competition (given the singer's common appearance in advertisements, she could be defined as an "ad hoc" competitor) or personality rights (alienation of the "right to one's own face"). The Supreme Court decided to qualify the conduct as unjust enrichment by the tabloid, which unlawfully (without a proper reason) took advantage of the singer's renowned in a parasitic fashion.

Economic literature seems to pay more attention to "negative externalities" than abuse of "positive externalities". Legal writings take note of that issue and recommend to bring claims on multiple legal grounds and overcome the obstacles (given, for instances, by varying jurisdiction) that prevent that.

France

19

Linda Arcelin, Sébastien Calmont, Arnaud Latil, and Aurélia Marie

19.1 Brand Image and Defence of Brand Image

19.1.1 Implicit Admission of the Concept of "Brand Image"

Though the concept of "brand image" is not expressly set down in French law in the Intellectual Property Code (IPC), and thus is not a "legal concept" *per se*, it is regularly used by French judges when taking into consideration the harm caused by trademark impairment to the rightholder.

A recent draft bill,[1] put forward by Senator Laurent Béteille on 17 May 2011, referred to the concept of "image of the deed of ownership" in Article 9 dealing with improvements to claims under civil law in terms of trademark law. They schedule the addition to the IPC of Article L. 716-4, drafted in the following terms: "In order to set damages, the jurisdiction (. . .) distinguishes between the negative economic consequences and the non-material harm endured by the injured party due to the impairment of their rights. Negative economic consequences cover shortfalls and losses incurred by the injured party. Non-material harm covers damage to the economic value of the property right or *image of the deed of ownership* (. . .)." However, this proposal has since been abandoned.

[1] Available at http://www.senat.fr/dossier-legislatif/ppl10-525.html.

L. Arcelin (✉)
Université de la Rochelle, La Rochelle, France
e-mail: linda.arcelin@wanadoo.fr

S. Calmont
Institut de recherche en propriété intellectuelle (IRPI), Paris, France

A. Latil
Université Paris-Sorbonne, Paris, France

A. Marie
Beau de Loménie, Paris, France

P. Këllezi et al. (eds.), *Antitrust for Small and Middle Size Undertakings and Image Protection from Non-Competitors*, LIDC Contributions on Antitrust Law, Intellectual Property and Unfair Competition, DOI 10.1007/978-3-642-54000-4_19, © Springer-Verlag Berlin Heidelberg 2014

The concept of "brand image" also occurs in Article L. 713-5 of the IPC, which stipulates that "The reproduction or imitation of a trademark which enjoys a reputation for goods or services not similar to those set out in the registration commits the civil liability of its perpetrator *if it is likely to harm the owner of the trademark* or if this reproduction or imitation constitutes unjustified exploitation of said.

The provisions of the previous indent apply to the reproduction or imitation of a trademark of wide repute in the sense of Article 6 (b) of the Paris Convention for the aforesaid protection of industrial property."

This Article widens the scope of protection for trademarks of wide repute by allowing free riding to be fought. It is indeed brand image impairment that is specifically sanctioned by this text.

19.1.2 Variable Contents of the Concept of "Brand Image"

There are relatively few specific doctrinal definitions of this concept. In an article dealing with brand image, Hervé Maccioni gives an interesting definition: 'Brand image is an intangible asset constituted by all representations tending to singularise, in the public's view, awareness of a brand – or of any other element that may have an economic value – which is the result of numerous investments (specifically in advertising and marketing)'.[2]

In terms of jurisprudence, it is through characterisation of brand image impairment that we can attempt to give a definition of brand image. In fact, brand image is a concept used frequently by judges when dealing with actions for infringement. Analysis of jurisprudence on this issue reveals 'that there is no coherent system to deal with brand image, but that brand images do indeed exist'.[3]

French jurisprudence distinguishes between several types of impairment that the holder of a trademark of wide repute may cite:

- *Damage to trademark reputation.* The reproduction or imitation of the trademark for different goods or services may harm the image of this trademark in terms of consumers if these goods or services are of poor quality or incompatible with the trademark's prestige. In a judgement given on 23 May 2001, the Paris Court of Appeal thus sanctioned the use of the *Olimpic* trademark to designate toilet paper[4] and the use of the *Régine* trademark to designate an adult chatline service via minitel.[5]
- In a judgement given by the Paris Court of Appeal on 22 March 1988 (*Chanel* case), magistrates sanctioned the debasing of a well-known trademark following the "discredit resulting from the use of the trademark for a product other than the

[2] H. Maccioni, Brand image. Emergence of a legal concept? JCP ed. G, No. 21, 22 May 1996, p. 3934.

[3] V. G. Cordier, Brand image and infringement impairment, JCP ed. E. No. 4, July-August 2007, p. 45 ff.

[4] V. G. Cordier, Brand image and infringement harm, JCP ed. E, no. 4, July-August 2007, p. 45 ff.

[5] CA Paris, 9 January 2002, Prop. Ind. 2002, com. 4, obs. P. Tréfigny.

one exploited by its legitimate owner". The conditions for commercialisation are, in this case, contrary to the values suggested by the trademark.[6]

- *Dilution of distinctive character*. This covers the trivialisation or popularisation of the trademark. We sometimes talk of dilution through interference[7] or loss of unicity, where the subsequent trademark causes dispersion in the identity of the prior trademark of wide repute. For instance, it is easy to imagine the sale at a lower price of articles reproducing the characteristics of a luxury product.

This brand image concept is also found in usage hypotheses of trademark parodies. It may be that the judge considers that the criticism levelled via a parody exceeds the bounds of freedom of expression and bases his ruling on brand image impairment to sanction the abusive parody.[8]

19.1.3 Use of the Action in Unfair Competition Irrespective of the Situation of the Protagonists

Generally speaking, brand image impairment is sanctioned by the courts essentially by bringing actions for unfair competition and free riding.

As we will see later,[9] a competitive relationship is not always required by the courts, specifically in terms of free riding.

As regards the protection laid down by Article L. 713-5 of the IPC, this is not, strictly speaking, an action for infringement but rather an action for specific liability. The likelihood of confusion was not proven in this case. In addition, the penal procedure for infringement cannot be given grounds to apply.

The idea of a competitive relationship between the companies in question, according to this hypothesis, is taken into consideration by judges. In a judgement given by the Douai Court of Appeal on 19 January 2010, magistrates did not uphold an impairment to "the brand image of the Scottish Terrier" (figurative trademark of the Agatha Diffusion company) since "the goods marketed (...) are so different in terms of their nature, their destination, and their distribution channels – they are

[6] See, in the same respect, Cass. com, 24/05/2011 (no. 10-18474) not published: "the goods in question were offered for sale and sold in a discount shop, in a commercial area accessible to the general public, among numerous loose items offered, sometimes still in their carriage packaging; [...] the conditions of exhibition for sale of Chanel goods were incompatible with the image of the Chanel trademark."

[7] For this issue, see M. Colonna, Special protection of well-known trademarks in light of the latest developments of community jurisprudence, Master's Dissertation II, University Panthéon-Assas, 2009.

[8] See, for instance, the ruling by the Paris District Court of 8 January 2002, SA Pernod Ricard v Verfaillie: "The use of the aforesaid trademarks for parody purposes, in order to illustrate different headings on a site playing on an ambiguous image of the plaintiff's goods constitutes an unjustified use of said trademarks when this use *impairs the image of the designated trademarks* and goods by linking them to jokes based on the misdemeanour of drinking pastis."

[9] See in particular Sect. 19.5.

sold in pet shops, while Agatha articles are sold in specialist stores – that they cannot *tarnish the brand image* of the Scottish Terrier (. . .).”

19.2 Trademark, Principle of Specialty, and Competitive Relationship

19.2.1 Extent of the Principle of Specialty

The principle of specialty reflects the requirement for a competitive relationship. The principle of specialty is the ‘principle by which the reservation of an element in terms of a distinctive mark is limited to the designation of one or more determined goods, services, or activities’.[10] This is laid down in Article L. 713-1 of the IPC for trademarks that are subject to registration. Although it is not intended for any distinctive marks other than the trademark, it is still given scope to apply.[11]

The principle of speciality allows the scope of protection offered to the trademark to be restricted to certain designated goods or services. It means that the mark is only distinctive as part of a competitive relationship. In this respect, the principle of speciality is synonymous with competitive relationship.

The principle of speciality constitutes at once a guarantee and a restriction to freedom of trade and industry: on the one hand, the principle of speciality ensures that the trademark owner can exercise freedom of trade and industry, allowing him to guarantee the origin of the goods or services to consumers. On the other, the principle of speciality restricts the freedom of trade and industry of competitors, prohibiting them from using a mark that has been subject to registration (trademark) or law (e.g., business name or mark).

The principle of speciality thus represents a ‘fulcrum’ in terms of achieving freedom of trade and industry.[12] It constitutes a “presumption” of likelihood of confusion between two identical or similar marks when operators are in a competitive situation. However, outside the speciality, in principle there is no likelihood of confusion.

Exceptions to the principle of speciality. However, hypothetical situations exist wherein the protection of a trademark falls outside a competitive relationship. This is the case for goods or services that are simply similar, and trademarks of wide repute.

– Similar goods or services. Article L.713-3 of the IPC gives protection to trademarks if a likelihood of confusion may result concerning “goods or services similar to those stipulated in the registration”. Jurisprudence in these cases examines whether or not an average consumer is likely to believe that goods or services come from the same manufacturer, service provider, distributor, or

[10] A. Bouvel, Principle of specialty and distinctive marks, Litec, 2004, no. 7.

[11] A. Bouvel, Principle of specialty and distinctive marks, Litec, 2004, no. 57 ff.

[12] A. Bouvel, Principle of specialty and distinctive marks, Litec, 2004, no. 6.

retailer. Thus, this rule does not provide a genuine exemption from the requirement for a competitive relationship insofar as apparent competition exists in consumers' eyes due to the similarity of the goods.

– Trademarks of wide repute. According to jurisprudence, this is 'a trademark that is known by a very wide cross-section of the general public that exercises its own drawing power independent of the goods or services it designates'.[13]

A trademark of wide repute is defined by the Court of Justice of the European Union as a trademark that is 'known by a significant part of the public, in a substantial part of the Union'.[14] The criteria selected by the French trial judges add interesting refinements to the nature of the "repute" similar to those upheld by the Paris Court of Appeal in its ruling of 19 May 2001[15]: market share, intensity of trademark exploitation, geographical scope, length of use, size of investment to which it gives rise. The judges may also use surveys.[16]

Trademarks of wide repute and well-known trademarks. Though for some authors, these terms are synonymous,[17] most of the doctrine considers that they are in fact separate. However, no agreement exists as to the elements distinguishing them. According to an 'egalitarian' theory, trademarks of wide repute and well-known trademarks enjoy an equivalent level of awareness but are distinguished by the absence of registration found regarding well-known trademarks.[18] The other notion, known as the 'hierarchical' notion, suggests a difference in the degree of awareness between the two trademarks.[19]

Separate system for infringement. Protection of a trademark of wide repute is based on the field of civil liability. Rules pertaining to actions for infringement are thus not applicable (referral of infringement, seizure of infringement, limitation in consequence of acquiescence, or opposition).

Exemption from principle of specialty. Protection of trademarks of wide repute is exempt from the principle of speciality. The protection of trademarks of wide repute outside the scope of a competitive relationship represents an exception to freedom of trade and industry.[20] Here, the object of protection is not the trademark owner, but the consumer.[21]

---

[13] CA Paris, 17 January 1996, Concorde, PIBD 1996, no. 607, III, 155.

[14] CJ, 14 September 1999, *General Motors*, RTD Com 2000, p. 87, note J.-Ch. Galloux; RTD Eur. 2000, 134, note G. Bonet.

[15] CA Paris, 18 May 2001, PIBD 2001, III, 576, *add.* CA Paris, division 5, ch. 2, 11 mars 2011, no. 10/06428.

[16] CA Paris, 25 February 2000, D. 2000, 227, B. Poisson note.

[17] G. Bonet, "Protection of well-known trademarks in the Intellectual Property Code," in Mélange Foyer, PUF, 1997, p.189.

[18] A. Bouvel, Principle of specialty and distinctive marks, Litec, 2004, no. 681, ff. *Add.* M.-A, Perot-Morel, "Awareness and repute: concept unicity or duality in trademark law?" Mélanges Burst, Litec, 2000, p. 463, P. Vivant, Well-known trademark and Trademark of wide repute: A distinction must be made: JCP E 2008, p. 1968.

[19] Ibid.

[20] J. Canlorbe, Using other people's brands, Litec, coll. Irpi, 2007, no. 98.

[21] G. Bonet, *op. cit.*

The doctrine analyses the protection of trademarks of wide repute outside the scope of speciality as an act of free riding.[22] The debate has now been superseded due to the existence of a legislative provision.[23]

Article L. 713-5 of the IPC in fact schedules protection for trademarks of wide repute in the field of civil liability for goods or services not similar to those designated in the registration.[24] Protection of the trademark of wide repute is subordinated to the proof of two alternative conditions pursuant to Article L. 713-5 of the IPC[25]:

- harm resulting from the reproduction or imitation of the trademark of wide repute: this may be actual or possible harm. It is a matter of no-fault liability, or
- unjustified exploitation of the trademark of wide repute: the condition of unjustified exploitation is characterised by an improper gain or a lack of justification.[26] It is regretful that the expression 'improper gain' is not present in the IPC, despite the drafting of the bill.[27] Gain is composed of the attraction of a customer base, the attraction represented by the trademark of wide repute or savings in advertising costs. However, this is irrespective of whether or not the exploitation creates a likelihood of confusion in consumers' minds.

The finality of the protection of trademarks of wide repute is based on the protection of the economic value represented by the trademark, specifically regarding its advertising function.[28]

Supplementary application of the liability scheme for unfair competition. Jurisprudence allows for a plurality of actions under Article L. 713-5 of the IPC, viz. the

---

[22] Y. Saint-Gal, 'Parasitic competition and free-riding acts', RIPIA 1956, 19, G. Bonet, 'Protection of trademarks of wide repute in the Intellectual Property Code', Mélange Foyer, PUF, 1997, p. 189, J. Canlorbe, no. 80, F. Pollaud-Dulian, 'On some avatars for civil liability action in business law', RTD Com 1997, p. 349, Ph. Le Tourneau, Free riding, Litec, 1998, no. 96.

[23] Article L. 713-5 IPC.

[24] This Article reads: "The reproduction or imitation of a trademark that enjoys repute for goods or services not similar to those designated in the registration commits the civil liability of its perpetrator if it is likely to harm the trade mark owner, or if this reproduction or imitation constitutes unjustified exploitation of said. The provisions of the previous indent are applicable to the reproduction or imitation of a brand that is widely known in the sense of Article 6 (b) of the Paris Convention for the aforesaid protection of industrial property."

Transposing Directive 89/104/EC, Article 5, § 2; mod Ord. no. 2008-1301, 11 December 2008.

[25] Drafting of this text is said to be the result of a "legislative failure" (see J. Foyer, *Legislative news*, *Dalloz* 1991, p. 65) when transposing the 1989 Directive. The text of the initial proposal scheduled that the use of a trademark of wide repute commits liability "if it is likely to harm the trademark owner, specifically when this use constitutes an unjustified exploitation of said trademark's awareness."

[26] A. Bouvel, *op. cit.*, no. 770.

[27] Colombet report, French National Assembly, 26 April 1990, National Assembly, session 1989–1990, doc. no. 1301, p. 47.

[28] F. Pollaud-Dulian, "Impairments to trademarks of wide repute. Regarding the Intel order of the ECJ of 27 November 2008" Gaz. Pal. 31 March 2009, no.90, p. 7.

protection of trademarks of wide repute, and the common civil liability law action of Article 1382 of the Civil Code in the event of separate facts.[29]

19.3 Consideration of the Context of the Use of the Trademark by Jurisprudence

The condition of use in the course of trade outlined at Article 16 of the TRIPS was taken into account by Directive 2008/95/EC,[30] which states in Article 5, paragraph 1: "The registered trade mark shall confer on the proprietor exclusive rights therein. The proprietor shall be entitled to prevent all third parties not having his consent from using them *in the course of trade* (. . .)".[31]

French trademark law has not however included this concept of use in the course of trade in the prohibitive measures it plans. In fact, Article L. 713-1 ff. of the Intellectual Property Code, which deals with the rights conferred by registration, forbids the reproduction or imitation of a trademark without outlining the context of said use.

Since European Directives are not subject to immediate application in Member States' legislations, it is thus the French judge's decision to interpret French law in the light of Directive 2008/95/EC, under the control of the Court of the EU. To this end, its *Arsenal* judgement of 12 November 2002[32] defines use in the course of trade to be that which 'takes place in the context of commercial activity with a view to economic advantage and not as a private matter.' Furthermore, the ECJ made two rulings in 2011 that enable further definition of the concept of use in the course of trade.

In *L'Oréal v eBay* ruling of 12 July 2011,[33] the Court makes clear that the fact that eBay enables users of its site to use a trademark-protected mark for economic transactions that the site itself does not perform, does not constitute, in respect of eBay, use in the course of trade. In addition, this ruling confirms the position adopted by the Court in the *Google* rulings of 23 March 2010.[34]

In a second *Winters* ruling of 15 December 2011,[35] the Court decided that the act of filling cans bearing a trademark at the request of third parties, with no link being

---

[29] Cass. com, 8 December 2000, PIBD 2001, III, 207.

[30] Directive 2008/95/EC of the European Parliament and of the Council of 22 October 2008 to approximate the laws of the Member States relating to trademarks.

[31] We emphasise.

[32] ECJ, case C-206/01, *Arsenal Football Club plc v Matthew Reed*, ECR 2002 I-10273.

[33] ECEU, case C-324/09, *L'Oréal SA and Others v eBay International AG and Others*, ECR 2011 I-6011.

[34] ECJ, joint cases C-236/08 to C-238/08, *Google France SARL and Google Inc. v Louis Vuitton Malletier SA, Viaticum SA and Luteciel SARL, Centre national de recherche en relations humaines (CNRRH) SARL and Others*, ECR 2010 I-2417.

[35] ECJ of 15 December 2011, case C-119/10, *Frisdranken Industrie Winters BV v Red Bull GmbH* (not yet published).

made apparent to consumers between the company performing the filling and the owner of said trademark, though this is by nature a commercial act, is not a technical act that may constitute use of said trademark in the course of trade.

In terms of the definition of the criterion of 'use in the course of trade' in France, in a ruling on 10 May 2011, the Court of Cassation was also led to make a decision about the concept of use in the course of trade[36]: "use occurring in the course of trade of a mark similar to a trademark during an activity aimed at obtaining an economic advantage, whether direct or indirect." It is evident here that the Court is going further than the ECJ, taking into consideration the concept of indirect economic advantage. It in fact moves away from a competitive relationship strictly speaking. In the case in point, the issue involved a trade union, which was a non-competitive third party, distributing a free newspaper in order to achieve an increase in the number of members and thus economic advantage due to an increase in subscriptions.

Examples taking into account the concept of 'use in the course of trade' have been increasing in France since 2008. Judges will in fact study the background of trademark use prior to the actual issue of infringement so as to provide a positive or negative response. For instance, the Court considered the purchase by a third party of a keyword on an online search engine, with a view to displaying an advertisement on a website, even if the brand in question does not appear on the site, as a 'use in the course of its economic business'.[37] The same thing goes for the use of a trademark on the cover of a book.[38]

Conversely, the judge will consider that use is outside the course of trade when it does not seek to obtain an economic advantage. For instance, this will be the case in terms of the use for the purposes of notification by an association alerting the public as to a company's attitude[39] or when the use is artistic in nature,[40] particularly when 'the use of the marks in question is solely designed to define the character traits of one of the characters (in a film)'.

French judges will thus focus on the issue of finding out whether the use made of the trademark is intended to obtain economic gain in any way whatsoever, even if its business does not intrinsically have an economic objective.

However, other actions in lieu of action for infringement are available to a trademark owner so as to intervene with regard to uses outside the course of

[36] Cass. Com., 10 May 2011, No. 10/18173.

[37] Paris Court of Appeal, Division 5, Chamber 1, 1 February 2012, No. 10/05322, *S.A.S. PETIT POUCET v SA BPCE and SE EURO RSCG C&CO*; Lyon Court of Appeal, Chamber 1 Civil A, 8 December 2011, *CDI-B v LA REDOUTE*; or else TGI Paris, 3rd Chamber, 4th Section, No. 10/16098, *Groupe Zenith v Kovitz Interactive*.

[38] TGI Paris, 3rd chamber, 1 April 2008, *CANAL+ v M.A. and Editions Privé*.

[39] Cass. Com. 8 April 2008, No. 06/10961, *ESSO v Greenpeace France*, or else TGI Paris, 23 November 2010, No. 09/11832, *M. Constantini and SARL LA MAISON D'ORIENT v SA France Télévisions*.

[40] Paris District Court, 10 November 2011, No. 10/09164, *Dolce & Gabbana and GADO srl v PATHE DISTRIBUTION and PULSAR PRODUCTIONS*.

trade. In fact, the owner may bring an action on common law principles resulting from civil liability.

As such, on 23 November 2010, the aforementioned Paris District Court ruling condemned the reproduction of a trademark in a report accompanied by disparaging comments on the grounds of civil liability in the absence of use in the course of trade, thus infringement.

In contrast, in the aforementioned *ESSO v Greenpeace* case, the Court considered that the ESSO brands, used outside the course of trade, represented in the form E$$O constituted a proportional use to the objective of said association, which was to denounce the allegedly greedy behaviour of this company. On the contrary, disproportionate use could have been sanctioned.

Thus in the case of *Areva v Greenpeace*,[41] the Court made clear that despite the absence of infringement, the fact of associating Areva's trademarks '(to a skull and crossbones and a sickly fish) did not target the company, rather the trademarks it had registered (...) in such a way that its business was impaired'. The improper use of a registered trademark, even if this does not constitute an act of impairment, can also be sanctioned under civil liability if the activity performed by a non-competitor impairs the trademarks of the owner bringing the action.

As regards use for artistic purposes, it is the motivation behind the use of the trademark by the third party that will be of interest to the judge. In its aforementioned judgement of 10 November 2011, the Court considered that the use of a trademark, in this case of *Dolce & Gabbana*, on clothing worn by the character in a film so as to reveal a personality trait, is not improper in the absence of trademark impairment, even though this personality trait is disadvantageous.

The liability of a party that does not use a trademark in the course of trade is thus not excluded under French law. However, this liability will be much more difficult for the judge to recognise than by using infringement liability. This solution may seem quite well adapted in the end. In fact, it appears that the non-competitor must not fall under the "systematic" sanction of infringement, on pain of breaching the principle of speciality and thus providing the trademark owner with a de facto monopoly in all sectors of the economy.

A sanction based on the grounds of civil liability for use made of a trademark by a non-competitor seems to allow the setting of limits that are more in line with the objectives of free competition. It in fact targets the sanctioning of improper behaviour, without calling into question the business undertaken by the perpetrator of the criticised behaviour.

[41] Cass. 1 Civ., 8 April 2008, Provision No. 07-11251, *Greenpeace v Areva*.

19.3.1 Incidences of the Introduction of New Functions of the Mark Regarding Infringement

In its *Arsenal* judgement of 12 November 2002, the ECJ[42] imposed the existence of impairment of one of the trademark's functions due to the use of a third party, in order to characterise infringement. The Court defines the essential function of the trademark as intended to "guarantee the identity of origin of the marked goods or services to the consumer or end user" (point 48), also known as the function of guarantee of origin. The other trademark functions outlined remain undefined.

This ruling has since been confirmed by the Court, specifically in the *Anheuser-Busch*[43] judgement of 16 November 2004, the *Adam Opel*[44] judgement of 25 January 2007, and the *Céline* judgement of 11 September 2007.[45]

It should be noted that French jurisdictions waited a long time before applying the criterion of impairment of an essential function of the trademark and then only did so in a non-systematic way.[46]

In its *Bellure* judgement of 18 June 2009,[47] the ECJ made clear that some of the other functions of the trademark were 'specifically those consisting of guaranteeing the quality of the goods or services in question, and those of communication, investment or advertising' (point 58). This ruling has since been confirmed by the Court in its *Google* judgement of 23 Mach 2010[48] and its *eBay* judgement of 12 July 2011.[49]

However, are these new functions of the same importance as the essential function set out in the *Arsenal* judgement of 12 November 2002, or in contrast, should they be more limited in their scope of interpretation and/or application?

The answer to this question was in fact specifically provided by the Court in the aforementioned Bellure judgement. In fact, the Court makes clear, immediately after acknowledging the existence of these new functions, that 'The protection

---

[42] ECJ, case C-206/01, *Arsenal Football Club plc v Matthew Reed*, ECR 2002 I-10273.

[43] ECJ, case C-245/02, *Anheuser-Busch Inc. v Budějovický Budvar, národní podnik*, ECR 2004 I-10989.

[44] ECJ, case C-48/05, *Adam Opel AG v Autec AG*, ECR 2007 I-1017.

[45] ECJ, case C-17/06, *Céline SARL v Céline SA*, ECR 2007 I-7041.

[46] To this end, see CA Paris, 4th Chamber Section A, 28 May 2008, No. 2007/03947, Les Choristes; CA Paris, 4th Chamber, Section B, 31 October 2008, No. 2007/06204, Bélem; CA Paris, Division 5 2nd Chamber, 2 April 2010, No. 2008/1440, PSG.

[47] ECJ, Case C-487/07, *L'Oréal SA, Lancôme parfums et beauté & Cie SNC and Laboratoire Garnier & Cie v Bellure NV, Malaika Investments Ltd and Starion International Ltd*, ECR 2009 I-5185.

[48] ECJ, jointed cases C-236/08 to 238/08, *Google France SARL and Google Inc. v Louis Vuitton Malletier SA, Viaticum SA and Luteciel SARL, Centre national de recherche en relations humaines (CNRRH) SARL and Others*, ECR 2010 I-2417; ECJ, case C-558/08, *Portakabin Ltd and Portakabin BV v Primakabin BV*, ECR 2010 I-6963.

[49] ECJ, case C-324/09, *L'Oréal SA and Others v eBay International AG and Others*, ECR 2011 I-6011.

conferred by Article 5(1)(a) of Directive 89/104 is thus broader than that provided by Article 5(1)(b), the application of which requires that there be a likelihood of confusion and accordingly the possibility that the essential function of the mark may be impaired.' Implementation of these newly defined functions thus seems limited in practice to the use by a third party of an identical trademark, for identical goods or services to those covered by the registration of said trademark, while the essential function will aim to apply not only in the event of an identical reproduction but also in the event of use of a similar mark for similar goods or services.

These other functions thus rekindle the traditional debate in that they entail a *de facto* difference in the appraisal of impairment of the trademark's function, since they will only apply in respect of Article 5, paragraph 1, sub a) of Directive 89/104, transposed into French law via Article L. 713-2 of the IPC. Furthermore, this interpretation has already found grounds for application in French jurisprudence.[50]

This distinction made by the Court is disputed by the doctrine. In fact, this difference in appraisal, and the subsequent broadening of action for infringements that are the result of consideration being given to impairments to other functions, not just the guarantee of origin function, regarding dual identical use (trademark and goods or services), leads us to observe that the *de facto* situation is sometimes rather imbalanced. This observation results specifically from the reading of two ECJ judgements.

In its *O2* judgement of 12 June 2008,[51] prior to the introduction of the new trademark functions via the aforementioned *Bellure* judgement of 18 June 2009, the Court actually considered that there was no likelihood of confusion in the absence of impairment of the essential function of guarantee of origin. In this case, the H3G company, a mobile telephony operator, used the bubble-shaped logo of the O2 company, another mobile telephony operator, as part of a comparative advertisement but said use was not identical to the brand of that company. National jurisdictions thus considered that the brand was not reproduced identically but only similarly. Application of the criteria set out in the *Bellure* judgement of 18 June 2009 to this *de facto* situation would mean that the impairment of the advertising function of the brand would not be taken into account, since there was no identical reproduction of the trademark, whereas the deeds concern a comparative advertisement.

The aforementioned *Portakabin* judgement of 23 March 2010 confirms this interpretation. The Primakabin company called on the fee-paying referencing services of Google to reserve keywords representing takeover of the trademarks of the Portakabin company, since these keywords included typing errors potentially made by online users when entering said terms. The Court, considering that these

[50] See, in particular, Paris District Court, 3rd Chamber, 4th Section, 26 January 2012, No. 10/16098; CA Lyon, Civil Chamber 1 A, 22 March 2012, No. 10/03392, *Google v Descroix-Vernier and others.*

[51] ECJ, Case C-533/06, *O2 Holdings Limited and O2 (UK) Limited v Hutchison 3G UK Limited*, ECR 2008 I-4231.

were in fact simple marks similar to the registered trademarks, once again excluded the consideration of the functions of communication, investment, and advertising in the case in point, and any possible impairment thereof.

The stance adopted by the ECJ, and subsequently adopted by national jurisdictions, may encourage third parties to avoid an identical takeover of the trademark they wish to use in order that they are only accused of impairment of the function of guarantee of origin of the trademark. In terms of the Internet, this may constitute a serious obstacle to actions for infringement.

Thus, we can see that in its aforementioned *L'Oréal v eBay* judgement of 12 July 2011, the Court made clear that impairment of the essential function of guarantee of origin was constituted solely "when advertising does not enable reasonably well-informed and reasonably observant internet users, or else enables them only with difficulty, to ascertain whether the goods or services referred to by the advertisement originate from the proprietor of the trade mark or from an undertaking economically linked to it or, on the contrary, originate from a third party" (point 94). This interpretation has since been used in France, specifically in the ruling of the Paris District Court of 26 January 2012 *Groupe Zénith v Kovitz Interactive*.[52] The Court made a *de facto* reduction in the scope of action for the trademark owner by requiring an impairment to the indication of origin by the use made by the third party, which could then easily bypass this obstacle.

The introduction of new functions of the trademark by the Court is thus likely to rekindle the traditional debate in terms of fighting infringement, both in legal terms, regarding the dual identity of infringement as seen in Article 5, paragraph 1, sub a) of Directive 89/104, and in practical terms due to the choices that may subsequently be made by third parties in order to promote their own business while continuing to avoid infringement.

19.4 Other Distinctive Marks

19.4.1 Examples of Sanction in Case of Use of Distinctive Signs by a Non-Competitor

A company's distinctive marks, other than the trademark, are mainly the following:

- the corporate name that enables the legal entity to be identified,
- the trade name that enables the business to be identified,
- the signage that enables the location of an establishment to be identified,
- the domain name that enables the company's website to be identified.

These distinctive signs have in common the fact that that they do not constitute "intellectual properties" in the sense of the IPC. As a result, actions for infringement are not applicable to them. Protection governing copying or imitation of these

[52] Paris District Court, 3rd Chamber, 4th Section, 26 January 2012, No. 10/16098.

distinctive marks by competitor or non-competitor companies is thus assured by other actions, essentially actions for unfair competition.

To begin with, it must be made clear that the protection of these distinctive signs presupposes that they have a sufficient degree of distinctiveness. A trivial mark is not subject to protection against use by a third party. In fact, although in the absence of a legal status no validity conditions exist for these marks, the success of an action for unfair competition is subject to the condition of their distinctiveness. This distinctive character then becomes more a condition for success of the action than a condition for validity of the distinctive marks.[53]

The success of a civil action for unfair competition in terms of the protection of distinctive marks other than the trademark is not subordinated to proof of a competitive relationship. However, an action in competition law requires that the companies be in a competitive situation.

Protection of distinctive signs without a competitive relationship using unfair competition law. French law for unfair competition is based on Article 1382 of the Civil Code. The action is in fact founded on common civil liability law. It then presupposes the proof of wrongdoing, harm, and causal link. Several types of action for unfair competition exist, according to the harm caused: disruption, likelihood of confusion, disparagement, and free riding. These actions offer protection to distinctive marks other than the trademark when such marks are copied or imitated.

The doctrine classifies the various hypotheses of unfair competition according to whether or not they require a competitive relationship.[54] As such, actions for unfair competition aimed at compensating for disruption or likelihood of confusion require that a competitive relationship exist between the companies. The likelihood of confusion between products or services of a company, or between the companies themselves, logically presupposes a competitive relationship, despite the absence of principle of speciality in respect of these distinctive marks.

Likelihood of confusion, proof of a competitive relationship. Trademark law is subject to a right of ownership according to a principle of speciality. The principle of specialty allows the trademark domain to be established and only offers protection to certain "classes" of goods or services. These "classes" thus reflect the competitive relationship between identical or similar trademarks. The principle of speciality does not exist for distinctive marks other than the trademark. The jurisprudential legal system of protection for these distinctive marks does however take account of competitive relationships, by requiring that the use of said marks must lead to the creation of a likelihood of confusion in the minds of customers. The condition of "likelihood of confusion" thus reflects the requirement of a competitive situation between the operators in litigation. When looking for a likelihood of confusion, account must in fact be taken of the sphere of business in which the goods or services are marketed.

[53] J. Passa, *Industrial property law*, t.1, 2nd ed., Litec, 2009, no. 470.

[54] L. Vogel, Treaty of business law. From trade law to economic law, LGDJ, 19th edition, 2010, no. 719.

Protection of the corporate name presupposes that the companies perform similar activities. By judgement of 21 May 2004, the Court of Cassation thus considered that 'Whereas by naming itself thusly, without seeking to find out whether or not the business carried out by the Créatis Evry company *was conducted in a field similar to computing*, thus making the term Créatis unavailable for the corporate name of a second company, due to the possible likelihood of confusion in the eyes of the general public, the Court of Appeal has not granted a legal basis for its ruling.'[55]

More generally, proof of the likelihood of confusion criterion presupposes that companies are targeting a common customer base. As such, the imitation of a distinctive mark does not have the force of unfair competition if the companies 'were not to target the same customer base and did not have the same purpose, one being destined for professional hair salons and the other for the general public'.[56]

Unfair competition actions in cases of absence of competitive relationship. However, a competitive relationship is not always required, even in terms of likelihood of confusion. Thus, the copying or imitation of a patronymic name by distinctive marks other than the trademark, constituting a likelihood of confusion, is sanctioned without requiring a competitive situation.[57] The aim is to prohibit advantage being taken of another party's reputation. In terms of a case whereby the distinctive mark is composed of the patronymic name of a former partner or employee, the outcome of the dispute is not dependent on the competitive situation but on the authorisation by the company's Articles of Association.[58]

That being the case, although a competitive relationship is required in these hypotheses so as to protect distinctive marks, such a criterion should still not apply in terms of free riding or well-known corporate names.[59]

Other types of action for unfair competition, free riding,[60] and disparagement[61] do however offer protection to distinctive marks other than the trademark outside a competitive relationship.

---

[55] Cass. com, 12 May 2004, Rev. Soc. 2004, p. 904 (we emphasise), note by J. Passa; *Adde*. Cass. com, 30 November 2004, no. 2-18731. Comp., the absence of a competitive relationship: CA Paris, 18 September 2002, RTD Com 2004, p. 92, obs. J. Azéma and J.-Ch. Galloux: "that the protection offered to a corporate name is not limited to the business sector of the legal entity, but itemises this in economic and corporate life as a whole; that the use of the name of a company may thus constitute injurious harm in terms of Article 1382 of the civil code when this use creates a likelihood of confusion independently of a competitive situation".

[56] Cass. Com., 25 April 2006, no. 04-12406.

[57] CA Paris, 5 October 1989, Rev. Soc. 1990, comm. 79, note Guyon.

[58] Cass. com, 12 March 1985, Bull. civ. IV, no. 95, 'Bordas'; Cass. com, 29 January 2008, PIBD 2008, no. 871, III, 221.

[59] J. Azéma and J.-Ch. Galloux, *Industrial property law*, Dalloz, 7th ed., 2012, no. 1693.

[60] Cass. com., 30 January 1996, no. 94-15.725, *Fleurs Éclairs company v Dutch office of milk products*, Contr. conc. consom. 1996, comm. 41, obs. L. Vogel; D. 1997, somm. p. 232, obs. Y. Serra.

[61] Cass. com., 20 November 2007, Contracts, conc. consom. 2008, comm. 51, obs. M. Malaurie-Vignal.

The Court of Cassation sometimes considered that competitive situation was a condition behind an action for unfair competition.[62] But jurisprudence has evolved and now excludes competitive situation from the conditions required for an action for unfair competition. Thus, an action for unfair competition based on Article 1382 of the Civil Code is applicable even in the absence of a competitive relationship between companies in dispute.

This is the case for the sanction for free riding, which outlines 'any illegitimate usurpation of third-party awareness'.[63] In the absence of a competitive relationship, as a result we most often talk of "parasitic acts" in contrast to cases where companies are competing, where the expression used is "parasitic competition."

In terms of free riding, the Court of Cassation considers thusly, for instance by judgement of 12 February 2008, that 'A direct or effective competitive situation between companies (. . .) is not a condition for an action for unfair competition which only requires the existence of proof of misconduct that causes harm'.[64]

In this case, the sanctioned misconduct consists of the misappropriation of another party's intellectual or financial investment, leading to the trivialisation of the image of the company subject to free riding. Since the copying or imitation of distinctive signs other than the trademark constitutes a parasitic act, they are subsequently sanctioned with no requirement for a competitive relationship.

Competitive situation also has no bearing in terms of disparagement. The Court of Cassation thus considers that the Court of Appeal 'added a condition to the law that it did not possess' by retaining the clause 'that the parties are not in a competitive situation' so as to reject the action.[65]

When a competitive relationship is not required, the objective sought via the sanction for impairments to these distinctive marks is to protect the market and the consumer. The risk of attracting new clients is in fact practically non-existent. The sanction of unfair competition thus enables fairness of business practice to be guaranteed, in addition to the protection offered to an economic operator that has been subject to harm.

Unfair business practices. Lastly, it is advisable to draw a parallel between these developments and the conditions of the action in Article L. 120-1 of the Consumer Code, which outlaws unfair business practices. This text sets out that "A business practice is unfair when it is contrary to the requirements of professional diligence and substantially alters, or is likely to alter, the economic behaviour of an averagely-informed consumer who is attentive and astute, with regard to specific goods or services".

---

[62] Cass. com., 19 November 2002, Bull. civ. IV, no. 171; JCP E 2003, no. 3, p. 107; RJDA 2003, no. 211.

[63] D. Legeais, "Unfair competition and free riding", Commercial Jurisprudence file, brochure 254, 2009, no. 1.

[64] Cass. com., 12 February 2008, D. 2008 (we emphasise), p. 2573, note by E. Chevrier, JCP E 2009, 1020, no. 1, obs. Ch. Caron. *Add.* Cass. com., 20 November 2007, no. 05-15.643, *Industrial property*. 2008, comm. 78.

[65] Cass. com., 20 November 2007, *op. cit.*

The text adds that "The unfair nature of a business practice aimed at a specific category of consumers or a group of vulnerable consumers due to their mental or physical infirmity, their age or their credulity, increases in respect of the average capacity for discernment of the category or group".

The Court of Cassation recently considered that a competitive relationship is not a condition for the implementation of said action.[66] Although it does not directly target distinctive marks other than trademarks, this ruling shows that the protection of fair business practices, an objective shared by actions for unfair competition, is not subordinated to proof of a competitive relationship.

Requirement of a competitive relationship. Alongside action for unfair competition, distinctive marks other than the trademark enjoy protection, thanks to an action set out in the Consumer Code. Article L. 121-1 of the Consumer Code, subsequent to the law of 3 January 2008 known as the "Chatel Law" relating to misleading commercial practices, adopted as a transposition of Directive 2005/29/EC of 11 May 2005, scheduling civil and penal action that allow a company's distinctive marks to be protected against misleading commercial practices. This text stipulates that "A commercial practice shall be regarded as misleading if it is committed under one of the following circumstances: 1. when it *creates confusion* with any products, trade marks, trade names or other distinctive marks *of a competitor* (. . .)".

Firstly, it should be noted that the competitive relationship is a requirement before any action can be brought. The distinctive marks ("trade name and others", with no further specific details) in question must belong to a "competitor" according to the terms of the text. The misleading commercial practice must then create confusion; simple risk is not sufficient. In contrast to an action for unfair competition, a competitive relationship is clearly required in order for this action to succeed.

Secondly, it must be noted that if the dispute targets a competitor, then the action may be brought by a consumer, a consumer association, or even a company that is not in a competitive situation.

19.4.2 The Issue of the Specific Nature of Domain Names and Web Addresses

The solutions chosen in terms of domain names seem to have partly brought to the fore the issue of the criterion of competitive relationship. As such, in terms of domain name protection in the field of actions for unfair competition, the Court of Cassation has, since the significant '*Locatour*' judgement of 13 December 2005, stipulated that takeover of a domain name risks creating confusion and that

[66] Cass. com., 29 November 2011, no. 10–27.402, FS-P+B, *SAS Kelkoo v SA Concurrence*, Industrial Property 2012, comm. 28.

companies are in a competitive situation.[67] Thus, in a conflict between two domain names, the registration of a domain name constitutes an impairment of prior right on a domain name provided that 'the companies in litigation carried out identical or competitive activities and if a likelihood of confusion resulted'.[68]

In the same respect, the Court of Cassation considered in its "Argus.fr" judgement of 23 January 2007 that 'Defending companies, that are not competitors of the publishing company (...) could not thus be held liable for acts of unfair competition in respect of said company'.[69]

The requirement of a competitive relationship in order to sanction domain names that copy or imitate distinctive marks is in contrast with other solutions in terms of unfair competition. The appearance of domain names in the "legal landscape" has thus reignited the problem of competitive relationship.

However, in line with common law, the protection of domain names in the event of free riding or disparagement should logically fall outside the scope of the principle of speciality. Furthermore, jurisprudence from trial judges has already ruled that a trademark is protected against similar or identical domain names even when the companies are not in a competitive situation.[70]

The principle of speciality in trademark law disappears when a domain name imitates a trademark. For instance, the imitation by a former intern of the 'SNCF' brand in a domain name ('sncf-usa.fr') is sanctioned without the requirement of a competitive relationship.[71]

In addition, Article L. 45-2 of the Postal and Electronic Communications Code relating to allocation rules for domain names, created by Law 2011-302 of 22 March 2011, does not refer to competitive relationships: "The registration or renewal of domain names can be refused or the domain name removed when the domain name is (...) likely to impair intellectual property or personal rights, unless the applicant justifies a legitimate interest and acts in good faith."

Domain names must not, in principle, impair intellectual property rights. However, it is accepted that in some situations, impairment of said rights is justified. These are

---

[67] E. Tardieu-Guigues, 'Allocation and disputes over domain names', Jurisclasseur Commercial, fasc. 805, 2011, no. 140.

[68] Cass. com, 13 December 2005, Com. 13 December 2005, Bull. civ. IV, no. 254; D. 2006. AJ. 63, obs. Manara; *ibid.* Pan. 2930, obs. Picod; JCP E 2006, no. 6–7, p. 289, note Ch. Caron; CCC 2006, no. 26, obs. Malaurie-Vignal; RJDA 2006, no. 472; RLDA Feb. 2006. 20, note Azéma; RDLC 2006, no. 2, p. 103, obs. Fasquelle and Morel.

[69] Cass. Com., January 2007, D. 2007. AJ. 794, obs. Manara; JCP E 2007, no. 20–21, p. 9, note Larrieu; CCC 2007, no. 100, obs. Malaurie-Vignal; RJDA 2007, no. 421; CCE 2007, no. 55, obs. Ch. Caron.

[70] CA Paris, 16 January 2008, *SNC Sté Sunshine v Dobosz*: Comm. com. electr. 2008, comm. 53, obs. Ch. Caron; Rev. Lamy dr. immat. 2008, no. 1147, comm. F. Sardain and no. 1148, comm. A. Nappey; D. 2008, p. 288, obs. C. Manara, A. Bouvel and F. Sardain, Intell Property. 2008, doctr. p. 37. This judgement was quashed by the Court of Cassation on the ground of application of laws over time (Cass. com, 9 June 2009, appeal no. 08-12904). *Adde*. CA Versailles, 12th ch., 1st sect., 22 November 2001, 'Zebank', Comm. com. electr. 2002, comm. 56, obs. Ch. Caron.

[71] District Court, Paris, 29 October 2010, 'SNCF' case, available at www.legalis.net.

cases in which the applicant demonstrates a legitimate interest and acts in good faith. The absence of any reference to the competitive relationship in this text, adopted in 2011, seems to confirm the turnaround seen in the *Locatour* jurisprudence.

However, application of this provision to distinctive marks other than the trademark is still doubtful, insofar as the text targets impairments of "intellectual property rights". The fact remains that distinctive marks other than the trademark are not, strictly speaking, intellectual property rights.[72]

19.4.3 Identical Questions Relating to Meta Tags and Sponsored Links

Meta tags (or "keywords") are used by search engines to display search results or sponsored links to online users. Most disputes concern the *Adwords* advertising system offered by the *Google* company. This company specifically uses brands as keywords enabling commercial links to be generated that are aligned with the online user's request.

When the action is taken within the free riding domain, a competitive relationship is not required.[73] This solution does not present any difficulties since a competitive relationship is never required in terms of free riding.

In a judgement given on 12 February 2008 in the field of unfair competition, the Court of Cassation considered that the use by the *Google* company of a well-known brand as a keyword with a view to generating business links does not require a competitive relationship: 'A competitive situation is not required to lodge an action for unfair competition, as this only requires misconduct'.[74]

This solution, provided in the field of unfair competition by way of the trademark, can be extended to other distinctive marks. The general nature of the phrasing employed by the Court of Cassation seems in fact to enable application to all distinctive marks.

19.4.4 Absence of Incidence of Alternative Modes or Settlement for Online Disputes Not Based on a Competitive Relationship Between a Cybersquatter and a Victim of Cybersquatter

Indifference in terms of the competitive relationship criterion does not seem to have notably influenced French law insofar as it already is, broadly speaking, indifferent

[72] N. Dreyfus, "New law on domain names on French territory: evolution or revolution?" Com. Com. Elect 2011, study 13.

[73] District Court Paris, 3rd ch., 12 December 2007, *Syndicat Français de la Literie v Google France*: Juriscom.net.

[74] Cass. com., 12 February 2008, *Yoplait v Sté La fermière*, CCC. 2008, comm. 103, obs. M. Malaurie-Vignal.

to said criterion. The extent and flexibility of an action for unfair competition already leads French judges to not require a competitive relationship in order to sanction impairments to distinctive marks other than the trademark.

The use of distinctive marks other than the trademark is sanctioned in the field of unfair competition outside the scope of any competitive relationship between companies in litigation. Sanction of free riding and disparagement actually enables the protection of distinctive marks to be guaranteed without the requirement of a competitive relationship.

Domain name protection is however subordinated to the existence of a competitive relationship, although practitioners of French law are divided on this point.

19.5 "Questionable" Acts and Absence of Competitive Relationship

19.5.1 Admissibility of an Unfair Competition Action in Relation to Common Customers and in the Absence of Competitive Relationship

For a long time, jurisprudence and the doctrine (Roubier) required as a condition of admissibility of any action that a common customer base existed between the perpetrator and the victim of an unfair act. This was a result of the very expression "unfair competition": a competitive situation had to exist, along with an unfair act. Jurisprudence gradually changed its view on this condition and today admits that a competitive situation is not a condition of an action for unfair competition, 'which only requires the existence of misconduct that causes harm',[75] even if we occasionally find jurisprudence that is apparently the reverse[76]: there is necessarily a competitive relationship between the perpetrator of the unfair act and its 'victim'.[77] Nevertheless, in the end the Court of Cassation reaffirmed its condition of absence of competition. Thus in its judgement of April 2011, we read[78]:

> Whereas Article 1382 of the civil code;
>
> Whereas to rule out the existence of any unfair competition by disparagement and parasitic competition, the judgement holds that there is no competition in the current state of affairs between a pharmacist who works in his pharmacy selling retail drugs, and large-scale distribution that markets over-the-counter pharmaceutical products;
>
> Whereas in ruling thusly, although the existence of a direct and effective competitive situation between the companies in question is not a condition of the action for unfair

[75] Cass. com., 30 May 2000: D. 2001, p. 2587, note Y. Serra; Contracts, conc., consom., 2000, comm. no. 161, obs. M. Malaurie-Vignal. – 17 July 2001, unpublished, appeal no. 99-16499. – 12 February 2008: D. 2008, p. 2573, note Y. Picod.

[76] Cass. com., April 25, 2006: Contracts, competition, consumption 2006, comm.. no. 141, obs. M. Malaurie-Vignal (import–export company and hypermarket).

[77] District Court, Paris, 3rd ch., 9 July 2008, GR no. 06/17243.

[78] Cass. Com., 27 April 2011, unpublished, no.10-15648.

competition or free riding, which simply requires the existence of misconduct causing harm, the Court of Appeal breached the abovementioned text.

However, this jurisprudence shows that a distinction must be made between a direct competitive situation and common customer base. It is traditionally taught that a competitive situation leads to the sharing of a common customer base, but the converse situation does not automatically occur. Operators may address identical targets without being in an objective competitive situation. This is where a difference exists in respect of parasitic acts, since the later target a different customer base.

Thus in the few cases that enabled the Court of Cassation to rule out the condition of competitive situation if there were no direct competition, we still cannot rule out the presence of a common customer base.

In fact, in the judgement of 30 May 2000, the unscrupulous operator was an association (*Europe Nautisme*) created by a former partner and manager of a limited company created to manage the business aspects of nautical races developed by a first association (*Transat des Alizés*). The limited company accused *Europe Nautisme* of acts of unfair competition consisting of the misappropriation of the customer base of the *Transat des Alizés* association. In this case, there is indeed an identical customer base.

In the judgement of 17 July 2001, the parties involved were a company manufacturing and marketing air-conditioning products and an economic interest group (EIG) whose purpose was the promotion of air conditioning. Here again, these parties do not operate at the same economic point. However, the fact remains that their businesses target a common customer base.

The judgement of 12 February 2008 continues in this vein: a company made yoghurts for Yoplait for the catering channel, which it also marketed under its own trademark to supermarkets. This manufacturer then decided to enter into an exclusive agreement with Danone to make yoghurt in the same range intended for supermarket distribution. In this case, there are effectively two different distribution channels and, by hypothesis, an absence of competition. However, the customer base may be common: catering customers may become supermarket customers.

Lastly, the hypothesis of the judgement of 27 April 2011 differs somewhat insofar as there was no actual competition or any common customer base between the distributor Leclerc (and its over-the-counter pharmaceuticals) and pharmacists selling products not reimbursed by the French social security body. However, a litigious "opinion" campaign was directed at the latter's customers, whom Leclerc hoped to capture following a subsequent change in regulations. Thus, there may have been a forthcoming common customer base and a sought-after competitive situation.

In these aforementioned cases, there was indeed an attitude that could create ambiguity in terms of the identity of the protagonists.

Consequently, in the 2000 judgement, ambiguity could exist in terms of the person founding the second association who previously took part in managing the limited company. In the 2001 case, the difficulty arises from the fact that the EIG represented the interests of air-conditioning product manufacturers who were themselves direct competitors of the "victim" company. In the 2008 affair, ambiguity was heightened by the similar presentation of the products (two-colour sandstone pots). A consumer from the catering channel could thus confuse it with the product sold in a supermarket. Lastly, in 2011, ambiguity existed in that Leclerc was already positioned as a potential competitor on the non-reimbursed drugs market and used this opinion campaign to advertise its over-the-counter pharmaceuticals (see in this respect L. Arcelin, *Leclerc's Campaign for the distribution of non-reimbursed drugs*: *This is not an advertisement...*: note under CA Colmar, 7 May 2008: JCP E 2008, 2499).

The Court of Cassation hardly justifies its position. It contents itself with setting out the principle and recapping the conditions of Article 1382 of the Civil Code, the fundament of the action: wrongdoing, harm, and causal link. The judge cannot add further conditions that are not set down in law (*Ubi lex non distinguit, nec nos distinguere debemus*).

19.5.2 Admission by Jurisprudence of the Concept of Parasitic Acts

French jurisprudence has indeed borne witness to parasitic acts for a long time. As confirmed by the Court of Cassation in a judgement given on 19 January 2010 (Céline), "free riding is characterised by the circumstance according to which a legal entity or private individual takes inspiration from or copies from another party for profit in an unjustified manner, an economic value that is individualised, and provides a competitive advantage thanks to know-how, intellectual work and investment". This echoes the idea developed by Professor Le Tourneau by which the takeover of owned distinctive marks can be a cause for conviction when it occurs 'in the search for profit in a commercial activity'.[79]

There is doubtlessly a distinction to be made between parasitic competition and parasitic acts, strictly speaking. The former involves a competitive situation; in other words, parasitic competition is unfair competition (CA Nîmes, 26 May 2009, GR no. 06/01115: 'parasitic or free-riding behaviour in the presence of a competitive situation constitutes an act of unfair competition'), which is implicitly acknowledged by the Court of Cassation when it confirms that 'recourse to an action for free riding or parasitic competition is not subordinated to the absence of a competitive situation between the parties'.[80] This is not the case for parasitic acts (on the absence of a competitive situation, see Paris District Court, 3rd Civil Chamber, 17 June 2008, GR no. 07/02500). Jurisprudence does sometimes employ the expression of parasitic acts in a very general sense, covering acts that deal with

[79] Ph. Le Tourneau, Free Riding, J-Cl. Competition – Consumption, brochure no. 227, 2010, no. 57.

[80] Cass. com., 15 November 2011.

parasitic competition.[81] We will focus on the concept of parasitic acts in a strict sense.

The theory was developed by Yves Saint-Gal in 1956, who defined them as "an act by a merchant or industrial partner, which even when no harm was intended, takes or tries to take advantage of the reputation acquired legitimately by a third party, without a likelihood of confusion existing under normal circumstances between the goods and establishments." The examples are numerous. The grounds can be found in the *Pontiac* case, where the Paris Court of Appeal judged—without using the term 'parasitic acts'—that use of the Pontiac trademark, which normally covered motor vehicles, constituted an offence when used to designate refrigerators.[82] In the aftermath came the famous *Comité interprofessionnel du vin de champagne* case against *Yves Saint Laurent Parfums*, which for the first time expressly developed the theory[83] or, indeed, the *Guerlain* case.[84]

The Pontiac jurisprudence was enshrined from a legislative perspective under Article L. 713-5 of the IPC, transposing directive 89/104/EEC of the Council of 21 December 1988 to approximate the legislations of the various Member States in terms of trademarks.[85]

In contrast to unfair competition, an action designed to sanction parasitic acts is not based on a competitive situation or even on a common customer base.

Furthermore, this jurisprudence relies on the concept of awareness, which is not the case for jurisprudence relating to unfair competition or free riding. In fact, any victim of an act of unfair competition may act on this basis regardless of the scope of its reputation. It is in no way a condition of admissibility for the action. For instance, in a judgement of 2 December 2010, the Court of Appeal in Versailles focuses on the wrongdoing without requiring a specific level of awareness of the victim or its goods: 'In view of the fact that the Professional Medical Accessories company also accuses the Ondes & Rayons company of acts of free riding,

[81] See e.g. Cass. com., 14 February 2012, unpublished, no. 10-27873. – 29 November 2011, unpublished, no. 10-25703. – 19 January 2010, unpublished, no. 08-15338 08-16459 08-16469.

[82] CA Paris, 8 December 1962, D. 1963, p. 406.

[83] CA Paris, 15 December 1993, D.1994, jur. p. 145; JCP 1994 E, II, 540.

[84] CA Paris, 29 September 1995, Gaz. Pal. 26–30 May 1996.

[85] OJEC 1989 L 40, p. 1. Article 5-2 reads as follows: "Any Member State may also provide that the proprietor shall be entitled to prevent all third parties not having his consent from using in the course of trade any sign which is identical with, or similar to, the trade mark in relation to goods or services which are not similar to those for which the trade mark is registered, where the latter has a reputation in the Member State and where use of that sign without due cause takes unfair advantage of, or is detrimental to, the distinctive character or the repute of the trade mark", and was amended by the Ordinance of 11 December 2008 on patents and trademarks: "The reproduction or imitation of a trademark that enjoys repute for goods or services not similar to those designated in the registration commits the civil liability of its perpetrator if it is likely to harm the trade mark owner, or if this reproduction or imitation constitutes unjustified exploitation of said. The provisions of the previous indent are applicable to the reproduction or imitation of a brand that is widely known in the sense of Article 6 (b) of the Paris Convention for the aforesaid protection of industrial property."

exposing the latter to take advantage of the former's intellectual work and financial investments; in view of the fact that economic free riding is characterised by the circumstance in which a private individual or legal entity takes inspiration from or copies from someone else for profit in an unjustified manner, an economic value that is individualised, and provides a competitive advantage thanks to know-how, intellectual work and investment; in the case in hand, this circumstance is not specifically characterised since the evidence produced by the Professional Medical Accessories company referring to catalogue design, printing and distribution costs are not sufficient to justify the nature of any know-how whatsoever.'[86]

An action for unfair competition and free riding is based more on the wrongdoing of the unscrupulous operator than the victim. In other words, it is above all a disciplinary action. This appears clearly in jurisprudence that deduces, from the existence of an act of unfair competition, the existence of harm that is sometimes simply described as disruption to business understood to be an autonomous form of harm covering all behaviours likely to disrupt the smooth running of the market. We thus see that it necessarily infers harm or disruption to business from the act of unfair competition.[87] However, the level of awareness will then be an important element in the appraisal and quantification of harm.

Lastly, confusion is not required when an action for parasitic acts is brought.[88]

Jurisprudence is based on the idea of usurpation of awareness of a third party, as set out in Article L. 713-5 of the IPC. The Court of Cassation seems to make this a condition in any action for free riding. Thus in an unpublished judgement of 29 January 2002 (no. 99-21396), it is observed that the means by which, according to the alleged victim, "the Mefran company may have behaved in a parasitic manner towards it are not valid insofar as they do not demonstrate that the model of the table marketed by the victim enjoys sufficient reputation or level of awareness to allow the Mefran company to seek to position itself in the wake of said product by bringing a similar product to market", lending full weight to the stance that if there is no proof of awareness attached to the product or brand, then an action for parasitic acts cannot be upheld.[89]

This requirement seems perfectly legitimate: due to the principle of free trade and industry, it is not possible to protect every single mark. However, a doubt may

---

[86] CA Versailles, 12th Ch. Section 1, 2 December 2010, GR no. 09/08768 See also CA Lyon, 28 May 2009, GR no. 07/03157.

[87] Cass. com., 22 October 1985: Bull. civ. IV, no. 245. – 25 January 2000: Contracts, conc. consom. 2000, comm. no. 62, obs. M. Malaurie-Vignal. – 22 February 2000: Contracts, conc, consom. 2000, comm. no. 81, obs. M. Malaurie-Vignal. – 9 October 2001: Contracts, conc. consom. 2002, comm. no. 6, obs. M. Malaurie-Vignal. – 1 July 2003: Industrial property, November 2003, comm.. no. 96, obs. J. Schmidty-Szalewski. – 12 December 2006: unpublished, appeal no. 04-11947. – 27 May 2008: unpublished, appeal no. 07-14422. – 28 September 2010, unpublished, no. 09-69272. – Cass. 1st civ., 6 July 2011, unpublished, no. 10-20588. – Paris Comm. Court, 8th Ch., 6 November 2002, SA Royal Canin v SNC Hill's Pet Nutrition.

[88] Cass. com., 11 March 2003: Bull. civ. IV, no. 44.

[89] District Court Paris, 3rd Ch. Civ., 18 June 2008, GR no. 06/10098.

remain in terms of the very concept of awareness. Is it specifically distinct from the neighbouring concept of repute?

The concept of awareness applied to free riding can base itself on industrial property law. Article 6 (b) of the Paris Convention, quoted in Article L. 713-5 of the IPC and Article L. 711-4 of the Intellectual Property Code, uses the concept but does not define it. We can reasonably assume that the trademark in question is known about by a large proportion of the public. In fact, according to jurisprudence, reference must be made to the knowledge the general public has and not the specialised public. In order to establish said awareness, several elements are used: the age of the trademark, the length of time it has been used, advertising investment, and the extent of distribution of goods. The repute of a trademark, as understood in Article 5-2 of Directive 89/104/EEC of the Council of 21 December 1988 to approximate the legislation of the Member States relating to trademarks[90] is one "known by a significant part of the public concerned by the products or services covered by that trade mark".[91] Both concepts are synonymous, so to speak. The difference is one based on system, in that the protection of a well-known trademark does not require registration, in application of the Paris Convention of 20 March 1883, while registration is necessary for the protection of a trademark of wide repute.[92]

Once awareness is established, jurisprudence requires that the plaintiff proves the wrongdoing of the perpetrator, that is to say the latter's will to position itself in the wake of the well-known trademarks or goods at no expense. This wide repute was in fact built using investment that the free rider (parasite) seeks to sidestep by simply copying the beneficiary of the repute.[93]

Thus in a ruling given by the District Court in Paris of 17 June 2008 (op. cit.), PSG's action for parasitic acts was dismissed insofar as it did not provide proof of the wrongdoing supposedly committed by a sports betting company: "Whereas an applicant who has had their applications for infringement rejected is admitted to pursue the same matters under unfair competition and commercial free riding on the basis of Article 1382 of the Civil Code; Whereas in the case in hand, the PSG company, citing acts of commercial free riding due to the labelling of bets, does not establish how the defendants are positioning themselves in its wake to take advantage of its efforts at no expense (...) Whereas it is not proven in what way, by specifically announcing matches in which the PSG team is to play, the defendants are taking advantage of investments made by PSG, insofar as the defendants make more profit if more bettors bet on these matches, even less so given that those sporting events in which the team of the applicant's company does not take part are

[90] OJEC, 1989 L 40, p. 1.

[91] ECJ, case C-375/97, *General Motors v Yplon*, ECR 1999 I-5421.

[92] See Ph. Le Tourneau, Free Riding, J-Cl. Competition – Consumption, brochure no. 227, 2010, no. 64.

[93] For a case of parasitic competition in which advertising investment has been taken into account, see CA Versailles, 12th Ch. Section 1, 18 February 2010.

highlighted to the same extent on the disputed sites; Whereas as a result, the deeds of commercial free riding are not proven, and all the applications made by the PSG company must be dismissed".

19.6 Infringement, Unfair Competition, and Free Riding

19.6.1 Conciliation Between Unfair Competitive Action and Infringement Action

The cumulative application of actions subordinated to the "separate fact" criterion. The IPC does not schedule any criteria allowing infringement and unfair competition/free riding actions to be linked. However, a link problem exists in terms of these two actions when the litigious acts can both constitute an act of infringement and an act of unfair competition/free riding.

Generally speaking, three links can be envisaged:

- autonomy of the action for unfair competition in respect of the action for infringement;
- subordination of the action for unfair competition to the action for infringement;
- cumulative application of both actions.

French law retains the cumulative application of actions for infringement and unfair competition/free riding. The consequence of this cumulative application is that trademark invalidity is not connected to the success of an action brought for unfair competition[94] or free riding.[95]

An exception to the plurality of actions is further application on appeal. However, an applicant in an action for infringement cannot invoke the existence of acts of unfair competition for the first time before an Appeal Court. In the same way, an applicant of an action for unfair competition cannot invoke the existence of acts of infringement for the first time on appeal.[96]

The "separate fact" criterion. Cumulative application means that the actions can be brought before a judge at the same time. However, jurisprudence considers that they must not cover identical acts. In order to be admitted, the action for unfair competition must be based on 'separate facts' from acts of infringement.[97] The requirement for separate facts seems to be widely approved by the doctrine. Sometimes, certain authors consider that the search for distinct deeds is unjust since it results in depriving the company from bringing an action for unfair

[94] Cass. com., 25 January 1977, Ann. propr. ind. 1977. 63, note P. Mathély.

[95] Cass. com., 22 October 2002, Metro v Cartier, JCP ed. E 2003, p. 563, note Mainguy, Intellectual property 2003, no. 6, p. 85, note J. Passa.

[96] Cass. com., 29 March 2011 (2 judgements), Propr. industr. 2011, comm. 49, P. Tréfigny-Goy; Comm. com. electr. 2011, comm., 53, C. Caron; Propr. intell. 2011, no. 40, p. 323, note M. Sabatier.

[97] Cass. com., 19 January 2010, *Comm. com. electr.* 2010, comm. 32, com. Ch. Caron, *Contr., conc. consom.* 2010, comm. 101, obs. M. Malaurie-Vignal.

competition when the deeds are identical, although the basis and subject of the actions are different.[98]

Exceptions to the "separate fact" condition: the licensee's action. However, the act of bringing an infringement action is exempt from demonstration of a separate fact when brought by a licensee. In fact, the licensee is admitted to act in unfair competition even when the facts on which his action is based are identical to those which the trademark owner may have opposed under infringement.[99]

Comparison of infringement acts and unfair/free-riding acts. In principle, the same fact can never constitute an unfair or free-riding act and an infringement act at the same time.[100] An "infringement" act may naturally be sanctioned in the field of unfair competition when the distinctive mark is not subject to any protection (no registration or invalidity of registration) and when the term of protection has expired. Thus, there is no conflict between two actions.

Difficulty arises when the action for unfair competition is admitted as a sanction to an offence of customer base misappropriation, trademark depreciation, or usurpation of the trade name or mark.[101] In fact, these deeds show the very essence of trademark law, sanctioned as such by an action for infringement.

Two types of acts create particular difficulties:

- *Likelihood of confusion.* The actions for infringement and unfair competition each requires proof of a likelihood of confusion. However, the same act cannot in principle be subject to two actions due to the 'separate fact' requirement.[102] As such, an action for unfair competition can only succeed if the likelihood of confusion covers trademarked goods, or their origin, but not the trademarks themselves. In the event of a plurality of actions, Professor Passa considers that the likelihood of confusion can only be accepted as an unfair or parasitic act when it deepens the likelihood of confusion by the reproduction or imitation of a distinguishing aspect that is not included in the trademark registration (presentation, graphical item, packaging, shape of goods) or external to the trademarked goods, such as means of advertising.[103]
- *Slavish imitation.* Can the slavish imitation of a trademark constitute both an unfair act and an infringement? In terms of an unprotected mark, jurisprudence considers that slavish imitation of an unprotected mark is not wrongdoing.[104] In terms of a protected creation, jurisprudence is divided. The first civil chamber of

[98] X. Desjeux, Civil liability law as a boundary to the principle of freedom of trade and industry (regarding sanctions for copying), JCP E 1985, 14490.

[99] Cass. com., 22 March 2005, prec. supra, no 579; 13 December 2005, Propr. ind., April 2006, comm. no. 40, note J. Schmidt-Szalewski, PIBD 2006. 825. III. 176.

[100] See the "separate fact" condition.

[101] J. Passa, Infringement and unfair competition, Litec, 1997, no. 269, S. Durrande, Relations between infringement and unfair competition, D. 1984, chron. 187.

[102] Cass. com., 11 February 2003, PIBD 2003. 762. III. 213.

[103] J. Passa, Infringement and unfair competition, Litec, 1997, no. 255.

[104] Cass. com., 18 June 2002, PIBD 2002, 754. III. 578; 9 July 2002 and 22 October 2002, Intell. Prop., January 2003, note J. Passa.

the Court of Cassation thus recognised that slavish imitation of a trademarked creation suffices to characterise free riding.[105] However, the Commercial Chamber considers that the copying of a trademarked model that has been the subject of substantial advertising investment does not suffice to establish separate facts.[106]

19.6.2 Lack of Substitution Between the Unfair Competition Action and the Infringement Action

An action for unfair competition or free riding does not represent a "substitute" to an infringement action, insofar as the basis for actions and the way in which they are brought are not the same.

"Substitution" of the infringement action with the unfair competition action faces two obstacles:

- a risk of re-establishing monopolies against the legislator's will,
- impairment of free trade and industry of the operator using a mark that does not enjoy right of ownership.

However, we cannot ignore that, in practice, an action for unfair competition provides the owner of a mark not covered by a trademark right (due to an absence of registration or invalidity) or one whose term of protection has expired a means by which to act against any impairment endured.

19.7 Extent of the Protection of Brands, Distinctive Signs, or Other Components of Image or Identity

The issue of protection of distinctive marks or other components of the image or identity of a company outside of a competitive relationship should, in our view, be led by the *function* pursued by the laws in question.

Determination of the scope of the protection of a company's distinctive marks actually depends very much on the *function* that is assigned to them.

The origin of the finalised approach to laws has its basis specifically in the work of Gény and Josserand.[107] Gény perfectly sums up the mechanism by which laws are finalised: the reference to the social functions of a law enables the moral, political, social, or economic considerations to be weighed up, which are engaged in the conflict of interest in operation.[108]

[105] Cass. 1st civ., 19 October 2004, *Prop. Ind.* 2005, comm. 27 note J.-P. Viennois.

[106] Cass. com., 19 January 2010, *op. cit.*

[107] Josserand, On the spirit of laws and their relativity. Theory known as the abuse of law, Dalloz, 2nd edition, 1939, repub. 2006, no. 305.

[108] GÉNY, Methods of interpretation and sources in positive private law, LGDJ, 1919, repub. 1996, no. 173.

This notion of property law as a finalised law is included as part of the contemporary doctrine.[109]

Furthermore, the notion of trademark as a finalised law has logically taken precedence over the past few years in jurisprudence. The ECJ thus makes a distinction between the function of identification of the origin of the goods or services,[110] the advertising function, and the investment function.[111] The OHIM considers in the same vein that the trademark specifically fulfils a function of goodwill protection, thus brand image.[112]

The requirement of a competitive relationship should logically differ according to the function pursued by the distinctive mark and the other components of its image and identity.

In our view, it is advisable to make a distinction as to whether the laws on distinctive marks and other components of a company's image and identity protect the company or else protect the consumer.

When the function pursued by laws on distinctive marks and other components of its image and identity target company protection, then the competitive relationship should have no bearing.

Here, the distinctive mark is considered as a means of protecting the company in its identity and its investments. The competitive relationship then has no bearing on the harm caused to the company, in terms of free riding, for example.

When the function pursued by laws on distinctive marks and other components of its image and identity target consumer protection, then a competitive relationship should always be required.

Here, the distinctive mark is considered as a guarantee of the correct operation of the market through consumer protection. In the absence of a competitive relationship, the use of a third party's distinctive mark does not harm the consumer (there is no likelihood of confusion as to the origin of the goods). By way of exception, consumer protection is at stake when the impairment covers a well-known trademark: it is thus logical that the protection of a well-known trademark can bypass a competitive relationship.

---

[109] J. Canlorbe, *op. cit.*, no. 97 ff. R. LIBCHABER, 'Property, a fundamental right', in R. Cabrillac, M.-A. Frison-Roche and Th. Revet, Fundamental rights and freedoms, Dalloz, 2010, 16th ed., p. 723, spec. p. 736., A. Pirovano, 'The social function of laws: Reflection on the fate of Josserand's theories", D. 1972, chron., p. 67.

[110] ECJ, joint cases C-236/08 to C-238/08, *Google France SARL and Google Inc. v Louis Vuitton Malletier SA, Viaticum SA and Luteciel SARL, Centre national de recherche en relations humaines (CNRRH) SARL and Others*, ECR 2010 I-2417.

[111] ECJ, Case C-487/07, *L'Oréal SA, Lancôme parfums et beauté & Cie SNC and Laboratoire Garnier & Cie v Bellure NV, Malaika Investments Ltd and Starion International Ltd*, ECR 2009 I-5185.

[112] OHIM, 1st ch. rec., 14 September 2000, Unilever, R 436/1999-1, PIBD 2001, 724-III-367.

Germany

20

Frauke Henning-Bodewig

20.1 Brand Image and Defence of the Brand Image

The term "brand image" is not used in German statutory law, nor can it be found in German court decisions. It is considered to belong to marketing literature where it indicates the psychological aspects attributed to a product or service. If used at all in legal literature, "branding" means quite broadly any strategy to distinguish an enterprise, a product (or service) from other enterprises' products (or services) by means of a mark, distinctive name, title, colour, getup, or domain name.[1]

Instead of "brand image", German statutory law speaks of the "reputation" of marks or other distinctive signs. As one of the (unwritten) criteria for assessing the exploitation of a reputation, German courts and literature refer to the "product image" and the "image transfer".

In Germany, the legal instruments to defend a "brand image" (as interpreted in the sense above) are twofold: (1) trademark law and (2) unfair competition law. Both are distinct fields of law of high economic importance that can look back on almost 100 years of application. Both sets of law have, however, been replaced by modern laws during the last two decades: the Trade Mark Act (hereinafter "TMA") in 1994 and the Act against Unfair Competition (hereinafter "UWG") in 2004. There is an interaction between both laws insofar as unfair competition law has a "gap filling" function—it steps in where IP law lacks in (justified) protection. Since 1994, many constellations that were previously decided under unfair competition law, e.g. the protection of well-known marks against the exploitation of the reputation, are now encompassed by trademark law. As a consequence, the legal protection of the "brand image" is not the same today as it was 20 years ago.

[1] See *Haupt, Stefan/Schmidt, Ronald*, Markenrecht und Branding, München 2007.

F. Henning-Bodewig (✉)
Max Planck Institute for Intellectual Property and Competition Law, Munich, Germany
e-mail: fhb@ip.mpg.de

P. Këllezi et al. (eds.), *Antitrust for Small and Middle Size Undertakings and Image Protection from Non-Competitors*, LIDC Contributions on Antitrust Law, Intellectual Property and Unfair Competition, DOI 10.1007/978-3-642-54000-4_20,

The *current statutory framework* for the protection of the "brand image" can be characterised as follows.

20.1.1 Trademark Law

The German Trade Marks Act of 1994[2] is extremely broad. It not only implemented the trade mark Directive 89/104/EC[3]—including all its optional provisions—but also extends protection to all distinctive signs, unregistered marks with secondary meaning, company names, work titles, geographical indications of origin etc. Trademark protection is open to names, pictures, designs, colours, shapes, etc. The scope of protection for trademarks is defined in Sect. 14 TMA. Similar to Sect. 6 of the Directive 89/104, trademarks can be infringed not only by the use of an identical sign for identical products or the use of an identical or similar sign for identical or similar products that causes the risk of confusion but also if the trademark is well known and

> the use of that sign, without there being a justifiable reason, unfairly exploits, or is detrimental to, the distinctive character or the repute of such trademark.

The statutory text speaks of "goods or services that are not similar to those with respect to which the trademark enjoys protection", but according to the "Davidoff" decision of the ECJ,[4] the extended protection also applies to cases where the products are identical or similar.

Other distinctive signs than trademarks that fulfil the requirements for "commercial designations" in the sense of Sect. 4 TMA (for instance, all company symbols, titles of works) enjoy similar protection. Section 15 TMA protects well-known designations even without any likelihood of confusion against unjustifiable use that unfairly exploits or is detrimental to the distinctive character or repute of such commercial designation.

As an unwritten statutory requirement, German courts additionally require the infringing sign (or commercial designation) to be used in *business and* "*as a mark*". The requirement of "trademark use" was originally interpreted as a use to name the infringers' own products. Following the decisions of the ECJ in "Céline" and "L'Oréal", the German Federal Supreme Court (BGH) has adopted a broader definition of trademark use: encompassed is any use that might impair the functions of the mark; it is sufficient that it evokes an association with the mark, even if it is used in a satirical or ornamental context.[5] This has extended the scope of trademark protection for well-known trademarks against the exploitation of their image

[2] Act on the Protection of Trade Marks and other Symbols of 25 October 1994. German trademark law is discussed in English by *Lange*, in Lange (ed.), International Trade Mark and Sign Protection, Beck/Hart/Nomos, 2010, p. 437*ff.*

[3] OJ 1989 L 40 p. 1 for a codified version see Directive 2008/95/EC.

[4] ECJ, case C-292/00, *Davidoff & Cie SA and Zino Davidoff SA v Gofkid Ltd.*, ECR 2003 I-389.

[5] Cf. the "violet postcard" case, discussed in detail under Sect 20.2.3.

considerably (but has not necessarily extended protection as such—because the cases now decided under trademark law were formerly decided under unfair competition).[6]

20.1.2 Unfair Competition Law

Unfair competition law is regulated in the *Act Against Unfair Competition* (UWG) of 2004.[7] Although originally derived from general tort law, it is now a distinct field of law that protects competitors, consumers, and the general public alike. As its predecessor, the UWG of 1909, it is of a high practical importance in Germany.

Centre piece of the UWG is a general clause in Sect. 3, prohibiting all unfair commercial practices. The term "unfair" is explained by a list of examples of unfair practices (Sect. 4) and three additional provisions on misleading, comparative and intrusive, harassing practices (Sect. 5 to 7 UWG). Pursuant to Sect. 8 ff. the UWG is enforced almost exclusively through civil law sanctions (injunctions, removal, damages, and confiscation of profit). In practice, the focus is on requests for injunctive relief, often enforced through interlocutory injunctions. Standing to sue is given to competitors, their organisations, consumer organisations, and the Chamber of Commerce.

There is no specific prohibition of "parasitic commercial behaviour" in the UWG. The element of parasitism can, however, be taken into account in the assessment of unfairness under the general clause (although German courts are increasingly reluctant to do so[8]).

This does not mean that the protection of the "brand image" is without basis in the UWG. So far, several provisions of the UWG can play a role:

- Pursuant to Sect. 5 II UWG, a commercial practice shall be deemed unfair (misleading) "if in connection with the marketing of goods or services, including comparative advertising, it creates a risk of confusion with other goods or services or with the trademark or other distinguishing mark of a competitor".
- Pursuant to Sect. 6 II No. 4 UWG, comparative advertising is not allowed if it "takes unfair advantage of the goods, services, activities or personal or business circumstances of a competitor".
- Pursuant to Sect. 4 no. 9 b UWG, it is considered unfair to market an imitation of a good or service if it "unreasonably exploits or impairs the assessment of the replicated goods or services".
- Pursuant to Sect. 4 no. 10 UWG, it is considered unfair to "impede a competitor through a targeted action".

---

[6] See Sect. 20.1.3.

[7] Act Against Unfair Competition of 3 July 2004; for an overview in English, see *Henning-Bodewig/Boesche*, in: Henning-Bodewig (ed.), International Handbook on Unfair Competition, Beck/Hart/Nomos 2013, p. 231*ff.*

[8] See BGH GRUR 2005, 349, *Lego*.

20.1.3 Competitive Relationship

For *trademark law*, a competitive relationship is *not a prerequisite for protection.* The protection against the exploitation of the reputation of well-known trademarks (Sect. 14 I 3 TDA) explicitly extends protection for the use of products that are not identical or similar to those for which the well-known mark is known. The factor that the products are in competition with each other can, however, be taken into consideration by the courts in the assessment of the "image transfer" necessary for the exploitation of a reputation or for the definition of the element of "unfair."

It can be different under *competition law*. Although the application of the UWG does not require a competitive relationship but only an action "objectively connected with the sale of goods or services" and most provisions of the UWG can be applied without any competitive relation (e.g., the general clause), some provisions explicitly refer to "a competitor". This is the case for all four statutory provisions named above. Furthermore, the right of action is granted to "competitors" (Sect. 8). Consequently, the protection of the "brand image" based on the prohibitions in Sect. 4 nos. 9, 10 and 5 II, 6 II UWG and enforced through the owner of the distinctive sign would require a competitive relationship.

Pursuant to Sect. 2 no. 3 UWG, a "competitor" is any person who is in a "concrete competitive" relationship with another person. As the ECJ has defined this for comparative advertising, the products must be interchangeable.[9] German courts have consistently used similarly broad concepts and also acknowledged so-called ad hoc competition. A "concrete competitor relationship" exists not only between enterprises that actually or potentially deal with goods or services in the same sector but also between enterprises on different levels and even between enterprises that compete in the licensing market for certain marks or products. The German Federal Supreme Court decided as early as 1982—in a case concerning the Rolls Royce trademark "Flying Lady" in an ad for whisky—that "it is sufficient that both parties (.....) come to the *advertising business* with the same offer, e.g. there is the possibility that they use pictures of Rolls Royce automobiles as a support for their own advertising" (...).

It should be noted that the decision of the German Federal Supreme Court that affirmed an unfair exploitation of the famous mark's reputation was before the passing of the 1995 Trade Mark Act and cannot any longer be considered the leading case in this field. The broad interpretation of the term "competitor", however, still applies in unfair competition law.

To sum up, the "competitive relation" is not a requirement for *trademark law* (but may be considered in assessing the unfairness of the exploitation of the reputation of a well-known mark or sign). It is required in *unfair competition law* for all provisions directed towards competitors and consequently for all provisions that might potentially protect the "brand image". It is further required for the

[9] ECJ, case C-381/05, *De Landtsheer Emmanuel SA v Comité Interprofessionnel du Vin de Champagne and Veuve Clicquot Ponsardin SA*, ECR 2007 I-3115.

competitor's right of action. The term "competition" is, however, interpreted quite broadly by established court decisions.

20.2 Trademark, Principle of Specialty, and Competitive Relationship

20.2.1 Connections Between the Principle of Specialty and Competitive Relationship

As mentioned, the German Trade Mark Act protects all trademarks and distinctive signs against (1) the use of an identical sign for identical products, (2) the use of an identical or similar sign for identical or similar products if there is risk of confusion, and (3) the use of a sign identical or similar to a well-known mark without due cause, which takes unfair advantage of the well-known mark's reputation or is detrimental to its distinctive character.

The principle of specialty is obviously irrelevant in relation to the protection of well-known marks. The principle of speciality is self evident in relation to the first case, i.e. in relation to identical signs and identical products. It is a legal requirement in relation to the second case, i.e. in relation to identical or similar signs/identical or similar products causing a risk of confusion.

Neither the notion of "similar products" nor the notion of "risk of confusion" requires a competitive relationship between the claimant and the respondent. However, in determining the likelihood of confusion—which in turn depends on the similarity of the products—all relevant factors have to be taken into account. Relevant factors are, for instance, the characteristics of the product, the intended purpose of use, the method of use, etc. The similarity (and the risk of confusion) is determined according to the perception of the average (actual or potential) user of the product. So far, courts may also take into account whether the products, according to their characteristics, are regarded as being in competition with each other or are considered as complementary products.

Although a competitive relationship is not a statutory requirement, in practice the risk of confusion will be more likely if the products compete with each other. Pursuant to ECJ case law,[10] there is an interaction between the degree of distinctiveness of the earlier trademark, the identity (similarity) of the mark and sign, and the identity (similarity) of the goods and products. A lesser degree of similarity between goods may, for instance, be offset by a greater degree of similarity between the marks (or secondary meaning) and vice versa. Although the common link will often be the risk of confusion, this is a broader notion than that of a "competitive

[10] See, for instance, ECJ, Case C-39/97, *Canon Kabushiki Kaisha v Metro-Goldwyn-Mayer Inc.*, ECR 1998 I-5507.

relation". "Similar products" were, for instance, seen in cigarettes and apparel for smoking[11]; tomato products, olive oil,[12] etc.

20.2.2 In Which Situations and Conditions May Trademark Rights Be Opposed to the Use of the Trademark by a Non-competing Undertaking?

As discussed above, German trademark law protects well-known marks against the exploitation of their reputation outside of the principle of speciality. A competitive relation between the undertakings is not required. The latter is considered as one of the several factors that the courts may take into account while assessing the risk of confusion/similarity of goods or the extended protection for well-known marks (exploitation of the repute).

20.2.3 Protection of Well-Known Marks Against Exploitation of Repute or Lessening of Distinctive Character

Again, it has to be distinguished between protection provided by trademark law and protection provided by unfair competition law. Although in most cases the outcome will be similar, the requirements for protection can be different.

20.2.3.1 Trademark Protection

Section 14 of the German Trade Mark Act corresponds to Article 5(2) of the Directive 2008/95/EC. Consequently, the statutory text requires a well-known mark that has a reputation in Germany, and a use of a sign that "without due cause" either takes "unfair advantage of the repute of the trademark" or is "detrimental to its distinctive character". As discussed above, German courts further require the infringing sign to be used in business and "as a trademark".

According to the ECJ,[13] an exploitation of reputation adheres to the principle of correlation—the more distinctive the trademark is and the more it tends to resemble a famous mark, the more likely there seems to be an image transfer and thus an appropriation of its reputation.

The "taking advantage" of the repute of a well-known mark is considered as evident if there is an *image transfer*. An image transfer is not restricted to competing products. On the contrary, German courts have frequently dealt with cases in which the products were totally different, e.g. the Rolls Royce trademark (Flying Lady) used in an ad for whisky. There only has to be the possibility that the buyers

[11] BGH GRUR 1999, 496, *Tiffany*.

[12] BPatG Mitt. 2001, 7, *DelMonte*.

[13] See, e.g., the 2007 "Chevy" case, Case C-375/97, *General Motors Corporation v Yplon SA*, ECR 1999 I-5421.

of one product come into contact with the other product (assumed with "Dimple" buyers of whisky and cosmetics[14]). The well-known mark has to be original *per se* or must have acquired a strong secondary meaning; it must have a concise image. This was, e.g., denied in the case of McDonalds as the image as an efficient franchise was considered too vague[15].

The protection granted to well-known trademarks under Sect. 14 TMA is, however, not restricted to cases of an image transfer. Equally important are constellations where well-known marks are used as an *attention-getter*. The use of the (in Germany, famous) mark "TÜV" (for technical testing services) in "Erster privater TÜV" ("first private TÜV") for services offered on the internet without any risk of confusion was considered to be a trademark infringement because of the unfair exploitation of the well-known mark's reputation.[16]

The exploitation of a product's reputation in order to obtain attention for one's own product often implies a surprising, *satirical use* of the mark (which in turn can be highly *unpleasant* for the famous mark[17]).

Another group of cases concerns the so-called *ornamental use*, in which, for instance, a trademark is used as a pattern of a sweater.[18]

It should be kept in mind, however, that not every reference to a well-known trademark is considered a trademark violation. The mark has to be used "as a trademark", "without due cause" and "unfairly". "Unfair" means that according to a balance of interests considering all relevant aspects, in particular all aspects that might justify the respondent's use of the mark, one cannot expect that such use be acceptable to the trademark owner. So far, *constitutional aspects* may also play a role.

The attitude of German courts towards all the above-mentioned criteria is best demonstrated in the *violet postcard* case, decided by the BGH in 2005 (published in English in 38 IIC 119 (2007)):

> The case concerned a well-known colored trademark in a specific shade of lavender, registered for chocolate by the producer of "Milka", and often used for a "lilac cow". The same shade of lilac was used for a commercially marketed postcard with a satirical adaptation of a famous German poem by Rainer Maria Rilke. The first line of the poem "Über allen Gipfeln ist Ruh" was supplemented with the line "irgendwo blökt eine Kuh Muh"[19] and the author's name was changed into "Rainer Maria Milka."

As to a violation of Sect. 14 TMA, the Federal Supreme Court (BGH) stated:

---

[14] See BGH GRUR 1985, 550.

[15] OLG München, GRUR 1996, 63, *MacFish*.

[16] BGH GRUR 2011, 1043.

[17] See, for instance BGH GRUR 1995, 57 – use of the well-known mark Nivea for cosmetics for condoms; in the same direction, GRUR 1994, 808, *Mars*; GRUR 1986, 759, *BMW* – which considered the "satirical use" as illicit.

[18] BGH GRUR 1994, 635, *Pulloverbeschriftung*.

[19] In free translation: "There is silence above all troops", "somewhere a cow makes Muh".

aa) A use as a trademark is to be assumed if the sign is used in a manner such that it distinguishes the goods and services bearing the sign from the goods or services of other enterprises within the framework of the marketing of the product. ... For the scope of application of Article 5(2) of the Trade Mark Directive (Sec. 14 (2) No. 3 of the Trade Mark Act), it is also sufficient according to the judicial practice of the ECJ for the public concerned to regard the conflicting sign as decoration while associating it mentally with the famous trade mark on the grounds of the high degree of similarity.

bb) The question whether a use is a use in the manner of a sign is a question of law, but the answer depends largely on the findings of fact concerning the interpretation of the averagely informed, attentive and reasonable consumer as determined by the trial judge (...).

In the case at issue, there is no need to determine whether the target public, as the appeal court assumed and as contested by the appeal on the law as being contrary to experience, assumes that the postcard in question originated from the plaintiff's enterprise. Even if the public interprets the term "Milka" and the violet colour of the postcard purely as a product get up, it will mentally associate these elements with the plaintiff's trademark on the grounds of the plaintiff's identical word trademark and the background colour of the defendant's postcard, which is very similar to the plaintiff's colour mark. The appeal court rightly held that the stylistic means used by the defendant unmistakably refer to the plaintiff's trademarks. The association between the design of the postcard and the plaintiff's trademarks is precisely what constitutes the joke of the postcard. Thus, a use as a trademark within the meaning of Sec. 4(2) No. 3 of the Trade Mark Act is to be assumed in the case of the issue.

As the appeal court also assumed, the defendant exploits the particular degree of attentiveness that is associated with the use of the plaintiff's trademarks in the form of the name of a fictitious poet and the violet-coloured background of the postcard. The humorous character that the defendant aims to achieve through the design of the postcard can only be obtained if the target public recognises the reference to the plaintiff's trademarks, which presupposes that they have a reputation. In this way, the defendant exploits the particular attentiveness aroused by the association between a designation and a trademark with a reputation.

cc) However, the appeal on the law successfully contests the appeal court's assumption that the defendant was dishonestly using the plaintiff's signs without due cause.

dd) Nevertheless, where a trademark with a reputation is used in identical or similar form for the purpose of exploiting the attentiveness associated with its use, a conduct establishing dishonesty within the meaning of Sec. 14(2) No. 3 of the Trade Mark Act is to be assumed as a rule.

ee) In the case at issue, however, a trademark infringement by the defendant's postcard in question can be excluded by taking into account the defendant's right to the freedom of art as protected by Article 5(3) of the Constitution. The protection of the freedom of art applies not only, as the appeal court apparently assumed, to works that have a certain creative level (...).

20.2.3.2 Unfair Competition Law

As mentioned, there is an interaction between IP laws and unfair competition law insofar as the "gap filling function" of the UWG becomes less important the more protection is granted through IP laws. This can also be seen in the protection of well-known marks. Before the enactment of the Trade Mark Act 1994, no protection outside of the principle of specialty existed. Consequently, the appropriation of a famous mark's reputation without any risk of confusion could only be dealt with on the basis of the general clause in Sect. 1 UWG 1909 (prohibition of all acts of competition that were against "bones mores"). On this basis, the BGH decided, for instance, the famous "Rolls Royce" case cited above, where the use of the Rolls Royce in an ad for whisky was declared unfair competition. After the enactment of Sect. 14 TMA and its extended protection for well-known marks, constellations like this are mainly decided under trademark law.

Unfair competition law, however, still plays a role in constellations where *trademark use* is missing.

Other cases concern *comparative advertising*. Pursuant to Sect. 6 II UWG, comparative advertising is not allowed if it exploits the competitor's mark—which, contrary to trademark law, has not necessarily to be a well-known mark. German case law emphasises that the use of a competitor's mark as such in a comparison, even one with a strong image, is not an exploitation of reputation. There has to be an additional element of unfairness, e.g. an unusual focus on the competitor's mark that is not justified by the comparison itself or consumer interests. As the ECJ has indicated in its L'Oréal-decision,[20] the notion of unfair exploitation is determined in accordance with the criteria developed in trademark law. Consequently, the outcome of a case decided under unfair competition law and under trademark law will often be similar. For instance, in a recent decision on the basis of Sect. 6 UWG, the Federal Supreme Court denied a denigration of the trademark "Bild" (registered for a daily yellow paper) although the—humorous—comparison between its readers and those of the advertiser's newspaper presented the "Bild" reader as extremely primitive.[21] The arguments used in this decision were quite similar to those of the "violet postcard" decision cited above.

Outside of comparative advertising, the Supreme Federal Court (GRUR 2005, 163) had decided that the use of a picture of a famous sports car in an ad for car wheels is not an unfair exploitation of reputation because it is justified by the consumer's interest to be informed about the concrete use of the wheels and the fact that the image of the car's mark was not unnecessarily put forward (as to a different assessment, see the "Rolls Royce" case).

Unfair competition law further can be applied in cases of *product imitation* that lead to an exploitation of the reputation of the original (Sect. 4 no. 9 lit. b UWG). As early as 1985, the BGH has decided that the mass marketing of cheap copies of a luxury product (Rolex watch) can constitute unfair competition because it may destroy the exclusivity of the famous mark.[22] Recent decisions, however, have been more restrictive. In a case that concerned the imitation of the famous handbags of Hermès (which were, however, marketed under a different brand), the BGH neither saw a risk of confusion nor an exploitation of reputation—it was assumed that the buyers of such products are well aware of copies and thus pay close attention also to minor differences; consequently, there is no "post sale confusion" and no image

[20] ECJ, Case 487/07, *L'Oréal SA, Lancôme parfums et beauté & Cie SNC and Laboratoire Garnier & Cie v Bellure NV, Malaika Investments Ltd and Starion International Ltd.*, ECR 2009 I-5185.

[21] BGH GRUR 2010, 161, *Gib' Zeitung*.

[22] BGH GRUR 1985, *Tschibo/Rolex*.

transfer.[23] The imitation of famous sports cars as toys was equally not considered unfair.[24]

As to the offence of the *impediment of an individual competitor* through a targeted action (Sect. 4 no. 9 UG), German jurisprudence considers trademark protection as *lex specialis*. The BGH, for instance, refused to examine this point in the "lilac postcard" case, discussed above. It can be different if there is no "trademark use" so that a protection based on Sect. 14 TMA fails.[25]

20.2.4 Overlaps Between Trademark Law and Unfair Completion Law

Although Sect. 2 of the German Trade Mark Act explicitly states that additional protection on the basis of other statutory provisions, e.g. unfair competition law, is not excluded, the exact demarcation between both areas of law is more disputed than ever. Until recently, the prevailing view considered trademark protection as *lex specialis* so that unfair competition law was restricted to its function of filling the gap or to incidences where the requirements for trademark protection were not met (e.g., infringement without "trademark use") or additional aspects that play no role in trademark law were involved (e.g., deception). Since Directive 2005/29/EC[26] introduced a prohibition of so-called "imitation marketing" (deception through confusion between signs or marks), it is emphasised that both laws can *in principle be applied side by side* because they pursue different goals and have at least partly different requirements.[27] It is, however, equally stressed that unfair competition law may not undermine the principles of trademark law, in particular, not its conditions and terms of protection and it's right of action that is much broader in unfair competition law than in trademark law.

The outcome of this discussion is still open. In areas without any European harmonisation, like the impediment of competitors, which is regulated in Sect. 4 no. 10 UWG, the Federal Supreme Court still sees trademark law as *lex specialis*.

20.3 Trademark, Economy of the Trademark, and Relations with Competition

Section 14 TMA requires the trademark to be used in the course of trade and as a "trademark." Consequently, trademark law does not apply to any use "outside business". It was already mentioned that the German courts, following the ECJ,

---

[23] BGH GRUR 2007, 795.

[24] BGH GRUR 1994, 732, *MacLaren*.

[25] For Adwords, see Sect. 20.4.

[26] Directive 2005/29/EC of the European Parliament and of the Council of 11.5.2005 concerning unfair business-to-consumer commercial practices in the internal market, OJ 2005 L 149, p. 22.

[27] BGH GRUR 2013, 1161, Hard Rock Café.

have quite broadly interpreted the notion of trademark use. However, a behaviour that is purely private, political, etc. is not encompassed by trademark law, e.g. politically motivated boycotts against certain enterprises or marks or the use of a trademark as a motto for a private party or the modification of a branded watch by a private person.[28]

The same rule applies to unfair competition law. Purely private or social behaviour is not "objectively connected" with the sale of goods (although it may have an effect on the sale of goods). The offer of goods on the internet (Ebay) by private persons is neither trademark use nor a commercial practice under the UWG.[29]

The first three functions (origin, quality, communication) are undisputed. As to the fourth function (investment and advertising), it can be argued that the explicit recognition of investments as a function might strengthen the property right character of a trademark to a degree that endangers the mark's traditional function to guide consumers through an increasingly complex consumer world.

20.4 Other Distinctive Signs

Distinctive corporate signs can be infringed through all other signs, including marks. The prevailing view (at least before the ECJ's "Céline" decision)[30] sees the use as a trademark and a company name as intertwined because the business name at least indirectly also identifies the commercial source of the goods or services.

As mentioned, distinctive corporate signs and work titles enjoy protection against the exploitation of their reputation even if the infringing sign is not used for similar goods (Sect. 15 TMA). As with the extended protection for well-known marks, the use has to be unfair, which is determined according to a balance of interest. This is not restricted to any competitive relationship. For example, the use of "Dr. Sommer" for a rock band was regarded as an unfair exploitation of the title "Dr. Sommer" for a well-known column in a magazine.

The registration of a *domain name* is considered as "trademark use" (or use of a distinctive corporate sign) if it is used in relation to goods or services and not purely as a private address. According to the Federal Supreme Court, the use of *Adwords* as such is not a trademark use.[31] It can be different if the "Adword" is taken up in the ad of the respondent so that there is a clear reference to the mark.[32] If trademark protection fails, unfair competition law becomes crucial. In its "Adwords" decision, the German Supreme Federal Court denied, however, any impediment to the owner

[28] OLG Karlsruhe GRUR 1995, 417, *Rolex*.

[29] For Adwords, see Sect. 20.4.

[30] ECJ, Case C-17/06, *Céline SARL v Céline SA*, ECR 2007 I-7041.

[31] BGH 13 January 2011, MMR 2011, 590, *Bananabay II*.

[32] LG Nürnberg-Fürth 29 February 2012, WRP 2012, 879.

of the mark, as well as any deception of the public (mainly because there was no image transfer and recognisable reference to the mark).

The reputation of well-known marks and other distinctive signs can be exploited through the use of domain names, even for not similar goods or services. It is considered to be "unfair" if the owner of a well-known company name is prevented from using his name as a domain because this has been registered by another undertaking in order to attract attention. For instance, the domain "shell.de" registered for translation services was considered an exploitation of the famous mark and company name "Shell".[33]

20.5 Reprehensible Conduct and Lack of Relation of Competition

Trademark protection against the exploitation of the reputation of well-known marks and other distinctive signs does not require a competitive relationship. Unfair competition law requires it only for those provisions that refer to "a competitor"; for other provisions, e.g. the general clause in Sect. 3 UWG, it is not a prerequisite. If neither trademark law nor unfair competition law applies, mainly because the behaviour is not within business, the general tort clause (Sect. 823 BGB) or the protection for names (Sect. 12 BGB) may step in.

20.6 Infringement, Unfair Competition, and Parasitism

As to the relation between trademark law and unfair competition law, see above.

20.7 To Conclude

In general, enterprises are well protected against the exploitation of the reputation of their trademarks, even against the use for totally different products. The German Trade Mark Act is very broad and protects marks and all distinctive signs alike. Recent case law has found a convincing way to separate "fair" from "unfair" behaviour, e.g. in cases of "humorous" use. Unfair competition law grants equally broad protection but is restricted to those cases that cannot be solved under trademark law. Whether this traditional view can be upheld in the light of Article 6 of Directive 2005/29/EC (imitation marketing) remains to be seen. In general, it is to be regretted that Community law increasingly blurs the demarcation between IP laws and unfair competition law by introducing provisions that overlap with the existing "Acquis Communautaire".

[33] BGH 22 November 2001, MMR 2002, 382.

Hungary

21

Péter Lukácsi, Gusztáv Bacher, Ágnes Eszter Komári, Zsófia Lendvai, Ádám Liber, Boglárka Priskin, Katalin Szamosi, Izabella Szoboszlai, and Alexander Vida

21.1 The Status of the Brand Image

21.1.1 Legal Definition of the Brand Image

From a marketing point of view, brand image can be defined as the view of customers about a brand. Brand image, as the overall impression in the consumer's mind, is developed over time through the brand owner's continuous efforts (i.e., product quality, advertising campaigns) and is authenticated through the consumer's direct experience.

Brand image cannot be regarded as a legal notion in the Hungarian legal system. However, in our view, the significance of brand image, in relation to consumers, ought to be taken into consideration in unfair competition matters.

Péter Lukácsi is Head of the Working Committee.

P. Lukácsi (✉) • K. Szamosi
SBGK Law Office, Budapest, Hungary
e-mail: Lukacsi@sbgk.hu

G. Bacher
Szecskay Law Office, Budapest, Hungary

Á.E. Komári
Ministry of Rural Development, Budapest, Hungary

Zs. Lendvai
Baker & McKenzie, Budapest, Hungary

Á. Liber
Bogsch & Partners, Budapest, Hungary

B. Priskin • I. Szoboszlai
Hungarian Competition Authority, Budapest, Hungary

A. Vida
Danubia Patent and Trademark Ltd., Budapest, Hungary

P. Këllezi et al. (eds.), *Antitrust for Small and Middle Size Undertakings and Image Protection from Non-Competitors*, LIDC Contributions on Antitrust Law, Intellectual Property and Unfair Competition, DOI 10.1007/978-3-642-54000-4_21,

21.1.2 The Notion of "Brand Image" Through Case Law or Academic Writing

Brand image has not been defined in Hungarian law (neither in codified law nor in case law). By analogy, we refer to the concept of the trademark family. In case of a 'family' or 'series' of trademarks, the likelihood of confusion results from the possibility that the consumer may be mistaken as to the provenance or origin of goods or services covered by the later trademark applied for by third party or considers erroneously that such trademark is part of that family or series of marks. The risk that the public might believe that the goods or services in question come from the same undertaking or, as the case may be, from economically linked undertakings constitutes a likelihood of confusion.[1] In a similar way to the ECJ practice, the Hungarian Supreme Court has established that the trademark family constitutes an existing concept in the trademark law and means that the trademark owner holds several similar trademarks. The trademark family shall be taken into consideration as a factor in analysing the likelihood of confusion, in particular, by way of association.[2]

21.1.3 The Legal Instruments Used to Defend the "Brand Image" and the Implementation of the Notion of the Competitive Relations

Pursuant to Section 6 of the Competition Act,[3] "it shall be prohibited to manufacture, distribute or advertise goods and services (hereinafter together: goods) without the consent of competitor with such typical outside appearance, packaging or labelling (including designation of origin), or to use a name, mark or designation, by which a competitor or its goods are usually recognised". In legal practice, this is called "infringement of the characteristic appearance" or "slavish imitation" (although the scope of Section 6 is broader). This provision is the Hungarian passing-off rule.

The rationale for prohibiting imitations of a competitor's well-known and characteristic goods or signs is to prevent the competitor from unjustifiably drawing any profit from others' investments in promoting the goods. The exploitation of such successful economic activities (parasitism) constitutes unfair market practice.[4]

[1] ECJ, case C-234/06 P, *Il Ponte Finanziaria SpA v Office for Harmonisation in the Internal Market (Trade Marks and Designs) (OHIM)*, ECR 2007 I-733, para 63.

[2] Legfelsőbb Bíróság (Hungarian Supreme Court) Pfv.IV.21.975/2009/6.; in Hungarian legal literature, see Akos Süle, A védjegycsaládok, mint relatív kizáró okok; in Iparjogvédelmi és Szerzői Jogi Szemle, 2009/2, p. 42 and Alexander Vida, Protection of trademark families in Hungary, in: Hungarian Trademark News, 2010., p. 9.

[3] Act LVII of 1996 on the Prohibition of Unfair Trading Practices and Unfair Competition (hereinafter: "Competition Act").

[4] EBH 2003. 861.

The infringer would like to benefit from transferring the image of the well-known brand to its own goods. The protection against the confusion serves the interests of consumers as well. The basis of the protection is exclusively whether the sign or the appearance of the goods has already become well-known on the Hungarian market among consumers and if such a reputation involves positive evaluation by the consumers. If any sign or product appearance complies with these requirements, protection under competition law shall be granted.[5] The following aspects shall be taken into consideration in deciding whether or not an infringement exists:

1. Is the appearance of the allegedly copied product characteristic?
2. Is this characteristic appearance known by consumers?
3. Is the appearance of the competing product identical or similar to such an extent that consumers would associate such a competing product with the original product, thus resulting in the existence of an actual likelihood of confusion?

However, the first requirement for the application of Section 6 is whether the parties are competitors.

An example from court practice is the following: A foreign undertaking may start an unfair competition lawsuit if it qualifies as a competitor under the Competition Act. This issue is relevant in the case of services offered on the internet. When the operator of "Casino de Monte-Carlo" commenced litigation against the Hungarian operator of a casino and online gambling services under the name of "Monte-Carlo Budapest", the court established lack of a competitive situation because, with its seat outside Hungary, the plaintiff did not carry out any economic activity in Hungary. In general, the scope of the application of the Competition Act covers actions abroad if they affect the Hungarian market. However, this rule does not apply to unfair competition.[6] The plaintiff did not provide online gambling, and the plaintiff's market activity in Hungary cannot be established merely on the basis that its website was accessible from Hungary. Although the plaintiff's activities in Monaco are well known in Hungary, it is not present on the Hungarian market.[7]

If the specific provision on passing off is not applicable (Section 6), the injured party may seek protection under the general clause against unfair competition.

Section 2 of the Competition Act provides that "it is prohibited to conduct economic activities in an unfair manner and, in particular, in a manner which violates or jeopardises the lawful interests of competitors, business partners and consumers, or in a way which is in conflict with the requirements of business integrity".

The general clause establishing the general prohibition on unfair competition in Section 2 is a so-called subsidiary provision. If the market practice that is the

---

[5] BDT 2005. 1258.

[6] Section 1 of the Competition Act.

[7] BH 2011. 39, note: the factual situation was delicate since the services of both parties were available via the internet, but in the lack of real competing e-commerce services, the business activities could be territorially delineated. It should be noted that the judgment did not analyse the specific rules on e-commerce.

subject of litigation does not fall under any specific provisions, it shall be evaluated under this subsidiary provision and Section 2 can be used as an independent legal ground. Nevertheless, court practice considers the general clause not only as a general fallback rule behind the specific provisions on unfair competition but also as a *sui generis* provision, similar to the specific provisions of the Competition Act.[8]

Section 2 is applicable even if the parties are not competitors.[9]

The Competition Act does not define unfairness. Section 2 contains examples on unfair practices and the interests to be protected; however, this list is not exhaustive.

Therefore, in the lack of a normative definition of unfairness, it is the task of the judge to define the concept of "fairness" in light of the specific behaviours subject to the legal dispute. Fairness is interpreted as the prevalence of "good morals" among market participants. In the course of adjudicating whether a practice is fair, in particular, social expectations, usages, and standards shall be decisive factors. The Competition Act provides a list of market activities that are considered by the legislator *per se* as being unfair because they violate or jeopardise the legitimate interest of competitors, business partners, and consumers or because they are contrary to the requirement of business fairness. The violation or jeopardising of any of these interests is sufficient in itself for the application of Section 2 of the Competition Act, because practices that do not fall within one of the specific provisions can nevertheless be qualified as unfair competition. However, the alleged unfairness must have an impact on market participants (which is broader in scope than the concept of "competitors") that is equal to the expressly named stated occurrences; causing confusion, discrediting a competitor, or making false allegations about a product are reasonably harmful practices, and in order for any commercial conduct to be prohibited directly under the general clause, it has to be equally serious and harmful to competitors.

Here is an example from court practice: if the competitor uses a product name that does not comply with the legal requirements for using such a name, this constitutes unfair market practice. The basis of the unfairness is that the infringing party gains a competitive advantage over his competitors who comply with legal rules, and he saves on the investment costs necessary for the production of goods complying with the legal requirements.[10]

---

[8] BDT 2011/4/61, Szegedi Ítélőtábla (Szeged Court of Appeal) Gf.I.30056/2010.

[9] See Sect. 21.5.1.

[10] BDT 2005. 1087.

21.2 The Link Between the Rule of Speciality Applicable in Trademarks Law and the Possibility to Act Against Non-competitors

The rule of speciality defined in the law of trademarks means that, in principle, the scope of protection of a trademark shall only cover those goods and services for which the trademark is registered. This chapter deals with the question of whether being registered for certain goods and services automatically means that the trademark proprietor may only act against producers and distributors of identical or similar goods and services or whether national law permits, under given circumstances, action to be taken against non-competitors as well.

21.2.1 The Link Between the Rule of Speciality and Competitive Relations

It is apparent that trademark protection is granted through the registration of a given sign in relation to a certain group of goods and/or services. This has the effect that the proprietor may, in general, only exercise his trademark rights against the use or attempt of registration of an identical or similar sign in relation to identical or similar services. Accordingly, this may lead to conclude that trademark protection principally extends to providing a legal basis for actions against competing undertakings in competitive relations.

However, while applying the principle of speciality, Hungarian trademark law also provides for the enhanced protection of trademarks with reputation, in compliance with the Trademark Directive.

Pursuant to Section 4 (1) c) of Act XI of 1997 on the Protection of Trademarks and Geographical Indications (hereinafter the "Trademark Act"), "a sign with later priority registered for different goods or services that is identical or similar to an earlier trademark enjoying a good reputation in the domestic market may not be granted trademark protection, where the use of the later trademark without due cause would take unfair advantage of, or be detrimental to, the distinctive character or the repute of the earlier trademark".

As regards trademark infringement, Section 12 (2) c) of the Trademark Act provides the following: "[o]n the basis of this exclusive right of use, the proprietor may initiate proceedings against any party who, without his consent, uses in its business operations any sign identical or similar to the trademark in connection with goods or services that are not listed in the specification of goods for which the trademark is registered, to the extent that such trademark has a good reputation in the domestic market and the use of the sign without due cause would be detrimental to or unfairly exploit the trademark's distinctive character or reputation".

It is therefore clear that the protection of reputed trademarks goes beyond identical/similar goods and services and shall thus be applicable in case the concerned undertakings are not in competition with one another.

The legal requirements in this regard correspond with the European practice, i.e. a trademark enjoys reputation if it is known by a substantial part of the relevant public in Hungary. The same applies for the detriment caused to, or the unfair advantage that is gained from, the distinctive character or repute of the trademark without due cause: there is no specific Hungarian jurisprudence that would deviate from the general rules and guidelines of European trademark law and practice.

21.2.2 Influence on the Rules of Civil Liability

In case of any type of trademark infringement—including an infringement of a reputed trademark, as specified above—sanctions apply in accordance with Section 27 (2) and (3) of the Trademark Act.[11]

In case of a breach of the Competition Act, practically the same sanctions shall apply.

It can be concluded from the above that almost all of the above sanctions concern objective liability, regardless of the fact whether the infringement was committed by a competitor or a non-competitor. The only exception is the liability for damages, which is at all times dependent on subjective conditions such as the culpability of the infringer.

The general clause of civil liability for damages is defined in Section 339 (1) of the Hungarian Civil Code as follows: "A person who causes damage to another person in violation of the law shall be liable for such damage. He shall be relieved of liability if he is able to prove that he has acted in a manner that can generally be expected in the given situation."

[11] Section 27 (2) and (3) reads as follows: "(2) In the event of trademark infringement, the trademark proprietor may – in accordance with the circumstances of the case – lodge the following civil law claims:

a) he may demand a court ruling establishing that trademark infringement has occurred;

b) he may demand cessation of the trademark infringement or threat of infringement and inhibition of the infringer from further infringement;

c) he may demand that the infringer provide information on parties taking part in the manufacture of and trade in goods or performance of services which infringe on the trademark, as well as on business relationships established for the use of the infringer;

d) he may demand that the infringer make amends for his action – by declaration or in some other appropriate manner – and, if necessary, that such amends should be given due publicity by and at the expense of the infringer;

e) he may demand restitution of the economic gains achieved through infringement of the trademark;

f) he may demand seizure of those assets and materials used exclusively or primarily in the infringement of the trademark, as well as of the goods infringing on the trademark or their packaging, or demand that they are delivered to a particular person, recalled and definitively withdrawn from commercial circulation, or destroyed.

(3) In the event of trademark infringement the trademark proprietor may demand compensation for damages in accordance with the provisions of civil liability."

Consequently, it follows that the establishment of infringement is generally to be distinguished from the liability for damages on the basis of the objective nature of the former and the subjective character of the latter. In other words, the establishment of the infringement is not necessarily followed by the establishment of a liability for damages; additional conditions shall be fulfilled.

Overall, the establishment of infringement may influence the liability for damages in one aspect, i.e. the fact that the presumption of unlawfulness contained in the general provisions of tort law turns into an undisputable fact once the decision on the infringement becomes final and legally binding. Thus, there may be no room for an infringer to prove the lawfulness of his conduct; he may only argue that there was no causal link or culpability.

21.3 Trademark, "Economy" of the Trademark, and Relation of Competition

21.3.1 The Liability of a Non-competitor Who Uses a Previous Trademark "Outside Business"

The liability of someone who uses a trademark "outside business" is not excluded in the law of Hungary. Examples include the following:

a) The act of denigrating the mark of a competitor or the competitor itself is an injury in the term of Section 3 of the Competition Act.
b) If the denigrating is damaging, the committer ought not be competitor, he can be sued in the terms of Section 339 of the Civil Code.

A case of this kind was adjudged by the Hungarian courts. The trademark HYUNDAI was used by the former retailers of cars and the registrar of the identical domain name. Both were condemned to discontinue the use of the HYUNDAI mark even though the registrar had not been in any kind of business relationship with the trademark owner, nor had they been competitors.[12]

21.3.2 The Future of the Community Case Law Regarding the Trademark Functions and the Grounds of Trademark Infringement

The initial approach of the European Court of Justice was made 10 years ago in ARSENAL (C-206/01), namely an approach stressing on indication of origin. This function was not invented by the European Court of Justice; it was known for a long time in the common opinion of the international profession. We think that statements of the European Court of Justice on the functions of trademark are not

[12] See a report in English in Acta Juridica Hungarica 2011, No 4. p. 343.

constitutive but declarative ones. As a result, these statements do not "renew" the traditional problem.

The Hungarian courts seek to apply in trademark matters also the "acquis communautaire"; as a result, reference to the functions of trademarks occurs rather often in judgments.

Sanctioning the "undermining" of the trademark functions is, in some kind, based on Section 5 (2) of the Trademark Directive protecting reputed marks that may be protected only by law of unfair competition outside the European Union.

21.4 Other Distinctive Signs

21.4.1 Possible Concrete Examples of the Liability of a Non-competitor Who Uses Other Signs as Company Names, Brand Names

Rules that may provide legal basis for sanctioning the infringing use of distinctive signs by a non-competing undertaking do exist in the Hungarian legal system.

Firstly, company names are initially protected by Section 77 of the Civil Code, as well as Sections 3 (4) and 4 (4) of Act V of 2006 on Public Company Information, Company Registration and Winding-up Proceeding, according to which "The corporate name (concise name) of a company must clearly differ from the name of any other company already registered in the country, and from the name referred to in Subsection (3) of Section 6—irrespective of the company form—and it must not suggest any misleading implications, in particular as relating to the scope of activities and the form of the company. The names of outstanding historical figures may only be included in a corporate name by authorisation of the Hungarian Academy of Sciences, and a name the rights of which are owned by others may be included in a corporate name only with the consent of the party holding such right".

Pursuant to Section 2 of the Competition Act, "it is prohibited to conduct economic activities in an unfair manner and, in particular, in a manner which violates or jeopardizes the lawful interests of competitors, business partners and consumers, or in a way which is in conflict with the requirements of business integrity". This provision sets out the general prohibition of unfair competition and may be applicable to non-competitors as well. Unfair economic activity may consist of the misuse of distinctive signs by a non-competitor. Based on this rule, the injured party may seek protection in court proceeding.

There are other legal grounds based on which action can be brought in case of misuse, however, not by the injured party itself but by different administrative authorities. These provisions protect primarily the common interest of consumers and business partners; their application is therefore available for sanctioning the misuse of distinctive signs by both competing and non-competing undertakings. These provisions are presented below.

According to Section 8 of the Competition Act, "deception of trading shall be presumed, in particular, if false declarations are made or facts are declared in a manner which is likely to deceive with respect to prices or essential features of the goods, including, in particular, the composition, use, effects on health or the environment, as well as their handling, origin or place of origin, source or method of the procurement; if the designation of goods is likely to deceive, or if any other information which is likely to deceive pertaining to the essential features of the goods is disseminated". In this respect, distinctive signs may be considered essential features of the goods.

Furthermore, Section 12 of Act XLVIII of 2008 on Essential Conditions of and Certain Limitations to Business Advertising Activity[13] prohibits misleading advertising, which may also consist in the infringing use of distinctive signs by a non-competing entity.

Finally, provisions of Act XLVII of 2008 on the prohibition of the unfair business to consumer commercial practices (hereinafter "UCPA"), which implemented Directive 2005/29/EC concerning unfair business-to-consumer commercial practices in the internal market[14] (the "Unfair Commercial Practices Directive" or "UCP Directive") into the Hungarian law, protect the general interest of consumers and prohibit the misleading or deceptive commercial practice of an entity. The provisions of this Act apply to non-competitors as well and may apply in relation to the misuse of a distinctive sign by a non-competitor. Besides Section 3 of the UCPA, which generally prohibits unfair commercial practices, Section 6 (2) a)[15] sets forth special prohibition in relation to distinctive signs. In addition,

[13] Section 12:

"(1) Misleading advertising shall be prohibited. (2) In determining whether advertising is misleading, account shall be taken in particular of any information and communication it contains concerning:

a) The characteristics of goods,

b) The price of goods or the manner in which the price is calculated, and the other contractual terms and conditions on which the goods are purchased or used,

c) The appraisal of the advertiser, such as his nature, attributes and rights, his assets, qualifications, awards and distinctions.

(3) For the purposes of point a) of Section (2), characteristics of goods are in particular their design, composition, technical specification, quantity, geographical and commercial origin, method and date of manufacture or provision, availability, delivery, usage, the knowledge needed for their use and maintenance, fitness for purpose, the results to be expected from their use, the danger and risks attached to their use, their impact on health, their environmental effects, energy consumption characteristics, tests and checks on them or the results of those tests and checks."

[14] OJ 2005 L 149, p. 22.

[15] Section 6 (2):

"a) the commercial practice shall also be regarded as misleading if it may create confusion with another undertaking or any trade names, goods, designations of goods or other distinguishing marks of another undertaking; if, in the factual context of the commercial practice, taking account of all its features and circumstances, this causes or is likely to cause the consumer to take a transactional decision that he would not have taken otherwise".

Annex Point 3 and Point 14 of the UCPA define special commercial practices concerning the misuse of other distinctive signs that may be considered per se unfair according to Section 3 (4) of the same Act. Pursuant to Annex Point 3, "displaying a trust mark, quality mark or similar distinctive labeling without having obtained the necessary authorization is a prohibited commercial practice". Annex Point 14 stipulates that "advertising goods that are similar to goods made by a particular undertaking in such a manner as deliberately to mislead the consumer into believing that the goods are made by the same undertaking when they are not is prohibited".

21.4.2 Same Question Concerning the Use of Domain Names

While the Trademark Act does not deal with domain name as such, i.e. does not specify the use of a trademark in a domain name as trademark infringement, the Domain Registration Rules that apply to the registration of .hu ccTLD domain names do. This means that the registration of a domain name will not constitute in itself trademark infringement without the use of the domain name in the course of business activity. However, pursuant to the Rules that are binding on domain name holders (as well as on the registrars), registering a domain name that is the trademark of a third party may constitute registration against the Rules and thus might be subject to revocation or transfer of the domain name to the trademark holder. According to the Rules, as well as the trademark holder, any third party who has a right or legal interest in a domain name can object to the registration of such a name.

We are of the view that the specificity of domain names and/or the Internet should not justify any particular treatment. This is in accordance with the consequent court practice that regards the domain name as a type of trade name.[16] The relevant court practice also states that instead of the context of misuse of the name, the infringing nature of the use has decisive importance if "infringement of the characteristic appearance" is committed by domain name use.

The Hungarian court practice gives regard to the competition relationship when deciding on infringing domain names. The court practice established that the so-called infringement of the characteristic appearance, which constitutes an unfair economic activity as defined in Section 6 of the Competition Act,[17] may be committed by domain name use. In a recent case,[18] the online operator providing accommodation advertising services that registered and used the domain name

[16] BDT 2010. 2216, BDT 2009. 1960 and BDT 2008. 1740.

[17] Section 6:

"It shall be prohibited to manufacture, distribute or advertise goods and services (hereinafter together: goods) without the consent of competitors if such goods have a characteristic presentation, packaging or labeling (including designation of origin), or to use a name, mark or designation, by which a competitor or its goods are usually recognized."

[18] Fővárosi Ítélőtábla (Metropolitan Court of Appeal) 14. Gf. 40 601/2010/3.

szallasinfo.hu brought lawsuit against the operator who provided the same services under the domain name *szallasinfo.info*. The defendant, who was the competitor of the plaintiff, registered its domain name and launched its business activity after several years of that of the plaintiff. In this case, the judges established that the defendant violated the prohibition of unfair economic activities defined in Section 2 and Section 6 of the Competition Act by committing "infringement of the characteristic appearance" of its competitor. Although the plaintiff's domain name was a part of the plaintiff's registered figurative trademark, the court decision did not mention the existence of a trademark as a criterion for establishing an "infringement of the characteristic appearance".

21.4.3 Same Questions Concerning Meta Tags and Sponsored Links

Meta tags and sponsored links do not constitute a subject matter of special legal regulation as such and do not appear in the published Hungarian court practice. Thus, the general Hungarian trademark and competition rules shall apply to them.

The recent judgment of the Court of Justice of the European Union in the case Interflora[19] may give some guidance in this matter, but the judgment is based on the trademark approach since the case was brought on, and consequently the Court founded its reasoning on the Trademark Directive and did not examine the question from the point of view of EU competition law.

21.4.4 Possible Implication of Alternative Dispute Resolution Systems

Alternative Dispute Resolution (ADR) exists in Hungary, where the competitive relation between the opposing parties is given weight. During such procedure, the ADR body may decide to revoke or transfer the infringing domain name by applying its Rules of Procedures. The Rules define that the revocation or the transfer of a domain name may be ordered if the domain name has been applied for or is being used in bad faith [Point 31 b)]. The use of a domain name in bad faith may—among other things—be established if the domain name was primarily registered for the purpose of disrupting the professional activity of the competing undertaking [Point 33 c)].

---

[19] Case C-323/09, *Interflora Inc. and Interflora British Unit v Marks & Spencer plc et Flowers Direct Online Ltd.*, ECR 2011 I-8625.

21.5 "Reprehensible" Conduct and Lack of Competitive Relations

21.5.1 Unfair Competition by Non-competitors

According to the court practice, the rules on unfair competition are applicable not only in legal disputes between competitors. In the judgment published under No. BDT 2011. 2444, it was established that—as opposed to the earlier regulation—Part I Chapter II of the Competition Act regulates not only those acts that can be committed by competitors against each other. Accordingly, there are provisions that can be applied in individual, civil procedures between the injured undertaking and the infringer, irrespective of whether or not they are competitors.

Under the prohibition on unfair competition, Chapter II of the Competition Act generally sets forth the prohibition on unfair competition (Section 2) and, within this area, separately enumerates the following prohibitions: to violate or jeopardise the good reputation or credit-worthiness of a competitor (Section 3), to gain access to or use business secrets in an unfair manner (Section 4), to make an unfair appeal to another party to cease a business relationship (boycott) (Section 5), to make slavish imitation (Section 6); to interfere with the fairness of a bidding process (in particular, public tender, invitation to tender) (Section 7). According to Hungarian law, these behaviours are considered as unfair competition in a narrow sense, which entitle the injured party to seek protection from the court.

Although Section 3 and Section 6 are applicable between competitors, Sections 2, 4 and 5 can be referred to by the injured party even if it is not a competitor.

21.5.2 Parasitism and Non-competitive Relations

As presented in Sect. 21.1.3, the court practice has set forth that the reason for the prohibition on the imitation of competitor's well-known and characteristic goods or signs (Section 6 of the Competition Act) is to prevent the competitor from drawing without any grounds any profit from others' investments in promoting the goods. The exploitation of such successful economic activities constitutes unfair market practice (parasitism).

In our view, this approach shall be applicable, in general, to all unfair market practices.

In view of the Hungarian group, any undertaking shall be entitled to prevent all third parties not having its consent from acting in the course of trade in such a manner that aims or results at—without due cause—taking unfair advantage of, or being detrimental to, the achievements or the repute of that undertaking. This type of protection shall be similar to the protection of trademarks with good reputation.

21.6 The Links Between Infringement, Unfair Competition, and Parasitism in a Legal Action

We note that this question has been thoroughly answered by the report of the Hungarian Group to Question A in 2005; see the summary of our standpoint below.

21.6.1 Articulation of Those Various Legal Grounds

Under Hungarian law, unfair competition claims are *secondary* in relation to claims based on industrial property rights.[20] However, this does not exclude claimants from asserting claims simultaneously based on two separate legal grounds, including infringement and unfair competition claims. In that regard, competition law might complement the protection conferred to by IP rights where industrial property rights (e.g., trademark, design) do not provide full-scope protection. This may be the case where, due to the lack of specific intellectual property rights, unfair competition law grants protection to well-known characteristic of goods or their packaging. Conversely, Hungarian law does not exclude the possibility of violation of competition rights in cases where the infringement of IP rights in itself could not be established, as the general clause of competition law makes protection possible even in cases where no specific form of protection provided by law is available.

In a trademark or design infringement lawsuit, it is sufficient to rely on the respective trademark/design as registered, which has to be compared with the allegedly infringing sign when assessing infringement.

In its unfair competition claim, the claimant must assert before a court that

1. the imitated product has a characteristic appearance,
2. the characteristic appearance is known by the consumers, and
3. the appearance of the competing product is identical with, or similar to, the imitated product to such an extent that consumers would associate the competing product with the original and, for instance, whether there exists a risk of confusion.[21]

In assessing the risk of confusion, both unfair competition law and trademark law take as a benchmark the notion of the average consumer who is reasonably well informed and reasonably observant. Further, it is also generally acknowledged by the Hungarian judicial practice that consumers do not analyse the various details of the product but take the transactional decision after the first impression.[22] Notably, in trademark law the registered sign is compared to the infringing use; however, in case of an unfair competition claim, not the registration but the imitated product (its actual use) shall be compared to the imitation as a whole whether the impression

[20] See Competition Law/"Commentaries of Economic Laws" Series (Versenyjog/Gazdasági törvények kommentárjai sorozat), HVG-ORAC, 2001, p. 78.

[21] Section 6 of the Competition Act.

[22] Legfelsőbb Bíróság (Supreme Court) BH 1993. 25.

given by the products is likely to deceive the consumer, i.e. as regards the source of the product or economic relationship of its manufacturer. In that regard, it is of significant importance that the nature of the products is identical.[23]

21.6.2 Possible Substitution of Unfair Competition Legal Action Instead of Infringement Legal Action

In Hungary, "unfair competition law" and "trademark law" are in the relationship of general versus specific rules; therefore, as a rule, unfair competition can be seen as a substitute for trademark infringement, even though the law does not exclude the possibility of an unfair competition violation where the infringement of trademark rights in itself could not be established.

According to local practice, the parallel enforcement of rights may be justified if trademark protection has not yet been granted,[24] trademark protection has lapsed,[25] or proprietor of the trademark is a foreign person and the product is distributed by a domestic distributor. In this latter case, the proprietor of the trademark may institute proceedings for trademark infringement, whereas the distributor may proceed as a co-claimant on the basis of competition law harm. Finally, unfair competition law may grant protection to the characteristic of goods or their packaging if the claimant could not rely upon a specific trademark right. This may be the case where the trademark (the list of goods) does not enjoy protection with respect to the imitated goods.[26]

With a view to the above, it is legitimate to use the action for unfair competition (parasitic practices) as a substitute for infringement proceedings where the scope of protection of the rights in unfair competition is independent from the intellectual property right.

We are not aware of any legal literature on the undue exploitation of "positive externalities".

The general clause[27] of the Competition Act declares a general prohibition of unfair economic activities. The scope of the prohibition is not limited to the economic activities of competitors: "It shall be prohibited to engage in unfair economic activities, particularly in a manner that infringes or jeopardises the legitimate interests of competitors, trading parties or consumers or is contrary to the requirements of business fairness."

---

[23] Legfelsőbb Bíróság (Supreme Court) No. Pfv.IV.20.791/2011/4.; Fővárosi Ítélőtábla (Metropolitan Court of Appeal) No 8.Pf.21.705/2011/4.

[24] BH 1993. 25.

[25] BH 1995. 20.

[26] See Dr. Boytha Györgyné, Dr. Rácz László, Dr. Szamosi Katalin, Dr. Vida Sándor: Versenyjog és iparjogvédelem (Competition Law and Industrial Property Rights), October 1997, Iparjogvédelmi és Szerzői Jogi Szemle.

[27] Section 2.

Contrary to the above-stated provision, the Competition Act[28] contains a special prohibition that gives protection to a competitor in the event that another competitor is using its distinctive signs. On the other hand, the provisions of the UCPA[29] directly protect the general interests of consumers and therefore provide broader protection for all market players.

Since safeguarding fair competition for the sake of the common interest is considered to be the main and utmost goal of both of the above-mentioned acts, all other market actors are consequently protected *indirectly and generally* by both the Competition Act and the UCPA.

The enforcement system that is in operation justifies the above-mentioned distinction—while claims stemming from the infringement of Section 6 of the Competition Act (such as imitation[30]) shall be enforced before the Courts,[31] the authorities have the power to act[32] under the provisions of the UCPA to protect consumers against unfair commercial practices. In the latter case, it is assumed that the broader public interest is affected by the commercial practice in question.

Before presenting the relevant UCPA provisions, it must be mentioned that Hungarian law also provides protection against unfair practices for vertical business partners. However, in such cases, a higher level of awareness in the decision-

[28] Section 6: "It shall be prohibited to manufacture, distribute or advertise goods and services (hereinafter together: goods) without the consent of competitors if such goods have a characteristic presentation, packaging or labelling (including designation of origin), or to use a name, mark or designation, by which a competitor or its goods are usually recognised."

[29] Which came into force on 1 September 2008.

[30] Section 6 of the Competition Act.

[31] The court shall have the power to hear and decide cases conducted against violations of the provisions contained in Sections 2 to 7 of the Competition Act.

[32] Section 10 of UPCA reads as following:

(1) The consumer protection authority shall have the power to proceed against infringements of the prohibition of unfair commercial practices, with the exceptions defined in Sections (2) and (3).

(2) The Hungarian Financial Supervisory Authority shall have the power to proceed against infringements of the prohibition of unfair commercial practices, with the exception defined in Section (3), where the commercial practice concerned relates to an activity of the undertaking, which is supervised, under Act CXXXV of 2007 on the Hungarian Financial Supervisory Authority (hereinafter: "FSAA"), by the Hungarian Supervisory Authority.

(3) The Hungarian Competition Authority shall have the power to proceed against infringements of the prohibition of unfair commercial practices, where the commercial practice is capable of materially affecting competition.

(4) Section (3) shall not apply where the unfair commercial practice is displayed only on the product or on the packaging of the product, or fixed to the product by other means (hereinafter referred to collectively as "label"), or is apparent from manual guides or directions for use provided with the product or from the warranty note, or if it is carried out by the infringement of the information requirement set out in Section 7 (3).

(5) Where the commercial practice displayed on the label is also carried out by other means of communication represented in the same way and with the same content, and where with respect to the latter commercial practice the Hungarian Competition Authority has the power to proceed in view of its material effect on competition, the Hungarian Competition Authority shall also have the power to assess the infringement committed by the commercial practice displayed on the label.

making process is expected of the trading parties than is expected of public consumers. Chapter III of the Competition Act prohibits unfair manipulation of business decisions; however, the scope of this chapter does not cover practices that qualify as misleading advertising under the provisions of Act XLVIII of 2008 on Essential Conditions of and Certain Limitations to Business Advertising Activity (hereinafter: *Advertising Act*).

According the Competition Act's wording,[33] *deception of trading parties shall be presumed, in particular, if*

a) false declarations are made or facts are declared in a manner which is likely to deceive with respect to prices or essential features of the goods, including, in particular, the composition, use, effects on health or the environment, as well as their handling, origin or place of origin, source or method of the procurement; if the designation of goods is likely to deceive, or if any other information which is likely to deceive pertaining to the essential features of the goods is disseminated;

b) it is concealed that the goods fail to meet legal or other usual requirements for such goods, or that the use of the goods requires conditions which are significantly different from what is customary;

c) information that is deceptive or may possibly be deceptive is given about factors related to the sale and distribution of the goods influencing the decision of trading parties, in particular, about the method of distribution, terms of payment, gifts associated with the goods, discounts, or the chance of winning;

d) a false impression of especially advantageous purchase is created.

Even without relevant decisions regarding the above-mentioned sections, it can be stated that distinctive signs are essential features of the goods—unless the businesses would not use them.

In fact the trading parties may behave deceptively through their advertisements, and therefore Section 12 of the Advertising Act[34] should be applied on a more regular basis in the case of the misleading use of distinctive signs in business-to-business relations.

---

[33] Section 8.

[34] Pursuant to Section 12 of the Advertising Act:

(1) Misleading advertising shall be prohibited.

(2) In determining whether advertising is misleading, account shall be taken in particular of any information and communication it contains concerning:

a) The characteristics of goods,

b) The price of goods or the manner in which the price is calculated, and the other contractual terms and conditions on which the goods are purchased or used,

c) The appraisal of the advertiser, such as his nature, attributes and rights, his assets, qualifications, awards and distinctions.

(3) For the purposes of point a) of Section (2), *characteristics of goods are in particular their design, composition, technical specification, quantity, geographical and commercial origin, method and date of manufacture or provision, availability, delivery, usage, the knowledge needed for their use and maintenance, fitness for purpose, the results to be expected from their use, the danger and risks attached to their use, their impact on health, their environmental effects, energy consumption characteristics, tests and checks on them or the results of those tests and checks.*

Nevertheless, any false or deceptive use of a distinctive sign may be misleading, regardless of whether it is applied by a competitor or a non-competing company.

In 2012, the Hungarian Competition Authority (hereinafter "GVH") commenced six competition supervision proceedings against different companies supplying online or printed registers. The companies involved were sending invoices to different, non-competitor companies without real orders. As a result of this behaviour, some of these companies may have been under the impression that the service had been ordered before.

Moreover, one of companies against which the competition supervision proceeding was launched used magenta as a dominant colour on the invoice, which referred to one of the biggest telecom companies in the Hungarian market. By using magenta on the invoices, the targeted clients may have believed that the company's service belonged to the trusted company. The above-mentioned proceeding is still in process.

Due to the asymmetry of information that exists in business-to-consumer relations, misleading or deceptive commercial practices may occur on a more regular basis in that context than in a business-to-business context. In contrast to this, abuse of distinctive signs is more likely to be caught between competitors than at other levels of the supply chain. It can be presumed that the misuse of some well-known and reliable signs that are familiar to consumers might be an effective marketing method even for a non-competing market player.

According to Article 14 of the preamble to the UCP Directive, it "is not the intention of this Directive to reduce consumer choice by prohibiting the promotion of products which look similar to other products unless this similarity confuses consumers as to the commercial origin of the product and is therefore misleading".

The general clause of the UCPA says that "this Act determines the requirements for commercial practices followed in regard to consumers before, during and after a commercial transaction in relation to goods and for the codes of conduct applied to such commercial practices, furthermore, it determines the rules for the procedures conducted against infringements of those requirements".[35]

Unfair commercial practices are prohibited by Section 3 of the UPCA. Two general conditions must be met by the commercial practice in question in order for it to qualify as an unfair commercial practice:

a) it fails to meet the standard of special skill and care, which a person carrying out that commercial practice may reasonably be expected to exercise, commensurate with the fundamental principle of good faith and fairness (hereinafter referred to as the "requirement of professional diligence"), and
b) it appreciably reduces or is likely to appreciably reduce the possibility for the consumer to whom it is directed, whom it reaches, or whom it is addressed to make an informed decision with regard to the goods based on the necessary information and thereby causes the consumer or is likely to cause him to take a

[35] Section 1 (1) of UCPA.

transactional decision that he would not have taken otherwise (hereinafter referred to as "distortion of the behaviour of consumers").

For example, if a webshop uses a well-known sign of a product or any trust mark of a service as a reference without having any right or ground that would justify its use of the sign, the requirement of professional diligence may be infringed as the operator of the webshop should be aware of the need to gain the authorisation or consent of the right holder to use the sign. Distortion of the transactional decisions[36] of consumers may be proved if they are buying products from the webshop because they are trusting in the misused signs that imply that the products in question are of a high quality when in fact the consumers actually receive products of a significantly lower quality.

In particular, commercial practices shall be unfair if they are misleading, as set out in Sections 6 and 7, or are aggressive, as set out in Section 8 of the UPCA.[37]

In addition to the general prohibition of misleading commercial practices that are laid down in the UCPA, it also adopts special provisions concerning distinctive signs. The above-mentioned provisions are set out in Section 6 (2) a) of the UCPA and points 3 and 13 of the Annex of the UCPA. Pursuant to Section 6 (2) a), the commercial practice shall also be regarded as misleading if it may create confusion with another undertaking or any trade names, goods, designations of goods, or other distinguishing marks of another undertaking if, in the factual context of the commercial practice, taking account of all its features and circumstances, this causes or is likely to cause the consumer to take a transactional decision that he would not have taken otherwise.

In addition, there are two commercial practices in the Annex that may be infringed by means of the misuse of distinctive signs by a non-competitor enterprise. The commercial practices listed in the Annex shall be considered as *per se* unfair.[38]

Point 3 of the Annex stipulates "displaying a trust mark, quality mark or similar distinctive labelling without having obtained the necessary authorisation is a prohibited commercial practice".

The following commercial practices may fall under the scope of Point 3 of the Annex, according to the brochure that introduced the UCP directive[39]:

- claiming to be a signatory to a code of conduct when the trader is not;
- displaying a trust mark, quality mark, or equivalent without having obtained the necessary authorisation;
- claiming that a code of conduct has an endorsement from a public or other body that it does not have.

[36] A transactional decision means any decision taken by a consumer concerning whether, how, and on what terms to conclude a contract or to exercise a right in relation to the goods. Section 2 h) UCPA.

[37] Section 3 (3) of UCPA.

[38] Section 3 (4) of UCPA.

[39] See also http://ec.europa.eu/consumers/cons_int/safe_shop/fair_bus_pract/ucp_en.pdf.

- claiming that a trader (including its commercial practices) or a product has been approved, endorsed, or authorised by a public or private body when it has not or making such a claim without complying with the terms of the approval, endorsement, or authorisation.

A "Guidance on the UCP directive"[40] adopted by the European Commission gives the following example for the commercial practice laid down in Point 3 of the Annex: "Using any community or national label (e.g. Nordic Swan label, Blue angel, or NF environment) without authorisation."

Notably, the scope of Point 3 of the Annex is not limited to a failure to obtain authorisation from the relevant public or private body but also covers the misuse of trust marks or quality marks of any kind.

According to Point 13 of the Annex, "advertising goods that are similar to goods made by a particular undertaking in such a manner as deliberately to mislead the consumer into believing that the goods are made by that same undertaking when they are not" is prohibited.

The above-mentioned brochure contains[41] the following explanation with respect to Annex point 13 "promoting a product similar to a product made by a particular manufacturer in such a manner as deliberately to mislead the consumer into believing that the product is made by that same manufacturer when it is not".

Thus far, the GVH has very little case law on the application of the provisions of the UCPA mentioned above.

The GVH[42] ruled that by displaying the trademark "Biokontroll" in the commercial communication that was subject to the investigation, the party to the proceeding had infringed the prohibition of unfair commercial practices against consumers. The GVH held that by displaying the trademark "Biokontroll"[43] in the relevant commercial communication, the party to the proceeding had implied to the consumers that the cosmetics in question were certified by "Biokontroll" and that they consequently qualified as bio-products. The commercial practice in question simultaneously implied that the whole production process, including the use of organic ingredients, could be considered as bio. The GVH concluded that none of the products of the party to the proceeding were endorsed by "Biokontroll" and that only the cultivation processes of some of the ingredients made out of plants were authorised. The GVH said in its resolution that the display of the trademark in question constituted the infringement. The GVH found the additional explanatory

---

[40] See Commission, 2009, Guidance on the implementation/application of directive 2005/29/EC on unfair commercial practices, SEC(2009) 1666, available at http://ec.europa.eu/consumers/rights/docs/Guidance_UCP_Directive_en.pdf.

[41] See also http://ec.europa.eu/consumers/cons_int/safe_shop/fair_bus_pract/ucp_en.pdf.

[42] The Resolution of the GVH in a competition proceeding, which was initiated for a suspected infringement of the prohibition of unfair commercial practices against consumers. See case No Vj-103/2009, Ilcsi Szépítő Füvek Biokozmetikai Kft.

[43] The trademark holder is Biokontroll Hungária Nonprofit Kft., which pursues endorsement activity with regard to agricultural products.

information that was displayed on the website of the party in connection with the trademark to be insufficient to eliminate the infringement in question.

Over past 4–5 years, the GVH has launched dozen of competition supervision proceedings against so-called consumer groups. Consumer groups do not provide any financial service; consequently, the consumers do not receive any loan when the contracts are concluded, and therefore they do not compete with financial service companies (such as banks). Thus, the consumers of consumer groups only get a so-called purchase right: it is decided monthly by draw which consumer of the group will be able to purchase the targeted item. At the same time, they launched an aggressive advertising campaign in the printed media. Their advertisements failed to provide complete information on the true nature of these consumer groups, and their advertisements suggested that their services were similar to financial services. Even their names implied financial activity and contained words that referred to financial services such as "invest", "euro correct", or "group saving".

If the Competition Council declares the commercial practice in question illegal, besides imposing a fine it may simultaneously:[44]

- order the termination of any illegal conduct,
- prohibit the continuation of any illegal conduct,
- order the publication of a statement of correction in connection with any unlawful communication of information.

Consequently, if distinctive signs are used by non-competitors whose commercial practices infringe the provisions of the UCPA, this behaviour may give rise to the sanctions discussed above.

Nevertheless, in any case, in relation to the potential misleading or misused name, prior to the intervention of competition law, as a filter, Section 3 (4) and Section 4 (5) of the Act V of 2006 on Public Company Information, Company Registration and Winding-up Proceedings should be considered. The provisions referred to above set forth the following: "The corporate name (concise name) of a company must clearly differ from the name of any other company already registered in the country, and from the name referred to in Subsection (3) of Section 6—irrespective of the company form—and it must not suggest any misleading implications, in particular as relating to the scope of activities and the form of the company. The names of outstanding historical figures may only be included in a corporate name by authorisation of the Hungarian Academy of Sciences, and a name the rights of which are owned by others may be included in a corporate name only with the consent of the party holding such right."

Conclusions and Policy Recommendations

As presented above, the Hungarian court practice has set forth that the reason for the prohibition on the imitation of competitor's well-known and characteristic goods or signs is to prevent the competitor from drawing without any grounds

[44] Section 77 of the Competition Act.

any profit from others' investments in promoting the goods. The exploitation of such successful economic activities constitutes unfair market practice.

In our view, this approach shall be applicable in general to all unfair market practices, including those between non-competitors.

Thus, any undertaking shall be entitled to prevent all third parties not having his consent from acting in the course of trade in such a manner that aims or results at—without due cause—taking unfair advantage of, or being detrimental to, the achievements or the repute of that undertaking. This type of protection shall be similar to the protection of trademarks with good reputation.

Italy

22

Francesca La Rocca

22.1 The Status of Brand Image

22.1.1 Legal Definition of Brand Image

Under Italian law, there is no specific legal definition and notion of brand image. However, in relation to trademarks with a reputation, which are regulated by Article 20.1*c* Code of Intellectual Property (hereinafter CIP), case law recognises the importance of protecting the goodwill of trademarks when referring to "blurring of the image of the trademark", "product not in line with the image of the trademark".[1]

22.1.2 The Notion of "Brand Image" Through Case Law or Academic Writing

Italian case law mainly refers to the concept of "company image"[2] rather than "brand image", but the two concepts can probably be assimilated. Even if there is no express definition of "company image", we may conclude that the concept is similar to the one of the "image of a person" protected by Italian Law under Article 10 of the Italian Civil Code (hereinafter CC). However, recently, the Italian Supreme Court expressly recognised "the protection of the right to the image and denomination of a product identified by a trademark".[3]

---

[1] Court of Venice, 10/4/2006.

[2] Cass. 4/6/2007 n. 12929; Court of Milan 9 March 1987; Court of Naples 13 July 1998; Court of Milan 19 April 2010; *Giurì codice autodisciplina pubblicitaria* 19 December 2002.

[3] Cass. 11 August 2009 n. 18218.

F. La Rocca (✉)
Sena e Tarchini, Milano, Italy
e-mail: senatarchini@senatarchini.com

P. Këllezi et al. (eds.), *Antitrust for Small and Middle Size Undertakings and Image Protection from Non-Competitors*, LIDC Contributions on Antitrust Law, Intellectual Property and Unfair Competition, DOI 10.1007/978-3-642-54000-4_22, © Springer-Verlag Berlin Heidelberg 2014

22.1.3 The Legal Instruments Available to Defend "Brand Image" and the Implementation of the Notion of the Competitive Relations

Under Italian intellectual property law there are no specific rules that protect "brand image", but Article 2043 CC may apply that provides for a general tort rule prohibiting behaviours that cause unlawful damages, regardless of the existence of a competitive relationship between the parties.[4] Furthermore, Article 2598 (2) and (3) CC, regarding unfair competition behaviours, may mainly apply in the case of competing undertakings. Lastly, in the hypothesis of a trademark with a reputation, Article 20.1*c* CIP may be applied, which provides protection to trademark owners also regardless of the existence of competitive relations.

22.2 The Link Between the Rule of Specialty Applicable in Trademarks Law and the Possibility to File Suit Against Non-competitors

22.2.1 The Link Between the Rule of Speciality and Competitive Relationships

Under Italian law, according to the principle of speciality, confusion between signs may subsist and involve only either identical or similar (*affini*) goods or services; therefore, a competitive relationship is usually implicitly assumed (Article 20.1*a-b*, 12.1*b-c* CIP). Case law of the Italian Supreme Court underlines that goods and services, to be similar, should be directed to the same group of consumers.[5] Regarding the competitive relation, the Supreme Court held that "the commonality of clients is a sufficient requirement to have competitive relations between parties".[6] Therefore, the rule of speciality and the concept of competitive relationship are based on the same principle.

22.2.2 Influence on the Rules of Civil Liability

Article 20.1*c* CIP, which recalls Article 5.2 of the European Directive 08/95/EC,[7] protects trademarks with a reputation regardless of any actual competition between the products or services of the trademark owner and the infringer. It allows a trademark proprietor to claim infringement of his registered trademark even against

[4] Cass. 11 August 2009 n. 18218; Cass. 4 June 2007 n. 12929.

[5] *Inter alia*, Cass.19 March 1991 n. 2942; Cass. 22 January 1993 n. 782; Cass. 15 May 1997 n. 4295.

[6] Cass. 2 April 2007 n. 8215.

[7] Directive 2008/95/EC of the European Parliament and of the Council.

trademarks of non-competing undertakings. Indeed, this Article prohibits any use of that trademark that causes unfair advantage of, or is detrimental to, the distinctive character or reputation of the trademark. Italian Courts have held that the undue advantage may consist in positive effects, acquired by the users, which derive from their parasitic behaviour. Moreover, the damage suffered by the proprietor of the trademark has been identified as that damage resulting from the blurring of the image of the trademark due to the use of a confusingly similar trademark by a competitor on goods that do not conform to the image of the proprietor's trademark.[8]

Furthermore, according to Article 21.1 CIP, specific uses of a registered trademark by a third party may be allowed in cases where the trademark corresponds to the name of this person or the trademark is used in a descriptive way or the use of the trademark is necessary to indicate the intended purpose of a product or service. However, these uses will give rise to an infringement if they are not in accordance with honest practices in industrial or commercial matters. Therefore, a descriptive use of the trademark, by a third party, that dilutes or tarnishes the registered trademark will be illicit, regardless of whether the use is made by a competitor or non-competitor.[9] Furthermore, there may be cases where a third party uses a registered trademark, without the consent of the trademark owner, not to identify its own products or services but to identify the original products or services. This hypothesis is usually lawful, but the trademark owner may have a right to oppose to such use of its trademark if this behaviour causes damage to the image of the trademark amongst the consumers.[10]

Recently, the function of a trademark has expanded. A trademark is not just a badge of origin, but it communicates a message to the consumer. It is a guarantee of quality and has power of advertising. Therefore, nowadays, a trademark has a value *per se*. If such value is undermined, Article 2598.3 CC and Article 2043 CC may apply.[11]

Article 2598 CC pertains to unfair competition practices (*concorrenza sleale*). In relation to the topic discussed here, Article 2598.2 prohibits allegations that discredit the products or the activity of a competitor and those acts that will allow a third party to take unfair advantage; thus, it specifically refers to competing relations. On the other hand, Article 2598.3 CC prohibits all acts that are contrary to honest practices (*correttezza professionale*). The majority of Courts[12] in interpreting Article 2598 CC stated that a competitive relationship between

---

[8] Court of Bologna 27 January 1996; Court of Milan 4 March 1999; Court of Milan 30 May 2005; Court of Venice 10 April 2006; Court of Turin 26 October 2007; Court of Milan 31 December 2009.

[9] Court of Milan 4 July 1998; Court of Rome 18 December 2007; Cass. n. 17734, 30 July 2009.

[10] Court of Milan 11 October 1976; Court of Appeal of Milan 26 May 1978; Court of Appeal of Milan 13 July 1979; Cass. 28 June 1980 n. 4090; Cass. 7 May 1983 n. 3109.

[11] Court of Bari, *ord.*1 February 2010.

[12] *Inter alia*, Cass. 2 April 2007 n. 8215.

undertakings is essential in order to have unfair competition. However, a case law has established that this rule applies even if the undertakings involved are non-competitors, but they must be commercial undertaking. Indeed, case law stated that the behaviour of a commercial undertaking that takes unfair advantage from or is detrimental to the reputation or image of a third party infringes Article 2598.3 CC, irrespective of the competitive relationship between the parties.[13] It must be specified that the interpretation of Article 2598.3 CC is still under debate and no unanimous solution has yet been reached.

Article 2043 CC states that one who commits an unlawful behaviour is liable to pay damages. This rule has been applied also in the hypothesis where the behaviour of an undertaking that does not infringe a trademark nor constitute unfair competition tarnishes or dilutes the economic reputation of another non-competing party.[14]

22.3 Trademark, "Economy" of the Trademark, and Relation of Competition

22.3.1 The Liability of a Non-competitor Who Uses a Previous Trademark "Outside Business"

Article 20 CIP, which states the principles of trademark infringement, requires the infringer to be a commercial undertaking. The same requirement is established under the unfair competition provisions contained in Article 2598.3 CC. On the other hand, Article 2043 CC states a general clause of tort law that may be applied to prohibit the use of a trademark outside of the context of commercial activity. As mentioned in Sect. 22.2.2, a trademark owner may have a right to oppose a third party's use of its registered trademark even when the use of the trademark is to identify the original products or services. This hypothesis may include cases where the trademark is not used for commercial purposes (i.e., parodist use of trademark). In particular, we may consider the decision of the Court of Milan,[15] which held that the third party who uses such trademark as a sponsor link without the consent of the trademark owner is taking unfair advantage of the repute of the trademark. The Court continued noting that this behaviour will not just cause confusion, unfair advantage, and acts of dishonest practice but also represents trademark infringement.

[13] Court of Milan 9 March 1987.

[14] Cass. 25 July 1986 n. 4755; *Pretura* of Rome, *ord.* 4 July 1987.

[15] Court of Milan 11 March 2009.

22.3.2 The Future of Community Case Law Regarding Trademarks Infringement

Italian case law expressly referred to the "new" functions of the trademark (such as guarantee of quality and advertising) and its goodwill; moreover, it recognised that trademarks communicate to consumers the image of the undertaking.[16] The Court of Venice ruled that the detriment to the distinctive character of a trademark with repute is caused by the use by a third party of an identical or similar sign for products of an inferior quality than those of the trademark owner. In this way, the Court recognised the function of the trademark as guarantee of quality.

We may conclude that, also according to Italian case law, the function of a trademark has moved beyond its role as a badge of origin to embody other meanings.

22.4 Other Distinctive Signs

22.4.1 Possible Concrete Examples of the Liability for a Non-competitor Who Uses Other Signs as Company Names, Brand Names, Domain Names, Meta Tags, and Sponsored Links

Article 2.4 CIP states that rules on registered trademarks are applicable also to other distinctive signs (company names, domain names, meta tags, and sponsored links). Article 22 CIP establishes the "unity principle of distinctive signs" under which the same rules of trademark law are applicable to company names, domain names, and other signs used in business activities. Specifically, the use, as a domain name or meta tag of a trademark with reputation is forbidden regardless of the existence of a competitive relationship (Article 22.2 CIP). Furthermore, even Article 2598 CC may apply when the necessary requirements are met.[17] However, those decisions concern competitors.

On the other hand, in the so-called domain-grabbing cases there is no need for a competitive relationship between the parties, even when the trademark used as domain name does not have a repute; indeed in such cases, it would suffice to prove the bad faith of the party who registered the domain name in order to qualify the behaviour as being illegal.

[16] Court of Milan 7 October 2010; Court of Bologna 6 February 2009; Court of Venice, 10 April 2006.

[17] Regarding domain names and meta tags: Court of Milan 20 February 2009; Court of Milan 14 November 2005; Court of Naples 20 December 2002; on sponsored links: Court of Milan 11 March 2009.

22.4.2 Possible Implication of Alternative Dispute Resolution Systems

Disputes regarding the assignment of "country code Top Level Domain.it" may be decided through arbitration. This is an alternative resolution system with respect to the ordinary procedure, and it is regulated by establishing an administrative procedure to resign the domain names. These disputes may also involve non-competitors.[18]

22.5 "Reprehensible" Conduct and Lack of Competitive Relationship

22.5.1 Unfair Competition by Non-competing Undertakings

Unfair competition under Italian law is regulated by Article 2598 CC. Particularly, Article 2598.2 CC prohibits allegations that discredit the products or the activity of a competitor and those acts that will allow a third party to derive an unfair advantage. In this case, Italian law recognises as unfair and unlawful the behaviour of a third party that uses a trademark of another undertaking in order to refer to the original product, but not as a source identifier. However, this rule requires the undertaking to be a competitor and a commercial undertaking. Article 2598.3 CC prohibits all the uses of a trademark and other distinctive signs that are contrary to honest practices (*correttezza professionale*). It must be underlined that according to the latter Article, part of the jurisprudence has argued that there is no need for a competitive relationship between the undertakings. Therefore, such interpretation, followed by a part of the jurisprudence, would allow a wider application of unfair competition rules. However, it must be highlighted that it is disputed whether Article 2598.3 CC requires the existence of a competitive relationship between the parties. For this reason, in the case of damage caused by the unlawful conduct of a non-competing undertaking, it is advisable for the damaged party to claim an infringement under Article 2043 CC.

22.5.2 Parasitism and Non-competitive Relationship

Under Italian law, initially, the concept of "parasitic practice" as defined by the French Supreme Court did not exist. Indeed, parasitic practice under Italian law has a different meaning. However, recently, case law has expressly adopted the term "parasitic practice" also to identify those conducts of an economic agent that sets itself in the wake of another in order to gain an advantage from the reputation and

[18] C.r.d.d. 1/8/2009 regarding the domain name "missitalia.it".

goodwill of a competitor.[19] Those cases identify "parasitic practices" as infringements of the unfair competition rule, thus generally requiring the existence of a competitive relation between the parties. But more recently, the Supreme Court held that a "parasitic practice" by a non-competing party amounts to a violation of Article 2043 CC.[20]

22.6 The Links Between Infringement, Unfair Competition, and Parasitism in a Legal Action

22.6.1 Articulation of These Different Legal Grounds

There is no action that is better suited to apprehend offending behaviour of non-competitors; in order to decide which rule should be applied, it is important to look at the facts on a case-by-case basis. However, generally, Courts require a competitive relationship between undertakings when applying Article 2598 (2) and (3) CC. Nevertheless, a case law argues that Article 2598.3 CC does not require a competitive relationship between the parties.[21] This is an interpretation given only by a few courts. Usually, in the case of non-competing parties, it would be advisable to apply the general tort rule under Article 2043 CC.

22.6.2 Possible Substitution of Unfair Competition Legal Action Instead of Infringement Legal Action

The prohibition of unfair competition and parasitic practices may be applied where, in light of the facts of the specific case, there is no trademark infringement under Article 20.1 CIP but the image of the trademark is undermined by the behaviour of a third party. More precisely, these rules may be useful to prohibit allegations that discredit the products or the activity of a trademark owner and those acts that allow a third party to take unfair advantage. Depending on the circumstances of the case, either Article 2598 n. 2 or n. 3 CC may apply, mostly, where a competitive relation exists between the undertakings or Article 2043 CC where there is no such relationship.

Conclusions and Policy Recommendations

Under Italian law, trademark owners may obtain protection against the use, by non-competing undertakings, not only of their trademark but also of other

[19] *Inter alia*, Court of Viterbo 22 April 2002; Court of Milan, 24 July 2003; Court of Venice, 3 March 2005; Court of Bologna, 5 March 2008; Court of Rome, 4 February 2010.

[20] Cass. 11 August 2009 n. 18218.

[21] Court of Milan 9 March 1987.

components of their image. We can identify three different types of protection that may apply according to the specific case.

To begin, when a non-competitor uses as source identifier of its own goods and services a sign identical or similar to a reputable registered trademark, and this causes unfair advantage or is detrimental to the distinctive character or repute of the registered trademark, the trademark owner can claim infringement of its trademark under Article 20.1 *c* CPI. The Italian provision recalls Article 5.2 of European Directive No. 2008/95 and Article 8.5 Council Regulation No. 207/09.[22] The same rule is applied to distinctive signs. Indeed, a trademark with a reputation, given its communicative function, has a value *per se* independently from the products on which it is affixed.

Article 2598.2 of the Italian Civil Code prohibits allegations that discredit the products or the activity of a competitor and those acts that will allow a third party to take unfair advantage. In this case, Italian law recognises as unfair and unlawful behaviour a third party who uses a trademark of another undertaking in order to refer to the original product, but not as a source identifier. This rule may be applied to trademarks, distinctive signs, and also to other components of their image. However, in this case, the law specifically requires the undertakings to be competitors; thus, this Article cannot apply in the event of non-competing undertakings.

On the other hand, Article 2598.3 CC, which prohibits all acts that are contrary to honest practice (*correttezza professionale*), requires the undertakings to be involved in commercial activities, but according to some Courts, they could also be non-competitors. The latter interpretation of Article 2598.3C. C. is still under discussion among the jurisprudence and doctrine.

Furthermore, when an undertaking suffers a damage caused by the unlawful use of its trademark, distinctive sign, or other component of its image by a third party, it could claim a violation of Article 2043 CC. This article, which establishes a general tort, does not require the third party to be a competitor of the trademark owner and or a commercial undertaking.

[22] Council Regulation (EC) No. 207/2009.

Luxembourg 23

Nicolas Decker and Marianne Decker

23.1 The Status of Brand Image

23.1.1 Legal Definition of Brand Image

There is no legal definition of brand image in Luxembourg.

23.1.2 The Notion of "Brand Image" Through Case Law or Academic Writing

The notion of "brand image" has not been defined through case law or academic writing either.

23.1.3 The Legal Instruments Used to Defend "Brand Image" and the Implementation of the Notion of the Competitive Relationship

The notion of "brand image" does not have a specific legal status.

However, certain legal provisions can be used to protect "brand image".

First, the Benelux Convention on Intellectual Property (BCIP) contains two provisions that, under certain circumstances, prohibit the use of trademarks without due cause and take unfair advantage of, or are detrimental to, the distinctive character or the reputation of the earlier trademark.[1]

---

[1] See Articles 2.20, 1° c) and d) of the Benelux Convention on Intellectual Property Rights (BCIP); see Sects. 23.2.1 and 23.3.1.

N. Decker (✉) • M. Decker
Decker & Braun, Luxembourg, Luxembourg
e-mail: decker.braun@pt.lu

P. Këllezi et al. (eds.), *Antitrust for Small and Middle Size Undertakings and Image Protection from Non-Competitors*, LIDC Contributions on Antitrust Law, Intellectual Property and Unfair Competition, DOI 10.1007/978-3-642-54000-4_23,

Second, public disparagement of a competitor and/or its products is considered an act of unfair competition by case law and therefore falls under the scope of Article 14 of the Unfair Competition Act of 30 July 2002.[2]

Last, the provisions setting the framework for comparative advertising provide, among others, that the advertisement must not

- lead to the disparagement of the trademarks, company names, other distinctive signs, goods, services, activities, or situation of a competitor;
- take unfair advantage of the reputation attached to a trademark, a company name, or other distinctive signs of a competitor or the designation of origin of competing products;
- present a good or a service as an imitation or reproduction of a good or service bearing a protected trademark or company name.[3]

It will be seen below that trademark law may be applicable to non-competitive relationships, whereas unfair competition strictly applies to competitors only.

23.2 The Link Between the Rule of Speciality Applicable to Trademarks Law and the Possibility to Act Against Non-competitors

23.2.1 The Link Between the Rule of Speciality and Competitive Relationships

In Luxembourg, trademark law is regulated by the Benelux Convention on Intellectual Property (BCIP).

The BCIP contains a specific regime for trademarks with reputation where an exception is made to the principle of specialty.

Article 2.20, 1°, c) of the BCIP enables the holder of trademarks with reputation to prohibit any third party

> to use in the course of trade, a sign identical or similar to the trade mark, for goods or services which are not similar to those the trade mark is registered for if this trade mark has a reputation in the Benelux territory and where the use without due cause of the trade mark applied for would take unfair advantage of, or be detrimental to, the distinctive character or the reputation of the earlier trade mark.

[2] According to Article 14 of the Unfair Competition Act of 30 July 2002, "commits an unfair competition act every person, who is exercising a commercial, industrial, skilled crafts or self-employed activity and who, by acts contrary to honest purposes in commercial, industrial, skilled crafts or self-employed activities, or to a contractual agreement, takes away or tries to take away from his competitors or one of them part of their clients or who interferes or tries to interfere with their competitive capacity".

[3] See Article 18 (2) e), g) and h) of the Unfair Competition Act of 30 July 2002.

This provision does not require a competitive relationship between the right holder and the infringer since their goods or services do not have to be identical or similar.

The right holder must however suffer some kind of detriment, although the Benelux Court of Justice and the Luxembourg courts are not very demanding concerning the prejudice.

The Benelux Court of Justice has decided that "the prejudice referred to in Article 13 A 2 of the Benelux Uniform Law on Trade Marks" (currently Article 2.20, 1°, c) of the BCIP "can also consist in a decrease of the power to incite the purchase of such products for which the claimant's trademark was registered, decrease arising from any circumstance (...) so that the attractiveness of the trademark is reduced for the kind of products for which it was registered".[4]

In Luxembourg, the use of the sign "DIOR" for an equestrian club was declared to be capable of causing prejudice to the holder of the trademark "CHRISTIAN DIOR" because the said trademark would be "weakened following the dilution of the trademark in the public".[5]

The same applies to the use of a sign similar to the figurative trademark "monogram canvas" of the company Louis Vuitton for condoms.[6]

By using in its company name the word "ROLLS", a prestige car rental company causes prejudice to the English company "ROLLS ROYCE PLC", owner of the trademark "ROLLS ROYCE" for products in classes 7 (engines) and 12 (cars).[7]

23.2.2 Influence on the Rules of Civil Liability

Although in theory tort law could be used against a non-competitor using a similar trademark, it has never been used in Luxembourg, and there is hence no case law on this question.

However, unlike the above-mentioned protection granted to trademarks with reputation by the BCIP, the threshold concerning the prejudice would be much higher and an actual damage in most cases would be difficult to prove.

---

[4] Benelux Court of Justice, 22 May 1985, SA Lever c/ International Metals SA, Case. LUX c. LUX-TALC), Recueil 1985, p. 1.

[5] Commercial Court of Luxembourg, 15 July 1994, Christian Dior S.A. c/ Club hippique Dior a.s.b. l., not published.

[6] Commercial Court of Luxembourg, 23 December 1992, Louis Vuitton S.A. c/ Nobilis Choserie, not published.

[7] Commercial Court of Luxembourg, 19 October 1990, Rolls Royce PLC c/ Luxembourg Rolls Service S.A., not published.

23.3 Trademark, "Economy" of the Trademark, and Relation of Competition

23.3.1 The Liability of a Non-competitor That Uses a Previous Trademark "Outside Business"

The BCIP only forbids use of an infringing trademark in the course of trade.

However, Article 2.20, 1° d) of the BCIP also protects the publicity function of the trademark and provides that a trademark holder can prohibit any third party "to use a sign for a mean other than to distinguish goods or services where the use is done without due cause or would take unfair advantage of, or be detrimental to, the distinctive character or the reputation of the earlier trademark".

As an example, one can cite the use of the trademark "COKE" in a movie that has been sanctioned by the Court of Amsterdam.[8] Even if the trademark was not used to distinguish products or services of the trademark owner, the use was still considered as use in the course of trade.

According to EU case law, a use can be considered to be made in the course of trade when it is made in the context of a commercial activity aiming at an economic advantage, i.e. not made in the private field.[9]

Hence, the liability of a non-competitor cannot and should not be excluded in such cases.

23.3.2 The Future of the Community Case Law Regarding the Grounds for Trademarks Infringement

The view taken by the Court of Justice of the European Union to extend the protection of the trademark rights is welcome and enhances the general protection granted to trademark holders to some extent.

The fact that the Court has recently put an emphasis on the different functions of the trademark (origin, quality, communication, investment, and publicity) could however reopen the traditional problem concerning the scope of trademark protection in Europe.

In any case, one must not lose sight of the fact that the digital and Internet environment are a huge challenge for the right holders (as well as for the judges and lawyers). Since these cases very often include trademark use by non-competitors, it is important that the issue of the scope of trademark protection is addressed more generally to adapt case law and/or legislation.

---

[8] Court of Amsterdam, 18 December1975, Bulletin Industriële Eigendom, 1975, p. 214.

[9] ECJ, Case C-206/01, *Arsenal Football Club plc v Matthew Reed*, ECR 2002 I-10273.

23.4 Other Distinctive Signs

23.4.1 Possible Concrete Examples of the Liability of a Non-competitor That Uses Other Signs as Company Names, Brand Names

Company names are protected by the unfair competition legislation as well as, to a lesser extent, by Article 25 of the modified law of 10 August 1915 on commercial companies.

According to the Unfair Competition Act,[10] the owner of a distinctive sign other than a trademark or design can launch an unfair competition action against a third party using the same or a similar sign only if the alleged infringer is a competitor.

The competitive relation is the most important condition in this respect.

Article 25 of the above-mentioned Commercial Companies Act provides that each company name must be different from the name of any other company.

If a company name is identical or similar so as to cause a likelihood of confusion with an existing company name, the first company can request that the second be enjoined from using such company name and be condemned to pay damages.

This provision does not require a competitive relation between the parties.

23.4.2 Same Question Concerning the Use of Domain Names

In Luxembourg, the appropriation of a domain name by a reseller of a trademark has been declared illicit and forbidden pursuant to Article 2.20, 1°, d) of the BCIP.[11]

In this case, the Luxembourg distributor of FIAT cars had registered the domain name www.fiat.lu without the consent of the holder of the trademark "FIAT".

The claimant could not base the action on unfair competition law because according to Luxembourg case law, the manufacturer is not in a competitive relation with a distributor. Vertical relations on a same market are indeed not considered as competitive by Luxembourg case law.

The Court decided however that this constituted use of a trademark in the course of trade.

In conclusion, there is no need for a specific regulation concerning domain names in Luxembourg.

---

[10] Unfair Competition Act of 30 July 2002, in French: loi du 30 juillet 2002 *réglementant certaines pratiques commerciales, sanctionnant la concurrence déloyale et transposant la directive 97/55CE du Parlement européen et du Conseil modifiant la directive 84/450CEE sur la publicité trompeuse afin d'y inclure la publicité trompeuse.*

[11] President of District Court Luxembourg, 20 October 2000, Ingénieur Conseil, 2000, p. 406.

23.4.3 Same Question Concerning Meta Tags and Sponsored Links

There is no case law on meta tags and sponsored links in Luxembourg.

Usage of a trademark in a meta tag or sponsored link by a competitor of the trademark holder would probably be handled the same way as in Belgium and would be considered an unfair competition act.[12]

Such use would probably also be considered a trademark infringement pursuant to Article 2.20, 1°, d) of the BCIP.

23.4.4 Possible Implication of Alternative Dispute Resolution Systems

The existence of alternative dispute resolution systems concerning, among others, domain name conflicts does not have any particular impact on Luxembourg law.

It can be added that the Luxembourg domain name system (.lu) does not include any alternative dispute resolution system like ICANN.

23.5 "Reprehensible" Conduct and Lack of Competitive Relationship

23.5.1 Unfair Competition by Non-competing Undertakings

According to Article 14 of the Unfair Competition Act of 30 July 2002, "commits an unfair competition act every person, who is exercising a commercial, industrial, skilled crafts or self-employed activity and who, by acts contrary to honest purposes in commercial, industrial, skilled crafts or self-employed activities, or to a contractual agreement, takes away or tries to take away *from its competitors*[13] or one of them part of their clients or who interferes or tries to interfere with their competitive capacity".

In Luxembourg, unfair competition cannot be sanctioned outside competitive relations. This results from the wording of the provision itself as highlighted above.

The notion of competitive relation is moreover analysed quite strictly by the Courts.

According to a very constant case law, competition is a state that only exists if two business men offer directly, to whole or part of the same customers, comparable goods or services for the satisfaction of the same needs.

[12] See Antwerp Court, 09.10.2000, R.D.C., 2001, p. 407, cited by Antoine Braun and Emmanuel Cornu, Précis des marques, Larcier, 5th ed., 2009, No. 415bis).

[13] Highlighted by the authors.

23.5.2 Parasitism and Non-competitive Relationship

Parasitism is considered as a form of unfair competition in Luxembourg, which hence falls under the scope of Article 14 of the Unfair Competition Act of 30 July 2002.

A competitive relation is hence also necessary in case of parasitism.

Economic parasitism is defined by case law as "the behaviour of a person who follows the wake of another person to take advantage, without spending any money, of the know-how which results from the intellectual effort and the investments of this other person".[14]

The main criterion describing economic parasitism is when the copying plagiarist is taking over the substance and the form of the work of the victim.

In the above-mentioned case, the systematic copying by a newspaper of obituary, wedding, and birth information published in a competing newspaper the day before was considered as economic parasitism and, hence, an unfair competition act.

In another case, the slavish copying by a competitor of a plan of a machine used in a blast furnace was considered as economic parasitism.[15]

There is currently no case law concerning the usurpation of a third party's reputation or "brand image". But in a competitive relationship, such action could, in certain circumstances, constitute an unfair competition act.

23.6 The Links Between Infringement, Unfair Competition, and Parasitism in a Legal Action

23.6.1 Articulation of Those Various Legal Grounds

Unfair competition and, hence, also parasitism actions cannot be filed against non-competitors. It is only if the claimant is also the holder of an intellectual property right that it will, under certain circumstances, be able to act against a non-competitor.

From a procedural point of view, Luxembourg case law clearly states that trademark infringement and unfair competition actions are not cumulative.

Trademark infringements cannot be sanctioned via an unfair competition action; the trademark holder must, in such cases, sue on the basis of trademark law.[16]

---

[14] Luxembourg Court of Appeal, 14 November 2007, Saint-Paul Luxembourg S.A. c/ Editpress Luxembourg S.A., not published.

[15] President of Commercial Court Luxembourg, 11 April 2008, n° 508/08, not published.

[16] President Commercial Court Luxembourg, 20 March 1982; President Commercial Court Luxembourg, 28 November 1986; Luxembourg Court of Appeal, 15 May 1986 in Pasicrisie 28, La concurrence déloyale en jurisprudence luxembourgeoise, p. 76.

23.6.2 Possible Substitution of Unfair Competition Legal Action Instead of Infringement Legal Action

For the reasons outlined above, an unfair competition action can hardly be considered as a substitute for a trademark infringement action.

If an act is only contrary to honest commercial practices because it constitutes a mean to indirectly defend an intellectual property right such as a trademark, the judges will declare themselves incompetent and reject the action.

The trademark holder who intends to file an unfair competition action must hence be very careful concerning the description and designation of the unfair competition act he wants to forbid.

There are currently no discussions on this point in Luxembourg, and the courts do not seem inclined to change their position on this.

Conclusions and Policy Recommendations

Trademarks, as well as the image or identity of companies, have become an increasingly important element of such companies and their marketing strategies. This goes far beyond the simple origin function of the trademark.

Concerning trademark law, case law has acknowledged that today trademarks bear far more than just the origin function. This is a welcome development, although the issue of the scope of protection of trademarks, in particular, in the digital and Internet environment should be addressed more generally to ensure effective protection.

The present report proves however that it can be quite difficult for companies to protect themselves against non-competitors that use their trademarks or other distinctive signs or components such as their identity or brand image.

The Unfair Competition Act, which is a very flexible and effective tool to deal with many different behaviours on the market in Luxembourg, cannot be used against non-competitors.

Therefore, the notion of "competitive relation" should either be broadened or ideally deleted by the Luxembourg legislator and/or case law. It also seems that there are disparities between the different Member States concerning the application of unfair competition rules and/or parasitism to non-competitors, which raises the question of a European harmonisation in this respect.

Sweden 24

Alexander Jute

24.1 The Status of Brand Image

24.1.1 Legal Definition of Brand Image

The notion "brand image" has a broader meaning than trademark and is primarily regulated through marketing law. According to Article 10 in the Swedish Marketing Act (2008:486) (the Swedish Marketing Act or SMA), a trader may not, in marketing, make use of false claims or other statements that are misleading with regard to the trader's own or someone else's business. This especially applies to the trader's own or another trader's business qualifications, market position, commitments, trademarks, trade names, features, and other rights.

24.1.2 The Notion of "Brand Image" Through Case Law or Academic Writing

Actions that are covered by the Swedish Marketing Act can be litigated in the Swedish Market Court. The Market Court has, as a main rule, no standing to decide on intellectual property disputes—such disputes are handled by the general courts. The assessment according to the marketing regulation shall be independent of intellectual property considerations. For instance it is, as a main rule, not possible to issue a prohibition under the Swedish Marketing Act on the ground that a practice constitutes, for instance, a trademark infringement.[1] However, in a recent decision from the Swedish Market Court,[2] the court has decided to take a stand in an

[1] An example is the decision MD 1994:25 from the Swedish Market Court.

[2] MD 2012:15, see about this case under Sect. 24.2.2.

A. Jute (✉)
Marlaw Lawfirm, Stockholm, Sweden
e-mail: alexander.jute@marlaw.se

P. Këllezi et al. (eds.), *Antitrust for Small and Middle Size Undertakings and Image Protection from Non-Competitors*, LIDC Contributions on Antitrust Law, Intellectual Property and Unfair Competition, DOI 10.1007/978-3-642-54000-4_24, © Springer-Verlag Berlin Heidelberg 2014

intellectual property dispute concerning trademarks by referring to the principle of legality. The principle states that an act that is in conflict with another law can also, when the act is used in marketing, be regarded as being in conflict with the Swedish Marketing Act. The principle has a broader scope than bullet point 9 in Annex I to the Unfair Commercial Practices Directive.[3] Actions that are in conflict with the principle are regarded as being in conflict with the general clause regarding good marketing practice, Article 5 of the Swedish Marketing Act. When claiming that an action is in conflict with the principle of legality, the court first assesses whether the action constitutes an intellectual property infringement. If so, the court then refers to the principle of legality and states that the actions are in conflict with Swedish law; hence, the actions are regarded as being in conflict with good marketing practice.

Marketing that is not in accordance with good marketing practice according to Article 5 in the Swedish Marketing Act is to be regarded as unfair only if it appreciably affects or is likely to affect the recipient's ability to make a well-founded transaction decision. Actions that involve unfair advantage of another trader's reputation or discredit is likely to be regarded as being in violation of the general clause against unfair marketing since the consumer's ability to make a well-founded transaction decision is likely to be affected (the transactional test). Since the transactional test demands an affection on the consumer's ability to make a well-founded transaction decision, there may be "parasitic marketing", which in practice is not considered to affect buyers and therefore not being regarded as unfair.

If one would consider that a certain activity is causing damage on a trader's sign/brand but it cannot be established whether the activity affects the ability to make a well-founded transaction decision or not, it is possible to use 1st chapter 10th Article 1st paragraph 3rd point of the Swedish Trademark Act (2010:1877) (the Swedish Trademark Act). But, as mentioned above, actions such as trademark infringements are, as a main rule, handled by general courts. This means that a separate legal action is needed. A case decided under the Swedish Marketing Act in the Swedish Market Court cannot, as a main rule, be combined or handled together with a legal action under the Swedish Trademark Act. As a main rule, intellectual property disputes are handled by the general courts. But according to recent case law, an illegitimate use of a trademark, which would be regarded as being in conflict with the Swedish Trademark Act, can be regarded as being in conflict with the principle of legality. Hence, it is possible to use the Swedish Marketing Act, and the legal proceedings before the Swedish Market Court, in order to "catch" a trademark infringement (or other intellectual property infringements).[4]

---

[3] Directive 2005/29/EC of the European Parliament and of the Council of 11 May 2005 concerning unfair business-to-consumer commercial practices in the internal market and amending Council Directive 84/450/EEC, Directives 97/7/EC, 98/27/EC and 2002/65/EC of the European Parliament and of the Council and Regulation (EC) No 2006/2004 of the European Parliament and of the Council ('Unfair Commercial Practices Directive'): ("Stating or otherwise creating the impression that a product can legally be sold when it cannot.")

[4] In MD 2011:29, the court issued a ban against a company for selling illegal firmware for a media console. The court's assessment was based on the fact that the actions by the infringer was constituting copyright infringement. With regard to the principle of legality, the court found that the actions were in conflict with good marketing practice, and a ban with a fine was issued.

Another kind of use of a brand image can be found in Article 18 of the Swedish Marketing Act concerning comparative advertising. The provision states that a trader may, in its advertising, directly or indirectly point to another business or its products only if the comparison does not take unfair advantage of another trader's reputation associated with the trader's trademark, trade, or other features or the product's origin. This provision is based on the EC Directive 2006/114/EC on comparative marketing, which does not involve a transactional test.

There are numerous cases from the Swedish Market Court in which the court has established that it is not permissible to take advantage of another trader's reputation.[5] The case law clearly shows that the exploitation of goodwill is an independent ground of unfairness. In order to establish an unfair advantage of another trader's reputation, it is not required to show any element of misleading aspects to the marketing. The use of another trader's sign/brand or the like can also lead to conflict with Article 18 Section 7.[6]

24.1.3 The Swedish Marketing Act, Article 14 "Misleading Imitations"

There is also another kind of use of a brand that is regarded as being in conflict with the Swedish Marketing Act, and that is when a trader is using imitations of another trader's products, packages, and other distinctive brand notions. The provision, found in Article 14 of the Swedish Marketing Act, requires that the product/brand is "known" and "distinctive" and also that there is "risk of confusion" between the trader's brands. The meaning of "product" includes the product itself, as well as its packaging and advertising of the product. The provision does not only refer to pure copying but "also" designs that are confusingly similar.[7] According to case law, it has to be a very blatant imitation. There are, for example, numerous cases regarding taxis and the logotype of the different taxi companies.[8]

A recent case from the Swedish Market Court[9] concerned the company Marabou AB (which was purchased by Kraft Group). Kraft Group had been promoting chocolate-coated peanuts under the mark "m" in Sweden since 1957. Another company, the American company Mars Inc., had been selling its product "M&M's" since 1941 in a number of countries. In 2009, Mars' Swedish subsidiary introduced "M&M's" on the Swedish market. Kraft Group claimed that the

[5] See, e.g., MD 1999:21, MD 2000:25 and MD 2001:16.

[6] See ECJ, Case C-487/07, *L'Oréal SA, Lancôme parfums et beauté & Cie SNC and Laboratoire Garnier & Cie v Bellure NV, Malaika Investments Ltd and Starion International Ltd*, Rec 2009 I-5185.

[7] Case MD 2005:12 on snuff packages.

[8] In case MD 2011:17, the design of a taxicab was found to be confusingly similar with another taxi company's known and embossed design. See, for example, MD 2008:20, MD 2007:29 and MD 2007:25.

[9] MD 2010:29.

"M&M" packages should not be allowed to be dominated by the letter "M". On both companies' packaging, the letter "M" (in a very similar style) had a prominent placement. However, on Kraft's packages, it was only one "M", and on Mars', there were two "Ms". According to the Market Court's opinion, the packages gave different overall impressions, and the court found that there was no risk of confusion between "M's" packaging and "M&M's" packaging.

The necessary conditions "distinctive" and "known" on the market are crucial. What determines whether a product is "distinctive" is that the design has a main distinguishing feature, i.e. has the objective to give the product an appearance that, from an aesthetic viewpoint, distinguishes it from other products. "Known" means that the product should be well established on the market (more or less the same assessment as in the trademark regulation). The requirement of *well establishment* is strict, and the fact that the product is known on the market has to be proven unless this is notorious. If a trader's sign/brand is not found to be well known, the actions are not in conflict with the provision. One example from the Swedish Market Court is a case concerning the pear-liqueur Xanté,[10] which was not considered to be "known" on the market. Another example concerned supposedly offending lights.[11] However, the lights deviated from the right holder's lights so strongly that they were not confusingly similar and therefore could not be associated with the right holder or the products in a way required according to the provision.

The association according to Article 14 of the Swedish Marketing Act shall transfer the positive brand image on to another brand/trader. By doing so, the trader using another trader's brand image acquires an undeserved economic advantage, while the exposed trader/company may be damaged by having his reputation diluted.

24.1.4 The Legal Instruments Used to Defend "Brand Image" and the Implementation of the Notion of Competitive Relationship

The notion of competitive relationship between the involved undertakings is taken into consideration, but it is not necessary in order to commence legal proceedings. If there is a competitive relationship, the risk of causing confusions regarding the origin of a brand/product is most likely higher and, hence, could be regarded as misleading actions, as well as unfair advantage of another trader's reputation.[12]

---

[10] MD 2009:12.

[11] MD 2008:15.

[12] See court cases from the Swedish Market Court, inter alia, MD 1999:21 – Robinson Crisps and MD 2002:20 – Champagne; for a summary of the cases, see Sect. 24.5.1.

24.2 The Link Between the Rule of Speciality Applicable in Trademark Law and the Possibility to File Suit Against Non-competitors

24.2.1 The Link Between the Rule of Speciality and Competitive Relationships

The Swedish Trademark Act states[13] that a registered or well-established trademark takes precedence over younger, identical or similar, trademarks for goods or services of the same kind.[14] Accordingly, the holder of the trademark may prevent the use of a younger identical or similar (similarity of marks) trademark that is registered or protected for the same or similar goods or services (similarity of goods or services, the so-called principle of speciality). Trademarks that are well known (well-known trademarks) enjoy extended protection against younger identical or similar marks that are used for other goods or services. When making assessments of whether two marks are confusingly similar, one has to make an overall assessment of the similarity between the marks and between the goods or services. It is sufficient that the use of a younger mark leads the public to the conclusion that there is an economic relationship (likelihood of association) between two different companies (indirect confusion).[15]

24.2.2 Influence on the Rules of Civil Liability

The protection granted by the Swedish Trademark Act is found in Article 10. The holder of a trademark enjoys protection against anyone who, in a commercial context, is trying to use an identical or a similar trademark/brand name for the same goods or services as the protected trademark. Trademarks that are well-known have an extended protection. Such trademarks are protected against anyone who, in a commercial context, is trying to use an identical or similar trademark, irrespective of what kind of goods or services it is used for. In order to obtain such protection, the following two requisites have to be fulfilled (1) the trader who uses the trademark that is similar to the protected mark has to take unfair advantage of the well-known trademark, or (2) the use of the trademark that is similar to the well-known mark must be harmful to the well-known trademark's reputation or distinctiveness.

There are a number of cases where holders of well-known trademarks have successfully opposed to another trader's use of their trademark. One case that is illustrative regarding the use of another trader's trademarks and unfair marketing is

[13] In 1st chapter 10th Article the Swedish Trademark Act (the provision is commented in the following preparatory work: prop. 2009/10:225 s. 403 f. and 117 f. and in SOU 2001:26 s. 247 f.).

[14] Please see 1st chapter 10th Article 1st and 2nd sections of the Swedish Trademark Act.

[15] Bernitz et al, Immaterialrätt och otillbörlig konkurrens, Jure förlag, 12th ed., 2011, p 271 ff.

a case[16] concerning the company Svenska Tobaks AB (Swedish Tobacco Ltd), owner of the trademark "Blend". The tobacco company was using a package picturing a sun on the front of the package. Another trader, Nils Adamssons Försäljnings AB (Nils Adamssons Sales Ltd), started using a package design for condoms alluding to various cigarette brands (inter alia, Marlboro, Blend, and Gitanes). The tobacco company claimed that the use by Nils Adamsson was an infringement of the tobacco company's trademark rights irrespective of the difference in goods.[17] In order to acclaim such a wide protection, the trademark must be particularly well established and known within large areas of the public. Recognition of the trademark has to be established not only within a smaller group of people but also for a larger group of people who are not the target group (the target group being smokers). The tobacco company presented market surveys showing a very high recognition not only among smokers but also among the public. Due to the high recognition also outside the target group, the court found that the cigarette brand should be granted a broader protection. The court found that despite the differences between the cigarette and condom packages, there was still a risk of confusion since it could actually lead consumers to get the impression that there was a connection between the companies despite differences in the goods provided, especially since both products were sold in the same point of sales. The court found that the condom packages constituted trademark infringement of the tobacco company's trademark.

The same action could also be regarded as an unfair advantage of another trader's reputation according to the Swedish Marketing Act. The condom packages, as mentioned in the section above, were also target for legal proceedings by another tobacco company. Philip Morris AB (Philip Morris Ltd) also initiated legal proceedings but on the grounds of unfair competition in the Swedish Market Court.[18] The Swedish Market Court found that the condom packages showed essential similarities with the Marlboro package. According to the Court, the marketing did not appear to be an especially arguable usage of Philip Morris' product or trademark. The Court found that the condom company's marketing was creating associations with many different cigarette brands, and more generally, with the whole tobacco industry. As a result, the court found that Philip Morris did not suffer any damage. The court found that the condom company's marketing was acceptable according to the Swedish Marketing Act. In our opinion, it is unlikely that the court would reach the same decision today, but the two cases show that the same kind of action can result in two different outcomes depending on the legal option, either according to the Swedish Trademark Act or according to the Swedish Marketing Act.[19]

[16] The Court of Appeal in Stockholm of 1987 June 24.

[17] The claim in the case was based on § 6 section 2 in the old Swedish Trademark Act, now replaced by 1st chapter 10th Article 1 section, number 3 in the new Swedish Trademark Act.

[18] MD 1985:11.

[19] See Sect. 24.1.2 for further information on what circumstances that could constitute unfair advantage of reputation according to the Swedish Marketing Act. Svensson et al, Praktisk marknadsrätt, Norstedts Juridik, 8th ed., 2010, p 435ff.

In the case from the Swedish Market Court,[20] mentioned under Sect. 24.1.2, the court has taken a stand in an act that involved alleged trademark infringement, as well as alleged actions in conflict with good marketing practice. The case concerned companies Elskling AB (Elskling) and Kundkraft Sweden AB (Kundkraft). The two companies run competing websites where consumers can compare prices on different electric utilities. Elskling owns the trademark "elskling" and is the holder of the registered domain [www.elskling.se]. Kundkraft bought the word "Elskling" as a keyword in Google AdWords, which meant that an advertisement for Kundkraft appeared at the top search results by searching on the word "Elskling". Elskling filed a lawsuit against Kundkraft to the Swedish Market Court, claiming that Kundkraft should be prohibited under penalty to use Elskling as a keyword in a way that led consumers to get the impression that Elskling was behind the website or that there was a commercial relationship between the two competitors. The Swedish Market Court noted that according to the EU Court of Justice,[21] a trader may use a competitor's trademark as a keyword in services such as Google AdWords, as long as it does not cause damage to any of the brand's functions. One of these is the function of indicating origin, which means that Internet users should not be misled about the advertisement's origin. The court found that the advertisement for Kundkraft was not designed in such a way that it was difficult for an average internet user to understand the advertisement's origin. In addition to the function of indicating origin, the Court found that the use was not causing damage to the brand's investment or advertising function. Hence, the Court found that there was no trademark infringement that would have been contrary to good marketing practice.

24.3 Trademark, "Economy" of the Trademark, and Relation of Competition

24.3.1 The Liability of a Non-competitor That Uses a Previous Trademark "Outside Business"

General principles state that damages may only be claimed if there has been a criminal action or if there is a personal injury or property damage. Reimbursement for pure economical damages requires a statutory basis. Such statutory law

[20] MD 2012:15.

[21] ECJ, case C-323/09, *Interflora Inc. and Interflora British Unit v Marks & Spencer plc et Flowers Direct Online Ltd*, ECR 2011 I-8625; ECJ, case C 278/08, *Die BergSpechte Outdoor Reisen und Alpinschule Edi Koblmüller GmbH vs. Günther Guni and trekking.at Reisen GmbH*, ECR 2010 I-2517; ECJ, case C-487/07, *L'Oréal SA, Lancôme parfums et beauté & Cie SNC and Laboratoire Garnier & Cie v Bellure NV, Malaika Investments Ltd and Starion International Ltd.*, ECR 2009 I-05185; ECJ, joint cases C-236/08 to C-238/08, *Google France SARL and Google Inc. v Louis Vuitton Malletier SA, Viaticum SA and Luteciel SARL, Centre national de recherche en relations humaines (CNRRH) SARL and Others*, ECR 2010 I-2417.

foundation may be found in the intellectual property laws of Sweden (for instance, the Swedish Trademark Act 8th chapter 4th Article). According to Swedish law, a legal protection for unfair competition does not exist unless there is support from special regulation. In the fields of law, where such protection does not exist, it is possible to cause economic damage to competitors by means of competitive measures. Pure economic damage is, according to Swedish law, only possible to claim when the damages are caused through criminal actions or in contract law. The intellectual property laws include various provisions regarding liability in non-criminal situations. The same applies for marketing law and competition law. In the preparatory work for the Swedish tort law, the legislator noted that the courts should have the possibility to decide that an action should be regarded as pure economic damage even outside the statuary law. However, the courts have rarely used this possibility. This was used in one case, decided by the Swedish Supreme Court, NJA 1953 s 775, regarding a lapsed patent. In that decision, one trader had claimed that another trader was committing infringement of a patent belonging to the former trader. The latter trader then stopped production (to avoid further possible patent infringement) and sought legal advice. The latter trader then found out that the patent had lapsed and decided to initiate court proceedings against the former trader in order to claim damages.[22]

Another case is from the Uppsala District Court,[23] in which a manufacturer of olive oil claimed damages due to the use of his trademark/company name by the Swedish food administration. Because such use was not a commercial use, trademark law was not applicable and the claimant had to refer to tort law in order to claim damages. The claimant was successful and received compensation according to the District Court's decision. The judgment was appealed to the Court of Appeal and finally settled out of court.

24.3.2 The Future of the Community Case Law Regarding the Grounds of Trademark Infringement

The future holds many big issues. As we have already seen today, the Internet provides numerous possibilities, such as social media, blogs, etc., to infringe upon the rights of other companies'/employees' "undercover" (e.g., employees of one company can write damaging messages regarding other companies on social forums, blogs, etc.). This can also be the case for a non-competitor—but the damages caused could still be of major scale due to the fast circulation of the Internet. Therefore, if it is possible to determine that a company is engaging in such activities, whatever the reason, it is recommended that the legal system holds a

[22] Bernitz et al., Immaterialrätt och otillbörlig konkurrens, Jure förlag, 12th edition, 2011, p. 327 f. and 412 ff.

[23] Uppsala District Court, case number T 2089-02.

possibility to make such company liable irrespective of the presence or absence of competitive relationships.

24.4 Other Distinctive Signs

24.4.1 Liability of a Non-competitor That Uses Other Signs as Company Names, Brand Names

"Natural trademarks" are quite commonly referred to in Swedish doctrine. For example, 1st chapter 11th Article 2nd paragraph of the Swedish Trademark Act states that anyone may, in line with good business practice, use its firm, name or address, information regarding the goods and services in respect of art, quality, intended use, value, geographical origin, or other characteristics. A trader can also make use of other traders' trademarks, but only if it is necessary in order to inform the intended user of the goods/services provided by the trader. One example is when a trader wants to inform that the company's products are spare parts to another company's products.

There are also other commercial marks/signs that fill the same role as trademarks but that are covered by other legislation. One of the most important such laws is the Swedish Firm Act (1974:156). The relationship between the Swedish Trademark Act and the Swedish Firm Act has been established by the European Court of Justice.[24] According to EU case law, it is only when a company name is used as a trademark that the trademark regulation could be applied. According to Swedish law, it is not the same outcome.[25] In the case referred to in footnote 25, the court stated that when there is a legal dispute regarding company names and trademarks, the scope of the legal protection for a company name is to be assessed in the same way as a trademark. The case concerned the trademark owner Guccio Gucci S.p.A., whose registration of a figurative trademark with the letters "GG" was refused due to a small Swedish firm registered as "GG Sömnadsindustri". The court found that even though both the company name and the trademark application had the letters "GG", the scope of protection must be considered as narrow. In addition, the two companies' signs/marks were visually different. In an overall assessment, the court found that there was no risk that the public would be under the impression that there was a connection between the two companies.

There are also provisions in the Swedish Marketing Act, which give similar protection. For example, misleading marketing (Article 10 of the Swedish Marketing Act) states that a trader may not, in marketing, use false claims or other statements that are misleading with regard to the trader's own or someone else's business. This is especially applicable to presentations concerning the trader's own

[24] See ECJ, case C-120/04, *Medion AG vs. Thomson multimedia Sales Germany and Austria GmbH*, ECR 2005 I-8551; ECJ, case C-17/06, *Céline SARL v Céline SA*, ECR 2007 I-7041.

[25] See the Swedish Supreme Administrative Court case no 2561-2562-09 (Gucci).

or other traders' qualifications, market positions, commitments, trademarks, trade names, features, and other trademark rights. Hence, a non-competing company that uses signs similar to another trader could be brought before the Swedish Market Court due to misleading actions in the form of use of another trader's trademark or the like.[26]

24.4.2 Liability of a Non-competitor That Uses Domain Names

When it first was possible to register domain names, there were some problems regarding the scope of the Swedish Trademark Act and the ownership of a domain name (which could be regarded as a private asset). However, conflicts with trademarks shall be solved according to the intellectual property rights principles.

Further to this, trademarks have universal validity.[27] If a foreign trademark is well known, it should also be respected in Sweden,[28] although the rule is of limited significance because it only covers goods of similar nature. However, according to the TRIPS Article 16.3, the protection is broadened beyond the similarity between the goods or services if there is a risk that the brand is damaged. This is further emphasised by the Swedish Trademark Act,[29] where another trader's use takes unfair advantage of, or without due cause can be detrimental to, the trademark's distinctive character or reputation.[30]

WIPO has been interested in the distinction between universality and territoriality, which resulted in the adoption of the "Joint Recommendation Concerning Protection of Marks and Other Industrial Property Rights on Signs on the Internet". The "Joint Recommendation on Provisions on the Protection of Well-Known Marks" was also adopted, under which Member States should adopt a mechanism for the removal of domain name registrations that are in conflict with well-known brands (Article 6). However, this is not possible in Sweden since a court cannot issue bans to be implemented by anyone who is not a party to the proceedings. In Sweden, it is the Swedish Foundation for the Internet Infrastructure (.SE) that handles the registrations.[31] According to .SE's terms, a domain name can be deleted or transferred to a claimant if the domain name is (1) identical/or similar to a trademark, (2) the holder of the domain name has no legitimate interest in the domain name, and (3) the domain name was registered in bad faith.

[26] Levin, Lärobok i immaterialrätt, Norstedts juridik, 10th edition, 2011, pp. 393–396.

[27] Paris Convention Articles 6 and 6bis-6septies.

[28] Paris Convention 6bis.

[29] 1st chapter 10th Article 1st and 3rd points and 2nd chapter 8th Article 1st point, no 3 of the Swedish Trademark Act.

[30] Levin, Lärobok i immaterialrätt, Norstedts juridik, 10th edition, 2011, p. 387 ff.

[31] Ibid pp. 396 f. and 387 ff.

24.4.3 Liability of a Non-competitor Concerning Meta Tags and Sponsored Links

Both meta tags and sponsored links are handled and controlled by the trader using them. There is a case from the Swedish Market Court[32] where a trader had used meta tags in order to get certain search results in Google. The court found that the trader had full control of this and hence was responsible for the content in the meta tags. A trader is responsible for all actions that it takes; this applies both to meta tags and sponsored links. There are several court rulings from the ECJ[33] regarding sponsored links but only a few from the Swedish courts[34]—the legal aspects are quite clear on this.

24.4.4 Possible Implication of Alternative Dispute Resolution Systems

In Sweden, the country code top-level domain is ".se", and there is an option for an alternative dispute resolution (ADR) within the .SE system. A trademark owner can choose to initiate an ADR proceeding or legal proceedings on the ground of trademark infringement. The ADR system has been quite popular, and one of the reasons is that it is usually much faster than a legal proceeding in the general courts.

24.5 "Reprehensible" Conduct and Lack of Competitive Relationship

24.5.1 Unfair Competition by Non-competing Undertakings

There are several court rulings regarding unfair competition by a non-competing undertaking. The notion of unfair competition is found in Article 5 of the Swedish Marketing Act. Two examples are the following. In the first case,[35] the background was that the Swedish public service broadcaster "Sveriges Television" (SVT) produced a TV series called Robinson—a reference to the novel Robinson Crusoe

---

[32] MD 2010:30.

[33] ECJ, case C-323/09, *Interflora Inc. and Interflora British Unit v Marks & Spencer plc et Flowers Direct Online Ltd*, ECR 2011 I-8625; ECJ, case C 278/08, Die BergSpechte Outdoor Reisen und Alpinschule Edi Koblmüller GmbH vs. Günther Guni and trekking.at Reisen GmbH, ECR 2010 I-2517; ECJ, Case C-487/07, *L'Oréal SA, Lancôme parfums et beauté & Cie SNC and Laboratoire Garnier & Cie v Bellure NV, Malaika Investments Ltd and Starion International Ltd*, ECR 2009 I-5185; ECJ, joint cases C-236/08 to C-238/08, *Google France SARL and Google Inc. v Louis Vuitton Malletier SA, Viaticum SA and Luteciel SARL, Centre national de recherche en relations humaines (CNRRH) SARL and Others*, ECR 2010 I-2417.

[34] Gothenburg's District Court, case T 1889-12, MD 2010:30.

[35] MD 1999:21.

by Daniel Defoe. The programme quickly became popular. OLW—a snack manufacturer—noticed the immediate popularity of the show and started selling "Robinson crisps". SVT brought OLW to the Swedish Market Court and claimed that OLW had made unfair use of SVT's programme's reputation. The Court ruled in favour of SVT, and OLW was found to take unfair use of the reputation that SVT had built from the attention and publicity of the show. Even though the show had not run for long, the court found that it had gained a widespread reputation.

In another case,[36] the Swedish food manufacturer, Arla, had started selling yoghurt with "Champagne flavour". Two trade organisations representing the Champagne producers brought suit against Arla before the Swedish Market Court claiming that Arla had made unfair use of the Champagne brand. The Court stated that "Champagne" is a geographical origin and also a well-known name of the beverage. Arla was found to have made unfair use of the Champagne trademark and the goodwill connected to it.

The necessary conditions for unfair advantage of another's reputation are when another trader, in marketing, uses the reputation of another trader's business, products, trademarks, or other symbols, figures, or specific concepts. This applies even if there is no risk of confusion or other kind of misleading element in order to establish unfair use. The trader claiming that another trader is using his reputation is the owner of a trademark/sign that the other party is taking advantage of, and the trademark/sign must be well known in a way that it is regarded as having a reputation that is worth taking advantage of.

Both the Robinson and the Champagne cases show that competition between traders is not a necessary condition; rather, using the publicity and the attention that another trader have built is regarded as unfair competition.

24.6 The Links Between Infringement, Unfair Competition, and Parasitism in a Legal Action

24.6.1 Articulation of These Different Legal Grounds

Both actions are overlapping. For instance, a case of trademark infringement could also be regarded as unfair competition in the form of misleading advertising according to the Swedish Marketing Act. However, the assessment according to the marketing regulation does not depend on intellectual property law and trademark regulation. The assessment according to the marketing regulation shall be independent of intellectual property considerations. However, as referred to above in Sect. 24.1.2 and 24.2.2, the Swedish Market Court can assess intellectual property infringements. In such a case, the court has to use the principle of legality. The procedure means that the first step is to prove that an intellectual property

[36] MD 2002:20.

infringement is at hand and that the action is in conflict with the law and thus also in conflict with the Swedish Marketing Act.

24.6.2 Possible Substitution of Unfair Competition Legal Action Instead of Infringement Legal Action

Since there are two separate systems, there exist quite good options for a trader being exposed to unfair competition and/or infringement. A good example can be found in the above-referred cases regarding the tobacco companies and the condom company. The two different tobacco companies initiated two legal proceedings, one based on the trademark regulation for infringement and one based on the marketing regulation for unfair competition. In the infringement case, the court found that there was an infringement. But in the unfair competition case, the court found that the condom company was not causing damage to a specific company but rather was associating to the tobacco industry as a whole. It shall be noticed that it is far from certain that the court would rule this way today. Further to this, an interesting option is that if a trader finds that another trader is committing intellectual property infringement, e.g. trademark infringement, due to the fact that the trader is using a confusingly similar trademark, the first trader can bring such infringement before the Swedish Market Court claiming the principle of legality.[37]

Conclusions and Policy Recommendations

In order to give some conclusions and recommendation, I would start with a short summary of the judicial aspects. The protection granted by the Swedish Trademark Act is found in the 1st chapter 10th Article. It provides trademark holders with a protection against anyone who, in a commercial context, is trying to use an identical or similar trademark/brand name for the same goods or services as the protected trademark. Trademarks that are well known have further protection. Such trademarks are protected against anyone who, in a commercial context, uses an identical or similar trademark, irrespective of what kind of goods or services it is used for. In order to obtain such protection, one of the following two requisites has to be fulfilled: (1) the trader who uses the trademark, which is similar to the protected mark, has to take an unfair advantage of the well-known trademark, or (2) the use of the trademark that is similar to the well-known mark must be harmful to the well-known trademark's reputation or distinctiveness.

Further to the protection granted by the Swedish Trademark Act, the Swedish Marketing Act also protects a trader's brand image, etc. As we have seen above, there are quite good alternatives in order to act against infringements and illegitimate use of another trader's reputation. As previously mentioned

[37] See Sects. 24.1.2 and 24.2.2.

(Sects. 24.1.2 and 24.2.2), it is also possible to use the Swedish Market Court in matters concerning intellectual property infringements.

An undertaking that has a well-established reputation/trademark/brand is always exposed to traders willing to take advantage of that reputation/trademark/brand in order to gain access to the market or strengthen their position on the market. In situations where a trader has a well-established reputation regarding certain goods or services and another trader is using that reputation for other kinds of goods/services, it would not be fair if the well-known trader was prevented from stopping such action since the well-known trader could very well be interested in gaining access to that new market in the future. Even if that is not the case, it is still not fair to use a well-known trader's reputation to gain access to or strengthen one's position in a market because it is likely to cause damage to the well-known trader, who loses control over its trademark. However, it is of utmost importance that the trader benefitting of a well-known reputation can actually prove its reputation or notoriety—otherwise, it would be too easy to block other traders from starting up businesses arguing that the newcomer is taking unfair advantage of the incumbent's reputation. This would eventually harm competition in the market and the consumers as well.

Switzerland 25

Leila Ghassemi Farreras

25.1 The Status of Brand Image

25.1.1 Legal Definition of Brand Image

Under Swiss law, the concept of brand image is not defined as such in the law. The dictionary defines the expression "brand image" as being the "impression the public has of a product, firm or commercial trademark, and by extension, the collective impression of an institution, [or of] a person".[1] In trademark law, this expression refers to the notion of reputation.

25.1.2 The Notion of "Brand Image" Through Case Law or Academic Writing

Swiss case law relating to distinctive signs does not expressly refer to the term "brand image" but rather to the exploitation of the reputation of another. Thus, an imitator acts unfairly when it uses "improper or underhand conduct to achieve its ends, when it systematically or cunningly seeks to take advantage of the good reputation of a competitor or exploits that reputation in a parasitic manner [. . .]. The unlawful exploitation of the services of another consists in the fact that the holder is deprived of the fruits of its successful efforts, because the defendant acquires them directly by not having to make the investments that would be objectively necessary and exploits them to its advantage on the market".[2] In another decision, the Swiss Supreme Court (SC) held that "in order to meet the conditions required for unfair

[1] Le Nouveau Petit Robert, 1995.

[2] Judgment of the Cantonal Court of Vaud of 12 January 2009, in sic! 2009, 431 ("Ferrari II").

L.G. Farreras (✉)
University of Neuchâtel, Neuchâtel, Switzerland
e-mail: ghassemi.leila@gmail.com

P. Këllezi et al. (eds.), *Antitrust for Small and Middle Size Undertakings and Image Protection from Non-Competitors*, LIDC Contributions on Antitrust Law, Intellectual Property and Unfair Competition, DOI 10.1007/978-3-642-54000-4_25, © Springer-Verlag Berlin Heidelberg 2014

exploitation of the reputation of another or parasitic conduct, it is enough for a sign to be used in such a way that it is objectively likely, given all the circumstances, to create in the intended audience an association of ideas with the product designated by another sign that has a certain reputation".[3] The same applies "when a holder has succeeded in generating such a reputation for its trademark that it possesses an advertising power that is useful not only in the category of goods or services in the area of which it was established but that it is now likely to promote the sale of other goods or other services".[4] Case law also refers to the "positive impressions" that famous trademarks generate within the public. "These positive impressions might tempt third parties to make use of them in their own interest."[5]

25.1.3 The Legal Instruments Used to Defend "Brand Image" and the Implementation of the Notion of the Competitive Relations

The Trademark Protection Law (hereafter referred to as "LPM") and the Law against Unfair Competition (hereafter referred to as "LCD") both refer to the notion of "reputation" linked to the brand.[6] However, in Switzerland, exploiting the reputation of a distinctive sign is only sanctioned by trademark law under Article 15 LPM, which specifically targets famous trademarks. Rights relating to personality, including the right to a name (Article 29 Swiss Civil Code) also protect the reputation attached to a name, particularly if it is used as a trademark. The same is true of rights relating to a business name (Article 956 Swiss Code of Obligations).[7]

In trademark law, the competitive relationship between businesses is taken into consideration, except for famous trademarks governed in Article 15 LPM.[8] Thus, for brands that are not famous, the distinctive function and the origin function are the only ones to enjoy legal protection, properly speaking.[9] Exploitation of the reputation of a distinctive sign is consequently only penalised in trademark law under Article 15 LPM. In all other cases, exploitation of the reputation of a distinctive sign comes under the LCD, which, contrary to trademark law, is not governed by the principle of speciality. Contrary to what one might think, the competitive relationship between businesses is not a decisive factor in applying the Law against Unfair Competition.

[3] Judgment of the Supreme Court, 4A_103/2008, in sic ! 2008, 907 ("Botox/Botoina II").

[4] Supreme Court (SC), ATF 124 III 277, para 1 = JdT 1998 I 324 ("Nike").

[5] FC, ATF 124 III 277, para 1 = JdT 1998 I 324 ("Nike").

[6] Article 9 para. 1 of the Law against Unfair Competition (LCD; RS 241) and Article 15 para. 1 of the Trademark Protection Law (LPM; RS 232.11).

[7] Article 29 of the Civil Code (CC; Systematic Compilation SC 210) and Article 957 of the Code of Obligations (CO; SC 220).

[8] See point 2 in relation to the principle of speciality.

[9] Message of the Federal Council concerning a federal law on the protection of trademarks and indications of provenance of 21 November 1990, Official Journal (Feuille Fédéral/FF) 1991 I 18 ff. particularly 18.

In relation to rights of personality or rights relating to a business name, a competitive relationship is not a *sine qua non* condition. However, it can be taken into account in the outcome of the analysis.[10] The better known is a name in the public, the more extended will be its protection.[11]

25.2 The Link Between the Rule of Speciality Applicable in Trademark Law and the Possibility to File Suit Against Non-competitors

25.2.1 The Link Between the Rule of Speciality and Competitive Relationship

Trademark Protection Law is governed by the principle of speciality under which the protection of a trademark only extends to the goods or services for which the trademark is registered.[12] The Swiss Supreme Court held that fashion Articles or products that might be within the same class of products cannot, in themselves, be considered to be similar. They are considered to be similar if there is some proximity between them and not when, in order to respond to diversification strategies, they are included in the same class.[13] Protection under trademark law only applies to the categories of goods and services actually used. Article 3 LPM lists three exclusionary grounds for which trademark protection is excluded.

In all cases referred to in this Article, a sign that is identical or similar to an earlier trademark can only be excluded from protection if it is intended for identical or similar products or services. Consequently, a sign that is identical or similar to an earlier trademark is admissible when it is intended for different products or services. According to case law, there is an interaction between the similitude of the signs and that of the products and services. The closer the goods and services for which the trademarks are registered, greater are the risk of confusion and the more the later sign must differ from the prior and vice versa. If there is no similarity between the goods or services, the holder of a trademark cannot invoke protection based on trademark law.[14] Similitude of goods or services is assessed based on criteria such as same technologies, same specific know-how, same general purpose,

---

[10] Troller Patrick, Kollisionen zwischen Firmen, Handelsnamen und Marken [Conflicts between company names, trade names and trademarks], academic paper Basel 1980, p. 158; also Gilliéron Philippe, Les divers régimes de protection des signs distinctifs et leurs rapports avec le droit des marques [Various systems for protecting distinctive signs and their relationship with trademark law], dissertation, Staempfli, Berne, 2000, p. 243.

[11] FC, ATF 102 II 161 = JdT 1978 I 237 ("Naegeli").

[12] Article 3 LPM; ATF 128 III 96 (Orfina); FC, sic! 2010, 353 ("Coolwater/Cool water").

[13] FC, sic! 2008, 44, Recital 2.2.2; ATF 128 III 96, Recital. 2d (Orfina).

[14] FC, sic! 2010, 353 ("Coolwater/cool water").

substitutability,[15] complementarity, similar customer group, or same distribution channels.[16]

Under Article 3 LPM, the principle of speciality and the risk of confusion are the key conditions for the holder of the earlier trademark to be able to exercise its right. It should be recalled that the likelihood of confusion analysis is unnecessary when a sign that is identical to an earlier trademark is intended for identical goods or services.[17]

Such a risk would exist when the public buying the goods or services might be led to believe, given the identity or similitude of the trademarks, that the goods or services come from the same business (risk of direct confusion) or that they come from businesses that have financial ties with each other (risk of indirect confusion). A risk of confusion is sufficient, and a potential competitive relationship between the goods or services is not decisive.[18] The risk of confusion is a question of law that the courts assess as they think fit.[19]

In addition, Article 15 LPM expressly refers to famous trademarks but does not provide a definition: "The holder of a famous trademark may prohibit third parties from using said trademark for all goods or services where such use threatens the distinctive character of the trademark, exploits its reputation or harms it."

According to case law, "a famous trademark is characterised by the fact that its promotional power represents a major economic value in a wide variety of areas". Fame for its part assumes that this trademark is generally well known by a large number of people.[20] Thus, in a judgment dated 24 March 1998 relating to the Nike brand, the Swiss Supreme Court referred to a "trademark cult".[21] A famous trademark is defined primarily by its celebrity, which enables it to be known beyond just the goods or services for which it is used.[22] This celebrity is assessed with regard to the Swiss public as a whole by comparing it with the assessment of the risk of confusion in the environments specifically concerned for ordinary trademarks and trademarks that have notoriety. It should also be noted that before this Article

[15] Marbach Eugène, Markenrecht [Trademark Law], in: SIWR III/1, 2nd ed., Basel 2009, p. 108.

[16] Federal Commission of appeals relating to intellectual property, in sic! 2004, 418: "Similarity of goods is verified using indicators which, as a rule of thumb, are taken into the balance either in favour or against similarity: substitutability, the same technology or related indications and the case of an accessory that is added to the principal good are arguments in favour of similarity whereas separate distribution channels within the same layer of buyers and goods that are auxiliary to the principal good are to be considered as indications that the goods are not similar."

[17] Article 3 para. 1 letter a LPM.

[18] Cherpillod Ivan, le droit suisse des marques [Trademark Law], Lausanne 2007, p. 107.

[19] FC, ATF 119 II 473 = JdT 1994 I 358 (Radion/Radomat).

[20] FC, ATF 124 III 277, trad. = JdT 1998 I 324 ("Nike").

[21] FC, ATF 124 III 277, para 1a = JdT 1998 I 324 ("Nike").

[22] FC, ATF 124 III 277, para 1a = JdT 1998 I 324 ("Nike"): "Fame is predicated on the fact that the trademark enjoys general acclaim by a broad segment of the public."

was introduced,[23] famous trademarks used to be protected by the law against unfair competition and protection of personality.[24]

Thus, Article 15 LPM shatters the principle of speciality, which dominates trademark law. Contrary to ordinary trademarks, a trademark that is famous is protected both in terms of its distinctive character and its reputation.[25] In other words, Article 15 LPM grants the holder protection against the attempts by third parties to benefit from the reputation of the famous trademark for goods or services other than those for which their holder uses them, i.e. for goods or services for which the two businesses are not in principle in a competitive relationship.

Consequently, if the fame of a trademark is acknowledged, Article 15 LPM will allow the holder to invoke its exclusive right in the following cases:

a) The trademark must firstly be a famous trademark, which implies that it is very well known and the public associates high quality goods or services with it.
b) The famous trademark is only protected if one of the following sub-conditions is met:
    (i) The use of the trademark by the third party must threaten the distinctive character of the trademark. The type of usage does not matter; the law actually targets any use that might be made of the famous trademark.

    A considerable body of legal literature and recent case law holds that it is thus not necessary for there to be a risk of confusion; a simple association of ideas is enough when the later trademark conveys a message such as "as good as" or "surrogate of".[26] In other words, there must be an image transfer, where using a famous trademark enables the usurping party to advertise its goods and to sell them more easily, and this is so even if the goods or services are different.[27] This extended protection is justified by the fact that famous trademarks generate "positive impressions or inspire spontaneous confidence in the public".[28] Since trademark law is governed by the principle of specialty, in the absence of such a provision, any third party would be tempted to make use of the positive impressions generated by the brand in its own interest.[29]

---

[23] On 1 April 1993.

[24] FC, ATF 116 II 463, trad. *in* JdT 1991 I 599; ATF 116 II 614, trad. *in* JdT 1991 I 605.

[25] FC, ATF 130 III 748; Gilliéron Philippe, Les divers régimes de protection des signes distinctifs et leurs rapports avec le droit des marques [The various systems of protection of distinctive signs and their relationship with trademark law], academic paper, Staempfli, Berne, 2000, p. 243.

[26] Judgment of the Federal Court, 4A_128/2012 ("Vogue"); Hilti Christian, in: SIWR III/2, Basel 2005, p. 127, see also Gilliéron Philippe, Les divers régimes de protection des signes distinctifs et leurs rapports avec le droit des marques [the various systems of protection of distinctive signs and their relationship with trademark law], academic paper, Staempfli, Berne, 2000, p. 271.

[27] FC, ATF 124 III 277, para 1 = JdT 1998 I 324 ("Nike").

[28] Brandt Dominique, la protection élargie de la marque de haute renommée au-delà des produits identiques et similaires [expanded protection of famous trademarks beyond identical and similar products]. Comparative law study, Comparativa collection, Droz Geneva, 1985, pp. 183 ss.

[29] FC, ATF 124 III 277, para 1 ("Nike").

(ii) The third party must seek to exploit the reputation of the famous trademark.

Case law tends to examine in each case if the third party is really taking advantage of the reputation of the famous trademark.[30]

(iii) The holder of a famous trademark can also prohibit any third party from making any other use of this trademark when said use harms it. In fact, the holder of a famous trademark may invoke its exclusive right against any use that harms it for defamatory parodies or when its trademark is associated with goods or services that would run the risk of creating a negative image in the mind of the public.[31]

In order to determine if there is harm, the situation must be examined with regard to personality law or unfair competition law.

Notorious trademarks, on the other hand, do not have more extended protection. The LPM contains no provision upon which a preferential system would be based.

25.2.2 Influence on the Rules of Civil Liability

Article 55 paragraph 2 LPM contains a general reference to the Code of Obligations (CO), which includes the general part of tort law that specifically affects damages claims. Consequently, the general liability clause (Article 41 CO) may be invoked if the general conditions (damage, illegal infringement, causal link between conduct and damage) are met.[32]

25.3 Trademark, "Economy" of the Trademark, and Relation of Competition

25.3.1 The Liability of a Non-competitor That Uses a Previous Trademark "Outside Business"

Generally, the right to a trademark confers on the holder the exclusive right to make use of the trademark to distinguish the goods or services registered and to dispose of them (Article 13 paragraph 1 LPM). Article 13 paragraph 2 *lit.* e LPM gives the holder of the trademark the right to prohibit third parties from affixing the trademark on business papers, using it for promotional purposes or otherwise making use of it in business.

Private use is not covered by the LPM. Only serious use that is in accordance with the commercial uses in force in the sector in question constitutes legally valid use. This will not be the case for symbolic use or use for advertising purposes.

[30] FC, ATF 124 III 277 = JdT 1998 I 324 ("Nike").

[31] Cherpillod Ivan, le droit suisse des marques [Swiss trademark law], CEDIDAC, Lausanne 2007, p. 184.

[32] FC, ATF 132 III 379 (damages in the case of patent rights infringement).

However, in one judgment, the Federal Court found that the risk of confusion, as a condition for trademarks infringement, would not be affected by private use.[33]

The Law against Unfair Competition and the remedies derived from the right to a name confer protection to the trademark holder in the case of denigration, for example, if the trademark is parodied or pirated. The term “commercial use” must be interpreted in the broad sense. Distributing goods free of charge to loyal customers will thus be deemed to be marketing and use as a trademark.[34]

In Switzerland, the problem associated with AdWords is controversial. Some writers feel that using the trademark of a third party as a key word is unlawful when the party making such use does not offer the goods of the brand in question,[35] while others consider that using the trademark of another party in AdWords is in principle never an infringement.[36] For ordinary trademarks, it does not seem possible to simply automatically transpose into Swiss law the criterion of being misled advanced by the ECJ because it does not match the Swiss notion of risk of confusion. As regards famous trademarks, on the other hand, “their use as “bait” in Google AdWords will almost always constitute, in our view, exploitation of their reputation as defined in Article 15 LPM, such that it can be generally accepted that there is an infringement thereof.”[37]

25.3.2 The Future of the Community Case Law Regarding Trademarks Infringement

Whereas the Community Case law seems to be oriented towards an extension of trademark’s functions, only the indication of origin and the distinctive function are expressly considered under Swiss trademark law. The promotional function associated with the reputation of a brand is only protected when there is a famous trademark.[38]

[33] FC, sic! 2005, 392.

[34] FC, ATF 116 II 463.

[35] Reinle Michael/Obrecht Matthias, Markenrechtsverletzung durch Google AdWords [Trademark infringement by Google], in: sic! 2009, 112.

[36] Kohli Thomas, Keine Markenrechtverletzung durch Google AdWords. Eine Replik zum Diskussionsbeitrag von Michael Reinle und Matthias Obrecht [No trademark infringement by Google AdWords. A response to the contribution made by Michael REINLE and Matthias OBRECHT to the debate] in: sic! 2009, 629; Gilliéron Philippe, Online advertising business models and distinctive signs – should one rethink the concept of confusion, IIC 2008, 70.

[37] Schlosser Ralph, Usage d’une marque dans les Google AdWords: violation du droit à la marque [Use of a trademark in Google AdWords; infringement of trademark law], in InfoLex 2/10, at: http://www.kasser-schlosser.ch/InfoLex03.html.

[38] Message of Federal Council concerning the federal law on protection of trademarks and indications of provenance dated 21 November 1990, Official Journal (Feuille fédérale/FF) 1991 I 18 ff. partic. 18.

25.4 Other Distinctive Signs

25.4.1 Possible Concrete Examples of the Liability of a Non-competitor That Uses Other Signs as Company Names, Brand Names

Articles 944 and 956 of the Code of Obligations apply respectively to the creation and to the protection of business names. Article 956 CO can only be invoked by a business that is registered in the Trade Register (hereafter referred to as "RC"). Thus, the application of Article 956 paragraph 2 CO is subject to the unfair use of a business name. This use would cause detriment, which is assessed based on the existence of a risk of confusion. The concept of risk of confusion is identical for the entire law relating to distinctive signs.

Unlike trademark law, a company name guarantees the identity of the person referred to in all business life, and this justifies protection outside that person's particular sector of activity. Hence, the principle of speciality does not apply under business name law.[39]

Similarly, Article 956 only applies if the usurping party makes use of the sign in question as a business name. Said use comprises any use of the sign, regardless of whether it is on business documents, price lists, prospectuses, or telephone directories.[40] In fact, according to Article 13 paragraph 2 *lit.* e LPM, only the use of a trademark as such allows the owner of the business name to invoke Article 956 CO. This is not so for the use of a sign, a commercial name, or the name of an association or foundation. In fact, given these situations, the beneficiary of a business name may only invoke competition law or Article 29 paragraph 2 of the Civil Code relating to the protection of a name.[41]

Lastly, the purpose of a name is to identify a legal subject. This will be the case if the name has distinctive power. Otherwise, protection will only be granted if the sign becomes notorious as a result of long use.[42] Protection of the right to a name is subject to three conditions: (1) presence of a name, (2) unfair use of the name (usurping practice), (3) detriment caused to the holder of the name that has been usurped. The right to protection of the name may only be invoked to the extent that there is an interest worthy of protection. The harm caused to the interests of the injured party and consequently the detriment that it might incur will be examined by the judge in the light of the risk of confusion.[43]

[39] FC, ATF 118 II 322 = JdT 1993 I 357 ("Ferosped"); ATF 92 II 98 = JdT 1966 I 618.

[40] FC, ATF 103 IV 202 = JdT 1979 IV 11.

[41] Judgment of the Federal Court in JdT 1965 I 262.

[42] FC, ATF 90 II 461 = JdT 1965 U 262 ("Gotthard").

[43] FC, ATF 117 II 513 ("ASTAG").

25.4.2 Same Question Concerning the Use of Domain Names

The Trademark Protection Law only provides protection for goods or services that are similar to the priority trademark. The Swiss Supreme Court confirmed the application of the principle of speciality.[44] While derogations were admitted in relation to famous trademarks, the Swiss Supreme Court confirmed the application of speciality in relation to trademark infringements by domain names, i.e. protection is provided only if the goods or services are identical or similar to those pertaining to the prior trademark.[45]

Article 3 *lit.* d LDC prohibits any measure that might create confusion with the goods, services, or business of another party. Choosing a domain name that is close to the business name or trademarks of another party may fall within the ambit of this provision. It will not be necessary for the parties to be in a competitive relationship. However, the conduct of the party using the trademark or business name for its domain name must affect a market of goods or services.[46] Where this provision cannot apply for these grounds, Articles 29 and 28 Swiss Civil Code (CC) concerning protection of the name and personality may be applicable.[47] Finally, the general principle dominating the resolution of disputes between non-registered distinctive signs lies in priority of use, whereas trademark law is based on priority of registration.

25.4.3 Same Question Concerning Meta Tags and Sponsored Links

Meta tags are markers attached to a webpage that are not visible to the consumer surfing the internet. In Germany, the *Bundesgerichtshof* (BGH) held that using someone else's trademark as a meta tag to offer competing goods or services[48] constitutes use for distinctive purposes and can be sanctioned by trademark law.[49] However, the Court finds that the principle of speciality must be complied with. Some writers are of the view that the decision of the BGH is debatable: "a meta-tag, which is not perceptible for the user, is not used to distinguish or identify that offer of goods or services; it is used to distort the search results in order to include a reference there to the competing site although it does not offer goods or services of that trademark, but competing services. It is therefore a process that constitutes

[44] FC, ATF 125 III 91 ("Rytz"). TF in sic! 2005, p. 200.

[45] FC, in sic! 2005, p. 390 ("maggi.com").

[46] Sic! 2009, p. 793, Recital 4.1 ("Maltesers").

[47] FC, ATF 128 III 401 ("luzern.ch"); FC, ATF 128 III 250 ("montana.ch").

[48] In fact, the BGH (German Federal Court of Justice) considers that the principle of speciality must be respected.

[49] BGH, 26 May 2006, in: GRUR 2007, 65.

unfair competition".[50] This would be parasitic conduct. Thus, the owner of a domain name that is the subject of parasitic conduct can sue on the basis of the LCD. The key criterion is how visible the trademark is to the consumer, without which distinctive character of the trademark could not be achieved. It is different for cases in which the trademark appears in a link to the competing site; in such cases, this would be the use of another party's trademark and consequently use for distinctive purposes.

Offering sponsored links provides the possibility of buying keywords in a search engine. If a user clicks on the said keyword, a link appears in the search engine indicating the site of the party who has reserved the key word (typically the Google system AdWords). In trademark language, this technique enables the party who has reserved the key word to use the trademark of a third party to offer its own competing goods. This represents use of the trademark for distinctive purposes. Thus, if the trademark is used by competing businesses, the party using this technique is infringing the LPM. If the key word is a famous trademark and is used by a business that offers different services or goods, said use falls under Article 15 LPM.

25.4.4 Possible Implication of Alternative Dispute Resolution Systems

25.4.4.1 Uniform Domain Name Dispute Resolution (UDRP) Principles

Unlike a legal action brought pursuant to trademark law, neither the principle of territoriality nor the principle of speciality is decisive. Hence, it is sufficient for the plaintiff to have rights to a trademark in any given country in order to be able to act pursuant to the UDRP procedure.[51] However, under the UDRP principles, the parties may decide to have recourse to the ordinary courts with a view to obtaining another decision.

25.4.4.2 Rules Relating to .ch Domain Names

From a substantive standpoint, the application can only be received if "the registration or use of the domain name clearly constitutes an infraction of a right attached to a distinctive sign granted to the petitioner in accordance with the law of Switzerland or Liechtenstein".[52] These rights can thus fall within exclusive rights, particularly trademark law and also unfair competition law, the right to a name and company name. The principle of speciality will thus be complied with if one invokes the

[50] Cherpillod Ivan, le droit suisse des marques [Swiss trademark law], Lausanne 2007, p. 261; Gilliéron Philippe, Publicité en ligne: des modèles aux enjeux juridiques [Online advertising: models with legal challenges], in: medialex 2009, p. 3, 6.

[51] Paragraph 4 let. a of UDRP.

[52] Article 24 letter c of the Provisions relating to the procedure for resolving disputes relating to the domain names .ch and .li, available at: https://www.nic.ch/reg/cm/wcm-page/index.html?res=EF6GW2JBPVTG67DLNIQWUZ35PZ5XU235EF6HWYTLPVIXQPZAMR6X4.

LPM, subject to the case of famous trademarks.[53] Thus, the applicable principles, contrary to the UDRP principles, are unlikely to influence the issue at stake.

As regards case law, the Federal Court in a recent decision indicated that "The two decisions that the petitioner claims the cantonal court arbitrarily made no mention of are not likely to influence the outcome of the dispute, regardless of what that party says. Firstly, they were handed down in an administrative proceeding of a summary nature, expressly reserving the right to apply to the competent state courts for a legal remedy.[54] The petitioner itself concedes, incidentally, that the Court of Justice was not bound by the two aforementioned decisions. Each of them moreover contains an explicit comment as to the limited scope of its effects [...]".[55]

It can finally be assumed that with regard to cybersquatting, the victims are, in principle, holders of a famous trademark (Article 15 LPM), and in this case the principle of speciality no longer applies.

25.5 "Reprehensible" Conduct and Lack of Competitive Relationship

25.5.1 Unfair Competition by Non-competing Undertakings

Swiss competition law no longer requires a competitive relationship to exist between the infringer and the injured party.[56] The unfair commercial practices referred to are mentioned in the general clause (Article 2 LCD) and described through a series of constituent components (Article 3–8 LCD).

Someone who fails to comply with the rules of a certain professional ethical code of conduct that applies to all participants in a given market is thus seen to be acting unfairly. Article 2 LCD stipulates that an action for unfair competition must influence the relations between competitors or between suppliers and customers.

[53] de Werra Jacques, Domain-Dispute.ch Le service de règlement des différends pour les domain names ".CH" [Domain name dispute resolution department], in: FDBM 2005 I p. 149; Cherpillod Ivan, le droit suisse des marques [Swiss trademark law], Lausanne 2007, p. 257.

[54] ICANN's Uniform Domain Name Dispute Resolution Policy, adopted on 26 August 1999, ch. 4K, available at: http://www.wipo.int/amc/fr/domains/rules/index.html); Article 14g paragraph 4 Ordinance of 6 October 1997 on Addressing Resources in the Telecommunications Sector (ORAT; RS 784.104); No 4.2, paragraph 2, of the General Conditions of SWITCH relating to the registration and management of domain names based on the domain ".ch" or ".li".

[55] Judgment of the Federal Court, 4A_2168/2010, Recital 3.2 ("Pneus-online").

[56] Troller Alois, IGR, Vol. II, p. 922; Perret François, la protection des prestations en droit privé Suisse [Protection of services in Swiss private law], in RDS 1977, 239; Lucas David, Schweizerisches Wettbewerbsrecht [Swiss Competition Law], 3rd ed., Berne 1997, N 4; CARL BAUDENBACHER, Lauterkeitsrecht, Kommentar zum Gesetz gegen den unlauterenWettbewerb (UWG) [Purity Law, Commentary on Unfair Competition Law (UCL)], Basel/Geneva/Munich/St. Gallen/Berlin 2001, n. 1 above Article 2 LCD; see also Judgment of the Cantonal Court of Vaud of 12 January 2009, in sic! 2009 431 ("Ferrari II").

Any conduct or commercial practice that is misleading or that contravenes in any other way the rules of good faith and that influences relations between competitors or between suppliers and customers (Article 2 LCD) is therefore unfair and unlawful. In other words, the unfair conduct must influence the way competition plays out or the way the market operates. Competition, therefore, assumes the market exists. "Although it is not necessary for the perpetrator of the act to himself be a competitor or for him to have the intention of influencing the economic activity, the act must, however, be objectively likely to advantage or disadvantage a business in its struggle to acquire customers, or to increase or reduce its market shares as the case may be."[57]

The protection of consumers from false signals such as fallacious statements or misleading methods also contributes to ensuring that competition runs smoothly. These market disruptions create distortions in competition and contribute nothing economically. Combating deceptive practices of all kinds improves the general competitive framework and the efficient use of resources.[58]

Eventually, denigrating conducts that might fall within the ambit of the provisions of the LCD may result from persons, organisations, or associations that are not in any competitive relationship with the injured party. Thus, for example, it will have to be determined if fallacious or needlessly hurtful allegations compromise to an unacceptable degree the commercial position of the party targeted.[59]

25.5.2 Parasitism and Non-competitive Relationship

Swiss courts sanction parasitic actions and generally distinguish between two types of conduct. Exploiting another party's reputation can thus come about in two ways: either the third party expressly refers to the sign of the plaintiff through comparative advertising or express references such as "equivalent to" or "as good as" (direct parasitic practices provided in Article 3 *lit.* e LCD) or the third party exploits the reputation of the plaintiff by creating a transfer of image in its favour (indirect parasitic practices provided in Articles 2 and 3 *lit.* e LCD).

The key criterion for assessing whether parasitic practices prevail has long been the risk of confusion. Indeed, for a long time the Swiss Supreme Court has examined the situation under Article 3 *lit.* d LCD, which sanctions a party who "takes measures likely to generate confusion with the goods, works, services or business of another".[60] Under that provision, the likelihood of confusion is the key

[57] FC 4A_313/2008 du 27 November 2008, cons.3; ATF 126 III 198, para 2c; ATF 120 II 76 Recital 3a; Judgment of the Federal Court, 4P_291/2000, in sic! 2001 317 ("Central Perk").

[58] Message of the Federal Council of 18 May 1983, Official Journal (Feuille fédérale/FF) 1983 II 1037 ff., particularly 1091; FC, ATF 129 III 426, para 2.2.

[59] FC, ATF 117 IV 193 ("Bernina"); FC, sic! 2000, 712 ("Club de l'Economie").

[60] FC, ATF 116 II 365 = JdT 1991 I 613 ("Nivea").

criterion for assessing whether the conduct is unfair. It was only in a recent decision that the Swiss Supreme Court held that the absence of a risk of confusion does not mean that action could not be taken under the LCD for exploitation of another party's reputation or a parasitic act, particularly if the later sign conveys the idea that the related product is "a substitute for" or "as good as".[61] Since the IWC/WWC judgment,[62] exploitation of another party's reputation or services as stated in Article 3 *lit.* 2 LCD seems to have acquired an independent scope.

25.6 The Links Between Infringement, Unfair Competition, and Parasitism in a Legal Action

25.6.1 Articulation of Those Various Legal Grounds

Infringement is characterised by the servile reproduction of the trademark of another.[63]

Contrary to an action for infringement, which aim is to penalise the infringement of an intellectual property right, an action for unfair competition, pursuant to Article 9 LCD, sanctions unfair conduct. The goal of the LCD is to ensure, in the interest of all parties concerned, competition that is fair and is not distorted.[64]

Article 2 LCD actually defines *a contrario* what constitutes economically acceptable conduct: "Any conduct or practice which is misleading or which in any other way contravenes the rules of good faith and which influences relationships between competitors or between suppliers and customers is unfair and unlawful." The law then provides a non-exhaustive list of conduct that is considered to be unfair in Articles 3–8 LCD. Parasitic actions for their part are constituted either from comparative advertising or from indirect references to the sign or product of the trademark holder.

25.6.2 Possible Substitution of Unfair Competition Legal Action to Infringement Legal Action

An action for unfair competition may be invoked alone or in addition to an action for infringement, but it does not seem that it can be stated generally that the first is a

[61] Judgment of the Federal Court, 4A_467/2007, in sic! 2008 454, Recital 4.2 and 5.2.

[62] Judgment of the Federal Court, 4A_467/2007 et 4A_469/2007, in sic! 2008 454 ("IWC/WWC"); Schlosser Ralph, comments on the "IWC/WWC" judgment in sic! 2008 454, p. 461 which applauds the decision of the FC.

[63] Killias Pierre-Alain, La mise en œuvre de la protection des signs distinctifs [Enforcing protection of distinctive signs], CEDIDAC Lausanne, 2002, p. 161.

[64] Article 1 LCD; FC, ATF of 4 September 2004, in sic! 2004, 430.

substitute for the second. The overall functions of each law should be analysed, as well as those specific to each provision that might apply to a particular case.

Legal actions for unfair competition can be based on two types of unfair conduct:

1. the creation of a risk of confusion (Article 3 *lit.* d LCD),
2. the parasitic exploitation of another party's reputation (Article 2s and 3 *lit.* e LCD):
   - direct parasitic practices (Article 3 *lit.* e LCD)—comparative advertising,
   - indirect parasitic practices (Articles 2 and 3 *lit.* e LCD)—systematic and cunning imitation that results in the exploitation of the reputation of another party through a transfer of image.

Thus, case law in relation to parasitic practices is rendered pursuant to the LCD, hence the term parasitic competition (subject to parasitic practices against famous trademarks as stated in Article 15 LPM).

Generally, competition law and trademark law have independent functions; whereas the first pertains to practices that distort competition, the second protects the distinctive character of the brand. Some writers, relying on the different purposes of these laws, consider therefore that competition law may apply, along with trademark law, when this is in line with the purposes of unfair competition law. In other words, these two legal grounds are distinct and independent from each other. Consequently, where one is not applicable, the other one may apply, provided its conditions are met. Another school of thought considers that the cumulative application of the two laws has become impossible since the 1993 Trademark Protection Act came into force.[65] One of the main reasons advanced has to do with the principle of registration of the trademark. Thus, allowing cumulative application would impede this principle if the party who has not registered its sign were able to object to the trademark holder pursuant to Article 3 *lit.* d LCD.[66] Another school of thought considers that trademark law is a *lex specialis* compared to competition law as regards distinctive signs.[67] Finally, some writers, although they accept that the functions of the two laws differ, are of the opinion that each of the provisions of the LCD (particularly Articles 2, 3 *lit.* d and *lit.* e LCD) has a specific function.[68]

Two specific provisions of the LCD, which can be used as the basis for an action for unfair competition and an action for infringement, are briefly mentioned in the following paragraphs.

---

[65] Cherpillod Ivan, la notion de marque, in: La nouvelle loi fédérale sur la protection des marques, CEDIDAC n° 27, Lausanne 1994, p. 31; Dessemontet François, Droit à la marque, Pratique Juridique Actuelle (PJA), 1993 p. 49.

[66] ATF 116 II 471 = JdT 1991 I 594 ("Volvo").

[67] Arnet Ruth, die Formmarke, thesis, Zürich1993, p. 171.

[68] Gilliéron Philippe, Les divers régimes de protection des signs distinctifs et leurs rapports avec le droit des marques [The various systems of protection of distinctive signs and their relationship with trademark law], academic paper, Staempfli, Berne, 2000, p. 312.

25.6.2.1 Action for Infringement Pursuant to Article 3 Paragraph 1 LPM and Article 3 *lit.* d LCD

The intent of both Article 3 let. d LCD and Article 3 paragraph 1 *lit.* c LPM is to protect distinctive signs from any risk of confusion.[69] This assumes that the earlier product has a certain distinctive character. The result is that the functions of these two provisions overlap. The purpose of amending the Trademark Protection Law was to ensure a certain consistency in the system, specifically to prevent exclusive rights not envisaged by trademark law being created through Article 3 *lit.* d LCD.[70] Pursuant to the opinion of the SC and some writers, an action for infringement pursuant to the LPM ranks above an action pursuant to Article 3 *lit.* d LCD in the area of distinctive signs. Thus, where there are unregistered signs, Article 3 *lit.* d LCD could apply without any restriction imposed by exclusive rights. In this case, a party who cannot invoke the LPM and, consequently, Article 3 *lit.* d LCD can initiate an action based on the general clause of the law on unfair competition (Article 2 LCD).[71]

25.6.2.2 Action for Infringement Pursuant to Article 3 Paragraph 1 LPM and Article 3 *lit.* e LCD

Article 3 lit. e LCD and infringement claims have different functions. The aim of the former is to protect the reputation of the injured party from any exploitation resulting from a comparison that is inaccurate, fallacious, needlessly hurtful, or parasitic. Recent case law shows that the creation of the risk of confusion is no longer necessary for parasitic practices. As soon as the conditions of Article 3 *lit.* e LCD are met, it may be applied autonomously. However, this does not mean that the risk of confusion is automatically excluded. The outcome of the IWC/WMC judgment[72] is that parasitic competition seems to have acquired an independent scope.

Positive externalities mean situations where a party benefits from the action of third parties without having to pay anything. It should be recalled that a trademark is defined as a sign that enables a distinction to be made between the goods or services of one business and those of other businesses.[73] The SC notes that the economic role of the trademark is to give the consumer the means to find a product among the plethora of goods offered.[74] The trademark not only makes it easier for consumers to look for something among the huge array of goods offered to them but

---

[69] Gilliéron Philippe, Les divers régimes de protection des signs distinctifs et leurs rapports avec le droit des marques [The various systems of protection of distinctive signs and their relationship with trademark law], academic paper, Staempfli, Berne, 2000, p. 315.

[70] FC, ATF 116 II 471, para 3a aa = JdT 1991 I 594 ("Volvo").

[71] Gilliéron Philippe, Les divers régimes de protection des signs distinctifs et leurs rapports avec le droit des marques [The various systems of protection of distinctive signs and their relationship with trademark law], academic paper, Staempfli, Berne, 2000, p. 329.

[72] Cited in footnote 60.

[73] Article 1 LPM.

[74] FC, ATF 119 II 473 = JdT 1994 I 358.

also reduces the search costs. Before the new LPM came into force, only the distinctive function and the origin function of the trademark enjoyed legal protection. The groups interested in protection being extended to scenarios where no risk of confusion existed have actively supported the special protection currently enjoyed by so-called famous trademarks. From an economic standpoint, like other intellectual property rights, a famous trademark is an intangible asset requiring considerable prior investments to be made, such as promotional investments.

In the light of the above, positive externalities are still allowed as long as the protection enjoyed by the trademark is confined to the risk of confusion, whether it is comparative advertising or the use of a trademark by a retailer to promote original goods or replacements. However, as soon as the determining criterion is no longer the risk of confusion (implicitly a competitive relationship) but exploitation of the reputation associated with a trademark and its value as an asset, the exploitation of the positive externalities might be penalised due to the protection being extended to famous trademarks.[75]

Conclusions and Policy Recommendations

Only famous trademarks should enjoy enhanced protection. This enhanced protection, in trademark law, aims to penalise parasitic conduct, i.e. conduct consisting of using or reproducing an earlier trademark of repute, but for goods or services that are not similar to those for which the famous trademark has been registered.

Apart from this case, Swiss legislation provides that anyone may use the services or results of the work of others who have no intellectual property protection. The LCD contains no general prohibition against copying the services of others; on the contrary, there is freedom to copy. The LCD seeks to ensure fairness of competition, while it is reserved to special intellectual property laws to protect particular services as such. The services are not therefore protected by the LCD against reproduction and copying as such but solely when there are relevant circumstances in unfair competition law, for example avoidable confusion as to the provenance of the goods, the risk of confusion, or parasitic conduct.[76]

---

[75] Landes William M. and Posner Ricard A., The Economics Structure Of Intellectual Property Law", Harvard University Press, London 2003, p. 168.

[76] FC, ATF 131 III 384, para 5.1 = JdT 2005 I 434.

United Kingdom

26

Ben Longstaff

26.1 Introduction

For the purposes of this contribution, the discussions are confined to the law of England and Wales (with apologies to practitioners in the jurisdictions of Scotland and Northern Ireland).

Any report on the protection within the UK of trademarks, distinctive signs, and so on must of course examine Community law and other supranational provisions, in addition to the forms of legal protection specific (at least in their detail) to this jurisdiction. The latter may perhaps be of the greater interest to lawyers in other jurisdictions, while the former aspects are arguably already well known (certainly to practitioners in Europe) by dint of the of Community law in this area over the past two decades. Accordingly, and to avoid the risk of duplicating what may be contained in the reports of other Member States, this report focuses more on national provisions, but it does also attempt to survey at least broadly the implications of wider law as between non-competing undertakings.

It is important to make clear at the start that this report has taken "trademarks" to refer to registered trademarks and "distinctive signs and other components" to mean signs outside of the system of registered marks.

It is also important to consider what is to be understood by the term "non-competing". The difficulty is that in this context it seems too restrictive to give a rigid definition of competition in terms such as substitutability of goods or services, or geographical overlap of markets, when one is also considering the effect of trading styles upon consumer behaviour towards, say, dissimilar but not entirely non-competing undertakings. Accordingly, this report assumes the context of a "sliding scale" of competition rather than trying to define "non-competing" in absolute terms.

B. Longstaff (✉)
Hogarth Chambers, London, UK
e-mail: blongstaff@hogarthchambers.com

P. Këllezi et al. (eds.), *Antitrust for Small and Middle Size Undertakings and Image Protection from Non-Competitors*, LIDC Contributions on Antitrust Law, Intellectual Property and Unfair Competition, DOI 10.1007/978-3-642-54000-4_26, © Springer-Verlag Berlin Heidelberg 2014

26.2 The Status of Brand Image

26.2.1 Legal Definition of Brand Image

Brand image is of course a central concern of the law of registered trademarks within the European Community, and that branch of protection is discussed in due course below in relation to registered rights. However, brand image also offers a convenient entry point into the discussion of unregistered rights and their protection in national law, and so the remainder of this first section will consider the legal status of "brand image" in that respect.

Brand image is a natural starting point for such a discussion because it is more or less equivalent to the notion of "goodwill" in English law, which in turn is a cornerstone of the long-standing (though gradually evolving) tort of passing off. Before exploring the nature and protection of brand image within this tort, it is therefore worth outlining very briefly the essence of passing off itself.

Passing off is essentially the common law protection of unregistered trademark rights and is a species of unfair competition law. Its principles are contained in a vast and somewhat unwieldy body of case law, but the title of one key practitioner work on the subject provides an instructive summary: *The Law of Passing Off: Unfair Competition by Misrepresentation.*[1] As will be seen, it is a tort of deception. The underlying principle was summarised as follows (more than 100 years ago):

> For myself, I believe the principle of law may be very plainly stated, and that is that nobody has any right to represent his goods as the goods of somebody else. How far the use of particular words, signs, or pictures does or does not come up to the proposition ... must always be a question of evidence.[2]

It remains true today that each case turns on its own particular facts, but fortunately the case law has also clarified the applicable principles in establishing whether the tort has been committed. These ingredients have commonly been reduced to the "classical trinity" of (1) goodwill attaching to a business or undertaking, (2) misrepresentation causing (or likely to cause) deception among consumers, and (3) consequent damage to the goodwill of the business.

26.2.2 The Notion of Brand Image in Case Law

Turning to the relationship between passing off and brand image specifically, the case law on passing off has provided a classic statement about what constitutes goodwill, which is still widely cited by the courts to this day:

[1] Wadlow C. (2011), 4th ed. Sweet & Maxwell.

[2] *Reddaway v Banham* (1896) 13 R.P.C. 218 at 224.

> It is a thing very easy to describe, very difficult to define. It is the benefit and advantage of the good name, reputation and connection of a business. It is the attractive force which brings in custom.[3]

Thus, it can be seen that brand image has much in common with the legal concept of goodwill, since it is by brand that consumers generally distinguish the offerings of one undertaking from those of another, and the value of a brand image is typically the value of attracting and retaining custom. This notion of brand image as goodwill also squares well with the essential (and other) functions of registered trademarks insofar as they too protect brands. The key difference in the tort of passing off is that there is no need for registration. In that sense, the tort potentially offers wider protection than trademark rights, however, the counterbalance is that a would-be claimant must establish goodwill through evidence rather than simply pointing to a registration.

The passing-off cases establish a number of propositions about the nature of brand image (as goodwill) under English law:

(1) The threshold for protectable goodwill is not a high or onerous one, though mere reputation will not suffice: a business or trading goodwill is required. This is particularly relevant in relation to international undertakings, which may have a reputation in the UK but no goodwill as such (see for example, *NASA*[4]). The leading authority on this latter point is now *Hotel Cipriani*.[5]

(2) Goodwill in a new business usually extends initially only to the claimant's actual business, and to its geographical area of trading, so that protection accordingly extends only to those in direct competition for the same goods or services in the same approximate locality. However, over time goodwill may flourish in both scale of renown and geographical extent to such a degree that a distant undertaking marketing entirely different goods and services may make an operative misrepresentation by reference to the claimant's name or branding or other embodiment of goodwill.

(3) Goodwill may persist in a residual form for a substantial period of time even after an undertaking has ceased trading, as long as it has not been definitively abandoned.

(4) Goodwill may be embodied (in the sense of vesting in something that is recognised as such by the relevant public) in all sorts of ways, including business name, trading name, packaging,[6] getup, colourways, slogans, or trading style. There is no limit in principle to the variety of possible embodiments.

(5) Goodwill may accrue to one or more proprietors jointly; only the owner or owners of the goodwill can bring an action for passing off.

---

[3] *IRC v Muller & Co's Margarine Ltd* [1901] A.C. 217 at 223.

[4] *Nice and Safe Attitude Ltd v Piers Flook* (*trading as Slaam Clothing Co*) [1997] F.S.R. 14.

[5] *Hotel Cipriani Srl v Cipriani* (*Grosvenor Street*) *Ltd* [2010] R.P.C. 16.

[6] Famously in the "Jif Lemon" case: *Reckitt & Colman Products Ltd v Borden Inc* [1990] R.P.C. 341.

(6) Goodwill may vest in *non-trading* undertakings, such as charities or political parties.
(7) Goodwill may also vest in an open-ended class of undertakings rather than being owned by a particular one, so that any undertaking in the class has a right to prevent others making misrepresentations damaging to the collective goodwill. This is the basis of the so-called extended form of passing off, in which a category of producers (e.g., champagne makers) is entitled to prevent others from passing off their goods as being the real thing. There is a long line of English cases (many to do with drinks producers), establishing this species of the tort.[7]

26.2.3 The Legal Instruments Used to Defend Brand Image and the Role of Competitive Relations

26.2.3.1 Limits on the Tort of Passing Off: Need for Deception and Damage?

The scope of protection is fundamentally defined by the requirement for deception or a likelihood of deception, leading to damage, which at least notionally places a limit on the tort of passing off. In *Hodgkinson*,[8] Jacob J made clear that there is no tort of taking another undertaking's customers or business or in copying a business product or other idea. Crucially, he emphasised that there is no tort of competition and stated (at p. 175):

> At the heart of passing off lies deception or its likelihood, deception of the ultimate consumer in particular. . . . Never has the tort shown even a slight tendency to stray beyond cases of deception. Were it to do so it would enter the field of honest competition, declared unlawful for some reason other than deceptiveness. Why there should be any such reason I cannot imagine. It would serve only to stifle competition.

Thus, the focus in passing off is very much on the nature of the scope and extent of the goodwill and whether the acts complained of amount to an operative misrepresentation giving rise to damage. It is for this reason that the tort is so fact-sensitive.

Despite the ostensible need for deception and damage, however, Jennifer Davis has argued that the tort of passing off has been extended to (or is capable of covering) situations where there is no real deception or likelihood of any damage, despite the protestations of the Court of Appeal in *L'Oréal v Bellure*.[9] She argues

---

[7] See, e.g., *Diageo North America Inc v Intercontinental Brands Ltd* [2010] R.P.C. 12 for a summary of the case law; the decision itself established goodwill in vodka (and was upheld on appeal).

[8] *Hodgkinson and Corby Ltd v Wards Mobility Services Ltd* [1995] F.S.R. 169.

[9] Davis J. (2010) Why the United Kingdom should have a law against misappropriation. C.L.J. 69 (3): 561–581. *L'Oréal v Bellure* [2008] R.P.C. 9, at [160]-[161]. See in response Carty H. (2012) Passing off: frameworks of liability debated. I.P.Q. 2: 106–122.

that because the UK courts have tended to find that damage follows almost automatically where there is a misrepresentation (e.g., damage in nebulous forms such as dilution of exclusivity), and since claimants are often not put to proof to show any actual damage, the law of passing off has become a way of preventing "pure misappropriation"—a form of general unfair competition law.

26.2.3.2 Is There a Need for Competition?

This is the key aspect of the tort for consideration here: is the notion of competitive relations taken into account in passing off? The answer is broadly yes, the notion of competition is at least considered, but crucially it is not a *necessary* ingredient of the tort, as will be seen. Although the issues of misrepresentation and confusion do not explicitly refer to the competitive status of the parties, the notion is introduced obliquely in that the court will consider whether or not there is a "common field of activity" as between claimant and defendant.

For a long time, it appeared to be thought that unless there was some common field of activity as between claimant and defendant, there could not be passing off.[10] However, this theory was finally dispelled by the Court of Appeal in *Harrods*[11]:

> There is no requirement that the defendant should be carrying on a business which competes with that of the plaintiff or which would compete with any natural extension of the plaintiff's business. . . . What the plaintiff in an action for passing off must prove is not the existence of a common field of activity but likely confusion among the common customers of the parties.

From this and subsequent cases, it is now clear that a likelihood of deception does not require any threshold level of overlap in terms of competition between the parties.[12] Indeed, they may operate in entirely distinct spheres. However, the directness or otherwise of competition will almost certainly be a very important factor in assessing the likelihood of confusion. The court in *Harrods* went on:

> The absence of a common field of activity, therefore, is not fatal; but it is not irrelevant either. In deciding whether there is a likelihood of confusion, it is an important and highly relevant consideration '. . .whether there is any kind of association, or could be in the minds of the public any kind of association, between the field of activities of the plaintiff and the field of activities of the defendant' . . .
>
> In the *Lego* case Falconer J. likewise held that the proximity of the defendant's field of activity to that of the plaintiff was a factor to be taken into account when deciding whether the defendant's conduct would cause the necessary confusion.

It may be noted at this point that there is an analogue here with the principle of interdependency between similarity of marks and similarity of goods/services when assessing likelihood of confusion in the European jurisprudence on registered trademarks—see the discussion further below.

---

[10] See, e.g., *Muculloch v Lewis A. May (Produce Distributors) Ltd* (1948) 65 R.P.C. 58.

[11] *Harrods Ltd v Harrodian School Ltd* [1996] R.P.C. 697.

[12] See e.g. the judgment of Arnold J in *Och-Ziff Management Europe Ltd v Och Capital LLP* [2011] F.S.R. 11 at [159].

The position today, as summarised by Professor Wadlow, is that the existence or otherwise of a common field of activity is "no more than a rule of thumb" that may offer a useful starting point.[13]

Two specific cases illustrate the point that there is no hard-and-fast rule about whether the absence of competition will be decisive in a given situation. In *Stringfellows*,[14] the defendant (selling oven chips) was plainly taking advantage of the claimant's reputation (for nightclubs) in its advertising, yet such use did not amount to passing off because there was no suggestion that anyone would be deceived into thinking that the defendant's chips were anything to do with the claimant. In contrast, in *Lego*[15] the claimant made children's plastic building blocks and succeeded against a manufacturer of plastic irrigation equipment, since this was held to be a line of goods into which the claimant might be perceived to have diversified, thus giving rise to a risk of deception.

26.2.3.3 Instruments of Deception

The risk of deception in passing off is closely related to the doctrine of "instruments of deception" or "instruments of fraud"—things that, in the right hands or in the right circumstances, become tools of deception for the commission of acts such as fraud or passing off.[16] The production or distribution of such instruments of fraud is a significant source of potential liability for those who are commissioned to make goods that another party intends to pass off.

26.2.3.4 Conclusions About Protection of Brand Image as Goodwill

The law of passing off clearly provides significant protection for undertakings with unregistered trademarks, i.e. a "brand image" with a suitable trading reputation. The protection against passing off may be considered wider than that for trademark infringement in the sense that there is no need for registration and that following cessation of trading, residual goodwill may persist long after the point at which a registered trademark would be liable to revocation for non-use. In addition, the wide range of embodiments in which goodwill may subsist is arguably far wider than the range of "signs" that would be registrable as trademarks in European law—an undertaking's trading style is a good example.[17] On the other hand, it can be awkward (as a matter of evidence) to establish the requisite goodwill and/or to demonstrate actual deception or a likelihood of deception.

---

[13] *Supra* at 4-109.

[14] *Stringfellow v McCain Foods (GB) Ltd* [1984] R.P.C. 501.

[15] *Lego System A/S v Lego M Lemelstritch Ltd* [1983] F.S.R. 155, referred to in the earlier quote from *Harrods*.

[16] See, e.g., *BT v One in a Million* [1999] FSR 1, and *L'Oréal v Bellure* [2008] R.P.C. 9.

[17] See also alluding to an advertising campaign: *Cadbury-Schweppes Pty Ltd v Pub Squash Co Ltd* [1981] 1 W.L.R. 193; or slogans: *United Biscuits (UK) Ltd v Asda Stores Ltd* [1997] R.P.C. 513, relating to "P. . .P. . .P. . . Pick up a Penguin".

Most significantly, it seems that passing off does offer an undertaking the ability to obtain relief against a non-competitor. Although this is tempered by the need to establish a likelihood of deception, it is clear that an undertaking with a substantial goodwill may obtain relief against even non-competing undertakings where there is some element of misrepresentation liable to deceive and thereby take advantage of the former party's reputation. In that sense, of course, there is no such thing as a non-competitor: even though the respective customers may form disjoint classes, any attempt to obtain custom by utilising another's goodwill is de facto competition of a sort.

In addition, it should also be remembered that goodwill may accrue to non trading parties such as charities or political parties. As such, any undertaking that trespasses on that goodwill is *ex hypothesi* not a competitor in the usual core commercial sense yet is still liable to be restrained by the law of passing off.

It is interesting that, as will be seen with distinctiveness or reputation in registered trademarks, the protection available to an undertaking as against non-competitors appears to grow disproportionately strong as the magnitude of their goodwill increases.

26.2.3.5 Effect of the Unfair Commercial Practices Directive (UCPD)[18]

Professor Wadlow notes the possibility that the UCPD, which harmonises the law relating to unfair business-to-consumer practices, might in principle have some effect on passing off.[19] The reason is that the UCPD's aim of harmonisation (see Article 4) means that Member States are not free to impose their own stricter standards of liability in the sphere of the directive. The professor states his belief that although that directive takes precedence in its area of concern, there is little risk that it will cause any problems for the national law of passing off, in particular, since Article 6 of the UCPD prohibits what is arguably a far wider range of misleading conduct. He concludes that it is hard to conceive of something prohibited by passing off that would, under the UCPD, be permissible.

However, that is rather to presume that the law of passing off is not capable of producing anomalous effects. Where an undertaking's goodwill enables it to prevent the free movement of goods that are not in direct competition with its own, the law is arguably producing an impermissible distortion of the internal market. As yet, though, there does not appear to be any case law on this point.

---

[18] Directive 2005/29 of the European Parliament and of the Council of May 11, 2005 concerning unfair business-to-consumer commercial practices in the internal market.

[19] Wadlow C., *supra*, at 1-073 *et seq*.

26.3 The Principle of Speciality Versus Legal Action Between Non-competitors

26.3.1 The Link Between Speciality and Competitive Relations

The principle of speciality in trademark law is concerned with the subdivision of monopoly rights so that a given sign or similar signs should not be prevented from being used simultaneously by undertakings with prima facie dissimilar markets, i.e. those not in direct competition. It should be noted that while the courts and practitioners in the UK are familiar with this concept, the term "principle of speciality" itself appears to be little used. The connection with competitive relations is clear: in order to apply the principle of speciality, one must ask in every case whether two given undertakings operate in sufficiently similar markets or in a sufficient degree of competition that their trademark rights can no longer harmoniously coexist. That interplay is best explored by considering how the law of registered trademarks deals with the problem (but without attempting an exhaustive summary of the law).

26.3.2 Influence on Civil Liability

The national law of registered trademarks has been largely harmonised by Council Directive 89/104/EEC, now codified as Directive 2008/95/EC ("the Directive"). The relevant provisions of the Directive are reflected in the Trade Marks Act 1994 ("the 1994 Act"). The provisions of the Directive are mirrored in Council Regulation (EC) 40/94, now consolidated as Regulation (EC) 207/2009. As such, the law of the United Kingdom now follows the jurisprudence of the Court of Justice and the General Court, in addition to national case law established under the same harmonised principles. For convenience, this report will refer to the provisions of the Directive.

It can be seen that the interaction between competition and the principle of speciality is dealt with by Article 5(1)(b) and 5(2) of the Directive.[20]

---

[20] Those provisions state: *5(1). The registered trade mark shall confer on the proprietor exclusive rights therein. The proprietor shall be entitled to prevent all third parties not having his consent from using in the course of trade*:

(*a*) . . .;

(*b*) *any sign where, because of its identity with, or similarity to, the trade mark and the identity or similarity of the goods or services covered by the trade mark and the sign, there exists a likelihood of confusion on the part of the public; the likelihood of confusion includes the likelihood of association between the sign and the trade mark.*

5(2) Any Member State may also provide that the proprietor shall be entitled to prevent all third parties not having his consent from using in the course of trade any sign which is identical with, or similar to, the trade mark in relation to goods or services which are not similar to those for which the trade mark is registered, where the latter has a reputation in the Member State and where use

26.3.2.1 Article 5(1)(b): Identical or Similar Marks, Identical or Similar Goods

This provision deals with the question of proximity between undertakings by asking whether there is a likelihood of confusion, taking into account the level of similarity of the marks, and the degree of competition between the respective undertakings, as gauged by the similarity of the goods or services in question. The applicable principles are well known (see, for example, the recent summary by Arnold J in *Och-Ziff*[21] drawing together the numerous European cases on this aspect of the harmonised legislation). Most of those principles relate more to the perception of the marks themselves, but the following two are perhaps particularly relevant to competition:

(1) There is an interdependency between the two limbs of similarity, such that a greater degree of similarity in one may be offset by a lesser degree in the other[22];
(2) A high degree of distinctiveness leads to a greater likelihood of confusion: such marks enjoy a broader degree of protection.[23]

Thus, it may be argued that Article 5(1)(b) certainly leans towards affording protection as between non-competing undertakings, and it comes closest in the case of highly distinctive marks. Where a mark is so famous (for example, Coca-Cola) that it has attained an extremely high level of distinctiveness, it is easy to conceive that the proprietor of such a mark would be able to stop virtually any other undertaking from using a similar mark. Such marks may be relatively rare, but for less distinctive marks there is also the protection offered by Article 5(2), discussed below.

There is also a significant territorial dimension to the issue of trademark conflicts between non-competing undertakings. Since the clash of the marks must be considered in relation to the territory over which the rights in question subsist, there is always the prospect that a "local" undertaking may nonetheless obtain protection against another undertaking that is no real sense in competition but is simply within the same jurisdiction. This is most pronounced in relation to Community Trade Marks (as governed by the Regulation), where the relevant territory is the whole of the Community. Since use of the mark in question within a single Member State is enough to avoid revocation for non-use, the undertaking against whom the rights are being enforced may find it has little recourse even where the proprietor operates on only a relatively small scale in a distant part of the Community.

---

of that sign without due cause takes unfair advantage of, or is detrimental to, the distinctive character or the repute of the trade mark.

[21] *Supra*, at [173].

[22] *Canon Kabushiki Kaisha v Metro-Goldwyn-Mayer Inc*, Case C-39/97 [1999] R.P.C. 117

[23] *Sabel BV v Puma AG*, Case C-251/95, [1998] R.P.C. 199; *Canon, supra*.

26.3.2.2 Article 5(2): Trademarks with a Reputation

This provision dispenses with the requirement that the undertakings are, to at least some degree, in competition (as judged by the similarity of the relevant goods and services). Instead, the touchstone is that the mark has a "reputation" and that the use by another undertaking of the same or a similar mark takes unfair advantage of, or is detrimental to, the distinctive character or repute of the proprietor's mark. (Note that although the legislation refers to dissimilar goods or services, the Court of Justice has confirmed that the provision applies equally to similar goods and/or services; the 1994 Act has been amended accordingly.)

The case law establishes, inter alia, the following principles on the operation of Article 5(2):

(1) To establish the requisite reputation, the registered mark must be known by a significant proportion of the public, taking into account all relevant factors.[24]
(2) A national mark must have a reputation in the relevant Member State. For CTMs, the reputation must be in the Community, but for these purposes it may suffice to establish that the mark has a reputation throughout just one Member State.[25]
(3) Article 5(2) covers three types of damage: (i) detriment to distinctive character, (ii) detriment to repute, and (iii) taking unfair advantage of the mark's distinctive character or repute.[26]
(4) In relation to (i) and (ii), there is no need for a likelihood of confusion per se: the formation of a link in the minds of the relevant public may be enough. The assessment of whether such a link is established will involve considering a similar range of factors as in relation to likelihood of confusion, but the threshold for finding a link would seem to be lower.
(5) In *Intel*, the Court of Justice further stated:

> 50. Accordingly, the nature of the goods or services for which the conflicting marks are registered must be taken into consideration for the purposes of assessing whether there is a link between those marks.
>
> 51. It must also be pointed out that certain marks may have acquired such a reputation that it goes beyond the relevant public as regards the goods or services for which those marks were registered.
>
> 52. In such a case, it is possible that the relevant section of the public as regards the goods or services for which the later mark is registered will make a connection between the conflicting marks, even though that public is wholly distinct from the relevant section of the public as regards goods or services for which the earlier mark was registered.

However, it was also said that for the purposes of showing detriment, some evidence of change (or a serious likelihood of change) in economic behaviour is needed.

---

[24] *General Motors v Yplon*, Case C-375/97. [2000] R.P.C. 572.

[25] See *PAGO*, Case C-301/07.

[26] *Intel Corp Inv v CPM United Kingdom Ltd*, Case C-252/07, [2009] R.P.C. 15

(6) The Court of Justice considered unfair advantage in *L'Oréal v Bellure*.[27] It held that an unfair advantage is taken where any undertaking seeks to "free-ride on the coat-tails" of the proprietor undertaking's repute in the mark without paying compensation.

Thus, the detriment limb of Article 5(2) may allow an undertaking to obtain protection against non-competing undertakings where the reputation of the former's registered mark(s) is sufficiently great, but only as long as there is some evidence of economic effect, i.e. a change in consumer behaviour. Whether this is truly an example of brand protection extending between non-competing undertakings depends to some extent on one's definition of competition. However, since the *Intel* test contemplates not just actual economic effect but also a serious likelihood of change in future, it may be argued that the protection extends to non-competing undertakings so long as the proprietor of the mark can persuade a court that some element of competition will probably arise in due course. That may be enough to stifle a non-competitor.[28]

In light of *L'Oréal v Bellure*, the unfair advantage limb of Article 5(2) arguably provides even greater protection against non-competing undertakings, at least in principle, since free-riding need not involve offering goods in direct competition. Moreover, and as with Article 5(1)(b), where a mark has a very significant reputation, the degree of protection available may overreach the scope of true competition. The requirement that the advantage taken be unfair appears to add little in the way of checks or balances, since if the use of the mark is deemed without due cause, it will automatically be unfair.

26.3.2.3 Well-Known Marks: Section 56 of the 1994 Act

There is an additional provision within the 1994 Act for "well-known marks", corresponding to the protection contemplated by Article 6*bis* of the Paris Convention.[29] The protection thus afforded subsists whether or not the proprietor carries on business or has any goodwill in the United Kingdom, which is a remarkably wide right; however, the Court of Justice has indicated that an exceptional degree of reputation is required.[30] The proprietor of the well-known mark must also establish a likelihood of confusion along the same lines as per Article 5(1)(b) of the Directive, so it seems likely that the same considerations apply as in relation to non-competing undertakings. Note also that the remedy available under s. 56 is confined to an injunction, not damages.

---

[27] ECJ, Case C-487/07, *L'Oréal SA, Lancôme parfums et beauté & Cie SNC and Laboratoire Garnier & Cie v Bellure NV, Malaika Investments Ltd and Starion International Ltd.*, R.P.C. 2010 I-5185.

[28] In addition, it is arguable that the Court of Justice has recently weakened the *Intel* requirement for a change (or risk of change) in economic behaviour to something more akin to mere dilution – see *Environmental Manufacturing LLP v OHIM, Société Elmar Wolf*, Case C-570/10, at [51]*ff.*

[29] For more detail, see Mostert F. (2004) Famous and Well-Known Marks. INTA.

[30] See *General Motors v Yplon, supra.*

26.3.2.4 Cumulation of Rights

Lastly in this section, it should be noted that the rights above are all cumulative with the national common law rights, in particular the rights afforded by the law of passing off, which are outlined above.[31] In other words, the provisions of the harmonised legislation are without prejudice to such rights. However, note that if it turns out in a particular case that the legislative provisions no longer apply, on account of some underlying circumstance, it may well be that the same underlying reasons (e.g. acquiescence) would prevent an undertaking from bringing an action in passing off as well. See, e.g., Pumfrey J's comments in *Merc*[32]:

> I should just add that there must come a time after which the court would not interfere with a continued course of trading which might have involved passing off at its inception but no longer did so: logically, this point would come six years after it could safely be said that there was no deception and independent goodwill had been established in the market by the protagonists. There must also be doubt as to the availability of injunctive relief if there is no passing-off at the date the action is commenced.

26.4 Trademarks, Use in Business, and the Relation of Competition

26.4.1 The Liability of Non-competitors Using a Trademark "Outside Business"

The wording of Article 16 TRIPS is reflected in the harmonised trademark legislation of the Community by the requirement in Article 5 of the Directive (and in the equivalent parts of the Regulation and the 1994 Act) that the use complained of be "in the course of trade".

The scope of such business use has been explored both by national courts and by the Court of Justice, notably in cases concerning online transactions. From such cases, we glean the following:

(1) The use of a sign identical with a trade mark constitutes use in the course of trade where it occurs in the context of commercial activity with a view to economic advantage and not as a private matter.[33]
(2) Use in the course of trade means use in the course of a business even if not as a trade mark per se, so that the provisions of the legislation apply to the use of trade marks in "cyber-squatting" cases.[34]
(3) Use of a trade mark as an advertising keyword by an advertiser on a search engine does amount to use in the course of trade, but such use does not extend to the service provider.[35]

---

[31] See recitals (5) and (7) of the Directive and Article 14 of the Regulation.

[32] *Daimler Chrysler v Alavi* (*t/a Merc*) [2001] R.P.C. 42 at [67].

[33] Case C-238/08 *Google France* [2010] E.T.M.R. 30 at [50].

[34] *British Telecommunications Plc v One in a Million Ltd* [1998] F.S.R. 265, upheld on appeal.

[35] *Google France*, *supra*.

(4) Sale by an individual of a single item bearing a trade mark on an online market place such as eBay does not amount to use in the course of trade, unless such sales go beyond private activity by virtue of their volume, frequency or other characteristics.[36]

These and the related propositions of the case law do not immediately suggest any great danger that an undertaking will be able to use the Directive to suppress non-competing undertakings, since they appear to impose quite reasonable limits on the operation of the legislation. In particular, the requirement of "commercial activity for economic advantage" appears to protect those operating outside business, so that non-business use appears very unlikely to be caught under the harmonised regime.

However, there is no doubt that genuinely non-business use of a trademark or other sign may be objectionable. For example, use of a mark or sign outside of business might still cause detriment to the distinctive character or repute of a registered mark, yet not be actionable under Article 5(2) of the Directive. In such cases, it seems more likely that another branch of law will offer the proprietor of the mark some protection, depending on the use that is being made of the mark.[37]

26.4.2 The Future of Community Law on Infringement

While it is true that the Court of Justice appears to be continuing to expand and particularise the concepts of trademark functions beyond the original "essential function",[38] the requirement that infringing use be in the course of trade appears to keeping the trademark proprietor's rights in check as against non-competitors, for the reasons outlined above.

On the other hand, differences seem to be emerging in the scope of protection arising from the different types of trademark functions. In *Interflora*, the Court of Justice stated that trademark rights should not interfere with practices inherent in competition, such that the use of an Adword need not adversely affect the advertising function. Yet the Court also went on to say that the potential harm to the investment function must be considered separately, asking whether the use complained of "substantially interferes with the proprietor's use of its trademark to acquire or preserve a reputation capable of attracting consumers and retaining their loyalty". It remains to be seen how these developments will continue and whether the trademark functions will evolve to such an extent that even some non-business uses may end up infringing.

[36] *L'Oréal v eBay* Case C-324/09 [2011] E.T.M.R. 52 at [55].

[37] See Sect. 26.5.

[38] See, e.g., *Interflora Inc v Marks & Spencer Plc* Case C-323/09, [2012] F.S.R. 3.

26.5 Other Distinctive Signs

26.5.1 Liability of a Non-competitor That Uses Other Signs

The protection of other distinctive signs (i.e., signs other than registered trademarks) is dealt with by the law of passing off, discussed above in Sect. 26.2. As already mentioned, one key feature of passing off is that the requisite goodwill may be embodied in a wide variety of forms or "badges" that would frequently be outside the scope of registration. For example, a business with a particular getup or trading style to its premises might be able to prevent the use of similar indicia by another undertaking.

It is of course possible that such rights might allow an undertaking to take action against a non-competitor, but in reality the desire to imitate is likely to reflect an imperative to compete for business. A notable exception might be satire or parody, where the manufacturer of the spoof product does not compete with the product it is parodying but which may nonetheless be liable to an injunction.[39]

26.5.2 Liability in Respect of Domain Names

The appearance of domain names has certainly brought the issue back to the fore. This area is of particular interest in relation to the principle of speciality because of the differing functions of trademarks and domain names. The former are subject to that principle, whereas domain names may be said to defy these principles.

26.5.2.1 Domain Names and Passing Off

The English courts have dealt with this problem by adopting a broad approach to the harm, or potential harm, done by cybersquatters. In *One in a Million*, the Court of Appeal established that such activity was liable to be prevented under the tort of passing off and, in particular, by reference to the doctrine of instruments of fraud (discussed above).[40] Where an undertaking obtains a domain name registration for which the registrant has no conceivable use other than passing off (whether actual or threatened) or extracting money from the organisation that has the bona fide interest in the registration, the courts will grant an injunction. The court also held that even where there is no actual use of the mark—such as would be necessary to constitute trademark infringement—there may still be a threat to infringe.

[39] Since there is no defence of parody in English law.

[40] See *BT v One in a Million*, *supra*. Cf the dicta of the Court of Appeal in *L'Oréal v Bellure* [2008] R.P.C. 9, which played down the extent of the doctrine: "If what is complained of does not inherently tell a lie, it is not an instrument of deception. If it does tell a lie, it is no answer to say, as in effect the defendants in BT . . . were arguing: 'but there may be circumstances where the lie will not in fact be understood as such.' If a third party down the line says something dishonest about a product honest in itself, the vendor of the honest product is not liable in passing off."

Moreover, registration to exploit the distinctive character and reputation of the marks may be unfair and harmful.

Professor Wadlow has argued that the doctrine of instruments of deception is an inappropriate way in which to deal with domain names.[41] In his view, the better approach is to rely on either or both of (1) the court's equitable jurisdiction to order even innocent parties to surrender materials (whether tangible or intangible) insofar as that is required to prevent infringement and (2) joint tortfeasorship. On the other hand, it has also been noted that the courts appear reluctant to make a finding of contributory liability in the sphere of the internet.[42]

As regards domain names and cybersquatters specifically, it is submitted that the courts remain ready and willing to offer protection against cybersquatters, without worrying unduly about which is the most appropriate legal basis for such remedies. The principle of speciality seems to be disregarded in such cases, presumably because the focus is on the threat rather than the actual sphere of business and perhaps also because the courts take a dim view of the typical defendant in such cases: sophisticated, knowledgeable, and deliberately targeting the owner of a well-known brand.

26.5.2.2 Domain Name Registration Disputes

More problematic is the case where two undertakings both have a prima facie good case for owning a particular registration. In such cases, the first-come-first-served rule of registration can leave one or more parties feeling aggrieved, and in such cases domain name providers and/or overseers such as ICANN provide dispute resolution services.

The company that manages .uk domain name registrations is Nominet UK Limited, and its dispute resolution service policy is available online.[43] At the heart of Nominet's policy is the requirement that the complainant demonstrate that the contested registration is an "Abusive Registration". Paragraph 3 of the policy provides a non-exhaustive list of criteria that may be evidence of an Abusive Registration.[44]

Although that paragraph contains no express consideration of the notion of competitive relations, paragraph 4 sets out a non-exhaustive list of factors that may mitigate against a finding of an Abusive Registration. From these, it seems clear that a complainant has little hope of disturbing the registration so long as the registrant got there first and had a bona fide reason for obtaining and/or retaining the

[41] Wadlow C., *supra*, 4-137 et seq.

[42] Davis J. (2011) Passing off and joint liability: the rise and fall of 'instruments of deception'. E.I.P.R. 33(4): 204–209.

[43] Nominet (2012) Dispute Resolution Service Policy. http://www.nominet.org.uk/disputes/drs/?contentId=5239 (accessed 10 July 2012).

[44] The scenarios contemplated in paragraph 3.a.i and ii of the policy seem to be ones that would also be dealt with by reference to trademark infringement and/or passing off and/or malicious falsehood or interference with contractual relations.

registration. In that respect, there is little or no application of the principle of specialty.

26.6 "Reprehensible Conduct" and Non-competitors

26.6.1 Unfair Competition by Non-competing Undertakings: Other Modes of Protection

In addition to the modes of protection already discussed above, English law offers other avenues of redress that relate to what might broadly be called "reprehensible" conduct.

26.6.1.1 Malicious Falsehood

Damaging comments about a business made by reference to any aspect of its brand or image may (if untrue or not justifiable) give rise to an action in libel or malicious falsehood.[45] The latter cause of action is commonly deployed in the United Kingdom as an adjunct to trademark infringement (although not always successfully[46]). It is a tort of common law rather than legislation, in which the following elements must be made out:

(1) the defendant has published an untrue statement to a third party (other than the claimant).
(2) the statement was made maliciously, and
(3) as a result of the statement the claimant has suffered special damage.[47]

It seems unlikely that malicious falsehood might well be "misused" as between non-competing undertakings. Any organisation in a position to be labelled an "undertaking" is likely to be deemed to be operating in the course of trade, and so it seems probable that in circumstances where there is sufficient basis for malicious falsehood, say, the necessary criteria for an action in passing off or infringement will also be made out. If the non-competing undertaking is genuinely not acting in the course of trade, it is submitted that it is still correct that the law should enable the proprietor of the mark or goodwill to prevent such harmful use. The basis for such causes of action is not unfair competition so much as unfair behaviour generally.

26.6.1.2 Interference with Contractual Relations

A non-competitor might also be in a position to rely on the tort of interference with contractual relations—see *OBG v Allan*.[48] This tort has no particular requirement of

[45] Also known as trade libel, injurious falsehood, or slander of goods.

[46] E.g., *Kingspan v Rockwool* [2011] EWHC 250 (Ch).

[47] Note that the need for special damage is removed where the statement takes the form of words published in writing or some other permanent form and where it is calculated to cause pecuniary damage to the claimant – see s. 3(1) Defamation Act 1952.

[48] *OBG Ltd v Allan* [2008] 1 A.C. 1.

competition, although the parties to such an action will often be known to each other in some kind of competitive context.

26.6.1.3 Joint Tortfeasorship

It is important also to note that the principle of joint tortfeasorship may be invoked by an undertaking to sue defendants who are not in any sense competitors but who are involved in the acts of the primary tortfeasor or of others who may or may not compete.[49]

26.6.1.4 Criminal Offences

The 1994 Act also provides a variety of criminal sanctions relating to trademarks.[50] However, it is suggested that these provisions are most likely to catch undertakings seeking to compete directly with the owner of the registered mark or marks in question by selling counterfeit goods.

26.6.2 Parasitism and Non-competitive Relations

English law has no special principle of protecting against "parasitic practices" *per se*, in contrast to other civil codes—see, for example, the French decision in *L'Oréal v Bellure*.[51] Nonetheless, clearly some notion of parasitism is inherent in the law of both trademark infringement and passing off, and as noted above, it has been argued that passing off does in fact introduce a law of pure misappropriation or parasitism.

26.7 Coexistence of Infringement, Unfair Competition and "Parasitism"

26.7.1 Interplay Between the Various Legal Bases

Section 2 of the 1994 Act states that "nothing in this Act affects the law relating to passing off", and indeed, the action for passing off is widely seen as a useful alternative or adjunct to an action for trademark infringement in the United Kingdom. The differences between the two species of protection have already been outlined above. There is also the plurality of remedies available in relation to domain names, as well as the alternatives discussed in Sect. 26.5.

[49] See the discussion of joint tortfeasorship by Arnold J in *L'Oréal v eBay, supra*.

[50] See Sections 92 to 96.

[51] *L'Oréal SA v Bellure NV* Case 04/18300 [2006] E.C.D.R. 16.

26.7.2 Unfair Competition as a Substitute for Trademark Infringement?

It is certainly perfectly legitimate to bring an action for passing off as an alternative to infringement proceedings. Indeed, passing off may be the only option where a claimant has no registered rights but has a substantial reputation. Passing off has also proved a powerful tool in its "extended" form, affording protection to a wide range of products that fall under particular designations or quality marks unsuitable for trademark registration on account of the absolute grounds of refusal in Article 3 of the Directive (e.g. "vodka", "whisky", "Swiss chocolate").

While it is true that passing off can apply to situations that would scarcely be covered by the law of registered trademarks, it is generally considered that reliance on registered rights, perhaps with a parallel cause of action in passing off, is a far safer bet than bringing an action in passing off alone. It is suggested that registered trademarks offer more reliable protection against "pure misappropriation", in view of the jurisprudence on Article 5(s) of the Directive and the dicta of the Court of Appeal in *L'Oréal v Bellure*.[52]

Conclusions

The legal principles outlined above are certainly capable of allowing an undertaking to obtain protection against a non-competing undertaking that uses any of the former party's trademarks or other signs. The possibility of such protection also appears to increase dramatically with the size of what may be called the undertaking's brand distinctiveness (whether embodied in registered marks or goodwill or both). This creates scope for abuse or at least a heavy-handed approach by brand owners. On the other hand, protection against non-competitors may be perfectly justified, as in the case of genuinely unfair free-riding, denigration, or malicious falsehood.

Whether the use of passing off or extended passing off sidesteps the safety measures that are present in the legislation is something the courts must consider as part of their evaluation of any given case. There is cause for concern that the question of damage in passing off is arguably accepted as doctrine by the UK courts, such that litigation risks being conducted as an academic exercise in which an injunction follows without the need ever to prove any real-world harm.

Concerns about the use of unfair competition law between non-competing undertakings are tempered slightly by the fact that in reality, non-competing undertakings often have very little interest in spending time and money on attacking each other. However, that is little comfort for the small enterprise threatened by a famous brand. There is no obvious reason why the law should allow companies to turn brand ownership into a licence to intimidate or injunct other undertakings when those other undertakings are not competing and are not otherwise harming the brand or unfairly exploiting it. Of course, deciding who

[52] *L'Oréal v Bellure* [2008] R.P.C. 9.

(if anyone) is exploiting or acting unfairly is the heart of the problem. It is probably inevitable that any legal system that provides halfway adequate protection against genuine unfair competition is going to throw up the occasional instance of misuse; what it should seek to avoid is systematic abuse.

Acknowledgement The Author wishes to thank Dr Jennifer Davis and Professor Alison Firth for their invaluable input and suggestions during the preparation of this report. Any errors, omissions, or oversights remain entirely the Author's own.

The manufacturer's authorised representative in the EU is Springer Nature Customer Service Centre GmbH, Europaplatz 3, 69115 Heidelberg, Germany. If you have any concerns regarding our products, please contact ProductSafety@springernature.com

Printed and bound by CPI Group (UK) Ltd, Croydon, CR0 4YY
25/09/2026
02222882-0006